then trade them on Stock–Trak!

Standard & Poor's Educational Version of Market Insight

A free (with each new text purchased) exclusive partnership through McGraw-Hill/Irwin and the Institutional Market Services division of Standard & Poor's allows you to access this rich online database. Containing six years of fundamental financial data for over 1,000 companies, you can use this database to research and help answer the corresponding end-of-chapter S&P problems. For more details and to register, please see the bound-in card inside the front cover of this text or visit **www.mhhe.com/edumarketinsight.**

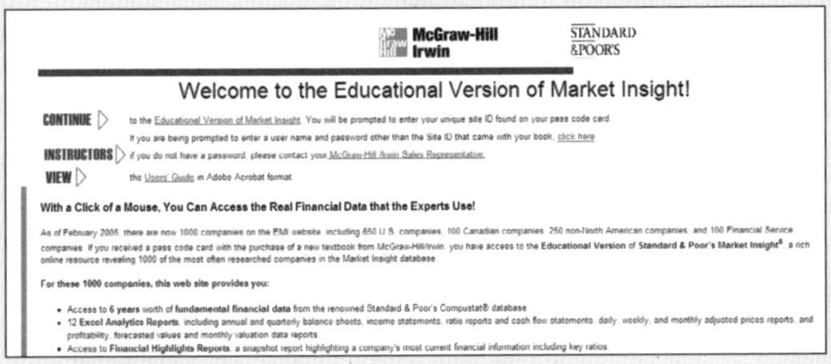

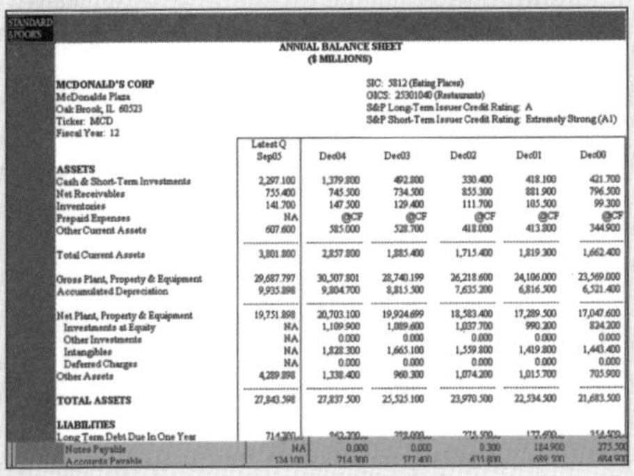

Fundamentals of Investments

VALUATION AND MANAGEMENT

The McGraw-Hill/Irwin Series in Finance, Insurance and Real Estate

Stephen A. Ross
Franco Modigliani Professor of Finance and Economics
Sloan School of Management
Massachusetts Institute of Technology
Consulting Editor

Financial Management

Adair
Excel Applications for Corporate Finance
First Edition

Block, Hirt, and Danielsen
Foundations of Financial Management
Thirteenth Edition

Brealey, Myers, and Allen
Principles of Corporate Finance
Ninth Edition

Brealey, Myers, and Allen
Principles of Corporate Finance, Concise Edition
First Edition

Brealey, Myers, and Marcus
Fundamentals of Corporate Finance
Sixth Edition

Brooks
FinGame Online 5.0

Bruner
Case Studies in Finance: Managing for Corporate Value Creation
Fifth Edition

Chew
The New Corporate Finance: Where Theory Meets Practice
Third Edition

Cornett, Adair, and Nofsinger
Finance: Applications and Theory
First Edition

DeMello
Cases in Finance
Second Edition

Grinblatt (editor)
Stephen A. Ross, Mentor: Influence through Generations

Grinblatt and Titman
Financial Markets and Corporate Strategy
Second Edition

Higgins
Analysis for Financial Management
Ninth Edition

Kellison
Theory of Interest
Third Edition

Kester, Ruback, and Tufano
Case Problems in Finance
Twelfth Edition

Ross, Westerfield, and Jaffe
Corporate Finance
Eighth Edition

Ross, Westerfield, Jaffe, and Jordan
Corporate Finance: Core Principles and Applications
Second Edition

Ross, Westerfield, and Jordan
Essentials of Corporate Finance
Sixth Edition

Ross, Westerfield, and Jordan
Fundamentals of Corporate Finance
Eighth Edition

Shefrin
Behavioral Corporate Finance: Decisions that Create Value
First Edition

White
Financial Analysis with an Electronic Calculator
Sixth Edition

Investments

Bodie, Kane, and Marcus
Essentials of Investments
Seventh Edition

Bodie, Kane, and Marcus
Investments
Eighth Edition

Hirschey and Nofsinger
Investments: Analysis and Behavior
First Edition

Hirt and Block
Fundamentals of Investment Management
Ninth Edition

Jordan and Miller
Fundamentals of Investments: Valuation and Management
Fifth Edition

Financial Institutions and Markets

Rose and Hudgins
Bank Management and Financial Services
Seventh Edition

Rose and Marquis
Money and Capital Markets: Financial Institutions and Instruments in a Global Marketplace
Tenth Edition

Saunders and Cornett
Financial Institutions Management: A Risk Management Approach
Sixth Edition

Saunders and Cornett
Financial Markets and Institutions: An Introduction to the Risk Management Approach
Fourth Edition

International Finance

Eun and Resnick
International Financial Management
Fifth Edition

Kuemmerle
Case Studies in International Entrepreneurship: Managing and Financing Ventures in the Global Economy
First Edition

Real Estate

Brueggeman and Fisher
Real Estate Finance and Investments
Thirteenth Edition

Ling and Archer
Real Estate Principles: A Value Approach
Second Edition

Financial Planning and Insurance

Allen, Melone, Rosenbloom, and Mahoney
Retirement Plans: 401(k)s, IRAs, and Other Deferred Compensation Approaches
Tenth Edition

Altfest
Personal Financial Planning
First Edition

Harrington and Niehaus
Risk Management and Insurance
Second Edition

Kapoor, Dlabay, and Hughes
Focus on Personal Finance: An Active Approach to Help You Develop Successful Financial Skills
Second Edition

Kapoor, Dlabay, and Hughes
Personal Finance
Ninth Edition

Fifth Edition

Fundamentals of Investments

VALUATION AND MANAGEMENT

Bradford D. Jordan
University of Kentucky

Thomas W. Miller Jr.
Saint Louis University

McGraw-Hill Irwin

Boston Burr Ridge, IL Dubuque, IA New York San Francisco St. Louis
Bangkok Bogotá Caracas Kuala Lumpur Lisbon London Madrid Mexico City
Milan Montreal New Delhi Santiago Seoul Singapore Sydney Taipei Toronto

The McGraw-Hill Companies

McGraw-Hill Irwin

FUNDAMENTALS OF INVESTMENTS

Published by McGraw-Hill/Irwin, a business unit of The McGraw-Hill Companies, Inc., 1221 Avenue of the Americas, New York, NY, 10020.

This book is printed on acid-free paper.
1 2 3 4 5 6 7 8 9 0 VNH/VNH 0 9 8

ISBN 978-0-07-338235-7
MHID 0-07-338235-3

Vice president and editor-in-chief: *Brent Gordon*
Executive editor: *Michele Janicek*
Developmental editor I: *Elizabeth Hughes*
Marketing manager: *Ashley Smith*
Senior project manager: *Bruce Gin*
Production supervisor: *Gina Hangos*
Lead designer: *Matthew Baldwin*
Lead media project manager: *Brian Nacik*
Cover design: *Cara Hawthorne*
Interior design: *Kiera Pohl*
Typeface: *10/12 Times Roman*
Compositor: *ICC Macmillan Inc.*
Printer: *R.R. Donnelley*

Library of Congress Cataloging-in-Publication Data

Jordan, Bradford D.
Fundamentals of investments : valuation and management / Bradford D. Jordan, Thomas W. Miller. -- 5th ed.
p. cm. -- (The McGraw-Hill/Irwin series in finance, insurance and real estate)
Includes index.
ISBN-13: 978-0-07-338235-7 (alk. paper)
ISBN-10: 0-07-338235-3 (alk. paper)
1. Investments. I. Miller, Thomas W. II. Title.
HG4521.C66 2009
332.6--dc22

2008023316

www.mhhe.com

To my late father, S. Kelly Jordan Sr.,
a great stock picker.

BDJ

To my parents, Tom and Kathy Miller,
my wife Carolyn, and #21
—Thomas W. Miller III.

TWM Jr.

About the Authors

Bradford D. Jordan

Gatton College of Business and Economics, University of Kentucky

Bradford D. Jordan is Professor of Finance and holder of the Richard W. and Janis H. Furst Endowed Chair in Finance at the University of Kentucky. He has a long-standing interest in both applied and theoretical issues in investments, and he has extensive experience teaching all levels of investments. Professor Jordan has published numerous research articles on issues such as valuation of fixed-income securities, tax effects in investments analysis, the behavior of security prices, IPO valuation, and pricing of exotic options. He is co-author of *Fundamentals of Corporate Finance* and *Essentials of Corporate Finance*, two of the most widely used finance textbooks in the world.

Thomas W. Miller Jr.

John Cook School of Business, Saint Louis University

Tom Miller is the Senior Associate Dean for Academic Programs and Professor of Finance at the John Cook School of Business at Saint Louis University. Professor Miller has a long-standing interest in derivative securities and investments and has published numerous articles on various topics in these areas. Professor Miller has been honored with many research and teaching awards. Professor Miller is a co-author (with David Dubofsky) of *Derivatives: Valuation and Risk Management* (Oxford University Press). Professor Miller's interests include golf, skiing, and American saddlebred horses.

Preface

So why *did* we write this book?

As we toiled away, we asked ourselves this question many times, and the answer was always the same: *Our students made us.*

Traditionally, investments textbooks tend to fall into one of two camps. The first type has a greater focus on portfolio management and covers a significant amount of portfolio theory. The second type is more concerned with security analysis and generally contains fairly detailed coverage of fundamental analysis as a tool for equity valuation. Today, most texts try to cover all the bases by including some chapters drawn from one camp and some from another.

The result of trying to cover everything is either a very long book or one that forces the instructor to bounce back and forth between chapters. This frequently leads to a noticeable lack of consistency in treatment. Different chapters have completely different approaches: Some are computational, some are theoretical, and some are descriptive. Some do macroeconomic forecasting, some do mean-variance portfolio theory and beta estimation, and some do financial statements analysis. Options and futures are often essentially tacked on the back to round out this disconnected assortment.

The goal of these books is different from the goal of our students. Our students told us they come into an investments course wanting to learn how to make investment decisions. As time went by, we found ourselves supplying more and more supplemental materials to the texts we were using and constantly varying chapter sequences while chasing this elusive goal. We finally came to realize that the financial world had changed tremendously, and investments textbooks had fallen far behind in content and relevance.

What we really wanted, and what our students really needed, was a book that would do several key things:

- Focus on the students as investment managers by giving them information they can act on instead of concentrating on theories and research without the proper context.
- Offer strong, consistent pedagogy, including a balanced, unified treatment of the main types of financial investments as mirrored in the investment world.
- Organize topics in a way that would make them easy to apply—whether to a portfolio simulation or to real life—and support these topics with hands-on activities.

We made these three goals the guiding principles in writing this book. The next several sections explain our approach to each and why we think they are so important.

Who Is This Book For?

This book is aimed at introductory investments classes with students who have relatively little familiarity with investments. A typical student may have taken a principles of finance class and had some exposure to stocks and bonds, but not much beyond the basics. The introductory investments class is often a required course for finance majors, but students from other areas often take it as an elective. One fact of which we are acutely aware is that this may be the only investments class many students will ever take.

We intentionally wrote this book in a relaxed, informal style that engages the student and treats him or her as an active participant rather than a passive information absorber. We think the world of investments is exciting and fascinating, and we hope to share our considerable enthusiasm for investing with the student. We appeal to intuition and basic principles whenever possible because we have found that this approach effectively promotes understanding. We also make extensive use of examples throughout, drawing on material from the world around us and using familiar companies wherever appropriate.

By design, the text is not encyclopedic. As the table of contents indicates, we have a total of 20 chapters. Chapter length is about 30 to 40 pages, so the text is aimed at a single-term course; most of the book can be covered in a typical quarter or semester.

Aiming the book at a one-semester course necessarily means some picking and choosing, with regard to both topics and depth of coverage. Throughout, we strike a balance by introducing and covering the essentials while leaving some of the details to follow-up courses in security analysis, portfolio management, and options and futures.

How Does the Fifth Edition of This Book Expand upon the Goals Described Above?

Based on user feedback, we have made numerous improvements and refinements in the fifth edition of *Fundamentals of Investments: Valuation and Management*. We have included an appendix containing useful formulas. We updated every chapter to reflect current market practices and conditions, and we significantly expanded and improved the end-of-chapter material. Also, our chapters devoted to market efficiency and to behavioral finance continue to rate highly among readers.

To give some examples of our additional new content:

- Chapter 2 contains a greatly expanded section on investment fraud and the Security Investors Protection Corporation (SIPC). In addition, a new section has been added to show students one way to form an investment portfolio.
- Chapter 4 contains a new section on the advantages and drawbacks of mutual fund investing and a greatly expanded section on exchange-traded funds, which includes exchange-traded notes (ETNs).
- Chapter 5 includes a greatly expanded section on private equity versus selling securities to the public. In addition, discussion of the current structure of the NYSE and the NASDAQ is enhanced with new material.
- Chapter 6 contains a section on how we get the formula for constant perpetual growth. Also, a detailed discussion of the two-stage dividend growth model is presented.
- Chapter 7 contains new material on an event study using actual events surrounding Advanced Medical Optics.
- Chapter 10 contains a greatly revamped section on dedicated portfolios and reinvestment risk.
- Chapter 14 now includes a detailed example of how to hedge an inventory using futures contracts.
- Chapter 15 contains an expanded discussion of the Options Clearing Corporation (OCC). In addition, the chapter has been extensively reorganized so that it naturally culminates in the put-call parity condition.
- Chapter 16 has been extensively reworked. It now contains sections on a simple way to value options; the one-period binomial option pricing model; the two-period option pricing model; the binomial option pricing model with many periods; and the Black-Scholes model. This chapter also describes employee stock options (ESOs) and their valuation using a modified Black-Scholes-Merton model.
- Chapter 20 (*Web site only*) includes a discussion of reverse mortgages.

In addition, we have written a set of learning objectives for each chapter. We have extensively reworked our chapter summaries to reflect the chapter's learning objectives.

For the fifth edition, we significantly expanded and improved the end-of-chapter material. We added new problems throughout, and we increased the number of CFA questions. We created new questions that test understanding of concepts with no calculations involved. In addition, our *What's on the Web?* questions give students assignments to perform based on information they retrieve from various Web sites. Our *S&P Problems* require the use of the educational version of Market Insight, which provides access to S&P's well-known Compustat database, and they provide instructors with an easy way to incorporate current, real-world data. Finally, in selected chapters, we have created spreadsheet assignments, which ask students to create certain types of spreadsheets to solve problems.

We continue to emphasize the use of the Web in investments analysis, and we integrate Web-based content in several ways. First, wherever appropriate, we provide a commented link in the margin. These links send readers to selected, particularly relevant Web sites. Second, our *Work the Web* feature, expanded and completely updated for this edition, appears in most chapters. These boxed readings use screen shots to show students how to access, use, and interpret various types of key financial and market data. Finally, as previously noted, new end-of-chapter problems rely on data retrieved from the Web.

We continue to provide *Spreadsheet Analysis* exhibits, which we have enhanced for this edition. These exhibits illustrate directly how to use spreadsheets to do certain types of important problems, including such computationally intensive tasks as calculating Macaulay duration, finding Black-Scholes option prices, and determining optimal portfolios based on Sharpe ratios. We also continue to provide, where relevant, readings from *The Wall Street Journal*, which have been thoroughly updated for this edition.

Assurance-of-Learning Ready

Many educational institutions today are focused on the notion of assurance of learning, an important element of some accreditation standards. This edition is designed specifically to support your assurance-of-learning initiatives with a simple, yet powerful, solution. Listed below are the learning objectives for each chapter.

Each test bank question for this book maps to a specific chapter learning objective listed in the text. You can use the test bank software to easily query for learning outcomes and objectives that directly relate to the learning objectives for your course. You can then use the reporting features of the software to aggregate student results in similar fashion, making the collection and presentation of assurance-of-learning data simple and easy.

Chapter Learning Objectives

Chapter 1: A Brief History of Risk and Return

To become a wise investor (maybe even one with too much money), you need to know:

1. How to calculate the return on an investment using different methods.
2. The historical returns on various important types of investments.
3. The historical risks on various important types of investments.
4. The relationship between risk and return.

Chapter 2: Buying and Selling Securities

Don't sell yourself short. Instead, learn about these key investment subjects:

1. The various types of securities brokers and brokerage accounts.
2. How to calculate initial and maintenance margin.
3. The workings of short sales.
4. The importance of investor objectives, constraints, and strategies.

Chapter 3: Overview of Security Types

Price quotes for all types of investments are easy to find, but what do they mean? Learn the answer for:

1. Various types of interest-bearing assets.
2. Equity securities.
3. Futures contracts.
4. Option contracts.

Chapter 4: Mutual Funds

You're probably going to be a mutual fund investor very soon, so you should definitely know the following:

1. The different types of mutual funds.
2. How mutual funds operate.
3. How to find information about how mutual funds have performed.
4. The workings of exchange-traded funds.

Chapter 5: The Stock Market

Take stock in yourself. Make sure you have a good understanding of:

1. The difference between primary and secondary stock markets.
2. The workings of the New York Stock Exchange.
3. How NASDAQ operates.
4. How to calculate index returns.

Chapter 6: Common Stock Valuation

Separate yourself from the commoners by having a good understanding of these security valuation methods:

1. The basic dividend discount model.
2. The two-stage dividend growth model.
3. The residual income model.
4. Price ratio analysis.

Chapter 7: Stock Price Behavior and Market Efficiency

You should strive to have your investment knowledge fully reflect:

1. The foundations of market efficiency.
2. The implications of the forms of market efficiency.
3. Market efficiency and the performance of professional money managers.
4. What stock market anomalies, bubbles, and crashes mean for market efficiency.

Chapter 8: Behavioral Finance and the Psychology of Investing

Psych yourself up and get to know something about:

1. Prospect theory.
2. The implications of investor overconfidence and misperceptions of randomness.
3. Sentiment-based risk and limits to arbitrage.
4. The wide array of technical analysis methods used by investors.

Chapter 9: Interest Rates

It will be worth your time to increase your rate of interest in these topics:

1. Money market prices and rates.
2. Rates and yields on fixed-income securities.
3. Treasury STRIPS and the term structure of interest rates.
4. Nominal versus real interest rates.

Chapter 10: Bond Prices and Yields

Singing "The Bonds Song" will help you learn:

1. How to calculate bond prices and yields.
2. The importance of yield to maturity.
3. Interest rate risk and Malkiel's theorems.
4. How to measure the impact of interest rate changes on bond prices.

Chapter 11: Diversification and Risky Asset Allocation
To get the most out of this chapter, spread your study time across:

1. How to calculate expected returns and variances for a security.
2. How to calculate expected returns and variances for a portfolio.
3. The importance of portfolio diversification.
4. The efficient frontier and importance of asset allocation.

Chapter 12: Return, Risk, and the Security Market Line
Studying some topics will yield an expected reward. For example, make sure you know:

1. The difference between expected and unexpected returns.
2. The difference between systematic risk and unsystematic risk.
3. The security market line and the capital asset pricing model.
4. The importance of beta.

Chapter 13: Performance Evaluation and Risk Management
To get a high evaluation of your performance, make sure you know:

1. How to calculate the three best-known portfolio evaluation measures.
2. The strengths and weaknesses of these three portfolio evaluation measures.
3. How to calculate a Sharpe-optimal portfolio.
4. How to calculate and interpret Value-at-Risk.

Chapter 14: Futures Contracts
You will derive many future benefits if you have a good understanding of:

1. The basics of futures markets and how to obtain price quotes for futures contracts.
2. The risks involved in futures market speculation.
3. How cash prices and futures prices are linked.
4. How futures contracts can be used to transfer price risk.

Chapter 15: Stock Options
Give yourself some in-the-money academic and professional options by understanding:

1. The basics of option contracts and how to obtain price quotes.
2. The difference between option payoffs and option profits.
3. The workings of some basic option trading strategies.
4. The logic behind the put-call parity condition.

Chapter 16: Option Valuation
Make sure the price is right by making sure that you have a good understanding of:

1. How to price options using the one-period and two-period binomial model.
2. How to price options using the Black-Scholes model.
3. How to hedge a stock portfolio using options.
4. The workings of employee stock options.

Chapter 17: Projecting Cash Flow and Earnings
Help yourself grow as a stock analyst by knowing:

1. How to obtain financial information about companies.
2. How to read basic financial statements.
3. How to use performance and price ratios.
4. How to use the percentage of sales method in financial forecasting.

Chapter 18: Corporate Bonds

Conform to your fixed-income knowledge covenants by learning:

1. The basic types of corporate bonds.
2. How callable bonds function.
3. The workings of convertible bonds.
4. The basics of bond ratings.

Chapter 19: Government Bonds

Before you loan money to Uncle Sam (and his relatives), you should know:

1. The basics of U.S. Treasury securities and how they are sold.
2. The workings of the STRIPS program and pricing Treasury bonds.
3. How federal agencies borrow money.
4. How municipalities borrow money.

Chapter 20 (*Web site only*): Mortgage-Backed Securities

Before you mortgage your future, you should know:

1. The workings of a fixed-rate mortgage.
2. Government's role in the secondary market for home mortgages.
3. The impact of mortgage prepayments.
4. How collateralized mortgage obligations are created and divided.

How Is This Book Relevant to the Student?

Fundamental changes in the investments universe drive our attention to relevance. The first major change is that individuals are being asked to make investment decisions for their own portfolios more often than ever before. There is, thankfully, a growing recognition that traditional "savings account" approaches to investing are decidedly inferior. At the same time, the use of employer-sponsored "investment accounts" has expanded enormously. The second major change is that the investments universe has exploded with an ever-increasing number of investment vehicles available to individual investors. As a result, investors must choose from an array of products, many of which are very complex, and they must strive to choose wisely.

Beyond this, students are more interested in subjects that affect them directly (as are we all). By taking the point of view of the student as an investor, we are better able to illustrate and emphasize the relevance and importance of the material.

Our approach is evident in the table of contents. Our first chapter is motivational; we have found that this material effectively "hooks" students and even motivates a semester-long discourse on risk and return. Our second chapter answers the student's next natural question: "How do I get started investing and how do I buy and sell securities?" The third chapter surveys the different types of investments available. After only three chapters, very early in the term, students have learned something about the risks and rewards from investing, how to get started investing, and what investment choices are available.

We close the first part of the text with a detailed examination of mutual funds. Without a doubt, mutual funds have become the most popular investment vehicles for individual investors. There are now more mutual funds than there are stocks on the NYSE! Given the size and enormous growth in the mutual fund industry, this material is important for investors. Even so, investments texts typically cover mutual funds in a cursory way, often banishing the material to a back chapter under the obscure (and obsolete) heading of "investment companies." Our early placement lets students quickly explore a topic they have heard a lot about and are typically interested in learning more about.

How Does This Book Allow Students to Apply the Investments Knowledge They Learn?

After studying this text, students will have the basic knowledge needed to move forward and actually act on what they have learned. We have developed two features to encourage students in making decisions as an investment manager. Learning to make good investment decisions comes with experience, while experience (regrettably) comes from making bad investment decisions. As much as possible, we press our students to get those bad decisions out of their systems before they start managing real money!

Not surprisingly, most students don't know how to get started in buying and selling securities. We have learned that providing some structure, especially with a portfolio simulation, greatly enhances the experience. Therefore, we have a series of *Get Real!* boxes. These boxes (at the end of each chapter) usually describe actual trades for students to explore. The intention is to show students how to gain real experience with the principles and instruments covered in the chapter. The second feature is a series of *Stock-Trak* exercises that take students through specific trading situations using *Stock-Trak Portfolio Simulations,* which can be found in the book's Web site, www.mhhe.com/jm5e.

Because we feel that portfolio simulations are so valuable, we have taken steps to assist instructors who, like us, plan to integrate portfolio simulations into their courses. Beyond the features mentioned above, we have organized the text so that the essential material needed before participating in a simulation is covered at the front of the book. Most notably, with every book, we have included a *free* subscription to *Stock-Trak Portfolio Simulations. Stock-Trak* is the leading provider of investment simulation services to the academic community; providing *Stock-Trak* free represents a significant cost savings to students. To our knowledge, ours is the first (and only) investments text to directly offer a full-featured online brokerage account simulation with the book at no incremental cost.

How Does This Book Maintain a Consistent, Unified Treatment?

In most investments texts, depth of treatment and presentation vary dramatically from instrument to instrument, which leaves the student without an overall framework for understanding the many types of investments. We stress early on that there are essentially only four basic types of financial investments—stocks, bonds, options, and futures. In parts 2 through 6, our simple goal is to take a closer look at each of these instruments. We take a unified approach to each by answering these basic questions:

1. What are the essential features of the instrument?
2. What are the possible rewards?
3. What are the risks?
4. What are the basic determinants of investment value?
5. For whom is the investment appropriate and under what circumstances?
6. How is the instrument bought and sold, and how does the market for the instrument operate?

By covering investment instruments in this way, we teach the students what questions to ask when looking at any potential investment.

Unlike other introductory investments texts, we devote several chapters beyond the basics to the different types of fixed-income investments. Students are often surprised to learn that the fixed-income markets are so much bigger than the equity markets and that money management opportunities are much more common in the fixed-income arena. Possibly the best way to see this is to look at recent CFA exams and materials and note the extensive coverage of fixed-income topics. We have placed these chapters toward the back of the text because we recognize not everyone will want to cover all this material. We have also separated the subject into several shorter chapters to make it more digestible for students and to allow instructors more control over what is covered.

Acknowledgments

We have received extensive feedback from reviewers at each step along the way, and we are very grateful to the following dedicated scholars and teachers for their time and expertise:

Aaron Phillips, California State University - Bakersfield
Allan O'Bryan, Rochester Community & Technical College
Allan Zebedee, San Diego State University
Ann Hackert, Idaho State University
Carl R. Chen, University of Dayton
Carla Rich, Pensacola Junior College
Caroline Fulmer, University of Alabama
Charles Appeadu, University of Wisconsin–Madison
Christos Giannikos, Bernard M. Baruch College
David Dubofsky, University of Louisville
David Louton, Bryant College
David Loy, Illinois State University
David Peterson, Florida State University
David Stewart, Winston-Salem State University
Deborah Murphy, University of Tennessee–Knoxville
Donald Wort, California State University–East Bay
Dwight Giles, Jefferson State Community College
Edward Miller, University of New Orleans
Felix Ayadi, Fayetteville State University
Gay B. Hatfield, University of Mississippi
Gioia Bales, Hofstra University
Howard Van Auken, Iowa State University
Howard W. Bohnen, St. Cloud State University
It-Keong Chew, University of Kentucky
Jeff Edwards, Portland Community College
Jeff Manzi, Ohio University
Jennifer Morton, Ivy Technical Community College of Indiana
Ji Chen, University of Colorado
Jim Tipton, Baylor University
Joe Brocato, Tarleton State University
Joe Walker, University of Alabama–Birmingham
Johnny Chan, University of Dayton
John Bockino, Suffolk County Community College
John Clinebell, University of Northern Colorado
John Ledgerwood, Bethune-Cookman College
John Paul Broussard, Rutgers, The State University of New Jersey
John Romps, St. Anselm College
John Wingender, Creighton University
Jorge Omar R. Brusa, University of Arkansas
Karen Bonding, University of Virginia
Kerri McMillan, Clemson University
Lalatendu Misra, University of Texas at San Antonio
Linda Martin, Arizona State University
Lisa Schwartz, Wingate University

M. J. Murray, Winona State University
Marc LeFebvre, Creighton University
Margo Kraft, Heidelberg College
Matthew Fung, Saint Peter's College
Michael C. Ehrhardt, University of Tennessee–Knoxville
Michael Gordinier, Washington University
Michael Nugent, SUNY–Stony Brook
Nolan Lickey, Utah Valley State College
Nozar Hashemzadeh, Radford University
Patricia Clarke, Simmons College
Paul Bolster, Northeastern University
Percy S. Poon, University of Nevada, Las Vegas
Randall Wade, Rogue Community College
Richard Lee Kitchen, Tallahassee Community College
Richard W. Taylor, Arkansas State University
Robert Friederichs, Alexandria Technical College
Robert Kozub, University of Wisconsin—Milwaukee
Ronald Christner, Loyola University–New Orleans
Samira Hussein, Johnson County Community College
Sammie Root, Texas State University—San Marcos
Samuel H. Penkar, University of Houston
Scott Barnhart, Clemson University
Scott Beyer, University of Wisconsin–Oshkosh
Stephen Chambers, Johnson County Community College
Steven Lifland, High Point University
Stuart Michelson, University of Central Florida
Thomas M. Krueger, University of Wisconsin–La Crosse
Tim Samolis, Pittsburgh Technical Institute
Vernon Stauble, San Bernardino Valley College
Ward Hooker, Orangeburg-Calhoun Technical College
William Compton, University of North Carolina–Wilmington
William Elliott, Oklahoma State University
William Lepley, University of Wisconsin–Green Bay
Yvette Harman, Miami University of Ohio
Zekeriah Eser, Eastern Kentucky University

We'd like to thank Kay Johnson, Penn State University–Erie, for developing the Test Bank, Scott Beyer, University of Wisconsin, Oshkosh, for his work on the Instructor's Manual, and Lynn Phillips Kugele, University of Mississippi, for creating the Student Narrated Power Point.

The following doctoral and MBA students did outstanding work on this text: Steve Hailey, Jared Jones MD, and Brett Carney; to them fell the unenviable task of technical proofreading and, in particular, careful checking of each calculation throughout the text and supplements.

We are deeply grateful to the select group of professionals who served as our development team on this edition: Michele Janicek, Executive Editor; Elizabeth Hughes, Development Editor; Ashley Smith, Marketing Manager; Bruce Gin, Project Manager; Matt Baldwin, Designer; Gina Hangos, Production Supervisor, and Brian Nacik, Media Project Manager.

Bradford D. Jordan

Thomas W. Miller, Jr.

Coverage

This book was designed and developed explicitly for a first course in investments taken by either finance majors or nonfinance majors. In terms of background or prerequisites, the book is nearly self-contained, but some familiarity with basic algebra and accounting is assumed. The organization of the text has been designed to give instructors the flexibility they need to teach a quarter-long or semester-long course.

To present an idea of the breadth of coverage in the fifth edition of *Fundamentals of Investments*, the following grid is presented chapter by chapter. This grid contains some of the most significant new features and a few selected chapter highlights. Of course, for each chapter, features like opening vignettes, *Work the Web, Spreadsheet Analyses, Get Real, Investment Updates*, and end-of-chapter material have been thoroughly reviewed and updated.

Chapters and Learning Outcomes	Selected Topics of Interest	Learning Outcome/Comment
PART ONE Introduction		
Chapter 1		
A Brief History of Risk and Return	Dollar returns and percentage returns.	Average returns differ by asset class.
	Return variability and calculating variance and standard deviation.	Return variability also differs by asset class.
	Arithmetic versus geometric returns.	Geometric average tells you what you actually earned per year, compounded annually. Arithmetic returns tells you what you earned in a typical year.
	The risk-return trade-off.	Historically, higher returns are associated with higher risk.
Chapter 2		
Buying and Selling Securities	Brokerage accounts and choosing a broker.	Discussion of the different types of brokers and accounts available to an individual investor.
	Expanded Material: Investment Fraud and the Security Investors Protection Corporation (SIPC).	"Insurance" for investment fraud does not exist in the United States. The SIPC restores funds to investors who have securities in the hands of bankrupt brokerage firms.
	Short sales.	Description of the process of short-selling stock.
	Investor objectives, constraints, and strategies.	Presentation of issues like risk and return, resource constraints, market timing, and asset allocation.
	New Section: Forming an Investment Portfolio.	An investment portfolio must account for an investor's risk tolerance, objectives, constraints, and strategies.

Chapters and Learning Outcomes	Selected Topics of Interest	Learning Outcome/Comment
Chapter 3		
Overview of Security Types	Classifying securities.	Interest-bearing, equity, and derivative securities.
	NASD's new TRACE system and transparency in the corporate bond market.	Up-to-date discussion of new developments in fixed income with respect to price, volume, and transactions reporting.
	Equity securities	Obtaining price quotes for equity securities.
	Derivative securities: Obtaining futures contract and option contract price quotes using the Internet.	Defining the types of derivative securities, interpreting their price quotes, and calculating gains and losses from these securities.
Chapter 4		
Mutual Funds	Investment companies and types of funds. *New Section:* The Advantages and Drawbacks of Mutual Fund Investing.	Covers concepts like open-end versus closed-end funds and net asset value.
	Mutual fund organization, creation, costs, and fees.	Presents types of expenses and fees like front-end loads, 12b-1 fees, management fees, and turnover.
	Short-term funds, long-term funds, and fund performance.	Discussion of money market mutual funds versus the variety of available stock and bond funds and how to find their performance.
	Special funds like closed-end funds, exchange-traded funds (*expanded material*), and hedge funds (*expanded material*). *New Material:* exchange traded notes (ETNs).	The closed-end fund discount mystery and a discussion of exchange-traded funds (ETFs) and exchange-traded notes (ETNs).
PART TWO Stock Markets		
Chapter 5		
The Stock Market	The primary stock market. *Expanded Material:* Seasoned equity offerings (SEOs).	The workings of an initial public offering (IPO), a seasoned equity offering (SEO), the role of investment bankers, the role of the Securities and Exchange Commission (SEC).
	The secondary stock market. *New Material:* The current structure of the NYSE and NASDAQ.	The role of dealers and brokers, the operation of the New York Stock Exchange (NYSE), NASDAQ market operations.
	Stock indexes, including the Dow Jones Industrial Average (DJIA) and the Standard & Poor's 500 Index (S&P 500).	The difference between price-weighted indexes and value-weighted indexes.
Chapter 6		
Common Stock Valuation	The basic dividend discount model (DDM) and several of its variants. *New Material:* How we get the formula for constant perpetual growth. *New Material:* The two-stage dividend growth model.	Valuation using constant and nonconstant growth.
	Expanded Section: Residual Income Model (RIM).	Valuation of non-dividend-paying stocks.
	Price ratio analysis.	Valuation using price-earnings, price-cash flow.
	New Material: Updated McGraw-Hill valuation detailed example.	Using *Value Line* information to value a stock using methods presented earlier in the chapter.

Chapters and Learning Outcomes	Selected Topics of Interest	Learning Outcome/Comment
Chapter 7		
Stock Price Behavior and Market Efficiency	Forms of market efficiency.	The effects of information on stock prices with respect to market efficiency.
	New Material: Event studies using actual events surrounding Advanced Medical Optics.	Explains how new information gets into stock prices and how researchers measure it.
	Informed traders, insider trading, and illegal insider trading.	*New Example:* Martha Stewart and ImClone.
	Expanded Material: Market efficiency and the performance of professional money managers.	Discuss the performance of professional money managers versus static benchmarks.
	Expanded Material: Anomalies.	Presentation of the day-of-the-week effect, the amazing January effect, the turn-of-the-year effect, and the turn-of-the-month effect.
	Bubbles and crashes.	Shows the extent of famous events like the crash of 1929, the crash of October 1987, the Asian market crash, and the "dot-com" bubble and crash.
Chapter 8		
Behavioral Finance and the Psychology of Investing	Introduction to behavioral finance.	The influence of reasoning errors on investor decisions.
	Prospect theory.	How investors tend to behave differently when faced with prospective gains and losses.
	Overconfidence, misperceiving randomness, and overreacting to chance events.	Examines the consequences of these serious errors in judgment.
	Sentiment-based risk and limits to arbitrage.	*New Examples:* 3Com/Palm mispricing, the Royal Dutch/Shell Price Ratio.
	Expanded Material: Technical analysis.	*New Material:* Elliott Waves, expanded discussions of charting, moving averages, MACD, money flow, and Fibonacci numbers.
PART THREE Interest Rates and Bond Valuation		
Chapter 9		
Interest Rates	Interest rate history and a quick review of the time value of money.	A graphical presentation of the long-term history of interest rates.
	Money market rates and their prices.	Important money market concepts including pricing U.S. Treasury bills, bank discount yields versus bond equivalent yields, annual percentage rates, and effective annual returns.
	Rates and yields on fixed-income securities.	The Treasury yield curve, the term structure of interest rates, and Treasury STRIPS.
	Nominal versus real interest rates.	The Fisher hypothesis.
	Determinants of nominal interest rates.	Problems with traditional theories and modern term structure theory.
Chapter 10		
Bond Prices and Yields	Straight bond prices and yield to maturity (YTM).	Calculate straight bond prices, calculate yield to maturity.
	The concept of duration and bond risk measures based on duration.	Calculate and interpret a bond's duration. The dollar value of an "01," yield value of a 32nd.
	Expanded Material: Dedicated portfolios and reinvestment risk.	Learn how to create a dedicated portfolio and show its exposure to reinvestment risk.
	Immunization.	Minimize the uncertainty concerning the value of a bond portfolio at its target date.

Chapters and Learning Outcomes	Selected Topics of Interest	Learning Outcome/Comment
PART FOUR Portfolio Management		
Chapter 11		
Diversification and Risky Asset Allocation	Expected returns and variances.	Calculating expected returns and variances using equal and unequal probabilities.
	Portfolios and the effect of diversification on portfolio risk.	Compute portfolio weights, expected returns, variances, and why diversification works.
	The importance of asset allocation.	The effect of correlation on the risk-return trade-off.
	The Markowitz efficient frontier and illustrating the importance of asset allocation using three securities.	Compute risk-return combinations using various portfolio weights for three assets.
Chapter 12		
Return, Risk, and the Security Market Line	Diversification, systematic and unsystematic risk.	Total risk is comprised of unsystematic and systematic risk and only unsystematic risk can be reduced through diversification.
	Measuring systematic risk with beta.	The average beta is 1.00. Assets with a beta greater than 1.00 have more than average systematic risk.
	The security market line and the reward-to-risk ratio.	The security market line describes how the market rewards risk. All assets will have the same reward-to-risk ratio in competitive financial markets.
	The capital asset pricing model (CAPM).	Expected return depends on the amount and reward for bearing systematic risk as well as the pure time value of money.
	Extending CAPM.	One of the most important extensions of the CAPM is the Fama-French three-factor model.
Chapter 13		
Performance Evaluation and Risk Management	Performance evaluation measures.	Calculate and interpret the Sharpe ratio, the Treynor ratio, and Jensen's alpha.
	Sharpe-optimal portfolios.	The portfolio with the highest possible Sharpe ratio given the assets comprising the portfolio is Sharpe optimal.
	Value-at-Risk (VaR)	VaR is the evaluation of the probability of a significant loss.
	Example showing how to calculate a Sharpe-optimal portfolio.	Combines the concepts of a Sharpe ratio, a Sharpe-optimal portfolio, and VaR.
PART FIVE Futures and Options		
Chapter 14		
Futures Contracts	The basics of futures contracts and using them to hedge price risk. *New Material:* Hedging an inventory using futures markets.	Futures quotes from the Internet and financial press, short and long hedging, futures accounts.
	Spot-futures parity.	Basis, cash markets, and cash-futures arbitrage.
	Stock index futures. *Expanded Example:* Changing the beta of a stock portfolio using stock index futures.	Index arbitrage, speculating with stock index futures, and hedging stock market risk with stock index futures.
	Hedging interest rate risk with futures.	Shows how to use portfolio duration when deciding how many futures contracts to use to hedge a bond portfolio.

Chapters and Learning Outcomes	Selected Topics of Interest	Learning Outcome/Comment
Chapter 15		
Stock Options	Option basics and option price quotes.	The difference between call and put options, European and American options, online option price quotes, option chains.
	Option payoffs and profits.	Diagram long and short option payoffs and profits for calls and puts.
	Option strategies. *New Material:* Using options to manage risk. *Enhanced Material:* Spreads and combinations.	Protective puts, covered calls, straddles.
	Option intrinsic value.	Know how to calculate this important aspect of option prices.
	Put-call parity.	Shows how a call option price equals a put option price, the price of an underlying share of stock, and appropriate borrowing.
PART SIX Topics in Investments		
Chapter 16		
Option Valuation	*New Material:* The one-period and two-period binomial option pricing model.	How to compute option prices using this option pricing model—by hand and by using an online option calculator.
	New Material: The Black-Scholes option pricing model.	How to compute option prices using this famous option pricing model—by hand and by using an online option calculator.
	Measuring the impact of changes in option inputs.	Computing call and put option deltas.
	Hedging stock with stock options.	Using option deltas to decide how many option contracts are needed to protect a stock's price from feared declines in value.
	Employee stock options (ESOs) and their valuation. *Enhanced Material:* Black-Scholes-Merton option pricing model.	Features of ESOs, repricing ESOs, and ESO valuation.
Chapter 17		
Projecting Cash Flow and Earnings	The basics of financial statements.	Income statement, balance sheet, cash flow statement, performance and price ratios.
	Financial statement forecasting using the percentage of sales approach.	Preparing pro forma income statements and balance sheets to examine the potential amount of external financing needed.
	Updated Material: A detailed case study valuing Starbucks Corporation.	Using actual financial data to prepare pro forma income statements and balance sheets using different sales growth scenarios.
Chapter 18		
Corporate Bonds	Corporate bond basics and types of corporate bonds.	Become familiarized with the basics of the various types of corporate bonds.
	Bond indentures and callable bonds. *Enhanced Material:* Make-whole call provisions.	Bond seniority provisions, call provisions, and make-whole call provisions.
	Corporate bond credit ratings. *Enhanced Material:* Bond yield spreads.	Assessing the credit quality of the bond issue.

Chapters and Learning Outcomes	Selected Topics of Interest	Learning Outcome/Comment
Chapter 19		
Government Bonds	Government bonds basics emphasizing U.S. government debt.	Details of U.S. Treasury bills, notes, bonds, and STRIPS.
	U.S. savings bonds.	Covers important changes to these investment vehicles.
	Municipal bonds and their credit ratings.	Reviews important features of bonds issued by municipal governments.
Chapter 20 (*Web site only*)		
Mortgage-Backed Securities	Fixed-rate mortgages and prepayment.	Presents home mortgage principal and interest calculations.
	Secondary mortgage markets. *New Material:* Reverse mortgages.	The function of GNMA and its clones, the PSA mortgage prepayment model.
	Collateralized mortgage obligations, CMOs.	Describing how cash flows from mortgage pools are carved up and distributed to investors.

Features

Pedagogical Features

From your feedback, we have included many pedagogical features in this text that will be valuable learning tools for your students. This walkthrough highlights some of the most important elements.

Chapter Openers

These one-paragraph introductions for each chapter present scenarios and common misconceptions that may surprise you. An explanation is more fully developed in the chapter.

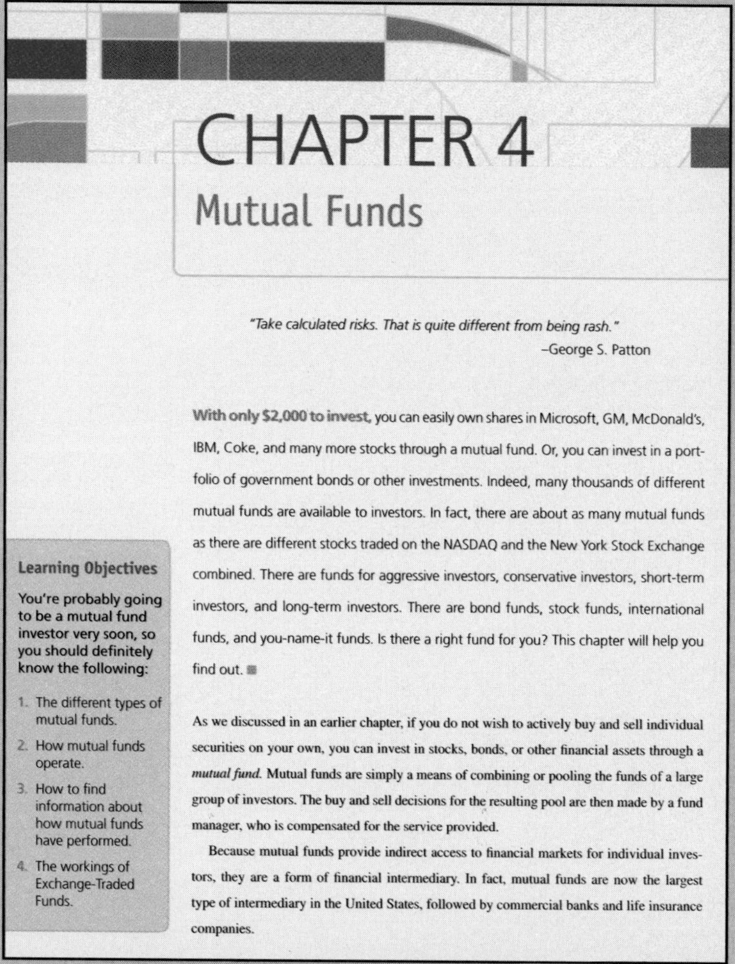

CHAPTER 4
Mutual Funds

"Take calculated risks. That is quite different from being rash."
–George S. Patton

With only $2,000 to invest, you can easily own shares in Microsoft, GM, McDonald's, IBM, Coke, and many more stocks through a mutual fund. Or, you can invest in a portfolio of government bonds or other investments. Indeed, many thousands of different mutual funds are available to investors. In fact, there are about as many mutual funds as there are different stocks traded on the NASDAQ and the New York Stock Exchange combined. There are funds for aggressive investors, conservative investors, short-term investors, and long-term investors. There are bond funds, stock funds, international funds, and you-name-it funds. Is there a right fund for you? This chapter will help you find out. ■

Learning Objectives

You're probably going to be a mutual fund investor very soon, so you should definitely know the following:

1. The different types of mutual funds.
2. How mutual funds operate.
3. How to find information about how mutual funds have performed.
4. The workings of Exchange-Traded Funds.

As we discussed in an earlier chapter, if you do not wish to actively buy and sell individual securities on your own, you can invest in stocks, bonds, or other financial assets through a *mutual fund.* Mutual funds are simply a means of combining or pooling the funds of a large group of investors. The buy and sell decisions for the resulting pool are then made by a fund manager, who is compensated for the service provided.

Because mutual funds provide indirect access to financial markets for individual investors, they are a form of financial intermediary. In fact, mutual funds are now the largest type of intermediary in the United States, followed by commercial banks and life insurance companies.

Check This!

Every major section in each chapter ends with questions for review. This feature helps students test their understanding of the material before moving on to the next section.

CHECK THIS

4.4a What is the difference between a load fund and a no-load fund?

4.4b What are 12b-1 fees?

Key Terms

Key terms are indicated in bold and defined in the margin. The running glossary in the margin helps students quickly review the basic terminology for the chapter.

MONEY MARKET MUTUAL FUNDS

money market mutual fund
A mutual fund specializing in money market instruments.

As the name suggests, **money market mutual funds**, or MMMFs, specialize in money market instruments. As we describe elsewhere, these are short-term debt obligations issued by governments and corporations. Money market funds were introduced in the early 1970s and have grown tremendously. At the end of 2006, about 850 money market funds managed almost $2.3 trillion in assets. All money market funds are open-end funds.

Web Addresses

Web sites are called out in the margins, along with a notation of how they relate to the chapter material.

WWW
Visit
www.mfea.com
for info on thousands of funds, including MMMFs.

MONEY MARKET FUND ACCOUNTING A unique feature of money market funds is that their net asset values are always $1 per share. This is purely an accounting gimmick, however. A money market fund simply sets the number of shares equal to the fund's assets. In other words, if the fund has $100 million in assets, then it has 100 million shares. As the fund earns interest on its investments, the fund owners are simply given more shares.

The reason money market mutual funds always maintain a $1 net asset value is to make them resemble bank accounts. As long as a money market fund invests in very safe,

Investment Updates

These boxed readings, reprinted from various business press sources, provide additional real-world events and examples to illustrate the material in the chapter. Some articles from the past two years highlight very recent events, and others present events of more historical significance.

INVESTMENT UPDATES

GET A FRESH ANGLE ON YOUR FINANCES

Not sure whether you're saving enough or whether you have the right investment mix? To get a better handle on your portfolio, it sometimes helps to look at your finances from another angle.

1 How Much Do You Need in Conservative Investments to Feel Safe?

Investment advisers and Wall Street firms constantly exhort investors to consider their risk tolerance. For instance, we are often prodded to fill out those irritating questionnaires where we are asked whether our goal is "growth" or "capital preservation."

The answer, of course, is that we want both. Even retirees need growth from their portfolios. Even freshly minted college graduates hanker after some stability.

My advice: Forget risk tolerance. Instead, divide your high-quality corporate bonds, municipals, money-market funds, and savings accounts. But don't stop there.

I would expand the list to include Social Security retirement benefits, pension income, mortgage debt, and any other loans you have. After all, you regularly receive income from Social Security and your pension, just as you would from a bond. Meanwhile, your debts involve making regular payments to other folks.

All these dealings affect your sense of financial security, and they should influence how you structure your portfolio. For instance, if you expect a traditional company pension when you retire, you effectively have a huge position in bonds and thus you might want to load up on stocks in your investment portfolio.

On the other hand, if you have a heap of debts, your financial position is much more precarious and you may want to take less risk with your investments. On that

Work the Web

Various screenshots appear throughout the text. These exercises illustrate how to access specific features of selected Web sites in order to expand students' knowledge of current investment topics.

WORK THE WEB

Here is a stock quote and an option chain for Starbucks Corp. (SBUX) from Yahoo! Finance (finance.yahoo.com).

STARBUCKS CP (NasdaqGS:SBUX) Edit

Last Trade:	**26.45**	Day's Range:	26.43 - 26.75
Trade Time:	12:05PM ET	52wk Range:	25.22 - 40.01
Change:	↓ 0.39 (1.45%)	Volume:	3,054,091
Prev Close:	26.84	Avg Vol (3m):	12,407,200
Open:	26.68	Market Cap:	19.74B
Bid:	26.45 x 15400	P/E (ttm):	32.53
Ask:	26.46 x 12600	EPS (ttm):	0.81
1y Target Est:	34.82	Div & Yield:	N/A (N/A)

New! Try our new Charts in Beta

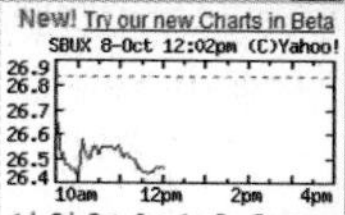

1d 5d 3m 6m 1y 2y 5y max

Market Updates Hourly from Fox Business Now. Watch.

NEW Add Quotes to Your Web Site   Add SBUX to Portfolio   Set Alert   Download Data

Quotes delayed, except where indicated otherwise. For consolidated real-time quotes (including real-time pre/post market data), sign up for a free trial of Real-time Quotes.

View By Expiration: Oct 07 | Nov 07 | Jan 08 | Apr 08 | Jan 09 | Jan 10

CALL OPTIONS Expire at close Fri, Oct 19, 2007

Strike	Symbol	Last	Chg	Bid	Ask	Vol	Open Int
15.00	SQXJC.X	12.30	0.00	11.40	11.60	50	73
17.50	SQXJW.X	9.20	0.00	8.90	9.10	50	87
22.50	SQXJX.X	4.10	↓ 0.30	3.90	4.10	1	719
25.00	SQXJE.X	1.50	↓ 0.45	1.55	1.60	78	8,642
27.50	SQXJY.X	0.15	↓ 0.04	0.10	0.15	44	32,043
30.00	SQXJF.X	0.05	0.00	N/A	0.05	2	22,625
32.50	SQXJZ.X	0.05	0.00	N/A	0.05	9	12,699
35.00	SQXJG.X	0.02	0.00	N/A	0.05	3	7,180
37.50	SQXJU.X	0.01	0.00	N/A	0.05	4	2,133
40.00	SQXJH.X	0.05	0.00	N/A	0.05	100	734
42.50	SQXJV.X	0.05	0.00	N/A	0.05	0	273

PUT OPTIONS Expire at close Fri, Oct 19, 2007

Strike	Symbol	Last	Chg	Bid	Ask	Vol	Open Int
17.50	SQXVW.X	0.05	0.00	N/A	0.05	0	30
22.50	SQXVX.X	0.03	0.00	N/A	0.05	5	3,790
25.00	SQXVE.X	0.10	0.00	0.05	0.10	42	23,717
27.50	SQXVY.X	1.10	↑ 0.30	1.10	1.15	46	31,422
30.00	SQXVF.X	3.50	↑ 0.30	3.50	3.60	10	6,854
32.50	SQXVZ.X	5.80	0.00	6.00	6.10	10	3,200
35.00	SQXVG.X	8.35	0.00	8.40	8.60	31	100

Highlighted options are in-the-money.

Numbered Examples

Example boxes are integrated throughout the chapters to reinforce the content and demonstrate to students how to apply what they've learned. Each example displays an intuitive or mathematical application in a step-by-step format. There is enough detail in the explanations so that the student doesn't have to look elsewhere for additional information.

EXAMPLE 10.1 **Calculating Straight Bond Prices**

Suppose a bond has 20 years to maturity and a coupon rate of 8 percent. The bond's yield to maturity is 7 percent. What's the price?

In this case, the coupon rate is 8 percent and the face value is $1,000, so the annual coupon is $80. The bond's price is calculated as follows:

1. Present value of semiannual coupons:

$$\frac{\$80}{.07}\left[1 - \frac{1}{(1.035)^{40}}\right] = \$854.20289$$

2. Present value of $1,000 principal:

$$\frac{\$1,000}{(1.035)^{40}} = \$252.57247$$

The bond's price is the sum of coupon and principal present values:

$$\text{Bond price} = \$854.20 + \$252.57 = \$1,106.77$$

This bond sells for $1,106.77.

Straight bond prices may be calculated using a built-in spreadsheet function. An example of how to use an Excel™ spreadsheet to calculate a bond price is shown in the nearby *Spreadsheet Analysis* box.

Spreadsheet Analysis

Self-contained spreadsheet examples show students how to set up spreadsheets to solve problems—a vital part of every business student's education.

SPREADSHEET ANALYSIS

	A–H
1	
2	**Calculating the Price of a Coupon Bond**
3	
4	A Treasury bond traded on March 30, 2008 matures in 20 years on March 30, 2028.
5	Assuming an 8 percent coupon rate and a 7 percent yield to maturity, what is the
6	price of this bond?
7	Hint: Use the Excel function PRICE.
8	
9	$110.6775 = PRICE("3/30/2008","3/30/2028",0.08,0.07,100,2,3)
10	
11	For a bond with $1,000 face value, multiply the price by 10 to get $1,106.78.
12	
13	This function uses the following arguments:
14	
15	=PRICE("Now","Maturity", Coupon,Yield,100,2,3)
16	
17	The 100 indicates redemption value as a percent of face value.
18	The 2 indicates semi-annual coupons.
19	The 3 specifies an actual day count with 365 days per year.
20	
21	

Numbered Equations

Key equations are highlighted and numbered sequentially. For easy reference, a new appendix at the end of the book lists these key equations by chapter.

$$\text{American put option price} \geq \text{MAX}[K - S, 0] \quad (15.4)$$

EUROPEAN CALLS Because European options cannot be exercised before expiration, we cannot use the arbitrage strategies that we used to set lower bounds for American options. We must use a different approach (which can be found in many textbooks that focus on options). It turns out that the lower bound for a European call option is greater than its intrinsic value.

$$\text{European call option price} \geq \text{MAX}[S - K/(1 + r)^T, 0] \quad (15.5)$$

EUROPEAN PUTS The lower bound for a European put option price is less than its intrinsic value. In fact, in-the-money European puts will frequently sell for less than their intrinsic value. How much less? Using an arbitrage strategy that accounts for the fact that European put options cannot be exercised before expiration, the lower bound for a European put option is:

$$\text{European put option price} \geq \text{MAX}[K/(1 + r)^T - S, 0] \quad (15.6)$$

To give you some intuition, let's look at an extreme case. Suppose the stock price falls to zero before expiration and there is absolutely no chance that the stock price will recover

Figures and Tables

This text makes extensive use of real data and presents them in various figures and tables. Explanations in the narrative, examples, and end-of-chapter problems refer to many of these exhibits.

FIGURE 1.9 The Normal Distribution: Illustrated Returns Based on the Historical Return and Standard Deviation for a Portfolio of Large-Company Common Stocks

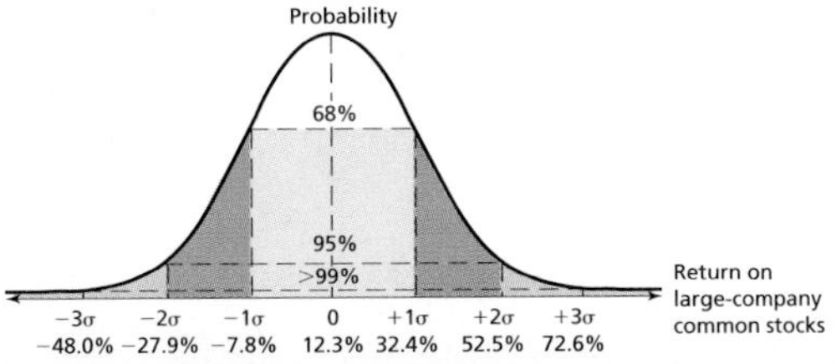

Summary and Conclusions

Each chapter ends with a summary that highlights the important points of the chapter. This provides a handy checklist for students when they review the chapter.

3.6 Summary and Conclusions

In this chapter we examine the basic types of financial assets. We discuss three broad classes: interest-bearing assets, equity securities, and derivative assets—futures and options. For each of the broad classes, we ask three questions. First, what is its basic nature and what are its distinguishing characteristics? Second, what are the potential gains and losses from owning it? Third, how are its prices quoted online and in the financial press? We cover many aspects of these investments. We provide a brief description of these investments broken down by the chapter's important concepts.

1. Various types of interest-bearing assets.

A. Each of these major groups can be further subdivided. Interest-bearing assets include money market instruments and fixed-income securities.

B. Money market instruments generally have the following two properties: (1) they are essentially IOUs sold by large corporations or governments to borrow money; and (2) they mature in less than one year from the time they are sold, meaning that the loan must be repaid within one year.

Get Real!

For instructors looking to give their students a taste of what it means to be an investment manager, this feature (at the end of each chapter) acts as a first step by explaining to students how to apply the material they just learned. The *Get Real* boxes encourage students—whether for practice in a trading simulation, or with real money—to make investment decisions, and they also give some helpful tips to keep in mind.

GET REAL

This chapter added to your understanding of put and call options by covering the rights, obligations, and potential gains and losses involved in trading options. How should you put this information to work? You need to buy and sell options to experience the gains and losses that options can provide. So, with a simulated brokerage account (such as Stock-Trak), you should first execute each of the basic option transactions: buy a call, sell a call, buy a put, and sell a put.

For help getting started, you can find an enormous amount of information about options on the Internet. Useful places to start are the options exchanges: Chicago Board Options Exchange (www.cboe.com), American Stock Exchange (www.amex.com), Pacific Stock Exchange (www.pacificex.com), and Philadelphia Stock Exchange (www.phlx.com). Excellent Web sites devoted to options education are the Options Industry Council (www.optionscentral.com) and the Options Clearing Corporation (www.optionsclearing.com). You might also look at the options section of Trading Markets (www.tradingmarkets.com) or Investor Links (www.investorlinks.com).

For information on option trading strategies, try entering the strategy name into an Internet search engine. For example, enter the search phrases "covered calls" or "protective puts" for online information about those strategies. For more general information, try the search phrase "options trading strategies" to find sites like Commodity World (www.commodityworld.com). For a sales pitch on writing covered calls, check out Write Call (www.writecall.com).

If you're having trouble understanding options ticker symbols, don't feel alone because almost everyone has trouble at first. For help on the net, try the search phrases "option symbols" or "options symbols" to find sites like www.optionscentral.com. Of course, the options exchanges listed above also provide complete information on the option ticker symbols they use.

Chapter Review Problems and Self-Test

Students are provided with one to three practice problems per chapter with worked-out solutions to test their abilities in solving key problems related to the content of the chapter.

Chapter Review Problems and Self-Test

1. **Call Option Payoffs** You purchase 25 call option contracts on Blue Ox stock. The strike price is $22, and the premium is $1. If the stock is selling for $24 per share at expiration, what are your call options worth? What is your net profit? What if the stock were selling for $23? $22?
2. **Stock versus Options** Stock in Bunyan Brewery is currently priced at $20 per share. A call option with a $20 strike and 60 days to maturity is quoted at $2. Compare the percentage gains and losses from a $2,000 investment in the stock versus the option in 60 days for stock prices of $26, $20, and $18.
3. **Put-Call Parity** A call option sells for $8. It has a strike price of $80 and six months until expiration. If the underlying stock sells for $60 per share, what is the price of a put option with an $80 strike price and six months until expiration? The risk-free interest rate is 6 percent per year.

Answers to Self-Test Problems

1. Blue Ox stock is selling for $24. You own 25 contracts, each of which gives you the right to buy 100 shares at $22. Your options are thus worth $2 per share on 2,500 shares, or $5,000. The option premium was $1, so you paid $100 per contract, or $2,500 total. Your net profit is $2,500. If the stock is selling for $23, your options are worth $2,500, so your net profit is exactly zero. If the stock is selling for $22, your options are worthless, and you lose the entire $2,500 you paid.
2. Bunyan stock costs $20 per share, so if you invest $2,000, you'll get 100 shares. The option premium is $2, so an option contract costs $200. If you invest $2,000, you'll get $2,000/$200 = 10 contracts. If the stock is selling for $26 in 60 days, your profit on the stock is $6 per share, or $600 total. The percentage gain is $600/$2,000 = 30%.

Test Your IQ

An average of 15 multiple-choice questions are included for each chapter, many of which are taken from past CFA exams. This text is unique in that it is the only text that presents CFA questions in multiple-choice format—which is how they appear on the actual exam. Answers to these questions appear in Appendix A.

Test Your Investment Quotient

IQ

CFA® PROBLEMS

For the remaining questions and problems, the circled numbers in the margin refer to the corresponding learning objective in this chapter.

(2) 1. **Balance Sheet Assets** White Company assets as of December 31, 2007:

Cash and cash equivalents	$ 150
Operating assets	$1,190
Property, plant, and equipment	$1,460
Total assets	$2,800

White Co. experienced the following events in 2008:

Old equipment that cost $120 and that was fully depreciated was scrapped

Depreciation expense was $125

Cash payments for new equipment were $200

Based on the information above, what was White Co.'s net amount of property, plant, and equipment at the end of 2008?

a. $1,415
b. $1,535
c. $1,655
d. $1,660

(2) 2. **Cash Flow** Cash flow per share is calculated as

a. Net cash flow/Shares outstanding.
b. Operating cash flow/Shares outstanding.
c. Investing cash flow/Shares outstanding.
d. Financing cash flow/Shares outstanding.

Concept Questions

At the end of every chapter are 10 to 15 concept questions that further reinforce key concepts found throughout the chapter.

Concept Questions

(1) 1. **Money Market Instruments** What are the distinguishing features of a money market instrument?

(2) 2. **Preferred Stock** Why is preferred stock "preferred"?

(2) 3. ***WSJ* Stock Quotes** What is the PE ratio reported for stocks in *The Wall Street Journal*? In particular, how is it computed?

(1) 4. **Yields** The current yield on a bond is the coupon rate divided by the price. Thus, it is very similar to what number reported for common and preferred stocks?

Questions and Problems

A variety of problems (average of 20 per chapter) are included in each chapter to test students' understanding of the conceptual and mathematical elements. Each problem is labeled with the subject and the level—core or intermediate. Selected answers appear in Appendix B, and complete solutions are included in the Instructor Web site.

Questions and Problems

Core Questions

(2) 1. **Stock Quotations** You found the following stock quote for DRK Enterprises, Inc., at your favorite Web site. You also find that the stock paid an annual dividend of $0.86, which resulted in a dividend yield of 1.30 percent. What was the closing price for this stock yesterday? How many round lots of stock were traded yesterday?

		DAILY				YTD	52 WEEK		
Company	Symbol	Vol	Close	Chg	%Chg	%Chg	High	Low	%Chg
DRK Enterprises	DRK	18,649,130	??	0.26	−0.39%	8.73%	78.19	51.74	27.4%

S&P Problems

Now included in the end-of-chapter material are problems directly incorporating the Educational Version of Market Insight, a service based on Standard & Poor's renowned Compustat database. These problems provide an easy method of including current real-world data in the course.

S&P Problems

STANDARD &POOR'S

www.mhhe.com/edumarketinsight

1. **Industry Comparison** On the Market Insight Home Page, follow the "Industry" link to go to the industry home page. The drop down menu allows you to select different industries. Answer the following questions for these industries: Air Freight & Logistics, Apparel Retail, Department Stores, Electric Utilities, Home Improvement Retail, Investment Banking & Brokerage, and Regional Banks.

a. How many companies are in each industry?
b. What are the total sales in each industry?
c. Do the industries with the largest total sales have the most companies in the industry? What does this tell you about competition in the various industries?

Chapter 1 ■ A Brief History of Risk and Return 35

What's on the Web?

These end-of-chapter activities show students how to use and learn from the vast amount of financial resources available on the Internet.

What's on the Web?

1. **Ticker Symbols** Go to finance.yahoo.com and look up the ticker symbols for the following companies: 3M Company, International Business Machines, Dell Computer, Advanced Micro Devices, American Standard Company, and Bed, Bath & Beyond.
2. **Average Return and Standard Deviation** Go to finance.yahoo.com and enter the ticker symbol for your favorite stock. Now, look for the historical prices and find the monthly closing stock price for the last six years. Calculate the annual arithmetic average return, the standard deviation, and the geometric return for this period.

Stock-Trak Exercises

STOCK | TRAK
GLOBAL PORTFOLIO SIMULATIONS

To access the Stock-Trak Exercise for this chapter, please visit the book Web site at www.mhhe.com/jm5e and choose the corresponding chapter.

Stock-Trak Exercises

Unique to this text! This text is the only book that incorporates Stock-Trak Portfolio Simulations® exercises. Stock-Trak is one of the most successful trading simulations with over 30,000 college students having trading accounts each semester (see Supplements for more information). Go to the next level in teaching your students about investments management by encouraging your students to use this product. Chapters with Stock-Trak Exercises will have the logo and the URL for the book's Web site. The actual exercise and questions related to the chapter will be presented in both the Student and Instructor portions of the Web site. Instructors and Students must be registered for Stock-Trak in order to make trades (see the Supplement Section of the Preface or the insert card for more information).

Resources

Teaching and Learning Supplements

We have developed a number of supplements for both teaching and learning to accompany this text. Each product has been significantly revised for the fifth edition.

For Instructors

Instructor's Resource CD-ROM

ISBN 0-07-3363804

The Instructor's Resource CD-ROM contains the following assets:

PowerPoint Presentation, *prepared by Thomas W. Miller Jr.*, Saint Louis University

This product, created by one of the authors, contains over 300 slides with lecture outlines, examples, and images and tables from the text.

Instructor's Manual, *prepared by Scott Beyer*, University of Wisconsin, Oshkosh

Developed to clearly outline the chapter material as well as provide extra teaching support, the first section of the Instructor's Manual includes an annotated outline of each chapter with suggested Web sites, references to PowerPoint slides, teaching tips, additional examples, and current events references.

Solutions Manual, *Prepared by Joe Smolira,* Belmont University

The Solutions Manual contains the complete worked-out solutions for the end-of-chapter questions and problems.

Test Bank, *prepared by Kay Johnson,* Penn State University–Erie

With almost 1,500 questions, this Test Bank, in Microsoft Word, provides a variety of question formats (true-false, multiple choice, fill-in-the-blank, and problems) and levels of difficulty to meet any instructor's testing needs.

Computerized Test Bank (Windows) This computerized version of the Test Bank utilizes McGraw-Hill's EZ Test testing software to quickly create customized exams. This user-friendly program allows instructors to sort questions by format; edit existing questions or add new ones; and scramble questions for multiple versions of the same test.

Videos ISBN 0-07-3363790 (DVD format)

The McGraw-Hill/Irwin series of finance videos are 10-minute case studies on topics such as Financial Markets, Stocks, Bonds, Portfolio Management, Derivatives, and Going Public.

Digital Solutions

Online Learning Center (OLC):

Online Support at www.mhhe.com/jm5e

The Online Learning Center (OLC) contains FREE access to additional Web-based study and teaching aids created for this text, such as:

Student Support

New! Student-Narrated PowerPoints *created by Lynn Phillips Kugele,* The University of Mississippi.

Students all learn differently and these chapter PowerPoints were created with that rationale in mind. The interactive presentations provide detailed examples demonstrating how to solve key problems from the text. The slides are accompanied by an audio narration. They can be purchased as part of the premium content package available for $10 and then viewed online or uploaded onto an iPod.

Excel Templates

Corresponding to most end-of-chapter problems, each template allows the student to work through the problem using Excel, reinforcing each concept. Each end-of-chapter problem with a template is indicated by an Excel icon in the margin beside it.

Self-Study Chapter Quizzes

Quizzes consist of 10–15 multiple-choice questions on various chapter topics. They reveal a score instantly and provide feedback to help students study.

Other Features

Be sure to check out the other helpful features found on the OLC including key-term flashcards, helpful Web links, and more!

Teaching Support

Along with having access to all of the same material your students can view on the book's OLC, you also have password-protected access to the Instructor's Manual, Solutions to end-of-chapter problems, Instructor's PowerPoint, Excel Template Solutions, Video clips, and Video projects and questions.

OLCs can be delivered in multiple ways—through the textbook Web site (www.mhhe.com/jm5e), through PageOut (see Packages below), or within a course management system like Blackboard, WebCT, TopClass, or eCollege. Ask your campus representative for more details.

PageOut at www.pageout.net

Free to adopters, this Web page generation software is designed to help you create your own course Web site, without all of the hassle. In just a few minutes, even the most novice computer user can have a functioning course Web site.

Simply type your material into the template provided and PageOut instantly converts it to HTML. Next, choose your favorite of three easy-to-navigate designs and your class Web home page is created, complete with online syllabus, lecture notes, and bookmarks. You can even include a separate instructor page and an assignment page.

PageOut offers enhanced point-and-click features, including a Syllabus Page that applies a real-world link to original text material, an automatic grade book, and a discussion board where you and your students can exchange questions and post announcements. Ask your campus representative to show you a demo.

Additional Resources Packaged with Your New Text

Stock-Trak Portfolio Simulation

Give your students investment management experience! McGraw-Hill/Irwin has partnered with *Stock-Trak* and is providing a **free** subscription to the *Stock-Trak Portfolio Simulation* for one semester with the purchase of every new copy of *Fundamentals of Investments: Valuation and Management, Fifth Edition* by Jordan and Miller. *Stock-Trak* gives students $500,000 and allows them to trade stocks, options, futures, bonds, mutual funds, and international stocks—no other simulation offers all these types of securities! More than 600 professors have used this service, and around 30,000 college students each semester participate. All trades are done on the Web at www.stocktrak.com/cj. See this site for more information or use the Stock-Trak card bound into this text. Stock-Trak exercises are available on the book Web site, www.mhhe.com/jm5e.

Standard & Poor's Educational Version of Market Insight

McGraw-Hill/Irwin and the Institutional Market Services division of Standard & Poor's are pleased to announce an exclusive partnership that offers instructors and students **free** access to the educational version of Standard & Poor's Market Insight with each new textbook. The Educational Version of Market Insight is a rich online resource that provides six years of fundamental financial data for more than 1,000 companies in the database. S&P-specific problems can be found at the end of almost all chapters in this text. For more details, please see the bound-in card inside the front cover of this text, or visit www.mhhe.com/edumarketinsight.

Brief Contents

Contents

Part 1

CHAPTER 1

A Brief History of Risk and Return

"All I ask is for the chance to prove that money can't make me happy."
–Spike Milligan

Who wants to be a millionaire? Actually, anyone can retire as a millionaire. How? Consider this: Suppose you, on your 25th birthday, invest $3,000. You have the discipline to invest $3,000 for the next 39 birthdays. You retire on your 65th birthday. How much will you have? The answer might surprise you. If you earn 10 percent per year, you will have about $1.46 million. Are these numbers realistic? Based on the history of financial markets, the answer appears to be yes. For example, over the last 81 or so years, the widely followed Standard & Poor's index of large-company common stocks has actually yielded about 12 percent per year. ■

Learning Objectives

To become a wise investor (maybe even one with too much money), you need to know:

1. How to calculate the return on an investment using different methods.
2. The historical returns on various important types of investments.
3. The historical risks on various important types of investments.
4. The relationship between risk and return.

The study of investments could begin in many places. After thinking it over, we decided that a brief history lesson is in order, so we start our discussion of risk and return by looking back at what has happened to investors in U.S. financial markets since 1925. In 1931, for example, the stock market lost 43 percent of its value. Just two years later, the market reversed itself and gained 54 percent. In more recent times, the stock market lost about 25 percent of its value on October 19, 1987, alone, and it gained almost 40 percent in 1995. Very recently, following nine years of consecutive gains, the stock market lost value in three straight years, 2000 through 2002. From the end of 2002 through July of 2007, however, the market gained about 58 percent.

So what should you, as a stock market investor, expect when you invest your own money? In this chapter, we study more than eight decades of market history to find out.

In this chapter, we present the historical relation between risk and return. As you will see, this chapter has a lot of very practical information for anyone thinking of investing in financial assets such as stocks and bonds. For example, suppose you were to start investing in stocks today. Do you think your money would grow at an average rate of 5 percent per year? Or 10 percent? Or 20 percent? This chapter gives you an idea of what to expect (the answer may surprise you). The chapter also shows how risky certain investments can be, and it gives you the tools to think about risk in an objective way.

Our primary goal in this chapter is to see what financial market history can tell us about risk and return. One of the most important things to get out of this discussion is a perspective on the numbers. What is a high return? What is a low return? More generally, what returns should we expect from financial assets such as stocks and bonds, and what are the risks from such investments? Beyond this, we hope that by studying what *did* happen in the past, we will at least gain some insight into what *can* happen in the future.

The history of risk and return is made day by day in global financial markets. The Internet is an excellent source of information on financial markets. Visit our Web site (at www.mhhe.com/jm5e) for suggestions on where to find information on recent financial market events. We will suggest other sites later in the chapter.

Not everyone agrees on the value of studying history. On the one hand, there is philosopher George Santayana's famous comment, "Those who do not remember the past are condemned to repeat it." On the other hand, there is industrialist Henry Ford's equally famous comment, "History is more or less bunk." These extremes aside, perhaps everyone would agree with Mark Twain, who observed, with remarkable foresight (and poor grammar), that "October. This is one of the peculiarly dangerous months to speculate in stocks in. The others are July, January, September, April, November, May, March, June, December, August, and February."

Two key observations emerge from a study of financial market history. First, there is a reward for bearing risk, and, at least on average, that reward has been substantial. That's the good news. The bad news is that greater rewards are accompanied by greater risks. The fact that risk and return go together is probably the single most important fact to understand about investments, and it is a point to which we will return many times.

1.1 Returns

We wish to discuss historical returns on different types of financial assets. First, we need to know how to compute the return from an investment. We will consider buying shares of stock in this section, but the basic calculations are the same for any investment.

DOLLAR RETURNS

If you buy an asset of any type, your gain (or loss) from that investment is called the *return* on your investment. This return will usually have two components. First, you may receive some cash directly while you own the investment. Second, the value of the asset you purchase may change. In this case, you have a capital gain or capital loss on your investment.[1]

To illustrate, suppose you purchased 100 shares of stock in Harley-Davidson (ticker symbol: HOG) on January 1. At that time, Harley was selling for $50 per share, so your 100 shares cost you $5,000. At the end of the year, you want to see how you did with your investment.

[1] As a practical matter, what is and what is not a capital gain (or loss) is determined by the Internal Revenue Service. Even so, as is commonly done, we use these terms to refer to a change in value.

The first thing to consider is that over the year, a company may pay cash dividends to its shareholders. As a stockholder in Harley, you are a part owner of the company, and you are entitled to a portion of any money distributed. So if Harley chooses to pay a dividend, you will receive some cash for every share you own.

In addition to the dividend, the other part of your return is the capital gain or loss on the stock. This part arises from changes in the value of your investment. For example, consider these two cases:

WWW

Our favorite investments Web site is Yahoo! Finance at finance.yahoo.com Visit this site and look around!

	Case 1	Case 2
Ending Stock Price	$69.96	$39.78
January 1 value	$5,000	$5,000
December 31 value	$6,996	$3,978
Dividend income	$ 81	$ 81
Capital gain or loss	$1,996	−$1,022

At the beginning of the year, on January 1, the stock is selling for $50 per share, and, as we calculated above, your total outlay for 100 shares is $5,000. Over the year, Harley pays dividends of $.81 per share. By the end of the year, then, you received dividend income of

$$\text{Dividend income} = \$.81 \times 100 = \$81$$

In Case 1, suppose that as of December 31, Harley was selling for $69.96, meaning that the value of your stock increased by $19.96 per share. Your 100 shares are now worth $6,996, so you have a capital gain of

$$\text{Capital gain} = (\$69.96 - \$50) \times 100 = \$1{,}996$$

On the other hand, if the price had dropped to, say, $39.78 (Case 2), you would have a capital loss of

$$\text{Capital loss} = (\$39.78 - \$50) \times 100 = -\$1{,}022$$

Notice that a capital loss is the same thing as a negative capital gain.

total dollar return
The return on an investment measured in dollars that accounts for all cash flows and capital gains or losses.

The **total dollar return** on your investment is the sum of the dividend and the capital gain (or loss):

$$\text{Total dollar return} = \text{Dividend income} + \text{Capital gain (or loss)}$$

In Case 1, the total dollar return is thus given by

$$\text{Total dollar return} = \$81 + \$1{,}996 = \$2{,}077$$

Overall, between the dividends you received and the increase in the price of the stock, the value of your investment increased from $5,000 to $5,000 + $2,077 = $7,077.

A common misconception often arises in this context. Suppose you hold on to your Harley-Davidson stock and don't sell it at the end of the year. Should you still consider the capital gain as part of your return? Isn't this only a "paper" gain and not really a cash gain if you don't sell it?

The answer to the first question is a strong yes, and the answer to the second is an equally strong no. The capital gain is every bit as much a part of your return as the dividend, and you should certainly count it as part of your return. The fact that you decide to keep the stock and don't sell (you don't "realize" the gain) is irrelevant because you could have converted it to cash if you had wanted to. Whether you choose to do so is up to you.

After all, if you insist on converting your gain to cash, you could always sell the stock and immediately reinvest by buying the stock back. There is no difference between doing this and just not selling (assuming, of course, that there are no transaction costs or tax consequences from selling the stock). Again, the point is that whether you actually cash out and buy pizzas (or whatever) or continue to hold the investment doesn't affect the return you actually earn.

PERCENTAGE RETURNS

It is usually more convenient to summarize information about returns in percentage terms than in dollar terms, because that way your return doesn't depend on how much you actually invested. With percentage returns the question we want to answer is: How much do we get *for each dollar* we invest?

To answer this question, let P_t be the price of the stock at the beginning of the year. Let D_{t+1} be the dividend paid on the stock during the year. The following cash flows are the same as those shown earlier, except that we have now expressed everything on a per-share basis:

	Case 1	Case 2
January 1 stock price, P_t	\$50.00	\$50.00
December 31 stock price, P_{t+1}	\$69.96	\$39.78
Dividend income, D_{t+1}	\$ .81	\$ .81
Capital gain or loss	\$19.96	−\$10.22

dividend yield
The annual stock dividend as a percentage of the initial stock price.

In our example, the price at the beginning of the year was \$50 per share and the dividend paid during the year on each share was \$.81. If we divide the dividend by the beginning stock price, the result is the **dividend yield**:

$$\begin{aligned}\text{Dividend yield} &= D_{t+1} / P_t \\ &= \$.81 / \$50 = .0162 = 1.62\%\end{aligned} \tag{1.1}$$

This calculation says that for each dollar we invested we received 1.62 cents in dividends.

capital gains yield
The change in stock price as a percentage of the initial stock price.

The second component of our percentage return is the **capital gains yield**. This yield is calculated as the change in the price during the year (the capital gain) divided by the beginning price. With the Case 1 ending price, we get:

$$\begin{aligned}\text{Capital gains yield} &= (P_{t+1} - P_t) / P_t \\ &= (\$69.96 - \$50) / \$50 \\ &= \$19.96 / \$50 = .3992 = 39.92\%\end{aligned} \tag{1.2}$$

This 39.92 percent yield means that for each dollar invested we got about 40 cents in capital gains (HOG heaven).

total percent return
The return on an investment measured as a percentage that accounts for all cash flows and capital gains or losses.

Putting it all together, per dollar invested, we get 1.62 cents in dividends and 39.92 cents in capital gains for a total of 41.54 cents. Our **total percent return** is 41.54 cents on the dollar, or 41.54 percent. When a return is expressed on a percentage basis, we often refer to it as the *rate of return,* or just "return," on the investment. Notice that if we combine the formulas for the dividend yield and capital gains yield, we get a single formula for the total percentage return:

$$\begin{aligned}\text{Percentage return} &= \text{Dividend yield} + \text{Capital gains yield} \\ &= D_{t+1} / P_t + (P_{t+1} - P_t) / P_t \\ &= (D_{t+1} + P_{t+1} - P_t) / P_t\end{aligned} \tag{1.3}$$

To check our calculations, notice that we invested \$5,000 and ended up with \$7,077. By what percentage did our \$5,000 increase? As we saw, our gain was \$7,077 − \$5,000 = \$2,077. This is an increase of \$2,077 / \$5,000, or 41.54 percent.

WORK THE WEB

To look up information on common stocks using the Web, you need to know the "ticker" symbol for the stocks in which you are interested. You can look up ticker symbols in many places, including one of our favorite sites, finance.yahoo.com. Here we have looked up (using the "Symbol Lookup" link) and entered ticker symbols for some well-known "tech" stocks: Dell, Cisco, Intel, and Microsoft.

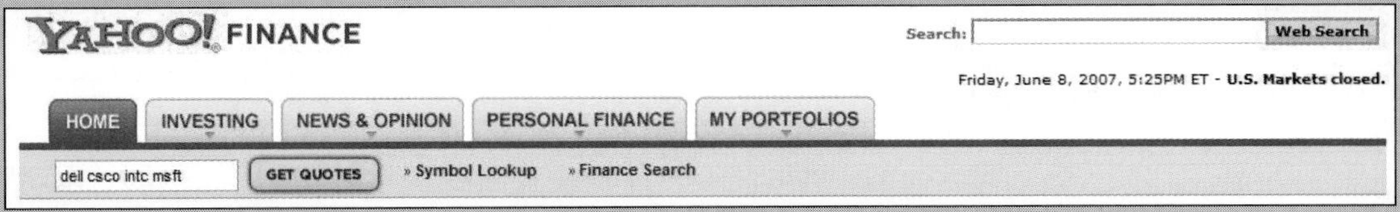

Once we hit "Get Quotes," this is what we got:

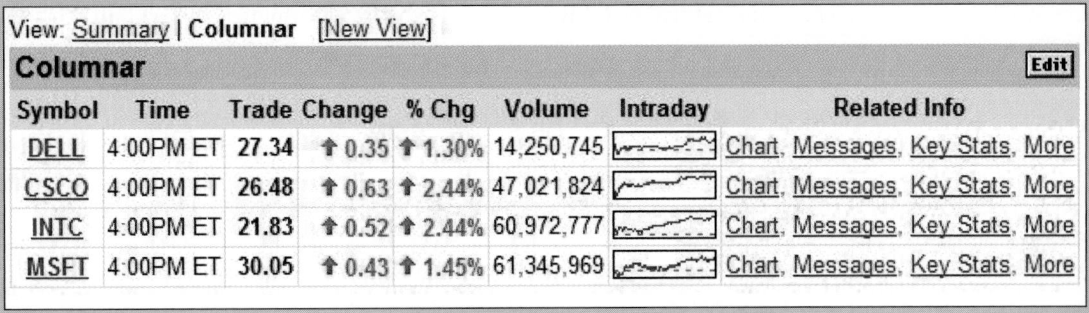

View: Summary | Columnar [New View]

Columnar Edit

Symbol	Time	Trade	Change	% Chg	Volume	Intraday	Related Info
DELL	4:00PM ET	27.34	↑ 0.35	↑ 1.30%	14,250,745		Chart, Messages, Key Stats, More
CSCO	4:00PM ET	26.48	↑ 0.63	↑ 2.44%	47,021,824		Chart, Messages, Key Stats, More
INTC	4:00PM ET	21.83	↑ 0.52	↑ 2.44%	60,972,777		Chart, Messages, Key Stats, More
MSFT	4:00PM ET	30.05	↑ 0.43	↑ 1.45%	61,345,969		Chart, Messages, Key Stats, More

As you can see, we get the price for each stock, along with information about the change in price and volume (number of shares traded). You will find a lot of links to hit and learn more, so have at it!

EXAMPLE 1.1

Calculating Percentage Returns

Suppose you buy some stock in Concannon Plastics for \$35 per share. After one year, the price is \$49 per share. During the year, you received a \$1.40 dividend per share. What is the dividend yield? The capital gains yield? The percentage return? If your total investment was \$1,400, how much do you have at the end of the year?

Your \$1.40 dividend per share works out to a dividend yield of

$$\begin{aligned}\text{Dividend yield} &= D_{t+1} / P_t \\ &= \$1.40 / \$35 \\ &= 4\%\end{aligned}$$

The per-share capital gain is \$14, so the capital gains yield is

$$\begin{aligned}\text{Capital gains yield} &= (P_{t+1} - P_t) / P_t \\ &= (\$49 - \$35) / \$35 \\ &= \$14 / \$35 \\ &= 40\%\end{aligned}$$

The total percentage return is thus 4% + 40% = 44%.

If you had invested \$1,400, you would have \$2,016 at the end of the year. To check this, note that your \$1,400 would have bought you \$1,400 / \$35 = 40 shares. Your 40 shares would then have paid you a total of 40 × \$1.40 = \$56 in cash dividends. Your \$14 per share gain would give you a total capital gain of \$14 × 40 = \$560. Add these together and you get \$616, which is a 44 percent total return on your \$1,400 investment.

A NOTE ON ANNUALIZING RETURNS

So far, we have only considered annual returns. Of course, the actual length of time you own an investment will almost never be exactly a year. To compare investments, however, we will usually need to express returns on a per-year or "annualized" basis, so we need to do a little bit more work.

For example, suppose you bought 200 shares of Lowe's Companies, Inc. (LOW) at a price of \$48 per share. In three months, you sell your stock for \$51. You didn't receive any dividends. What is your return for the three months? What is your annualized return?

In this case, we say that your *holding period,* which is the length of time you own the stock, is three months. With a zero dividend, you know that the percentage return can be calculated as:

$$\text{Percentage return} = (P_{t+1} - P_t)/P_t = (\$51 - \$48)/\$48 = .0625 = 6.25\%$$

This 6.25 percent is your return for the three-month holding period, but what does this return amount to on a per-year basis? To find out, we need to convert this to an annualized return, meaning a return expressed on a per-year basis. Such a return is often called an **effective annual return**, or **EAR** for short. The general formula is this:

effective annual return (EAR)
The return on an investment expressed on a per-year, or "annualized," basis.

$$1 + EAR = (1 + \text{holding period percentage return})^m \quad (1.4)$$

where m is the number of holding periods in a year.

In our example, the holding period percentage return is 6.25 percent, or .0625. The holding period is three months, so there are four (12 months/3 months) periods in a year. We calculate the annualized return, or EAR, as follows:

$$\begin{aligned} 1 + EAR &= (1 + \text{holding period percentage return})^m \\ &= (1 + .0625)^4 \\ &= 1.2744 \end{aligned}$$

So, your annualized return is 27.44 percent.

EXAMPLE 1.2 A "QWEST" for Returns

Suppose you buy some stock in Qwest (no, that's not a typo, that's how the company spells it) at a price of \$8 per share. Four months later, you sell it for \$8.40. No dividend is paid. What is your annualized return on this investment?

For the four-month holding period, your return is:

$$\text{Percentage return} = (P_{t+1} - P_t) / P_t = (\$8.40 - \$8) / \$8 = .05 = 5\%$$

There are three four-month periods in a year, so the annualized return is:

$$1 + EAR = (1 + \text{holding period percentage return})^m = (1 + .05)^3 = 1.1576$$

Subtracting the one, we get an annualized return of .1576, or 15.76 percent.

EXAMPLE 1.3 More Annualized Returns

Suppose you buy some stock in Johnson & Johnson (JNJ) at a price of \$50 per share. Three *years* later, you sell it for \$62.50. No dividends were paid. What is your annualized return on this investment?

The situation here is a bit different because your holding period is now longer than a year, but the calculation is basically the same. For the three-year holding period, your return is:

$$\text{Percentage return} = (P_{t+1} - P_t) / P_t = (\$62.50 - \$50) / \$50 = .25 = 25\%$$

(continued)

How many three-year holding periods are there in a single year? The answer is one-third, so m in this case is 1/3. The annualized return is:

$$\begin{aligned} 1 + EAR &= (1 + \text{holding period percentage return})^m \\ &= (1 + .25)^{1/3} \\ &= 1.0772 \end{aligned}$$

Subtracting the one, we get an annualized return of .0772, or 7.72 percent.

Now that you know how to calculate returns on a hypothetical stock, you should begin looking at real stocks. The nearby *Work the Web* box using finance.yahoo.com describes how to get going. Meanwhile, in the next several sections, we will take a look at the returns that some common types of investments have earned over the last 81 years.

CHECK THIS

1.1a What are the two parts of total return?

1.1b What is the difference between a dollar return and a percentage return? Why are percentage returns usually more convenient?

1.1c What is an effective annual return (EAR)?

1.2 The Historical Record

We now examine year-to-year historical rates of return on five important categories of financial investments. These returns can be interpreted as what you would have earned if you had invested in portfolios of the following asset categories:

WWW

Annual historical financial market data can be downloaded (but not for free) at www.globalfindata.com

1. Large-company stocks. The large-company stock portfolio is based on the Standard & Poor's (S&P's) 500 Index, which contains 500 of the largest companies (in terms of total market value of outstanding stock) in the United States.
2. Small-company stocks. This is a portfolio composed of stock of smaller companies, where "small" corresponds to the smallest 20 percent of the companies listed on the New York Stock Exchange, again as measured by market value of outstanding stock.
3. Long-term corporate bonds. This is a portfolio of high-quality bonds with 20 years to maturity.
4. Long-term U.S. government bonds. This is a portfolio of U.S. government bonds with 20 years to maturity.
5. U.S. Treasury bills. This is a portfolio of Treasury bills (T-bills for short) with a three-month maturity.

If you are not entirely certain what these investments are, don't be overly concerned. We will have much more to say about each in later chapters. For now, just take as given that these are some of the things that you could have put your money into in years gone by. In addition to the year-to-year returns on these financial instruments, the year-to-year percentage changes in the Consumer Price Index (CPI) are also computed. The CPI is a standard measure of consumer goods price inflation.

Here is a bit of market jargon for you. A company's *total market capitalization* (or market "cap" for short) is equal to its stock price multiplied by the number of shares of stock. In other words, it's the total value of the company's stock. Large companies are often called "large-cap" stocks, and small companies are called "small-cap" stocks. We'll use these terms frequently.

FIGURE 1.1 A $1 Investment in Different Types of Portfolios: 1926–2006 (Year-end 1925 = $1)

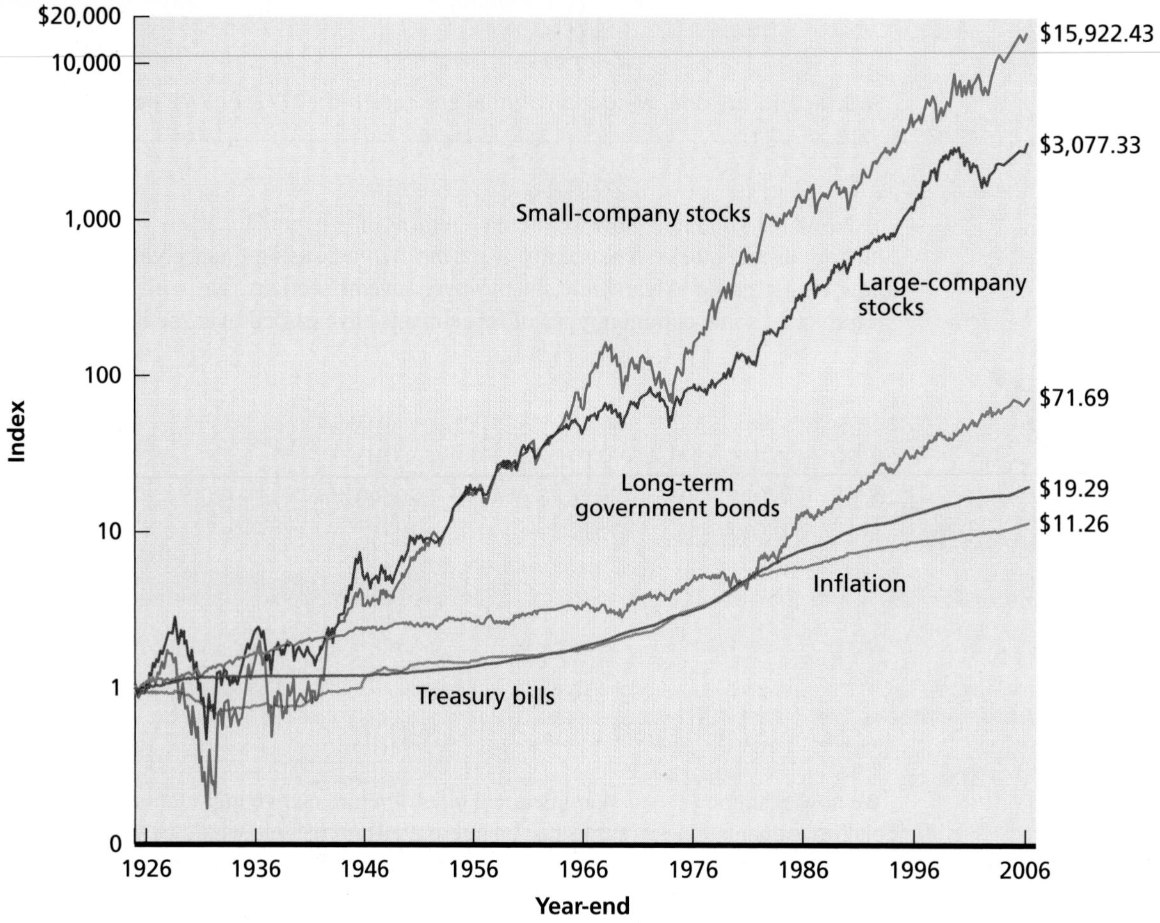

Source: *Stocks, Bonds, Bills, and Inflation Yearbook*™, Ibbotson Associates, Inc., Chicago (annually updates work by Roger G. Ibbotson and Rex Sinquefield). All rights reserved.

A FIRST LOOK

Before examining the different portfolio returns, we first take a look at the "big picture." Figure 1.1 shows what happened to $1 invested in these different portfolios at the beginning of 1926 and held over the 81-year period ending in 2006 (for clarity, the long-term corporate bonds are omitted). To fit all the information on a single graph, some modification in scaling is used. As is commonly done with financial time series, the vertical axis is scaled so that equal distances measure equal percentage (as opposed to dollar) changes in value. Thus, the distance between $10 and $100 is the same as that between $100 and $1,000, since both distances represent the same 900 percent increases.

Looking at Figure 1.1, we see that the small-company investment did the best overall. Every dollar invested grew to a remarkable $15,922.43 over the 81 years. The larger common stock portfolio did less well; a dollar invested in it grew to $3,077.33.

At the other end, the T-bill portfolio grew to only $19.29. This is even less impressive when we consider the inflation over this period. As illustrated, the increase in the price level was such that $11.26 is needed just to replace the original $1.

Given the historical record, why would anybody buy anything other than small-company stocks? If you look closely at Figure 1.1, you will probably see the answer—risk. The T-bill portfolio and the long-term government bond portfolio grew more slowly than did the stock portfolios, but they also grew much more steadily. The small stocks ended up on top, but, as you can see, they grew quite erratically at times. For example, the small stocks were the

FIGURE 1.2 Financial Market History

Total return indexes (1801–2007)

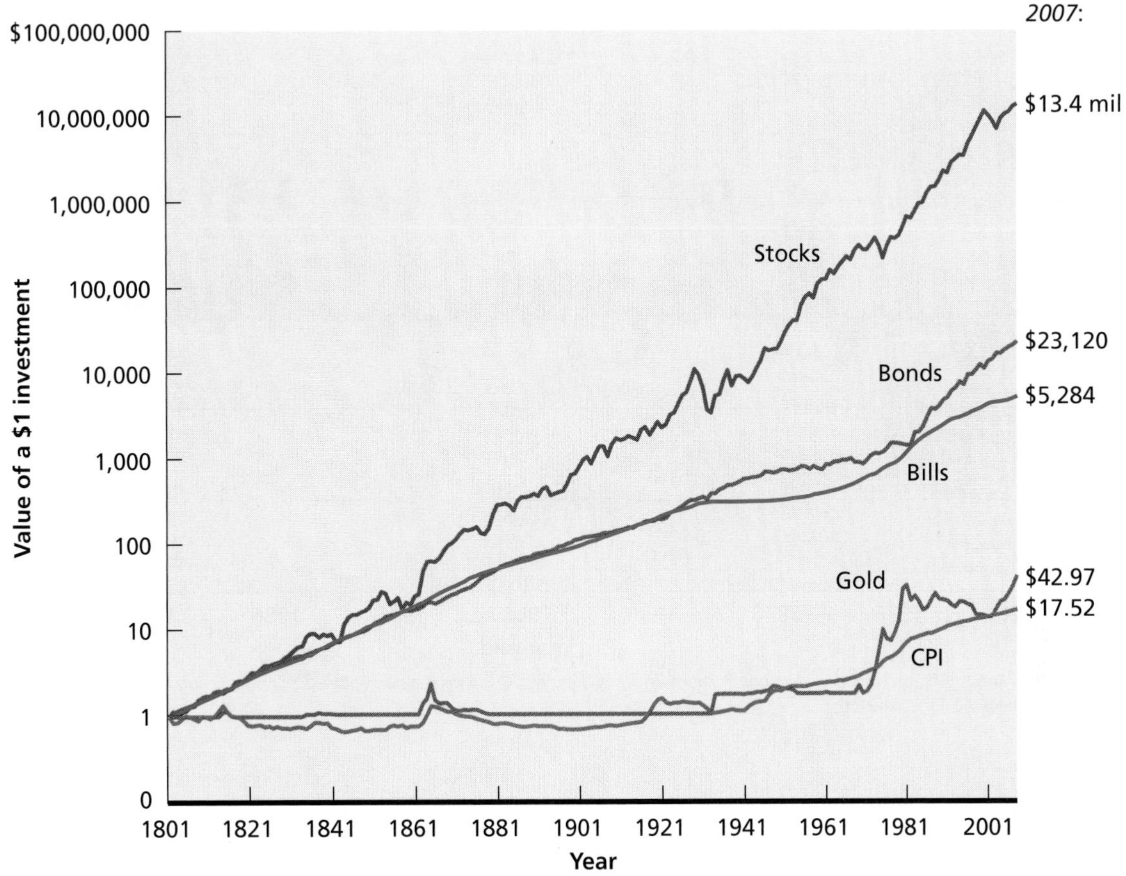

Source: Jeremy J. Siegel, *Stocks for the Long Run*, 3rd ed. (New York: McGraw-Hill, 2003). Update through 2007 provided by Jeremy J. Siegel.

worst performers for about the first 10 years and had a smaller return than long-term government bonds for almost 15 years.

A LONGER RANGE LOOK

The data available on the stock returns before 1925 are not comprehensive, but it is nonetheless possible to trace reasonably accurate returns in U.S. financial markets as far back as 1801. Figure 1.2 shows the values, in 2007, of $1 invested in stocks, long-term bonds, short-term bills, and gold. The CPI is also included for reference.

Inspecting Figure 1.2, we see that $1 invested in stocks grew to an astounding $13.4 million over this 207-year period. During this time, the returns from investing in stocks dwarf those earned on other investments. Notice also in Figure 1.2 that, after two centuries, gold has managed to keep up with inflation, but that is about it.

What we see thus far is that there has been a powerful financial incentive for long-term investing. The real moral of the story is this: Get an early start!

A CLOSER LOOK

To illustrate the variability of the different investments, Figures 1.3 through 1.6 plot the year-to-year percentage returns in the form of vertical bars drawn from the horizontal axis. The height of a bar tells us the return for the particular year. For example, looking at the long-term government bonds (Figure 1.5), we see that the largest historical return (40.35 percent) occurred in 1982. This year was a good year for bonds. In comparing these charts, notice the differences in the vertical axis scales. With these differences in mind,

FIGURE 1.3 Year-to-Year Total Returns on Large-Company Stocks: 1926–2006

Large-company stocks
Return indices, returns, and dividend yields

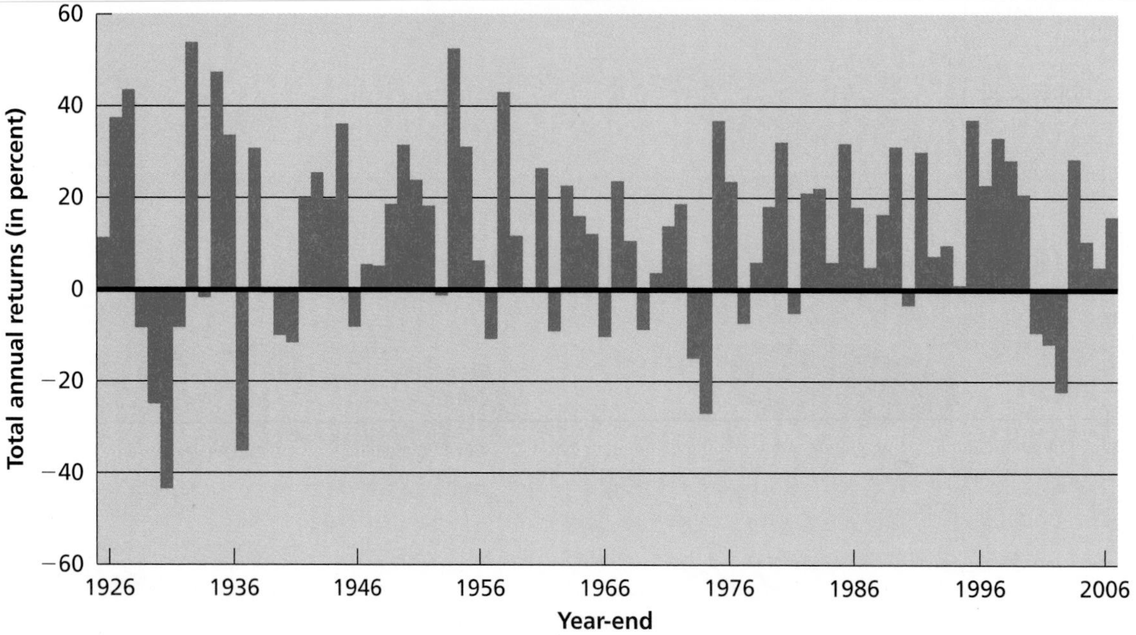

Source: *Stocks, Bonds, Bills, and Inflation Yearbook*™, Ibbotson Associates, Inc., Chicago (annually updated by Roger G. Ibbotson and Rex A. Sinquefield). All rights reserved.

FIGURE 1.4 Year-to-Year Total Returns on Small-Company Stocks: 1926–2006

Small-company stocks
Return index and returns

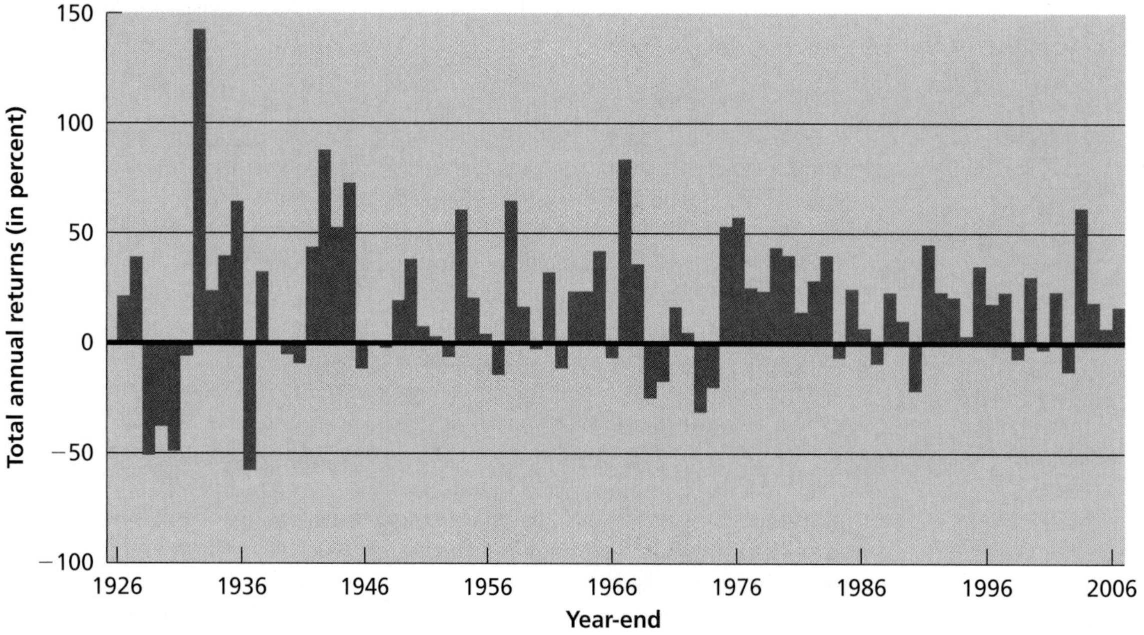

Source: *Stocks, Bonds, Bills, and Inflation Yearbook*™, Ibbotson Associates, Inc., Chicago (annually updated by Roger G. Ibbotson and Rex A. Sinquefield). All rights reserved.

FIGURE 1.5 Year-to-Year Total Returns on Bonds and Bills: 1926–2006

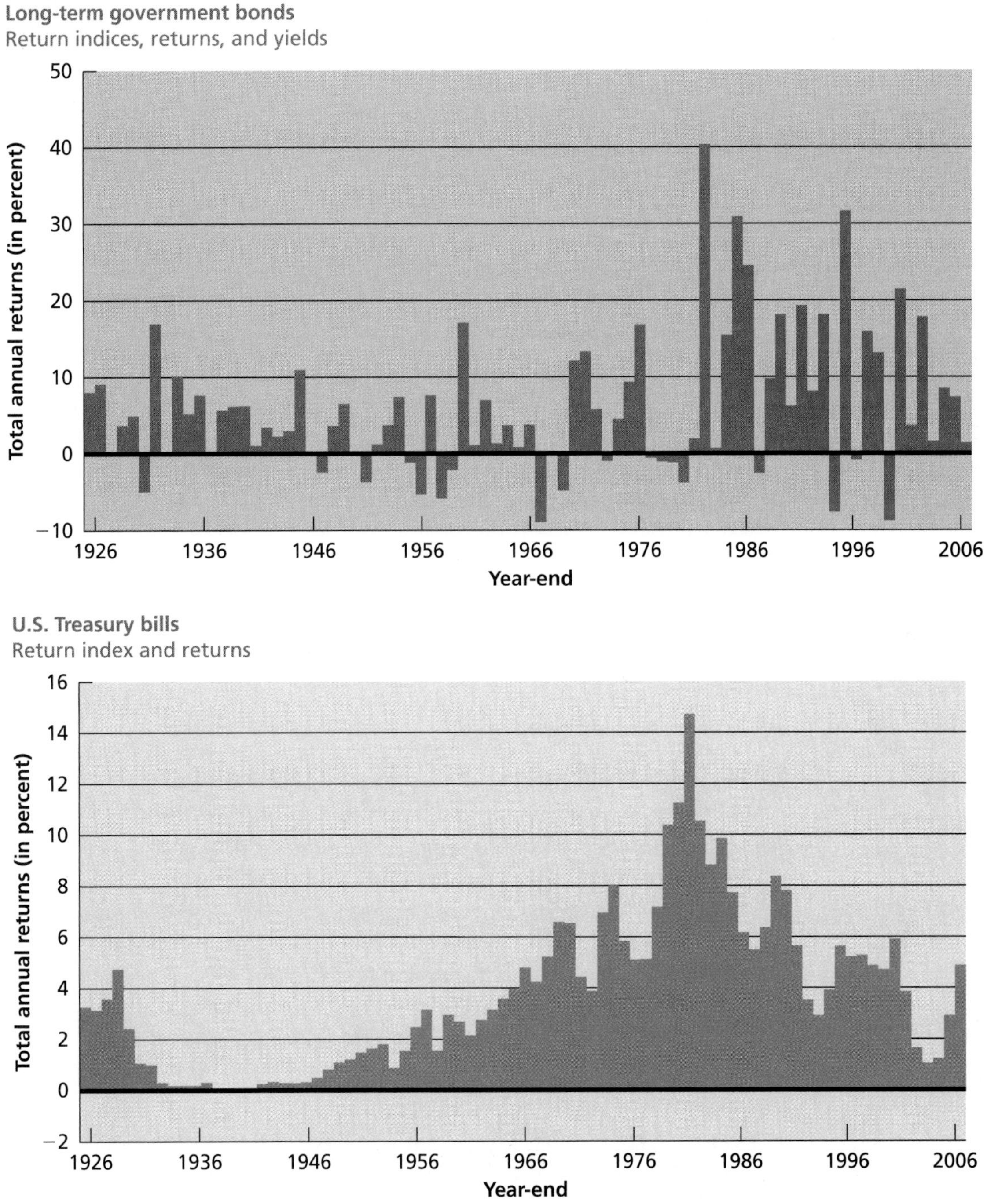

Source: *Stocks, Bonds, Bills, and Inflation Yearbook*™, Ibbotson Associates, Inc., Chicago (annually updated by Roger G. Ibbotson and Rex A. Sinquefield). All rights reserved.

you can see how predictably the Treasury bills (bottom of Figure 1.5) behaved compared to the small stocks (Figure 1.4).

The returns shown in these bar graphs are sometimes very large. Looking at the graphs, we see, for example, that the largest single-year return was a remarkable 143 percent for the small-cap stocks in 1933. In the same year, the large-company stocks returned "only" 53 percent. In contrast, the largest Treasury bill return was 15 percent, in 1981. For future reference, the actual year-to-year returns for the S&P 500, long-term government bonds, Treasury bills, and the CPI are shown in Table 1.1 on page 13.

FIGURE 1.6 Year-to-Year Inflation: 1926–2006

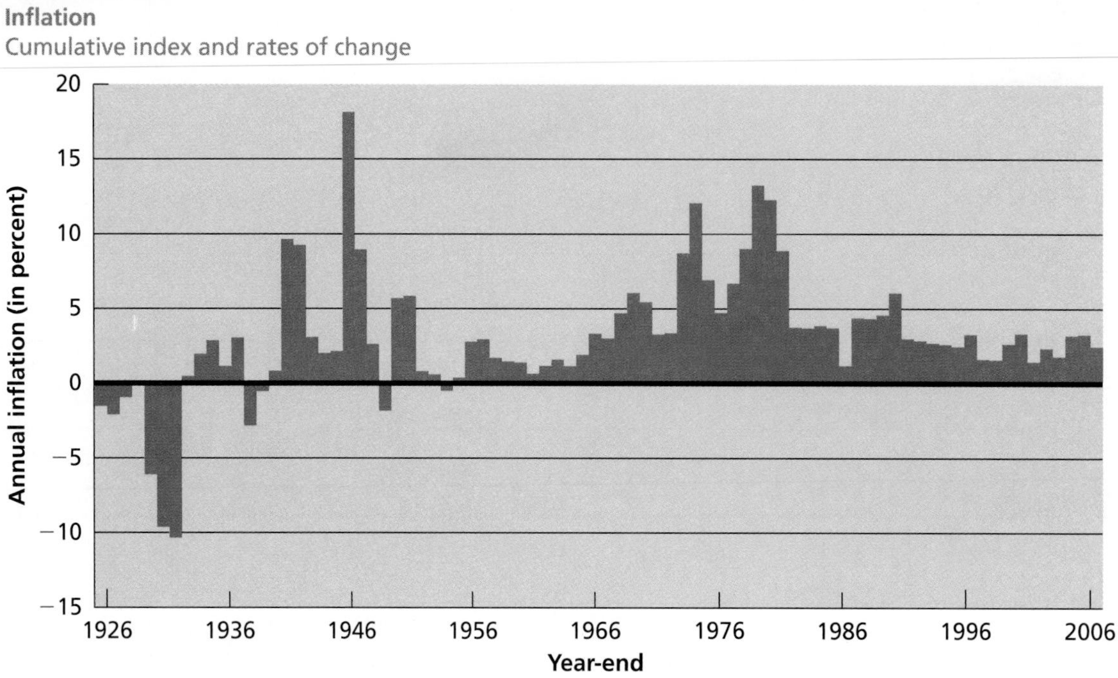

Source: *Stocks, Bonds, Bills, and Inflation Yearbook*™, Ibbotson Associates, Inc., Chicago (annually updated by Roger G. Ibbotson and Rex A. Sinquefield). All rights reserved.

CHECK THIS

1.2a With 20-20 hindsight, what was the best investment for the period 1926–35?

1.2b Why doesn't everyone just buy small stocks as investments?

1.2c What was the smallest return observed over the 81 years for each of these investments? Approximately when did it occur?

1.2d About how many times did large stocks (common stocks) return more than 30 percent? How many times did they return less than −20 percent?

1.2e What was the longest "winning streak" (years without a negative return) for large stocks? For long-term government bonds?

1.2f How often did the T-bill portfolio have a negative return?

1.3 Average Returns: The First Lesson

As you've probably begun to notice, the history of financial market returns in an undigested form is complicated. What we need are simple measures to accurately summarize and describe all these numbers. Accordingly, we discuss how to go about condensing detailed numerical data. We start by calculating average returns.

CALCULATING AVERAGE RETURNS

The obvious way to calculate average returns on the different investments in Figures 1.3 to 1.6 is to simply add up the yearly returns and divide by 81. The result is the historical average of the individual values. For example, if you add the returns for large-company common stocks for the 81 years, you will get about 996 percent. The average annual return is thus 996/81 = 12.3%. You can interpret this 12.3 percent just like any other average.

TABLE 1.1 Year-to-Year Total Returns: 1926–2006

Year	Large-Company Stocks	Long-Term Government Bonds	U.S. Treasury Bills	Consumer Price Index	Year	Large-Company Stocks	Long-Term Government Bonds	U.S. Treasury Bills	Consumer Price Index
1926	11.14%	7.90%	3.30%	−1.12%	1966	−10.10%	−1.61%	4.94%	3.46%
1927	37.13	10.36	3.15	−2.26	1967	23.94	−6.38	4.39	3.04
1928	43.31	−1.37	4.05	−1.16	1968	11.00	5.33	5.49	4.72
1929	−8.91	5.23	4.47	0.58	1969	−8.47	−7.45	6.90	6.20
1930	−25.26	5.80	2.27	−6.40	1970	3.94	12.24	6.50	5.57
1931	−43.86	−8.04	1.15	−9.32	1971	14.30	12.67	4.36	3.27
1932	−8.85	14.11	0.88	−10.27	1972	18.99	9.15	4.23	3.41
1933	52.88	0.31	0.52	0.76	1973	−14.69	−12.66	7.29	8.71
1934	−2.34	12.98	0.27	1.52	1974	−26.47	−3.28	7.99	12.34
1935	47.22	5.88	0.17	2.99	1975	37.23	4.67	5.87	6.94
1936	32.80	8.22	0.17	1.45	1976	23.93	18.34	5.07	4.86
1937	−35.26	−0.13	0.27	2.86	1977	−7.16	2.31	5.45	6.70
1938	33.20	6.26	0.06	−2.78	1978	6.57	−2.07	7.64	9.02
1939	−0.91	5.71	0.04	0.00	1979	18.61	−2.76	10.56	13.29
1940	−10.08	10.34	0.04	0.71	1980	32.50	−5.91	12.10	12.52
1941	−11.77	−8.66	0.14	9.93	1981	−4.92	−0.16	14.60	8.92
1942	21.07	2.67	0.34	9.03	1982	21.55	49.99	10.94	3.83
1943	25.76	2.50	0.38	2.96	1983	22.56	−2.11	8.99	3.79
1944	19.69	2.88	0.38	2.30	1984	6.27	16.53	9.90	3.95
1945	36.46	5.17	0.38	2.25	1985	31.73	39.03	7.71	3.80
1946	−8.18	4.07	0.38	18.13	1986	18.67	32.51	6.09	1.10
1947	5.24	−1.15	0.62	8.84	1987	5.25	−8.09	5.88	4.43
1948	5.10	2.10	1.06	2.99	1988	16.61	8.71	6.94	4.42
1949	18.06	7.02	1.12	−2.07	1989	31.69	22.15	8.44	4.65
1950	30.58	−1.44	1.22	5.93	1990	−3.10	5.44	7.69	6.11
1951	24.55	−3.53	1.56	6.00	1991	30.46	20.04	5.43	3.06
1952	18.50	1.82	1.75	0.75	1992	7.62	8.09	3.48	2.90
1953	−1.10	−0.88	1.87	0.75	1993	10.08	22.32	3.03	2.75
1954	52.40	7.89	0.93	−0.74	1994	1.32	−11.46	4.39	2.67
1955	31.43	−1.03	1.80	0.37	1995	37.58	37.28	5.61	2.54
1956	6.63	−3.14	2.66	2.99	1996	22.96	−2.59	5.14	3.32
1957	−10.85	5.25	3.28	2.90	1997	33.36	17.70	5.19	1.70
1958	43.34	−6.70	1.71	1.76	1998	28.58	19.22	4.86	1.61
1959	11.90	−1.35	3.48	1.73	1999	21.04	−12.76	4.80	2.68
1960	0.48	7.74	2.81	1.36	2000	−9.10	22.16	5.98	3.39
1961	26.81	3.02	2.40	0.67	2001	−11.89	5.30	3.33	1.55
1962	−8.78	4.63	2.82	1.33	2002	−22.10	14.08	1.61	2.38
1963	22.69	1.37	3.23	1.64	2003	28.68	1.62	1.03	1.88
1964	16.36	4.43	3.62	0.97	2004	10.88	10.34	1.43	3.26
1965	12.36	1.40	4.06	1.92	2005	4.91	10.35	3.30	3.42
					2006	15.79	0.28	4.97	2.54

Source: Author calculations based on data obtained from *Global Financial Data* and other sources.

INVESTMENT UPDATES

AFTER 30 YEARS OF INVESTING, MARKET HAS NO SURE THING

The stock market exists to enrich investors, while utterly humiliating them. With great regularity, I receive e-mails from readers who are convinced that you should own only blue-chip companies, or only high-dividend stocks, or only technology companies. And all I can think about is the market's litany of once-sure things. It happens again and again. Hot stocks turn cold. Highflying stock funds crash and burn. Time-tested stock-picking strategies suddenly falter. To understand just how capricious the market can be, consider results from the past three decades.

As the Decades Turn

Take a look at the accompanying table (Swings and Roundabouts), which shows returns calculated by Baltimore's T. Rowe Price Associates using data from Chicago's Ibbotson Associates. In particular, focus on the performance of large, small and foreign stocks in each of the past three decades. I think of these as the three key stock-market sectors.

As you will see, large-company stocks—which are so beloved after their dazzling gains in the 1990s—didn't fare quite so well in the prior two decades. They ranked second behind foreign stocks in the 1980s and they lagged behind both small and foreign stocks in the 1970s. Similarly, small stocks ranked first in the 1970s, second in the 1990s and third in the 1980s. Meanwhile, foreign stocks were first in the 1980s, second in the 1970s and third in the 1990s.

In other words, none of the sectors consistently ranked as the top performer and all had periods of dreadful performance. Moreover, if you look at results for the 30 years through December 2001, there isn't a huge difference between the average annual returns for large, small and foreign stocks. Of course, if you were really clever, you would figure out which sector was going to be the decade's top performer, and then invest everything in that sector. But I am not smart enough to make that sort of market call, and I don't think anybody else is, either.

Gerald Perritt, a money manager in Largo, Fla., and editor of the Mutual Fund Letter, a monthly newsletter, says he has lately met many investors who got themselves into financial trouble. All have one thing in common: They failed to diversify and instead made big investment bets that turned sour. "Diversification is good," Mr. Perritt says. "But if it's so good, why don't more people practice it? Return is the most visible element in the investing process. The least visible is risk. People see the return they miss by diversifying. We don't think about what will happen if a big bet goes in the wrong direction."

My hunch is that the current decade will be a lackluster one for blue-chip shares. Large-company stocks have been dazzling performers over the past two decades, and now they are burdened by lofty share price-to-earnings multiples and boast only skimpy dividend yields. Indeed, I suspect foreign and small stocks will prove to be the market's new darlings. But I am unwilling to invest based on such hunches. So what should an investor do? Owning a little bit of everything has worked well in the past, and it still seems like a mighty fine strategy to me.

Glancing at the performance of narrower market sectors strengthens the case for humility. In the past two years, three of the market's best-performing segments have been gold, bargain-priced "value" stocks and real estate investment trusts, or REITs. Meanwhile, "growth" stocks, including once-sparkling technology shares, have been crushed. But look at the accompanying table to see results from earlier decades. Unfortunately, data aren't available for all time periods. Still, there are enough results to see how unpredictable market returns can be. Sure, value stocks were strong performers in 2000 and 2001. But they lagged behind growth stocks in the 1990s. True, REITs have generated great results recently. But they didn't do

If you picked a year at random from the 81-year history and you had to guess the return in that year, the best guess is 12.3 percent.

AVERAGE RETURNS: THE HISTORICAL RECORD

Table 1.2 shows the average returns for the investments we have discussed. These averages don't reflect the impact of inflation. Notice that over this 81-year period the average inflation rate was 3.1 percent per year while the average return on U.S. Treasury bills was 3.8 percent per year. Thus, the average return on Treasury bills exceeded the average rate of inflation by only .7 percent per year. At the other extreme, the return on small-cap common stocks exceeded the rate of inflation by about $17.4\% - 3.1\% = 14.3\%$. The real return of the large-cap common stocks averaged $12.3\% - 3.1\% = 9.2\%$ per year.

Our analysis thus far has covered market history going back to the end of 1925. You might be wondering about the more recent past. The nearby *Investment Updates* box provides more detail on the stock market's ups and downs since 1970.

Swings and Roundabouts All market sectors enjoy periods of dazzling gains. But none performs well all the time.						
	Bear Markets		Long-Run Annual Performance			
	1973–74	2000–01	1970s	1980s	1990s	30 Years*
Large-company stocks	−42.6%	−29.3%	5.9%	17.6%	18.2%	12.2%
Small-company stocks	−43.2	−19.4	11.5	15.8	15.1	14.9
Foreign markets	−35.2	−36.6	10.1	22.8	7.3	11.2
Growth stocks	NA	−42.2	NA	16.3	20.6	NA
Value stocks	NA	−13.4	NA	18.3	15.4	NA
Real-estate trusts	−52.6	35.2	NA	12.5	8.1	9.4
Intermediate bonds	4.9	19.4	7.0	11.9	7.2	8.5
Treasury bills	13.5	7.9	6.3	8.9	4.9	6.7
Gold	133.1	5.9	30.7	−2.5	−3.1	6.4

*Through December 31, 2001.

Note: All returns are annualized, except for the two bear markets, for which cumulative performance is shown.

NA: Not available.

much better than intermediate-term government bonds in the 1990s. And gold? You have to go back to the 1970s to find a decent decade for the yellow metal.

When the Bear Growls

To get a handle on down-market performance, I had T. Rowe Price calculate returns for the two most-searing bear markets of recent decades, the 1973–74 debacle and the 2000–01 tech wreck. In both stock-market declines, gold, bonds, and Treasury bills posted gains, even as other sectors were crushed. Clearly, if you want a little bear-market protection, these are good assets to own.

But how did different stock-market sectors fare? Consider the 1973–74 crash. The two hardest-hit sectors were REITs and small-company stocks. If you were worried about a bear market and you had taken your cues from the 1973–74 crash, you would have avoided both sectors. Yet REITs, the hardest-hit sector in the 1973–74 crash, were the biggest winners in the recent bear market. Small-company stocks, meanwhile, didn't perform quite so impressively in the 2000–01 market decline. Nonetheless, they lost far less money than large-company stocks.

As the data make clear, there aren't many sure things in investing. But that doesn't mean you can't make good money over time. If you simply build a well-diversified portfolio and hang on for the long haul, history suggests you will be handsomely rewarded. "Here's a 30-year period that includes two grueling bear markets and one awful decade, the 1970s," notes Steven Norwitz, a T. Rowe Price vice president. "But if you invested through the whole period, you got pretty attractive returns."

Source: Jonathan Clements, *The Wall Street Journal,* April 28, 2002.

TABLE 1.2 Average Annual Returns: 1926–2006

Investment	Average Return
Large stocks	12.3%
Small stocks	17.4
Long-term corporate bonds	6.2
Long-term government bonds	5.8
U.S. Treasury bills	3.8
Inflation	3.1

Source: *Stocks, Bonds, Bills, and Inflation Yearbook*™, Ibbotson Associates, Inc., Chicago (annually updated by Roger G. Ibbotson and Rex A. Sinquefield). All rights reserved.

TABLE 1.3 Average Annual Returns and Risk Premiums: 1926–2006

Investment	Average Return	Risk Premium
Large stocks	12.3%	8.5%
Small stocks	17.4	13.6
Long-term corporate bonds	6.2	2.4
Long-term government bonds	5.8	2.0
U.S. Treasury bills	3.8	0.0

Source: *Stocks, Bonds, Bills, and Inflation Yearbook™*, Ibbotson Associates, Inc., Chicago (annually updated by Roger G. Ibbotson and Rex A. Sinquefield). All rights reserved.

RISK PREMIUMS

Now that we have computed some average returns, it seems logical to see how they compare with each other. Based on our discussion above, one such comparison involves government-issued securities. These are free of much of the variability we see in, for example, the stock market.

The government borrows money by issuing debt, that is, bonds. These bonds come in different forms. The ones we focus on are Treasury bills. Treasury bills have the shortest time to maturity of the different types of government debt. Because the government can always raise taxes or print money to pay its expenses, Treasury bills are virtually free of any default risk. Thus, we will call the rate of return on such debt the **risk-free rate**, and we will use it as a kind of investing benchmark.

risk-free rate
The rate of return on a riskless investment.

A particularly interesting comparison involves the virtually risk-free return on T-bills and the risky return on common stocks. The difference between these two returns can be interpreted as a measure of the *excess return* on the average risky asset (assuming that the stock of a large U.S. corporation has about average risk compared to all risky assets).

We call this the "excess" return because it is the additional return we earn by moving from a virtually risk-free investment to a risky one. Because this excess return can be interpreted as a reward for bearing risk, we will call it a **risk premium**.

risk premium
The extra return on a risky asset over the risk-free rate; the reward for bearing risk.

THE FIRST LESSON

From the data in Table 1.2, we can calculate risk premiums for the five different categories of investments. The results are shown in Table 1.3. Notice that the risk premium on T-bills is shown as zero in the table because they are our riskless benchmark. Looking at Table 1.3, we see that the average risk premium earned by the large-cap common stock portfolio is $12.3\% - 3.8\% = 8.5\%$. This difference is a significant reward. The fact that it exists historically is an important observation, and it is the basis for our first lesson: Risky assets, on average, earn a risk premium. Put another way, there is a reward, on average, for bearing risk.

Why is this so? Why, for example, is the risk premium for small stocks so much larger than the risk premium for large stocks? More generally, what determines the relative sizes of the risk premiums for the different assets? These questions are at the heart of the modern theory of investments. We will discuss the issues involved many times in the chapters ahead. For now, part of the answer can be found by looking at the historical variability of the returns of these different investments. So, to get started, we now turn our attention to measuring variability in returns.

CHECK THIS

1.3a What do we mean by excess return and risk premium?

1.3b What is the historical risk premium on small-company stocks? On U.S. Treasury bonds?

1.3c What is the first lesson from financial market history?

1.4 Return Variability: The Second Lesson

We have already seen that the year-to-year returns on common stocks tend to be more volatile than returns on, say, long-term government bonds. We now discuss measuring this variability so we can begin examining the subject of risk.

FREQUENCY DISTRIBUTIONS AND VARIABILITY

To get started, we can draw a *frequency distribution* for large-company stock returns like the one in Figure 1.7. What we have done here is to count the number of times that an annual return on the large-company stock portfolio falls within each 10 percent range. For example, in Figure 1.7, the height of 15 for the bar within the interval 10 percent to 20 percent means that 15 of the 81 annual returns are in that range. Notice also that most of the returns are in the −10 to 40 percent range.

What we need to do now is to actually measure the spread in these returns. We know, for example, that the return on the S&P 500 index of common stocks in a typical year was 12.3 percent. We now want to know by how much the actual return differs from this average in a typical year. In other words, we need a measure of the volatility of returns. The **variance** and its square root, the **standard deviation**, are the most commonly used measures of volatility. We describe how to calculate them next. If you've already studied basic statistics, you should notice that we are simply calculating an ordinary sample variance and standard deviation, just as you may have done many times before.

variance
A common measure of volatility.

standard deviation
The square root of the variance.

THE HISTORICAL VARIANCE AND STANDARD DEVIATION

The variance essentially measures the average squared difference between the actual returns and the average return. The bigger this number is, the more the actual returns tend to differ from the average return. Also, the larger the variance or standard deviation is, the more spread out the returns will be.

FIGURE 1.7 Frequency Distribution of Returns on Large-Company Common Stocks: 1926–2006

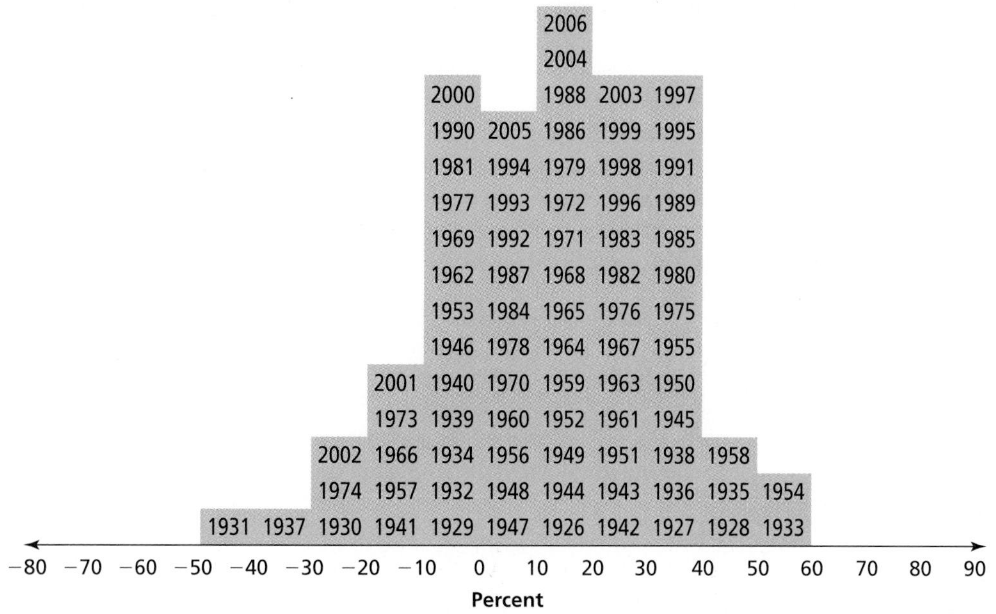

Source: *Stocks, Bonds, Bills, and Inflation Yearbook*™, Ibbotson Associates, Inc., Chicago (annually updated by Roger G. Ibbotson and Rex A. Sinquefield). All rights reserved.

The way we calculate the variance and standard deviation depends on the specific situation. In this chapter, we are looking at historical returns. Therefore, the procedure we describe here is the correct one for calculating the *historical* variance and standard deviation. If we were examining projected future returns, then the procedure would be different. We describe this procedure in a later chapter.

To illustrate how we calculate the historical variance, suppose a particular investment had returns of 10 percent, 12 percent, 3 percent, and −9 percent over the last four years. The average return is $(.10 + .12 + .03 - .09)/4 = .04$, or 4 percent.

Notice that the return is never actually equal to 4 percent. Instead, the first return deviates from the average by $.10 - .04 = .06$, the second return deviates from the average by $.12 - .04 = .08$, and so on. To compute the variance, we square each of these deviations, add them up, and divide the result by the number of returns less one, or three in this case.[2] These calculations are summarized in the following table.

WWW

For an easy-to-read review of basic statistics, see www.robertniles.com/stats/

Year	(1) Actual Return	(2) Average Return	(3) Deviation (1) − (2)	(4) Squared Deviation
1	.10	.04	.06	.0036
2	.12	.04	.08	.0064
3	.03	.04	−.01	.0001
4	−.09	.04	−.13	.0169
Totals	.16		.00	.0270

In the first column, we write down the four actual returns. In the third column, we calculate the difference between the actual returns and the average by subtracting out 4 percent. Finally, in the fourth column, we square the numbers in Column 3 to get the squared deviations from the average.

The variance can now be calculated by dividing .0270, the sum of the squared deviations, by the number of returns less 1. Let Var(R) or σ^2 (read this as "sigma squared") stand for the variance of the return:

$$\text{Var}(R) = \sigma^2 = .027/(4 - 1) = .009$$

The standard deviation is the square root of the variance. So, if SD(R) or σ stands for the standard deviation of the return:

$$\text{SD}(R) = \sigma = \sqrt{.009} = .09487$$

The square root of the variance is used because the variance is measured in "squared" percentages and thus is hard to interpret. The standard deviation is an ordinary percentage, so the answer here could be written as 9.487 percent.

In the table above, notice that the sum of the deviations is equal to zero. This will always be the case, and it provides a good way to check your work. In general, if we have N historical returns, where N is some number, we can write the historical variance as:

$$\text{Var}(R) = \frac{1}{N - 1}[(R_1 - \overline{R})^2 + \cdots + (R_N - \overline{R})^2]$$

This formula tells us to do just what we did above: Take each of the N individual returns ($R_1, R_2, \ldots, R_N$) and subtract the average return, $\overline{R}$; square the results, and add up all these squares; and finally, divide this total by the number of returns less 1 (i.e., $N - 1$). The standard deviation is the square root of Var(R). Standard deviations are a widely used measure of volatility.

[2] The reason for dividing by $N - 1$ rather than simply N is based on statistical sampling theory, which is beyond the scope of this book. Just remember that to calculate a variance about a sample average, you need to divide the sum of squared deviations from the average by $N - 1$.

EXAMPLE 1.4 Calculating the Variance and Standard Deviation

From Table 1.1, we see that the large-company stocks and long-term government bonds had these returns for the past four years:

Year	Large-Company Stocks	Long-Term Government Bonds
2003	0.2868	0.0162
2004	0.1088	0.1034
2005	0.0491	0.1035
2006	0.1579	0.0028

What are the average returns? The variances? The standard deviations?

To calculate the average returns, we add up the returns and divide by four. The results are:

$$\text{Large-company stocks, average return} = \bar{R} = .6026/4 = .15065$$
$$\text{Long-term government bonds, average return} = \bar{R} = .2259/4 = .056475$$

To calculate the variance for large-company stocks, we can summarize the relevant calculations as follows:

Year	(1) Actual Return	(2) Average Return	(3) Deviation (1) − (2)	(4) Squared Deviation
2003	.2868	.15065	.13615	.01854
2004	.1088	.15065	−.04185	.00175
2005	.0491	.15065	−.10155	.01031
2006	.1579	.15065	.00725	.00005
Totals	.6026		.00000	.03065

Because there are four years of returns, we calculate the variance by dividing .03065 by (4 − 1) = 3:

	Large-Company Stocks	Long-Term Government Bonds
Variance (σ^2)	.03065/3 = .010217	.00892/3 = .002973
Standard deviation (σ)	$\sqrt{.010217}$ = .1011	$\sqrt{.002973}$ = .0545

For practice, verify that you get the same answers that we do for long-term government bonds. Notice that the standard deviation for large-company stocks, 10.11 percent, is about twice as much as the standard deviation for long-term government bonds, 5.45 percent. What does this difference mean?

THE HISTORICAL RECORD

Figure 1.8 summarizes much of our discussion of capital market history so far. It displays average returns, standard deviations, and frequency distributions of annual returns on a common scale. In Figure 1.8, notice, for example, that the standard deviation for the small-stock portfolio (32.7 percent per year) is more than 10 times larger than the T-bill

FIGURE 1.8 Historical Returns, Standard Deviations, and Frequency Distributions: 1926–2006

Series	Average return	Standard deviation	Distribution
Large-company stocks	12.3%	20.1%	
Small-company stocks	17.4	32.7	
Long-term corporate bonds	6.2	8.5	
Long-term government	5.8	9.2	
Intermediate-term government	5.4	5.7	
U.S. Treasury bills	3.8	3.1	
Inflation	3.1	4.3	

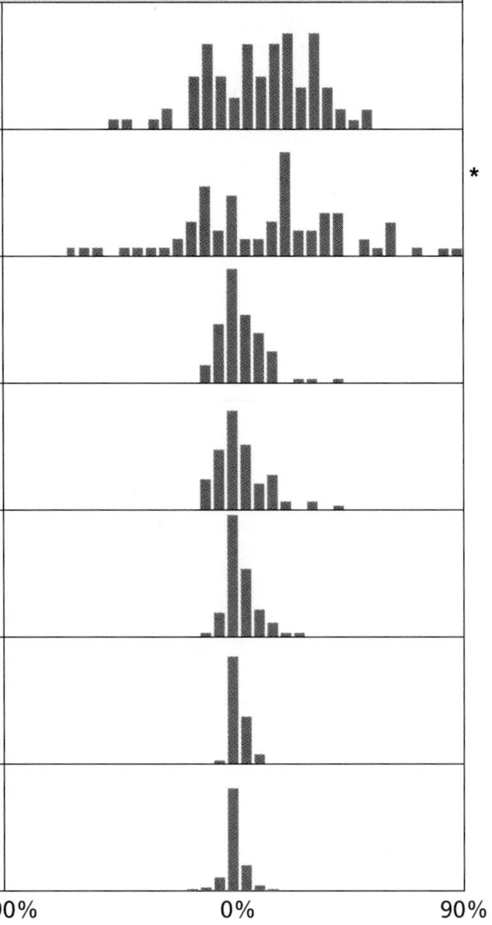

*The 1933 small-company stocks total return was 142.9 percent.

Source: *Stocks, Bonds, Bills, and Inflation Yearbook*™, Ibbotson Associates, Inc., Chicago (annually updated by Roger G. Ibbotson and Rex A. Sinquefield).

portfolio's standard deviation (3.1 percent per year). We will return to discuss these facts momentarily.

NORMAL DISTRIBUTION

normal distribution
A symmetric, bell-shaped frequency distribution that is completely defined by its average and standard deviation.

For many different random events in nature, a particular frequency distribution, the **normal distribution** (or *bell curve*) is useful for describing the probability of ending up in a given range. For example, the idea behind "grading on a curve" comes from the fact that exam scores often resemble a bell curve.

Figure 1.9 illustrates a normal distribution and its distinctive bell shape. As you can see, this distribution has a much cleaner appearance than the actual return distributions illustrated in Figure 1.7. Even so, like the normal distribution, the actual distributions do appear to be at least roughly mound shaped and symmetric. When this is true, the normal distribution is often a very good approximation.

Also, keep in mind that the distributions in Figure 1.8 are based on only 81 yearly observations, while Figure 1.9 is, in principle, based on an infinite number. So, if we had been able

FIGURE 1.9 The Normal Distribution: Illustrated Returns Based on the Historical Return and Standard Deviation for a Portfolio of Large-Company Common Stocks

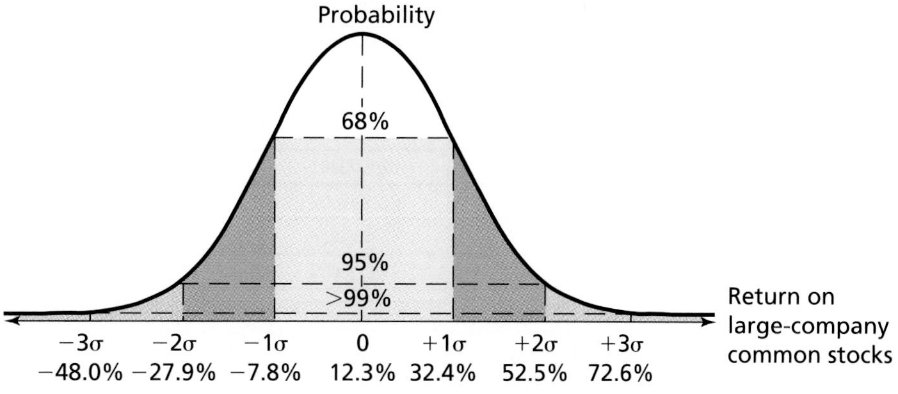

to observe returns for, say, 1,000 years, we might have filled in a lot of the irregularities and ended up with a much smoother picture. For our purposes, it is enough to observe that the returns are at least roughly normally distributed.

The usefulness of the normal distribution stems from the fact that it is completely described by the average and the standard deviation. If you have these two numbers, then there is nothing else you need to know. For example, with a normal distribution, the probability that we end up within one standard deviation of the average is 68 percent, or about 2/3. The probability that we end up within two standard deviations is about 95 percent. Finally, the probability of being more than three standard deviations away from the average is less than 1 percent. These ranges and the probabilities are illustrated in Figure 1.9.

To see why this range is useful, recall from Figure 1.8 that the standard deviation of returns on the large-company common stocks is 20.1 percent. The average return is 12.3 percent. So, assuming that the frequency distribution is at least approximately normal, the probability that the return in a given year is in the range of –7.8 percent to 32.4 percent (12.3 percent plus or minus one standard deviation, 20.1 percent) is about 2/3. This range is illustrated in Figure 1.9. In other words, there is about one chance in three that the return will be *outside* this range. This literally tells you that, if you buy stocks in large companies, you should expect to be outside this range in one year out of every three. This reinforces our earlier observations about stock market volatility. However, there is only a 5 percent chance (approximately) that we would end up outside the range of −27.9 percent to 52.5 percent (12.3 percent plus or minus 2 × 20.1%). These points are also illustrated in Figure 1.9.

THE SECOND LESSON

Our observations concerning the year-to-year variability in returns are the basis for our second lesson from capital market history. On average, bearing risk is handsomely rewarded, but, in a given year, there is a significant chance of a dramatic change in value. Thus, our second lesson is this: The greater the potential reward, the greater is the risk.

Thus far in this chapter, we have emphasized the year-to-year variability in returns. We should note that even day-to-day movements can exhibit considerable volatility. For example, on September 17, 2001, the Dow Jones Industrial Average (DJIA) plummeted 684.81 points, or 7.13 percent. By historical standards, it was one of the worst days ever for the 30 stocks that comprise the DJIA (as well as for a majority of stocks in the market). Still, while the drop was the largest one-day decrease in the DJIA ever in terms of points, it actually wasn't quite in the top 10 largest one-day percentage decreases in history, as illustrated in the following table:

Days with Greatest Net Loss				
Rank	Date	Close	Net Change	% Change
1	09/17/2001	8920.70	−684.81	−7.13
2	04/14/2000	10305.77	−617.78	−5.66
3	10/27/1997	7161.15	−554.26	−7.19
4	08/31/1998	7539.07	−512.61	−6.37
5	10/19/1987	1738.74	−508.00	−22.61
6	03/12/2001	10208.25	−436.37	−4.10
7	02/27/2007	12216.24	−416.02	−3.29
8	07/19/2002	8019.26	−390.23	−4.63
9	08/09/2007	13270.68	−387.18	−2.83
10	09/20/2001	8376.21	−382.92	−4.37

Days with Greatest Percentage Loss				
Rank	Date	Close	Net Change	% Change
1	10/19/1987	1738.74	−508.00	−22.61
2	10/28/1929	260.64	−38.33	−12.82
3	10/29/1929	230.07	−30.57	−11.73
4	11/06/1929	232.13	−25.55	−9.92
5	12/18/1899	58.27	−5.57	−8.72
6	08/12/1932	63.11	−5.79	−8.40
7	03/14/1907	76.23	−6.89	−8.29
8	10/26/1987	1793.93	−156.83	−8.04
9	07/21/1933	88.71	−7.55	−7.84
10	10/18/1937	125.73	−10.57	−7.75

Source: Dow Jones (http://www.djindexes.com/mdsidx/index.cfm?event=showAvgStats#no4).

This discussion highlights the importance of looking at returns in terms of percentages rather than dollar amounts or index points. For example, before 2001, the biggest one-day loss in terms of points was on April 14, 2000, when the DJIA declined by about 618 points. The second worst was the 554-point drop of October 27, 1997. By contrast, the 5.57-point drop in the DJIA on December 18, 1899, marked the fifth worst day in the history of the index, but a 5.57-point loss in the DJIA in today's market would hardly be noticed. This is precisely why we relied on percentage returns when we examined market history in this chapter.[3]

[3] By the way, as you may have noticed, what's kind of weird is that 6 of the 12 worst days in the history of the DJIA occurred in October, including the top 3. We have no clue as to why. Furthermore, looking back at the Mark Twain quote near the beginning of the chapter, how do you suppose he knew? Sounds like a case for *CSI: Wall Street.*

EXAMPLE 1.5

Investing in Growth Stocks

The term *growth stock* is frequently a euphemism for small-company stock. Are such investments suitable for "widows and orphans"? Before answering, you should consider the historical volatility. For example, from the historical record, what is the approximate probability that you will actually lose 16 percent or more of your money in a single year if you buy a portfolio of such companies?

Looking back at Figure 1.8, we see that the average return on small stocks is 17.4 percent and the standard deviation is 32.7 percent. Assuming that the returns are approximately normal, there is about a 1/3 probability that you will experience a return outside the range of −15.3 percent to 50.1 percent (17.4% ± 32.7%).

(continued)

Because the normal distribution is symmetric, the odds of being above or below this range are equal. There is thus a 1/6 chance (half of 1/3) that you will lose more than 15.3 percent. So, you should expect this to happen once in every six years, on average. Such investments can thus be *very* volatile, and they are not well suited for those who cannot afford the risk.

Now that you know how to calculate and, more importantly, interpret average returns and standard deviations, the nearby *Spreadsheet Analysis* box shows how to do the calculations using Excel, which can really speed up things when we have a lot of data.

SPREADSHEET ANALYSIS

Using a Spreadsheet to Calculate Average Returns and Volatilities

Here is an Excel spreadsheet summarizing the formulas and analysis needed to calculate average returns and standard deviations using the 1990s as an example:

	A	B	C	D	E	F	G	H
1								
2	**Using a spreadsheet to calculate average returns and standard deviations**							
3								
4	Looking back in the chapter, the data suggest that the 1990s were one							
5	of the best decades for stock market investors. We will find out just how good by							
6	calculating the average returns and standard deviations for this period. Here are the							
7	year-by-year returns on the large-company S&P 500 Index:							
8								
9		*Year*	*Return(%)*	*Year*	*Return(%)*			
10		1990	−3.10	1995	37.58			
11		1991	30.46	1996	22.96			
12		1992	7.62	1997	33.36			
13		1993	10.08	1998	28.58			
14		1994	1.32	1999	21.04			
15								
16		Average return (%):		18.99				
17		Standard deviation (%):		14.16				
18								
19	The formulas we used to do the calculations are just =AVERAGE(C10:C14;E10:E14)							
20	and =STDEV(C10:C14;E10:E14). Notice that the average return in the 1990s was 18.99							
21	percent per year, which is larger than the long-run average of 12.3 percent. At the same							
22	time, the standard deviation, 14.16 percent, was smaller than the 20.1 percent long-run value.							

CHECK THIS

1.4a In words, how do we calculate a variance? A standard deviation?

1.4b What is the second lesson from financial market history?

1.5 More on Average Returns

Thus far in this chapter, we have looked closely at simple average returns. But there is another way of computing an average return. The fact that average returns are calculated two different ways leads to some confusion, so our goal in this section is to explain the two approaches and also explain the circumstances under which each is appropriate.

ARITHMETIC VERSUS GEOMETRIC AVERAGES

Let's start with a simple example. Suppose you buy a particular stock for \$100. Unfortunately, the first year you own it, it falls to \$50. The second year you own it, it rises back to \$100, leaving you where you started (no dividends were paid).

What was your average return on this investment? Common sense seems to say that your average return must be exactly zero since you started with \$100 and ended with \$100. But if we calculate the returns year-by-year, we see that you lost 50 percent the first year (you lost half of your money). The second year, you made 100 percent (you doubled your money). Your average return over the two years was thus $(-50\% + 100\%)/2 = 25\%$! So which is correct, 0 percent or 25 percent?

geometric average return
The average compound return earned per year over a multiyear period.

arithmetic average return
The return earned in an average year over a multiyear period.

The answer is that both are correct; they just answer different questions. The 0 percent is called the **geometric average return**. The geometric average return answers the question *"What was your average compound return per year over a particular period?"*

The 25 percent is called the **arithmetic average return**. The arithmetic average return answers the question *"What was your return in an average year over a particular period?"*

Notice that, in previous sections, the average returns we calculated were all arithmetic averages, so you already know how to calculate them. What we need to do now is (1) learn how to calculate geometric averages and (2) learn the circumstances under which one average is more meaningful than the other.

CALCULATING GEOMETRIC AVERAGE RETURNS

If we have N years of returns, the geometric average return over these N years is calculated using this formula:

$$\text{Geometric average return} = [(1 + R_1) \times (1 + R_2) \times \cdots \times (1 + R_N)]^{1/N} - 1 \quad (1.5)$$

This formula tells us that four steps are required:

1. Take each of the N annual returns $R_1, R_2, \ldots, R_N$ and add a one to each (after converting them to decimals!).
2. Multiply all the numbers from step 1 together.
3. Take the result from step 2 and raise it to the power of $1/N$.
4. Finally, subtract one from the result of step 3. The result is the geometric average return.

To illustrate how we calculate a geometric average return, suppose a particular investment had annual returns of 10 percent, 12 percent, 3 percent, and –9 percent over the last four years. The geometric average return over this four-year period is calculated as $(1.10 \times 1.12 \times 1.03 \times .91)^{1/4} - 1 = 3.66\%$. In contrast, the average arithmetic return is $(.10 + .12 + .03 - .09)/4 = 4.0\%$.

One thing you may have noticed in our examples thus far is that the geometric average returns seem to be smaller. It turns out that this will always be true (as long as the returns are not all identical, in which case the two "averages" would be the same). To illustrate, Table 1.4 shows the arithmetic averages and standard deviations from Figure 1.8, along with the geometric average returns.

As shown in Table 1.4, the geometric averages are all smaller, but the magnitude of the difference varies quite a bit. The reason is that the difference is greater for more volatile investments. In fact, there is a useful approximation. Assuming all the numbers

TABLE 1.4 Geometric versus Arithmetic Average Returns: 1926–2006

Series	Geometric Mean	Arithmetic Mean	Standard Deviation
Large-company stocks	10.4%	12.3%	20.1%
Small-company stocks	12.7	17.4	32.7
Long-term corporate bonds	5.9	6.2	8.5
Long-term government bonds	5.4	5.8	9.2
Intermediate-term government bonds	5.3	5.4	5.7
U.S. Treasury bills	3.7	3.8	3.1
Inflation	3.0	3.1	4.3

are expressed in decimals (as opposed to percentages), the geometric average return is approximately equal to the arithmetic average return minus half the variance. For example, looking at the large-company stocks, the arithmetic average is .123 and the standard deviation is .201, implying that the variance is .040401. The approximate geometric average is thus $.123 - .040401/2 = .1028$, which is quite close to the actual value.

EXAMPLE 1.6 Calculating the Geometric Average Return

Calculate the geometric average return for the large-company stocks for the last four years in Table 1.1, 2003–2006.

First, convert percentages to decimal returns, add one, and then calculate their product.

Year	Large-Company Stocks	Product
2003	28.68	1.2868
2004	10.88	× 1.1088
2005	4.91	× 1.0491
2006	15.79	× 1.1579
		1.7332

Notice that the number 1.7332 is what our investment is worth after five years if we started with a one-dollar investment. The geometric average return is then calculated as

$$\text{Geometric average return} = 1.7332^{1/4} - 1 = .1474, \text{ or } 14.74\%$$

Thus the geometric average return is about 14.74 percent in this example. In contrast, in Example 1.4, the average arithmetic return was calculated as 15.07 percent. Here is a tip: If you are using a financial calculator, you can put $1 in as the present value, $1.7332 as the future value, and 4 as the number of periods. Then, solve for the unknown rate. You should get the same answer we did.

EXAMPLE 1.7 More Geometric Averages

Take a look back at Figure 1.1. There, we showed the value of a $1 investment after 81 years. Use the value for the large-company stock investment to check the geometric average in Table 1.4.

(continued)

In Figure 1.1, the large-company investment grew to \$3,077.33 over 81 years. The geometric average return is thus

$$\text{Geometric average return} = 3{,}077.33^{1/81} - 1 = .1042, \text{ or about } 10.4\%$$

This 10.4% is the value shown in Table 1.4. For practice, check some of the other numbers in Table 1.4 the same way.

ARITHMETIC AVERAGE RETURN OR GEOMETRIC AVERAGE RETURN?

When we look at historical returns, the difference between the geometric and arithmetic average returns isn't too hard to understand. To put it slightly differently, the geometric average tells you what you actually earned per year on average, compounded annually. The arithmetic average tells you what you earned in a typical year. You should use whichever one answers the question you want answered.

A somewhat trickier question concerns forecasting the future, and there is a lot of confusion about this point among analysts and financial planners. The problem is the following. If we have *estimates* of both the arithmetic and geometric average returns, then the arithmetic average is probably too high for longer periods and the geometric average is probably too low for shorter periods.

The good news is that there is a simple way of combining the two averages, which we will call *Blume's formula*.[4] Suppose we calculated geometric and arithmetic return averages from N years of data and we wish to use these averages to form a T-year average return forecast, $R(T)$, where T is less than N. Here's how we do it:

$$R(T) = \frac{T-1}{N-1} \times \textit{Geometric average} + \frac{N-T}{N-1} \times \textit{Arithmetic average}$$

For example, suppose that, from 25 years of annual returns data, we calculate an arithmetic average return of 12 percent and a geometric average return of 9 percent. From these averages, we wish to make 1-year, 5-year, and 10-year average return forecasts. These three average return forecasts are calculated as follows:

$$R(1) = \frac{1-1}{24} \times 9\% + \frac{25-1}{24} \times 12\% = 12\%$$

$$R(5) = \frac{5-1}{24} \times 9\% + \frac{25-5}{24} \times 12\% = 11.5\%$$

$$R(10) = \frac{10-1}{24} \times 9\% + \frac{25-10}{24} \times 12\% = 10.875\%$$

Thus, we see that 1-year, 5-year, and 10-year forecasts are 12 percent, 11.5 percent, and 10.875 percent, respectively.

This concludes our discussion of geometric versus arithmetic averages. One last note: In the future, when we say "average return," we mean arithmetic average unless we explicitly say otherwise.

[4] This elegant result is due to Marshal Blume. ("Unbiased Estimates of Long-Run Expected Rates of Return," *Journal of the American Statistical Association,* September 1974, pp. 634–638.)

EXAMPLE 1.8

Forecasting Average Returns

Over the 81-year period 1926–2006, the geometric average return for the large-company stocks was 10.4 percent and the arithmetic average return was 12.3 percent. Calculate average return forecasts for 1, 5, 10, and 25 years into the future.

In this case, we would use Blume's formula with values of T = 1, 5, 10, and 25 and N = 81:

$$R(T) = \frac{T-1}{80} \times 10.4\% + \frac{81-T}{80} \times 12.3\%$$

(continued)

T	$R(T)$
1	12.3%
5	12.2
10	12.1
25	11.7
81	10.4

Notice that short-term forecasts are closer to the arithmetic average return and long-term forecasts are closer to the geometric average return.

CHECK THIS

1.5a Over a five-year period, an investment in a broad market index yielded annual returns of 10, 16, −5, −8, and 7 percent. What were the arithmetic and geometric average annual returns for this index?

1.5b Over a 25-year period, an investment in a broad market index yielded an arithmetic average return of 4 percent and a geometric average return of 3.6 percent. Using Blume's formula, what would be the 5-year and 10-year average return forecasts?

1.6 Risk and Return

In previous sections we explored financial market history to see what we could learn about risk and return. In this section we summarize our findings and then conclude our discussion by looking ahead at the subjects we will be examining in later chapters.

THE RISK-RETURN TRADE-OFF

Figure 1.10 is a way of putting together our findings on risk and return. What it shows is that there is a risk-return trade-off. At one extreme, if we are unwilling to bear any risk at all, but we are willing to forgo the use of our money for a while, then we can earn the

FIGURE 1.10 Risk-Return Trade-Off

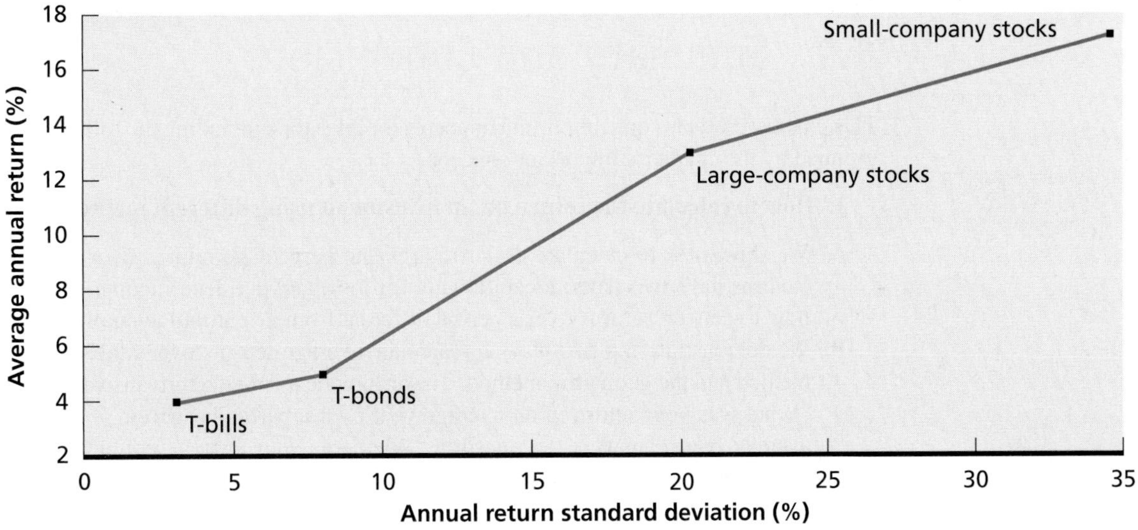

risk-free rate. Because the risk-free rate represents compensation for just waiting, it is often called the *time value of money*.

If we are willing to bear risk, then we can expect to earn a risk premium, at least on average. Further, the more risk we are willing to bear, the greater is the risk premium. Investment advisers like to say that an investment has a "wait" component and a "worry" component. In our figure, the time value of money is the compensation for waiting, and the risk premium is the compensation for worrying.

There are two important caveats to this discussion. First, risky investments do not *always* pay more than risk-free investments. Indeed, that is precisely what makes them risky. In other words, there is a risk premium *on average,* but, over any particular time interval, there is no guarantee. Second, we have intentionally been a little imprecise about what we mean exactly by risk. As we will discuss in the chapters ahead, investors are not compensated for all risks. Some risks are cheaply and easily avoidable, and there is no expected reward for bearing them. It is only those risks that cannot be easily avoided that are compensated (on average).

A LOOK AHEAD

In the remainder of this text, we focus exclusively on financial assets. An advantage of this approach is that it is limited to four major types: stocks, bonds, futures, and options, in the order that we cover them. This means that we won't be discussing collectibles such as classic automobiles, baseball cards, coins, fine art, or stamps. We also won't be discussing real estate or precious metals such as gold and platinum. It's not that these are unimportant; rather, they are very specialized. So, instead of treating them superficially, we leave a discussion of them for another day (and another book).

As we've indicated, to understand the potential reward from an investment, it is critical to first understand the risk involved. There is an old saying that goes like this: It's easy to make a small fortune investing in_____ (put your favorite investment here)—just start with a large fortune! The moral is that the key to successful investing is to make informed, intelligent decisions about risk. For this reason, we are going to pay particular attention to the factors that determine the value of the different assets we discuss and the nature of the associated risks.

One common characteristic that these assets have is that they are bought and sold around the clock and around the world in vast quantities. The way they are traded can be very different, however. We think it is important and interesting to understand exactly what happens when you buy or sell one of these assets, so we will be discussing the different trading mechanisms and the way the different markets function. We will also describe actual buying and selling at various points along the way to show you the steps involved and the results of placing buy and sell orders and having them executed.

1.7 Summary and Conclusions

This chapter presents some important concepts for investors, including the following items—grouped by the chapter's important concepts.

1. How to calculate the return on an investment using different methods.

A. We show how to calculate dollar returns and percentage returns over a time period. Returns have two parts: a capital gain (or loss) and dividend income. We also show how to convert returns over a period different from a year into annualized returns.

B. We demonstrate the two ways to calculate average returns over time: the arithmetic method and the geometric method. The arithmetic average return answers the question "What was your return in an average year over a particular period?" The geometric average return answers the question "What was your average compound return per year over a particular period?" Generally, when investors say "average return," they are referring to arithmetic average unless they explicitly say otherwise.

2. The historical returns on various important types of investments.

A. In order of their historical return from highest to lowest, we discuss returns on some important portfolios, including:

- *Small-company stocks.* This is a portfolio composed of the smallest (in terms of total market value of outstanding stock) of the companies listed on the New York Stock Exchange.
- *Large-company stocks.* This portfolio is based on the Standard & Poor's 500 Index. This index contains 500 of the largest companies (in terms of total market value of outstanding stock) in the United States.
- *Long-term U.S. government bonds.* This is a portfolio of U.S. government bonds with 20 years to maturity.
- *U.S. Treasury bills.* This is a portfolio of Treasury bills (T-bills for short) with a three-month maturity.

B. One important historical return fact is that U.S. T-bill returns have barely outpaced inflation. Therefore, an investor must invest in stocks or bonds to earn a return higher than the inflation rate.

3. The historical risks on various important types of investments.

A. Historically, the risk (as measured by standard deviation of returns) of the portfolios described above is highest for small-company stocks. The next highest risk is for large-company stocks, followed by long-term government bonds and Treasury bills.

B. We draw two key lessons from historical risk:

- Risky assets, on average, earn a risk premium. That is, there is a reward for bearing risk. However, this expected reward is not realized each year.
- The greater the potential reward from a risky investment, the greater is the risk.

4. The relationship between risk and return.

A. When we put these two key lessons together, we concluded that there is a risk-return trade-off.

B. The only way to earn a higher return is to take on greater risk.

GET REAL

This chapter took you through some basic, but important, investment-related calculations. We then walked through the modern history of risk and return. How should you, as an investor or investment manager, put this information to work?

The answer is that you now have a rational, objective basis for thinking about what you stand to make from investing in some important broad asset classes. For the stock market as a whole, as measured by the performance of large-company stocks, you know that you might realistically expect to make 12 percent or so per year on average.

Equally important, you know that you won't make 12 percent in any one year; instead, you'll make more or less. You know that the standard deviation is about 20-percent per year, and you should know what that means in terms of risk. In particular, you need to understand that in one year out of every six, you should expect to lose more than 8 percent (12 percent minus one standard deviation), so this will be a relatively common event. The good news is that in one year out of six, you can realistically expect to earn more than 32 percent (12 percent plus one standard deviation).

The other important, practical thing to understand from this chapter is that a strategy of investing in very low-risk assets (such as T-bills) has historically barely kept up with inflation. This might be sufficient for some investors, but if your goal is to do better than that, then you will have to bear some amount of risk to achieve it.

Key Terms

arithmetic average return 24
capital gains yield 4
dividend yield 4
effective annual return (EAR) 6
geometric average return 24
normal distribution 20
risk-free rate 16
risk premium 16
standard deviation 17
total dollar return 3
total percent return 4
variance 17

Chapter Review Problems and Self-Test

1. **Calculating Returns** You bought 400 shares of Metallica Heavy Metal, Inc., at $30 per share. Over the year, you received $.75 per share in dividends. If the stock sold for $33 at the end of the year, what was your dollar return? Your percentage return?
2. **Calculating Returns and Variability** Using the following returns, calculate the arithmetic average returns, the variances, the standard deviations, and the geometric returns for the following stocks:

Year	Michele, Inc.	Janicek Co.
1	12%	5%
2	−4	−15
3	0	10
4	20	38
5	2	17

3. **Forecasting Returns** Over a 30-year period an asset had an arithmetic return of 12.8 percent and a geometric return of 10.7 percent. Using Blume's formula, what is your best estimate of the future annual returns over the next 5 years? 10 years? 20 years?

Answers to Self-Test Problems

1. Your dollar return is just your gain or loss in dollars. Here, we receive $.75 in dividends on each of our 400 shares, for a total of $300. In addition, each share rose from $30 to $33, so we make $3 × 400 shares = $1,200. Our total dollar return is thus $300 + $1,200 = $1,500.

   Our percentage return (or just "return" for short) is equal to the $1,500 we made divided by our initial outlay of $30 × 400 shares = $12,000; so $1,500/12,000 = .125 = 12.5%. Equivalently, we could have just noted that each share paid a $.75 dividend and each share gained $3, so the total dollar gain per share was $3.75. As a percentage of the cost of one share ($30), we get $3.75/30 = .125 = 12.5%.
2. First, calculate arithmetic averages as follows:

Michele, Inc.	Janicek Co.
12%	5%
−4	−15
0	10
20	38
2	17
30%	55%
Average return: 30/5 = 6%	55/5 = 11%

www.mhhe.com/jm5e

Using the arithmetic averages above, calculate the squared deviations from the arithmetic average returns and sum the squared deviations as follows:

Michele, Inc.	Janicek Co.
$(12 - 6)^2 = 36$	$(5 - 11)^2 = 36$
$(-4 - 6)^2 = 100$	$(-15 - 11)^2 = 676$
$(0 - 6)^2 = 36$	$(10 - 11)^2 = 1$
$(20 - 6)^2 = 196$	$(38 - 11)^2 = 729$
$(2 - 6)^2 = 16$	$(17 - 11)^2 = 36$
384	1,478

Calculate return variances by dividing the sums of squared deviations by four, which is the number of returns less one.

$$\text{Michele: } 384/4 = 96 \qquad \text{Janicek: } 1{,}478/4 = 369.5$$

Standard deviations are then calculated as the square root of the variance.

$$\text{Michele: } \sqrt{96} = 9.8\% \qquad \text{Janicek: } \sqrt{369.5} = 19.22\%$$

Geometric returns are then calculated as:

$$\text{Michele: } [(1 + .12)(1 - .04)(1 + .00)(1 + .20)(1 + .02)]^{1/5} - 1 = 5.65\%$$

$$\text{Janicek: } [(1 + .05)(1 - .15)(1 + .10)(1 + .38)(1 + .17)]^{1/5} - 1 = 9.65\%$$

3. To find the best forecast, we apply Blume's formula as follows:

$$R(5) = \frac{5 - 1}{29} \times 10.7\% + \frac{30 - 5}{29} \times 12.8\% = 12.51\%$$

$$R(10) = \frac{10 - 1}{29} \times 10.7\% + \frac{30 - 10}{29} \times 12.8\% = 12.15\%$$

$$R(20) = \frac{20 - 1}{29} \times 10.7\% + \frac{30 - 20}{29} \times 12.8\% = 11.42\%$$

Test Your Investment Quotient

For the remaining questions and problems, the circled numbers in the margin refer to the corresponding learning objective in this chapter.

IQ

CFA® PROBLEMS

(1) 1. **Prices and Returns** You plan to buy a common stock and hold it for one year. You expect to receive both $1.50 from dividends and $26 from the sale of the stock at the end of the year. If you wanted to earn a 15 percent rate of return, what is the maximum price you would pay for the stock today?

a. $22.61
b. $23.91
c. $24.50
d. $27.50

CFA® PROBLEMS

(1) 2. **Returns** A portfolio of non-dividend-paying stocks earned a geometric mean return of 5 percent between January 1, 1994, and December 31, 2000. The arithmetic mean return for the same period was 6 percent. If the market value of the portfolio at the beginning of 1994 was $100,000, the market value of the portfolio at the end of 2000 was *closest* to:

a. $135,000
b. $140,710
c. $142,000
d. $150,363

CFA® PROBLEMS

(4) 3. **Standard Deviation** Which of the following statements about standard deviation is true? Standard deviation

a. Is the square of the variance.
b. Can be a positive or negative number.
c. Is denominated in the same units as the original data.
d. Is the arithmetic mean of the squared deviations from the mean.

CFA® PROBLEMS

(4) **4. Normal Distribution** An investment strategy has an expected return of 12 percent and a standard deviation of 10 percent. If the investment returns are normally distributed, the probability of earning a return less than 2 percent is closest to:

a. 10 percent
b. 16 percent
c. 32 percent
d. 34 percent

CFA® PROBLEMS

(4) **5. Normal Distribution** What are the mean and standard deviation of a standard normal distribution?

	Mean	Standard Deviation
a.	0	0
b.	0	1
c.	1	0
d.	1	1

CFA® PROBLEMS

(4) **6. Normal Distribution** Given a data series that is normally distributed with a mean of 100 and a standard deviation of 10, about 95 percent of the numbers in the series will fall within which of the following ranges?

a. 60 to 140
b. 70 to 130
c. 80 to 120
d. 90 to 110

(3) **7. Asset Types** Stocks, bonds, options, and futures are the four major types of

a. Debt
b. Real assets
c. Equity
d. Financial assets

(1) **8. Investment Returns** Suppose the value of an investment doubles in a one-year period. In this case, the rate of return on this investment over that one-year period is what amount?

a. 100 percent even if the gain is not actually realized.
b. 200 percent even if the gain is not actually realized.
c. 100 percent only if the gain is actually realized.
d. 200 percent only if the gain is actually realized.

(2) **9. Historical Returns** Which of the following asset categories has an annual returns history most closely linked to historical annual rates of inflation?

a. U.S. Treasury bills
b. Corporate bonds
c. Large-company stocks
d. Small-company stocks

(2) **10. Historical Returns** Based on the annual returns history since 1926, which asset category, on average, has yielded the highest risk premium?

a. U.S. government bonds
b. Corporate bonds
c. Large-company stocks
d. Small-company stocks

(1) **11. Stat 101** Over a four-year period, an investment in Outa'Synch common stock yields returns of −10, 40, 0, and 20. What is the arithmetic return over this period?

a. 5 percent
b. 7.5 percent
c. 10 percent
d. 12.5 percent

(4) **12. Stat 101** You calculate an average historical return of 20 percent and a standard deviation of return of 10 percent for an investment in Stonehenge Construction Co. You believe these values well represent the future distribution of returns. Assuming that returns are normally distributed, what is the probability that Stonehenge Construction will yield a negative return?

a. 17 percent
b. 33 percent

c. 5 percent
d. 2.5 percent

(4) **13. Stat 101** Which of the following statements about a normal distribution is incorrect?

a. A normal distribution is symmetrically centered on its mean.
b. The probability of being within one standard deviation from the mean is about 68 percent.
c. The probability of being within two standard deviations from the mean is about 95 percent.
d. The probability of a negative value is always one-half.

CFA® PROBLEMS

(4) **14. Normal Distribution** Based on a normal distribution with a mean of 500 and a standard deviation of 150, the z-value for an observation of 200 is closest to:

a. –2.00
b. –1.75
c. 1.75
d. 2.00

CFA® PROBLEMS

(4) **15. Normal Distribution** A normal distribution would least likely be described as:

a. Asymptotic.
b. A discrete probability distribution.
c. A symmetrical or bell-shaped distribution.
d. A curve that theoretically extends from negative infinity to positive infinity.

Concept Questions

(3) **1. Risk versus Return** Based on the historical record, rank the following investments in increasing order of risk. Rank the investments in increasing order of average returns. What do you conclude about the relationship between the risk of an investment and the return you expect to earn on it?

a. Large stocks
b. Treasury bills
c. Long-term government bonds
d. Small stocks

(1) **2. Return Calculations** A particular stock had a return last year of 4 percent. However, you look at the stock price and notice that it actually didn't change at all last year. How is this possible?

(4) **3. Returns Distributions** What is the probability that the return on small stocks will be less than –100 percent in a single year (think about it)? What are the implications for the distribution of returns?

(1) **4. Arithmetic versus Geometric Returns** What is the difference between arithmetic and geometric returns? Suppose you have invested in a stock for the last 10 years. Which number is more important to you, the arithmetic or geometric return?

(1) **5. Blume's Formula** What is Blume's formula? When would you want to use it in practice?

(1) **6. Inflation and Returns** Look at Table 1.1 and Figures 1.5 and 1.6. When were T-bill rates at their highest? Why do you think they were so high during this period?

(1) **7. Inflation and Returns** The returns we have examined are not adjusted for inflation. What do you suppose would happen to our estimated risk premiums if we did account for inflation?

(1) **8. Taxes and Returns** The returns we have examined are not adjusted for taxes. What do you suppose would happen to our estimated returns and risk premiums if we did account for taxes? What would happen to our volatility measures?

(1) **9. Taxes and Treasury Bills** As a practical matter, most of the return you earn from investing in Treasury bills is taxed right away as ordinary income. Thus, if you are in a 40 percent tax bracket and you earn 5 percent on a Treasury bill, your aftertax return is only $.05 \times (1 - .40) = .03$, or 3 percent. In other words, 40 percent of your return goes to pay taxes, leaving you with just 3 percent. Once you consider inflation and taxes, how does the long-term return from Treasury bills look?

(4) **10. The Long Run** Given your answer to the last question and the discussion in the chapter, why would any rational person do anything other than load up on 100 percent small stocks?

Questions and Problems

Core Questions

(1) **1. Calculating Returns** Suppose you bought 100 shares of stock at an initial price of $73 per share. The stock paid a dividend of $0.88 per share during the following year, and the share price at the end of the year was $82. Compute your total dollar return on this investment. Does your answer change if you keep the stock instead of selling it? Why or why not?

(1) **2. Calculating Yields** In the previous problem, what is the capital gains yield? The dividend yield? What is the total rate of return on the investment?

(1) **3. Calculating Returns** Rework Problems 1 and 2 assuming that you buy 750 shares of the stock and the ending share price is $68.40.

(3) **4. Historical Returns** What is the historical rate of return on each of the following investments? What is the historical risk premium on these investments?

a. Long-term government bonds
b. Treasury bills
c. Large stocks
d. Small stocks

(1) **5. Calculating Average Returns** The rate of return on Cherry Jalopies, Inc., stock over the last five years was 7 percent, 21 percent, −8 percent, −5 percent, and 31 percent. Over the same period, the return on Straw Construction Company's stock was 12 percent, 34 percent, −11 percent, −7 percent, and 41 percent. What was the arithmetic average return on each stock over this period?

(4) **6. Calculating Returns and Variability** Using the following returns, calculate the arithmetic average returns, the variances, and the standard deviations for stocks A and B.

Year	A	B
1	17%	21%
2	9	7
3	−14	−10
4	24	26
5	13	15

(1) **7. Return Calculations** A particular stock has a dividend yield of 1.7 percent. Last year, the stock price fell from $65 to $59. What was the return for the year?

(1) **8. Geometric Returns** A stock has had returns of 16 percent, −19 percent, 4 percent, 34 percent, and 22 percent over the last five years. What is the geometric return for the stock?

(1) **9. Arithmetic and Geometric Returns** A stock has had returns of 31 percent, 9 percent, 17 percent, −3 percent, −21 percent, and 37 percent over the last six years. What are the arithmetic and geometric returns for the stock?

Intermediate Questions

(4) **10. Returns and the Bell Curve** An investment has an expected return of 11 percent per year with a standard deviation of 26 percent. Assuming that the returns on this investment are at least roughly normally distributed, how frequently do you expect to earn between −15 percent and 37 percent? How often do you expect to earn less than −15 percent?

(4) **11. Returns and the Bell Curve** An investment has an expected return of 7 percent per year with a standard deviation of 3.5 percent. Assuming that the returns on this investment are at least roughly normally distributed, how frequently do you expect to lose money?

(2) **12. Using Returns Distributions** Based on the historical record, if you invest in long-term U.S. Treasury bonds, what is the approximate probability that your return will be less than −3.4 percent in a given year? What range of returns would you expect to see 95 percent of the time? 99 percent of the time?

(2) **13. Using Returns Distributions** Based on the historical record, what is the approximate probability that an investment in small stocks will double in value in a single year? How about triple in a single year?

(2) **14. Risk Premiums** Refer to Table 1.1 for large-stock and T-bill returns for the period 1973–1977:

a. Calculate the observed risk premium in each year for the common stocks.
b. Calculate the average returns and the average risk premium over this period.

c. Calculate the standard deviation of returns and the standard deviation of the risk premium.
d. Is it possible that the observed risk premium can be negative? Explain how this can happen and what it means.

1 **15. Geometric Return** Your grandfather invested $1,000 in a stock 52 years ago. Currently the value of his account is $193,000. What is his geometric return over this period?

1 **16. Forecasting Returns** You have found an asset with a 12.20 percent arithmetic average return and a 9.95 percent geometric return. Your observation period is 40 years. What is your best estimate of the return of the asset over the next 5 years? 10 years? 20 years?

2 **17. Geometric Averages** Look back to Figure 1.1 and find the value of $1 invested in each asset class over this 81-year period. Calculate the geometric return for small-company stocks, long-term government bonds, Treasury bills, and inflation.

1 **18. Arithmetic and Geometric Returns** A stock has returns of −15 percent, 12 percent, 15 percent, 22 percent, and 11 percent. What are the arithmetic and geometric returns?

1 **19. Arithmetic and Geometric Returns** A stock has had the following year-end prices and dividends:

Year	Price	Dividend
0	$ 77.50	$ –
1	92.68	0.64
2	98.58	0.72
3	82.20	0.80
4	97.15	1.20
5	110.19	1.60

What are the arithmetic and geometric returns for the stock?

1 **20. Arithmetic versus Geometric Returns** You are given the returns for the following three stocks:

Year	Stock A	Stock B	Stock C
1	12%	7%	−20%
2	12	17	41
3	12	11	18
4	12	9	13
5	12	16	8

Calculate the arithmetic return, geometric return, and standard deviation for each stock. Do you notice anything about the relationship between an asset's arithmetic return, standard deviation, and geometric return? Do you think this relationship will always hold?

Spreadsheet Problems

4 **21. Return and Standard Deviation** The 1980s was a good decade for investors in S&P 500 stocks. To find out how good, construct a spreadsheet that calculates the arithmetic average return, variance, and standard deviation for the S&P 500 returns during the 1980s using spreadsheet functions.

S&P Problems

www.mhhe.com/edumarketinsight

STANDARD & POOR'S

1. **Industry Comparison** On the Market Insight Home Page, follow the "Industry" link to go to the industry home page. The drop down menu allows you to select different industries. Answer the following questions for these industries: Air Freight & Logistics, Apparel Retail, Department Stores, Electric Utilities, Home Improvement Retail, Investment Banking & Brokerage, and Regional Banks.
   a. How many companies are in each industry?
   b. What are the total sales in each industry?
   c. Do the industries with the largest total sales have the most companies in the industry? What does this tell you about competition in the various industries?

2. **Calculating Returns** Download the historical stock prices for Boeing (BA) under the "Mthly. Adj. Prices" link. Use the closing stock prices to calculate the monthly return each month for the last 12 months. Do your calculations match the return calculations given in the file? Why or why not? Now calculate the dividends paid each month.
3. **Calculating Standard Deviation** Download the historical stock prices for Canon (CAJ) under the "Mthly. Adj. Prices" link. Using the monthly returns in the file, calculate the monthly standard deviation of Canon stock for the past 12 months.

What's on the Web?

1. **Ticker Symbols** Go to finance.yahoo.com and look up the ticker symbols for the following companies: 3M Company, International Business Machines, Dell Computer, Advanced Micro Devices, American Standard Company, and Bed, Bath & Beyond.
2. **Average Return and Standard Deviation** Go to finance.yahoo.com and enter the ticker symbol for your favorite stock. Now, look for the historical prices and find the monthly closing stock price for the last six years. Calculate the annual arithmetic average return, the standard deviation, and the geometric return for this period.

Stock-Trak Exercises

STOCK | TRAK
GLOBAL PORTFOLIO SIMULATIONS

To access the Stock-Trak Exercise for this chapter, please visit the book Web site at www.mhhe.com/jm5e and choose the corresponding chapter.

CHAPTER 2

Buying and Selling Securities

"Don't gamble! Take all your savings and buy some good stock and hold it till it goes up. If it don't go up, don't buy it."

–Will Rogers

Learning Objectives

Don't sell yourself short. Instead, learn about these key investment subjects:

1. The various types of securities brokers and brokerage accounts.
2. How to calculate initial and maintenance margin.
3. The workings of short sales.
4. The importance of investor objectives, constraints, and strategies.

You might wish to try Will Rogers's well-known stock market advice, but first you must know the basics of securities trading. Fortunately, trading is a relatively simple task, as attested to by the billions of shares of stocks that trade among investors on a typical day. Essentially, you begin the process by opening a trading account with a brokerage firm and then submitting trading orders. But you should know about some important details beforehand. ■

We hope reading about the history of risk and return in our previous chapter generated some interest in investing on your own. To help you get started, this chapter covers the basics of the investing process. We begin by describing how you go about buying and selling securities such as stocks and bonds. We then outline some of the most important considerations and constraints to keep in mind as you get more involved in the investing process.

2.1 Getting Started

Suppose you have some money that you want to invest. One way to get started is to open an account with a securities broker, such as Edward Jones or Merrill Lynch. Such accounts are often called *brokerage* or *trading accounts*. Opening a trading account is straightforward and really much like opening a bank account. You will be asked to supply some basic information about yourself and to sign an agreement (often simply called a customer's agreement) that spells out your rights and obligations and those of your broker. You then give your broker a check and instructions on how you want the money invested.

To illustrate, suppose that instead of going to Disneyland, you would rather own part of it. You therefore open an account with $10,000. You instruct your broker to purchase 100 shares of Walt Disney stock and to retain any remaining funds in your account. Your broker will locate a seller and purchase the stock on your behalf. Say shares of stock in Walt Disney Corporation are selling for about $33 per share, so your 100 shares will cost $3,300. In addition, for providing this service, your broker will charge you a commission. How much depends on a number of things, including the type of broker and the size of your order, but on this order, $50 wouldn't be an unusual commission charge. After paying for the stock and paying the commission, you would have $6,650 left in your account. Your broker will hold your stock for you or deliver the shares to you, whichever you wish. At a later date, you can sell your stock by instructing your broker to do so. You would receive the proceeds from the sale, less another commission charge. You can always add money to your account and purchase additional securities, and you can withdraw money from your account or even close it altogether.

In broad terms, this basic explanation is really all there is to it. As we begin to discuss in the next section, however, there is a range of services available to you, and there are important considerations that you need to take into account before you actually begin investing.

CHOOSING A BROKER

The first step in opening an account is choosing a broker. Brokers are traditionally divided into three groups: full-service brokers, discount brokers, and deep-discount brokers. What distinguishes the three groups is the level of service they provide and the resulting commissions they charge.

With a deep-discount broker, essentially the only services provided are account maintenance and order execution—that is, buying and selling. You generally deal with a deep-discount broker over the telephone or, increasingly, using a Web browser (see the next section on online brokers).

At the other extreme, a full-service broker will provide investment advice regarding the types of securities and investment strategies that might be appropriate for you to consider (or avoid). The larger brokerage firms do extensive research on individual companies and securities and maintain lists of recommended (and not recommended) securities. They maintain offices throughout the country, so, depending on where you live, you can actually stop in and speak to the person assigned to your account. A full-service broker will even manage your account for you if you wish.

Today, many full-service brokers are trying to specialize in wealth management. That is, these brokers manage many aspects of financial planning for high net worth investors. These high net worth accounts are exactly what you think they are—accounts with a lot of money in them.

Discount brokers fall somewhere between the two cases we have discussed so far, offering more investment counseling than the deep-discounters and lower commissions than the full-service brokers. Which type of broker should you choose? It depends on how much advice and service you need or want. If you are the do-it-yourself type, then you may seek out the lower commissions. If you are not, then a full-service broker might be more suitable. Often investors begin with a full-service broker, and then, as they gain experience and confidence, move on to a discount broker or a deep-discount broker.

We should note that the brokerage industry is very competitive, and differences between broker types seem to be blurring. Full-service brokers frequently discount commissions to attract new customers (particularly those with large accounts), and you should not hesitate to ask about commission rates. Similarly, discount brokers have begun to offer securities research and extensive account management services. Basic brokerage services have become almost commoditylike, and, more and more, brokerage firms are competing by offering financial services such as retirement planning, credit cards, and check-writing privileges, to name a few.

ONLINE BROKERS

The most important recent change in the brokerage industry is the rapid growth of online brokers, also known as e-brokers or cyberbrokers. With an online broker, you place buy and sell orders over the Internet using a Web browser.

Before 1995, online accounts essentially did not exist; by 2007, many millions of investors were buying and selling securities online. Online investing has fundamentally changed the discount and deep-discount brokerage industry by slashing costs dramatically. In a typical online trade, no human intervention is needed by the broker as the entire process is handled electronically, so operating costs are held to a minimum. As costs have fallen, so have commissions. Even for relatively large trades, online brokers typically charge less than $20 per trade. For budget-minded investors and active stock traders, the attraction is clear.

Competition among online brokers is fierce. Some take a no-frills approach, offering only basic services and very low commission rates. Others, particularly the larger ones, charge a little more but offer a variety of services, including research and various banking services such as check-writing privileges, credit cards, debit cards, and even mortgages. As technology continues to improve and investors become more comfortable using it, online brokerages will almost surely become the dominant form because of their enormous convenience—and the low commission rates.

INVESTOR PROTECTION

THE FEDERAL DEPOSIT INSURANCE CORPORATION You probably know that a U.S. government agency called the Federal Deposit Insurance Corporation, or FDIC, protects money deposited into bank accounts. In fact, the FDIC insures deposits (up to $100,000 per account) in nearly every bank and thrift in the United States. However, savers have not always had deposit insurance.

In the 1920s and early 1930s, many banks failed. When these banks failed, the money held in bank accounts vanished. To help restore faith in the banking system, the U.S. Congress created the FDIC in 1933. So far, so good. Since the start of FDIC insurance on January 1, 1934, no depositor has lost a single cent of insured funds as a result of a bank failure.

However, the FDIC insures only bank deposits. That is, the FDIC does *not* insure stocks, bonds, mutual funds, or other investments offered by banks, thrift institutions, and brokerage firms—even those calling themselves investment banks.

INVESTMENT FRAUD Suppose someone swindles you by selling you shares in a fictitious company. Or suppose someone sells you shares in a real company, but does not transfer ownership to you. These two situations are examples of investment fraud.

Experts estimate that losses from investment fraud in the United States ranges from $10 billion to $40 billion a year. You should know that "insurance" for investment fraud does not exist in the United States, but state and federal securities agencies were established to help investors deal with cases of investment fraud. Of course, investors can help protect themselves against fraud simply by dealing with reputable brokerage firms.

THE SECURITIES INVESTOR PROTECTION CORPORATION Even reputable brokerage firms can go bankrupt or suffer financial difficulties. Fortunately for investors, all reputable brokerage firms belong to the **Securities Investor Protection Corporation**, or **SIPC**. In fact, almost all brokerage firms operating in the United States are required to be members of the SIPC. The SIPC insures your brokerage account for up to $500,000 in cash and securities, with a $100,000 cash maximum.

Securities Investor Protection Corporation (SIPC)
Insurance fund covering investors' brokerage accounts with member firms.

Congress chartered the SIPC in 1970, but SIPC is not a government agency; SIPC is a private insurance fund supported by the securities industry. SIPC has a narrow, but important, focus: restore funds to investors who have securities in the hands of bankrupt or financially troubled brokerage firms. When a brokerage firm is closed as a result of financial difficulties,

WWW

If you want to learn more about the SIPC, go to www.sipc.org and surf to the Answers to the Seven Most Asked Questions.

sometimes customer assets are missing. In this case, the SIPC works to return customers' cash, bonds, stock, and other eligible securities. Without SIPC, investors at financially troubled brokerage firms might lose their securities or money forever.

Not every loss is protected by the SIPC. For example, the SIPC does not guarantee the value of securities held in an SIPC-covered brokerage account. In other words, you can still lose everything in an SIPC-covered account if the value of your securities falls to zero.

BROKER–CUSTOMER RELATIONS

There are several other important things to keep in mind when dealing with a broker. First, any advice you receive is *not* guaranteed. Far from it—buy and sell recommendations carry the explicit warning that you rely on them at your own risk. Your broker does have a duty to exercise reasonable care in formulating recommendations and not recommend anything grossly unsuitable, but that is essentially the extent of it.

Second, your broker works as your agent and has a legal duty to act in your best interest; however, brokerage firms are in the business of generating brokerage commissions. This fact will probably be spelled out in the account agreement that you sign. There is, therefore, the potential for a conflict of interest. On rare occasions, a broker is accused of "churning" an account, which refers to excessive trading for the sole purpose of generating commissions. In general, you are responsible for checking your account statements and notifying your broker in the event of any problems, and you should certainly do so.

WWW

To learn more about dispute resolution, visit www.finra.org

Finally, in the unlikely event of a significant problem, your account agreement will probably specify very clearly that you must waive your right to sue and/or seek a jury trial. Instead, you agree that any disputes will be settled by arbitration and that arbitration is final and binding. Arbitration is not a legal proceeding, and the rules are much less formal. In essence, a panel is appointed by a self-regulatory body of the securities industry to review the case. The panel will be composed of a small number of individuals who are knowledgeable about the securities industry, but a majority of them will not be associated with the industry. The panel makes a finding, and, absent extraordinary circumstances, its findings cannot be appealed. The panel does not have to disclose factual findings or legal reasoning.

CHECK THIS

2.1a What are the differences between full-service and deep-discount brokers?

2.1b What is the SIPC? How does SIPC coverage differ from FDIC coverage?

2.2 Brokerage Accounts

The account agreement that you sign has a number of important provisions and details specifying the types of trades that can be made and who can make them. Another important concern is whether the broker will extend credit and, if so, the terms under which credit will be extended. We discuss these issues next.

cash account
A brokerage account in which all transactions are made on a strictly cash basis.

margin account
A brokerage account in which, subject to limits, securities can be bought and sold on credit.

call money rate
The interest rate brokers pay to borrow bank funds for lending to customer margin accounts.

CASH ACCOUNTS

A **cash account** is the simplest arrangement. Securities can be purchased to the extent that sufficient cash is available in the account. If additional purchases are desired, then the needed funds must be promptly supplied.

MARGIN ACCOUNTS

With a **margin account**, you can, subject to limits, purchase securities on credit using money loaned to you by your broker. Such a purchase is called a *margin purchase*. The interest rate you pay on the money you borrow is based on the broker's **call money rate**, which is, loosely, the rate the broker pays to borrow the money. You pay some amount over the call money rate, called the *spread;* the exact spread depends on your broker and the size of the loan. Suppose the call money rate has been hovering around 7 percent. If a brokerage firm charges a 2.5 percent spread above this rate on loan amounts under $10,000, then you would pay a total of about 9.5 percent. However, this is usually reduced for larger loan amounts. For example, the spread may decline to .75 percent for amounts over $100,000.

Several important concepts and rules are involved in a margin purchase. For concreteness, we focus on stocks in our discussion. The specific margin rules for other investments can be quite different, but the principles and terminology are usually similar.

margin
The portion of the value of an investment that is *not* borrowed.

In general, when you purchase securities on credit, some of the money is yours and the rest is borrowed. The amount that is yours is called the **margin**. Margin is usually expressed as a percentage. For example, if you take $7,000 of your own money and borrow an additional $3,000 from your broker, your total investment will be $10,000. Of this $10,000, $7,000 is yours, so the margin is $7,000/$10,000 = .70, or 70 percent.

It is useful to create an account balance sheet when thinking about margin purchases (and some other issues we'll get to in just a moment). To illustrate, suppose you open a margin account with $5,000. You tell your broker to buy 100 shares of 3M Company (MMM). Shares in 3M Company are selling for $80 per share, so the total cost will be $8,000. Because you have only $5,000 in the account, you borrow the remaining $3,000. Immediately following the purchase, your account balance sheet would look like this:

Assets		Liabilities and Account Equity	
100 shares of 3M	$8,000	Margin loan	$3,000
		Account equity	5,000
Total	$8,000	Total	$8,000

On the left-hand side of this balance sheet, we list the account assets, which, in this case, consist of the $8,000 in 3M stock you purchased. On the right-hand side, we first list the $3,000 loan you took out to help you pay for the stock. This amount is a liability because, at some point, the loan must be repaid. The difference between the value of the assets held in the account and the loan amount is $5,000. This amount is your *account equity,* that is, the net value of your investment. Notice that your margin is equal to the account equity divided by the value of the stock owned and held in the account: $5,000/$8,000 = .625, or 62.5 percent.

EXAMPLE 2.1

The Account Balance Sheet

You want to buy 1,000 shares of Pfizer (PFE) at a price of $24 per share. You put up $18,000 and borrow the rest. What does your account balance sheet look like? What is your margin?

The 1,000 shares of Pfizer cost $24,000. You supply $18,000, so you must borrow $6,000. The account balance sheet looks like this:

Assets		Liabilities and Account Equity	
1,000 shares of Pfizer	$24,000	Margin loan	$ 6,000
		Account equity	18,000
Total	$24,000	Total	$24,000

Your margin is the account equity divided by the value of the stock owned:

$$\begin{aligned} \text{Margin} &= \$18{,}000/\$24{,}000 \\ &= .75 \text{ or } 75 \text{ percent} \end{aligned}$$

initial margin
The minimum margin that must be supplied on a securities purchase.

INITIAL MARGIN When you first purchase securities on credit, there is a minimum margin that you must supply. This percentage is called the **initial margin**. The minimum percentage (for stock purchases) is set by the Federal Reserve (the "Fed"). However, the exchanges and individual brokerage firms may require higher initial margin amounts.

The Fed's power to set initial margin requirements was established in the Securities Exchange Act of 1934. In subsequent years, initial margin requirements ranged from a low of 45 percent to a high of 100 percent. Since 1974, the minimum has been 50 percent (for stock purchases). In other words, if you have $10,000 of your own cash, you can borrow up to an additional $10,000, but no more.

We emphasize that these initial margin requirements apply to stocks. In contrast, for the most part, there is little initial margin requirement for government bonds. On the other hand, margin is not allowed at all on certain other types of securities.

EXAMPLE 2.2

Calculating Initial Margin

Suppose you have $3,000 in cash in a trading account with a 50 percent initial margin requirement. What is the largest order you can place (ignoring commissions)? If the initial margin were 60 percent, how would your answer change?

When the initial margin is 50 percent, you must supply half of the total (and you borrow the other half). So, $6,000 is the largest order you could place. When the initial margin is 60 percent, your $3,000 must equal 60 percent of the total. In other words, it must be the case that

$$\begin{aligned} \$3{,}000 &= 0.60 \times \text{Total order} \\ \text{Total order} &= \$3{,}000/.60 \\ &= \$5{,}000 \end{aligned}$$

As this example illustrates, the higher the initial margin required, the less you can borrow. When the margin is 50 percent, you could borrow $3,000. When the margin is 60 percent, you can borrow only $2,000.

maintenance margin
The minimum margin that must be present at all times in a margin account.

margin call
A demand for more funds that occurs when the margin in an account drops below the maintenance margin.

MAINTENANCE MARGIN In addition to the initial margin requirement set by the Fed, brokerage firms and exchanges generally have a **maintenance margin** requirement. For example, the New York Stock Exchange (NYSE) requires a minimum of 25 percent maintenance margin. This amount is the minimum margin required at all times after the purchase.

The maintenance margin set by your broker is sometimes called the "house" margin requirement. The level is established by your broker, who may vary it depending on what you are buying. For low-priced and very volatile stocks, the house margin can be as high as 100 percent, meaning no margin at all.

A typical maintenance margin would be 30 percent. If your margin falls below 30 percent, then you may be subject to a **margin call**, which is a demand by your broker to add to your account, pay off part of the loan, or sell enough securities to bring your margin back up to an acceptable level. In some cases, you will be asked to restore your account to the initial margin level. In other cases, you will be asked to restore your account to the maintenance margin level. If you do not or cannot comply, your securities may be sold. The loan will be repaid out of the proceeds, and any remaining amounts will be credited to your account.

To illustrate, suppose your account has a 50 percent initial margin requirement and a 30 percent maintenance margin. Suppose stock in Vandelay Industries is selling for $50 per share. You have $20,000, and you want to buy as much of this stock as you possibly can. With a 50 percent initial margin, you can buy up to $40,000 worth, or 800 shares. The account balance sheet looks like this:

Assets		Liabilities and Account Equity	
800 shares @$50/share	$40,000	Margin loan	$20,000
		Account equity	20,000
Total	$40,000	Total	$40,000

Unfortunately, right after your purchase, Vandelay Industries reveals that it has been artificially inflating earnings for the last three years (this is not good). Share prices plummet to $35 per share. What does the account balance sheet look like when this happens? Are you subject to a margin call?

To create the new account balance sheet, we recalculate the total value of the stock. The margin loan stays the same, so the account equity is adjusted as needed:

Assets		Liabilities and Account Equity	
800 shares @$35/share	$28,000	Margin loan	$20,000
		Account equity	8,000
Total	$28,000	Total	$28,000

As shown, the total value of your "position" (i.e., the stock you hold) falls to $28,000, a $12,000 loss. You still owe $20,000 to your broker, so your account equity is $28,000 − $20,000 = $8,000. Your margin is therefore $8,000/$28,000 = .286, or 28.6 percent. You are below the 30 percent minimum, so you are subject to a margin call.

THE EFFECTS OF MARGIN Margin is a form of *financial leverage*. Any time you borrow money to make an investment, the impact is to magnify both your gains and losses, hence the use of the term "leverage." The easiest way to see this is through an example. Imagine that you have $30,000 in an account with a 60 percent initial margin. You now know that you can borrow up to an additional $20,000 and buy $50,000 worth of stock (why?). The call money rate is 5.50 percent; you must pay this rate plus a .50 percent spread. Suppose you buy 1,000 shares of Coca-Cola Co. (KO) at $50 per share. One year later, shares in Coca-Cola Co. are selling for $60 per share. Assuming the call money rate does not change and ignoring dividends, what is your return on this investment?

At the end of the year, your 1,000 shares are worth $60,000. You owe 6 percent interest on the $20,000 you borrowed, or $1,200. If you pay off the loan with interest, you will have $60,000 − $21,200 = $38,800. You started with $30,000 and ended with $38,800, so your net gain is $8,800. In percentage terms, your return was $8,800/$30,000 = .2933, or 29.33 percent.

How would you have done without the financial leverage created from the margin purchase? In this case, you would have invested just $30,000. At $50 per share, you would have purchased 600 shares. At the end of the year, your 600 shares would be worth $60 apiece, or $36,000 total. Your dollar profit is $6,000, so your percentage return would be $6,000/$30,000 = .20, or 20 percent. If we compare this to the 29.33 percent that you made above, it's clear that you did substantially better by leveraging.

The downside is that you would do much worse if Coca-Cola's stock price fell (or didn't rise very much). For example, if Coca-Cola shares had fallen to $40 a share, you would have lost (check these calculations for practice) $11,200, or 37.33 percent on your margin investment, compared to $6,000, or 20 percent on the unmargined investment. This example illustrates how leveraging an investment through a margin account can cut both ways.

EXAMPLE 2.3 A Marginal Investment?

A year ago, you bought 300 shares of Pepsico, Inc. (PEP) at $55 per share. You put up the 60 percent initial margin. The call money rate plus the spread you paid was 8 percent. What is your return if the price today is $50? Compare this to the return you would have earned if you had not invested on margin.

Your total investment was 300 shares at $55 per share, or $16,500. You supplied 60 percent, or $9,900, and you borrowed the remaining $6,600. At the end of the year, you owe $6,600 plus 8 percent interest, or $7,128. If the stock sells for $50, then your position is worth 300 × $50 = $15,000. Deducting the $7,128 leaves $7,872 for you. Since you originally invested $9,900, your dollar loss is $9,900 − $7,872 = $2,028. Your percentage return is − $2,028/$9,900 = −20.48 percent.

If you had not leveraged your investment, you would have purchased $9,900/$55 = 180 shares. These would have been worth 180 × $50 = $9,000. You therefore would have lost $900; your percentage return would have been −$900/$9,900 = −9.09 percent, compared to the −20.48 percent that you lost on your leveraged position.

EXAMPLE 2.4 How Low Can It Go?

In our previous example (Example 2.3), suppose the maintenance margin was 40 percent. At what price per share would you have been subject to a margin call?

To answer, let P^* be the critical price. You own 300 shares, so, at that price, your stock is worth $300 \times P^*$. You borrowed $6,600, so your account equity is equal to the value of your stock less the $6,600 you owe, or $300 \times P^* - \$6{,}600$. We can summarize this information as follows:

$$\text{Amount borrowed} = \$6{,}600$$

$$\text{Value of stock} = 300 \times P^*$$

$$\text{Account equity} = 300 \times P^* - \$6{,}600$$

From our preceding discussion, your percentage margin is your dollar margin (or account equity) divided by the value of the stock:

$$\text{Margin} = \frac{\text{Account equity}}{\text{Value of stock}}$$

$$= \frac{300 \times P^* - \$6{,}600}{300 \times P^*}$$

To find the critical price, we will set this margin to the maintenance margin and solve for P^*:

$$\text{Maintenance margin} = \frac{\text{Number of shares} \times P^* - \text{Amount borrowed}}{\text{Number of shares} \times P^*}$$

Solving for P^* yields

$$P^* = \frac{\text{Amount borrowed/Number of shares}}{1 - \text{Maintenance margin}}$$

Finally, setting the maintenance margin equal to 40 percent, we obtain this critical price, P^*:

$$P^* = \frac{\$6{,}600/300}{1 - .40}$$

$$= \frac{\$6{,}600}{180} = \$36.67$$

At any price below $36.67, your margin will be less than 40 percent, and you will be subject to a margin call. So, $36.67 is the lowest possible price that could be reached before you are subject to a margin call.

As Example 2.4 shows, you can calculate the critical price (the lowest price before you get a margin call) as follows:

$$P^* = \frac{\text{Amount borrowed/Number of shares}}{1 - \text{Maintenance margin}} \tag{2.1}$$

For example, suppose you had a margin loan of $40,000, which you used to purchase, in part, 1,000 shares. The maintenance margin is 37.5 percent. What's the critical stock price, and how do you interpret it?

See if you don't agree that the critical stock price, P^*, is $40/.625 = $64. The interpretation is straightforward: If the stock price falls below $64, you are subject to a margin call.

ANNUALIZING RETURNS ON A MARGIN PURCHASE

Things get a little more complicated when we consider holding periods different from a year on a margin purchase. For example, suppose the call money rate is 9 percent, and you pay a spread of 2 percent over that. You buy 1,000 shares of Costco (COST) at $60 per share, but you put up only half the money. In three months, Costco is selling for $63 per share, and you sell your Costco shares. What is your annualized return assuming no dividends are paid?

In this case, you invested $60,000, half of which, $30,000, is borrowed. How much do you have to repay in three months? Here we have to adjust for the fact that the interest rate is 11 percent per year, but you only borrowed the money for three months. In this case, the amount you repay is equal to:

$$\text{Amount repaid} = \text{Amount borrowed} \times (1 + \text{interest rate year})^t$$

where t is the fraction of a year. In our case, t would be 3 months/12 months, or .25. So, plugging in our numbers, we get:

$$\begin{aligned}\text{Amount repaid} &= \text{Amount borrowed} \times (1 + \text{interest rate per year})^t \\ &= \$30{,}000 \times (1 + .11)^{.25} \\ &= \$30{,}000 \times 1.02643 \\ &= \$30{,}792.90\end{aligned}$$

So, when you sell your stock, you get $63,000, of which $30,792.90 is used to pay off the loan, leaving you with $32,207.10. You invested $30,000, so your dollar gain is $2,207.10, and your percentage return for your three-month holding period is $2,207.10/$30,000 = .0736, or 7.36 percent.

Finally, we have to convert this 7.36 percent to an annualized return. There are four three-month periods in a year, so:

$$\begin{aligned}1 + EAR &= (1 + \text{holding period percentage return})^m \\ &= (1 + .0736)^4 \\ &= 1.3285\end{aligned}$$

So, your annualized return is 32.85 percent.

HYPOTHECATION AND STREET NAME REGISTRATION

As part of your margin account agreement, you must agree to various conditions. We discuss two of the most important next.

HYPOTHECATION Any securities you purchase in your margin account will be held by your broker as collateral against the loan made to you. This practice protects the broker because the securities can be sold by the broker if the customer is unwilling or unable to meet a margin call. Putting securities up as collateral against a loan is called **hypothecation**. In fact, a margin agreement is sometimes called a hypothecation agreement. In addition, to borrow the money that it loans to you, your broker will often

hypothecation
Pledging securities as collateral against a loan.

re-hypothecate your securities, meaning that your broker will pledge them as collateral with its lender, normally a bank.

STREET NAME REGISTRATION Securities in a margin account are normally held in **street name**. This means that the brokerage firm is actually the registered owner. If this were not the case, the brokerage firm could not legally sell the securities should a customer refuse to meet a margin call or otherwise fail to live up to the terms of the margin agreement. With this arrangement, the brokerage firm is the "owner of record," but the account holder is the "beneficial owner."

street name
An arrangement under which a broker is the registered owner of a security.

When a security is held in street name, anything mailed to the security owner, such as an annual report or a dividend check, goes to the brokerage firm. The brokerage firm then passes these on to the account holder. Street name ownership is actually a great convenience to the owner. In fact, because it is usually a free service, even customers with cash accounts generally choose street name ownership. Some of the benefits are:

1. Since the broker holds the security, there is no danger of theft or other loss of the security. This is important because a stolen or lost security cannot be easily or cheaply replaced.
2. Any dividends or interest payments are automatically credited, and they are often credited more quickly (and conveniently) than they would be if the owner received the check in the mail.
3. The broker provides regular account statements showing the value of securities held in the account and any payments received. Also, for tax purposes, the broker will provide all the needed information on a single form at the end of the year, greatly reducing the owner's record-keeping requirements.

OTHER ACCOUNT ISSUES

If you do not wish to manage your account yourself, you can set up an *advisory account*. In this case, you pay someone else to make buy and sell decisions on your behalf. You are responsible for paying any commissions or other costs, as well as a management fee.

In a relatively recent innovation, brokerage firms have begun to offer *wrap accounts*. In such an account, you choose a money manager or a set of money managers from a group offered by the brokerage firm. All of the costs, commissions, and expenses associated with your account are "wrapped" into a single fee that you pay, hence the name. If you simply authorize your broker to trade for you, then there is no management fee, but you are still responsible for any commissions. This arrangement is termed a *discretionary account*.

Most of the large brokerage firms offer accounts that provide for complete money management, including check-writing privileges, credit cards, and margin loans, especially for larger investors. Such accounts are generally called *asset management accounts*. The terms of these accounts differ from broker to broker, and the services provided frequently change in response to competition.

Finally, if you want to buy and sell a broad variety of individual securities, then a brokerage account is almost a requirement. It is true that some companies and other entities (such as the U.S. government) do sell directly to the public, at least at certain times and subject to various restrictions, so you can buy securities directly in some cases. In fact, you could buy and sell through the want ads in your local paper if you were so inclined, but given the modest commissions charged by deep-discount brokers, this hardly seems worth the trouble.

However, you should be aware that if you do not wish to actively buy and sell securities, but you do want to own stocks, bonds, or other financial assets, there is an alternative to a brokerage account: a *mutual fund*. Mutual funds are a means of combining or pooling the funds of a large group of investors. The buy and sell decisions for the resulting pool are then made by a fund manager, who is compensated for the service. Mutual funds have become so important that we devote an entire chapter to them (Chapter 4).

CHECK THIS

2.2a What is the difference between a cash and margin account?

2.2b What is the effect of a margin purchase on gains and losses?

2.2c What is a margin call?

2.3 Short Sales

An investor who buys and owns shares of stock is said to be *long* in the stock or to have a *long position*. An investor with a long position will make money if the price of the stock increases and lose money if it goes down. In other words, a long investor hopes that the price will increase.

Now consider a different situation. Suppose you thought, for some reason, that the stock in a particular company was likely to *decrease* in value. You obviously wouldn't want to buy any of it. If you already owned some, you might choose to sell it.

short sale
A sale in which the seller does not actually own the security that is sold.

Beyond this, you might decide to engage in a **short sale**. In a short sale, you actually sell a security that you do not own. This is referred to as *shorting* the stock. After the short sale, the investor is said to have a *short position* in the security.

Financial assets of all kinds are sold short, not just shares of stock, and the terms "long" and "short" are universal. However, the mechanics of a short sale differ quite a bit across security types. Even so, regardless of how the short sale is executed, the essence is the same. An investor with a long position benefits from price increases, and, as we will see, an investor with a short position benefits from price decreases. For the sake of illustration, we focus here on shorting shares of stock. Procedures for shorting other types of securities are discussed in later chapters.

BASICS OF A SHORT SALE

How can you sell stock you don't own? It is easier than you might think: You borrow the shares of stock from your broker and then you sell them. At some future date, you will buy the same number of shares that you originally borrowed and return them, thereby eliminating the short position. Eliminating the short position is often called *covering the position* or, less commonly, *curing the short*.

You might wonder where your broker will get the stock to loan you. Normally, it will simply come from other margin accounts. Often, when you open a margin account, you are asked to sign a loan-consent agreement, which gives your broker the right to loan shares held in the account. If shares you own are loaned out, you still receive any dividends or other distributions and you can sell the stock if you wish. In other words, the fact that some of your stock may have been loaned out is of little or no consequence as far as you are concerned.

An investor with a short position will profit if the security declines in value. For example, assume that you short 1,000 shares of Xerox Corp. (XRX) at a price of $20 per share. You receive $20,000 from the sale (more on this in a moment). A month later, the stock is selling for $16 per share. You buy 1,000 shares for $16,000 and return the stock to your broker, thereby covering your short position. Because you received $20,000 from the sale and it cost you only $16,000 to cover, you made $4,000.

Conventional Wall Street wisdom states that the way to make money is to "buy low, sell high." With a short sale, we hope to do exactly that, just in opposite order—"sell high, buy low." If a short sale strikes you as a little confusing, it might help to think about the everyday use of the terms. Whenever we say that we are "running short" on something, we mean we don't have enough of it. Similarly, when someone says "don't sell me short," they mean don't bet on them not to succeed. A nearby *Investment Updates* box describes the world of short sellers.

INVESTMENT UPDATES

IT'S A TOUGH JOB, SO WHY DO THEY DO IT? THE BACKWARD BUSINESS OF SHORT SELLING

The shorting life is nasty and brutish. It's a wonder anyone does it at all.

Shorts make a bet that a stock will sink, and nobody else wants that: Not company executives, employees, investment banks nor most investors. That's why most manipulation is on the other side; fewer people object when share prices are being pumped up. For most on Wall Street, the debate is whether shorts are anti-American or merely un-American.

Yet in all the paranoia about evil short-sellers bad-mouthing companies, what is lost is how agonizingly difficult their business is. They borrow stock and sell it, hoping to replace the borrowed shares with cheaper ones bought later so they can pocket the price difference as profit. It's a chronologically backward version of the typical long trade: sell high and then buy low.

For one, companies targeted by shorts try to silence attempts to publicize negative information. Two long-standing targets, discount Internet retailer Overstock.com and drug maker Biovail, are suing short-sellers, accusing them of conspiring to spread misinformation to drive down their stocks. The Securities and Exchange Commission subpoenaed journalists—and then quickly retreated—to investigate the relationship between short-selling hedge funds, the media and a small independent research firm.

Many hedge funds—the sophisticated investors who are the bogeymen du jour—try to avoid shorting. They simply can't stomach the pain. Often, hedge funds only do it to be able to call themselves "hedge" funds—shorting is the classic way to hedge risk on long buys, after all—and charge those fat fees. Assets at hedge funds almost tripled in the past five years, yet short activity on the major exchanges hasn't even doubled.

The biggest problem with the business is that the market is stacked against the technique. Stocks tend to go up over time. Shorts swim against this tide.

There is also theoretically no ceiling on potential profits from a long position. A stock bought at $10 can go to $20 for a 100 percent gain and then to $30 for a 200 percent gain. But 100 percent decline is as good as it gets for a short. The opposite is true, too: long losses are finite but short losses can be infinite. Many hedge funds have reduced their shorting for this reason. Why put so much time and energy into something that can inherently not pay off with a multiple bagger?

What's more, shorting can be expensive when the shares available to borrow are scarce. Prime brokers, the investment-bank folks who facilitate hedge-fund trading, charge interest on popular shorts. Look at this week's rates: It cost 25 percent to short Martha Stewart Living Omnimedia and 24 percent to borrow Overstock. So, you wouldn't make a dime shorting Overstock unless shares tank by almost a fourth of its value over the course of a year.

Given all that, how do the shorts fare? A study by Yale's Roger Ibbotson and his eponymous research

EXAMPLE 2.5 **The Long and Short of It**

Suppose you short 2,000 shares of Alcoa, Inc. (AA), at $35 per share. Six months later you cover your short. If Alcoa is selling for $30 per share at that time, did you make money or lose money? How much? What if you covered at $40?

If you shorted at $35 per share and covered at $30, you originally sold 2,000 shares at $35 and later bought them back at $30, so you made $5 per share, or $10,000. If you covered at $40, you lost $10,000.

SHORT SALES: SOME DETAILS

When you short a stock, you must borrow it from your broker, so there are various requirements you must fulfill. First, there is an initial margin and a maintenance margin. Second, after you sell the borrowed stock, the proceeds from the sale are credited to your account, but you cannot use them. They are, in effect, frozen until you return the stock. Finally, if any dividends are paid on the stock while you have a short position, you must pay them.

To illustrate, we will again create an account balance sheet. Suppose you want to short 100 shares of Texas Instruments, Inc. (TXN), when the price is $30 per share. This means firm's chief investment officer, Peng Chen, found that short-biased hedge funds fell 2.3 percent per year on a compounded basis after fees from 1995 through March 2004.

Sounds like a lousy business to me. So why bother?

The curious thing is those negative returns are actually quite impressive when you consider what shorts are supposed to do—hedge risk. The researchers calculated that the market, measured by the appropriate benchmarks, was up 5.9 percent a year in that period. That means short-sellers started each year trying to climb out of a hole almost 6 percent deep. And, on average, they did, by 3.6 percent. That shows their stock-picking skill and ability to reduce market risks for clients, who presumably invested in those funds to hedge their long positions elsewhere.

Short-sellers obviously are in it for the money, but in talking to them for many years, I can tell you they are a quirky bunch who love ferreting out bad guys. The dirty secret of the SEC enforcement is that the major financial frauds are frequently uncovered by short-sellers. The shorts had Enron and Tyco in the cross hairs before anyone else.

Shorts aren't always right. They shorted Sears, trumpeting its struggling retailing and troubled credit-card divisions. They shorted Amazon and eBay in the bubble years, failing to see that some Internet wonders wouldn't go bankrupt. But it is a myth that shorts can easily profit from misinformation because the market is merciless in dealing with erroneous information.

Amid all of the targets' litigiousness and outcry, short-sellers' influence over the markets is vastly overstated. Here's an example: Gradient, the independent stock-research firm being sued by Overstock and Biovail, started covering Overstock in June 2003 when its shares were traded around $13 and the company was expected to be profitable in 2005. Over the next year and a half, as short-sellers and Gradient bashed the company to anyone who would listen, the stock topped $76 a share. The company ended up losing $1.29 a share last year—yet the stock remains above $22, higher than where Gradient first picked it up. That's some market-moving power.

Mr. Patrick Byrne, Overstock's CEO, has been the most vocal in his assault against shorts. But it isn't the short-sellers who cause Overstock to lose money or to miss earnings estimates. It isn't the shorts who screwed up Overstock's information-technology installation. It isn't the shorts who caused Overstock—just yesterday—to restate its financials going back to 2002.

By seeming to side with Overstock when it started seeking information about its complaints against the shorts, the SEC chills its best sources and hinders the market from doing its job. It was the shorts who lost money in Overstock for months and months—until most investors realized they were right.

Source: Jesse Eisinger, *The Wall Street Journal,* March 1, 2006.

you will borrow shares of stock worth a total of $30 × 100 = $3,000. Your broker has a 50 percent initial margin and a 40 percent maintenance margin on short sales.

An important thing to keep in mind with a margin purchase of securities is that margin is calculated as the value of your account equity relative to the value of the securities purchased. With a short sale, margin is calculated as the value of your account equity relative to the value of the securities sold short. Thus, in both cases, margin is equal to equity value divided by security value.

In our Texas Instruments example, the initial value of the securities sold short is $3,000 and the initial margin is 50 percent, so you must deposit at least half of $3,000, or $1,500, in your account. With this in mind, after the short sale, your account balance sheet is as follows:

Assets		**Liabilities and Account Equity**	
Proceeds from sale	$3,000	Short position	$3,000
Initial margin deposit	1,500	Account equity	1,500
Total	$4,500	Total	$4,500

WWW

There are many sites devoted to the fine art of short selling. Try www.bearmarketcentral.com

As shown, four items appear on the account balance sheet:

1. *Proceeds from sale*. This is the $3,000 you received when you sold the stock. This amount will remain in your account until you cover your position. Note that you will not earn interest on this amount—it will just sit there as far as you are concerned.
2. *Margin deposit*. This is the 50 percent margin that you had to post. This amount will not change unless there is a margin call. Depending on the circumstances and your particular account agreement, you may earn interest on the initial margin deposit.
3. *Short position*. Because you must eventually buy back the stock and return it, you have a liability. The current cost of eliminating that liability is $3,000.
4. *Account equity*. As always, the account equity is the difference between the total account value ($4,500) and the total liabilities ($3,000).

We now examine two scenarios: (1) the stock price falls to $20 per share, and (2) the stock price rises to $40 per share.

If the stock price falls to $20 per share, then you are still liable for 100 shares, but the cost of those shares is now just $2,000. Your account balance sheet becomes:

Assets		Liabilities and Account Equity	
Proceeds from sale	$3,000	Short position	$2,000
Initial margin deposit	1,500	Account equity	2,500
Total	$4,500	Total	$4,500

Notice that the left-hand side doesn't change. The same $3,000 you originally received is still held, and the $1,500 margin you deposited is still there also. On the right-hand side, the short position is now a $2,000 liability, down from $3,000. Finally, the good news is that the account equity rises by $1,000, so this is your gain. Your margin is equal to account equity divided by the security value (the value of the short position), $2,500/$2,000 = 1.25, or 125 percent.

However, if the stock price rises to $40, things are not so rosy. Now, the 100 shares for which you are liable are worth $4,000:

Assets		Liabilities and Account Equity	
Proceeds from sale	$3,000	Short position	$4,000
Initial margin deposit	1,500	Account equity	500
Total	$4,500	Total	$4,500

Again, the left-hand side doesn't change. The short liability rises by $1,000, and, unfortunately for you, the account equity declines by $1,000, the amount of your loss.

To make matters worse, when the stock price rises to $40, you are severely undermargined. The account equity is $500, but the value of the stock sold short is $4,000. Your margin is $500/$4,000 = 12.5 percent. Since this is well below the 40 percent maintenance margin, you are subject to a margin call. You have two options: (1) buy back some or all of the stock and return it, or (2) add funds to your account.

EXAMPLE 2.6 A Case of The Shorts

You shorted 5,000 shares of a particular stock at a price of $30 per share. The initial margin is 50 percent, and the maintenance margin is 40 percent. What does your account balance sheet look like following the short?

Following the short, your account becomes:

Assets		Liabilities and Account Equity	
Proceeds from sale	$150,000	Short position	$150,000
Initial margin deposit	75,000	Account equity	75,000
Total	$225,000	Total	$225,000

Notice that you shorted $150,000 worth of stock, so, with a 50 percent margin requirement, you deposited $75,000.

EXAMPLE 2.7 Margin Calls

In our previous example (Example 2.6), at what price per share would you be subject to a margin call?

To answer this one, let P^* be the critical price. The short liability then is 5,000 shares at a price of P^*, or $5{,}000 \times P^*$. The total account value is $225,000, so the account equity is $\$225{,}000 - 5{,}000 \times P^*$. We can summarize this information as follows:

$$\text{Short position} = 5{,}000 \times P^*$$

$$\text{Account equity} = \$225{,}000 - 5{,}000 \times P^*$$

Notice that the total account value, $225,000, is the sum of your initial margin deposit plus the proceeds from the sale, and this amount does not change. Your margin is the account equity relative to the short liability:

$$\begin{aligned}\text{Margin} &= \frac{\text{Account equity}}{\text{Value of stock}} \\ &= \frac{\text{Initial margin deposit} + \text{Short proceeds} - \text{Number of shares} \times P^*}{\text{Number of shares} \times P^*} \\ &= \frac{\$150{,}000 + 75{,}000 - 5{,}000 \times P^*}{5{,}000 \times P^*}\end{aligned}$$

To find the critical price, we will set this margin equal to the maintenance margin and solve for P^*:

$$\text{Maintenance margin} = \frac{\text{Initial margin deposit} + \text{Short proceeds} - \text{Number of shares} \times P^*}{\text{Number of shares} \times P^*}$$

Solving for P^* yields:

$$P^* = \frac{(\text{Initial margin deposit} + \text{Short proceeds})/\text{Number of shares}}{1 + \text{Maintenance margin}}$$

Finally, setting the maintenance margin equal to 40 percent, we obtain this critical price, P^*:

$$P^* = \frac{\$225{,}000/5{,}000}{1.40} = \$32.14$$

At any price *above* $32.14, your margin will be less than 40 percent, so you will be subject to a margin call. So $32.14 is the highest possible price that could be reached before you are subject to a margin call.

INVESTMENT UPDATES

NYSE BEARISH BETS HIT ANOTHER HIGH

Short-selling activity rose to a fifth consecutive monthly record at the New York Stock Exchange as interest-rate jitters roiled the market, then gave way to optimism about earnings and the economy.

For the monthly period ending July 13, the number of short-selling positions not yet closed out at the NYSE—so-called short interest—rose 3.9% to 12,950,726,148 shares from 12,467,283,409 shares in mid-June.

Marketwide, the short ratio, or number of days' average volume represented by the short positions outstanding at the exchange, rose to 8.4 from 8.0.

Investors who "short" shares borrow them and sell them, betting the price will fall and they will be able to buy the shares back later at a lower price for return to the lender. In general, the higher the short interest, the more investors expect a downturn. Short positions rise in value as stocks fall, and vise versa.

During the period covered by the latest report, the Dow Jones Industrial Average was off 1.1% at its lows in late June—the sort of pullback that generally emboldens bearish investors. However, the market recovered to post a 3.2% gain for the month ended July 13.

Source: Peter A. McKay, *The Wall Street Journal*, July 20, 2007.

The Long and Short of It

"Short" shares are borrowed and then sold in the hope that the share price will fall before the borrowed shares have to be purchased and replaced. A high level of short interest could indicate that a share price is ready to fall, but can also be a hedge, or counterbet, for an investor who has gone "long," or bought a lot of shares of a company thinking that the share price will rise.

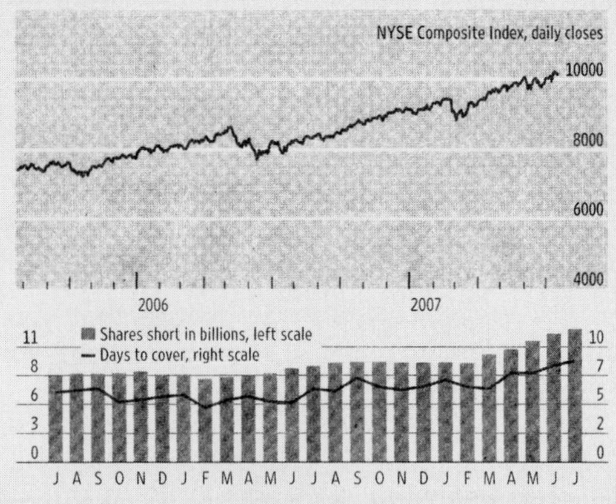

Biggest short positions
Companies with the biggest number of shares that are shorted

Shares shorted (000s)	% float	Days to cover	Avg daily volume (000s)	Name	Symbol	Close	Market value, in millions ($)	52-WEEK RANGE ($) Low	Close (●)	High
301,305.9	n.a.	n.a.	n.a.	iShrRus2000	IWM	84.58	3,603.11	66.35		85.74
212,917.2	14.4	4	50,427	Ford Motor Co	F	8.63	15,689.70	6.06		9.70
207,908.0	52.6	2	137,429	SPDR 500	SPY	155.07	41,028.58	123.82		156.00
128,408.3	5.6	6	23,019	Motorola Inc	MOT	18.22	42,172.35	17.32		26.30
82,090.3	5.1	6	13,879	Qwest Comm Int'l	Q	9.54	17,814.10	7.41		10.45
81,250.1	14.7	4	22,804	Advanced Micro Dev	AMD	15.78	8,657.01	12.60		27.90
70,396.2	1.9	3	25,362	Time Warner	TWX	20.71	78,477.13	15.77		23.15
66,836.2	n.a.	n.a.	n.a.	Fin'l Sel SPDR	XLF	36.08	824.50	32.17		38.15
59,997.4	8.0	2	24,897	Micron Technol	MU	13.60	10,259.56	10.88		18.65
59,367.1	19.0	9	6,888	Natl Semiconductor	NSM	28.27	8,862.65	20.56		29.69
59,152.1	5.8	1	42,017	General Electric	GE	40.71	418,626.22	32.20		40.95
58,762.5	3.8	6	9,343	CVS Caremark	CVS	35.69	55,823.80	27.09		39.44
57,369.7	10.2	3	16,980	Gen'l Mtr	GM	35.38	20,006.54	28.09		38.66
53,723.8	1.6	5	11,221	Wells Fargo	WFC	35.54	118,863.10	33.01		36.99
51,421.5	8.7	8	6,622	Countrywide Fin'l	CFC	34.77	20,507.94	32.20		45.26
50,692.1	10.7	9	5,930	Tenet Healthcare	THC	6.31	2,984.69	5.77		8.69
50,307.0	12.3	6	7,826	Chesapeake Engy	CHK	36.96	17,054.88	27.27		37.75
50,159.9	1.8	3	18,657	Sprint Nextel	S	22.01	61,132.30	15.92		23.42
49,890.5	0.7	1	40,490	Pfizer Inc	PFE	24.99	177,102.03	23.50		28.60
49,754.5	6.6	3	15,354	LSI Corp	LSI	8.00	6,123.25	7.40		11.08

As Example 2.7 shows, you can calculate the critical price on a short sale (the highest price before you get a margin call) as follows:

$$P* = \frac{\text{(Initial margin deposit + Short proceeds)/Number of shares}}{1 + \text{Maintenance margin}}$$

For example, suppose you shorted 1,000 shares at \$50. The initial margin is 50 percent, and the maintenance margin is 40 percent. What's the critical stock price, and how do you interpret it?

Noting that the initial margin deposit is \$25,000 (50 percent of the short proceeds), see if you don't agree that the critical stock price, $P*$, is \$75/1.4 = \$53.57. So, if the stock price rises above \$53.57, you're subject to a margin call.

short interest
The amount of common stock held in short positions.

At this point, you might wonder whether short selling is a common practice among investors. Actually, it is quite common and a substantial volume of stock sales are initiated by short sellers. The nearby *Investment Updates* box is a sample *Wall Street Journal* box reporting **short interest**. Short interest is the amount of common stock held in short

WORK THE WEB

You can find the short interest for the current month in many financial publications. But what if you want a longer history of the shares sold short for a particular company? At www.nasdaq.com, you can find the short interest for companies listed on the NASDAQ for the previous 11 months. We went to the site and looked up Yahoo!, and here is what we found:

YAHOO! YHOO
Yahoo! Inc. NASDAQ-GS

Settlement Date	Short Interest	Avg Daily Share Volume	Days to Cover
Jun. 15, 2007	72,588,303	21,777,099	3.33
May 15, 2007	79,288,212	41,477,295	1.91
Apr. 13, 2007	79,040,213	13,195,754	5.99
Mar. 15, 2007	82,317,698	22,093,195	3.73
Feb. 15, 2007	79,932,271	24,306,105	3.29
Jan. 12, 2007	84,085,547	24,709,446	3.40
Dec. 15, 2006	78,124,708	22,374,852	3.49
Nov. 15, 2006	84,338,150	35,008,741	2.41
Oct. 13, 2006	77,929,435	32,789,977	2.38
Sep. 15, 2006	87,245,548	12,331,933	7.07
Aug. 15, 2006	92,308,836	30,109,315	3.07

As you can see, the short interest in Yahoo! fell from about 82 million shares in March 2007 to about 72.5 million shares in June 2007. Why would you want a history of short sales? Some investors use short sales as a technical indicator, which we discuss in a later chapter. Here's a question for you: What do you think "Days to Cover" means?

positions. As shown, the amount of stock held short for some companies can be several tens of millions of shares, and the total number of shares held short across all companies can be several billion shares. A nearby *Work the Web* box shows how to find short interest for a particular company.

We conclude our discussion of short sales with a *very* important observation. With a long position, the most you can ever lose is your total investment. In other words, if you buy $10,000 worth of stock, $10,000 is the most you can lose because the worst that can happen is the stock price drops to zero. However, if you short $10,000 in stock, you can lose *much more* than $10,000 because the stock price can keep rising without any particular limit. In fact, as our previous chapter showed, stock prices do tend to rise, at least on average. With this in mind, potential short sellers should remember the following classic bit of Wall Street wisdom: "He that sells what isn't his'n, must buy it back or go to prison!"[1]

CHECK THIS

2.3a What is a short sale?

2.3b Why might an investor choose to short a stock?

2.3c What is the maximum possible loss on a short sale? Explain.

[1] Of course, the same is true for "she that sells what isn't hers'n"; it just doesn't rhyme as well.

2.4 Investor Objectives, Constraints, and Strategies

Different investors will have very different investment objectives and strategies. For example, some will be very active, buying and selling frequently; others will be relatively inactive, buying and holding for long periods of time. Some will be willing to bear substantial risk in seeking out returns; for others, safety is a primary concern. In this section, we describe, in general terms, some strategies that are commonly pursued and their relationship to investor constraints and objectives.

In thinking about investor objectives, the most fundamental question is: Why invest at all? For the most part, the only sensible answer is that we invest today to have more tomorrow. In other words, investment is simply deferred consumption; instead of spending today, we choose to wait because we wish to have (or need to have) more to spend later. There is no difference, really, between investing and saving.

Given that we invest now to have more later, the particular investment strategy chosen will depend on, among other things, willingness to bear risk, the time horizon, and taxes. We discuss these and other issues next.

RISK AND RETURN

Probably the most fundamental decision that an investor must make concerns the amount of risk to take. Most investors are *risk-averse,* meaning that, all else equal, they dislike risk and want to expose themselves to the minimum risk level possible. However, as our previous chapter indicated, larger returns are generally associated with larger risks, so there is a trade-off. In formulating investment objectives, the individual must therefore balance return objectives with risk tolerance.

WWW

How else can you build a portfolio? Go to moneycentral.msn.com and search the site for "Prepare to Invest"

Attitudes toward risk are strictly personal preferences, and individuals with very similar economic circumstances can have very different degrees of risk aversion. For this reason, the first thing that must be assessed in evaluating the suitability of an investment strategy is risk tolerance. Unfortunately, this is not an easy thing to do. Most individuals have a difficult time articulating in any precise way their attitude toward risk (what's yours?). One reason is that risk is not a simple concept; it is not easily defined or measured. Nevertheless, the nearby *Investment Updates* box contains an article from *The Wall Street Journal* about risk tolerance that has a short quiz that might help you assess your attitude toward risk. When you take the quiz, remember there are no right or wrong answers. Afterwards, score your risk tolerance as shown at the end of the article.

INVESTOR CONSTRAINTS

In addition to attitude toward risk, an investor's investment strategy will be affected by various constraints. We discuss five of the most common and important constraints next.

WWW

Can you open a brokerage account with no money? See www.sharebuilder.com and www.buyandhold.com

RESOURCES Probably the most obvious constraint, and the one to which many students can most easily relate, is *resources*. Obviously, if you have no money, you cannot invest at all. Beyond that, certain types of investments and investment strategies generally have minimum requirements. For example, a margin account must normally have a minimum of $2,000 when it is established.

What is the minimum resource level needed? The answer to this question depends on the investment strategy, so there is no precise answer. Through mutual funds, initial investments in the stock market can be made for as little as $500, with subsequent investments as small as $100 or less. However, because minimum commission levels, account fees, and other costs are frequently associated with buying and selling securities, an investor interested in actively trading on her own would probably need an account in the $5,000 to $50,000 range.

HORIZON The investment *horizon* refers to the planned life of the investment. For example, individuals frequently save for retirement, where the investment horizon, depending on your age, can be very long. On the other hand, you might be saving to buy a house in the near future, implying a relatively short horizon.

The reason that horizon is important is evident in our previous chapter. It is true that stocks outperformed the other investments in the long run, but there were short periods over which they did much worse. This fact means that, if you have to pay tuition in 30 days, stocks are probably not the best investment for that money. Thus, in thinking about the riskiness of an investment, one important consideration is when the money will be needed.

LIQUIDITY Some investors have to sell an asset quickly. In such cases, the asset's *liquidity* is particularly important. An asset with a high degree of liquidity is one that can be sold quickly without a significant price concession. Such an asset is said to be liquid.

Liquidity has two related parts. One part of liquidity is the ease with which an asset can be sold. The other part is how much you have to lower the price to sell the asset quickly. Liquidity is difficult to measure precisely, but some assets are clearly much more liquid than others. A good way to think about liquidity is to imagine buying an asset and then immediately reselling it. The less you would lose on this "round-trip" transaction, the more liquid is the asset.

TAXES Different types of investments are taxed very differently. When we talk about the return on an investment, what is really relevant is the *aftertax* return. As a result, taxes are a vital consideration. Higher tax bracket investors will naturally seek investment strategies with favorable tax treatments, while lower tax bracket (or tax-exempt) investors will focus more on pretax returns.

In addition, the way in which an investment is held can dramatically affect its tax status. The tax laws and other rules are in a constant state of flux, so we will stick to broad principles. The general idea is that certain types of accounts, particularly retirement savings accounts, receive preferential tax treatment. The tax break can be enormous, and, as a result, the amount you can invest each year in these accounts is strictly limited. There are also lots of rules regarding when you can withdraw the money, and it is important to pay careful attention to them.

In terms of tax treatment, there are basically two types of retirement savings accounts. With the first type, you pay taxes today on money you earn. If you then invest these aftertax dollars in a retirement savings account, you pay no taxes at all when you take the money out later. This means that dividends, interest, and capital gains are not taxed, a big break. Currently, this type of account is called a Roth Individual Retirement Account (Roth IRA).

With the second type of account, you do not pay taxes on the money you earn today if you invest it. Such accounts are "tax-deferred" and are the way most employer-sponsored retirement accounts (such as so-called 401(k) plans) are set up. Later, when you retire, you owe income taxes on whatever you take out of the account.

The two types of accounts really come down to this: You either pay taxes today and do not pay taxes later, or vice versa. It would be great if you could invest pretax dollars and never pay taxes. Alas, this is tax avoidance—which is illegal. Therefore, investors must decide whether to pay taxes now or pay taxes later.

SPECIAL CIRCUMSTANCES Almost everyone will have some special or unique requirements or opportunities. For example, many companies will match certain types of investments made by employees on a dollar-for-dollar basis (typically up to some maximum per year). In other words, you double your money immediately with complete certainty. It is difficult to envision any other investment with such a favorable payoff. Therefore, investors should probably seize this opportunity even though there could be some undesirable liquidity, tax, or horizon considerations.

A list of possible special circumstances is essentially endless. To give a few examples, however, the number of dependents and their needs will vary from investor to investor. Therefore, the need to provide for dependents will be an important constraint for some investors. Some investors want to invest only in companies whose products and activities they consider to be socially or politically suitable. Some investors want to invest primarily in their own community or state. Other investors, such as corporate insiders, face regulatory and legal restrictions on their investing. Elected officials may have to avoid (or at least ethically *should* avoid) some types of investments out of conflict of interest concerns.

STRATEGIES AND POLICIES

Investors need to address four key areas when they devise their investment strategy. These key areas are investment management, market timing, asset allocation, and security selection. We discuss each of these next.

INVESTMENT MANAGEMENT A basic decision that all investors make is who manages their investments. At one extreme, investors make all of the buy and sell decisions themselves. At the other extreme, investors make no buy and sell decisions. Instead, the investor hires someone to manage his or her investments.

Often investors make some investment decisions and hire professional managers to make other investment decisions. For example, suppose you divide your money among four different mutual funds. In this case, you have hired four different money managers. However, you decided what types of mutual funds to buy. Also, you chose the particular funds within each type. Finally, you decided how to divide your money among the funds.

At first blush, managing your money yourself might seem to be the cheapest way to go because you do not pay management fees. Upon reflection, this is not a cheap decision. First, you must consider the value of your time. For some investors, researching investments and making investment decisions is something of a hobby. For most investors, however, it is too time-consuming. The value of your time is a powerful incentive to hire professional money managers. Also, for some strategies, the costs of doing it yourself can exceed those of hiring someone even after considering fees. This higher cost is simply due to the higher level of commissions and other fees that individual investors generally have to pay. For example, it might not be a bad idea for some of your investment to be in real estate, but a small investor will find it very difficult to directly acquire a sound real estate investment at reasonable cost.

An interesting question regarding professional money managers concerns their performance. It certainly seems logical to argue that by hiring a professional investor to manage your money, you would earn more, at least on average. Surely the pros make better investment decisions than the amateurs! Surprisingly, this is not necessarily true. We will return to this subject in a later chapter. For now, we simply note that the possibility of a superior return might not be a compelling reason to prefer professional management.

MARKET TIMING A second basic investment decision you must make is whether you will try to buy and sell in anticipation of the future direction of the overall market. For example, you might move money into the stock market when you think stock prices will rise. Or you might move money out of the stock market when you think stock prices will fall. This trading activity is called **market timing**. Some investors actively move money around to try to time short-term market movements. Other investors are much less active, but they still try to time long-term market movements. At the extreme, a fully passive strategy is one in which you make no attempt to time the market.

market timing
Buying and selling in anticipation of the overall direction of a market.

Market timing certainly seems like a reasonable thing to do. After all, why leave money in an investment if you expect it to decrease in value? You might be surprised that a common recommendation is that investors *avoid* trying to time the market. Why? As we discuss in more detail in a later chapter, the simple reason is that successful market timing is, to put it mildly, extremely difficult. To outperform a completely passive strategy, you must be able to accurately predict the future. If you make even a small number of bad calls, you will likely never catch up.

ASSET ALLOCATION Another fundamental decision that you must make concerns the distribution of your investment across different types of assets. We saw in Chapter 1 that

asset allocation
The distribution of investment funds among broad classes of assets.

different asset types—small stocks, large stocks, bonds—have distinct risk and return characteristics. In formulating your investment strategy, you must decide what percentage of your money will be placed in each of these broad categories. This decision is called **asset allocation**.

An important asset allocation decision for many investors is how much to invest in common stocks and how much to invest in bonds. There are some basic rules of thumb for this decision, one of the simplest being to split the portfolio into 60 percent stocks and 40 percent bonds. A slightly more sophisticated rule of thumb is that your equity percentage should be equal to your age subtracted from 100 (or 110, depending on the source). Under this rule, a 22-year-old college student should have $100 - 22 = 78$ percent (or $110 - 22 = 88$ percent) of her portfolio in stocks. This approach gradually reduces your exposure to stocks as you get older. Most of the major investment firms and many Web sites maintain recommended asset allocation schemes, which can be custom-tailored for individuals depending on their risk tolerance, wealth, and retirement goals.

security selection
Selection of specific securities within a particular class.

SECURITY SELECTION Finally, after deciding who will manage your investment, whether you will try to time the market, and the various asset classes you wish to hold, you must decide which specific securities to buy within each class. This is termed **security selection**.

For example, you might decide that you want 30 percent of your money in small stocks. This is an asset allocation decision. Next, however, you must decide *which* small stocks to buy. Here again you must choose an active strategy or a passive strategy. With an active strategy, you would try to identify those small stocks that you think will perform best in the future. In other words, you are trying to pick "winners." Investigating particular securities within a broad class in an attempt to identify superior performers is often called *security analysis*.

With a passive security selection strategy, you might just acquire a diverse group of small stocks, perhaps by buying a mutual fund that holds shares in hundreds of small companies (such funds are discussed in detail in a later chapter).

A useful way to distinguish asset allocation from security selection is to note that asset allocation is a macro-level activity. That is, the focus is on whole markets or classes of assets. Security selection is a much more micro-level activity. The focus of security selection is on individual securities.

If we consider the active versus passive aspects of asset allocation and security selection simultaneously, four distinct investment strategies emerge. These strategies appear in the following two-by-two table:

	Security Selection	
Asset Allocation	**Active**	**Passive**
Active	I	II
Passive	III	IV

With strategy I, we actively move money between asset classes based on our beliefs and expectations about future performance. In addition, we try to pick the best performers in each class. This is a fully active strategy. At the other extreme, strategy IV is a fully passive strategy. In this strategy, we seldom change asset allocations or attempt to choose the likely best performers from a set of individual securities.

With strategy II, we actively vary our holdings by class, but we do not try to choose particular securities within each class. With this strategy, we might move back and forth between short-term government bonds and small stocks in an attempt to time the market. Finally, with strategy III, we do not vary our asset allocations, but we do select individual securities. A diehard stock picker would fall into this category. Such an investor holds 100 percent stocks and concentrates solely on buying and selling individual companies.

BUMPY MARKET REMINDS INVESTORS TO ASSESS THEIR RISK TOLERANCE

Do-It-Yourself Crowd Has Quizzes to Rate Courage on Finances

Risk

For many investors, it's a word that has all but disappeared from the lexicon. Throughout much of the 1990s, stocks mostly went up. And even when they went down, many investors saw the slump as just another buying opportunity because stocks soon would go up again.

But the bumpy ride of the past six months finally has woken investors up to the fact that, with stocks more volatile these days than anytime in history, risk is playing an increasingly significant role in their lives.

Did you root the NASDAQ Composite Index higher when it bested 5000 earlier this year, but secretly fear for your overbloated technology shares? Did you panic when the NASDAQ subsequently plummeted in March and April, then kick yourself for not investing more when the market rebounded days later?

These dueling visions of fear and greed reflect the fact that many of today's do-it-yourself investors haven't assessed their own tolerance for risk, captivated instead by the lure of what seems to be easy, almost riskless, riches.

The current, and often myopic, quest for market wealth has spawned "a willingness to take risks that [average investors] haven't had in the past," says Robert J. Shiller, an economics professor at Yale University and author of a new market tome, "Irrational Exuberance." In the process, he says, "investors haven't stopped to think about what risk is at all."

Until the recent market drop, "people had no clue what [risk] is about," agrees Joanna Bickel, a project manager at TIAA-CREF, the big New York provider of retirement services, which is working to bring a more sophisticated risk-assessment tool to its Web site later this year so that its investors can better gauge their own risk profile.

There once was a time when risk assessment was the duty of stockbrokers or financial planners, who questioned clients to gauge their comfort level for volatility and potential losses. But with the explosion of online trading, investors have taken control of their own finances. In the process, they have cast aside the mental due diligence that ultimately determines whether they're sleepless in Cisco or bored by Boeing.

It's an age-old quest for balance. Investors who structure their portfolios so that they are comfortable with both the rewards and risks are the ones who sleep best when market downdrafts keep others awake at night. Moreover, they aren't the ones berating themselves for missing out on big gains when the market rebounds.

To help investors determine the level of risk they're most comfortable with, here's a statistically based risk-tolerance quiz constructed with the help of Investment Technologies Inc., a New York firm that provides investment tools and risk-assessment instruments to financial institutions such as banks and investment firms.

Financial companies increasingly rely on risk quizzes similar to this one, though often far more detailed, to better assess a client's true tolerance for market vicissitudes. As investors continue to take on increasing responsibility for their own money—through online trading or in self-managed 401(k) and IRA retirement accounts—"the issue of how individual investors make investment decisions is becoming a huge issue," says Brian Rom, president of Investment Technologies.

All manner of risk-assessment quizzes are available. Some are posted on financial Web sites, others are available from financial planners and investment companies. Some are relatively simple and are designed to match an investor with particular mutual funds or annuities.

The more sophisticated quizzes are based on statistical research that quantifies the psychological behavior of people and their money habits. Such "behavioral finance" studies have determined that many people typically aren't rational but are irrational when it comes to money and risk.

For example, research has shown that most people fear loss more than they value comparable gain. Offer someone a sure $50 or, on the flip of a coin, the possibility of winning $100 or winning nothing, and chances are they'll pocket the sure thing. Conversely, penalize them $50 to start, then offer a flip of a coin to lose $100 or lose nothing, and they'll invariably take the coin toss. Both scenarios are statistically equivalent, yet people tend to view "the possibility of recouping a loss as more important than the possibility of greater gain," even though the coin flip could mean an even greater loss, says James Corter, associate professor of statistics and education at New York's Columbia University.

The accompanying quiz is based on research done by Mr. Corter. At just eight questions, it is short, but it is backed by empirical studies and "has adequate reliability and validity," says Mr. Corter.

The quiz is designed to reveal where an individual falls along the risk spectrum. It is accompanied by a chart detailing where a variety of stock and bond investments, based on historical performance and volatility, fall along the risk spectrum, to give quiz takers an idea of the class of investments most likely to match an investor's temperament.

Certainly, no risk quiz can tell you everything about your financial courage, and your score here doesn't mean that if you fall into a more conservative category that you can't stomach a little exposure to volatile tech stocks. "But if you answer the questions candidly," says Ms. Bickel at TIAA-CREF, "and don't worry about whether you come out conservative or a swinger, you'll have an accurate portrayal of your risk level that you can use when building your portfolio."

Risk Advisor

Do you know your risk tolerance? This short questionnaire can help you gain a better understanding of your tolerance for market vicissitudes. Answer the questions, tally the results and match the score to the Suitable Investments.*

1. Choose the statement that best describes your interests in an investment program.
   - A My primary aim is to achieve high long-term return in the value of my portfolio, even if that means accepting some significant short-term swings in values.
   - B My primary interest is in stable growth in the value of my portfolio, even if that means somewhat lower returns over time.
   - C I attach equal value to maximizing long-term returns and minimizing fluctuations in value.
2. How important are the following factors when you decide to purchase a stock or mutual fund?
   - a) Short-term potential for the price to appreciate.
   - b) Long-term potential for the price to appreciate.
   - c) If a stock, the potential that the company will be bought or taken over.
   - d) Gain or loss in the price over the past six months.
   - e) Gain or loss in the price over the past five years.
   - f) Stock was recommended by a friend or coworker.
   - g) Risk that the price could drop.
   - h) Potential that the investment will pay dividends.

Very Important	Somewhat Important	Not At All Important
A	B	C
A	B	C
A	B	C
A	B	C
A	B	C
A	B	C
A	B	C
A	B	C

3. a) Would you put $5,000 of your assets into an investment where you have a 70% chance of doubling your money (to $10,000) and a 30% chance of losing the entire $5,000?

   Yes__ No__

   b) How about an 80% chance of doubling to $10,000 and a 20% chance of losing the entire $5,000?

   Yes__ No__

   c) How about a 60% chance of doubling to $10,000 and a 40% chance of losing the entire $5,000?

   Yes__ No__

4. Suppose you have a choice between two mutual funds, both of which are broadly diversified into 6 asset classes (e.g., stocks, bonds, real estate, etc.). The charts below show the changes in value over the past 12 months for the assets in each portfolio. Which portfolio of assets do you prefer to invest in?

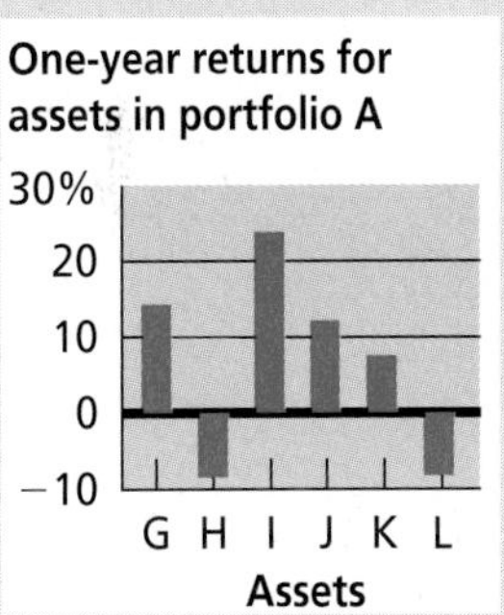

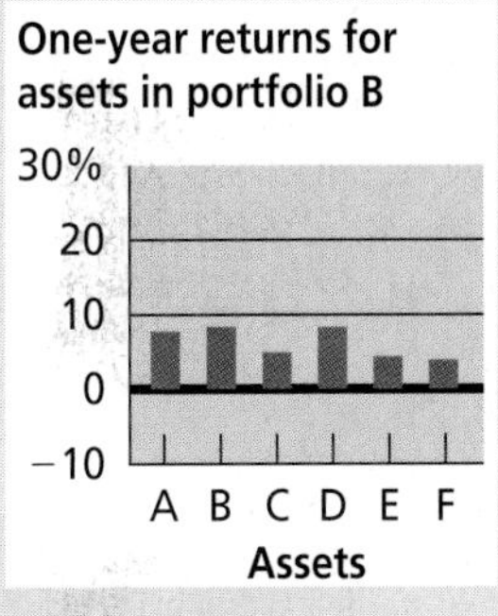

5. Assume that you have made an investment that has dropped in value by $2,000 and you find yourself faced with the following choice (please circle only one option):
   - A Sell and take the immediate $2,000 loss (a 100% chance of loss).
   - B Hold on to it with a 50% chance of recouping the $2,000 and a 50% chance of losing an additional $2,000.
   - C No preference.
6. Assume that you have recently invested $10,000 in a stock and that the value of this stock has dropped 15% in value in one week. You can discover no reason for this decline, and the broader market has not dipped accordingly. Which of the following actions would you be most likely to take? (Circle one answer only.)
   - A Buy more.
   - B Sell all your holdings in the fund immediately and put the money into a less volatile investment.

(continued)

C Sell half of your holdings in the fund immediately and put the money elsewhere.

D Wait for the price to recover and then sell all your holdings in the fund.

E Do nothing (occasional dips in price are to be expected).

7. The following charts show quarterly performance of two equity mutual funds over the past two years. Which do you prefer to invest in?

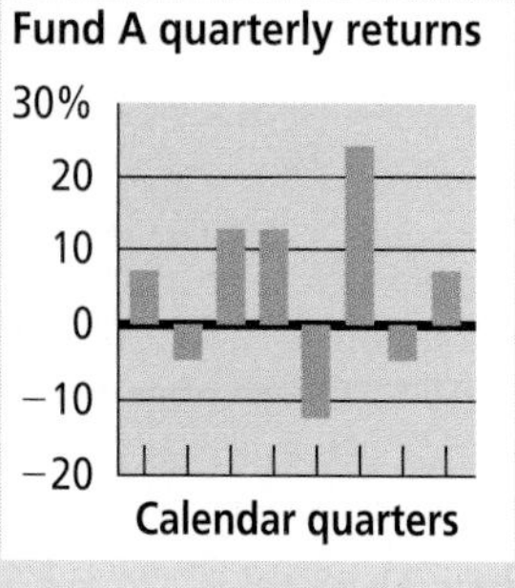

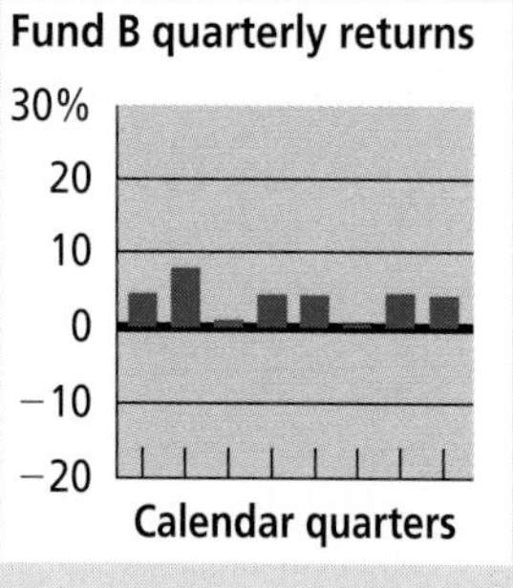

8. As an investor in stock and bond markets, how would you rate your degree of experience relative to other individual investors? (Please circle one.)

A Extremely experienced

B More than average experience

C Average experience

D Less than average experience

E Little or no experience

Source: Investment Technologies Inc.

Scoring

1 – A. 15; B. 0; C. 7

FOR EACH QUESTION:

2a) – A. 0; B. 1; C. 2

2b) through 2e)

A. 2; B. 1; C. 0

FOR EACH QUESTION:

2f) through 2h)

A. 0: B. 1; C. 2

FOR EACH QUESTION:

3a) through 3c)

Yes. 5; No. 0

4 – A. 10; B. 0

5 – A. 0; B. 10; C. 10

6 – A. 15; B. 0; C. 5; D. 0; E. 10

7 – A. 10; B. 0

8 – A. 20; B. 15; C. 10; D. 5; E. 0

Score in Points	Suitable Investments*
0–11	Avoid risk! Open a money-market account—or buy a bigger mattress.
12–33	Gentlemen (and ladies) prefer bonds, and are most at home with high-grade corporate and government bonds of an intermediate duration.
34–55	You're still a bond buyer. But you're willing to live a bit closer to the edge with interest-only U.S. Treasury STRIPS.
56–77	Mix it up. Convertible bonds and stocks are to your liking. But safer utilities and large blue chips are as risky as you go. Real-estate investment trusts fit too.
78–99	Stock up on stocks. At the low end, you're comfortable with larger value stocks; at the high end, riskier midcap and growth stocks work.
100+	Viva Las Vegas, baby! Place your bets on 'Net stocks and new-tech issues. Risks are high, but so are the payoffs.

*Suitable investments are based upon an analysis of the volatility of 75 various bond and stock indices, and apply to investment horizons of between 10 and 15 years.

Source: Jeff D. Opdyke, *The Wall Street Journal,* © 2003 Reprinted with permission of *The Wall Street Journal*, Dow Jones & Company. All Rights Reserved Worldwide.

CHECK THIS

2.4a What does the term "risk-averse" mean?

2.4b What are some of the constraints investors face in making investment decisions?

2.4c What is asset allocation?

2.5 Forming an Investment Portfolio

The nearby *Investment Updates* box contains a quiz to help you determine your risk tolerance. What was your score? The purpose of this section is to give you an example of how to use this score in forming an investment portfolio.

One way that an investor could go about forming an investment portfolio is to consider her objectives, constraints, and strategies as we discussed in the previous section. Of course, there are many other approaches, as we illustrate next.

SOME RISK TOLERANCE SCORES

To start, we gave the risk tolerance quiz to 10 students, staff, and faculty at a well-known private university in St. Louis. Their scores and some other information appear in Table 2.1 (their names are changed, but no one is innocent).

As you can see, the scores have a wide range: from 27 to 85. If you look closely, you will see that the average score for the males and females in this very small set of quiz takers is about the same. However, the average score for those investors with little or no investment experience is 47. Those with at least some investment experience have an average score of 61. What do these scores mean?

RISK AND RETURN

Risk tolerance is the first thing to assess in evaluating the suitability of an investment strategy. Let's look at the test results for Marie and Imelda.

Marie and Imelda have a sufficient cash reserve. That is, both Marie and Imelda have at least six months' living expenses readily available in a money market account. Of course, these amounts are not the same, largely because of housing and transportation cost differences. Having a sufficient cash reserve means that Marie and Imelda can proceed with building an investment portfolio.

MARIE Marie is a 21-year-old accounting student with more than average investment experience. According to the *Investment Updates* quiz, her score of 85 means Marie should: "Stock up on stocks. On the low end, you're comfortable with larger value stocks; at the high end, riskier midcap and growth stocks work." Okay, but how much of her portfolio should she devote to stock?

To help determine Marie's percentage stock allocation, we will use the rule of thumb from the previous section. That is, an investor's percentage allocation to stock should be equal to his or her age subtracted from 100. For Marie, this is 100 − 21 = 79 percent (let's call it 80 percent).

TABLE 2.1 Risk Tolerance Test Results

Name	Age	Sex	Investment Experience	Score
Lynn	23	F	Little or none	27
Lucy	50	F	Little or none	38
Isabel	28	F	Little or none	73
Brigit	38	F	Little or none	67
Lauren	22	F	Little or none	37
Patrick	29	M	Little or none	41
Imelda	59	F	Less than average	30
Homer	54	M	Average	52
Bart	25	M	Average	77
Marie	21	F	More than average	85

TABLE 2.2 Sample Asset Allocations

	Marie, 21		Imelda, 59	
Asset Class	Initial Allocation	Holding Limit	Initial Allocation	Holding Limit
Small-cap stock fund	40%	20–50%	10%	10–20%
Midcap stock fund	20	10–30	5	0–10
Large-cap stock fund	15	5–20	20	10–30
International stock fund	5	0–10	5	0–10
REIT fund	5	0–10	20	15–30
High-yield bond fund	5	0–15	0	0–5
High-quality bond fund	5	0–10	40	25–50
International bond fund	5	0–10	0	0–5

Marie has 30+ years to retirement, so she does not have to worry about short-term market volatility. In addition, she is studying diligently so that she can begin her auditing career and earn a steady and relatively high income. Therefore, for now, having 80 percent of her investments devoted to stock seems appropriate.

IMELDA Imelda is about 59. She is a college professor with many advanced degrees. Imelda's score of 30 means that: "Gentlemen (and ladies) prefer bonds, and are most at home with high-grade corporate and government bonds of an intermediate duration."

For Imelda, the rule of thumb shows that she should consider having a portfolio with $100 - 59 = 41$ percent in stocks (let's call it 40 percent). Imelda has 5+ years to retirement, but many years left to enjoy life. Therefore, Imelda has to worry about market volatility in the short term. Her worry stems from the fact that her lofty income will not be available to her when she retires. As a result, Imelda will really have to think long and hard about whether 40 is the appropriate percentage to have invested in stock.

INVESTOR CONSTRAINTS

In our example, both Marie and Imelda have sufficient *resources*[2] to set up the brokerage accounts that they will use for their investment portfolio, but they have different investment *horizons*. For simplicity, we will assume that both investors prefer highly *liquid* investments. With respect to *taxes,* Marie is currently in a low tax bracket. Therefore, she is likely to elect to pay taxes now and invest in a Roth IRA. Imelda will most likely defer taxes because she is currently in a high tax bracket. So Imelda will most likely try to invest as many pretax dollars as she can. Marie and Imelda will both have to factor in *special circumstances*. For example, Marie might very well have some dependents to support beginning in the next five years or so. Imelda has adult children, but her grandchildren will certainly appreciate her financial support in the years ahead.

STRATEGIES AND POLICIES

With respect to *investment management,* both Marie and Imelda want to avoid the time-consuming activities associated with managing her own investment portfolio. However, each will monitor her portfolio on a monthly basis. Marie and Imelda are convinced that attempts at *market timing* will result in investment underperformance. In addition, both think that *security selection* is a dangerous trap for the unwary. As a result, they both decide to invest in mutual funds (but they have not told us which ones).

Both investors have yet to decide on their *asset allocation.* The asset allocation strategy should provide the highest rate of return given the acceptable level of risk and after accounting for portfolio constraints. Based on their financial resources, financial goals, time horizon, tax status, and risk tolerance, our investors have selected the initial asset allocations seen in Table 2.2.

[2] All investor constraints, strategies, and policies appear in *italics*.

In addition, you can see that our investors have set holding limits on each asset class. That is, they want to make sure that they do not overinvest in any particular asset class. This can happen if an asset class performs well in relation to the rest.

REITS

REIT
A company that owns income-producing real estate

Some quiz results in the *Investment Updates* box suggested that investors consider REITs. REITs is an acronym for real estate investment trust(s). You might be unfamiliar with REITs. Briefly, a **REIT** is a company that owns income-producing real estate such as apartments, shopping centers, offices, hotels, and warehouses. The shares of many REITs trade on major stock exchanges. Therefore, REITS provide for a way to make a diversified investment in professionally managed income-producing real estate without having to deal directly with tenants. REITS are risky assets because cash flows from the properties are not guaranteed. However, the portfolio of properties varies from REIT to REIT. Therefore, not all REITs have the same risk.

WWW

To learn more about REITS, go to www.investinreits.com

CHECK THIS

2.5a Besides risk tolerance, what are some other constraints, strategies, and policies that investors use in forming an investment portfolio?

2.5b Why could two investors of the same age wind up with different investment portfolios?

2.6 Summary and Conclusions

In this chapter, we cover many aspects of the investing process—which we summarize by the chapter's important concepts.

1. The various types of securities brokers and brokerage accounts.

A. Opening a brokerage account is straightforward and really much like opening a bank account. You supply information and sign agreements with your broker. Then you write a check and provide instructions on how you want your money invested.

B. Brokers are traditionally divided into three groups: full-service brokers, discount brokers, and deep-discount brokers. What distinguishes the three groups is the level of service they provide and the resulting commissions they charge. In recent years, the boundaries among the groups have blurred.

C. Your broker does not have a duty to provide you with guaranteed purchase and sale recommendations. However, your broker does have a duty to exercise reasonable care in formulating recommendations. Your broker has a legal duty to act in your best interest. However, your broker relies on commissions generated from your account. Therefore, on rare occasions, a broker is accused of "churning" an account (i.e., promoting excessive trading). When you open your brokerage account, you generally agree that disputes will be resolved by binding arbitration.

2. How to calculate initial and maintenance margin.

A. If you have a "cash account," you can purchase securities only to the extent that you can pay for them in full. If you want to buy more stock, you must deposit more cash into your account.

B. If you have a "margin account," you can purchase securities on credit using money loaned to you by your broker. Generally, you can borrow only half the amount needed to buy the securities.

C. When you first purchase securities on credit, you must supply a specified minimum amount of money. This minimum amount of money is called initial margin.

D. After you have purchased securities on margin, the securities can decline in value. If they do, you must follow established rules concerning the amount of money you must keep in your account. This minimum is called maintenance margin. If your account balance falls below the maintenance margin level, you will receive a margin call. In this chapter, we show you how to calculate initial and maintenance margin levels and their effects on your returns.

3. The workings of short sales.

A. An investor who buys and owns shares of stock is said to be long in the stock, or to have a long position. An investor with a long position makes money only if the price of the stock increases.

B. If you think, for whatever reason, that shares of stock in a particular company are likely to decline in value, you can engage in a short sale. In a short sale, you actually sell a security that you do not own. This is referred to as shorting the stock. After the short sale, the investor is said to have a short position in the security. An investor with a short position makes money only if the shares decrease in value.

C. In this chapter we describe in detail the short sale process for shares of stock. We also stress the potentially unlimited losses that can arise from a short position.

4. The importance of investor objectives, constraints, and strategies.

A. We cover some of the constraints faced by investors. In addition, we briefly describe some basic investment strategy considerations, which include market timing, asset allocation, and security selection.

B. We present a detailed example of one way to form an investment portfolio. In this example, we use a sample of 10 potential investors. The example begins with some risk tolerance scores for these investors. Then the example goes through potential investor constraints and strategies.

GET REAL

This chapter covered the basics of brokerage accounts, some important trade types, and, finally, some big-picture issues regarding investment strategies and objectives. How should you, as an investor or investment manager, put this information to work?

The answer is that you need to open a brokerage account! Investing is like many activities; the best way to learn is by making mistakes. Unfortunately, making mistakes with real money is an expensive way to learn, so we don't recommend trying things like short sales with real money, at least not at first.

Instead, to learn about how to trade and gain some experience with making (and losing) money, you should open a Stock-Trak account (or a similar simulated brokerage account). Take it seriously. Try various trade types and strategies and see how they turn out. The important thing to do is to follow your trades and try to understand why you made or lost money and also why you made or lost the amount you did.

In a similar vein, you should carefully review your account statements to make sure you understand exactly what each item means and how your account equity is calculated.

After you have gained some experience trading "on paper," you should open a real account as soon as you can pull together enough money. Try visiting some online brokers such as Ameritrade to find out the minimum amount you need to open an account. The amount has been declining. In 2007, you could open a cash account for as little as $500, but to open a margin account, you need in the area of $2,000. Or, you can visit www.sharebuilder.com and www.buyandhold.com to open accounts with no money at all!

Looking back at Chapter 1, you know that it's important to get started early. Once you have a real account, however, it's still a good idea to keep a separate "play money" account to test trading ideas to make sure you really understand them before committing your precious real money.

Key Terms

Chapter Review Problems and Self-Test

1. **The Account Balance Sheet** Suppose you want to buy 10,000 shares of Intel Corporation at a price of $30 per share. You put up $200,000 and borrow the rest. What does your account balance sheet look like? What is your margin?
2. **Short Sales** Suppose that in the previous problem you shorted 10,000 shares instead of buying. The initial margin is 60 percent. What does the account balance sheet look like following the short?
3. **Margin Calls** You purchased 500 shares of stock at a price of $56 per share on 50 percent margin. If the maintenance margin is 30 percent, what is the critical stock price?

Answers to Self-Test Problems

1. The 10,000 shares of Intel cost $300,000. You supply $200,000, so you must borrow $100,000. The account balance sheet looks like this:

Assets		Liabilities and Account Equity	
10,000 shares of Intel	$300,000	Margin loan	$100,000
		Account equity	200,000
Total	$300,000	Total	$300,000

Your margin is the account equity divided by the value of the stock owned:

$$\begin{aligned} \text{Margin} &= \$200{,}000/\$300{,}000 \\ &= .666\ldots \\ &= 67\% \end{aligned}$$

2. Following the short, your account is as follows:

Assets		Liabilities and Account Equity	
Proceeds from sale	$300,000	Short position	$300,000
Initial margin deposit	180,000	Account equity	180,000
Total	$480,000	Total	$480,000

Notice that you shorted $300,000 worth of stock, so, with a 60 percent margin requirement, you deposited $180,000.

3. The lowest price the stock can drop before you receive a margin call is:

$$P^* = \frac{\text{Amount borrowed/Number of shares}}{1 - \text{Maintenance margin}}$$

You borrowed 500 × \$56 × .50 = \$14,000. Therefore:

$$P^* = \frac{14{,}000/500}{1 - .30} = \$40.00$$

You will receive a margin call if the stock drops below \$40.00.

Test Your Investment Quotient

For the remaining questions and problems, the circled numbers in the margin refer to the corresponding learning objective in this chapter.

IQ

CFA® PROBLEMS

CFA® PROBLEMS

(4) 1. **Investment Objectives** An individual investor's investment objectives should be expressed in terms of:

- **a.** Risk and return.
- **b.** Capital market expectations.
- **c.** Liquidity needs and time horizon.
- **d.** Tax factors and legal and regulatory constraints.

(4) 2. **Asset Allocation** Which of the following best reflects the importance of the asset allocation decision to the investment process? The asset allocation decision:

- **a.** Helps the investor decide on realistic investment goals.
- **b.** Identifies the specific securities to include in a portfolio.
- **c.** Determines most of the portfolio's returns and volatility over time.
- **d.** Creates a standard by which to establish an appropriate investment horizon.

(2) 3. **Leverage** You deposit \$100,000 cash in a brokerage account and purchase \$200,000 of stocks on margin by borrowing \$100,000 from your broker. Later, the value of your stock holdings falls to \$150,000, whereupon you get nervous and close your account. What is the percentage return on your investment (ignore interest paid)?

- **a.** 0 percent
- **b.** −25 percent
- **c.** −50 percent
- **d.** −75 percent

(3) 4. **Leverage** You deposit \$100,000 cash in a brokerage account and short sell \$200,000 of stocks. Later, the value of the stocks held short rises to \$250,000, whereupon you get nervous and close your account. What is the percentage return on your investment?

- **a.** 0 percent
- **b.** −25 percent
- **c.** −50 percent
- **d.** −75 percent

(2) 5. **Account Margin** You deposit \$100,000 cash in a brokerage account and purchase \$200,000 of stocks on margin by borrowing \$100,000 from your broker. Later, the value of your stock holdings falls to \$175,000. What is your account margin in dollars?

- **a.** \$50,000
- **b.** \$75,000
- **c.** \$100,000
- **d.** \$150,000

(2) 6. **Account Margin** You deposit \$100,000 cash in a brokerage account and purchase \$200,000 of stocks on margin by borrowing \$100,000 from your broker. Later, the value of your stock holdings falls to \$150,000. What is your account margin in percent?

- **a.** 25 percent
- **b.** 33 percent
- **c.** 50 percent
- **d.** 75 percent

(3) 7. **Account Margin** You deposit \$100,000 cash in a brokerage account and short sell \$200,000 of stocks on margin. Later, the value of the stocks held short rises to \$225,000. What is your account margin in dollars?

- **a.** \$50,000
- **b.** \$75,000
- **c.** \$100,000
- **d.** \$150,000

3 **8. Account Margin** You deposit $100,000 cash in a brokerage account and short sell $200,000 of stocks on margin. Later, the value of the stocks held short rises to $250,000. What is your account margin in percent?

a. 20 percent
b. 25 percent
c. 33 percent
d. 50 percent

2 **9. Margin Calls** You deposit $100,000 cash in a brokerage account and purchase $200,000 of stocks on margin by borrowing $100,000 from your broker, who requires a maintenance margin of 30 percent. Which of the following is the largest value for your stock holdings for which you will still receive a margin call?

a. $200,000
b. $160,000
c. $140,000
d. $120,000

3 **10. Margin Calls** You deposit $100,000 cash in a brokerage account and short sell $200,000 of stocks. Your broker requires a maintenance margin of 30 percent. Which of the following is the lowest value for the stocks you are holding short for which you will still receive a margin call?

a. $260,000
b. $240,000
c. $220,000
d. $200,000

4 **11. Investment Decisions** Which of the following investment factors, strategies, or tactics is the least relevant to a passive investment policy?

a. Market timing
b. Asset allocation
c. Political environment
d. Tax status

4 **12. Investment Decisions** Which of the following investment factors, strategies, or tactics is most associated with an active investment policy?

a. Market timing
b. Asset allocation
c. Security selection
d. Tax status

4 **13. Investment Decisions** Which of the following investment strategies or tactics will likely consume the greatest amount of resources, time, effort, and so on, when implementing an active investment policy?

a. Market timing
b. Asset allocation
c. Security selection
d. Tax strategy

4 **14. Investment Decisions** Which of the following investment strategies or tactics is likely the most relevant in the decision to short sell a particular stock?

a. Market timing
b. Asset allocation
c. Security selection
d. Tax strategy

4 **15. Investment Constraints** Which of the following investment constraints is expected to have the most fundamental impact on the investment decision process for a typical investor?

a. Investor's tax status
b. Investor's time horizon
c. Investor's need for liquidity
d. Investor's attitude toward risk

Concept Questions

(2) **1. Margin** What does it mean to purchase a security on margin? Why might you do it?

(3) **2. Short Sales** What does it mean to sell a security short? Why might you do it?

(2) **3. Margin Requirements** What is the reason margin requirements exist?

(4) **4. Allocation versus Selection** What is the difference between asset allocation and security selection?

(4) **5. Allocation versus Timing** Are market timing and active asset allocation similar? Why or why not?

(1) **6. Street Name Registration** Why is street name registration advantageous to investors? Under what circumstances is it required?

(1) **7. Broker–Customer Relations** Suppose your broker tips you on a hot stock. You invest heavily, but, to your considerable dismay, the stock plummets in value. What recourse do you have against your broker?

(3) **8. Long Profits** An important difference between a long position in stock and a short position concerns the potential gains and losses. Suppose a stock sells for $18 per share, and you buy 500 shares. What are your potential gains and losses?

(3) **9. Liquidity** The liquidity of an asset directly affects the risk of buying or selling that asset during adverse market conditions. Describe the liquidity risk you face with a short stock position during a market rally, and a long stock position during a market decline.

(3) **10. Short Sale Profits** Suppose you sell short 1,000 shares of a stock at $60 per share. Ignoring borrowing costs and fees, what is the maximum profit you can earn from this investment? What is the potential maximum loss?

Questions and Problems

Core Questions

(2) **1. Calculating Margin** Carson Corporation stock sells for $71 per share, and you've decided to purchase as many shares as you possibly can. You have $13,000 available to invest. What is the maximum number of shares you can buy if the initial margin is 60 percent?

(2) **2. Margin** You purchase 500 shares of 2nd Chance Co. stock on margin at a price of $53. Your broker requires you to deposit $11,000. What is your margin loan amount? What is the initial margin requirement?

(2) **3. Margin Return** In the previous problem, suppose you sell the stock at a price of $62. What is your return? What would your return have been had you purchased the stock without margin? What if the stock price is $44 when you sell the stock?

(2) **4. Margin** Repeat the previous two problems assuming the initial margin requirement is 30 percent. Does this suggest a relationship between the initial margin and returns?

(2) **5. Margin Purchases** You have $12,000 and decide to invest on margin. If the initial margin requirement is 55 percent, what is the maximum dollar purchase you can make?

(2) **6. Margin Calls** You buy 400 shares of stock at a price of $75 and an initial margin of 45 percent. If the maintenance margin is 30 percent, at what price will you receive a margin call?

(2) **7. Margin Calls** You decide to buy 600 shares of stock at a price of $43 and an initial margin of 55 percent. What is the maximum percentage decline in the stock before you will receive a margin call if the maintenance margin is 35 percent?

(3) **8. Margin Calls on Short Sales** The stock of Flop Industries is trading at $71. You feel the stock price will decline, so you short 900 shares at an initial margin of 60 percent. If the maintenance margin is 30 percent, at what share price will you receive a margin call?

(3) **9. Margin Calls on Short Sales** You short sold 1,000 shares of stock at a price of $63 and an initial margin of 55 percent. If the maintenance margin is 30 percent, at what share price will you receive a margin call? What is your account equity at this stock price?

(4) **10. Taxes and Returns** You purchase a stock at the beginning of the year at a price of $108. At the end of the year the stock pays a dividend of $1.80 and you sell the stock for $117. What is your return for the year? Now suppose that dividends are taxed at 15 percent and long-term capital gains (over 11 months) are taxed at 30 percent. What is your aftertax return for the year?

Intermediate Questions

11. **Calculating Margin** Using the information in Problem 1, construct your equity account balance sheet at the time of your purchase. What does your balance sheet look like if the share price rises to \$84? What if it falls to \$62 per share? What is your margin in both cases? Round the number of shares down to the nearest number of whole shares.

(2) 12. **Calculating Margin** You've just opened a margin account with \$11,000 at your local brokerage firm. You instruct your broker to purchase 600 shares of Smolira Golf stock, which currently sells for \$46 per share. What is your initial margin? Construct the equity account balance sheet for this position.

(2) 13. **Margin Call** Suppose you purchase 500 shares of stock at \$84 per share with an initial cash investment of \$15,000. If your broker requires a 30 percent maintenance margin, at what share price will you be subject to a margin call? If you want to keep your position open despite the stock price plunge, what alternatives do you have?

(2) 14. **Margin and Leverage** In the previous problem, suppose the call money rate is 5 percent and you are charged a 1.5 percent premium over this rate. Calculate your return on investment for each of the following share prices one year later. Ignore dividends.

   a. \$96
   b. \$84
   c. \$62

   Suppose instead you had simply purchased \$15,000 of stock with no margin. What would your rate of return have been now?

(2) 15. **Margin and Leverage** Suppose the call money rate is 6.8 percent, and you pay a spread of 1.9 percent over that. You buy 1,000 shares at \$51 per share with an initial margin of 40 percent. One year later, the stock is selling for \$57 per share, and you close out your position. What is your return assuming no dividends are paid?

(2) 16. **Margin and Leverage** Suppose the call money rate is 5.8 percent, and you pay a spread of 2.5 percent over that. You buy 800 shares of stock at \$43 per share. You put up \$15,000. One year later, the stock is selling for \$58 per share, and you close out your position. What is your return assuming a dividend of \$.64 per share is paid?

(2) 17. **Margin Interest** Suppose you take out a margin loan for \$30,000. The rate you pay is an 8.4 percent effective rate. If you repay the loan in six months, how much interest will you pay?

(2) 18. **Margin Interest** Suppose you take out a margin loan for \$39,000. You pay a 7.2 percent effective rate. If you repay the loan in two months, how much interest will you pay?

19. **Annualized Returns** Suppose you hold a particular investment for seven months. You calculate that your holding-period return is 9 percent. What is your annualized return?

20. **Annualized Returns** In the previous question, suppose your holding period was five months instead of seven. What is your annualized return? What do you conclude in general about the length of your holding period and your annualized return?

21. **Annualized Returns** Suppose you buy stock at a price of \$67 per share. Five months later, you sell it for \$61. You also received a dividend of \$.40 per share. What is your annualized return on this investment?

22. **Calculating Returns** Looking back at Problem 12, suppose the call money rate is 6 percent and your broker charges you a spread of 1.25 percent over this rate. You hold the stock for six months and sell at a price of \$53 per share. The company paid a dividend of \$.25 per share the day before you sold your stock. What is your total dollar return from this investment? What is your effective annual rate of return?

(3) 23. **Short Sales** You believe that Rose, Inc., stock is going to fall and you've decided to sell 1,500 shares short. If the current share price is \$47, construct the equity account balance sheet for this trade. Assume the initial margin is 100 percent.

(3) 24. **Short Sales** Repeat the previous problem assuming you short the 1,500 shares on 75 percent margin.

(3) 25. **Calculating Short Sale Returns** You just sold short 1,200 shares of Wetscope, Inc., a fledgling software firm, at \$96 per share. You cover your short when the price hits \$86.50 per share one year later. If the company paid \$.75 per share in dividends over this period, what is your rate of return on the investment? Assume an initial margin of 50 percent.

(3) 26. **Short Sales** You believe the stock in Freeze Frame Co. is going to fall, so you short 1,600 shares at a price of \$72. The initial margin is 50 percent. Construct the equity balance sheet for

the original trade. Now construct an equity balance sheet for a stock price of $63 and a stock price of $79. What is your margin at each of these stock prices? What is your effective annual return if you cover your short position at each of these prices in five months?

S&P Problems

www.mhhe.com/edumarketinsight

STANDARD &POOR'S

1. **Margin** Download the historical stock prices for Tootsie Roll Industries (TR) under the "Mthly. Adj. Prices" link. Assume you purchased 400 shares of Tootsie Roll stock at the closing price six months ago. The initial margin requirement is 50 percent and the maintenance margin is 30 percent. Show the account balance sheet based on monthly closing prices for the last five months. At what stock price will you receive a margin call? Are any margin deposits required over this period? What is your return on this investment?
2. **Short Sales** Download the historical stock prices for Ford (F) under the "Mthly. Adj. Prices" link. Assume you short sold 200 shares of Ford stock at the closing price six months ago. The initial margin requirement is 50 percent and the maintenance margin is 30 percent. Show the account balance sheet based on monthly closing prices for the last five months. At what stock price will you receive a margin call? Are any margin deposits required over this period? What is your return on this investment?

What's on the Web?

1. **Risk Tolerance** As we discussed in the chapter, risk tolerance is based on an individual's personality and investment goals. There are numerous risk tolerance questionnaires on the Web. One, provided by Merrill Lynch, is located at individual.ml.com. Go to the Web site, locate the questionnaire, and take the quiz. How conservative or aggressive are you?
2. **Short Interest** You can find the number of short sales on a particular stock at finance.yahoo.com. Go to the site and find the number of shares short sold for ExxonMobil (XOM) under the "Key Statistics" link. How many shares are sold short in the current month? What about the previous month? What do the "Percent of Float" and "Short Ratio" mean?
3. **Broker Call Money Rate** What is the current broker call money rate? To find out, go to www.money-rates.com and look up the call money rate.
4. **Margin Purchases** Suppose you have a margin account with TDAmeritrade. You purchase 1,000 shares of IBM stock on 50 percent margin at today's price. Go to finance.yahoo.com to find your purchase price. Ignoring transaction costs, how much will you borrow? Next, go to www.money-rates.com to find the current broker call money rate. Finally, go to www.TDAmeritrade.com to find out how much above the current broker call money rate you will pay. If you keep your investment for one year, how much will you pay in interest assuming the margin rate stays the same? What does the stock price have to be in one year for you to break even on your investment?

Stock-Trak Exercises

STOCK | TRAK
GLOBAL PORTFOLIO SIMULATIONS

To access the Stock-Trak Exercise for this chapter, please visit the book Web site at www.mhhe.com/jm5e and choose the corresponding chapter.

www.mhhe.com/jm5e

CHAPTER 3
Overview of Security Types

"An investment operation is one which upon thorough analysis promises safety of principal and an adequate return. Operations not meeting these requirements are speculative."

–Benjamin Graham

You invest $5,000 in Yahoo! common stock and just months later sell the shares for $7,500, realizing a 50 percent return. Not bad! At the same time, your neighbor invests $5,000 in Yahoo! stock options, which are worth $25,000 at expiration—a 400 percent return. Yahoo! Alternatively, your Yahoo! shares fall in value to $2,500, and you realize a 50 percent loss. Too bad! But at the same time your neighbor's Yahoo! stock options are now worthless. Clearly, there is a big difference between stock shares and stock options. Security type matters. ■

Learning Objectives

Price quotes for all types of investments are easy to find, but what do they mean? Learn the answers for:

1. Various types of interest-bearing assets.
2. Equity securities.
3. Futures contracts.
4. Option contracts.

Our goal in this chapter is to introduce you to some of the different types of securities that are routinely bought and sold in financial markets around the world. As we mentioned in Chapter 1, we will be focusing on financial assets such as bonds, stocks, futures, and options in this book, so these are the securities we briefly describe here. The securities we discuss are covered in much greater detail in the chapters ahead, so we touch on only some of their most essential features in this chapter.

For each of the securities we examine, we ask three questions. First, what is its basic nature and what are its distinguishing characteristics? Second, what are the potential gains and losses from owning it? Third, how are its prices quoted in the financial press?

3.1 Classifying Securities

To begin our overview of security types, we first develop a classification scheme for the different securities. As shown in Table 3.1, financial assets can be grouped into three broad categories, and each of these categories can be further subdivided into a few major subtypes. This classification is not exhaustive, but it covers the major types of financial assets. In the sections that follow, we describe these assets in the order they appear in Table 3.1.

When we examine some of these security types in more detail, we will see that the distinctions can become a little blurred, particularly with some recently created financial instruments; as a result, some financial assets are hard to classify. The primary reason is that some instruments are hybrids, meaning that they are combinations of the basic types.

As you may have noticed in our discussion, financial assets, such as bonds and stocks, are often called securities. They are often called financial "instruments" as well. In certain contexts, there are distinctions between these terms, but they are used more or less interchangeably in everyday discussion, so we will stick with common usage.

TABLE 3.1 Classification of Financial Assets

Basic Types	Major Subtypes
Interest-bearing	Money market instruments
	Fixed-income securities
Equities	Common stock
	Preferred stock
Derivatives	Futures
	Options

CHECK THIS

3.1a What are the three basic types of financial assets?

3.1b Why are some financial assets hard to classify?

3.2 Interest-Bearing Assets

Broadly speaking, interest-bearing assets (as the name suggests) pay interest. Some pay interest implicitly and some pay it explicitly, but the common denominator is that the value of these assets depends, at least for the most part, on interest rates. The reason that these assets pay interest is that they all begin life as a loan of some sort, so they are all debt obligations of some issuer.

There are many types of interest-bearing assets. They range from the relatively simple to the astoundingly complex. We discuss some basic types and their features next. The more complex types are discussed in later chapters.

MONEY MARKET INSTRUMENTS

money market instruments
Debt obligations of large corporations and governments with an original maturity of one year or less.

For the most part, **money market instruments** are the simplest form of interest-bearing asset. Money market instruments generally have the following two properties:

1. They are essentially IOUs sold by large corporations or governments to borrow money.
2. They mature in less than one year from the time they are sold, meaning that the loan must be repaid within one year.

Most money market instruments trade in very large denominations, and most, but not all, are quite liquid.

The most familiar example of a money market instrument is a Treasury bill, or T-bill for short. Every week, the U.S. Treasury borrows billions of dollars by selling T-bills to the public. Like many (but not all) money market instruments, T-bills are sold on a *discount basis*. This simply means that T-bills are sold at a price that is less than their stated face value. In other words, an investor buys a T-bill at one price and later, when the bill matures, receives the full face value. The difference is the interest earned.

U.S. Treasury bills are the most liquid type of money market instrument—that is, the type with the largest and most active market. Other types of money market instruments traded in active markets include bank certificates of deposit (or CDs) and corporate and municipal money market instruments.

The potential gain from buying a money market instrument is fixed because the owner is promised a fixed future payment. The most important risk is the risk of default, which is the possibility that the borrower will not repay the loan as promised. With a T-bill, there is no possibility of default, so, as we saw in Chapter 1, T-bills are essentially risk-free. In fact, most money market instruments have relatively low risk, but there are exceptions, and a few spectacular defaults have occurred in the past.

Prices for different money market instruments are quoted in the financial press in different ways. In fact, usually interest rates are quoted, not prices, so some calculation is necessary to convert rates to prices. The procedures are not complicated, but they involve a fair amount of detail, so we save them for another chapter.

FIXED-INCOME SECURITIES

fixed-income securities
Longer-term debt obligations, often of corporations and governments, that promise to make fixed payments according to a preset schedule.

Fixed-income securities are exactly what the name suggests: securities that promise to make fixed payments according to some preset schedule. The other key characteristic of a fixed-income security is that, like a money market instrument, it begins life as a loan of some sort. Fixed-income securities are therefore debt obligations. They are typically issued by corporations and governments. Unlike money market instruments, fixed-income securities have lives that exceed 12 months at the time they are issued.

The words "note" and "bond" are generic terms for fixed-income securities, but "fixed income" is more accurate. This term is being used more frequently as securities are increasingly being created that don't fit within traditional note or bond frameworks but are nonetheless fixed-income securities.

EXAMPLES OF FIXED-INCOME SECURITIES To give one particularly simple example of a fixed-income security, near the end of every month, the U.S. Treasury sells between $25 billion and $35 billion of two-year notes to the public. If you buy a two-year note when it is issued, you will receive a check every six months for two years for a fixed amount, called the bond's *coupon*, and in two years you will receive the face amount on the note.

Suppose you buy $1 million in face amount of a 4 percent, two-year note. The 4 percent is called the *coupon rate*, and it tells you that you will receive 4 percent of the $1 million face value each year, or $40,000, in two $20,000 semiannual "coupon" payments. In two years, in addition to your final $20,000 coupon payment, you will receive the $1 million face value. The price you would pay for this note depends on market conditions. U.S. government security prices are discussed in detail in a later chapter.

current yield
Annual coupon divided by the current bond price.

You must be careful not to confuse the *coupon rate* with **current yield**. The current yield is the annual coupon divided by the current bond price. For most bonds, the coupon rate never changes. But the current yield fluctuates with the price of the bond.

EXAMPLE 3.1 A "Note-Worthy" Investment?

Suppose you buy $100,000 in face amount of a just-issued five-year U.S. Treasury note. If the coupon rate is 5 percent, what will you receive over the next five years if you hold on to your investment?

You will receive 5 percent of $100,000, or $5,000, per year, paid in two semiannual coupons of $2,500. In five years, in addition to the final $2,500 coupon payment, you will receive the $100,000 face amount.

3.3 Equities

Equities are probably the most familiar type of security. They come in two forms: common stock and preferred stock. Of these, common stock is much more important, so we discuss it first.

COMMON STOCK

WWW

Are you a Foolish investor? Go to "Fool's School" at www.fool.com

Common stock represents ownership in a corporation. If you own 1,000 shares of IBM, for example, then you own about .0000685 percent of IBM (IBM has roughly 1.46 billion shares outstanding). It's really that simple. As a part owner, you are entitled to your pro rata share of anything paid out by IBM, and you have the right to vote on important matters regarding IBM. If IBM were to be sold or liquidated, you would receive your share of whatever was left over after all of IBM's debts and other obligations (such as wages) were paid.

The potential benefits from owning common stock come primarily in two forms. First, many companies (but not all) pay cash dividends to their shareholders. However, neither the timing nor the amount of any dividend is guaranteed. At any time, it can be increased, decreased, or omitted altogether. Dividends are paid strictly at the discretion of a company's board of directors, which is elected by the shareholders.

The second potential benefit from owning stock is that the value of your stock may rise because share values in general increase or because the future prospects for your particular company improve (or both). The downside is just the reverse: your shares may lose value if either the economy or your particular company falters. As we saw back in Chapter 1, both the potential rewards and the risks from owning common stock have been substantial, particularly shares of stock in smaller companies.

PREFERRED STOCK

The other type of equity security, preferred stock, differs from common stock in several important ways. First, the dividend on a preferred share is usually fixed at some amount and never changed. Further, in the event of liquidation, preferred shares have a particular face value. The reason that preferred stock (or preference stock, as it is sometimes termed) is called "preferred" is that a company must pay the fixed dividend on its preferred stock before any dividends can be paid to common shareholders. In other words, preferred shareholders must be paid first.

The dividend on a preferred stock can be omitted at the discretion of the board of directors, so, unlike a debt obligation, there is no legal requirement that the dividend be paid (as long as the common dividend is also skipped). However, some preferred stock is *cumulative,* meaning that any and all skipped dividends must be paid in full (although without interest) before common shareholders can receive a dividend.

Potential gains from owning preferred stock consist of the promised dividend plus any gains from price increases. The potential losses are just the reverse: the dividend may be skipped, and the value of your preferred shares may decline from either marketwide decreases in value or diminished prospects for your particular company's future business (or both).

Preferred stock issues are not rare, but they are much less frequently encountered than common stock issues. Most preferred stock is issued by large companies, particularly banks and public utilities.

In many ways, preferred stock resembles a fixed-income security; in fact, it is sometimes classified that way. In particular, preferred stocks usually have a fixed payment and a fixed liquidation value (but no fixed maturity date). The main difference is that preferred stock is not a debt obligation. Also, for accounting and tax purposes, preferred stock is treated as equity.

Having said this, preferred stock is a good example of why it is sometimes difficult to neatly and precisely classify every security type. To further complicate matters, some preferred stock issues have dividends that are not fixed. So it seems clear that these securities are not fixed-income securities. However, some bond issues make no fixed payments and allow the issuer to skip payments under certain circumstances. As we mentioned earlier, these are examples of hybrid securities.

To give a more difficult example, consider a *convertible bond*. Such a bond is an ordinary bond in every way except that it can be exchanged for a fixed number of shares of stock anytime at the bondholder's discretion. Whether this is really a debt or equity instrument is difficult (or even impossible) to say.

COMMON STOCK PRICE QUOTES

Unlike fixed-income securities, the price quotes on common and preferred stock are fairly uniform. Part of the common stock page found at www.wsj.com can be seen in Figure 3.2. Locate the entry for the Boeing Company (BA).

In the first column, you see a green arrow pointed upward. This arrow is a trend indicator that says the average price for Boeing stock over the past 20 days is higher than the average price for Boeing stock over the past 50 days. In addition, the average price for Boeing stock over the past 50 days is greater than the average price for Boeing stock over the past 100 days. We have much more to say about technical indicators, including trend indicators, in a later chapter.

The second and third columns contain the company name and its ticker symbol. The next piece of information, Volume, is the actual number of shares traded for the day: 6,196,160. Because investors usually trade stock in multiples of 100 shares, called "round lots," sometimes you will see volume figures reported in multiples of hundreds. For example, if you wanted to report Boeing's volume in round lots, you would report volume as 61,962.

The next three columns contain Boeing's share price at the close of trading, the share price change ("Chg") measured in dollars, and the percent change from the previous day's closing price ("% Chg"). You can see that Boeing shares closed at $104.53, which is $1.10 higher than the previous day. In percent change terms, you can verify that the closing price

FIGURE 3.2 Closing Prices: Most Widely Held

Most Widely Held: Closing Table

Wednesday, August 01, 2007

Alphabetical listing of stocks with the largest institutional ownership based on the most recent Form 13-F SEC filings.

Stocks' trends based on a comparison of three moving averages (20-day, 50-day and 100-day), as supplied by www.InvestorsIntelligence.com, based on the Dow Jones Wilshire 5000 universe. **Bullish (▲)** Shorter-term moving averages hold above longer-term (20-day>50-day>100-day). **Bearish (▼)** Shorter-term moving averages have crossed below longer-term (20-day<50-day<100-day). **No trend (◀▶)** No trend symbol means the company is not in the DJ Wilshire 5000 universe.

				DAILY				52 WEEK		
Trend	Company	Symbol	Volume	Close	Chg	% Chg	YTD % chg	High	Low	% Chg
◀▶	AT & T Inc	T	35,519,979	$40.23	1.07	2.73	12.5	$41.93	$29.82	31.6
▼	Abbott Labs	ABT	7,954,654	50.95	0.26	0.51	4.6	59.50	45.41	8.1
▲	Alcoa Inc	AA	25,446,464	37.95	-0.08	-0.21	26.5	48.77	26.39	28.0
◀▶	Altria Group Inc	MO	13,040,723	66.58	0.11	0.17	3.4	72.20	56.32	10.9
◀▶	American Express	AXP	10,718,649	59.63	1.09	1.86	-1.7	65.89	51.19	15.2
▼	Amer Int'l Group	AIG	38,422,947	64.57	0.39	0.61	-9.9	72.97	58.24	7.1
▼	Amgen Inc	AMGN	27,142,474	52.09	-1.65	-3.07	-23.7	77.00	50.30	-26.4
▲	Apple Inc	AAPL	61,263,300	135.00	3.24	2.46	59.1	148.92	62.58	98.1
▲	Applied Materials	AMAT	41,283,963	22.45	0.41	1.86	21.7	22.50	15.06	44.0
▼	Bank of America	BAC	48,211,553	47.63	0.21	0.44	-10.8	55.08	46.89	-8.3
◀▶	Bank of NY Mellon	BK	12,936,477	41.96	-0.59	-1.39	0.5	46.93	35.19	17.8
▲	Boeing Co	BA	6,196,160	104.53	1.10	1.06	17.7	107.83	72.13	33.0
▼	Boston Scientific	BSX	22,802,610	13.19	0.04	0.30	-23.2	18.69	12.96	-25.1
◀▶	Bristol-Myers	BMY	12,070,394	28.67	0.26	0.92	8.9	32.35	20.08	21.0
▲	CBS Corp B	CBS	6,377,433	31.97	0.25	0.79	2.5	35.75	25.53	17.8
◀▶	CVS Caremark	CVS	12,909,287	35.54	0.35	0.99	15.0	39.44	27.09	7.1
▼	Carnival Corp	CCL	5,643,024	44.80	0.49	1.11	-8.7	52.73	36.69	16.3
▲	Chevron Corp	CVX	21,436,036	85.17	-0.09	-0.11	15.8	95.00	60.72	29.1
▲	Cisco Systems	CSCO	58,195,321	29.77	0.86	2.97	8.9	30.39	17.10	70.3
▼	Citigroup Inc	C	59,098,611	46.85	0.28	0.60	-15.9	57.00	45.63	-3.8
▲	Coca-Cola Co	KO	12,337,403	53.27	1.16	2.23	10.4	54.49	43.48	20.2

Source: www.wsj.com, August 1, 2007. Reprinted by permission of *The Wall Street Journal*.

WORK THE WEB

Throughout this chapter, we have looked at information available online at www.wsj.com. One problem is that prices reported are sometimes from the previous day. Before you trade, you'll want more up-to-date prices, particularly in fast-moving markets. Using an Internet server, such as Yahoo!, let's get some intraday prices. Here, as in Chapter 1, we entered a ticker symbol ("HPQ" for Hewlett-Packard Co.).

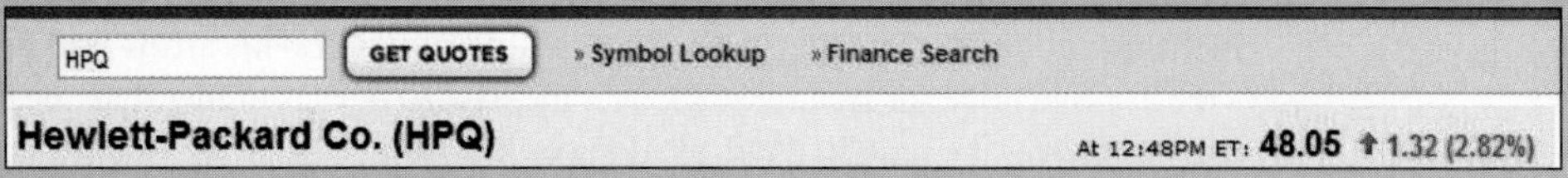

Most of the information here is self-explanatory. The abbreviation "Market Cap" is short for "market capitalization," which is the total value of all outstanding shares. Notice, on this particular day, HPQ was up 2.82 percent, compared to the $46.73 ("Prev Close") that you would see in the print version of *The Wall Street Journal*. We'll discuss other unfamiliar terms, such as "Bid" and "Ask," a little later in the book. For now, a good exercise is to select a detailed quote yourself and find out what information is in the links below the stock quote.

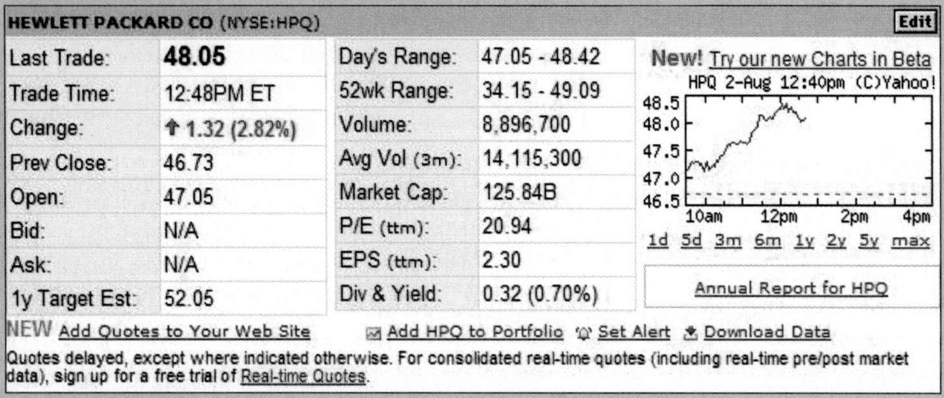

As noted, the free quotes available at finance.yahoo.com during the day are generally delayed by 20 minutes or so. These days, you can also see "real-time" quotes. After a free trial period, however, you must pay for this information.

is 1.06 percent higher than the previous closing price. The closing price is the last price at which a trade occurred before regular trading hours ended at 4:00 P.M. EST.

The last three numbers (labeled "52 WEEK High," "Low," and "% Chg") are the highest and lowest price per share that the stock has sold for over the past 52 weeks. Thus, Boeing's stock sold for as high as $107.83 per share and as low as $72.13 per share. Based on its share price 52 weeks ago, Boeing shares have increased by 33.0 percent.

You can also get preferred stock quotes at www.wsj.com. They appear in a separate section with a relatively simple format. Of course, the information contained in *The Wall Street Journal* and at www.wsj.com can be obtained online in many other places, too. The nearby *Work the Web* box describes one way.

To interpret this information, you will need to know the company's ticker symbol. The ticker symbol is a unique combination of letters assigned to each company. Hewlett-Packard's ticker symbol, for example, is HPQ.

Stock price information is also available all day long on television and on the Web. Our nearby *Investment Updates* box explains how to interpret a very common sight on television, the on-air ticker. As explained there, once you understand the display, you can actually create your own ticker to track the investments that interest you the most.

Some investors want a list of companies that pay dividends. A sample of such a list from www.wsj.com appears in Figure 3.3. Notice that much of the information is similar to the

INVESTMENT UPDATES

THE TALE OF THE TAPE

The on-air "ticker tape" is a familiar sight on television, particularly on financially oriented shows and networks. The most widely watched such channel is CNBC. All day long, at the bottom of the screen, two rolls of information scroll by.

On CNBC, the upper band shows trading on the New York Stock Exchange, and the lower band shows trading on the NASDAQ Stock Market. A lot of other information (too much, in fact, for us to cover here) will also scroll by.

To learn more, go to moneycentral.msn.com and scroll down to "Open MSN Money Streaming Ticker." Follow the installation instructions, and you will be able to create your own desktop ticker that you can display on your computer screen. A personalized ticker allows you to track just the stocks that interest you the most. We created our own ticker:

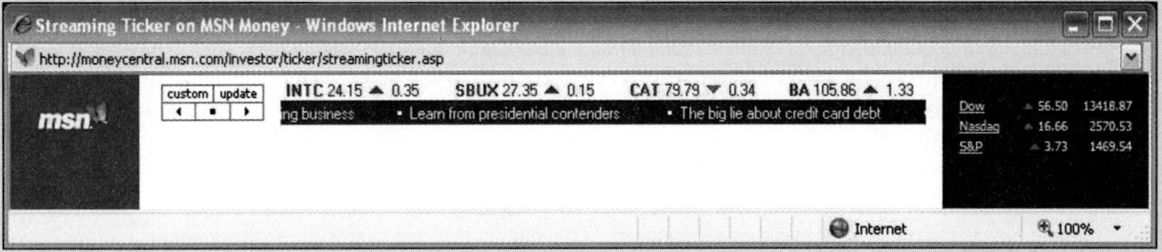

If you click on "custom," you can add your own list of stock symbols. You can make this ticker run forward or backward, and you can even pause it. If you see an interesting news headline flash by, you can click on it and read the pop-up window. Many other free stock tickers are available online. (We Googled "free stock ticker" and got about 26,000 results.)

The display is called a "ticker" because, at one time, it was printed on a thin strip of "ticker tape" (paper) by a "ticker" machine (so named because of the sound it made while printing). In fact, the reason for ticker symbols in the first place was to make information quicker and easier to print. Perhaps you have seen old film footage of a "ticker tape parade" in New York. The paper that rains down on the celebrities and dignitaries is ticker tape.

Ticker machines date to an era before television (if you can imagine such a time). The first one was introduced in 1867 and was later improved upon by none other than Thomas Edison. To learn more, visit the Web site www.stocktickercompany.com.

FIGURE 3.3 Top Yielding Stocks, Basic Resources Sector

Stock Scan: Dividend Stocks

TOP-YIELDING STOCKS

GO TO: WAYS TO INVEST FOR DIVIDENDS: Stocks With Fastest Dividend Growth | High-Yielding Mutual Funds | ETFs

Friday, August 17, 2007 — Find Historical Data | WHAT'S THIS?

Stocks with the highest dividend yields in the day's best performing U.S. sectors, ranked by dividend yield.

					DAILY				52-WEEK RANGE				
Div amt	Div % yld	Index/Core stock	Symbol	Mkt cap†	Close	Chg	% Chg	YTD % chg	Low	Close (●)	High	% Chg	P/E ratio
...	**1.43**	**Basic Resources**	...	...	2750.39	97.54	3.68	6.5	2138.59		3479.82	14.3	...
$2.24	**6.94**	Alliance Rsrc Prtn	ARLP	$1,170	$32.26	1.08	3.48	-6.5	$30.12		$45.50	-15.1	11
1.06	**4.43**	AllianceHldgGP LP	AHGP	1,433	23.94	0.45	1.92	21.2	18.41		33.73	10.4	16
0.32	**4.10**	Friedman Indus	FRD	52	7.81	0.36	4.83	-35.5	7.06		12.89	-14.0	8
0.80	**4.08**	Olin Corp	OLN	1,429	19.60	0.19	0.98	18.6	14.22		22.71	27.8	10
1.28	**3.87**	Compass Minerals	CMP	1,058	33.10	0.71	2.19	4.9	25.90		36.79	22.6	21
1.60	**3.76**	Pope Resources	POPEZ	199	42.50	1.42	3.46	23.8	30.50		50.01	35.4	9
2.40	**3.69**	Weyerhaeuser Co	WY	14,034	65.00	2.03	3.22	-8.0	56.95		87.09	12.1	11
0.68	**3.29**	Worthington Indus	WOR	1,764	20.70	0.20	0.98	16.8	16.41		23.40	0.4	16
0.20	**3.13**	Empire Resources	ERS	62	6.40	0.19	3.06	-41.5	5.54		16.90	-47.8	9
1.00	**3.02**	Int'l Paper Co	IP	14,404	33.07	0.75	2.32	-3.0	31.05		41.57	-5.1	5

Source: www.wsj.com, August 20, 2007. Reprinted by permission of *The Wall Street Journal*.

INVESTMENT UPDATES

REBALANCING YOUR PORTFOLIO

A year of major shifts in the world's financial markets is forcing investment advisers to overhaul some of their basic advice on asset allocation.

As a result, this fall as individual investors gear up for the ritual end-of-year reassessment and rebalancing of their portfolios, they might find they need to make bigger changes than in the past.

For instance, the longstanding 60%-in-stocks-and-40%-in-bonds rule for a medium-risk Baby Boomer portfolio is being tossed out the window at some firms. Instead, financial planners say, they are increasingly advising clients to test the waters of foreign investments, especially in Europe and Japan, as well as alternative investments such as hedge funds.

Portfolios that haven't been rebalanced this year most likely drifted toward U.S. real-estate related holdings, intermediate-term bonds, value stocks and small-capitalization stocks, all of which should be reined in, advisers say.

The shifting advice is the result of a range of the sometimes surprising changes in the investing landscape over the past year to 18 months. The federal-funds target rate has climbed to 4% from its nearly half-century low of 1% as recently as mid-2004, guiding short-term interest rates higher. That steady climb in itself is rapidly turning investors off debt investments, especially the riskiest so-called junk bonds, and instead increasing the appeal of cash-like investments such as money-market funds.

At the same time, the dollar has staged an unexpected surge. U.S. stocks, meanwhile, have been relatively flat this year, which has sent investors looking for better returns abroad.

Complicating matters: Energy prices remain high, an immediate concern that throws a wrench into investment planning because it is still unclear what the longer-term impact will be on the economy and the stock market. And real-estate prices have showed signs of softening in the past few months, perhaps signaling that the decade-long real-estate boom is cooling off. As a result, some once-popular real-estate investment trust stocks are now increasingly viewed as having topped out and run their course in recent months.

All this upheaval signals what some financial advisers believe is a turning point for investors. Namely, the changed landscape means people might need to make more than the usual small tune-up this year and possibly further down the road. "I think we're about to enter a multi-year shift," says David Darst, chief investment strategist at Morgan Stanley's individual investor group. "People should question how much their portfolios are returning," in a market in transition.

Investors need to be cautious about rebalancing. It is generally unwise to make significant changes to an investment strategy based on short-term market movements. And the current environment of relatively low returns across the board means it is crucial to minimize transaction costs and taxes, for example, taxes on capital-gains distributions from mutual funds at year-end.

One way to limit costs like these is to start rebalancing with a 401 (k) or other tax-deferred account, and use new money, like individual retirement account contributions, stock dividends and bond interest payments, to adjust existing holdings. Rebalancing now could also mean selling off stocks at a loss to offset gains, reducing year-end taxes in the process.

Interviews with 21 strategists nationwide indicated that there are a number of adjustments that investors should consider. Here is their advice on where the smart money may be headed.

Stocks

Many strategists now favor high-quality stocks over the lower-quality names that have led the market in recent years. Low-quality stocks are often smaller companies with substantial debt—but today, many have lofty stock valuations because investors were willing to make aggressive bets on them during the earlier stages of the

information in Figure 3.2. However, you can find some additional information on dividends, dividend yields, and price-earnings ratios.

You can see that this list is for a group of stocks in the "Basic Resources Sector." Locate the entry for Weyerhaeuser Company (WY). Weyerhaeuser Company is classified in the "Basic Resources Sector" because Weyerhaeuser grows and harvests timber and then manufactures and distributes a wide range of lumber and paper products.

The first two columns in Figure 3.3 are the dividend amount and dividend yield, $2.40 and 3.69 percent, respectively, for Weyerhaeuser. Like most dividend-paying companies, Weyerhaeuser pays dividends on a quarterly basis. The dividend number reported here, $2.40, is actually four times the most recent quarterly dividend. The dividend yield is this annualized dividend divided by the closing price.

bull market. For instance, many advisers recommend trimming holdings in energy and utilities, which are two lower-quality sectors that have been the S&P 500's top performers this year.

Instead, some advisers say that higher-quality sectors like health care and consumer staples are set to take the lead. The reason: Rising interest rates, inflation fears, and other market jitters will make investors look for surer bets, says Sam Stovall, chief investment strategist at Standard & Poor's. High-quality stocks, which normally command higher valuations, are now trading at a 10% discount to lower-quality stocks, says Mr. Stovall.

Strategists are especially bullish on health care and technology—areas that, like the broader market, have barely budged this year. Health-care companies stand to benefit from an aging population. And while the current wave of high energy prices might cause consumers to cut back on, say, new clothes or vacations, they will always spend money on medicine. "It's not a discretionary item," says Bryan Olson, vice president at Schwab's Center for Investment Research.

Thanks to strong performance in overseas markets, many investors may find their international-stock allocation has grown over the past year. Rather than cutting back, many strategists are raising their recommended foreign-stock allocations. They see a number of headwinds facing the U.S. stock market, including slowing profit growth and high energy prices, and good prospects for continued growth in emerging markets and Japan.

Bonds and Cash

One message rings loud and clear right now: Anything but bonds.

Many advisers say the expectation of rising interest rates and corresponding lower bond prices suggest investors aren't being rewarded to take on longer-term bond risk heading into next year.

That is why advisers are suggesting shorter-term U.S. bonds for medium-risk investors next year, with more-conservative investors being led into shorter-term U.S. municipal bonds. Some planners are calling for a mix that reduces bond holdings to as little as 15% of holdings, down from the more common 25% to 30% for a medium-risk and size portfolio. This might include more Treasury Inflation-Protected Securities, which offer investors upside with rising inflation.

"Fixed income as a whole is just not that attractive," and hasn't been for a while, says Nic Richard, head of asset allocation at Citigroup Private Bank.

In the five years ended 2004, cash or short-term fixed income investments held by U.S. households rose more than 41% to a record $5.7 trillion, while bond holdings declined, according to a Citigroup Private Bank investment-outlook bulletin released this month. While Citigroup cautions against "the risk of risk aversion," in the report, the trend mirrors many public companies hoarding cash these days amid restrained spending.

Cash was once seen as a place-holder: an idle bet that didn't generate returns but offered security. It is now being bumped up to 10% of holdings or more, especially as yields on some money-market accounts close in on the 4.57% yield on a 10-year Treasury note.

Alternative Investments

Alternative investments are taking up an ever-growing chunk of the pie even in medium-risk portfolios. Both Morgan Stanley and Citibank recommend 10% to 12% allocations to hedge funds, with another 4% or 5% devoted to private-equity, managed-futures funds and other, more opaque, items. The figure could ramp up to as much as 40% of a portfolio for more risk-friendly clients.

Upping holdings in alternative investments remains a more likely option for wealthier investors since categories like hedge funds often require $1 million of investable assets from the get-go.

Source: Diya Gullapalli and Eleanor Laise, *The Wall Street Journal*, November 12, 2005.

The last column contains the price-earnings ratio, or "P/E ratio." This ratio, as the name suggests, is equal to the price per share divided by earnings per share. Earnings per share is calculated as the sum of earnings per share over the last four quarters. We will discuss dividends, dividend yields, and price-earnings ratios in detail in a later chapter.

CHECK THIS

3.3a What are the two types of equity securities?

3.3b Why is preferred stock sometimes classified as a fixed-income security?

3.4 Derivatives

primary asset
Security originally sold by a business or government to raise money.

derivative asset
A financial asset that is derived from an existing traded asset rather than issued by a business or government to raise capital. More generally, any financial asset that is not a primary asset.

There is a clear distinction between real assets, which are essentially tangible items, and financial assets, which are pieces of paper describing legal claims. Financial assets can be further subdivided into primary and derivative assets. A **primary asset** (sometimes called a *primitive asset*) is a security that was originally sold by a business or government to raise money, and a primary asset represents a claim on the assets of the issuer. Thus, stocks and bonds are primary financial assets.

In contrast, as the name suggests, a **derivative asset** is a financial asset that is derived from an existing primary asset rather than issued by a business or government to raise capital. As we will see, derivative assets usually represent claims either on other financial assets, such as shares of stock or even other derivative assets, or on the future price of a real asset such as gold. Beyond this, it is difficult to give a general definition of the term "derivative asset" because there are so many different types, and new ones are created almost every day. On the most basic level, however, any financial asset that is not a primary asset is a derivative asset.

To give a simple example of a derivative asset, imagine that you and a friend buy 1,000 shares of a dividend-paying stock, perhaps the Weyerhaeuser stock we discussed. You each put up half the money, and you agree to sell your stock in one year. Furthermore, the two of you agree that you will get all the dividends paid while your friend gets all the gains or absorbs all the losses on the 1,000 shares.

This simple arrangement takes a primary asset, shares of Weyerhaeuser stock, and creates two derivative assets, the dividend-only shares that you hold and the no-dividend shares held by your friend. Derivative assets such as these actually exist, and there are many variations on this basic theme.

Two types of derivative assets, futures and options, are particularly important. Many other types exist, but they can usually be built up from these two basic types, possibly by combining them with other primary assets. Futures are the simpler of the two, so we discuss them first.

FUTURES CONTRACTS

futures contract
An agreement made today regarding the terms of a trade that will take place later.

In many ways, a futures contract is the simplest of all financial assets. A **futures contract** is just an agreement made today regarding the terms of a trade that will take place later. For example, suppose you know that you will want to buy 100 ounces of gold in six months. One thing you could do is to strike a deal today with a seller in which you promise to pay, say, $400 per ounce in six months for the 100 ounces of gold. In other words, you and the seller agree that six months from now, you will exchange $40,000 for 100 ounces of gold. The agreement that you have created is a futures contract.

WWW

You can download lots of basic futures information from the Knowledge Center at www.cmegroup.com

With your futures contract, you have locked in the price of gold six months from now. Suppose that gold is actually selling for $450 per ounce in six months. If this occurs, then you benefit from having entered into the futures contract because you have to pay only $400 per ounce. However, if gold is selling for $350, you lose because you are forced to pay $400 per ounce. Thus, a futures contract is essentially a bet on the future price of whatever is being bought or sold. Notice that with your futures contract, no money changes hands today.

After entering into the futures contract, what happens if you change your mind in, say, four months, and you want out of the contract? The answer is that you can sell your contract to someone else. You would generally have a gain or a loss when you sell. The contract still has two months to run. If market participants generally believe that gold will be worth more than $400 when the contract matures in two months, then your contract is valuable, and you would have a gain if you sold it. If, on the other hand, market participants think gold will not be worth $400, then you would have a loss on the contract if you sold it because you would have to pay someone else to take it off your hands.

Futures contracts are traded all over the world on many types of assets, and futures contracts can be traced back to ancient civilizations. As we discuss in detail in a later chapter, there are two broad categories of futures contracts: *financial futures* and *commodity futures*. The difference is that, with financial futures, the underlying asset is intangible, usually stocks, bonds, currencies, or money market instruments. With commodity futures, the underlying asset is a real asset, typically either an agricultural product (such as cattle or wheat) or a natural resource product (such as gold or oil).

FUTURES PRICE QUOTES

An important feature of traded futures contracts is that they are *standardized*, meaning that one contract calls for the purchase of a specific quantity of the underlying asset. Further, the contract specifies in detail what the underlying asset is and where it is to be delivered. For example, with a wheat contract, one contract specifies that 5,000 bushels of a particular type of wheat will be delivered at one of a few approved locations on a particular date in exchange for the agreed-upon futures price.

In Figure 3.4, futures price quotations for U.S. Treasury bonds (or "T-bonds" for short) are seen as they appear online at www.wsj.com. A nearby *Work the Web* contains links for futures price quotes. Looking at Figure 3.4, we see these are quotes for delivery of T-bonds with a total par, or face, value of $100,000. The letters CBT indicate to us where this contract is traded; in this case, it is the Chicago Board of Trade.

The first column in Figure 3.4 tells us the delivery date for the bond specified by the contract. For example, the "Sep 07" indicates that the first contract listed is for T-bond delivery in September 2007. The second is for delivery in December 2007. Following the delivery month, we have a series of prices. In order, we have the open price, the high price, the low price, and the settle price. The open price is the price at the start of the trading day, the high and low are highest and lowest prices for the day, and the settle is a price reflecting the trades at the end of the day. The "Chg" is the change in the settle price from the previous trading day.

The columns labeled "LIFETIME High" and "LIFETIME Low" refer to the highest and lowest prices over the life of this contract. Finally, the "Open Int" tells us how many contracts are currently outstanding.

To get a better idea of how futures contracts work, suppose you buy one September contract at the settle price. What you have done is agree to buy T-bonds with a total par value of $100,000 in September at a price of 110-02 per $100 of par value, where the "02" represents $\frac{2}{32}$. Thus, 110-02 can also be written as 110 $\frac{2}{32}$, which represents a price of

FIGURE 3.4 Futures Trading

Interest Rate Futures | Index | Agricultural | Currency | Metals & Petroleum

Wednesday, August 01, 2007 — Find Historical Data | WHAT'S THIS?

KEY TO EXCHANGES: CBT: Chicago Board of Trade; CME: Chicago Mercantile Exchange; CMX: Comex; DME: Dubai Mercantile Exchange;ENXT: Euronext.liffe; EUREX: EUREX; ICE: IntercontinentalExchange; KC: Kansas City Board of Trade; ME: Montreal Exchange; MPLS: Minneapolis Grain Exchange; NYBOT: New York Board of Trade; NYM: New York Mercantile Exchange, or Nymex; SGX-DT: Singapore Exchange Derivatives Trading Ltd

Treasury Bonds (CBT)-$100,000; pts 32nds of 100%

						LIFETIME			
	Open	High	Low	Settle	Chg	High	(▲▼)	Low	Open Int
Sep 07	110-11	110-25	109-26	**110-02**	...	114-06		104-16	998,171
Dec 07	110-12	110-21	109-24	**109-31**	...	114-17		104-18	7,624
Mar 08	110-15	110-15	110-15	**109-30**	...	113-15		105-03	495
Jun 08	110-08	110-08	110-08	**109-30**	...	112-26		105-30	6
Sep 08	110-00	110-00	110-00	**109-30**	...	110-00		108-31	10

Est vol 601,483; vol Tue 614,482; open int, 1,006,306, +1,320.

Sources: Reuters; WSJ Market Data Group

Source: www.wsj.com, August 1, 2007. Reprinted by permission of *The Wall Street Journal*.

WORK THE WEB

Futures price quotes have also become more available with the rise of the Internet. Sites where you can find futures price quotes currently include www.cbot.com, www.cme.com, and www.nymex.com.

At the Chicago Board of Trade (CBOT), futures contracts for grains (e.g., corn, wheat, soybeans), interest rates (U.S. Treasury notes and bonds, German bonds), and Dow Jones Index Futures are listed. Each futures contract has some unique aspects. For example, here is a sample soybean futures screen from the CBOT's Web site.

Soybeans Comp. - cbot

Data retrieved at Aug 02 17:36:27 GMT • All quotes are in Greenwich Mean Time • Data provided by eSignal

Contract	Month	Last	Chg	Open	High	Low	Volume	OpenInt	Exchange	Date	Time
SOYBEANS	Aug '07	**835'4**	9'6	827'0	835'4	826'6	4441	7405	CBT	08/02/07	17:17:57
SOYBEANS	Sep '07	**842'0**	9'4	832'0	844'4	832'0	5882	29758	CBT	08/02/07	17:25:45
SOYBEANS	Nov '07	**858'2**	9'4	851'2	860'6	849'4	30824	307529	CBT	08/02/07	17:26:25

Locate the line that starts with Nov '07. This is a very active futures contract that calls for November delivery of 5,000 bushels of soybeans. Note that these quotes are obtained at the end of the day's trading. By convention, soybean prices are still quoted in cents and eighths of a cent even though the minimum price change is one-fourth cent, or two-eighths of a cent. Under the "Last" column, you can see an entry of 858'2, which is 858 and 2/8 cents, or \$8.58¼. The daily low was 849'4, which is 849 and 4/8 cents, or \$8.49½.

At the Chicago Mercantile Exchange (CME), trading exists in a wide variety of markets including agricultural futures (live cattle, feeder cattle, lean hogs, frozen pork bellies), foreign exchange rate futures, S&P 500 futures, and interest rate futures (LIBOR, Eurodollar).

At the New York Mercantile Exchange (NYMEX), futures contracts for metals (copper, silver, gold, platinum) and energy (crude oil, heating oil, unleaded gasoline) are traded. A complete list of all the contracts traded at each commodity exchange can be found at the respective exchange's Web site.

Understanding futures markets, their use, and their quoting conventions takes a great deal of study. Your school might even offer a course where you can study futures markets in depth.

As this is written, the CBOT and the CME have agreed to merge their enterprises. This merger will create an extensive, diverse, and competitive global derivatives exchange. The combined company will be named CME Group Inc., a CME/Chicago Board of Trade Company. Corporate headquarters of the combined organization will remain in Chicago. Also, CME Group is exploring the purchase of NYMEX.

\$110,062.50 per \$100,000 face value. No money changes hands today. However, if you take no further action, when September rolls around your T-bonds will be delivered, and you must pay for them at that time.

Actually, most futures contracts don't result in delivery. Most buyers and sellers close out their contracts before the delivery date. To close out a contract, you take the opposite side. For example, suppose that with your one T-bond contract, you later decide you no longer wish to be in it. To get out, you simply sell one contract, thereby canceling your position.

GAINS AND LOSSES ON FUTURES CONTRACTS

Futures contracts have the potential for enormous gains and losses. To see why, let's consider again buying T-bond contracts based on the settle prices in Figure 3.4. To make matters somewhat more interesting, suppose you buy 15 September contracts at the settle price of 110-02 per \$100 of par value.

One month later, perhaps because of falling inflation, the futures price of T-bonds for September delivery rises five dollars to 115-02. This may not seem like a huge increase, but it generates a substantial profit for you. You have locked in a price of 110-02 per \$100 par value. The price has risen to 115-02, so you make a profit of \$5 per \$100 of par value, or \$5,000 per \$100,000 face value. With 15 contracts, each of which calls for delivery of

$100,000 in face value of T-bonds, you make a tidy profit of 15 × $5,000 = $75,000. Of course, if the price had decreased by five dollars, you would have lost $75,000 on your 15-contract position.

EXAMPLE 3.3

Future Shock

It is July. Suppose you purchase five September T-bond contracts at a settle price of 115-22. How much will you pay today? Suppose in one month you close your position and the September futures price at that time is 110-21. Did you make or lose money? How much?

When you purchase the five contracts, you pay nothing today because the transaction is for September. However, you have agreed to pay 115-22 per $100 par value. If, when you close your position in a month, the futures price is 110-21, you have a loss of 115-22 − 110-21 = $5\frac{1}{32}$ per $100 par value, or $5\frac{1}{32}$ × 1,000 = $5,031.25 per contract. Your total loss is thus $5,031.25 × 5 contracts, or $25,156.25 in all (ouch!).

CHECK THIS

3.4a What is a futures contract?

3.4b What are the general types of futures contracts?

3.4c Explain how you make or lose money on a futures contract.

3.5 Option Contracts

option contract
An agreement that gives the owner the right, but not the obligation, to buy or sell a specific asset at a specified price for a set period of time.

An **option contract** is an agreement that gives the owner the right, but not the obligation, to buy or sell (depending on the type of option) a specific asset at a specific price for a specific period of time. The most familiar options are stock options. These are options to buy or sell shares of stock, and they are the focus of our discussion here. Options are a very flexible investment tool, and a great deal is known about them. We present some of the most important concepts here; our detailed coverage begins in a later chapter.

OPTION TERMINOLOGY

call option
An option that gives the owner the right, but not the obligation, to buy an asset.

put option
An option that gives the owner the right, but not the obligation, to sell an asset.

Options come in two flavors, calls and puts. The owner of a **call option** has the right, but not the obligation, to *buy* an underlying asset at a fixed price for a specified time. The owner of a **put option** has the right, but not the obligation, to *sell* an underlying asset at a fixed price for a specified time.

Options occur frequently in everyday life. Suppose, for example, that you are interested in buying a used car. You and the seller agree that the price will be $3,000. You give the seller $100 to hold the car for one week, meaning that you have one week to come up with the $3,000 purchase price, or else you lose your $100.

This agreement is a call option. You paid the seller $100 for the right, but not the obligation, to buy the car for $3,000. If you change your mind because, for example, you find a better deal elsewhere, you can just walk away. You'll lose your $100, but that is the price you paid for the right, but not the obligation, to buy. The price you pay to purchase an option, the $100 in this example, is called the **option premium**.

option premium
The price you pay to buy an option.

strike price
The price specified in an option contract at which the underlying asset can be bought (for a call option) or sold (for a put option). Also called the striking price or exercise price.

A few other definitions will be useful. First, the specified price at which the underlying asset can be bought or sold with an option contract is called the **strike price**, the *striking price*, or the *exercise price*. Using an option to buy or sell an asset is called *exercising* the option.

The *last trading day* for all listed stock options in the United States is the third Friday of the option's expiration month (except when Friday falls on a holiday, in which case the last trading day is the third Thursday). The *expiration day* for stock options is the Saturday immediately following the last trading day. The expiration day is the last day (in the case of *American-style* options) or the only day (in the case of *European-style* options) on which an option may be *exercised.*

OPTIONS VERSUS FUTURES

Our discussion thus far illustrates the two crucial differences between an option contract and a futures contract. The first is that the purchaser of a futures contract is *obligated* to buy the underlying asset at the specified price (and the seller of a futures contract is obligated to sell). The owner of a call option has the right, but not the obligation, to buy.

The second important difference is that when you buy a futures contract you pay no money at the time of purchase (and you receive none if you sell). However, if you buy an option contract, you pay the premium at the time of the purchase; if you sell an option contract, you receive the premium at the time of the sale.

OPTION PRICE QUOTES

WWW

To learn more about options visit the Learning Center at www.cboe.com

Like futures contracts, most option contracts are standardized. One call option contract, for example, gives the owner the right to buy 100 shares (one round lot) of stock. Similarly, one put option contract gives the owner the right to sell 100 shares.

Figure 3.5 presents intraday 20-minute delay quotes for call and put options on Hewlett-Packard common stock. The data is from finance.yahoo.com. To obtain these option quotes, enter a ticker symbol (here: HPQ), then find and click the option link. At the time these quotes were obtained, Hewlett-Packard stock was trading at $47.80.

The first column in Figure 3.5 lists strike prices for options with August expiration. More precisely, these options expire at the close of trading on August 17, 2007. Option data for other expiration months can be obtained by clicking on other views.

The second column is the unique symbol for each option. For example, the symbol for the Hewlett-Packard August 47.50 call option is "HPQHW.X." The "HPQ" stands for Hewlett-Packard; the "H" represents August (for calls, expiration months correspond to the letters A through L, so, for calls, the eighth month gets the eighth letter of the alphabet, H); the "W" refers to the strike (W can be 17.50, 47.50, 77.50, etc.); and the "X" is the symbol Yahoo! uses for U.S. options. Note that the symbol for the Hewlett-Packard 47.50 put option is "HPQTW.X." For puts, expiration months correspond to the letters M through X. So, for puts, the eighth month gets the twentieth letter of the alphabet, T.

Columns three and four list last sale prices and the change from the previous close. Current bid and ask prices appear in the next two columns. The bid price is the price *you* will receive if you want to sell an option at the prevailing market price; the ask price is the price *you* will pay if you want to buy an option at the prevailing market price. Volume and open interest numbers appear in the last two columns. Volume is the number of contracts traded that day. Open interest is the number of contracts outstanding.

Referring to the Hewlett-Packard August 47.50 call options, we see that 2,081 call option contracts have been traded so far in this trading day, and the last transaction price for this option was $1.60 per share. Because each listed option contract actually involves 100 shares, the price per contract was $1.60 × 100 = $160.

The bid and ask prices reflect current market conditions, not the market conditions that prevailed at the time of the last transaction price. Based on the bid and ask prices, what price would you pay now for one of these call options? Remember, the ask price is the price *you* pay, so you would pay $1.65 per share, or $165 for the contract. If you were selling, you would sell at the bid price of $1.55 per share, or $155 for the contract.

Suppose you wanted the right to buy 500 shares of Hewlett-Packard for $45 sometime between now and August 17. What would you buy? Based on the information in Figure 3.5, how much would you have to pay?

You want the right to buy, so you want to purchase call options. Because each contract is for 100 shares, and you want the right to buy 500 shares, you need five contracts. The contract you want would be described as the Hewlett-Packard August 45 call option. From Figure 3.5, the option premium to buy the contract with a $45 strike and an August expiration is $3.40, so one contract would cost $3.40 × 100 = $340. The cost for five contracts would therefore be 5 × $340 = $1,700.

FIGURE 3.5 Options Trading

View By Expiration: **Aug 07** | Sep 07 | Nov 07 | Jan 08 | Feb 08 | Jan 09 | Jan 10

CALL OPTIONS Expire at close Fri, Aug 17, 2007

Strike	Symbol	Last	Chg	Bid	Ask	Vol	Open Int
27.50	HPQHY.X	**18.40**	**0.00**	20.30	20.50	52	390
30.00	HPQHF.X	**15.90**	**0.00**	17.80	18.00	40	595
32.50	HPQHZ.X	**13.40**	**0.00**	15.30	15.50	54	854
35.00	HPQHG.X	**11.30**	**0.00**	12.80	13.00	21	808
37.50	HPQHU.X	**10.70**	↑ 1.90	10.30	10.50	2	833
40.00	HPQHH.X	**8.40**	↑ 2.10	7.90	8.10	11	3,975
42.50	HPQHV.X	**5.60**	↑ 1.40	5.50	5.60	30	14,282
45.00	HPQHI.X	**3.28**	↑ 0.78	3.30	3.40	237	15,887
47.50	HPQHW.X	**1.60**	↑ 0.55	1.55	1.65	2,081	13,988
50.00	HPQHJ.X	**0.55**	↑ 0.20	0.50	0.60	1,458	16,907
52.50	HPQHX.X	**0.15**	↑ 0.07	0.10	0.20	91	3,844

PUT OPTIONS Expire at close Fri, Aug 17, 2007

Strike	Symbol	Last	Chg	Bid	Ask	Vol	Open Int
27.50	HPQTY.X	**0.10**	**0.00**	N/A	0.05	0	194
30.00	HPQTF.X	**0.05**	**0.00**	N/A	0.05	0	335
32.50	HPQTZ.X	**0.05**	**0.00**	N/A	0.05	5	822
35.00	HPQTG.X	**0.05**	**0.00**	N/A	0.05	1	1,675
37.50	HPQTU.X	**0.03**	**0.00**	N/A	0.05	13	9,213
40.00	HPQTH.X	**0.10**	↓ 0.05	N/A	0.05	35	10,744
42.50	HPQTV.X	**0.08**	↓ 0.27	0.10	0.15	212	12,412
45.00	HPQTI.X	**0.35**	↓ 0.45	0.35	0.45	56	9,663
47.50	HPQTW.X	**1.05**	↓ 0.85	1.10	1.20	239	8,783
50.00	HPQTJ.X	**2.60**	↓ 1.30	2.55	2.65	479	959
52.50	HPQTX.X	**4.50**	↓ 1.90	4.60	4.80	9	413

Highlighted options are in-the-money.

Source: finance.yahoo.com, August 2, 2007.

EXAMPLE 3.4 Put Options

Suppose you want the right to sell 200 shares of Hewlett-Packard between now and August 17 at a price of $50. In light of the information in Figure 3.5, what contract should you buy? How much will it cost you?

You want the right to sell stock at a fixed price, so you want to buy put options. Specifically, you want to buy two August 50 put contracts. In Figure 3.5, the ask premium for this contract is given as $2.65. Recalling that this is the premium per share, one contract will cost you $265, so two contracts would cost $530.

GAINS AND LOSSES ON OPTION CONTRACTS

As with futures contracts, option contracts have the potential for large gains and losses. To examine this, let's consider our previous example in which you paid $1,700 for five Hewlett-Packard August 45 call contracts. Suppose you hold on to your contracts until August rolls around, and they are just about to expire. What are your gains (or losses) if Hewlett-Packard is selling for $60 per share? $40 per share?

If Hewlett-Packard is selling for $60 per share, you will profit handsomely. You have the right to buy 500 shares at a price of $45 per share. Because the stock is worth $60, your options are worth $15 per share, or $7,500 in all. So you invested $1,700 and ended up with more than 4 times that. Not bad.

If the stock ends up at $40 per share, however, the result is not so pretty. You have the right to buy the stock for $45 when it is selling for $40, so your call options expire worthless. You lose the entire $1,700 you originally invested. In fact, if the stock price is anything less than $45, you lose $1,700.

EXAMPLE 3.5

More on Puts

In Example 3.4, you bought two Hewlett-Packard August 50 put contracts for $530. Suppose that August arrives, and Hewlett-Packard is selling for $35 per share. How did you do? What's the break-even stock price, that is, the price at which you just make enough to cover your $530 cost?

Your put contracts give you the right to sell 200 shares of Hewlett-Packard at a price of $50 per share. If the stock is worth only $35 per share, your put options are worth $15 per share, or $3,000 in all. To determine the break-even stock price, notice that you paid $2.65 per share for the option, so this is what you must make per share to break even. The break-even stock price is thus $50 − $2.65 = $47.35.

INVESTING IN STOCKS VERSUS OPTIONS

To get a better idea of the potential gains and losses from investing in stocks compared to investing in options, let's suppose you have $10,000 to invest. You're looking at Macron Technology, which is currently selling for $50 per share. You also notice that a call option with a $50 strike price and three months to maturity is available. The premium is $4. Macron pays no dividends.

You're considering investing all $10,000 either in the stock or in the call options. What is your return from these two investments, if, in three months, Macron is selling for $55 per share? What about $45 per share?

First, if you buy the stock, your $10,000 will purchase two round lots, meaning 200 shares. A call contract costs $400 (why?), so you can buy 25 of them. Notice that your 25 contracts give you the right to buy 2,500 shares at $50 per share.

If, in three months, Macron is selling for $55, your stock will be worth 200 shares × $55 = $11,000. Your dollar gain will be $11,000 less the $10,000 you invested, or $1,000. Because you invested $10,000, your return for the three-month period is $1,000/$10,000 = 10%. If Macron is selling for $45 per share, then you lose $1,000, and your return is −10 percent.

If Macron is selling for $55, your call options are worth $55 − $50 = $5 each, but now you control 2,500 shares, so your options are worth 2,500 shares × $5 = $12,500 total. You invested $10,000, so your dollar return is $12,500 − $10,000 = $2,500, and your percentage return is $2,500/$10,000 = 25%, compared to 10 percent on the stock investment. However, if Macron is selling for $45 when your options mature, then you lose everything, and your return is −100 percent.

EXAMPLE 3.6

Put Returns

In our example for Macron Technology, suppose a put option is also available with a premium of $2.50. Calculate your percentage return for the three-month holding period if the stock price declines to $47 per share. What is your annualized return?

(continued)

One put contract costs $250, so you can buy 40 of them. Notice that your 40 contracts give you the right to sell 4,000 shares at $50 per share.

If, in three months, Macron is selling for $47, your put options are worth $50 − $47 = $3 each. You control 4,000 shares, so your options are worth 4,000 shares × $3 = $12,000 total. You invested $10,000, so your dollar return is $12,000 − $10,000 = $2,000, and your percentage return is $2,000/$10,000 = 20%.

To annualize your return, we need to compute the effective annual return, recognizing that there are 4 three-month periods in a year:

$$1 + \text{EAR} = 1.20^4$$
$$1 + \text{EAR} = 2.0736$$
$$\text{EAR} = 1.0736 = 107.36\%$$

Your annualized return is thus about 107 percent.

CHECK THIS

3.5a What is a call option? A put option?

3.5b If you buy a call option, what do you hope will happen to the underlying stock? What if you buy a put option?

3.5c What are the two key differences between a futures contract and an option contract?

3.6 Summary and Conclusions

In this chapter we examine the basic types of financial assets. We discuss three broad classes: interest-bearing assets, equity securities, and derivative assets—futures and options. For each of the broad classes, we ask three questions. First, what is its basic nature and what are its distinguishing characteristics? Second, what are the potential gains and losses from owning it? Third, how are its prices quoted online and in the financial press? We cover many aspects of these investments. We provide a brief description of these investments broken down by the chapter's important concepts.

1. Various types of interest-bearing assets.

A. Each of these major groups can be further subdivided. Interest-bearing assets include money market instruments and fixed-income securities.

B. Money market instruments generally have the following two properties: (1) they are essentially IOUs sold by large corporations or governments to borrow money; and (2) they mature in less than one year from the time they are sold, meaning that the loan must be repaid within one year.

C. Fixed-income securities are securities that promise to make fixed payments according to some preset schedule. Another key characteristic of a fixed-income security is that it begins life as a loan of some sort. That is, fixed-income securities are debt obligations. Corporations and governments issue fixed-income securities. Unlike money market instruments, fixed-income securities have lives that exceed 12 months at the time they are issued.

2. Equity securities.

A. The two major equity types are common stock and preferred stock. Common stock represents ownership in a corporation. If you own 1,000 shares of General Electric, then you own a very small percentage of GE's outstanding shares. Nonetheless, you are a part-owner of GE. As a part-owner, you are entitled to your pro rata share of anything paid out by GE, and you have the right to vote on important matters regarding the company.

(1) 4. **Fixed-Income Securities** Your friend told you she just received her semiannual coupon payment on a U.S. Treasury note with a $100,000 face value that pays a 6 percent annual coupon. How much money did she receive from this coupon payment?

a. $3,000
b. $6,000
c. $30,000
d. $60,000

(2) 5. **Common Stock** A corporation with common stock issued to the public pays dividends

a. At the discretion of management, who are elected by the shareholders.
b. At the discretion of shareholders, since they own the corporation.
c. At the discretion of the company's board of directors, who are elected by shareholders.
d. At the discretion of the company's board of directors, who are appointed by management.

(3) 6. **Futures Contracts** You buy (go long) five copper futures contracts at 100 cents per pound, where the contract size is 25,000 pounds. At contract maturity, copper is selling for 102 cents per pound. What is your profit (+) or loss (−) on the transaction?

a. −$2,500
b. +$2,500
c. −$25,000
d. +$25,000

(3) 7. **Futures Contracts** You sell (go short) 10 gold futures contracts at $400 per ounce, where the contract size is 100 ounces. At contract maturity, gold is selling for $410 per ounce. What is your profit (+) or loss (−) on the transaction?

a. −$1,000
b. +$1,000
c. −$10,000
d. +$10,000

(4) 8. **Option Contracts** You buy 100 CJC call option contracts with a strike price of 95 at a quoted price of $1. At option expiration, CJC sells for $97. What is your net profit on the transaction?

a. $2,000
b. $5,000
c. $10,000
d. $20,000

(4) 9. **Option Contracts** You buy 100 CJC put option contracts with a strike price of 92 at a quoted price of $8. At option expiration, CJC sells for $83.80. What is your net profit on the transaction?

a. $200
b. $1,000
c. $2,000
d. $10,000

CFA® PROBLEMS

(4) 10. **Short Sales** Which of the following statements about short selling is true?

a. A short position may be hedged by writing call options.
b. A short position may be hedged by purchasing put options.
c. Short sellers may be subject to margin calls if the stock price increases.
d. Stocks that pay large dividends should be sold short before the ex-dividend date and bought afterward to take advantage of the large price declines in a short time period.

www.mhhe.com/jm5e

Concept Questions

(1) 1. **Money Market Instruments** What are the distinguishing features of a money market instrument?

(2) 2. **Preferred Stock** Why is preferred stock "preferred"?

(2) 3. ***WSJ* Stock Quotes** What is the PE ratio reported for stocks in *The Wall Street Journal*? In particular, how is it computed?

(1) 4. **Yields** The current yield on a bond is the coupon rate divided by the price. Thus, it is very similar to what number reported for common and preferred stocks?

(1) (2) (3) (4) 5. **Volume Quotations** Explain how volume is quoted for stocks, corporate bonds, futures, and options.

3 6. **Futures Contracts** Changes in what price lead to gains and/or losses in futures contracts?

3 7. **Futures Contracts** What is the open interest on a futures contract? What do you think will usually happen to open interest as maturity approaches?

3 8. **Futures versus Options** What is the difference between a futures contract and an option contract? Do the buyer of a futures contract and the buyer of an option contract have the same rights? What about the seller?

1 2 3 4 9. **Asset Types** What is the distinction between a real asset and a financial asset? What are the two basic types of financial assets, and what does each represent?

4 10. **Puts versus Calls** Suppose a share of stock is selling for $100. A put and a call are offered, both with $100 strike prices and nine months to maturity. Intuitively, which do you think is more valuable?

Questions and Problems

Core Questions

2 1. **Stock Quotations** You found the following stock quote for DRK Enterprises, Inc., at your favorite Web site. You also find that the stock paid an annual dividend of $0.86, which resulted in a dividend yield of 1.30 percent. What was the closing price for this stock yesterday? How many round lots of stock were traded yesterday?

		DAILY				YTD	52 WEEK		
Company	**Symbol**	**Vol**	**Close**	**Chg**	**%Chg**	**%Chg**	**High**	**Low**	**%Chg**
DRK Enterprises	DRK	18,649,130	??	0.26	−0.39%	8.73%	78.19	51.74	27.4%

2 2. **Stock Quotations** In the previous problem, assume the company has 95 million shares of stock outstanding and a PE ratio of 16. What was net income for the most recent four quarters?

2 3. **Dividend Yields** You find a stock selling for $96.40 that has a dividend yield of 2.8 percent. What was the last quarterly dividend paid?

2 4. **Earnings per Share** In the previous problem, if the company has a PE ratio of 21.5, what is the earnings per share (EPS) for the company?

1 5. **Bonds** You purchase 3,000 bonds with a par value of $1,000 for $940 each. The bonds have a coupon rate of 8.4 percent paid semiannually, and mature in 10 years. How much will you receive on the next coupon date? How much will you receive when the bonds mature?

3 6. **Futures Profits** The contract size for platinum futures is 50 troy ounces. Suppose you need 700 troy ounces of platinum and the current futures price is $1,530 per ounce. How many contracts do you need to purchase? How much will you pay for your platinum? What is your dollar profit if platinum sells for $1,595 a troy ounce when the futures contract expires? What if the price is $1,493 at expiration?

4 7. **Option Profits** You purchase 10 call option contracts with a strike price of $75 and a premium of $4.05. If the stock price at expiration is $83.61, what is your dollar profit? What if the stock price is $69.56?

2 8. **Stock Quotations** You found the following stock quote for Gigantus Corporation in today's newspaper. What was the stock selling for on January 1?

		DAILY				YTD	52 WEEK		
Company	**Symbol**	**Vol**	**Close**	**Chg**	**%Chg**	**%Chg**	**High**	**Low**	**%Chg**
Gigantus	GIG	12,805,325	53.87	0.72	1.34%	−2.70%	62.81	45.93	17.3%

Use the following bond quote for the next two questions:

Company	Symbol	Coupon	Maturity	Rating Moody's/ S&P/Fitch	High	Low	Last	Change	Yield%
Int'l Systems	ISU.GO	6.850%	May, 2032	Baa2/BBB/BB-	105.321	102.817	103.453	1.650	6.846%

(1) 9. **Bond Quotations** What is the yield to maturity of the bond? What is the current yield of the bond?

(1) 10. **Bond Quotations** If you currently own 25 of the bonds, how much will you receive on the next coupon date?

Intermediate Questions

Use the following corn futures quotes for the next three problems:

Corn 5,000 bushels	Open	High	Low	Settle	Chg	Open Int
Mar	455'1	457'0	451'6	452'0	−2'6	597,913
May	467'0	468'0	463'0	463'2	−2'6	137,547
July	477'0	477'0	472'4	473'0	−2'0	153,164
Sep	475'0	475'0	471'6	472'2	−2'0	29,258

(3) 11. **Futures Quotations** How many of the March contracts are currently open? How many of these contracts should you sell if you wish to deliver 150,000 bushels of corn in March? If you actually make delivery, how much will you receive? Assume you locked in the settle price.

(3) 12. **Futures Quotations** Suppose you sell 25 of the May corn futures at the high price of the day. You close your position later when the price is 460'4. Ignoring commission, what is your dollar profit on this transaction?

(3) 13. **Using Futures Quotations** Suppose you buy 15 of the September corn futures contracts at the last price of the day. One month from now, the futures price of this contract is 469'2, and you close out your position. Calculate your dollar profit on this investment.

Use the following quotes for JC Penney stock options for the next three problems:

View By Expiration: Jan 08 | Feb 08 | May 08 | **Aug 08** | Jan 09 | Jan 10

CALL OPTIONS — Expire at close Fri, Aug 15, 2008

Strike	Symbol	Last	Chg	Bid	Ask	Vol	Open Int
37.50	JCPHE.X	9.60	0.00	9.80	10.10	15	25
42.50	JCPHR.X	7.80	0.00	7.10	7.40	20	20
45.00	JCPHI.X	5.60	↓0.10	6.00	6.20	6	5
47.50	JCPHW.X	5.00	↓0.60	5.00	5.20	16	10
50.00	JCPHJ.X	3.80	↓0.90	4.10	4.30	17	13
52.50	JCPHX.X	3.30	0.00	3.30	3.50	5	5

PUT OPTIONS — Expire at close Fri, Aug 15, 2008

Strike	Symbol	Last	Chg	Bid	Ask	Vol	Open Int
37.50	JCPTE.X	3.60	0.00	3.30	3.50	22	27
40.00	JCPTH.X	4.60	0.00	4.30	4.50	13	13
42.50	JCPTR.X	5.50	0.00	5.50	5.70	17	17
45.00	JCPTI.X	6.70	0.00	6.80	7.00	10	10
47.50	JCPTW.X	8.20	0.00	8.20	8.40	10	10

(4) 14. **Options Quotations** If you wanted to purchase the right to sell 2,000 shares of JC Penney stock in August 2008 at a strike price of $45 per share, how much would this cost you?

(4) 15. **Options Quotations** Which put contract sells for the lowest price? Which one sells for the highest price? Explain why these respective options trade at such extreme prices.

(4) **16. Using Options Quotations** In Problem 14, suppose JC Penney stock sells for $38.13 per share immediately before your options' expiration. What is the rate of return on your investment? What is your rate of return if the stock sells for $47.85 per share (think about it)? Assume your holding period for this investment is exactly three months.

(4) **17. Options** You've located the following option quote for Eric-Cartman, Inc. (ECI):

ECI			Call		Put	
Option/Strike		Exp.	Vol.	Last	Vol.	Last
20.25	10	Sep	29	5.50	...	...
20.25	15	Sep	333	7	69	1
20.25	25	Dec	5	2	...	...
20.25	30	Sep	76	2	188	8.75
20.25	35	Oct	89	0.50	...	...

Two of the premiums shown can't possibly be correct. Which two? Why?

(2) (4) **18. Annualized Returns** Suppose you have $30,000 to invest. You're considering Miller-Moore Equine Enterprises (MMEE), which is currently selling for $50 per share. You also notice that a call option with a $50 strike price and six months to maturity is available. The premium is $7.50. MMEE pays no dividends. What is your annualized return from these two investments if, in six months, MMEE is selling for $63 per share? What about $44 per share?

(2) (4) **19. Annualized Returns** In the previous question, suppose a dividend of $.80 per share is paid. Comment on how the returns would be affected.

(4) **20. Option Returns** In Problem 18, suppose a put option with a $50 strike is also available with a premium of $6.25. Calculate your percentage return for the six-month holding period if the stock price declines to $40.37 per share.

What's on the Web?

1. **Option Prices** You want to find the option prices for ConAgra Foods (CAG). Go to finance.yahoo.com, get a stock quote, and follow the "Options" link. What is the option premium and strike price for the highest and lowest strike price options that are nearest to expiring? What are the option premium and strike price for the highest and lowest strike price options expiring next month?
2. **Futures Quotes** Go to www.cmegroup.com and find the contract specifications for corn futures. What is the size of the corn futures contract? On the CBOT Web site, find the settle price for the corn futures contract that will expire the soonest. If you go long 10 contracts, how much will the corn cost at the current price?
3. **LEAPS** Go to www.cboe.com, highlight the "Products" tab, then follow the "LEAPS" link. What are LEAPS? What are the two types of LEAPS? What are the benefits of equity LEAPS? What are the benefits of index LEAPS?
4. **FLEX Options** Go to www.cboe.com, highlight the "Institutional" tab, then follow the "FLEX Options" link. What is a FLEX option? When do FLEX options expire? What is the minimum size of a FLEX option?

Stock-Trak Exercises

STOCK | TRAK
GLOBAL PORTFOLIO SIMULATIONS

To access the Stock-Trak Exercise for this chapter, please visit the book Web site at www.mhhe.com/jm5e and choose the corresponding chapter.

www.mhhe.com/jm5e

CHAPTER 4
Mutual Funds

"Take calculated risks. That is quite different from being rash."

–George S. Patton

With only $2,000 to invest, you can easily own shares in Microsoft, GM, McDonald's, IBM, Coke, and many more stocks through a mutual fund. Or, you can invest in a portfolio of government bonds or other investments. Indeed, many thousands of different mutual funds are available to investors. In fact, there are about as many mutual funds as there are different stocks traded on the NASDAQ and the New York Stock Exchange combined. There are funds for aggressive investors, conservative investors, short-term investors, and long-term investors. There are bond funds, stock funds, international funds, and you-name-it funds. Is there a right fund for you? This chapter will help you find out. ■

Learning Objectives

You're probably going to be a mutual fund investor very soon, so you should definitely know the following:

1. The different types of mutual funds.
2. How mutual funds operate.
3. How to find information about how mutual funds have performed.
4. The workings of Exchange-Traded Funds.

As we discussed in an earlier chapter, if you do not wish to actively buy and sell individual securities on your own, you can invest in stocks, bonds, or other financial assets through a *mutual fund.* Mutual funds are simply a means of combining or pooling the funds of a large group of investors. The buy and sell decisions for the resulting pool are then made by a fund manager, who is compensated for the service provided.

Because mutual funds provide indirect access to financial markets for individual investors, they are a form of financial intermediary. In fact, mutual funds are now the largest type of intermediary in the United States, followed by commercial banks and life insurance companies.

WWW

For mutual fund facts and figures, visit www.ici.org

Mutual funds have become so important that we devote this entire chapter to them. The number of funds and the different fund types available have grown tremendously in recent years. As of the beginning of 2007, an estimated 96 million Americans in 55 million households owned mutual funds, up from just 5 million households in 1980. Investors contributed \$474 billion to mutual funds in 2006, and, by the end of the year, mutual fund assets totaled \$10.4 *trillion.*

One of the reasons for the proliferation of mutual funds and fund types is that mutual funds have become, on a very basic level, consumer products. They are created and marketed to the public in ways that are intended to promote buyer appeal. As every business student knows, product differentiation is a basic marketing tactic, and in recent years mutual funds have become increasingly adept at practicing this common marketing technique.

In fact, if you are not already a mutual fund investor, it is very likely that you will be in the near future. The reason has to do with a fundamental change in the way businesses of all types provide retirement benefits for employees. It used to be that most large employers offered so-called defined benefit pensions. With such a plan, when you retire, your employer pays you a pension typically based on years of service and salary. The key is that the pension benefit you receive is based on a predefined formula, hence the name.

Defined benefit plans are rapidly being replaced by "defined contribution" plans. With a defined contribution plan, your employer will contribute money each pay period to a retirement account on your behalf, but you have to select where the funds go. With this arrangement, the benefit you ultimately receive depends entirely on how your investments do; your employer only makes contributions. Most commonly, you must choose from a group of mutual funds for your investments, so it is very important that you understand the different types of mutual funds, as well as their risk and return characteristics.

4.1 Advantages and Drawbacks of Mutual Fund Investing

ADVANTAGES

Investing in mutual funds offers many advantages. Three of these are diversification, professional management, and the size of the initial investment.

DIVERSIFICATION When you invest in a mutual fund, you are investing in a portfolio, or basket, of securities. As you will learn in detail in later chapters, holding a diversified portfolio helps you reduce risk. How? A mutual fund might invest in hundreds (or thousands) of securities. If the value of one of them falls to zero, this decline will have a small impact on the mutual fund value. Diversification helps you reduce risk, but diversification does not eliminate risk. It is still possible for you to lose money when you invest in a mutual fund. Also note that not all mutual funds are diversified. For example, some intentionally specialize in specific industries or countries.

PROFESSIONAL MANAGEMENT Professional money managers make investment decisions for mutual funds. That is, the mutual fund manager makes the decision of when to add or remove particular securities from the mutual fund. This means that you, as the investor holding the mutual fund, do not have to make these crucial decisions.

MINIMUM INITIAL INVESTMENT Most mutual funds have a minimum initial purchase of \$2,500, but some are as low as \$1,000. After your initial purchase, subsequent purchases are sometimes as low as \$50. Of course, these amounts vary from fund to fund.

DRAWBACKS

As with any type of investment, some drawbacks are associated with mutual funds. In particular, three of them are risk, costs, and taxes.

RISK Let us start with a point that should be obvious. The value of your mutual fund investment, unlike a bank deposit, could fall and be worth less than your initial investment. You should also realize that no government or private agency guarantees the value of a mutual fund.

A not so obvious point is that some investors think that there is a cost to diversification. Diversification greatly reduces the risk of loss from holding one (or a few) securities. However, by spreading your investments over many securities, you limit your chances for large returns if one of these securities increases dramatically in value. We happen to think that this is a cost worth bearing.

COSTS Investing in mutual funds entails fees and expenses that do not usually accrue when purchasing individual securities directly. We detail most of these costs later in the chapter.

TAXES When you invest in a mutual fund, you will pay federal income tax (and state and local taxes, if applicable) on:

- Distributions (dividends and capital gains) made by the mutual fund.
- Profits you make when you sell mutual fund shares.

There are some exceptions. A notable one is the receipt of distributions in tax-deferred retirement accounts such as individual retirement accounts (IRAs).

CHECK THIS

4.1a What are some advantages of investing in mutual funds?

4.1b What are some drawbacks of investing in mutual funds?

4.2 Investment Companies and Fund Types

investment company
A business that specializes in pooling funds from individual investors and investing them.

At the most basic level, a company that pools funds obtained from individual investors and invests them is called an **investment company**. In other words, an investment company is a business that specializes in managing financial assets for individual investors. All mutual funds are, in fact, investment companies. As we will see, however, not all investment companies are mutual funds.

In the sections that follow, we will be discussing various aspects of mutual funds and related entities. Figure 4.1 is a big-picture overview of some of the different types of funds and how they are classified. It will serve as a guide for the next several sections. We will define the various terms that appear as we go along.

OPEN-END VERSUS CLOSED-END FUNDS

As Figure 4.1 shows, there are two fundamental types of investment companies, *open-end funds* and *closed-end funds*. The difference is very important. Whenever you invest in a mutual fund, you do so by buying shares in the fund. However, how shares are bought and sold depends on which type of fund you are considering.

open-end fund
An investment company that stands ready to buy and sell shares at any time.

closed-end fund
An investment company with a fixed number of shares that are bought and sold only in the open stock market.

With an **open-end fund**, the fund itself will sell new shares to anyone wishing to buy and will redeem (i.e., buy back) shares from anyone wishing to sell. When an investor wishes to buy open-end fund shares, the fund simply issues them and then invests the money received. When someone wishes to sell open-end fund shares, the fund sells some of its assets and uses the cash to redeem the shares. As a result, with an open-end fund, the number of shares outstanding fluctuates through time.

With a **closed-end fund**, the number of shares is fixed and never changes. If you want to buy shares, you must buy them from another investor. Similarly, if you wish to sell shares that you own, you must sell them to another investor.

FIGURE 4.1 Fund Types

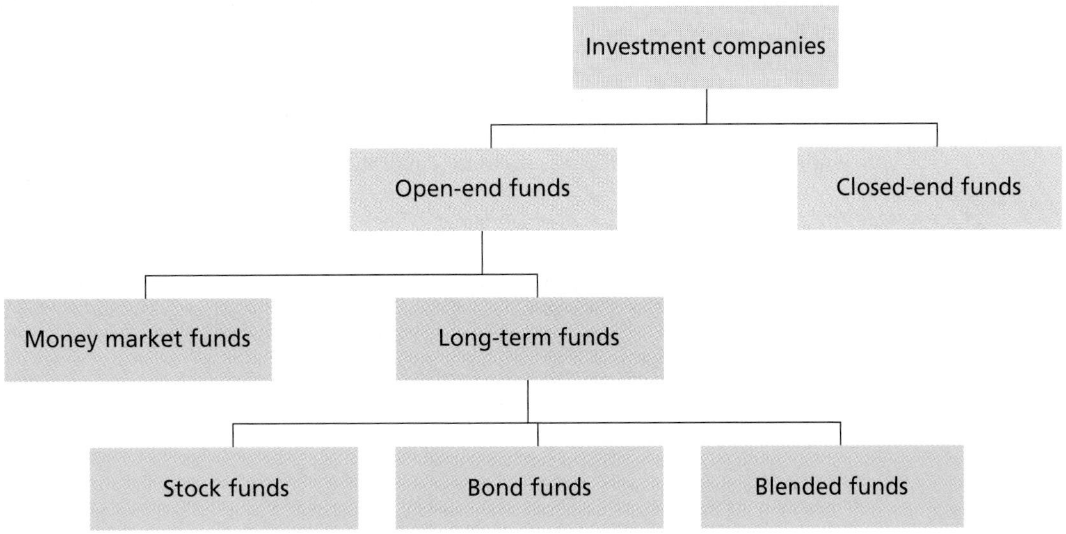

Thus, the key difference between an open-end fund and a closed-end fund is that, with a closed-end fund, the fund itself does not buy or sell shares. In fact, as we discuss below, shares in closed-end funds are listed on stock exchanges just like ordinary shares of stock, where their shares are bought and sold in the same way. Open-end funds are more popular among individual investors than closed-end funds.

Strictly speaking, the term "mutual fund" actually refers only to an open-end investment company. Thus, the phrase "closed-end fund" is a bit of an oxymoron, kind of like jumbo shrimp, and the phrase "open-end mutual fund" is a redundancy, an unnecessary repetition, or restatement. Nonetheless, particularly in recent years, the term "investment company" has all but disappeared from common use, and investment companies are now generically called mutual funds. We will stick with this common terminology to avoid any confusion.

NET ASSET VALUE

net asset value
The value of assets less liabilities held by a mutual fund, divided by the number of shares outstanding. Abbreviated NAV.

A mutual fund's **net asset value** is an important consideration. Net asset value is calculated by taking the total value of the assets held by the fund less any liabilities and then dividing by the number of outstanding shares. For example, suppose a mutual fund has $105 million in assets and $5 million in liabilities based on current market values and a total of 5 million shares outstanding. Based on the value of net assets held by the fund, $100 million, each share has a value of $100 million/5 million = $20. This $20 is the fund's net asset value, often abbreviated as NAV.

With one important exception, the net asset value of a mutual fund will change essentially every day simply because the value of the assets held by the fund fluctuates. The one exception concerns money market mutual funds, which we discuss in a later section.

EXAMPLE 4.1 Net Asset Value

The Fidelity Magellan Fund is one of the largest mutual funds in the United States with about $42.8 billion invested and approximately 465 million shares outstanding (as of mid-2007). What is its net asset value?

The net asset value is simply the asset value per share, or $42.8 billion/465 million = $92.04.

As we noted, an open-end fund will generally redeem or buy back shares at any time. The price you will receive for shares you sell is the net asset value. Thus, in our example above, you could sell your shares back to the fund and receive $20 each. Because the fund stands ready to redeem shares at any time, shares in an open-end fund are always worth their net asset value.

In contrast, because the shares of closed-end funds are bought and sold in the stock markets, their share prices at any point in time may or may not be equal to their net asset values. We examine this issue in more detail in a later section.

CHECK THIS

4.2a What is an investment company?

4.2b What is the difference between an open-end fund and a closed-end fund?

4.3 Mutual Fund Operations

In this section, we discuss some essentials of mutual fund operations. We focus on how mutual funds are created, marketed, regulated, and taxed. Our discussion here deals primarily with open-end funds, but much of it applies to closed-end funds as well. Further details on closed-end funds are provided in a later section.

MUTUAL FUND ORGANIZATION AND CREATION

A mutual fund is simply a corporation. Like a corporation, a mutual fund is owned by its shareholders. The shareholders elect a board of directors; the board of directors is responsible for hiring a manager to oversee the fund's operations. Although mutual funds often belong to a larger "family" of funds, every fund is a separate company owned by its shareholders.

WWW

All the major fund families have Web sites. Try, e.g., www.vanguard.com

Most mutual funds are created by investment advisory firms, which are businesses that specialize in managing mutual funds. Investment advisory firms are also called mutual fund companies. Increasingly, such firms have additional operations such as discount brokerages and other financial services.

There are hundreds of investment advisory firms in the United States. The largest, and probably best known, is Fidelity Investments, with more than 300 mutual funds, about $1.2 trillion in assets under management, and 22 million customers. Dreyfus, Franklin, and Vanguard are some other well-known examples. Many brokerage firms, such as Merrill Lynch and Charles Schwab, also have large investment advisory operations.

Investment advisory firms create mutual funds simply because they wish to manage them to earn fees. A typical management fee might be .75 percent of the total assets in the fund per year. A fund with $200 million in assets would not be especially large, but could nonetheless generate management fees of about $1.5 million per year. Thus, there is a significant economic incentive to create funds and attract investors to them.

For example, a company like Fidelity might one day decide that there is a demand for a fund that buys stock in companies that grow and process citrus fruits. Fidelity could form a mutual fund that specializes in such companies and call it something like the Fidelity Lemon Fund.[1] A fund manager would be appointed, and shares in the fund would be offered to the public. As shares are sold, the money received is invested. If the fund is a success, a large amount of money will be attracted and Fidelity would benefit from the fees it earns. If the fund is not a success, the board can vote to liquidate it and return shareholders' money or merge it with another fund.

[1] Fidelity would probably come up with a better name.

As our hypothetical example illustrates, an investment advisory firm such as Fidelity can (and often will) create new funds from time to time. Through time, this process leads to a family of funds all managed by the same advisory firm. Each fund in the family will have its own fund manager, but the advisory firm will generally handle the record keeping, marketing, and much of the research that underlies the fund's investment decisions.

In principle, the directors of a mutual fund in a particular family, acting on behalf of the fund shareholders, could vote to fire the investment advisory firm and hire a different one. As a practical matter, this rarely, if ever, occurs. At least part of the reason is that the directors are originally appointed by the fund's founder, and they are routinely reelected. Unhappy shareholders generally "vote with their feet"—that is, sell their shares and invest elsewhere.

TAXATION OF INVESTMENT COMPANIES

As long as an investment company meets certain rules set by the Internal Revenue Service, it is treated as a "regulated investment company" for tax purposes. This is important because a regulated investment company does not pay taxes on its investment income. Instead, the fund passes through all realized investment income to fund shareholders, who then pay taxes on these distributions as though they owned the securities directly. Essentially, the fund simply acts as a conduit, funneling gains and losses to fund owners.

To qualify as a regulated investment company, the fund must follow three basic rules. The first rule is that it must in fact be an investment company holding almost all of its assets as investments in stocks, bonds, and other securities. The second rule limits the fund to using no more than 5 percent of its assets when acquiring a particular security. This is a diversification rule. The third rule is that the fund must pass through all realized investment income to fund shareholders.

THE FUND PROSPECTUS AND ANNUAL REPORT

Mutual funds are required by law to produce a document known as a *prospectus*. The prospectus must be supplied to any investor wishing to purchase shares. Mutual funds must also provide an annual report to their shareholders. The annual report and the prospectus, which are sometimes combined, contain financial statements along with specific information concerning the fund's expenses, gains and losses, holdings, objectives, and management. We discuss many of these items in the next few sections.

CHECK THIS

4.3a How do mutual funds usually get started?

4.3b How are mutual funds taxed?

4.4 Mutual Fund Costs and Fees

All mutual funds have various expenses that are paid by the fund's shareholders. These expenses can vary considerably from fund to fund, however, and one of the most important considerations in evaluating a fund is its expense structure. All else the same, lower expenses are preferred, of course, but, as we discuss, matters are not quite that cut-and-dried.

TYPES OF EXPENSES AND FEES

Basically, there are four types of expenses or fees associated with buying and owning mutual fund shares:

1. Sales charges or "loads."
2. 12b-1 fees.

3. Management fees.
4. Trading costs.

We discuss each of these in turn.

front-end load
A sales charge levied on purchases of shares in some mutual funds.

SALES CHARGES Many mutual funds charge a fee whenever shares are purchased. These fees are generally called **front-end loads**. Funds that charge loads are called *load funds*. Funds that have no such charges are called *no-load funds*.

When you purchase shares in a load fund, you pay a price in excess of the net asset value, called the *offering price*. The difference between the offering price and the net asset value is the *load*. Shares in no-load funds are sold at net asset value.

Front-end loads can range as high as 8.5 percent, but 5 percent or so would be more typical. Some funds, with front-end loads in the 2 percent to 3 percent range, are described as *low-load funds*.

Front-end loads are expressed as a percentage of the offering price, not the net asset value. For example, suppose a load fund has an offering price of \$100 and a net asset value of \$98. The front-end load is \$2, which, as a percentage of the \$100 offering price, is \$2/\$100 = 2 percent. The way front-end loads are calculated understates the load slightly. In our example here, you are paying \$100 for something worth only \$98, so the load is really \$2/\$98 = 2.04 percent.

EXAMPLE 4.2

Front-End Loads

On a particular day, according to *The Wall Street Journal,* the Common Sense Growth fund had a net asset value of \$13.91. The offering price was \$15.20. Is this a load fund? What is the front-end load?

Because the offering price, which is the price you must pay to purchase shares, exceeds the net asset value, this is definitely a load fund. The load can be calculated by taking the difference between the offering price and the net asset value, \$1.29, and dividing by the \$15.20 offering price. The result is a hefty front-end load of 8.5 percent.

Some funds have "back-end" loads, which are charges levied on redemptions. These loads are often called *contingent deferred sales charges* and abbreviated CDSC. The CDSC usually declines through time. It might start out at 6 percent for shares held less than one year, then drop to 3 percent for shares held for two years, and disappear altogether on shares held for three or more years.

12b-1 fees
Named for SEC Rule 12b-1, which allows funds to spend up to 1 percent of fund assets annually to cover distribution and marketing costs.

12B-1 FEES So-called **12b-1 fees** are named after the Securities and Exchange Commission (SEC) rule that permits them. Mutual funds are allowed to use a portion of the fund's assets to cover distribution and marketing costs. Funds that market directly to the public may use 12b-1 fees to pay for advertising and direct mailing costs. Funds that rely on brokers and other sales force personnel often use 12b-1 fees to provide compensation for their services. The total amount of these fees could be .75 percent to 1.0 percent of the fund's assets per year.

Frequently, 12b-1 fees are used in conjunction with a CDSC. Such funds will often have no front-end load, but they effectively make it up through these other costs. Such funds may look like no-load funds, but they are really disguised load funds. Mutual funds with no front-end or back-end loads and no or minimal 12b-1 fees are often called "pure" no-load funds to distinguish them from the "not-so-pure" funds that may have no loads but still charge hefty 12b-1 fees.

MANAGEMENT FEES We briefly discussed management fees in an earlier section. Fees are usually based first on the size of the fund. Beyond this, there is often an incentive provision that increases the fee if the fund outperforms some benchmark, often the S&P 500 Index. Management fees generally range from .25 percent to 1.0 percent of total fund assets every year.

turnover
A measure of how much trading a fund does, calculated as the lesser of total purchases or sales during a year divided by average daily assets.

TRADING COSTS Mutual funds have brokerage expenses from trading just like individuals do. As a result, mutual funds that do a lot of trading will have relatively high trading costs.

Trading costs can be difficult to get a handle on because they are not reported directly. However, in the prospectus, funds are required to report something known as **turnover**. A fund's turnover is a measure of how much trading a fund does. It is calculated as the lesser of a fund's total purchases or sales during a year, divided by average daily assets.[2]

EXAMPLE 4.3 **Turnover**

Suppose a fund had average daily assets of $50 million during a particular year. It bought $80 million worth of stock and sold $70 million during the year. What is its turnover?

The lesser of purchases or sales is $70 million, and average daily assets are $50 million. Turnover is thus $70/$50 = 1.4 times.

A fund with a turnover of 1.0 has, in effect, sold off its entire portfolio and replaced it once during the year. Similarly, a turnover of .50 indicates that, loosely speaking, the fund replaced half of its holdings during the year. All else the same, a higher turnover indicates more frequent trading and higher trading costs.

EXPENSE REPORTING

Mutual funds are required to report expenses in a fairly standardized way in the prospectus. The exact format varies, but the information reported is generally the same. There are three parts to an expense statement. Figure 4.2 shows this information as it was reported for the Fidelity Low-Priced Stock Fund.

The first part of the statement shows shareholder transaction expenses, which are generally loads and deferred sales charges. As indicated, for this fund, there is no front-end load on shares purchased or on dividends received that are reinvested in the fund (it's common for mutual fund shareholders to simply reinvest any dividends received from the fund). The next item shows that there is no CDSC. The third item, labeled "redemption fee," refers to a back-end load that is applied under certain circumstances.

The second part of the statement, "Annual operating expenses," includes the management and 12b-1 fees. This fund's management fee was .67 percent of assets. There was no 12b-1 fee. The other expenses include things like legal, accounting, and reporting costs along with director fees. At .21 percent of assets, these costs are not trivial. The sum of these three items is the fund's total operating expense expressed as a percentage of assets, .88 percent in this case. To put this in perspective, this fund has about $35.8 billion in assets, so operating costs were about $315 million, of which about $240 million was paid to the fund manager.

The third part of the expense report gives a hypothetical example showing the total expense you would incur over time per $10,000 invested. The example is strictly hypothetical, however, and is only a rough guide. As shown here, your costs would amount to $1,084 after 10 years per $10,000 invested, assuming a return of 5 percent per year. This third part of the expense statement is not all that useful, really. What matters for this fund is that expenses appear to run about .88 percent per year, so that is what you pay (in addition to loads, if applicable).

One thing to watch out for is that funds may have 12b-1 fees but may choose not to incur any distribution or marketing costs. Similarly, the fund manager can choose to rebate some of the management fee in a particular year (especially if the fund has done poorly). These actions create a low expense figure for a given year, but this does not mean that expenses won't be higher in the future.

[2] Purchases and sales for a fund are usually different because of purchases and redemptions of fund shares by shareholders. For example, if a fund is growing, purchases will exceed sales.

FIGURE 4.2 Mutual Fund Expenses

Fidelity®

Low-Priced Stock Fund

(fund number 316, trading symbol FLPSX)

Prospectus

September 29, 2006

Fee Table

The following table describes the fees and expenses that are incurred when you buy, hold, or sell shares of the fund.

The annual fund operating expenses provided below for the fund do not reflect the effect of any reduction of certain expenses during the period.

Shareholder fees (paid by the investor directly)

Sales charge (load) on purchases and reinvested distributions[A]	None
Deferred sales charge (load) on redemptions	None
Redemption fee on shares held less than 90 days (as a % of amount redeemed)[B]	1.50%

[A] *The fund may impose a 3.00% sales charge on purchases upon 60 days notice to shareholders.*

[B] *A redemption fee may be charged when you sell your shares or if your shares are redeemed because your fund balance falls below the balance minimum for any reason, including solely due to declines in net asset value per share.*

Annual operating expenses (paid from fund assets)

Management fee	0.67%
Distribution and/or Service (12b-1) fees	None
Other expenses	0.21%
Total annual fund operating expenses	0.88%

This **example** helps you compare the cost of investing in the fund with the cost of investing in other mutual funds.

Let's say, hypothetically, that the fund's annual return is 5% and that your shareholder fees and the fund's annual operating expenses are exactly as described in the fee table. This example illustrates the effect of fees and expenses, but is not meant to suggest actual or expected fees and expenses or returns, all of which may vary. For every $10,000 you invested, here's how much you would pay in total expenses if you sell all of your shares at the end of each time period indicated:

1 year	$ 90
3 years	$ 281
5 years	$ 488
10 years	$ 1,084

WWW

Prospectuses are increasingly available online. Visit www.fidelity.com to see some examples.

WHY PAY LOADS AND FEES?

Given that pure no-load funds exist, you might wonder why anyone would buy load funds or funds with substantial CDSC or 12b-1 fees. It is becoming increasingly difficult to give a good answer to this question. At one time, there simply weren't many no-load funds, and those that existed weren't widely known. Today, there are many good no-load funds, and competition among funds is forcing many funds to lower or do away with loads and other fees.

Having said this, there are basically two reasons that you might want to consider a load fund or a fund with above-average fees. First, you may simply want a fund run by a particular manager. A good example of this is the Fidelity Magellan Fund we mentioned earlier. For many years, it was run by Peter Lynch, who is widely regarded as one of the most successful managers in the history of the business. The Magellan Fund was a load fund, leaving you no choice but to pay the load to obtain Lynch's expertise.

The other reason to consider paying a load is that you want a specialized type of fund. For example, you might be interested in investing in a fund that invests only in a particular foreign country, such as Brazil. We'll discuss such specialty funds in a later section, but for now we note that there is little competition among specialty funds, and, as a result, loads and fees tend to be higher.

CHECK THIS

4.4a What is the difference between a load fund and a no-load fund?

4.4b What are 12b-1 fees?

4.5 Short-Term Funds

Mutual funds are usually divided into two major groups, short-term funds and long-term funds. Short-term funds are collectively known as *money market mutual funds.* Long-term funds essentially include everything that is not a money market fund. We discuss long-term funds in our next section; here we focus on money market funds.

MONEY MARKET MUTUAL FUNDS

money market mutual fund
A mutual fund specializing in money market instruments.

As the name suggests, **money market mutual funds**, or MMMFs, specialize in money market instruments. As we describe elsewhere, these are short-term debt obligations issued by governments and corporations. Money market funds were introduced in the early 1970s and have grown tremendously. At the end of 2006, about 850 money market funds managed almost $2.3 trillion in assets. All money market funds are open-end funds.

Most money market funds invest in high-quality, low-risk instruments with maturities of less than 90 days. As a result, they have relatively little risk. However, some buy riskier assets or have longer maturities than others, so they do not all carry equally low risk. For example, some buy only very short-term U.S. government securities and are therefore essentially risk-free. Others buy mostly securities issued by corporations which entail some risk. We discuss the different types of money market instruments and their relative risks elsewhere in the book.

WWW
Visit www.mfea.com for info on thousands of funds, including MMMFs.

MONEY MARKET FUND ACCOUNTING A unique feature of money market funds is that their net asset values are always $1 per share. This is purely an accounting gimmick, however. A money market fund simply sets the number of shares equal to the fund's assets. In other words, if the fund has $100 million in assets, then it has 100 million shares. As the fund earns interest on its investments, the fund owners are simply given more shares.

The reason money market mutual funds always maintain a $1 net asset value is to make them resemble bank accounts. As long as a money market fund invests in very safe, interest-bearing, short-maturity assets, its net asset value will not drop below $1 per share. However, there is no guarantee that this will not happen, and the term "breaking the buck" is used to describe dropping below $1 in net asset value. This is a very rare occurrence, but, in 1994, several large money market funds experienced substantial losses because they purchased relatively risky derivative assets and broke the buck, so it definitely can happen.

TAXES AND MONEY MARKET FUNDS Money market funds are either taxable or tax-exempt. Taxable funds are more common; of the $2.3 trillion in total money market fund assets at the end of 2006, taxable funds accounted for about 84.4 percent. As the name suggests, the difference in the two fund types lies in their tax treatment. As a general rule, interest earned on state and local government (or "municipal") securities is exempt from federal income tax. Nontaxable money market funds therefore buy only these types of tax-exempt securities.

Some tax-exempt funds go even further. Interest paid by one state is often subject to state taxes in another. Some tax-exempt funds therefore buy only securities issued by a single state. For residents of that state, the interest earned is free of both federal and state taxes. For beleaguered New York City residents, there are even "triple-tax-free" funds that invest only in New York City obligations, thereby allowing residents to escape federal, state, and local income taxes on the interest received.

Because of their favorable tax treatment, tax-exempt money market instruments have much lower interest rates, or *yields*.[3] For example, in mid-2007, taxable money funds offered about 5.09 percent interest, whereas tax-exempt funds offered only 3.50 percent interest. Which is better depends on your individual tax bracket. If you're in a 40 percent bracket, then the taxable fund is paying only $.0509 \times (1 - .40) = .0305$, or 3.05 percent, on an aftertax basis, so you're better off with the tax-exempt fund.

EXAMPLE 4.4 **Taxes and Money Market Fund Yields**

In our discussion just above, suppose you were in a 20 percent tax bracket. Which type of fund is more attractive?

On an aftertax basis, the taxable fund is offering $.0509 \times (1 - .20) = .0407$, or 4.07 percent, so the taxable fund is more attractive.

MONEY MARKET DEPOSIT ACCOUNTS

Most banks offer what are called "money market" deposit accounts, or MMDAs, which are much like money market mutual funds. For example, both money market funds and money market deposit accounts generally have limited check-writing privileges.

There is a very important distinction between such a bank-offered money market account and a money market fund, however. A bank money market account is a bank deposit and offers FDIC protection, whereas a money market fund does not. A money market fund will generally offer SIPC protection, but this is not a perfect substitute. Confusingly, some banks offer both money market accounts and, through a separate, affiliated entity, money market funds.

CHECK THIS

4.5a What is a money market mutual fund? What are the two types?

4.5b How do money market mutual funds maintain a constant net asset value?

[3] We discuss how yields on money market instruments are calculated in another chapter.

4.6 Long-Term Funds

There are many different types of long-term funds. Historically, mutual funds were classified as stock, bond, or income funds. As a part of the rapid growth in mutual funds, however, it is becoming increasingly difficult to place all funds into these three categories. Also, providers of mutual fund information do not use the same classification schemes.

WWW

One of the best mutual fund sites is www.morningstar.com

Mutual funds have different goals, and a fund's objective is the major determinant of the fund type. All mutual funds must state the fund's objective in the prospectus. For example, the Fidelity Independence Fund states:

> The fund's objective is capital appreciation. Normally, the fund's strategy is to invest primarily in common stocks of domestic and foreign issuers. The fund strategy may result in the realization of capital gains without considering the tax consequences to shareholders. Fidelity Management & Research Company (FMR) is not constrained by any particular investment style and may invest in "growth" stocks, "value" stocks, or both, at any given time.

Thus, this fund invests in different types of stocks with the goal of capital appreciation. This fund is clearly a stock fund, and it might further be classified as a "capital appreciation" fund or "aggressive growth" fund, depending on whose classification scheme is used.

Mutual fund objectives are an important consideration; unfortunately, the truth is they frequently are too vague to provide useful information. For example, a very common objective reads like this: "The Big Bucks Fund seeks capital appreciation, income, and capital preservation." Translation: The fund seeks to (1) increase the value of its shares, (2) generate income for its shareholders, and (3) not lose money. Well, don't we all! More to the point, funds with very similar-sounding objectives can have very different portfolios and, consequently, very different risks. As a result, it is a mistake to look only at a fund's stated objective: Actual portfolio holdings speak louder than prospectus promises.

STOCK FUNDS

Stock funds exist in great variety. We consider nine separate general types and some subtypes. We also consider some new varieties that don't fit in any category.

CAPITAL APPRECIATION VERSUS INCOME The first four types of stock funds trade off capital appreciation and dividend income.

1. *Capital appreciation.* As in our example just above, these funds seek maximum capital appreciation. They generally invest in companies that have, in the opinion of the fund manager, the best prospects for share price appreciation without regard to dividends, company size, or, for some funds, country. Often this means investing in unproven companies or companies perceived to be out-of-favor.
2. *Growth.* These funds also seek capital appreciation, but they tend to invest in larger, more established companies. Such funds may be somewhat less volatile as a result. Dividends are not an important consideration.
3. *Growth and income.* Capital appreciation is still the main goal, but at least part of the focus is on dividend-paying companies.
4. *Equity income.* These funds focus almost exclusively on stocks with relatively high dividend yields, thereby maximizing the current income on the portfolio.

Among these four fund types, the greater the emphasis on growth, the greater the risk, at least as a general matter. Again, however, these are only rough classifications. Equity income funds, for example, frequently invest heavily in public utility stocks; such stocks had heavy losses in the first part of the 1990s.

COMPANY SIZE–BASED FUNDS These next three fund types focus on companies in a particular size range.

1. *Small company.* As the name suggests, these funds focus on stocks in small companies, where "small" refers to the total market value of the stock. Such funds are often called "small-cap" funds, where "cap" is short for total market value or capitalization. In Chapter 1, we saw that small stocks have traditionally performed very well, at least over the long run, hence the demand for funds that specialize in such stocks. With small-company mutual funds, what constitutes small is variable, ranging from perhaps $10 million up to $1 billion or so in total market value, and some funds specialize in smaller companies than others. Since most small companies don't pay dividends, these funds necessarily emphasize capital appreciation.
2. *Midcap.* These funds usually specialize in stocks that are too small to be in the S&P 500 Index but too large to be considered small cap stocks.
3. *Large Company.* Large-capitalization, or "large-cap", funds invest in companies with large market values. Most large-cap firms have a market value in excess of $8 billion.

INTERNATIONAL FUNDS Research has shown that diversifying internationally can significantly improve the risk-return trade-off for investors. The number of international funds grew rapidly during the 1980s and early 1990s. However, that growth slowed sharply in the late 1990s. Their number shrank in the early 2000s, but their numbers increased in 2005 and 2006. The two fund groups that invest outside the U.S. are:

1. *Global.* These funds have substantial international holdings but also maintain significant investments in U.S. stocks.
2. *International.* These funds are like global funds, except they focus on non-U.S. equities.

Among international funds, some specialize in specific regions of the world, such as Europe, the Pacific Rim, or South America. Others specialize in individual countries. Today, there is at least one mutual fund specializing in essentially every country in the world that has a stock market, however small.

International funds that specialize in countries with small or recently established stock markets are often called *emerging markets funds.* Almost all single-country funds, and especially emerging markets funds, are not well-diversified and have historically been extremely volatile.

Many funds that are not classified as international funds may actually have substantial overseas investments, so this is one thing to watch out for. It is not unusual for a fund to call itself a "growth" fund and actually invest heavily outside the United States.

SECTOR FUNDS Sector funds specialize in specific sectors of the economy and often focus on particular industries or particular commodities. There are far too many different types to list here. There are funds that only buy software companies, and funds that only buy hardware companies. There are funds that specialize in natural gas producers, oil producers, and precious metals producers. In fact, essentially every major industry in the U.S. economy is covered by at least one fund.

One thing to notice about sector funds is that, like single-country funds, they are obviously not well-diversified. Every year, many of the best performing mutual funds (in terms of total return) are sector funds simply because whatever sector of the economy is hottest will generally have the largest stock price increases. Funds specializing in that sector will do well. In the same vein, and for the same reason, the worst performing funds are also almost always some type of sector fund. When it comes to mutual funds, past performance is almost always an unreliable guide to future performance; nowhere is this more true than with sector funds.

OTHER FUND TYPES AND ISSUES Three other types of stock funds that don't fit easily into one of the above categories bear discussing: *index funds,* so-called *social conscience funds,* and *tax-managed funds.*

1. *Index funds.* Index funds simply hold the stocks that make up a particular index in the same relative proportions as the index. The most important index funds are S&P 500 funds, which are intended to track the performance of the S&P 500, the large stock index we discussed in Chapter 1. By their nature, index funds are passively managed, meaning that the fund manager trades only as necessary to match the

index. Such funds are appealing in part because they are generally characterized by low turnover and low operating expenses. Another reason index funds have grown rapidly is that there is considerable debate over whether mutual fund managers can consistently beat the averages. If they can't, the argument runs, why pay loads and management fees when it's cheaper just to buy the averages by indexing? To put the importance of index funds into perspective, as of mid-2007, the largest single stock mutual fund in the United States was the Vanguard 500 Index Fund, with $70.8 billion in assets. This fund, as the name suggests, is an S&P 500 Index fund.

WWW

To learn more about "social conscience" funds, visit www.socialinvest.org and www.domini.com

WWW

Is vice nice? Visit www.vicefund.com to find out.

2. *Social conscience funds.* These funds are a relatively new creation. They invest only in companies whose products, policies, or politics are viewed as socially desirable. The specific social objectives range from environmental issues to personnel policies. The Parnassus Fund is a well-known example, avoiding the alcoholic beverage, tobacco, gambling, weapons, and nuclear power industries. Of course, consensus on what is socially desirable or responsible is hard to find. In fact, there are so-called sin funds (and sector funds) that specialize in these very industries!
3. *Tax-managed funds.* Taxable mutual funds are generally managed without regard for the tax liabilities of fund owners. Fund managers focus on (and are frequently rewarded based on) total pretax returns. However, recent research has shown that some fairly simple strategies can greatly improve the aftertax returns to shareholders and that focusing just on pretax returns is not a good idea for taxable investors. Tax-managed funds try to hold down turnover to minimize realized capital gains, and they try to match realized gains with realized losses. Such strategies work particularly well for index funds. For example, the Schwab 1000 Fund is a fund that tracks the Russell 1000 Index, a widely followed 1,000-stock index. However, the fund will deviate from strictly following the index to a certain extent to avoid realizing taxable gains, and, as a result, the fund holds turnover to a minimum. Fund shareholders have largely escaped taxes as a result. We predict that funds promoting such strategies will become increasingly common as investors become more aware of the tax consequences of fund ownership.

TAXABLE AND MUNICIPAL BOND FUNDS

Most bond funds invest in domestic corporate and government securities, although some invest in foreign government and non-U.S. corporate bonds as well. As we will see, there are a relatively small number of bond fund types. Basically, five characteristics distinguish bond funds:

1. *Maturity range.* Different funds hold bonds of different maturities, ranging from quite short (2 years) to quite long (25–30 years).
2. *Credit quality.* Some bonds are much safer than others in terms of the possibility of default. United States government bonds have no default risk, while so-called junk bonds have significant default risk.
3. *Taxability.* Municipal bond funds buy only bonds that are free from federal income tax. Taxable funds buy only taxable issues.
4. *Type of bond.* Some funds specialize in particular types of fixed-income instruments such as mortgages.
5. *Country.* Most bond funds buy only domestic issues, but some buy foreign company and government issues.

SHORT-TERM AND INTERMEDIATE-TERM FUNDS As the names suggest, these two fund types focus on bonds in a specific maturity range. Short-term maturities are generally considered to be less than five years. Intermediate-term would be less than 10 years. There are both taxable and municipal bond funds with these maturity targets.

One thing to be careful of with these types of funds is that the credit quality of the issues can vary from fund to fund. One fund could hold very risky intermediate-term bonds, while another might hold only U.S. government issues with similar maturities.

GENERAL FUNDS For both taxable and municipal bonds, this fund category is kind of a catch-all. Funds in this category simply don't specialize in any particular way. Our warning just above concerning varied credit quality applies here. Maturities can differ substantially as well.

HIGH-YIELD FUNDS High-yield municipal and taxable funds specialize in low-credit quality issues. Such issues have higher yields because of their greater risks. As a result, high-yield bond funds can be quite volatile.

MORTGAGE FUNDS A number of funds specialize in so-called mortgage-backed securities such as GNMA (Government National Mortgage Association, referred to as "Ginnie Mae") issues. We discuss this important type of security in detail in a later chapter. There are no municipal mortgage-backed securities (yet), so these are all taxable bond funds.

WORLD FUNDS A relatively limited number of taxable funds invest worldwide. Some specialize in only government issues; others buy a variety of non-U.S. issues. These are all taxable funds.

INSURED FUNDS This is a type of municipal bond fund. Municipal bond issuers frequently purchase insurance that guarantees the bond's payments will be made. Such bonds have very little possibility of default, so some funds specialize in them.

SINGLE-STATE MUNICIPAL FUNDS Earlier we discussed how some money market funds specialize in issues from a single state. The same is true for some bond funds. Such funds are especially important in large states such as California and other high-tax states. Confusingly, this classification refers only to long-term funds. Short and intermediate single-state funds are classified with other maturity-based municipal funds.

STOCK AND BOND FUNDS

This last major fund group includes a variety of funds. The only common feature is that these funds don't invest exclusively in either stocks or bonds. For this reason, they are often called "blended" or "hybrid" funds. We discuss a few of the main types.

BALANCED FUNDS Balanced funds maintain a relatively fixed split between stocks and bonds. They emphasize relatively safe, high-quality investments. Such funds provide a kind of "one-stop" shopping for fund investors, particularly smaller investors, because they diversify into both stocks and bonds.

ASSET ALLOCATION FUNDS Two types of funds carry this label. The first is an extended version of a balanced fund. Such a fund holds relatively fixed proportional investments in stocks, bonds, money market instruments, and perhaps real estate or some other investment class. The target proportions may be updated or modified periodically.

The other type of asset allocation fund is often called a *flexible portfolio fund.* Here, the fund manager may hold up to 100 percent in stocks, bonds, or money market instruments, depending on her views about the likely performance of these investments. These funds essentially try to time the market, guessing which general type of investment will do well (or least poorly) over the months ahead.

CONVERTIBLE FUNDS Some bonds are convertible, meaning they can be swapped for a fixed number of shares of stock at the option of the bondholder. Some mutual funds specialize in these bonds.

INCOME FUNDS An income fund emphasizes generating dividend and coupon income on its investments, so it would hold a variety of dividend-paying common stocks, as well as preferred stocks and bonds of various maturities.

FIGURE 4.3 Mutual Fund Objectives

MUTUAL-FUND OBJECTIVES

Categories compiled by The Wall Street Journal, based on classifications by Lipper Inc.

STOCK FUNDS

Emerging Markets (EM): Funds investing in emerging-market equity securities, where the "emerging market" is defined by a country's GNP per capita and other economic measures.
Equity Income (EI): Funds seeking high current income and growth of income by investing in equities.
European Region (EU): Funds investing in markets or operations concentrated in the European region.
Global Stock (GL): Funds investing in securities traded outside of the U.S. and may own U.S. securities as well.
Gold Oriented (AU): Funds investing in gold mines, gold-mining finance houses, gold coins or bullion.
Health/Biotech (HB): Funds investing in companies related to health care, medicine and biotechnology.
International Stock (IL) (non-U.S.): Canadian; International; International Small Cap.
Latin American (LT): Funds investing in markets or operations concentrated in Latin American region.
Large-Cap Growth (LG): Funds investing in large companies with long-term earnings that are ex-pected to grow significantly faster than the earnings of stocks in major indexes. Funds normally have above-average price-to-earnings ratios, price-to-book ratios and three-year earnings growth.
Large-Cap Core (LC): Funds investing in large companies, with wide latitude in the type of shares they buy. On average, the price-to-earnings ratios, price-to-book ratios, and three-year earnings growth are in line with those of the U.S. diversified large-cap funds' universe average.
Large-Cap Value (LV): Funds investing in large companies that are considered undervalued relative to major stock indexes based on price-to-earnings ratios, price-to-book ratios or other factors.
Midcap Growth (MG): Funds investing in midsize companies with long-term earnings that are ex-pected to grow significantly faster than the earnings of stocks in major indexes. Funds normally have above-average price-to-earnings ratios, price-to-book ratios and three-year earnings growth.
Midcap Core (MC): Funds investing in midsize companies, with wide latitude in the type of shares they buy. On average, the price-to-earnings ratios, price-to-book ratios, and three-year earnings growth are in line with those of the U.S. diversified midcap funds' universe average.
Midcap Value (MV): Funds investing in midsize companies that are considered undervalued relative to major stock indexes based on price-to-earnings ratios, price-to-book ratios or other factors.
Multicap Growth (XG): Funds investing in companies of various sizes, with long-term earnings ex-pected to grow significantly faster than the earnings of stocks in major indexes. Funds normally have above-average price-to-earnings ratios, price-to-book ratios, and three-year earnings growth.
Multicap Core (XC): Funds investing in companies of various sizes with average price-to-earnings ratios, price-to-book ratios and earnings growth.
Multicap Value (XV): Funds investing in companies of various size, normally those that are consid-ered undervalued relative to major stock indexes based on price-to-earnings ratios, price-to-book ratios or other factors.
Natural Resources (NR): Funds investing in natural-resource stocks.
Pacific Region (PR): Funds that invest in China Region; Japan; Pacific Ex-Japan; Pacific Region.
Science & Technology (TK): Funds investing in science and technology stocks. Includes telecommunication funds.
Sector (SE): Funds investing in financial services; real estate; specialty & miscellaneous.
S&P 500 Index (SP): Funds that are passively managed and are designed to replicate the performance of the Standard & Poor's 500-stock Index on a reinvested basis.
Small-Cap Growth (SG): Funds investing in small companies with long-term earnings that are expected to grow significantly faster than the earnings of stocks in major indexes. Funds normally have above-average price-to-earnings ratios, price-to-book ratios, and three-year earnings growth.
Small-Cap Core (SC): Funds investing in small companies, with wide latitude in the type of shares they buy. On average, the price-to-earnings ratios, price-to-book ratios, and three-year earnings growth are in line with those of the U.S. diversified small-cap funds' universe average.
Small-Cap Value (SV): Funds investing in small companies that are considered undervalued relative to major stock indexes based on price-to-earnings ratios, price-to-book ratios or other factors.
Specialty Equity (SQ): Funds investing in all market-capitalization ranges, with no restrictions for any one range. May have strategies that are distinctly different from other diversified stock funds.
Utility (UT): Funds investing in utility stocks.

TAXABLE-BOND FUNDS

Short-Term Bond (SB): Ultra-short Obligation; Short Investment Grade Debt; Short-Intermediate Investment Grade Debt.
Short-Term U.S. (SU): Short U.S. Treasury; Short U.S. Government; Short-Intermediate U.S. Government debt.
Intermediate Bond (IB): Funds investing in investment-grade debt issues (rated in the top four grades) with dollar-weighted average maturities of five to 10 years.
Intermediate U.S. (IG): Intermediate U.S. Government; Intermediate U.S. Treasury.
Long-Term Bond (AB): Funds investing in corporate- and government-debt issues in the top grades.
Long-Term U.S. (LU): General U.S. Government; General U.S. Treasury; Target Maturity.
General U.S. Taxable (GT): Funds investing in general bonds.
High-Yield Taxable (HC): Funds aiming for high current yields from fixed-income securities and tend to invest in lower-grade debt.
Mortgage (MT): Adjustable Rate Mortgage; GNMA; U.S. Mortgage.
World Bond (WB): Emerging Markets Debt; Global Income; International Income; Short World MultiMarket Income.

MUNICIPAL-DEBT FUNDS

Short-Term Muni (SM): California Short-Intermediate Muni Debt; Other States Short-Intermediate Muni Debt; Short-Intermediate Muni Debt; Short Muni Debt.
Intermediate Muni (IM): Intermediate-term Muni Debt including single states.
General Muni (GM): Funds investing in muni-debt issues in the top-four credit ratings.
Single-State Municipal (SS): Funds investing in debt of individual states.
High-Yield Municipal (HM): Funds investing in lower-rated muni debt.
Insured Muni (NM): California Insured Muni Debt; Florida Insured Muni Debt; Insured Muni Debt; New York Insured Muni Debt.

STOCK & BOND FUNDS

Balanced (BL): Primary objective is to conserve principal, by maintaining a balanced portfolio of both stocks and bonds.
Stock/Bond Blend (MP): Multipurpose funds such as Balanced Target Maturity; Convertible Securities; Flexible Income; Flexible Portfolio; Global Flexible and Income funds, that invest in both stocks and bonds.

Source: Reprinted by permission of *The Wall Street Journal*, April 3, 2008.

MUTUAL FUND OBJECTIVES: RECENT DEVELOPMENTS

As we mentioned earlier, a mutual fund's stated objective may not be all that informative. In recent years, there has been a trend toward classifying a mutual fund's objective based on its actual holdings. For example, Figure 4.3 illustrates the classifications used by *The Wall Street Journal.*

A key thing to notice in Figure 4.3 is that most general-purpose funds (as opposed to specialized types such as sector funds) are classified based on the market "cap" of the stocks they hold (small, midsize, or large) and also on whether the fund tends to invest in either "growth" or "value" stocks (or both). We will discuss growth versus value stocks in a later chapter; for now, it is enough to know that "growth" stocks are those considered more likely to grow rapidly. "Value" stocks are those that look to be relatively undervalued and thus may

FIGURE 4.4 Mutual-Fund Yardsticks

Mutual Fund Yardsticks

Wednesday, August 01, 2007

Mutual-fund categories and their benchmarks ranked by one-year total return. Yardsticks are based on categories compiled by The Wall Street Journal, based on Lipper, Inc. fund investment objectives. Performance for Yardsticks is based on an arithmetic average of all the mutual funds in the category.

	DAILY		TOTAL RETURN (%)				
						Annualized	
Investment Objective	Chg	% Chg	4-wk	YTD	1-yr	3-yr	5-yr
Science & Technology	0.04	0.25	-2.23	10.34	30.31	13.76	16.36
European Region	-0.08	-0.16	-4.42	9.12	27.35	25.95	22.60
International	-0.15	-0.53	-3.58	9.06	24.95	23.00	19.83
Mid-Cap Growth Funds	unch.	0.01	-3.55	10.65	23.40	15.28	15.00
Dow Jones Ind Dly Reinv	248.53	1.15	-1.49	8.52	22.88	12.13	11.95
Utility	0.41	1.52	-3.83	9.46	22.76	22.42	20.02
Global Funds	-0.06	-0.19	-3.60	7.69	22.31	18.42	16.93
Multi-Cap Growth Funds	0.05	0.32	-2.83	8.33	21.82	13.40	13.90
Small-Cap Growth Funds	-0.02	-0.14	-5.53	6.50	20.53	13.30	14.87
Large-Cap Growth Funds	0.11	0.51	-2.40	6.58	19.02	9.88	9.78
Mid-Cap Core Funds	0.05	0.15	-5.59	6.79	18.95	14.88	15.57
Mid-Cap Value Funds	0.04	0.21	-6.56	5.21	18.67	15.64	17.33
S & P 500 Daily Reinv	16.55	0.73	-3.79	4.40	17.51	12.01	12.65
Multi-Cap Core Funds	0.08	0.29	-4.23	4.74	17.32	12.50	12.87
Large-Cap Core Funds	0.16	0.59	-3.84	4.26	16.86	11.05	11.17
Vanguard Small Co. index	0.05	0.15	-7.13	3.05	16.65	14.80	17.21
Equity Income	0.23	0.56	-4.42	4.14	15.62	13.42	13.11
Multi-Cap Value Funds	0.10	0.34	-5.63	3.05	15.50	13.25	14.05
Large-Cap Value Funds	0.27	0.54	-4.91	3.39	15.15	12.84	13.12
Small-Cap Core Funds	0.01	0.05	-7.33	1.96	15.05	13.53	15.93
Stock & Bond Funds	unch.	0.06	-2.97	4.64	14.97	10.78	11.58
Small-Cap Value Funds	0.01	0.04	-8.29	0.53	13.80	13.20	16.14
Balanced	0.04	0.17	-2.37	3.20	11.54	8.89	9.50
Health & Biotechnology	0.07	0.38	-3.50	2.70	8.77	9.01	10.97
General Taxable Bond	-0.01	-0.11	-1.07	1.15	5.91	5.70	7.90
High Yield Taxable Bond	-0.03	-0.34	-3.54	-0.67	5.45	6.22	9.89
Long Term Investment Grade Corporate Bond	unch.	-0.01	0.33	1.02	4.90	3.61	4.86
Lipper L-T Govt Bond Index	-0.17	-0.04	1.04	1.57	4.72	3.34	3.29
Intmdt Investment Grade Corporate Bond	unch.	0.01	0.52	1.14	4.72	3.38	4.06
Long Term US Treasury/Govt Bond	unch.	-0.01	1.30	1.32	4.68	3.14	3.28
Mortgage	unch.	0.05	0.62	1.38	4.56	3.24	3.12
Short Term Investment Grade Corp Bond	unch.	-0.02	0.38	2.14	4.55	3.02	3.05
Intermediate Term US Treasury/Govt Bond	-0.01	-0.08	1.60	2.64	4.03	3.21	3.53
Single State Municipal Debt	-0.01	-0.05	0.48	0.37	3.40	3.73	3.79
General Municipal Debt	-0.01	-0.06	0.39	0.25	3.33	3.80	3.85
Intermediate Term Municipal Debt	unch.	-0.01	0.62	0.62	3.09	2.69	2.96

Source: Lipper

Source: www.wsj.com, August 1, 2007. Reprinted by permission of *The Wall Street Journal*. © 2007 Dow Jones & Company, Inc. All Rights Reserved Worldwide.

Figure 4.5 is a small section of the mutual fund price quotations regularly reported by *The Wall Street Journal* online. All of the funds listed in Figure 4.5 belong to the very large family of funds managed by Fidelity Investments. We highlighted the Blue Chip Growth Fund (abbreviated BluCh). As its name suggests, the Blue Chip Fund has a large-cap focus.[6]

[6] A blue chip stock is a well-established, profitable, very-well regarded company. A good example might be GE. The term "blue chip" refers to the game of poker, in which chips are used for betting. The blue chips are the most valuable.

FIGURE 4.5 Mutual Funds: Closing Quotes

Mutual Funds: Closing Quotes

F

GO TO: A | B | C | D | E | G | H | I | J | K | L | M | N | O | P | Q | R | S | T | U | V | W | X | Y | Z

Wednesday, August 01, 2007

Alphabetical listing by fund family.

Family/ Fund	Symbol	NAV	Chg	YTD % return	3-yr % chg
Fidelity Invest					
100Index	FOHIX	10.37	-0.24	NS	NS
AggrGr r	FDEGX	21.43	-0.52	10.6	13.4
AggrInt	FIVFX	17.33	-0.28	3.6	17.3
AMgr20%	FASIX	12.68	-0.04	2.5	7.3
AMgr50%	FASMX	16.37	-0.17	3.0	7.2
AMgr70%	FASGX	16.79	-0.26	3.3	8.2
AMgr85%	FAMRX	13.85	-0.27	3.7	12.4
AZMun	FSAZX	11.05	0.03	-0.7	2.8
Balanc	FBALX	20.18	-0.34	4.8	12.8
BluCh	FBGRX	46.08	-1.08	4.0	7.4
BlueChipVal	FBCVX	15.10	-0.42	2.0	13.3
CAMun	FCTFX	11.95	0.03	-0.5	3.4
CAShITxFr t	FCSTX	10.00	0.01	1.6	NS
Canad r	FICDX	56.45	-1.43	17.0	28.1
CapAp	FDCAX	28.07	-0.74	3.5	12.5
CapDevA p	FDTTX	13.06	-0.29	5.5	10.8
CapDevO	FDETX	13.36	-0.29	5.8	11.4
ChinaReg	FHKCX	29.64	-0.92	20.9	26.5
CpInc r	FAGIX	8.69	-0.05	1.5	9.7
CngS	CNGRX	479.00	-9.54	5.0	10.5
Contra	FCNTX	68.84	-1.56	6.6	16.2

Source: www.wsj.com, August 1, 2007. Reprinted by permission of *The Wall Street Journal*.

The first piece of information given is the fund's symbol, FBGRX. Following the symbol is the latest net asset value, NAV, for the fund. Following the NAV are three performance measures. The first number is the daily change in the fund's NAV. In this case, the NAV of the Blue Chip Growth Fund fell $1.08 from the previous day's level. Next we have the year-to-date (YTD) return, 4.0 percent. The last column is the three-year annualized return for this fund, 7.4 percent. An "NS" in this column just means that the fund did not exist at the start of the period.

INVESTMENT UPDATES

TO CLOSE OR NOT TO CLOSE A FUND?

Turning Away Potential Investors Can Help Performance, But Letting Everyone In Could Boost Profits

"Go away" isn't what you want to hear from a company with which you'd like to do business.

But in the case of mutual-fund managers who are turning away potential investors in their funds, that message may be a signal to consider a firm's other offerings or watch for future reopenings.

Closing funds to prospective buyers can be a good thing for existing investors, fund researchers and financial advisers say, because performance can slip when funds grow so large that managers have trouble executing their strategies. Fund-management companies, however, have a financial incentive to keep the doors open even as portfolios swell: Their fees are figured as a percentage of those growing assets.

"Closing funds is one of the better indicators that a fund company is putting fund investors' long-term interests ahead of its own short-term profit goals," says Russel Kinnel, director of fund research at Morningstar Inc. in Chicago.

Turning away new investors is particularly critical with small-stock funds—since the limited supply of shares in small companies limits the dollars a manager can invest in a single stock. Some managers who invest in the tiniest stocks close their portfolios to new investors at $50 million or $100 million. When funds choose not to close, the managers usually end up buying a larger number of stocks or buying more and more larger stocks, thus changing the fund's profile.

Fund managers say there are no hard and fast rules about when to close; that depends on factors including whether the managers tend to trade frequently and how much money they are running outside of a particular mutual fund but in the same style.

A number of highly regarded fund families currently have at least half of their portfolios closed to most new investors. The largest such groups in total fund assets: Dodge & Cox, Artisan, Longleaf Partners, Third Avenue, and Hotchkis & Wiley. The fund managers generally say the closed funds are approaching capacity for their style or that they aren't finding sufficient opportunities to put new cash to work. (Some "closed" funds remain open to certain retirement-plan participants or to clients of financial planners who have relationships with the funds.)

"We manage money for the benefit of our existing clients," says Ken Olivier, a spokesman for Dodge & Cox, which closed two of its four funds to new investors last year. The San Francisco firm doesn't feel its Dodge & Cox Stock Fund and Dodge & Cox Balanced Fund are too large, at $46.3 billion and $22.5 billion, respectively, but wanted to slow the flow of new money to avoid realizing too late that that point had been reached. There are no current plans to reopen, Mr. Olivier says.

Dodge & Cox and other large firms with numerous closed funds are generally companies that are "focused on a few defined approaches to investing and not on being an asset-gathering operation," notes Tim Medley, a financial adviser in Jackson, Mississippi. Most of the firms are also privately owned. In contrast, "publicly owned management firms may have a quarterly earnings agenda" that makes them more reluctant to turn off the spigot of new investor cash, Mr. Medley says.

A willingness of fund managers to close portfolios before they become too bloated is one factor Morningstar

If you click on "BluCh," a screen appears with detailed performance measures. Figure 4.6 shows part of this screen. You can see in Figure 4.6 that this fund falls into the category of "Large-Cap Growth." Below the fund category, you can see a series of performance measures. The first number is the year-to-date return, 3.99 percent (which was rounded to 4.0 percent in Figure 4.5). Next we have annualized returns for the previous 1, 3, 5, and 10 years. Thus, the Blue Chip Fund averaged 4.09 percent per year over the previous 10 years. This return slightly exceeds the large-cap growth category but falls quite a bit short of the S&P 500 Index.

At the bottom of Figure 4.6, you see a letter grade assigned to each of the 1-, 3-, 5-, and 10-year returns. A grade of "A" means that the fund's return is in the top 20 percent of all funds in the same category. A grade of "B" means the next 20 percent, and so on. Notice that the grades are strictly relative, so mutual funds, in effect, are graded on the curve!

HOW USEFUL ARE FUND PERFORMANCE RATINGS?

If you look at the performance ratings reported in Figure 4.6, you might wonder why anyone would buy a fund in a category other than those with the highest returns. Well, the lessons learned in Chapter 1 suggest the answer is these historical returns do not consider the riskiness considers in assigning what it calls stewardship ratings that are intended to reflect how well a fund serves shareholders. At the 10 largest fund firms with at least half of their funds closed to new investors, all the funds that have been assigned those relatively new ratings are rated A or B on the A-to-F scale.

Morningstar has often criticized fund firms, including the nation's largest, for not closing funds as promptly as it believes they should. Mr. Kinnel points to Fidelity Magellan Fund and Fidelity Low-Priced Stock Fund, currently with $53.9 billion and $37.3 billion, respectively, in assets, as "good examples of funds that should have closed much sooner" than they did.

He names $53.4 billion Fidelity Contrafund and American Funds' $111 billion Growth Fund of America as two funds that are still delivering great performance but that he believes should close because ballooning assets are a growing handicap.

Fidelity Investments spokesman John Brockelman says the firm has "closed quite a number of funds" over the years, based on what is appropriate for each fund. "The decision of when to close is not a marketing decision. It is not a decision that is based on Fidelity's bottom line. It is a decision on what is in the best long-term interests of our shareholders," he says.

At American Funds, spokesman Chuck Freadhoff says closing Growth Fund is something that the firm looks at but "at this point, we don't see that shareholders are being disadvantaged by the size of the fund." The fund's portfolio is divided into portions that are managed independently by eight individual managers and a team of analysts.

Closing a fund is no guarantee of stellar future performance, of course. And while many funds close after a great run, others do so after less-thrilling results. A case in point: Tweedy, Browne Global Value Fund and Tweedy, Browne American Value Fund, which closed to new investors in May. The funds, with $7.2 billion and $628 million, respectively, in assets, rank in the bottom 10 percent of their Morningstar peer groups for the past three and five years.

In closing the funds, Tweedy cited a shortage of attractive investment opportunities and a desire not to dilute the existing investors' stakes in portfolio holdings. In a mid-July update to fund investors, the managers said cash positions in the funds are rising because "bargains remain scarce around the globe" and the managers are doing more selling than buying. Cash reserves at mid-year were about 21 percent of assets in the global fund and 18 percent in the U.S.-stock fund.

Tweedy officials could not be reached for comment.

While small-stock funds have always been among those most apt to close, such closures are particularly common these days, after several years in which small stocks have gained more than large ones. Seven of 11 funds are closed at small-stock specialist Wasatch Funds, for example, and six of those even bar new investments from existing shareholders. Wasatch Micro Cap Fund, now closed for the third time since its 1995 launch, had the best return among stock funds for the 10 years through August—up an average of 24.15 percent a year, according to Morningstar.

The firm has a policy of closing its small-stock funds at small sizes and "we will take what some may consider drastic measures to maintain that performance," says Eric Johnson, director of mutual funds.

Source: Karen Damato, *The Wall Street Journal*, September 9, 2005.

of the various fund categories. For example, if the market has done well, the best ranked funds may simply be the riskiest funds, since the riskiest funds normally perform the best in a rising market. In a market downturn, however, these best ranked funds are most likely to become the worst ranked funds, since the riskiest funds normally perform the worst in a falling market.

These problems with performance measures deal with the evaluation of historical performance. However, there is an even more fundamental criterion. Ultimately, we don't care about historical performance; we care about *future* performance. Whether historical performance is useful in predicting future performance is the subject of ongoing debate. However, one thing we can say is that some of the poorest-performing funds are those with very high costs. These costs act as a constant drag on performance, and such funds tend to have persistently poorer returns than otherwise similar funds.

CLOSED FUNDS

Sometimes, an open-end fund will choose to close, meaning that the fund will no longer sell shares to new investors. The use of the word "close" here should not be confused with "closed-end," because the number of shares can still fluctuate as existing owners buy and

FIGURE 4.6 Detailed Performance Measures

FIDELITY SECURITIES FUND: FIDELITY BLUE CHIP GROWTH FUND FBGRX

As of 8/28/07	1-Day Net Change	1-Day Return	YTD Total Return	Category
NAV: 46.08	▼ -1.08	▼ -2.29%	▲ 3.99%	Large-Cap Growth

LIPPER LEADER SCORECARD

TOTAL RETURN	CONSISTENT RETURN	PRESERVATION	TAX EFFICIENCY	EXPENSE
4	5	3	4	✓ (Leader)

LIPPER LEADER SCORECARD KEY: HIGHEST ✓ 2 3 4 5 LOWEST

More on Lipper Leaders

TOTAL RETURNS (%) 3, 5 and 10 year returns are annualized.

	YTD	1Yr	3Yr	5Yr	10Yr
Fund	**3.99**	11.67	7.36	7.78	4.09
Category	**4.32**	13.54	9.05	8.59	4.07
Index (S&P 500)	**2.20**	12.10	11.00	11.30	6.40
% Rank in Category	**55**	72	78	69	50
Quintile Rank	C	D	D	D	C

Source: www.wsj.com, August 1, 2007. Reprinted by permission of *The Wall Street Journal*. © 2007 Dow Jones & Company, Inc. All Rights Reserved Worldwide.

sell. Why would a fund choose to close? It usually happens when a fund grows so rapidly (due to good past performance) that the fund manager feels that the incoming cash is more than the fund can invest profitably. When this occurs, the fund in question is usually a small-cap fund, but large-cap funds have also closed on occasion. Funds that close often reopen at a later date. A nearby *Investment Updates* box has more on the issues surrounding closed funds.

CHECK THIS

4.7a Which mutual fund in Figure 4.5 had the best year-to-date return? The worst?

4.7b What are some of the problems with comparing historical performance numbers?

4.8 Closed-End Funds, Exchange-Traded Funds, and Hedge Funds

It is probably fitting that we close our mutual fund chapter with a discussion of closed-end funds and exchange-traded funds. As we will see, such funds have some unusual aspects.

CLOSED-END FUNDS PERFORMANCE INFORMATION

As we described earlier, the major difference between a closed-end fund and an open-end fund is that closed-end funds don't buy and sell shares. Instead, there is a fixed number of shares in the fund, and these shares are bought and sold on the open market. About 600 closed-end funds have their shares traded on U.S. stock exchanges, which is far fewer than the roughly 8,000 long-term, open-end mutual funds available to investors.

Figure 4.7 shows some quotes for a particular type of closed-end fund, "World Equity Funds." As the name suggests, these funds generally invest outside the United States, and they are a relatively common type (single-state municipal funds are the most common). The entry for the single-country China Fund is highlighted.

D. Investment advisory firms create mutual funds simply because they wish to manage them to earn fees. A typical management fee might be .75 percent of the total assets in the fund per year. A fund with $200 million in assets would not be especially large but could nonetheless generate management fees of about $1.5 million per year.

3. How to find information about mutual fund performance.

A. Funds have very different objectives and, as a result, very different risk and return potentials. Furthermore, funds with similar-sounding objectives can, in fact, be quite different. It is important to consider a fund's actual holdings and investment policies, not just read its stated objective.

B. Mutual fund information is widely available, but performance information should be used with caution. The best performing funds are often the ones with the greatest risks or the ones that just happened to be in the right investment at the right time.

4. The workings of Exchange-Traded Funds.

A. An Exchange-Traded Fund (ETF) is basically an index fund that seeks to achieve the same return as a particular market index. Therefore, when you buy an ETF, it is as if you are buying the basket of stocks that make up the index.

B. The most popular ETFs represent well-known indexes like the S&P 500, the NASDAQ 100, or the Dow Jones Industrial Average.

C. Many more specialized ETFs exist. For example, with an ETF, you can get a small piece of many small-cap stocks or mid-cap stocks, or you can invest in country-specific funds or in real estate.

GET REAL

This chapter covered the essentials of mutual funds. How should you, as an investor or investment manager, put this information to work?

The first thing to do is to start looking at mutual fund prospectuses. These are written to be accessible to novice investors (or, at least, they are *supposed* to be written that way). The best way to begin exploring is to visit Web sites. Almost any large mutual fund company will have extensive online information available. Links to some of the better known families are available at our Web page. It is important to look at different funds within a given family and also to look across families. Compare growth funds to growth funds, for example. This adventure will give you some of the real-life background you need to select the types of funds most suitable for you or someone else.

Once you have examined prospectuses on different funds, it's time to invest. Beginning with your simulated account, pick a few funds, invest, and observe the outcomes. Open-end mutual funds are probably the place most of you will begin investing real dollars. An initial purchase can be made with a relatively small amount, perhaps $500, and subsequent purchases can be made in amounts of as little as $100 or less.

Most important of all, as we discussed to start the chapter, most employers now provide employees with retirement plans. The way these work is that, typically, your employer will make a contribution to a mutual fund you select (often from a fairly limited set). Your employer may even match, or more than match, a contribution you make. Such plans may be the only retirement benefit offered, but they can be an extraordinary opportunity for those who take full advantage of them by getting the largest possible match and then investing in a suitable fund. It's an important choice, so the more knowledge you have regarding mutual funds, the better your outcome is likely to be.

Key Terms

12b-1 fees 102
closed-end fund 98
front-end load 102
hedge fund 123
investment company 98
money market mutual fund 105
net asset value 99
open-end fund 98
turnover 103

Chapter Review Problems and Self-Test

1. **Front-End Loads** The Madura HiGro Fund has a net asset value of $50 per share. It charges a 3 percent load. How much will you pay for 100 shares?
2. **Turnover** The Starks Income Fund's average daily total assets were $100 million for the year just completed. Its stock purchases for the year were $20 million, while its sales were $12.5 million. What was its turnover?

Answers to Self-Test Problems

1. You will pay 100 times the offering price. Since the load is computed as a percentage of the offering price, we can compute the offering price as follows:

   $$\text{Net asset value} = (1 - \text{Front-end load}) \times \text{Offering price}$$

   In other words, the NAV is 97 percent of the offering price. Since the NAV is $50, the offering price is $50/.97 = $51.55. You will pay $5,155 in all, of which $155 is a load.
2. Turnover is the lesser of purchases or sales divided by average daily assets. In this case, sales are smaller at $12.5, so turnover is $12.5/$100 = .125 times.

Test Your Investment Quotient

www.mhhe.com/jm5e

IQ

CFA® PROBLEMS

For the remaining questions and problems, the circled numbers in the margin refer to the corresponding learning objective in this chapter.

(2) 1. **Investment Companies** Which of the following statements typically does not characterize the structure of an investment company?
   - **a.** An investment company adopts a corporate form of organization.
   - **b.** An investment company invests a pool of funds belonging to many investors in a portfolio of individual investments.
   - **c.** An investment company receives an annual management fee ranging from 3 to 5 percent of the total value of the fund.
   - **d.** The board of directors of an investment company hires a separate investment management company to manage the portfolio of securities and handle other administrative duties.

(3) 2. **Expense Statement** Which of the following is *not* part of the expense statement?
   - **a.** Shareholder transactions expenses
   - **b.** Shareholder demographic profile
   - **c.** Annual operating expenses
   - **d.** A hypothetical example of expenses

(2) 3. **Mutual Fund Investing** Which of the following is the least likely advantage of mutual fund investing?
   - **a.** Diversification
   - **b.** Professional management
   - **c.** Convenience
   - **d.** Mutual fund returns are normally higher than market average returns

(2) 4. **Open-End Funds** An open-end mutual fund is owned by which of the following?
   - **a.** An investment company
   - **b.** An investment advisory firm
   - **c.** A "family of funds" mutual fund company
   - **d.** Its shareholders

(2) 5. **Closed-End Funds** Which of the following is most true of a closed-end investment company?

a. The fund's share price is usually greater than net asset value.
b. The fund's share price is set equal to net asset value.
c. Fund shares outstanding vary with purchases and redemptions by shareholders.
d. Fund shares outstanding are fixed at the issue date.

(2) 6. **Closed-End Funds** A closed-end fund is owned by which of the following?

a. An investment company
b. An investment advisory firm
c. A "family of funds" mutual fund company
d. Its shareholders

7. **Investment Advisory Firms** Which of the following is not true about the typical relationship between a mutual fund and an investment advisory firm? The investment advisory firm

a. Owns the mutual fund.
b. Manages the mutual fund's assets.
c. Manages shareholder purchase and redemption operations.
d. Receives a management fee for services rendered.

(1) 8. **Fund Types** Which mutual fund type is most likely to own stocks paying the highest dividend yields?

a. Capital appreciation fund
b. Equity income fund
c. Growth and income fund
d. Growth fund

(1) 9. **Fund Types** Which mutual fund type is most likely to own stocks paying the lowest dividend yields?

a. Capital appreciation fund
b. Equity income fund
c. Growth and income fund
d. Growth fund

(1) 10. **Fund Types** Which mutual fund type will most likely incur the greatest tax liability for its investors?

a. Index fund
b. Municipal bond fund
c. Income fund
d. Growth fund

(1) 11. **Fund Types** Which mutual fund type will most likely incur the smallest tax liability for its investors?

a. Index fund
b. Municipal bond fund
c. Income fund
d. Growth fund

(1) 12. **Fund Types** Which mutual fund type will most likely incur the greatest overall risk levels for its investors?

a. Large-cap index fund
b. Insured municipal bond fund
c. Money market mutual fund
d. Small-cap growth fund

(2) 13. **Mutual Fund Fees** Which of the following mutual fund fees is assessed on an annual basis?

a. 12b-1 fees
b. Front-end load
c. Back-end load
d. Contingent deferred sales charge (CDSC)

(2) 14. **Mutual Fund Fees** Which of the following mutual fund fees will most likely be the biggest expense for a long-term fund investor?

a. 12b-1 fees
b. Front-end load

c. Back-end load
d. Contingent deferred sales charge (CDSC)

(2) 15. **Mutual Fund Fees** Which of the following mutual fund fees and expenses is the most difficult for investors to assess?

a. Sales charges or "loads"
b. 12b-1 fees
c. Management fees
d. Trading costs

Concept Questions

(2) 1. **Fund Ownership** Who actually owns a mutual fund? Who runs it?

(2) 2. **Loads** Given that no-load funds are widely available, why would a rational investor pay a front-end load? More generally, why don't fund investors always seek out funds with the lowest loads, management fees, and other fees?

(2) 3. **Money Market Funds** Is it true that the NAV of a money market mutual fund never changes? How is this possible?

(2) 4. **Money Market Deposit Accounts** What is the difference between a money market deposit account and a money market mutual fund? Which is riskier?

(2) 5. **Front-End Loads** You are interested in investing in a mutual fund that charges a front-end load of 5 percent. If the length of your investment is one year, would you invest in this fund? Suppose the length of your investment is 20 years? How are the length of your investment and front-end loads related?

(2) 6. **Open versus Closed-End Funds** An open-end mutual fund typically keeps a percentage, often around 5 percent, of its assets in cash or liquid money market assets. How does this affect the fund's return in a year in which the market increases in value? How about during a bad year? Closed-end funds do not typically hold cash. What is it about the structure of open-end and closed-end funds that would influence this difference?

(2) 7. **12b-1 Fees** What are 12b-1 fees? What expenses are 12b-1 fees intended to cover? Many closed-end mutual funds charge a 12b-1 fee. Does this make sense to you? Why or why not?

(2) 8. **Open-versus Closed-End Funds** If you were concerned about the liquidity of mutual funds shares that you held, would you rather hold shares in a closed-end fund or an open-end fund? Why?

(3) 9. **Performance** Refer to Figure 4.5. Look at the 3-year performance for the funds listed. Why do you suppose there are so few poor performers? Hint: Think about the hit TV show *Survivor.*

(2) 10. **Mutual Fund Fees** Suppose you want to invest in a mutual fund and are given the choice of two share classes. Class U shares charge a fee as a percentage of the initial investment upfront. Class B shares charge the same fee, but the fee is taken out of the total assets at the end of the year. Which share class would provide you with the highest total return? Assume the fund makes no distributions prior to the fee assessment at the end of the year.

Questions and Problems

Core Questions

(2) 1. **Net Asset Value** The World Income Appreciation Fund has current assets with a market value of $5.8 billion and has 140 million shares outstanding. What is the net asset value (NAV) for this mutual fund?

(2) 2. **Front-End Loads** Suppose the mutual fund in the previous problem has a current market price quotation of $42.28. Is this a load fund? If so, calculate the front-end load.

(2) 3. **Calculating NAV** The Emerging Growth and Equity Fund is a "low-load" fund. The current offer price quotation for this mutual fund is $27.52, and the front-end load is 1.5 percent. What is the NAV? If there are 15.6 million shares outstanding, what is the current market value of assets owned by the fund?

(2) 4. **Money Market Funds** The Aqua Liquid Assets Money Market Mutual Fund has a NAV of \$1 per share. During the year, the assets held by this fund appreciated by 5.2 percent. If you had invested \$20,000 in this fund at the start of the year, how many shares would you own at the end of the year? What will the NAV of this fund be at the end of the year? Why?

(2) 5. **NAV** An open-end mutual fund has the following stocks:

Stock	Shares	Stock Price
A	9,000	\$68
B	13,000	39
C	8,600	49
D	12,500	82

If there are 50,000 shares of the market fund, what is the NAV?

(2) 6. **NAV** Suppose the fund in the previous problem has liabilities of \$110,000. What is the NAV of the fund now?

(2) 7. **Front-End Load** In the previous problem, assume the fund is sold with a 5 percent front-end load. What is the offering price of the fund?

(2) 8. **Turnover** A mutual fund sold \$63 million of assets during the year and purchased \$57 million in assets. If the average daily assets of the fund was \$130 million, what was the fund turnover?

(2) 9. **Closed-End Funds** A closed-end fund has total assets of \$420 million and liabilities of \$800,000. Currently, 19 million shares are outstanding. What is the NAV of the fund? If the shares currently sell for \$18.37, what is the premium or discount on the fund?

(2) 10. **Mutual Fund Returns** You invested \$10,000 in a mutual fund at the beginning of the year when the NAV was \$34.87. At the end of the year the fund paid \$.39 in short-term distributions and \$.98 in long-term distributions. If the NAV of the fund at the end of the year was \$38.21, what was your return for the year?

Intermediate Questions

(2) 11. **Calculating Turnover** A sector fund specializing in commercial bank stocks had average daily assets of \$3.4 billion during the year. This fund sold \$1.25 billion worth of stock during the year, and its turnover ratio was .42. How much stock did this mutual fund purchase during the year?

(2) 12. **Calculating Fees** In the previous problem, suppose the annual operating expense ratio for the mutual fund is 1.25 percent, and the management fee is .85 percent. How much money did the fund's management earn during the year? If the fund doesn't charge any 12b-1 fees, how much were miscellaneous and administrative expenses during the year?

(2) 13. **Calculating Fees** You purchased 2,000 shares in the New Pacific Growth Fund on January 2, 2008, at an offering price of \$53.82 per share. The front-end load for this fund is 5 percent, and the back-end load for redemptions within one year is 2 percent. The underlying assets in this mutual fund appreciate (including reinvested dividends) by 12 percent during 2008, and you sell back your shares at the end of the year. If the operating expense ratio for the New Pacific Growth Fund is 1.95 percent, what is your total return from this investment? What do you conclude about the impact of fees in evaluating mutual fund performance?

(2) 14. **Calculating Fees** Suppose in the previous problem that the mutual fund has no front-end load or back-end load. Further suppose that the operating expense ratio for the fund is .95 percent. What is your return on investment now?

(2) 15. **Front-End Loads and Returns** You are considering an investment in a mutual fund with a 5.5 percent front-end load. Assuming the fund return is 11 percent per year, what is your return in 1 year? 2 years? 5 years? 10 years? 20 years? 30 years? Graph and explain your answers.

(2) 16. **Expenses and Returns** The Bruin Stock Fund sells Class A shares that have a front-end load of 5.75 percent, a 12b-1 fee of .23 percent, and other fees of .73 percent. There are also Class B shares with a 5 percent CDSC that declines 1 percent per year, a 12b-1 fee of 1.00 percent, and other fees of .73 percent. If the portfolio return is 12 percent per year and you plan to sell after the third year, should you invest in Class A or Class B shares? What if your investment horizon is 20 years?

2 **17. Expenses and Returns** You are going to invest in a stock mutual fund with a 5 percent front-end load and a 1.30 percent expense ratio. You also can invest in a money market mutual fund with a 5.2 percent return and an expense ratio of .20 percent. If you plan to keep your investment for two years, what annual return must the stock mutual fund earn to exceed an investment in the money market fund? What if your investment horizon is 10 years?

2 **18. Taxes and MMMFs** Suppose you're evaluating three alternative MMMF investments. The first fund buys a diversified portfolio of municipal securities from across the country and yields 4.1 percent. The second fund buys only taxable, short-term commercial paper and yields 6.5 percent. The third fund specializes in the municipal debt from the state of New Jersey and yields 3.8 percent. If you are a New Jersey resident, your federal tax bracket is 35 percent, and your state tax bracket is 8 percent, which of these three MMMFs offers you the highest aftertax yield?

2 **19. Taxes and MMMFs** In the previous problem, which MMMF offers you the highest yield if you are a resident of Texas, which has no state income tax?

2 **20. Closed-End Funds** The Argentina Fund has $410 million in assets and sells at a 13.1 percent discount to NAV. If the quoted share price for this closed-end fund is $18.43, how many shares are outstanding? If you purchase 1,000 shares of this fund, what will the total shares outstanding be now?

2 **21. Closed-End Fund Discounts** Suppose you purchase 5,000 shares of a closed-end mutual fund at its initial public offering; the offer price is $28 per share. The offering prospectus discloses that the fund promoter gets an 8 percent fee from the offering. If this fund sells at a 12 percent discount to NAV the day after the initial public offering, what is the value of your investment?

What's on the Web?

1. **Bond Funds** One of the best Internet sites for information on mutual funds is www.morningstar.com. Go to the Web site and find the ticker symbol for the Harbor Bond Fund. Find all of the following information on the Web site for this fund: loads, expense ratio, top five holdings, bond quality ratings, the fund's rank in its category for the last seven years, and the Morningstar rating. Next, find out how the Morningstar star ranking system works.
2. **Stock Funds** Go to www.morningstar.com and find the ticker symbol for a domestic stock fund. Enter the ticker symbol and find the following information for the fund: manager and manager start date, year-to-date return, three-year return, five-year return, front-end or back-end loads, actual and maximum 12b-1 fees, management fees, expense ratio, the top 25 holdings, and the fund address and phone number.
3. **Morningstar Fund Selector** Find the Mutual Fund Screener on the Morningstar Web site. How many funds fit the following criteria: domestic stock fund, minimum initial purchase equal to or less than $500, expense ratio less than or equal to category average, and turnover less than 75 percent?
4. **ETFs** Go to www.amex.com. Once there, find out the advantages Amex lists for individuals buying ETFs. Now, find out how many ETFs AMEX lists. How many ETFs are international? What are Diamonds, Spiders, and Cubes (QQQQ)? What do each of these three invest in?

Stock-Trak Exercises

STOCK | TRAK
GLOBAL PORTFOLIO SIMULATIONS

To access the Stock-Trak Exercise for this chapter, please visit the book Web site at www.mhhe.com/jm5e and choose the corresponding chapter.

Part 2

CHAPTER 5

The Stock Market

"One of the funny things about the stock market is that every time one man buys, another sells, and both think they are astute."

–William Feather

"If you don't know who you are, the stock market is an expensive place to find out."

–Adam Smith (pseud. for George J. W. Goodman)

Learning Objectives

Take stock in yourself. Make sure you have a good understanding of:

1. The difference between primary and secondary stock markets.
2. The workings of the New York Stock Exchange.
3. How NASDAQ operates.
4. How to calculate index returns.

On May 17, 1792, a group of commodity brokers met and signed the now famous Buttonwood Tree Agreement, thereby establishing the forerunner of what soon became the New York Stock Exchange. On April 4, 2007, the NYSE and Euronext completed their merger. The new company, known as NYSE Euronext, operates large and liquid stock exchanges in Amsterdam, Brussels, Paris, New York, and other world cities. The NYSE is the world's best known stock exchange. It's big, too. On a typical day in 2007, trading volume at the NYSE is well over 2 billion shares. Established in 1971, and now famous as an arena for "tech" stock investing, daily trading volume at the NASDAQ is also about 2 billion shares. Together, the NYSE and NASDAQ account for the vast majority of stock trading in the United States. ■

With this chapter, we begin in earnest our study of stock markets. This chapter presents a "big picture" overview of how a stock market works and how to read and understand stock market information reported in the financial press.

5.1 Private Equity Versus Selling Securities to the Public

PRIVATE EQUITY

The broad term *private equity* is often used to label the rapidly growing area of equity financing for nonpublic companies. For example, one day, you and a friend have a great idea for a new computer software product that helps users communicate using the next generation Meganet. Filled with entrepreneurial zeal, you christen the product MegaComm and set about bringing it to market.

Working nights and weekends, you are able to create a prototype of your product. It doesn't actually work, but at least you can show it around to illustrate your idea. To develop a working product, you need to hire programmers, buy computers, rent office space, and so on. Unfortunately, because you are both college students, your combined assets are not sufficient to fund a pizza party, much less a start-up company. You need what is often referred to as OPM—other people's money.

Your first thought might be to approach a bank for a loan. You would probably discover, however, that banks are generally not interested in making loans to start-up companies with no assets (other than an idea) run by fledgling entrepreneurs with no track record. Instead, your search for capital would very likely lead you to the **venture capital (VC)** market, an important part of the private equity market.

venture capital (VC)
Financing for new, often high-risk ventures.

VENTURE CAPITAL

The term *venture capital* does not have a precise meaning, but it generally refers to financing for new, often high-risk ventures. For example, before it went public, Internet auctioneer eBay was venture capital financed. Individual venture capitalists invest their own money, whereas venture capital firms specialize in pooling funds from various sources and investing them. The underlying sources of funds for such firms include individuals, pension funds, insurance companies, large corporations, and even university endowment funds.

WWW

For a list of well-known VC firms, see www.vfinance.com.

Venture capitalists and venture capital firms recognize that many or even most new ventures will not fly, but the occasional one will. The potential profits are enormous in such cases. To limit their risk, venture capitalists generally provide financing in stages. At each stage, enough money is invested to reach the next milestone or planning stage. For example, the *first-stage* (or first "round") *financing* might be enough to get a prototype built and a manufacturing plan completed. Based on the results, the *second-stage financing* might be a major investment needed to actually begin manufacturing, marketing, and distribution. There might be many such stages, each of which represents a key step in the process of growing the company.

Venture capital firms often specialize in different stages. Some specialize in very early "seed money," or ground floor, financing. In contrast, financing in the later stages might come from venture capitalists specializing in so-called mezzanine level financing, where *mezzanine level* refers to the level just above the ground floor.

WWW

The Internet is a tremendous source of venture capital information, both for suppliers and demanders of capital. For example, see www.nvca.org

The fact that financing is available in stages and is contingent on specified goals being met is a powerful motivating force for the firm's founders. Often, the founders receive relatively little in the way of salary and have substantial portions of their personal assets tied up in the business. At each stage of financing, the value of the founder's stake grows and the probability of success rises. If goals are not met, the venture capitalist will withhold further financing, thereby limiting future losses.

In addition to providing financing, venture capitalists generally will actively participate in running the firm, providing the benefit of experience with previous start-ups as well as general business expertise. This is especially true when the firm's founders have little or no hands-on experience in running a company.

If a start-up succeeds, the big payoff frequently comes when the company is sold to another company or goes public. Either way, investment bankers are often involved in the process.

SELLING SECURITIES TO THE PUBLIC

primary market
The market in which new securities are originally sold to investors.

secondary market
The market in which previously issued securities trade among investors.

When we talk about the *stock market,* we are talking about securities that have been sold to the public. The stock market consists of a **primary market** and a **secondary market**. In the primary, or new-issue market, shares of stock are first brought to the market and sold to investors. In the secondary market, existing shares are traded among investors.

In the primary market, companies issue new securities to raise money. In the secondary market, investors are constantly appraising the values of companies by buying and selling shares previously issued by these companies. We next discuss the operation of the primary market for common stocks, and then we turn our attention to the secondary market for stocks.

THE PRIMARY MARKET FOR COMMON STOCK

initial public offering (IPO)
An initial public offering occurs when a company offers stock for sale to the public for the first time.

seasoned equity offering (SEO)
The sale of additional shares of stock by a company whose shares are already publicly traded.

general cash offer
An issue of securities offered for sale to the general public on a cash basis.

rights offer
A public issue of securities in which securities are first offered to existing shareholders (also called a rights offering).

investment banking firm
A firm specializing in arranging financing for companies.

The primary market for common stock is how new securities are first brought to market. It is best known as the market for **initial public offerings (IPOs)**. An IPO occurs when a company offers stock for sale to the public for the first time. Typically, the company is small and growing, and it needs to raise capital for further expansion.

An IPO is sometimes called an *unseasoned equity offering* because shares are not available to the public before the IPO. If a company already has shares owned by the public, it can raise equity with a **seasoned equity offering (SEO)**. The terms *secondary* and *follow-on offering* also refer to an SEO. A seasoned equity offering of common stock can be made using a general cash offer or a rights offer. In a **general cash offer**, securities are offered to the general public on a "first-come, first served" basis. With a **rights offer**, securities are initially offered only to existing owners. Rights offerings are rare in the United States but common in other countries.

Obviously, all initial public offerings are cash offers. To illustrate how an IPO occurs, let's look in on the software company that you started several years ago. Suppose your company was initially set up as a privately held corporation with 100,000 shares of stock, all sold for one dollar per share. The reason your company is privately held is that shares were not offered for sale to the general public. Instead, you bought 50,000 shares for yourself and sold the remaining 50,000 shares to a few supportive friends and relatives (who were taking the role of venture capitalists).

Fortunately, your company has prospered beyond all expectations. However, company growth is now hampered by a lack of capital. At an informal stockholders' meeting, it is agreed to take the company public. Not really knowing how to do this, you consult your accountant, who recommends an **investment banking firm**. An investment banking firm, among other things, specializes in arranging financing for companies by finding investors to buy newly issued securities.

After lengthy negotiations, including an examination of your company's current financial condition and plans for future growth, your investment banker suggests an issue of 4 million shares of common stock. Two million shares will be distributed to the original stockholders (you and your original investors) in exchange for their old shares. These 2 million shares distributed to the original stockholders ensure that effective control of the corporation will remain in their hands.

underwrite
To assume the risk of buying newly issued securities from a company and reselling them to investors.

underwriter spread
Compensation to the underwriter, determined by the difference between the underwriter's buying price and offering price.

syndicate
A group of underwriters formed to share the risk and to help sell an issue.

After much haggling, your investment banker agrees to **underwrite** the stock issue by purchasing the other 2 million shares from your company for $10 per share. The net effect of this transaction is that you have sold half the company to the underwriter for $20 million. The proceeds from the sale will allow your company to construct its own headquarters building and to double its staff of programmers and sales consultants.

Your investment banker will not keep the 2 million shares but instead will resell them in the primary market. She thinks the stock can probably be sold for $12 per share in an IPO. The difference between the $12 the underwriter sells the stock for and the $10 per share you received is called the **underwriter spread**, or discount. It is the basic compensation received by the underwriter. Sometimes the underwriter will get noncash compensation in the form of warrants and stock in addition to the spread.

Underwriters combine to form an underwriting group called a **syndicate** to share the risk and to help sell the issue. In a syndicate, one or more managers arrange the offering. This manager is designated as the lead manager, or principal manager. The lead manager typically has the responsibility of pricing the securities. The other underwriters in the syndicate serve primarily to distribute the issue.

Two basic types of underwriting are involved in a cash offer: firm commitment and best efforts. A third type of underwriting is Dutch auction underwriting.

firm commitment underwriting
The type of underwriting in which the underwriter buys the entire issue, assuming full financial responsibility for any unsold shares.

FIRM COMMITMENT UNDERWRITING In **firm commitment underwriting**, the issuer sells the entire issue to the underwriters, who then attempt to resell it. This is the most prevalent type of underwriting in the United States. This is really just a purchase-resale arrangement, and the underwriter's fee is the spread. For a new issue of seasoned equity, the underwriters can look at the market price to determine what the issue should sell for, and 95 percent of all such new issues are firm commitments.

If the underwriter cannot sell all of the issue at the agreed-upon offering price, it may have to lower the price on the unsold shares. Nonetheless, with firm commitment underwriting, the issuer receives the agreed-upon amount, and all the risk associated with selling the issue is transferred to the underwriter.

Because the offering price usually isn't set until the underwriters have investigated how receptive the market is to the issue, this risk is usually minimal. Also, because the offering price usually is not set until just before selling commences, the issuer doesn't know precisely what its net proceeds will be until that time.

best efforts underwriting
The type of underwriting in which the underwriter sells as much of the issue as possible, but can return any unsold shares to the issuer without financial responsibility.

BEST EFFORTS UNDERWRITING In **best efforts underwriting**, the underwriter is legally bound to use "best efforts" to sell the securities at the agreed-upon offering price. Beyond this, the underwriter does not guarantee any particular amount of money to the issuer. This form of underwriting has become very uncommon in recent years; firm commitments are now the dominant form.

Dutch auction underwriting
The type of underwriting in which the offer price is set based on competitive bidding by investors. Also known as a *uniform price auction.*

DUTCH AUCTION UNDERWRITING With **Dutch auction underwriting**, the underwriter does not set a fixed price for the shares to be sold. Instead, the underwriter conducts an auction in which investors bid for shares. The offer price is determined based on the submitted bids. A Dutch auction is also known by the more descriptive name *uniform price auction.* This approach to selling securities to the public is relatively new in the IPO market and has not been widely used there, but it is very common in the bond markets. For example, it is the sole procedure used by the U.S. Treasury to sell enormous quantities of notes, bonds, and bills to the public.

Dutch auction underwriting was much in the news in 2004 because Web search company Google elected to use this approach. The best way to understand a Dutch or uniform price auction is to consider a simple example. Suppose The Roserita Company wants to sell 400 shares to the public. The company receives five bids as follows:

Bidder	Quantity	Price
A	100 shares	$16
B	100 shares	14
C	200 shares	12
D	100 shares	12
E	200 shares	10

Thus, bidder A is willing to buy 100 shares at $16 each, bidder B is willing to buy 100 shares at $14, and so on. The Roserita Company examines the bids to determine the highest price that will result in all 400 shares being sold. So, for example, at $14, A and B would buy only 200 shares, so that price is too high. Working our way down, all 400 shares won't be sold until we hit a price of $12, so $12 will be the offer price in the IPO. Bidders A through D will receive shares; bidder E will not.

There are two additional important points to observe in our example: First, all the winning bidders will pay $12, even bidders A and B, who actually bid a higher price. The fact that all successful bidders pay the same price is the reason for the name "uniform price auction." The idea in such an auction is to encourage bidders to bid aggressively by providing some protection against bidding a price that is too high.

trades to a maximum of 1,099 shares. With the introduction of the NYSE Hybrid initiative, this restriction was eliminated and market orders and marketable DOT limit orders are now executed using the Direct+ logic.

floor traders
NYSE members who trade for their own accounts, trying to anticipate temporary price fluctuations.

Finally, a small number of NYSE members are **floor traders** who independently trade for their own accounts. Floor traders try to anticipate temporary price fluctuations and profit from them by buying low and selling high. In recent decades, the number of floor traders has declined substantially, suggesting that it has become increasingly difficult to profit from short-term trading on the exchange floor.

THE NYSE HYBRID MARKET

To keep pace with technology advances and innovations in global financial markets, the NYSE has been increasingly building an automated trading platform structure. The NYSE began rolling out phase three of a four-phase plan to initiate Hybrid trading in late 2006.

Hybrid trading combines the exchange's automated technology with the advantages of an auction market. In the Hybrid market, specialists and floor brokers interact with the market electronically as well as in person. This design allows the Hybrid market to offer more choice in how investor orders are executed on the exchange.

The Hybrid trading system has evolved because human judgment provided by the specialist is valuable (1) in less liquid stocks, (2) during the opening and closing of trading sessions, and (3) during times of market duress. In normal times for the average stock, however, the automated platform is an efficient option. Also, the NYSE Hybrid market allows investors to automatically execute up to 1 million shares.

NYSE-LISTED STOCKS

A company is said to be "listed" on the NYSE if its stock is traded there. At the end of December 2006, the total number of companies listed on the NYSE represented a total global market value of approximately $25 trillion. This total includes many large companies so well known that we easily recognize them by their initials—for example, IBM, GE, and GM. This total also includes many companies that are not so readily recognized. For example, relatively few investors would instantly recognize AEP as American Electric Power, but many would recognize AXP as American Express.

U.S. companies that wish to have their stock listed for trading on the Big Board must apply for the privilege. If the application is approved, the company must pay an initial listing fee. In 2006, this fee was $37,500, plus a per-share charge as follows. For the first 75 million shares, $4,800 per million shares. For the next 225 million shares, $3,750 per million shares. For each million shares above 300 million shares, the fee is $1,900. The maximum listing fee is $250,000.

In addition to an initial listing fee, the NYSE assesses an annual listing fee. In 2005, the annual listing fee was $930 per million shares (subject to a $38,000 minimum fee). In 2006, the NYSE filed a proposal with the SEC to eliminate the initial listing fee of any firm transferring from another equities market to the NYSE.

The NYSE has minimum requirements for companies wishing to apply for listing on the Big Board. Although the requirements might change from time to time, some examples of minimum requirements in effect in 2007 for U.S. domestic stocks included:

1. The company must have at least 2,200 shareholders, and average monthly trading volume for the most recent six months must be at least 100,000 shares.
2. At least 1.1 million stock shares must be held in public hands.
3. Publicly held shares must have at least $100 million in market value ($60 million for IPOs).
4. The company must have aggregate earnings of $10 million before taxes in the previous three years and $2 million pretax earnings in each of the preceding two years.

In practice, most companies with stock listed on the NYSE easily exceed these minimum listing requirements. Other listing standards can be found at the NYSE Web site, www.nyse.com, by following the "NYSE Regulation" link.

CHECK THIS

5.2a What are the types of members of the New York Stock Exchange?

5.2b Which NYSE member type is the most numerous? Which type is the second most numerous?

5.2c What is the NYSE Hybrid market?

5.3 Operation of the New York Stock Exchange

Now that we have a basic idea of how the NYSE is organized and who the major players are, we turn to the question of how trading actually takes place. Fundamentally, the business of the NYSE is to attract and process *order flow*—the flow of customer orders to buy and sell stocks. Customers of the NYSE are the millions of individual investors and tens of thousands of institutional investors who place their orders to buy and sell NYSE-listed stock shares with member-firm brokers.

Historically, the NYSE has been quite successful in attracting order flow. For example, in 2007, the average stock trading volume on the NYSE was well over 2 billion shares per day. In recent years, however, volume at the NYSE has decreased in proportion to the volume at the NASDAQ and Electronic Communication Networks (ECNs).

About one-third of all NYSE stock trading volume is attributable to individual investors, and almost half is derived from institutional investors. The remainder represents NYSE member trading, which is largely attributed to specialists acting as market makers.

NYSE FLOOR ACTIVITY

Quite likely you have seen film footage of the NYSE trading floor on television, or you may have visited the NYSE and viewed exchange floor activity from the gallery (when it was open). Either way, you saw a big room, about the size of a small basketball gym. This big room is aptly called "the big room." There are several other, smaller rooms that you normally do not see. Another is called "the garage" because that is what it was before it was taken over for securities trading. Two others were called the "blue room" because, well, the room is painted blue, and the "extended blue room." In November 2007, the NYSE closed the blue room and the extended blue room.

On the floor of the exchange are a number of stations, each with a roughly figure-eight shape. These stations have multiple counters with numerous computer terminal screens above and on the sides. People operate behind and in front of the counters in relatively stationary positions.

Other people move around on the exchange floor, frequently returning to the many telephone booths positioned along the exchange walls. In all, you may have been reminded of worker ants moving around an ant colony. It is natural to wonder: What are all those people doing down there (and why are so many wearing funny-looking coats)?

specialist's post
Fixed place on the exchange floor where the specialist operates.

As an overview of exchange floor activity, here is a quick look at what goes on. Each of the counters at the figure-eight shaped stations is a **specialist's post**. Specialists normally operate in front of their posts to monitor and manage trading in the stocks assigned to them. Clerical employees working for the specialists operate behind the counters. Moving from the many telephone booths out to the exchange floor and back again are swarms of floor brokers, receiving relayed customer orders, walking out to specialist posts where the orders can be executed, and returning to confirm order executions and receive new customer orders.

market order
A customer order to buy or sell securities marked for immediate execution at the current market price.

To better understand activity on the NYSE trading floor, imagine yourself as a floor broker. Your phone clerk has just handed you an order to sell 3,000 shares of KO (the ticker symbol for Coca-Cola common stock) for a customer of the brokerage company that employs you. The order is a **market order**, meaning that the customer wants to sell the stock at the best possible price as soon as possible. You immediately walk (running violates exchange rules) to the specialist's post where KO stock is traded.

Upon approaching the specialist's post where KO is traded, you check the terminal screen for information on the current market price for KO stock. The screen reveals that the last executed trade for KO was at 70.63 and that the specialist is bidding 70.50 per share. You could immediately sell to the specialist at 70.50, but that would be too easy.

Instead, as the customer's representative, you are obligated to get the best possible price. It is your job to "work" the order, and your job depends on providing satisfactory order execution service. So you look around for another broker who represents a customer who wants to buy KO stock. Luckily, you quickly find another broker at the specialist's post with a market order to buy 3,000 shares of KO. Noticing that the specialist is asking 70.76 per share, you both agree to execute your orders with each other at a price of 70.63. This price, halfway between the specialist's bid and ask prices, saves each of your customers approximately $\$.13 \times 3{,}000 = \$390$ compared to the specialist's prices.

In a trade of this type, in which one floor broker buys from another, the specialist acts only as a broker assisting in matching buy orders and sell orders. On an actively traded stock, many floor brokers can be buying and selling. In such cases, trading is said to occur "in the crowd." Thus, the specialist functions as a broker as long as buyers and sellers are available. The specialist steps in as a dealer only when necessary to fill an order that would otherwise go unfilled.

In reality, not all orders are executed so easily. For example, suppose you are unable to quickly find another broker with an order to buy 3,000 shares of KO. Because you have a market order, you may have no choice but to sell to the specialist at the bid price of 70.50. In this case, the need to execute an order quickly takes priority, and the specialist provides the necessary liquidity to allow immediate order execution.

In this situation, the specialist is often able to help floor brokers by agreeing to "stop" the stock. By stopping stock for a sell order, the specialist agrees to try to help you get a better price while also guaranteeing a minimum price. For your sell order, the specialist might guarantee a minimum price of 70.50 but try to get a better price, say, 70.63. So agreed, you leave the order with the specialist. If the next offer to buy KO is at a price of 70.63, the specialist will fill your order at that price. But if no better offer appears forthcoming, the specialist will execute the order at the guaranteed price of 70.50—if necessary, from the specialist's own inventory.

Stopping stock is also a goodwill gesture. The NYSE places great emphasis on the quality of performance by specialists, which is evaluated regularly through surveys of floor brokers' satisfaction. Specialists are expected to assist brokers in getting the best prices for customer orders, to provide liquidity to the market, and to maintain an orderly market for all securities assigned to them. Stopping stock helps accomplish these objectives.

Note an important caveat concerning this discussion of NYSE floor operations. If you think about it, there's no way that the NYSE could trade more than a billion shares a day using this system. It's just not physically possible. What actually happens is that over 99 percent of orders are processed electronically using the SuperDOT. Based on volume of orders submitted, however, that number drops to about 75 percent. The implication is that larger orders are handled by floor brokers, but smaller orders are not. In fact, with the introduction of the NYSE Hybrid initiative, much of the trading in liquid stocks during normal times happens completely electronically.

SPECIAL ORDER TYPES

limit order
Customer order to buy or sell securities with a specified "limit" price. The order can be executed only at the limit price or better.

Many orders are transmitted to the NYSE floor as **limit orders**. A limit order is an order to buy or sell stock, where the customer specifies a maximum price he is willing to pay in the case of a buy order, or a minimum price he will accept in the case of a sell order. For example, suppose that as a NYSE floor broker, you receive a limit order to sell 3,000 shares of KO stock at 70.75. This means that the customer is not willing to accept any price below 70.75 per share, even if it means missing the trade.

One strategy for handling limit orders is to hold the order and frequently check for potential buyers at the specialist post for KO stock. However, this is unnecessary because you can leave a limit order with the specialist. As a service to brokers, NYSE specialists display unfilled limit orders on the terminal screens at their posts for all approaching brokers to see. If another broker wants to buy KO at 70.75, the specialist will execute the sale for you. This service saves considerable time and energy for busy floor brokers. Indeed, monitoring and executing unfilled limit orders is a very important function of the NYSE specialist.

stop order
Customer order to buy or sell securities when a preset "stop" price is reached.

A **stop order** may appear similar to a limit order, but there is an important difference. With a stop order, the customer specifies a "stop" price. This stop price serves as a trigger point. No trade can occur until the stock price reaches this stop price. When the stock price reaches the stop price, the stop order is immediately converted into a market order. Since the order is now a market order, the customer may get a price that is better or worse than the stop price. Thus, the stop price only serves as a trigger point for conversion into a market order. Unlike a limit price, the stop price places no limit on the price at which a trade can occur. Once converted to a market order, the trade is executed just like any other market order.

The most common type of stop order is a *stop-sell* order, which is an order to sell shares if the stock price falls to a specified stop price below the current stock price. This type of order is generally called a *stop-loss* because it is usually intended to limit losses on a long position. The other type is a *stop-buy* order, which is an order to buy shares if the price rises to a specified stop price above the current stock price. Stop-buy orders are often placed in conjunction with short sales, again as means of limiting losses.

Placing stop-loss orders is frequently touted as a smart trading strategy, but there are a couple of issues we should mention. For concreteness, suppose you buy 1,000 shares of GoGo Corp. at $20. You simultaneously place a stop-sell order at $15. Thus you seem to have limited your potential loss to $5 per share.

Unfortunately, after the market closes, a rumor circulates that GoGo has uncovered a significant accounting fraud. The next morning, the stock opens at $8, meaning the first trade occurs at $8 per share. Because this price is below your $15 stop price, a market order to sell your stock will be placed and executed, and you'll lose much more than $5 per share. What you discover is that your stop-loss guarantees only that a market order to sell will be placed as soon as the stock trades at $15 *or below.*

Adding insult to injury, after your stock is sold, a creditable announcement is made indicating that the rumor is false. GoGo shares promptly bounce back to $20, but you were sold out at a big loss. Thus, a second danger in blindly using stop-loss orders is that volatile conditions can lead to an unfavorable stop sale. Table 5.1 summarizes the characteristics of limit and stop orders.

A limit price can be attached to a stop order to create a *stop-limit order.* This is different from a simple stop order in that once the stock price reaches the preset stop price the order is converted into a limit order. By contrast, a simple stop order is converted into a market order. At this point, the limit order is just like any other limit order. Notice that with a stop-limit order you must specify two prices, the stop and the limit. The two prices can be the same, or they can be different. In our GoGo Corp. example, you could place a stop-limit sell order at $15 stop, $12 limit. This order converts to a limit order to sell at $12 or better if the price ever hits $15 or below. Thus you will never sell below $12. Of course, you may never sell at all unless your limit price is reached! Our nearby *Work the Web* box shows how these orders are entered in an actual online brokerage account.

Another type of order that requires special attention is the *short-sale order.* As explained elsewhere, a short sale involves borrowing stock shares and then selling the borrowed

TABLE 5.1 Stock Market Order Types

Order Type	Buy	Sell
Market order	Buy at best price available for immediate execution.	Sell at best price available for immediate execution.
Limit order	Buy at best price available, but not more than the preset limit price. Forgo purchase if limit is not met.	Sell at best price available, but not less than the preset limit price. Forgo sale if limit is not met.
Stop order	Convert to a market order to buy when the stock price crosses the stop price from below.	Convert to a market order to sell when the stock price crosses the stop price from above. Also known as a "stop-loss."
Stop-limit order	Convert to a limit order to buy when the stock price crosses the stop price from below.	Convert to a limit order to sell when the stock price crosses the stop price from above.

WORK THE WEB

To illustrate the importance of getting order types straight, we captured the actual trading screen from one of the largest online brokers, eTrade. On the screen below, the ticker symbol entered is JWN, a purveyor of fine apparel, Nordstrom Inc. The order is a limit order to buy 200 shares at $46.50. That is, we want to purchase these shares for a price of $46.50 or lower. The limit order is good for the day only.

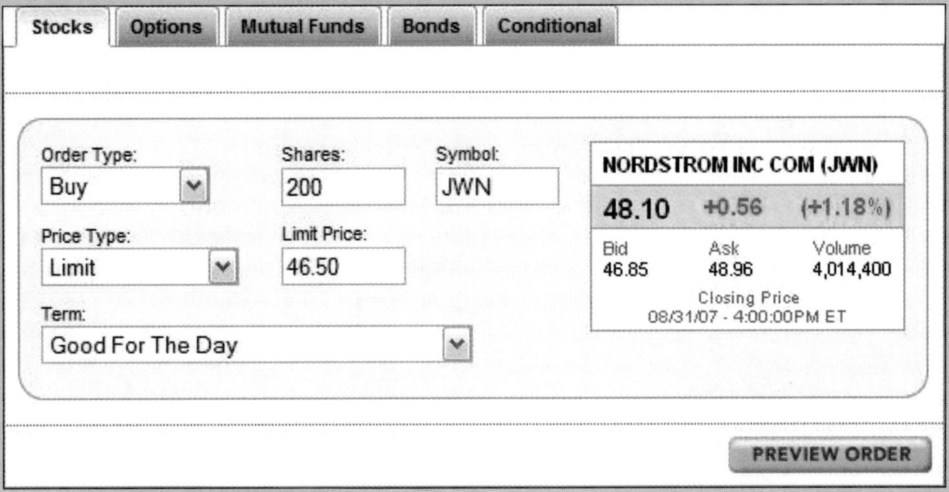

Clicking on the "Preview Order" button allows you to double-check your order before you submit it for transaction. Here is our preview screen:

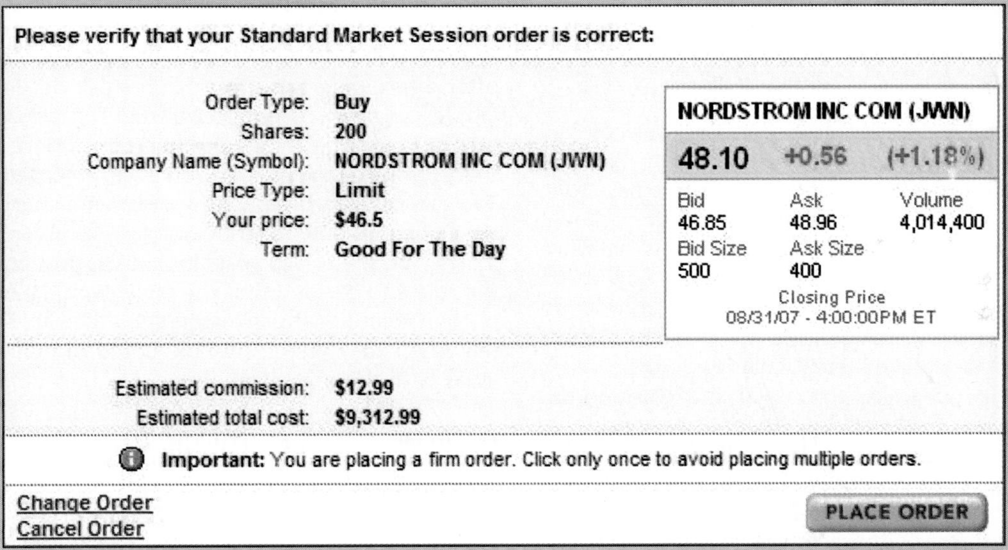

After checking to make sure we have entered everything correctly, we just hit the "Place Order" button to submit our order.

shares in the hope of buying them back later at a lower price. Short-sale loans are normally arranged through the customer's broker. New York Stock Exchange rules require that when shares are sold as part of a short-sale transaction, the order must be marked as a short-sale transaction when it is transmitted to the NYSE floor.

NYSE uptick rule
Rule for short sales requiring that before a short sale can be executed, the last price change must be an uptick.

Sell orders marked as short sales used to be subject to the **NYSE uptick rule**. According to the NYSE uptick rule, a short sale can be executed only if the last price change was an uptick. For example, suppose the last two trades were executed at 55.50 and then 55.63. The

INVESTMENT UPDATES

RULE CHANGE TICKS OFF SOME TRADERS

For most people, ticks are something that crop up at summer camp. This season, ticks of a different stripe are causing Wall Street traders to break out in a rash.

The markets have been in turmoil in recent weeks as the fallout from soaring defaults on riskier home-mortgage loans spread. Since hitting a record in late July, the Dow Jones Industrial Average has fallen more than 5 percent, and people looking to sell their holdings, especially bonds, have often had trouble finding buyers.

Dow Jones Industrials

Number of times the Dow Jones Industrial Average has closed at least 1% above or below its previous close

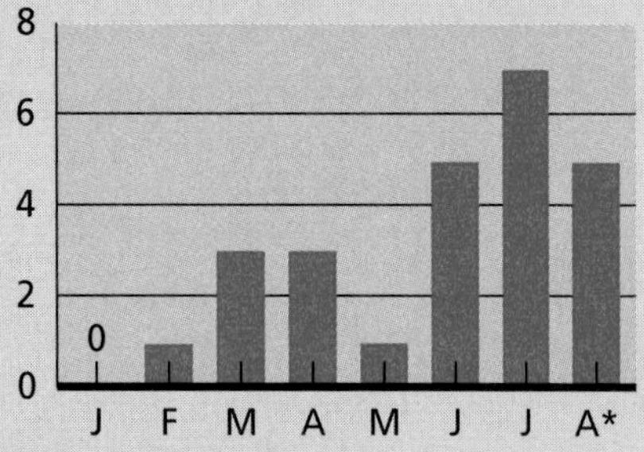

*As of Aug. 13

Source: WSJ Market Data Group

Some traders say another factor is causing turmoil: an arcane rule change—mockingly referred to as the "downtick" rule—that kicked into effect in July. This new rule makes it easier for investors to bet on stock-price declines. Before July, under the "uptick" rule, investors typically had to wait until a stock was rising to bet on its downfall.

Lots of selling can feed off itself, prompting nervous investors to sell more, which adds to volatility. Often, heavily shorted stocks can be particularly volatile.

The old rule generally prohibited the shorting of a stock while its price was falling, or experiencing a "downtick" in trader slang. The rule was instituted after the 1929 market crash in order to discourage avalanches of short sales to push a particular stock—or even the broader market—precipitously lower.

In a traditional short sale, investors borrow shares and sell them, betting the price will fall and that they will be able to buy the shares back later at a lower price for return to the lender. Short sellers are sometimes blamed for big rallies as well as stock declines. During one recent July rally in Intel Corp. shares, some investors blamed the move on a frantic exit by short sellers who had thrown in the towel on their bets.

At the New York Stock Exchange, traders pointed to the downtick rule on July 26, when the Dow Jones Industrial Average sank 311.50 points, or 2.3 percent, to finish at 13473.57. But instead of complaining about the Federal Reserve, the housing market or hedge funds, one trader directed his ire at the fact that the 1930s rule was recently revoked. "Appeal the repeal," he said, walking across the floor with a handheld computer.

Gary Lahey, a former chairman of the Chicago Board Options Exchange, says it's hard to quantify the added volatility given all the turmoil of late but there is no question it has had an impact. "You're going to get more volatility because it's easier to whack a stock," says Mr. Lahey, who nevertheless favors the rule change.

In recent years, proponents of abolishing the downtick rule argued that it had become obsolete in an era of electronic trading and new investment products that offer alternative ways to bet on stock declines. For example, an array of publicly traded options and futures contracts, which can be used to bet on a price decline for shares prior to a set expiration date, emerged in the last 30 years outside the purview of the old short-sales rule, which applies only to stocks.

The SEC spent two years looking at possibly scrapping the rule and decided that the move would have little impact on volatility and investors should be able to buy and sell when they want. The SEC voted in mid-June to do away with the rule altogether.

Source: Aaron Lucchetti and Peter A. McKay, *The Wall Street Journal,* August 14, 2007.

last price change was an uptick of .13, and a short sale can be executed at a price of 55.63 or higher. Alternatively, suppose the last two trades were executed at 55.50 and 55.25, where the last price change was a downtick of .25. In this case, a short sale can be executed only at a price higher than 55.25.

The NYSE originally enacted the uptick rule to make it more difficult for speculators to drive down a stock's price by repeated short sales. Interestingly, the uptick rule was a NYSE rule only and did not necessarily apply to short-sale transactions executed elsewhere. The uptick rule was repealed in June 2007. However, it could be reinstated someday. As you can read in our nearby *Investment Updates* box, strong opinions remain about the uptick rule.

Finally, colored coats are worn by many of the people on the floor of the exchange. The color of the coat indicates the person's job or position. Clerks, runners, visitors, exchange officials, and so on, wear particular colors to identify themselves. Also, since things can get a little hectic on a busy day with the result that good clothing may not last long, the cheap coats offer some protection. Nevertheless, many specialists and floor brokers wear a good business suit every day simply out of habit and pride.

CHECK THIS

5.3a What are the four main types of orders to buy and sell common stocks?

5.3b What do specialists do?

5.3c What is a limit order? How do limit and stop orders differ?

5.4 NASDAQ

In terms of total dollar volume of trading, the second largest stock market in the United States is NASDAQ (say "Naz-dak"). In fact, in terms of companies listed and, on most days recently, number of shares traded, NASDAQ is bigger than the NYSE. The somewhat odd name is derived from the acronym NASDAQ, which stands for National Association of Securities Dealers Automated Quotations system. But NASDAQ is now a proper name in its own right.

NASDAQ OPERATIONS

WWW

NASDAQ's Web site is www.nasdaq.com Click on "NASDAQ Corporate."

Introduced in 1971, the NASDAQ market is a computer network of securities dealers who disseminate timely security price quotes to NASDAQ subscribers. These dealers act as market makers for securities listed on NASDAQ. As market makers, NASDAQ dealers post bid and ask prices at which they accept sell and buy orders, respectively. With each price quote, they also post the number of stock shares that they obligate themselves to trade at their quoted prices.

Like NYSE specialists, NASDAQ market makers trade on an inventory basis, using their inventory as a buffer to absorb buy and sell order imbalances. Unlike the NYSE specialist system, NASDAQ features multiple market makers for actively traded stocks. Thus, there are two key differences between the NYSE and NASDAQ:

1. NASDAQ is a computer network and has no physical location where trading takes place.
2. NASDAQ has a multiple market maker system rather than a specialist system.

over-the-counter (OTC) market
Securities market in which trading is almost exclusively done through dealers who buy and sell for their own inventories.

Traditionally, a securities market largely characterized by dealers who buy and sell securities for their own inventories is called an **over-the-counter (OTC) market**. Consequently, NASDAQ is often referred to as an OTC market. However, in their efforts to promote a distinct image, NASDAQ officials prefer that the term OTC not be used when referring to the NASDAQ market. Nevertheless, old habits die hard, and many people still refer to NASDAQ as an OTC market.

The NASDAQ is actually made up of three separate markets: the NASDAQ Global Select Market, the NASDAQ Global Market, and the NASDAQ Capital Market. As the market for NASDAQ's larger and more actively traded securities, the NASDAQ Global Select Market lists about 1,200 securities (as of 2007), including some very well-known companies. The Global Market companies are somewhat smaller in size. NASDAQ lists about 1,450 of these companies. Finally, the smallest companies listed on NASDAQ are in the NASDAQ Capital Market. About 550 companies are listed in this market. As you might guess, an important difference among the markets is that the Global Select Market has the most stringent listing requirements. Of course, as Capital Market companies become more established, they may move up to the Global Market or the Global Select Market.

FIGURE 5.2 Dow Jones Industrial Average

Source: www.wsj.com, September 5, 2007. Reprinted by permission of Dow Jones & Company, Inc. via Copyright Clearance Center, Inc. © 2007 Dow Jones & Company, Inc. All Rights Reserved Worldwide.

Jones averages, a utilities average and a transportation average. We will focus on the industrial average. Figure 5.2 reproduces a chart of the DJIA from www.wsj.com.

Figure 5.2 shows daily high, low, and closing prices for the DJIA from March 2007 through August 2007. The vertical bars in the chart indicate the range of index high and low values on each trading day. The tick mark on the right side of each day's bar marks the closing value of the index on that day. We therefore see that, based on closing prices, the Dow reached a high of about 14,100 during this period compared to a low of about 12,000. Figure 5.3 contains a list of the 30 well-known companies in the DJIA and their dividend yields.

WWW

For more on the Dow, visit averages.dowjones.com Look for "Averages" under "Blue Chip Indexes."

Although the Dow is the most familiar stock market index, a number of other indexes are widely followed. In fact, as we begin to discuss next, the Dow is not the most representative index by any means, and the way it is computed presents various problems that can make it difficult to interpret.

STOCK MARKET INDEXES

WWW

What are the Russell indexes? Visit www.russell.com to find out.

The Dow Jones Industrial Average Web page is informative, but market watchers might be interested in more detail regarding recent stock market activity. A more comprehensive view of stock market trading is contained in Figure 5.4, which is also published daily at www.wsj.com.

The Web page we examine here, "Major Stock Indexes," reports information about a variety of stock market indexes in addition to the Dow Jones averages. Of the non–Dow Jones indexes shown, by far the best known and most widely followed is the Standard & Poor's Index of 500 stocks, commonly abbreviated as the S&P 500, or often just the S&P. We have seen this index before. In Chapter 1, we used it as a benchmark to track the performance of large-company common stocks for the last eight decades.

FIGURE 5.3 Yields on Dow Jones Industrial Average Component Stocks

Yields On Dow Stocks

Monday, March 31, 2008

Components of the Dow Jones Averages, ranked by dividend yield based on recent price and annualized dividend amount. This page is updated twice a month. (See charts of the Dow Jones Averages.)

DOW JONES INDUSTRIALS

Company	Indicated Yield	Indicated Annual Div	Price 3/31/2008	Change From 12/31/2007
Bank of America Corp	6.75	2.56	37.91	-3.35
Pfizer	6.12	1.28	20.93	-1.80
Citigroup	5.98	1.28	21.42	-8.02
General Motors	5.25	1.00	19.05	-5.84
Verizon	4.72	1.72	36.45	-7.24
AT&T Corp.	4.18	1.60	38.30	-3.26
Merck	4.01	1.52	37.95	-20.16
J.P. Morgan Chase	3.54	1.52	42.95	-0.70
DuPont	3.51	1.64	46.76	+2.67
General Electric	3.35	1.24	37.01	-0.06
Home Depot	3.22	0.90	27.97	+1.03
Chevron Corp	2.72	2.32	85.36	-7.97
McDonald's	2.69	1.50	55.77	-3.14
Intel	2.64	0.56	21.18	-5.48
Johnson & Johnson	2.56	1.66	64.87	-1.83
3M	2.53	2.00	79.15	-5.17
Coca-Cola	2.50	1.52	60.87	-0.50
Boeing	2.15	1.60	74.37	-13.09
Procter & Gamble	2.00	1.40	70.07	-3.35
Alcoa	1.89	0.68	36.06	-0.49
United Tech	1.86	1.28	68.82	-7.72
AIG	1.85	0.80	43.25	-15.05
Caterpillar	1.84	1.44	78.29	+5.73
Wal-Mart Stores	1.80	0.95	52.68	+5.15
Exxon-Mobil	1.66	1.40	84.58	-9.11
American Express	1.65	0.72	43.72	-8.30
Microsoft	1.55	0.44	28.38	-7.22
IBM	1.39	1.60	115.14	+7.04
Walt Disney	1.12	0.35	31.38	-0.90
Hewlett-Packard	0.70	0.32	45.66	-4.82

Source: www.wsj.com, April 4, 2008. Reprinted by permission of Dow Jones & Company, Inc., via Copyright Clearance Center, Inc.

If you were to scrutinize the various indexes in Figure 5.4, you would quickly find that there are essentially four differences between them: (1) the market covered; (2) the types of stocks included; (3) how many stocks are included; and (4) how the index is calculated.

FIGURE 5.4 Stock Market Major Indexes

Stock Indexes: Closing Data Bank

Friday, August 31, 2007 — Find Historical Data | WHAT'S THIS?

Index	DAILY High	DAILY Low	DAILY Close	DAILY Chg	DAILY % Chg	YTD % chg	52 WEEK High	52 WEEK Low	52 WEEK % Chg	3-yr % chg*
Dow Jones										
Industrial Average	13428.95	13240.84	13357.74	119.01	0.90	7.2	14000.41	11331.44	16.5	9.5
Transportation Average	4901.64	4786.56	4878.75	91.61	1.91	7.0	5446.49	4195.07	13.2	16.3
Utility Average	488.25	481.15	484.79	1.70	0.35	6.1	535.72	422.74	9.8	18.6
65 Composite	4427.10	4356.50	4404.17	47.51	1.09	6.9	4731.10	3804.61	14.0	13.3
Wilshire 5000	14916.09	14677.24	14847.70	170.46	1.16	4.1	15700.95	12948.96	13.1	11.5
Wilshire 2500	3534.36	3476.80	3517.60	40.80	1.17	4.3	3716.56	3069.86	13.0	13.3
Wilshire Large-Cap Growth	3049.62	3001.66	3036.93	35.34	1.18	6.5	3806.48	2603.72	14.8	11.3
Wilshire Large-Cap Value	3597.83	3538.51	3577.27	38.82	1.10	2.2	3803.47	3181.47	11.2	14.4
Wilshire Mid-Cap Growth	4143.32	4072.89	4131.85	59.21	1.45	10.2	4411.60	3368.01	20.5	19.4
Wilshire Mid-Cap Value	4783.54	4694.89	4760.62	65.99	1.41	0.5	5334.63	4309.38	8.8	12.6
Wilshire Small-Cap Growth	3770.99	3705.07	3760.11	55.08	1.49	8.5	4015.92	3114.06	18.1	17.7
Wilshire Small-Cap Vaue	5839.92	5736.26	5815.38	79.15	1.38	-0.2	6392.70	5290.81	8.0	14.2
Wilshire Micro	7641.33	7569.16	7625.23	56.08	0.74	-2.8	8328.01	7012.30	6.3	11.4
Wilshire REIT	237.52	230.32	235.22	4.93	2.14	-10.2	297.43	215.90	-1.5	17.9
Internet	104.80	103.09	104.53	1.44	1.40	7.9	115.24	85.07	18.9	18.8
Barron's 400	322.27	316.42	321.04	4.63	1.46	6.9	350.95	269.13	15.9	16.7
Nasdaq Stock Market										
Composite	2603.11	2579.79	2596.36	31.06	1.21	7.5	2720.04	2155.29	18.4	12.2
Nasdaq 100	1993.73	1975.83	1988.73	24.98	1.27	13.2	2052.99	1564.84	25.1	13.3
Biotech	816.25	808.28	813.67	7.57	0.94	1.9	857.98	734.23	7.3	5.6
Computer	1164.31	1154.04	1161.63	13.90	1.21	10.3	1225.15	933.43	22.7	13.4
Industrials	2244.26	2224.26	2237.58	27.98	1.27	7.0	2384.56	1853.27	18.8	13.5
Insurance	4124.34	4079.61	4111.95	45.87	1.13	0.1	4364.98	3777.36	8.2	11.0
Banks	3036.92	2999.20	3015.87	11.88	0.40	-11.7	3455.75	2819.81	-7.6	0.9
Telecommunications	276.03	273.37	275.55	4.78	1.77	17.2	279.63	194.04	37.5	17.5
Standard & Poor's										
500 Index	1481.47	1457.61	1473.99	16.35	1.12	3.9	1553.08	1294.02	12.4	10.1
100 Index	690.98	682.03	687.47	7.01	1.03	4.1	718.11	598.50	13.5	8.5
MidCap 400	866.24	850.65	863.00	12.32	1.45	7.3	926.23	738.41	14.5	14.4
SmallCap 600	419.08	412.32	417.61	5.29	1.28	4.4	445.19	363.23	12.9	14.6
SuperComp 1500	334.95	329.53	333.33	3.80	1.15	4.2	351.81	291.94	12.6	10.7
New York Stock Exchange										
Composite	9642.07	9456.67	9596.98	140.34	1.48	5.0	10220.67	8262.17	13.8	14.1
Arca Tech 100	948.30	935.75	945.78	10.09	1.08	8.0	992.47	793.90	17.3	13.2
Financial	9059.01	8870.11	9011.57	141.58	1.60	-5.7	9982.83	8526.67	3.3	10.3
Health Care	7052.73	6957.54	7026.58	69.04	0.99	1.0	7542.58	6726.47	1.1	6.3
Energy	13714.74	13412.96	13600.01	187.54	1.40	13.6	14739.52	10442.57	19.0	25.1

Source: www.wsj.com, September 3, 2007. Reprinted by permission of Dow Jones & Company, Inc., via Copyright Clearance Center, Inc.

The first three of these differences are straightforward. Some indexes listed in Figure 5.4, such as the Dow Jones Utilities, focus on specific industries. Others, such as the NASDAQ Composite, focus on particular markets. Some have a small number of stocks; others, such as the Wilshire 5000 (which actually has over 6,000 stocks), have a large number.

price-weighted index Stock market index in which stocks are held in proportion to their share price.

value-weighted index Stock market index in which stocks are held in proportion to the aggregate market value.

How stock market indexes are computed is not quite so straightforward, but it is important to understand. There are two major types of stock market index: price-weighted and value-weighted. With a **price-weighted index**, stocks are held in the index in proportion to their share prices. With a **value-weighted index**, stocks are held in proportion to the aggregate market value of the companies in the index.

The best way to understand the difference between price and value weighting is to consider an example. To keep things relatively simple, we suppose that there are only two companies in the entire market. We have the following information about their shares outstanding, share prices, and total market values:

		Price per Share		Total Market Value	
	Shares Outstanding	Beginning of Year	End of Year	Beginning of Year	End of Year
Company A	50 million	$10	$14	$500 million	$700 million
Company B	1 million	$50	$40	$ 50 million	$ 40 million

As shown, Company A has a lower share price but many more shares outstanding. Ignoring dividends, notice that Company A's stock price rose by 40 percent ($10 to $14) while Company B's stock price fell by 20 percent ($50 to $40).

The question we want to answer here is simply: How did the market do for the year? There are several ways we could answer this question. We could first focus on what happened to the average share price. The average share price was ($10 + $50)/2 = $30 at the beginning of the year, and ($14 + $40)/2 = $27 at the end, so the average share price fell. If we take the average share price as our index, then our index fell from 30 to 27, for a change of −3 points. Because the index began at 30, this is a −3/30 = −10% decrease. We might therefore say that the market was "off" by 10 percent.

This is an example of a price-weighted index. Because Company B's stock price is five times bigger than Company A's, it carries five times as much weight in the index. This explains why the index was down even though Company A's stock gained 40 percent whereas Company B's stock only lost 20 percent. The Dow Jones indexes are price weighted.

Alternatively, instead of focusing on the price of a typical share, we could look at what happened to the total value of a typical company. Here we notice that the average total value, in millions, rose from ($500 + $50)/2 = $275 to ($700 + $40)/2 = $370. If we take average total company value as our index, then our index rose from 275 to 370, a 35 percent *increase.*

WWW

Take a look at the "value" and "growth" indexes at www.mscibarra.com Click on "S&P/Barra Indexes" under products tab.

This is an example of a value-weighted index. The influence a company has in this case depends on its overall change in total market value, not just its stock price change. Because Company A has a much larger total value, it carries a much larger weight in the index. With the exception of the Dow Jones indexes, most of the other indexes in Figure 5.4, including the Standard & Poor's, are value weighted.

Now we have a problem. One index tells us the market was down by 10 percent, while the other tells us it was up by 35 percent. Which one is correct? The answer seems fairly obvious. The total value of the market as a whole grew from $550 million to $740 million, so the market as a whole increased in value. Put differently, investors as a whole owned stock worth $550 million at the beginning of the year and $740 million at the end of the year. So, on the whole, stock market investors earned 35 percent, even though the average share price went down.

This example shows that a price-weighted index can be misleading as an indicator of total market value. The basic flaw in a price-weighted index is that the effect a company has on the index depends on the price of a single share. However, the price of a single share is only part of the story. Unless the number of shares is also considered, the true impact on the overall market isn't known, and a distorted picture can emerge.

EXAMPLE 5.1

Caution: Indexes Under Construction

Suppose there are only two stocks in the market and the following information is given:

		Price per Share	
	Shares Outstanding	Beginning of Year	End of Year
Betty Co.	10 million	$10	$11
Gray Bull, Inc.	20 million	$20	$25

Construct price- and value-weighted indexes and calculate the percentage changes in each.

The average share price rose from $15 to $18, or $3, so the price-weighted index would be up by 3/15 = 20 percent. Average total market value, in millions, rose from $250 to $305, so the value-weighted index rose by 55/250 = 22 percent.

MORE ON PRICE-WEIGHTED INDEXES

Earlier we indicated that the Dow Jones averages are price weighted. Given this, you may wonder why the Dow Jones Industrial Average has such a high value when the stock prices used to calculate the average are much smaller. To answer this question, we must explain one last detail about price-weighted indexes.

The extra detail concerns the effects of stock splits on price-weighted indexes. For example, in a 2-for-1 stock split, all current shareholders receive two new shares in exchange for each old share that they own. However, the total value of the company does not change because it is still the same company after the stock split. There are just twice as many shares, each worth half as much.

A stock split has no effect on a value-weighted index since the total value of the company does not change. But it can have a dramatic effect on a price-weighted index. To see this, consider what happens to the price-weighted and value-weighted indexes we created above when Company B enacts a 2-for-1 stock split. Based on beginning prices, with a 2-for-1 split, Company B's shares fall to $25. The price-weighted index falls to (10 + 25)/2 = 17.50 from 30, even though nothing really happened.

For a price-weighted index, the problem of stock splits can be addressed by adjusting the divisor each time a split occurs. Once again, an example is the best way to illustrate. In the case stated just above, suppose we wanted the index value to stay at 30 even though B's price per share fell to $25 as a result of the split. The only way to accomplish this is to add together the new stock prices and divide by something less than 2.

This new number is called the *index divisor,* and it is adjusted as needed to remove the effect of stock splits. To find the new divisor in our case, the stock prices are $25 and $10, and we want the index to equal 30. We solve for the new divisor, d, as follows:

$$\text{Index level} = \frac{\text{Sum of stock prices}}{\text{Divisor}}$$

$$30 = \frac{25 + 10}{d}$$

$$d = \frac{35}{30} = 1.16666\ldots$$

The new divisor is thus approximately 1.17.

Adjusting the divisor takes care of the problem in one sense, but it creates another problem. Because we are no longer dividing the sum of the share prices by the number of companies in the index, we can no longer interpret the change in the index as the change in price of an average share.

EXAMPLE 5.2

Adjusting the Divisor

Take a look back at Example 5.1. Suppose that Gray Bull splits 5-for-1. Based on beginning information, what is the new divisor?

Following a 5-for-1 split, Gray Bull's share price will fall from $20 to $4. With no adjustment to the divisor, the price-weighted index would drop from 15 to (10 + 4)/2 = 7. To keep the index at its old level of 15, we need to solve for a new divisor such that (10 + 4)/d = 15. In this case, the new divisor would be 14/15 = .93333 . . ., illustrating that the divisor can drop below 1.0.

THE DOW JONES DIVISORS

The method we described of adjusting the divisor on a price-weighted index for stock splits is the method used to adjust the Dow Jones averages. Through time, with repeated adjustments for stock splits, the divisor becomes smaller and smaller. On February 19, 2008, Bank of America Corporation (BAC) and Chevron Corporation (CVX) replaced Altria Group Incorporated (MO) and Honeywell International, Incorporated (HON) in the DJIA. As of March 8, 2008, the DJIA divisor was a nice, round 0.122834016. Because there are 30 stocks in the index, the divisor on the DJIA would be 30 if it were never adjusted, so it has declined substantially. Divisors for the other Dow Jones averages have similarly odd values.

Given its shortcomings, you might wonder why the financial press continues to report the Dow Jones averages. The reason is tradition; the Dow Jones averages have been around for more than 100 years, and each new generation of investors becomes accustomed to its quirks.

MORE ON INDEX FORMATION: BASE-YEAR VALUES

We next discuss one or two more details about indexes. First, to ease interpretation, the starting value of an index is usually set equal to some simple base number, like 100 or 1,000. For example, if you were to create a value-weighted index for the NYSE, the actual value of the index would be very large and cumbersome, so adjusting it makes sense.

To illustrate, suppose we have a value-weighted index with a starting value of 1.4 million. If we want the starting value to be 100, we just divide the starting value, and every subsequent value, by 1.4 million and then multiply by 100. So, if the next value of the index is 1.6 million, the "reindexed" value would be 1.6 million/1.4 million × 100 = 114.29, which is easily interpreted as a 14.29 percent increase over a base of 100.

EXAMPLE 5.3 Reindexing

You've calculated values for an index over a four-year period as follows:

Year 1:	1,687 million
Year 2:	1,789 million
Year 3:	1,800 million
Year 4:	1,700 million

Suppose you wanted the index to start at 1,000. What would the reindexed values be?

To reindex these numbers, we need to (1) divide each of them by the starting value, 1,687 million, and then (2) multiply each by 1,000. Thus, we have:

Year 1:	1,687 million/1,687 million × 1,000 = 1,000.00
Year 2:	1,789 million/1,687 million × 1,000 = 1,060.46
Year 3:	1,800 million/1,687 million × 1,000 = 1,066.98
Year 4:	1,700 million/1,687 million × 1,000 = 1,007.71

Finally, an important consideration in looking at indexes is whether dividends are included. Most indexes don't include them. As a result, the change in an index measures only the capital gain (or loss) component of your return. When you're trying to evaluate how a particular type of stock market investment has done over time, dividends have to be included to get an accurate picture.

So which index is the best? The most popular alternative to the DJIA is the value-weighted S&P 500. You might further wonder, however, why this popular index limits itself to 500 stocks. The answer is timeliness and accuracy. Almost all stocks in the S&P 500 index trade every day, and therefore accurate daily updates of market prices are available each day. Stocks that do not trade every day can cause **index staleness**. Index staleness occurs when an index does not reflect all current price information because some of the stocks in the index have not traded recently. Also, as a practical matter, the largest 500 companies account for a very large portion of the value of the overall stock market.

index staleness
Condition that occurs when an index does not reflect all current price information because some of the stocks in the index have not traded recently.

CHECK THIS

5.6a What is the difference between price- and value-weighting in the construction of stock market indexes? Give an example of a well-known index of each type.

5.6b Which is better, price or value weighting? Why?

5.6c Which stock market index is likely to contain the greater degree of index staleness, the S&P 500 or the Wilshire 5000 index?

5.7 Summary and Conclusions

This chapter introduces you to stock markets. We discussed who owns stocks, how the stock exchanges operate, and how stock market indexes are constructed and interpreted. This chapter covers many important aspects of stock markets, including the following items—grouped by the chapter's important concepts.

1. The difference between primary and secondary stock markets.

A. Individual investors, directly or through mutual funds, own more than half of all traded stocks. The rest are owned mostly by financial institutions such as pension funds and insurance companies.

B. The stock market is composed of a primary market, where stock shares are first sold, and a secondary market, where investors trade shares among themselves. In the primary market, companies raise money for investment projects. Investment bankers specialize in arranging financing for companies in the primary market. Investment bankers often act as underwriters, buying newly issued stock from the company and then reselling the stock to the public. The primary market is best known as the market for initial public offerings (IPOs).

C. In the secondary market, investors trade securities with other investors. Secondary market transactions are directed through three channels: directly with other investors, indirectly through a broker, or directly with a dealer. We saw that a broker matches buyers and sellers; a dealer buys and sells out of inventory.

2. The workings of the New York Stock Exchange (NYSE).

A. Most common stock trading is directed through an organized stock exchange or through a trading network. The largest organized stock exchange in the United States is the New York Stock Exchange (NYSE). Popularly known as the Big Board, NYSE was once owned by its members. Today, however, the NYSE itself is a publicly traded company—so, it is owned by its shareholders.

B. The three major types of NYSE members are commission brokers, specialists, and floor traders. We discussed the role of each in the functioning of the exchange.

3. How NASDAQ operates.

A. The NASDAQ market is a computer network of securities dealers who post timely security price quotes to NASDAQ subscribers. These dealers act as market makers for securities listed on the NASDAQ.

B. Unlike the NYSE, the NASDAQ relies on multiple market makers instead of using a specialist system. Because it is a computer network, the NASDAQ has no physical location.

C. The NASDAQ network operates with three levels of information access:

- Level I provides timely and accurate price quotes which are feely available on the Internet.
- Level II allows users to view price quotes from all NASDAQ market makers. This level allows access to inside quotes. Inside quotes are the highest bid and lowest asked quote for a NASDAQ-listed security.
- Level III is for use by NASDAQ market makers only. With this access, market makers can change their quotes.

4. How to calculate index returns.

A. Investors interested in an overview of stock market activity refer to the returns on several stock market indexes.

B. The most widely followed barometer of day-to-day stock market activity is the Dow Jones Industrial Average (DJIA), often called the "Dow" for short. The DJIA is an index of the stock prices of 30 large companies representative of American industry. The DJIA is a price-weighted index.

C. Another widely followed index is the Standard & Poor's Index of 500 stocks, commonly abbreviated as the S&P 500, or often just the S&P. The S&P 500 Index is a value-weighted index.

D. Many newspapers and Web sites publish current price information for indexes as well as stocks. In the United States, the newspaper best known for reporting stock price information is *The Wall Street Journal*—with its companion Web site, www.wsj.com.

GET REAL

This chapter covered the operations and organization of the major stock markets. It also covered some of the most important order types and the construction of stock market indexes. How should you, as an investor or investment manager, put this information to work?

First, as in some previous chapters, you need to submit as many as possible of the different order types suggested by this chapter in a simulated brokerage account (note that not all simulated brokerage accounts allow all trade types). Your goal is to gain experience with the different order types and what they mean and accomplish for you as an investor or investment manager.

In each case, once you have placed the order, be sure to monitor the price of the stock in question to see if any of your orders should be executed. When an order is executed, compare the result to the stop or limit price to see how you did.

The second thing to do is to start observing the different indexes and learning how they are computed, what's in them, and what they are intended to cover. For example, the NASDAQ 100 is made up of the largest NASDAQ stocks. Is this index broadly representative of big stocks in general? Of NASDAQ stocks in general? Why is the Russell 2000 index widely followed (note that it *does not* contain 2,000 big stocks)? Visit www.russell.com to learn more.

Key Terms

ask price 139
best efforts underwriting 136
bid price 139
broker 139
commission brokers 140
dealer 139
Dutch auction underwriting 136
electronic communications network (ECN) 149
NYSE exchange member 140
firm commitment underwriting 136
floor brokers 140
floor traders 141
fourth market 149
general cash offer 135
index staleness 157
initial public offering (IPO) 135
inside quotes 149
investment banking firm 135
limit order 143
market order 142
NYSE uptick rule 145
over-the-counter (OTC) market 147
price-weighted index 154
primary market 135
prospectus 137
red herring 137
rights offer 135
seasoned equity offering (SEO) 135
secondary market 135
Securities and Exchange Commission (SEC) 137
specialist 140
specialist's post 142
spread 139
stop order 144
SuperDOT system 140
syndicate 135
third market 149
underwrite 135
underwriter spread 135
venture capital (VC) 134
value-weighted index 154

Chapter Review Problems and Self-Test

1. **Index Construction** Suppose there are only two stocks in the market and the following information is given:

		Price per Share	
	Shares Outstanding	Beginning of Year	End of Year
Ally Co.	100 million	$ 60	$ 66
McBeal, Inc.	400 million	$120	$100

Construct price- and value-weighted indexes and calculate the percentage changes in each.

2. **Stock Splits** In the previous problem, suppose that McBeal splits 3-for-1. Based on beginning information, what is the new divisor?

Answers to Self-Test Problems

1. The average share price at the beginning of the year is ($60 + 120)/2 = $90. At the end of the year, the average price is $83. Thus, the average price declined by $7 from $90, a percentage drop of −$7/$90 = −7.78%. Total market cap at the beginning of the year is $60 × 100 + $120 × 400 = $54 billion. It falls to $46.6 billion, a decline of $7.4 billion. The percentage decline is −$7.4 billion/$54 billion = −13.7%, or almost twice as much as the price-weighted index.
2. Following a 3-for-1 split, McBeal's share price falls from $120 to $40. To keep the price-weighted index at its old level of 90, we need a new divisor such that $(60 + 40)/d = 90$. In this case, the new divisor would be 100/90 = 1.1111.

Test Your Investment Quotient

For the remaining questions and problems, the circled numbers in the margin refer to the corresponding learning objective in this chapter.

IQ

(2) 1. **New York Stock Exchange** Which of the following is false?

   a. Specialists cannot trade for their own accounts.
   b. On the NYSE, all buy and sell orders are negotiated through a specialist.
   c. Specialists earn income from commissions and spreads in stocks prices.
   d. Specialists stand ready to trade at quoted bid and ask prices.

(2) 2. **Uptick Rule** You wish to sell short 100 shares of XYZ Corporation stock. Assume the uptick rule is in effect. If the last two transactions were $34.12 followed by $34.25, you can short on the next transaction only at a price of

   a. $34.12 or higher.
   b. $34.25 or higher.
   c. $34.25 or lower.
   d. $34.12 or lower.

CFA® PROBLEMS

(2) 3. **Uptick Rule** Which of the following is false regarding the NYSE uptick rule?

   a. The rule does not apply to short sales executed on other exchanges.
   b. The NYSE enacted the rule to make it more difficult for speculators to drive down a stock's price by repeated short sales.
   c. The rule has become less of a constraint than it once was.
   d. The rule applies when shorting a stock or when covering a short.

CFA® PROBLEMS

(4) 4. **Value-Weighted Index** An analyst gathered the following data about stocks J, K, and L, which together form a value-weighted index:

	December 31, Year 1		December 31, Year 2	
Stock	Price	Shares Outstanding	Price	Shares Outstanding
J	$40	10,000	$50	10,000
K	$30	6,000	$20	12,000*
L	$50	9,000	$40	9,000

*2-for-1 stock split.

The ending value-weighted index (base index = 100) is closest to:

a. 92.31
b. 93.64
c. 106.80
d. 108.33

CFA® PROBLEMS

4 **5. Dow Jones Index** The divisor for the Dow Jones Industrial Average (DJIA) is most likely to decrease when a stock in the DJIA

a. Has a stock split.
b. Has a reverse split.
c. Pays a cash dividend.
d. Is removed and replaced.

CFA® PROBLEMS

2 **6. New York Stock Exchange** Which of the following activities are *not* conducted by specialists on the NYSE?

a. Acting as dealers for their own accounts.
b. Monitoring compliance with margin requirements.
c. Providing liquidity to the market.
d. Monitoring and executing unfilled limit orders.

CFA® PROBLEMS

1 **7. Stock Markets** What is a securities market characterized by dealers who buy and sell securities for their own inventories called?

a. A primary market.
b. A secondary market.
c. An over-the-counter market.
d. An institutional market.

CFA® PROBLEMS

1 **8. Stock Markets** What is the over-the-counter market for exchange-listed securities called?

a. Third market
b. Fourth market
c. After-market
d. Block market

CFA® PROBLEMS

4 **9. Stock Indexes** If the market price of each of the 30 stocks in the Dow Jones Industrial Average changes by the same percentage amount during a given day, which stock will have the greatest impact on the DJIA?

a. The one whose stock trades at the highest dollar price per share.
b. The one whose total equity has the highest market value.
c. The one having the greatest amount of equity in its capital structure.
d. The one having the lowest volatility.

CFA® PROBLEMS

4 **10. Stock Indexes** In calculating the Standard & Poor's stock price indexes, how are adjustments for stock splits made?

a. By adjusting the divisor.
b. Automatically, due to the manner in which the index is calculated.
c. By adjusting the numerator.
d. Quarterly, on the last trading day of each quarter.

CFA® PROBLEMS

4 **11. Stock Indexes** Which of the following indexes includes the largest number of actively traded stocks?

a. The NASDAQ Composite Index.
b. The NYSE Composite Index.
c. The Wilshire 5000 Index.
d. The Value Line Composite Index.

2 **12. New York Stock Exchange** The largest number of NYSE members are registered as:

a. Stockholders
b. Floor brokers
c. Specialists
d. Floor traders

2 **13. New York Stock Exchange** The second largest number of NYSE members are registered as:

a. Stockholders
b. Floor brokers
c. Specialists
d. Floor traders

(2) **14. New York Stock Exchange** The effort by the NYSE to have market makers, specialists, and brokers interact with each other as well as the electronic market is known as

a. The Direct+ system.
b. The SuperDOT system.
c. NYSE Euronext.
d. The NYSE hybrid market.

(4) **15. Stock Indexes** Which one of the following statements regarding the Dow Jones Industrial Average is false?

a. The DJIA contains 30 well-known large-company stocks.
b. The DJIA is affected equally by dollar changes in low- and high-priced stocks.
c. The DJIA is affected equally by percentage changes in low- and high-priced stocks.
d. The DJIA divisor must be adjusted for stock splits.

Concept Questions

(1) **1. Primary and Secondary Markets** If you were to visit your local Chevrolet retailer, there is both a primary and a secondary market in action. Explain. Is the Chevy retailer a dealer or a broker?

(1) **2. Specialists** On the NYSE, does a specialist act as a dealer or a broker? Or both?

3. Market and Limit Orders What is the difference between a market order and a limit order? What is the potential downside to each type of order?

4. Stop That! What is a stop-loss order? Why might it be used? Is it sure to stop a loss?

5. Order Types Suppose Microsoft is currently trading at $100. You want to buy it if it reaches $120. What type of order should you submit?

6. Order Types Suppose Dell is currently trading at $65. You think that if it reaches $70, it will continue to climb, so you want to buy it if and when it gets there. Should you submit a limit order to buy at $70?

(3) **7. NASDAQ Quotes** With regard to the NASDAQ, what are inside quotes?

8. Index Composition There are basically four factors that differentiate stock market indexes. What are they? Comment on each.

9. Index Composition Is it necessarily true that, all else the same, an index with more stocks is better? What is the issue here?

(1) **10. Upticks** What is the uptick rule? Where does it apply? Why did it exist? Why was it eliminated?

www.mhhe.com/jm5e

Questions and Problems

Core Questions

(4) **1. Price-Weighted Divisor** Able, Baker, and Charlie are the only three stocks in an index. The stocks sell for $39, $132, and $87, respectively. If Baker undergoes a 2-for-1 stock split, what is the new divisor for the price-weighted index?

(4) **2. Price-Weighted Divisor** In the previous problem, assume that Baker undergoes a 3-for-1 stock split. What is the new divisor now?

(2) **3. Order Books** You find the following order book on a particular stock. The last trade on the stock was at $70.54.

Buy Orders		Sell Orders	
Shares	Price	Shares	Price
250	$70.53	100	$70.56
100	70.52	400	70.57
900	70.51	1,000	70.59
75	70.49	700	70.60
		900	70.61

a. If you place a market buy order for 100 shares, at what price will it be filled?
b. If you place a market sell order for 100 shares, at what price will it be filled?
c. Suppose you place a market order to buy 400 shares. At what price will it be filled?

4 **4. Price-Weighted Index** You are given the following information concerning two stocks that make up an index. What is the price-weighted return for the index?

		Price per Share	
	Shares Outstanding	Beginning of Year	End of Year
Kirk, Inc.	53,000	$73	$81
Picard Co.	62,000	48	63

4 **5. Value-Weighted Index** Calculate the index return for the information in the previous problem using a value-weighted index.

4 **6. Reindexing** In Problem 5, assume that you want to reindex with the index value at the beginning of the year equal to 100. What is the index level at the end of the year?

4 **7. Index Level** In Problem 5, assume the value-weighted index level was 408.16 at the beginning of the year. What is the index level at the end of the year?

4 **8. Reindexing** Suppose you calculated the total market value of the stocks in an index over a five-year period:

Year 1: 4,387 million
Year 2: 4,671 million
Year 3: 5,032 million
Year 4: 4,820 million
Year 5: 5,369 million

Suppose you wanted the index to start at 500. What would the reindexed values be?

Intermediate Questions

4 **9. Price-Weighted Divisor** Look back at Problem 1. Assume that Able undergoes a 1-for-3 reverse stock split. What is the new divisor?

4 **10. DJIA** On January 4, 2008, the DJIA closed at 12,800.18. The divisor at that time was .123017848. Suppose the next day the prices for 29 of the stocks remained unchanged and one stock increased $5.00. What would the DJIA level be the next day?

4 **11. DJIA** In January 2008, IBM was the highest priced stock in the DJIA and Intel was the lowest. The closing price for IBM on January 4, 2008, was $101.13 and the closing price for Intel was $22.67. Suppose the next day the other 29 stock prices remained unchanged and IBM increased 5 percent. What would the new DJIA level be? Now assume only Intel increased by 5 percent. Find the new DJIA level.

4 **12. DJIA** Looking back at the previous problems, what would the new index level be if all stocks on the DJIA increased by $1.00 per share on the next day?

4 **13. Price-Weighted Divisor** You construct a price-weighted index of 40 stocks. At the beginning of the day the index is 4,873.29. During the day, 39 stock prices remain the same, and one stock price increases $5.00. At the end of the day, your index value is 4,897.26. What is the divisor on your index?

4 **14. Price-Weighted Indexes** Suppose the following three defense stocks are to be combined into a stock index in January 2007 (perhaps a portfolio manager believes these stocks are an appropriate benchmark for his or her performance):

		Price		
	Shares (millions)	1/1/07	1/1/08	1/1/09
Douglas McDonnell	340	$103	$106	$118
Dynamics General	450	45	39	53
International Rockwell	410	74	63	79

a. Calculate the initial value of the index if a price-weighting scheme is used.
b. What is the rate of return on this index for the year ending December 31, 2008? For the year ending December 31, 2009?

4 **15. Price-Weighted Indexes** In the previous problem, suppose that Douglas McDonnell shareholders approve a 3-for-1 stock split on January 1, 2008. What is the new divisor for the index? Calculate the rate of return on the index for the year ending December 31, 2008, if Douglas McDonnell's share price on January 1, 2009, is $39.33 per share.

4 **16. Value-Weighted Indexes** Repeat Problem 14 if a value-weighted index is used. Assume the index is scaled by a factor of 10 million; that is, if the average firm's market value is $5 billion, the index would be quoted as 500.

4 **17. Value-Weighted Indexes** In the previous problem, will your answers change if Douglas McDonnell stock splits? Why or why not?

4 **18. Equally Weighted Indexes** In addition to price-weighted and value-weighted indexes, an equally weighted index is one in which the index value is computed from the average rate of return of the stocks comprising the index. Equally weighted indexes are frequently used by financial researchers to measure portfolio performance.

a. Using the information in Problem 14, compute the rate of return on an equally weighted index of the three defense stocks for the year ending December 31, 2007.
b. If the index value is set to 100 on January 1, 2007, what will the index value be on January 1, 2008? What is the rate of return on the index for 2008?

4 **19. Equally Weighted versus Value-Weighted Indexes** Historically there have been periods where a value-weighted index has a higher return than an equally weighted index and other periods where the opposite has occurred. Why do you suppose this would happen? Hint: Look back to Chapter 1.

4 **20. Geometric Indexes** Another type of index is the geometric index. The calculation of a geometric index is similar to the calculation of a geometric return:

$$1 + R_G = [(1 + R_1)(1 + R_2) \ldots (1 + R_N)]^{1/N}$$

The difference in the geometric index construction is the returns used are the returns for the different stocks in the index for a particular period, such as a day or year. Construct the geometric index returns for Problem 14 over each of the two years. Assume the beginning index level is 100.

21. Geometric Indexes We have seen the importance of geometric returns through time. A geometric index is formed across different stocks at a particular point in time, such as a day. Constructing a portfolio that exactly replicates a geometric index is thus impossible. Given this, why would you want to use a geometric index? In other words, what does a geometric index measure? Now consider the Value Line Arithmetic Index (VLA), which is equally weighted, and the Value Line Geometric Index (VLG). On February 1, 1988, both indexes were set to a value of 210.75. As of the close of the market on January 4, 2008, the VLA was at 2,118.61 and the VLG was at 414.98. Why would you expect to see such a disparity in the two index levels?

22. Interpreting Index Values Suppose you want to replicate the performance of several stock indexes, some of which are price-weighted, others value-weighted, and still others equally weighted. Describe the investment strategy you need for each of the index types. Are any of the three strategies passive, in that no portfolio rebalancing need be performed to perfectly replicate the index (assuming no stock splits or cash distributions)? Which of the three strategies do you think is most often followed by small investors? Which strategy is the most difficult to implement?

S&P Problem

www.mhhe.com/edumarketinsight

STANDARD & POOR'S

1. Index Construction You have decided that you want a stock market index that tracks publishing companies. The three constituent companies you have decided to use are McGraw-Hill Companies (MHP), Morningstar, Inc. (MORN), and Value Line Inc. (VALU). For each company, download the monthly stock prices. Under the "Financial Hlts" link you can find the number of shares outstanding. Construct a price-weighted and a value-weighted index for the publishing industry for the last six months. Use a beginning index value of 100 where appropriate. What are the monthly returns for each index?

What's on the Web?

1. **Specialists** Go to www.nyse.com and find the discussion of NYSE members. What are the five essential functions of the specialist according to the Web site?
2. **DJIA** As you have seen, in a price-weighted index, a stock with a higher price has a higher weight in the index return. To find out the weight of the stocks in the DJIA, go to www.djindexes.com. Which stock in the DJIA has the highest weight? The lowest weight?
3. **DJIA** You want to find the current divisor for the DJIA. Go to www.djindexes.com and look up the current divisor.
4. **S&P 500** To find out the most recent changes in the S&P 500, go to www2.standardandpoors.com. Once at the Web site, find the 10 most recent additions and deletions to the stocks in the index.
5. **Nikkei 225** The Nikkei 225 Index is a highly followed index that measures the performance of the Japanese stock market. Go to www.nni.nikkei.co.jp and find out if the Nikkei 225 is a price-weighted or value-weighted index. What is the divisor for this index? When was the latest reconstitution of the index? Which stocks were added? Which stocks were deleted? Hint: Look in the "Help" section.

Stock-Trak Exercises

STOCK | TRAK

GLOBAL PORTFOLIO SIMULATIONS

To access the Stock-Trak Exercise for this chapter, please visit the book Web site at www.mhhe.com/jm5e and choose the corresponding chapter.

CHAPTER 6
Common Stock Valuation

"If a business is worth a dollar and I can buy it for 40 cents, something good may happen to me."

–Warren Buffett

"Prediction is difficult, especially about the future."

–Niels Bohr[1]

Common stock valuation is one of the most challenging tasks in financial analysis. A fundamental assertion of finance holds that the value of an asset is based on the present value of its future cash flows. Accordingly, common stock valuation attempts the difficult task of predicting the future. Consider that the dividend yield for a typical large-company stock might be about 2 percent. This implies that the present value of dividends to be paid over the next 10 years constitutes only a portion of the current stock price. Thus, much of the value of a typical stock is derived from dividends to be paid more than 10 years away! ■

Learning Objectives

Separate yourself from the commoners by having a good understanding of these security valuation methods:

1. The basic dividend discount model.
2. The two-stage dividend growth model.
3. The residual income model.
4. Price ratio analysis.

In this chapter, we examine several methods commonly used by financial analysts to assess the economic value of common stocks. These methods are grouped into two categories: dividend discount models and price ratio models. After studying these models, we provide an analysis of a real company to illustrate the use of the methods discussed in this chapter.

[1] This quote has also been attributed to Yogi Berra, Samuel Goldwyn, and Mark Twain.

6.1 Security Analysis: Be Careful Out There

It may seem odd that we start our discussion with an admonition to be careful, but in this case, we think it is a good idea. The methods we discuss in this chapter are examples of those used by many investors and security analysts to assist in making buy and sell decisions for individual stocks. The basic idea is to identify both "undervalued" or "cheap" stocks to buy and "overvalued" or "rich" stocks to sell. In practice, however, many stocks that look cheap may in fact be correctly priced for reasons not immediately apparent to the analyst. Indeed, the hallmark of a good analyst is a cautious attitude and a willingness to probe further and deeper before committing to a final investment recommendation.

fundamental analysis
Examination of a firm's accounting statements and other financial and economic information to assess the economic value of a company's stock.

The type of security analysis we describe in this chapter falls under the heading of **fundamental analysis**. Numbers such as a company's earnings per share, cash flow, book equity value, and sales are often called *fundamentals* because they describe, on a basic level, a specific firm's operations and profits (or lack of profits).

Fundamental analysis represents the examination of these and other accounting statement-based company data used to assess the value of a company's stock. Information regarding such things as management quality, products, and product markets is often examined as well.

We urge you to be cautious when you apply these techniques. Further, the simpler the technique, the more cautious you should be. As our later chapter on market efficiency explains, there is good reason to believe that too-simple techniques that rely on widely available information are not likely to yield systematically superior investment results. In fact, they could lead to unnecessarily risky investment decisions. This is especially true for ordinary investors (like most of us) who do not have timely access to the information that a professional security analyst working for a major securities firm would possess.

WWW
Visit the New York Society of Security Analysts Web site at www.nyssa.org

As a result, our goal here is not to teach you how to "pick" stocks with a promise that you will become rich. Certainly, one chapter in an investments text is not likely to be sufficient to acquire that level of investment savvy. Still, an appreciation of the techniques in this chapter is important simply because buy and sell recommendations made by securities firms are frequently couched in the terms we introduce here. Much of the discussion of individual companies in the financial press relies on these concepts as well, so some background is necessary just to interpret commonly presented investment information. In essence, you must learn both the jargon and the concepts of security analysis.

CHECK THIS

6.1a What is fundamental analysis?

6.1b What is a "rich" stock? What is a "cheap" stock?

6.1c Why does valuing a stock necessarily involve predicting the future?

6.2 The Dividend Discount Model

dividend discount model (DDM)
Method of estimating the value of a share of stock as the present value of all expected future dividend payments.

A fundamental principle of finance says that the value of a security equals the sum of its future cash flows, where the cash flows are adjusted for risk and the time value of money. A popular model used to value common stock is the **dividend discount model**, or **DDM**. The dividend discount model values a share of stock as the sum of all expected future dividend payments, where the dividends are adjusted for risk and the time value of money.

For example, suppose a company pays a dividend at the end of each year. Let D_t denote a dividend to be paid t years from now, and let P_0 represent the present value of the future dividend stream. Also, let k denote the appropriate risk-adjusted discount rate. Using the dividend discount model, the present value of a share of this company's stock is measured as this sum of discounted future dividends:

$$P_0 = \frac{D_1}{(1+k)} + \frac{D_2}{(1+k)^2} + \frac{D_3}{(1+k)^3} + \cdots + \frac{D_T}{(1+k)^T} \quad (6.1)$$

In equation 6.1, we assume that the last dividend is paid T years from now. The value of T depends on the time of the *terminal,* or last, dividend. Thus, if $T = 3$ years and $D_1 = D_2 = D_3 = \$100$, the present value, P_0, is stated as:

WWW

Check out the American Association of Individual Investors Web site at www.aaii.com

$$P_0 = \frac{\$100}{(1+k)} + \frac{\$100}{(1+k)^2} + \frac{\$100}{(1+k)^3}$$

If the discount rate is $k = 10$ percent, then a quick calculation yields $P_0 = \$248.69$. Thus, the stock price should be about \$250 per share.

EXAMPLE 6.1

Using the Dividend Discount Model

Suppose again that a stock pays three annual dividends of \$100 per year and the discount rate is $k = 15$ percent. In this case, what is the price of the stock today?

With a 15 percent discount rate, we have:

$$P_0 = \frac{\$100}{(1.15)} + \frac{\$100}{(1.15)^2} + \frac{\$100}{(1.15)^3}$$

Check that the answer is $P_0 = \$228.32$.

EXAMPLE 6.2

Using the Dividend Discount Model Again

Suppose instead that the stock pays three annual dividends of \$10, \$20, and \$30 in years 1, 2, and 3, respectively, and the discount rate is $k = 10$ percent. What is the price of the stock today?

In this case, we have:

$$P_0 = \frac{\$10}{(1.10)} + \frac{\$20}{(1.10)^2} + \frac{\$30}{(1.10)^3}$$

Check that the answer is $P_0 = \$48.16$.

CONSTANT PERPETUAL GROWTH

constant perpetual growth model
A version of the dividend discount model in which dividends grow forever at a constant rate, and the growth rate is strictly less than the discount rate.

A particularly simple and useful form of the dividend discount model is called the **constant perpetual growth model**. In this case, we assume the firm will pay dividends that grow at the constant rate g forever. In the constant perpetual growth model, stock prices are calculated using this formula:

$$P_0 = \frac{D_0(1+g)}{k-g} \qquad (g < k) \quad (6.2)$$

Because $D_0(1+g) = D_1$, we can also write the constant perpetual growth model as:

WWW

Try surfing to the CFA Institute Web site at www.cfainstitute.org

$$P_0 = \frac{D_1}{k-g} \qquad (g < k) \quad (6.3)$$

Either way, we have a very simple, and very widely used, formula for the price of a share of stock based on its future dividend payments.

Notice that the constant perpetual growth model requires that the growth rate be strictly less than the discount rate, that is, $g < k$. It looks as if the share value would be negative if this were not true. Actually, the formula is simply not valid in this case. The reason is that a perpetual dividend growth rate greater than the discount rate implies an *infinite* value because the present value of the dividends keeps getting bigger and bigger. Because no security can have infinite value, the requirement that $g < k$ simply makes good economic sense.

To illustrate the constant perpetual growth model, suppose that the growth rate is g = 4 percent, the discount rate is k = 9 percent, and the current dividend is D_0 = \$10. In this case, a simple calculation yields:

$$P_0 = \frac{\$10(1.04)}{.09 - .04} = \$208$$

EXAMPLE 6.3

Using the Constant Perpetual Growth Model

Suppose dividends for a particular company are projected to grow at 5 percent forever. If the discount rate is 15 percent and the current dividend is \$10, what is the value of the stock?

$$P_0 = \frac{\$10(1.05)}{.15 - .05} = \$105$$

with these inputs, the stock should sell for \$105.

HOW DO WE GET THE FORMULA FOR CONSTANT PERPETUAL GROWTH? Good question. Many people wonder how such a simple-looking formula, equation (6.3), emerges when we add up an infinite number of dividends. Recall that perpetual dividend growth means that dividends will grow forever. This means today's stock price, P_0, equals

$$P_0 = \frac{D_1}{(1+k)} + \frac{D_1(1+g)}{(1+k)^2} + \frac{D_1(1+g)^2}{(1+k)^3} + \frac{D_1(1+g)^3}{(1+k)^4} \cdots \tag{6.4}$$

Equation (6.4) says that the stock price today is equal to the sum of the discounted amounts of all future dividends. To get the formula for today's stock price when assuming constant perpetual growth, we begin by multiplying both sides of equation (6.4) by the amount $[(1 + g)/(1 + k)]$. Equation (6.4) then becomes

$$P_0\left[\frac{(1+g)}{(1+k)}\right] = \frac{D_1}{(1+k)}\left[\frac{(1+g)}{(1+k)}\right] + \frac{D_1(1+g)}{(1+k)^2}\left[\frac{(1+g)}{(1+k)}\right] + \frac{D_1(1+g)^2}{(1+k)^3}\left[\frac{(1+g)}{(1+k)}\right] + \cdots \tag{6.5}$$

$$= \frac{D_1(1+g)}{(1+k)^2} + \frac{D_1(1+g)^2}{(1+k)^3} + \frac{D_1(1+g)^3}{(1+k)^4} + \cdots$$

Then we simply subtract equation (6.5) from equation (6.4). If you look closely, you can see that when we do this, we can cancel a lot of terms. In fact, we can cancel *all* the terms on the right side of equation (6.5) and all but the first term on the right side of equation (6.4). Using a little bit of algebra, we show what happens when we subtract equation (6.5) from equation (6.4):

$$P_0 - P_0\frac{(1+g)}{(1+k)} = \frac{D_1}{(1+k)} + \frac{D_1(1+g)}{(1+k)^2} - \frac{D_1(1+g)}{(1+k)^2} + \frac{D_1(1+g)^2}{(1+k)^3} - \frac{D_1(1+g)^2}{(1+k)^3} + \cdots \tag{6.6}$$

$$P_0\left[1 - \frac{(1+g)}{(1+k)}\right] = \frac{D_1}{(1+k)}$$

$$P_0\left[\frac{(1+k)}{(1+k)} - \frac{(1+g)}{(1+k)}\right] = \frac{D_1}{(1+k)}$$

$$P_0\left[\frac{(k-g)}{(1+k)}\right] = \frac{D_1}{(1+k)}$$

$$P_0 = \frac{D_1}{(1+k)} \cdot \frac{(1+k)}{(k-g)}$$

$$P_0 = \frac{D_1}{k-g}$$

There. Now you know how we get a formula for the price of a share of stock when we assume that dividends grow at a constant rate forever. We apply this formula in the following section.

WWW

Visit the AEP and DTE Web sites at
www.aep.com
www.dteenergy.com

APPLICATIONS OF THE CONSTANT PERPETUAL GROWTH MODEL In practice, the constant perpetual growth model is the most popular dividend discount model because it is so simple to use. Certainly, the model satisfies Einstein's famous dictum: "Simplify as much as possible, but no more." However, experienced financial analysts are keenly aware that the constant perpetual growth model can be usefully applied only to companies with a history of relatively stable earnings and if dividend growth is expected to continue into the distant future.

A standard example of an industry for which the constant perpetual growth model can often be usefully applied is the electric utility industry. Consider American Electric Power, which is traded on the New York Stock Exchange under the ticker symbol AEP. In mid-2007, AEP was paying an annual dividend of \$1.56; thus we set $D_0 = \$1.56$.

To use the constant perpetual growth model, we also need a discount rate and a growth rate. An old quick and dirty rule of thumb for a risk-adjusted discount rate for electric utility companies is the yield to maturity on 20-year maturity U.S. Treasury bonds, plus 2 percent. At the time this example was written, the yield on 20-year maturity T-bonds was about 4.70 percent. Adding 2 percent, we get a discount rate of $k = 6.70$ percent.

In 2007 and in 2006, AEP increased its dividend about 5.5 percent. However, a future growth rate this high for AEP might be unduly optimistic because earnings growth in the electric utilities industry was projected to be about 2 percent per year. Thus, a rate of, say, 2 percent might be more realistic as an estimate of future growth for AEP.

Putting it all together, we have $k = 6.70$ percent, $g = 2$ percent, and $D_0 = \$1.56$. Using these numbers, we obtain this estimate for the value of a share of AEP stock:

$$P_0 = \frac{\$1.56(1.02)}{.067 - .02} = \$33.86$$

This estimate is somewhat below the mid-2007 AEP stock price of \$44.48, possibly suggesting that AEP stock was overvalued.

We emphasize the word "possibly" here because we made several assumptions in the process of coming up with this estimate. A change in any of these assumptions could easily lead us to a different conclusion. In particular, we made assumptions about the discount rate, the growth rate, and the steady nature of dividend growth. What happens when we change these assumptions? We will return to this point several times in future discussions.

EXAMPLE 6.4

Valuing DTE Energy Co. (formerly Detroit ED)

In 2007, the utility company DTE Energy (DTE) paid a \$2.12 dividend. Using $D_0 = \$2.12$, $k = 6.70$ percent, and an industry average growth rate of $g = 2$ percent, calculate a present value estimate for DTE. Compare this with the mid-2007 DTE stock price of \$47.81.

Plugging in the relevant numbers, we immediately have:

$$P_0 = \frac{\$2.12(1.02)}{.067 - .02} = \$46.01$$

This estimate is a little below the mid-2007 DTE stock price of \$47.81, suggesting that DTE stock was slightly overvalued.

geometric average dividend growth rate
A dividend growth rate based on a geometric average of historical dividends.

arithmetic average dividend growth rate
A dividend growth rate based on an arithmetic average of historical dividends.

HISTORICAL GROWTH RATES

In the constant growth model, a company's historical average dividend growth rate is frequently taken as an estimate of future dividend growth. Sometimes historical growth rates are provided in published information about the company. Other times it is necessary to calculate a historical growth rate yourself. There are two ways to do this: (1) using a **geometric average dividend growth rate** or (2) using an **arithmetic average dividend growth rate**. Both methods are relatively easy to implement, as we will now illustrate.

To illustrate the difference between a geometric average and an arithmetic average of historical dividend growth, suppose that The Broadway Joe Company paid the following dividends at the end of each of the years indicated immediately below.

2007:	\$2.20	2004:	\$1.75
2006:	2.00	2003:	1.70
2005:	1.80	2002:	1.50

We begin with a geometric average growth rate because it is the easiest to calculate. Notice that five years elapsed between the \$1.50 dividend paid at the end of 2002 and the \$2.20 dividend paid at the end of 2007. A geometric average growth rate is equivalent to a constant rate of growth over the five-year period that would grow the dividend from \$1.50 to \$2.20. That is, it is the growth rate that solves this growth equation:

$$\$2.20 = \$1.50(1 + g)^5$$

$$g = \left(\frac{\$2.20}{\$1.50}\right)^{1/5} - 1 = .08$$

Thus, in this case, the five-year geometric average dividend growth rate is 8 percent. Notice that this calculation is similar to our calculation of the geometric average return in Chapter 1.

In general, if D_0 is the earliest dividend used and D_N is the latest dividend used to calculate a geometric average dividend growth rate over N years, the general equation used is:

$$g = \left[\frac{D_N}{D_0}\right]^{1/N} - 1 \tag{6.7}$$

In the above example, $D_0 = \$1.50$, $D_N = \$2.20$, and $N = 5$, which yields $g = 8\%$.

An arithmetic average growth rate takes a little more effort to calculate, because it requires that we first calculate each year's dividend growth rate separately and then calculate an arithmetic average of these annual growth rates. For our Broadway Joe example, the arithmetic average of five years of dividend growth is calculated as follows:

Year	Dividend	Yearly Growth Rates
2007	\$2.20	10.00% = (2.20 − 2.00)/2.00
2006	2.00	11.11% = (2.00 − 1.80)/1.80
2005	1.80	2.86% = (1.80 − 1.75)/1.75
2004	1.75	2.94% = (1.75 − 1.70)/1.70
2003	1.70	13.33% = (1.70 − 1.50)/1.50
2002	1.50	
		SUM/N = 40.24%/5 = 8.05%

The sum of the five yearly growth rates is 40.24%. Dividing by five yields an arithmetic average growth rate of 40.24%/5 = 8.05%. Notice that this arithmetic average growth rate is close to the geometric average growth rate of 8.0 percent. This is usually the case for dividend growth rates, but not always. A large difference between the two means that the dividend grew erratically, which calls into question the use of the constant growth formula.

EXAMPLE 6.5 Erratic Dividend Growth

To illustrate how the geometric average and the arithmetic average of historical dividend growth can differ, consider the following dividends paid by the Joltin' Joe Company:

2007:	\$2.20	2004:	\$2.00
2006:	2.00	2003:	1.50
2005:	1.80	2002:	1.50

(continued)

For Joltin' Joe, the arithmetic average of five years of dividend growth is calculated as follows:

Year	Dividend	Yearly Growth Rates
2007	$2.20	10.00% = (2.20 − 2.00)/2.00
2006	2.00	11.11% = (2.00 − 1.80)/1.80
2005	1.80	−10.00% = (1.80 − 2.00)/2.00
2004	2.00	33.33% = (2.00 − 1.50)/1.50
2003	1.50	0.00% = (1.50 − 1.50)/1.50
2002	1.50	
		44.44/5 = 8.89%

In this case, the sum of the five yearly growth rates is 44.44. Dividing by five yields an arithmetic average growth rate of 44.44/5 = 8.89%. Notice that this arithmetic average growth rate is somewhat larger than the geometric average growth rate of 8.0 percent, which you can verify using Equation (6.7).

As the Joltin' Joe example shows, sometimes the arithmetic and geometric growth rate averages can yield rather different results. In practice, most analysts prefer to use a geometric average when calculating an average historical dividend growth rate. In any case, a historical average growth rate may or may not be a reasonable estimate of future dividend growth. Many analysts adjust their estimates to reflect other information available to them, for example, whether the growth rate appears to be sustainable.

THE SUSTAINABLE GROWTH RATE

sustainable growth rate
A dividend growth rate that can be sustained by a company's earnings.

retained earnings
Earnings retained within the firm to finance growth.

payout ratio
Proportion of earnings paid out as dividends.

retention ratio
Proportion of earnings retained for reinvestment.

As we have seen, when using the constant perpetual growth model, it is necessary to come up with an estimate of g, the growth rate of dividends. In our previous discussions, we described two ways to do this: (1) using the company's historical average growth rate or (2) using an industry median or average growth rate. We now describe a third way, known as the **sustainable growth rate**, which involves using a company's earnings to estimate g.

As we have discussed, a limitation of the constant perpetual growth model is that it should be applied only to companies with stable dividend and earnings growth. Essentially, a company's earnings can be paid out as dividends to its stockholders or kept as **retained earnings** within the firm to finance future growth. The proportion of earnings paid to stockholders as dividends is called the **payout ratio**. The proportion of earnings retained for reinvestment is called the **retention ratio**.

If we let D stand for dividends and EPS stand for earnings per share, then the payout ratio is simply D/EPS. Because anything not paid out is retained, the retention ratio is just one minus the payout ratio. For example, if a company's current dividend is \$4 per share, and its earnings per share are currently \$10, then the payout ratio is \$4/\$10 = .40, or 40 percent, and the retention ratio is 1 − .40 = .60, or 60 percent.

A firm's sustainable growth rate is equal to its return on equity (ROE) times its retention ratio.[2]

$$\text{Sustainable growth rate} = \text{ROE} \times \text{Retention ratio} \qquad (6.8)$$
$$= \text{ROE} \times (1 - \text{Payout ratio})$$

[2] Strictly speaking, this formula is correct only if ROE is calculated using beginning-of-period shareholders' equity. If ending figures are used, then the precise formula is ROE × Retention ratio / [1 − (ROE × Retention ratio)]. However, the error from not using the precise formula is usually small, so most analysts do not bother with it.

Return on equity is commonly computed using an accounting-based performance measure and is calculated as a firm's net income divided by shareholders' equity:

$$\textbf{Return on equity (ROE)} = \textbf{Net Income / Equity} \qquad \textbf{(6.9)}$$

EXAMPLE 6.6

Calculating Sustainable Growth

In 2007, American Electric Power (AEP) had a return on equity (ROE) of 10.17 percent, earnings per share (EPS) of \$2.25, and paid dividends of D_0 = \$1.56. What was AEP's retention rate? Its sustainable growth rate?

AEP's dividend payout was \$1.56/\$2.25 = .693, or about 69.3 percent. Its retention ratio was thus 1 − .693 = .307, or 30.7 percent. Finally, AEP's sustainable growth rate was .1017 × .307 = .03122, or 3.122 percent.

EXAMPLE 6.7

Valuing American Electric Power (AEP)

Using AEP's sustainable growth rate of 3.122 percent (see Example 6.6) as an estimate of perpetual dividend growth and its current dividend of \$1.56, what is the value of AEP's stock assuming a discount rate of 6.7 percent?

If we plug the various numbers into the perpetual growth model, we obtain a value of P_0 = \$1.56(1.03122)/(.067 − .03122) = \$44.96.

In mid-2007, share prices for AEP were \$45.41. In this case, using the sustainable growth rate to value the stock gives a reasonably accurate estimate.

EXAMPLE 6.8

Valuing DTE Energy Co. (DTE)

In 2007, DTE had a return on equity (ROE) of 14.68 percent, earnings per share (EPS) of \$4.80, and a per-share dividend of D_0 = \$2.12. Assuming a 6.7 percent discount rate, what is the value of DTE's stock?

DTE's payout ratio was \$2.12/\$4.80 = .4417, or about 44.2 percent. Thus, DTE's retention ratio was 1 − .442 = .558, or 55.8 percent. DTE's sustainable growth rate is thus 14.68% × .558 = 8.19%. Finally, using the constant growth model, we obtain a value of \$2.12(1.0819)/(.067 − .0819) = −\$153.93! Clearly, something is wrong because we have a negative price. The problem is that the estimate of the sustainable growth rate (8.19%) is greater than the estimate of the discount rate (6.70%). So, if the discount rate is appropriate, we conclude the estimate of the sustainable growth rate is too high.

A common problem with sustainable growth rates is that they are sensitive to year-to-year fluctuations in earnings. As a result, security analysts routinely adjust sustainable growth rate estimates to smooth out the effects of earnings variations. Unfortunately, there is no universally standard method to adjust a sustainable growth rate, and analysts depend a great deal on personal experience and their own subjective judgment. Our nearby *Work the Web* box contains more information on analyst-estimated growth rates.

CHECK THIS

6.2a Compare the dividend discount model, the constant growth model, and the constant perpetual growth model. How are they alike? How do they differ?

6.2b What is a geometric average growth rate? How is it calculated?

6.2c What is a sustainable growth rate? How is it calculated?

WORK THE WEB

We discussed use of the sustainable growth formula to estimate a company's growth rate; however, the formula is not foolproof. Changes in the variables of the model can have a dramatic effect on growth rates. One of the most important tasks of an equity analyst is estimating future growth rates. These estimates require a detailed analysis of the company. One place to find earnings and sales growth rates on the Web is Yahoo! Finance at finance.yahoo.com. Here, we pulled up a quote for Coca-Cola (KO) and followed the "Analysts Estimates" link. Below you will see an abbreviated look at the results.

Earnings Est	Current Qtr Sep-07	Next Qtr Dec-07	Current Year Dec-07	Next Year Dec-08
Avg. Estimate	0.68	0.54	2.63	2.92
No. of Analysts	13	12	16	16
Low Estimate	0.67	0.51	2.59	2.83
High Estimate	0.69	0.58	2.66	2.97
Year Ago EPS	0.62	0.52	2.37	2.63

Revenue Est	Current Qtr Sep-07	Next Qtr Dec-07	Current Year Dec-07	Next Year Dec-08
Avg. Estimate	7.32B	6.73B	27.89B	30.28B
No. of Analysts	7	7	12	11
Low Estimate	6.86B	6.40B	27.14B	29.44B
High Estimate	7.79B	7.16B	28.79B	31.58B
Year Ago Sales	6.45B	5.93B	24.09B	27.89B
Sales Growth (year/est)	13.5%	13.5%	15.8%	8.6%

As shown, analysts expect revenue (sales) of $27.89 billion in 2007, growing to $30.28 billion in 2008, an increase of 8.6 percent. We also have the following table comparing Coca-Cola to some benchmarks:

Growth Est	KO	Industry	Sector	S&P 500
Current Qtr.	9.7%	8.7%	-2.7%	5.2%
Next Qtr.	3.8%	8.5%	20.8%	11.9%
This Year	11.0%	10.9%	-2.9%	8.2%
Next Year	11.0%	11.1%	21.0%	11.7%
Past 5 Years (per annum)	7.379%	N/A	N/A	N/A
Next 5 Years (per annum)	9.13%	9.68%	9.65%	N/A
Price/Earnings (avg. for comparison categories)	20.67	19.66	20.28	15.59
PEG Ratio (avg. for comparison categories)	2.26	2.03	2.1	N/A

As you can see, estimated earnings growth this year for KO is slightly higher than estimates for the industry and quite a bit higher than the S&P 500 estimate. What about next year? Here is an assignment for you: What is the PEG ratio? Locate a financial glossary on the Web (there are lots of them) to find out.

6.3 The Two-Stage Dividend Growth Model

In the previous section, the dividend discount model used one growth rate. You might have already thought that a single growth rate is often unrealistic. You might be thinking that companies experience temporary periods of unusually high or low growth, with growth eventually converging to an industry average or an economywide average. In these cases, financial analysts frequently use a **two-stage dividend growth model**.

two-stage dividend growth model
A dividend discount model that assumes a firm will temporarily grow at a rate different from its long-term growth rate.

A two-stage dividend growth model assumes that a firm will initially grow at a rate g_1 during a first stage of growth lasting T years and thereafter grow at a rate g_2 during a perpetual second stage of growth. The formula for the two-stage dividend growth model is stated as follows:

$$P_0 = \frac{D_0(1+g_1)}{k-g_1}\left[1-\left(\frac{1+g_1}{1+k}\right)^T\right] + \left(\frac{1+g_1}{1+k}\right)^T\left[\frac{D_0(1+g_2)}{k-g_2}\right] \quad \textbf{(6.10)}$$

At first glance, you might think that this expression looks a little complicated. Well, you are right. Let's make it easier by looking at each part of the formula. We'll start with the part of the formula to the left of the + sign in equation (6.10). To show how we get this part of the formula, we pretend that dividends grow at the constant rate g_1 forever. We do this because we want to know the value today of all the dividends beginning one date from now to Date T—the date where the dividend growth rate changes from g_1 to g_2. To begin, look at Figure 6.1.

You already know the formula for the value of the sum of all dividends that will be received beginning one date from now and growing at a constant rate g_1 in perpetuity. In Figure 6.1, (A_0) represents the value today of this set of cash flows. That is,

$$A_0 = \frac{D_0(1+g_1)}{k-g_1} \quad \textbf{(6.11)}$$

Now for something just a little bit different. Let us focus our attention on date T. Starting at date T, the value of the sum of all dividends that we will receive beginning one date from T (i.e., at date $T+1$) and growing at a constant rate g_1 in perpetuity is

$$B_T = \frac{D_0(1+g_1)^{T+1}}{k-g_1} \quad \textbf{(6.12)}$$

What is the value of these dividends today? To answer this, we discount this amount by $1/(1+k)^T$:

$$B_0 = \frac{1}{(1+k)^T}\left[\frac{D_0(1+g_1)^{T+1}}{k-g_1}\right] \quad \textbf{(6.13)}$$

What happens if we subtract B_0 from A_0? Looking at the timeline in Figure 6.1, you can see that we are left with the value of all dividends beginning one date from now and ending at Date T. That is,

$$C_0 = \frac{D_0(1+g_1)}{k-g_1} - \frac{1}{(1+k)^T}\left[\frac{D_0(1+g_1)^{T+1}}{k-g_1}\right] \quad \textbf{(6.14)}$$

FIGURE 6.1 A Handy Dividend Timeline

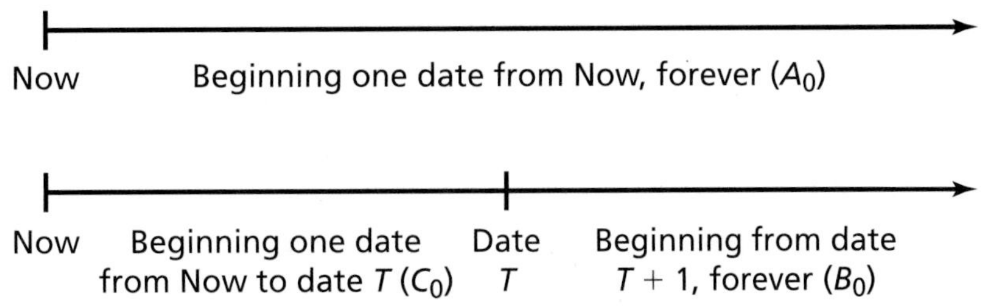

To help make equation (6.14) easier to calculate, recall that $D_0(1 + g_1)^{T+1}$ is $D_0(1 + g_1)(1 + g_1)^T$. Therefore, we can rewrite equation (6.14) as

$$C_0 = \frac{D_0(1 + g_1)}{k - g_1} - \frac{1}{(1 + k)^T}\left[\frac{D_0(1 + g_1)(1 + g_1)^T}{k - g_1}\right]$$

or, with some rearranging, we get

$$C_0 = \frac{D_0(1 + g_1)}{k - g_1} - \frac{D_0(1 + g_1)}{k - g_1}\left[\frac{(1 + g_1)^T}{(1+ k)^T}\right]$$

which is the term to the left of the + sign in equation (6.10):

$$C_0 = \frac{D_0(1 + g_1)}{k - g_1}\left[1 - \left(\frac{1 + g_1}{1 + k}\right)^T\right]$$

Now we have all the parts needed to write the term to the right of the + sign in equation (6.10). All we have to do is ask, what is the value now of all dividends received beginning at date $T + 1$ if dividends grow in perpetuity at the rate g_2 after Date T? To answer this question, we have to know what the dividend is at Date $T + 1$. We know the current dividend D_0 increases each date by $(1 + g_1)$ until Date T. Beginning at Date T, the growth rate becomes g_2. Therefore, the dividend at Date $T + 1$ is the amount $D_0(1 + g_1)^T(1 + g_2)$. We add an asterisk (*) to B_0 to alert us to the fact that the dividend growth rate has changed. So,

$$B_0^* = \frac{1}{(1 + k)^T}\left[\frac{D_0(1 + g_1)^T(1 + g_2)}{k - g_2}\right] \tag{6.15}$$

We see that equations (6.13) and (6.15) are quite similar. The difference is the value of the dividend at date $T + 1$. In equation (6.13), this dividend value is $D_0(1 + g_1)^{T+1}$, or $D_0(1 + g_1)(1 + g_1)^T$. In equation (6.15), this value is $D_0(1 + g_1)^T(1 + g_2)$.

With some rearranging, equation (6.15) becomes the term to the right of the + sign in equation (6.10). That is,

$$B_0^* = \frac{1}{(1 + k)^T}\left[\frac{D_0(1 + g_1)^T(1 + g_2)}{k - g_2}\right]$$

is

$$B_0^* = \left(\frac{1 + g_1}{1 + k}\right)^T\left[\frac{D_0(1 + g_2)}{k - g_2}\right]$$

To recap, equation (6.10) has two parts. The first term on the right-hand side measures the present value of the first T dividends, which is the value A_0 in equation (6.11). The second term then measures the present value of all subsequent dividends, assuming that the dividend growth rate changes from g_1 to g_2 at date T. We show that this value is B_0^* in equation (6.15).

Using the formula is mostly a matter of "plug and chug" with a calculator. For example, suppose a firm has a current dividend of \$2, and dividends are expected to grow at the rate $g_1 = 20$ percent for $T = 5$ years, and thereafter grow at the rate $g_2 = 5$ percent. With a discount rate of $k = 12$ percent, the stock price today, P_0, is calculated as:

$$\begin{aligned} P_0 &= \frac{\$2(1.20)}{.12 - .20}\left[1 - \left(\frac{1.20}{1.12}\right)^5\right] + \left(\frac{1.20}{1.12}\right)^5\left[\frac{\$2(1.05)}{.12 - .05}\right] \\ &= \$12.36 + \$42.36 \\ &= \$54.72 \end{aligned}$$

In this calculation, the total present value of \$54.72 is the sum of a \$12.36 present value for the first five dividends plus a \$42.36 present value for all subsequent dividends.

EXAMPLE 6.9 Using the Two-Stage Model

Suppose a firm has a current dividend of D_0 = $5, which is expected to "shrink" at the rate $g_1 = -10$ percent for $T = 5$ years and thereafter grow at the rate $g_2 = 4$ percent. With a discount rate of $k = 10$ percent, what is the value of the stock?

Using the two-stage model, the stock price today, P_0, is calculated as:

$$P_0 = \frac{\$5(.90)}{.10-(-.10)}\left[1-\left(\frac{.90}{1.10}\right)^5\right]+\left(\frac{.90}{1.10}\right)^5\left[\frac{\$5(1.04)}{.10-.04}\right]$$
$$= \$14.25 + \$31.78$$
$$= \$46.03$$

The total present value of $46.03 is the sum of a $14.25 present value of the first five dividends plus a $31.78 present value of all subsequent dividends.

The two-stage growth formula requires that the second-stage growth rate be strictly less than the discount rate, that is, $g_2 < k$. However, the first-stage growth rate g_1 can be greater than, less than, or equal to the discount rate.

EXAMPLE 6.10 Valuing American Express (AXP)

American Express trades on the New York Stock Exchange under the ticker symbol AXP. In 2007, AXP was paying a dividend of $.60 and analysts forecast five-year growth rates of 12.29 percent for AXP and 12.60 percent for the financial services industry. Assume the growth rate for the financial services industry will remain constant. Then, assuming AXP's growth rate will revert to the industry average after five years, what value would we place on AXP, if we use a discount rate of 14 percent?

$$P_0 = \frac{\$.60\,(1.1229)}{.14-.1229}\left[1-\left(\frac{1.1229}{1.14}\right)^5\right]+\left(\frac{1.1229}{1.14}\right)^5\left[\frac{\$.60(1.126)}{.14-.126}\right]$$
$$= \$39.40 \times .07278 + .92722 \times \$48.26$$
$$= \$2.87 + \$44.75$$
$$= \$47.62$$

This present value estimate is less than AXP's mid-2007 share price of $59.37. Is AXP overvalued? What other factors could explain the difference?

EXAMPLE 6.11 Have a Pepsi? (PEP)

Pepsi shares trade on the New York Stock Exchange under the ticker symbol PEP. In 2007, Pepsi was paying a dividend of $1.50 and analysts forecast a five-year growth rate of 10.96 percent for Pepsi and an 8.68 percent growth rate for the soft-drink industry. Suppose Pepsi grows at 11 percent for five years and then at 8.5 percent thereafter. Assuming a 10.5 percent discount rate, what value would we place on PEP?

Plugging this information into the two-stage dividend growth model, we get:

$$P_0 = \frac{\$1.50\,(1.11)}{.105-.11}\left[1-\left(\frac{1.11}{1.105}\right)^5\right]+\left(\frac{1.11}{1.105}\right)^5\left[\frac{\$1.50\,(1.085)}{.105-.085}\right]$$
$$= (-\$333.00) \times (-.02283) + 1.02283 \times \$81.38$$
$$= \$7.60 + \$83.24$$
$$= \$90.84$$

(continued)

This estimate is about 34 percent higher than PEP's mid-2007 share price of $67.74. Suppose we try a second-stage growth rate of 7.75 percent. Then, we get:

$$P_0 = \frac{\$1.50\,(1.11)}{.105 - .11}\left[1 - \left(\frac{1.11}{1.105}\right)^5\right] + \left(\frac{1.11}{1.105}\right)^5\left[\frac{\$1.50\,(1.0775)}{.105 - .0775}\right]$$

$$= (-\$333.00) \times (-.02283) + 1.02283 \times \$58.77$$

$$= \$7.60 + \$60.11$$

$$= \$67.71$$

This yields a much more realistic stock price estimate and illustrates how sensitive dividend growth price formulas can be to small changes in estimated growth rates.

NONCONSTANT GROWTH IN THE FIRST STAGE

WWW

Visit AXP and PEP Web sites at www.americanexpress.com and www.pepsico.com

The last case we consider is nonconstant growth in the first stage. As a simple example of nonconstant growth, consider the case of a company that is currently not paying dividends. You predict that, in five years, the company will pay a dividend for the first time. The dividend will be $.50 per share. You expect that this dividend will then grow at a rate of 10 percent per year indefinitely. The required return on companies such as this one is 20 percent. What is the price of the stock today?

To see what the stock is worth today, we first find out what it will be worth once dividends are paid. We can then calculate the present value of that future price to get today's price. The first dividend will be paid in five years, and the dividend will grow steadily from then on. Using the dividend growth model, we can say that the price in four years will be:

$$P_4 = D_4 \times (1 + g)/(k - g)$$

$$= D_5/(k - g)$$

$$= \$.50/(.20 - .10)$$

$$= \$5$$

If the stock will be worth $5 in four years, then we can get the current value by discounting this price back four years at 20 percent:

$$P_0 = \$5/1.20^4 = \$5/2.0736 = \$2.41$$

The stock is therefore worth $2.41 today.

The problem of nonconstant growth is only slightly more complicated if the dividends are not zero for the first several years. For example, suppose that you have come up with the following dividend forecasts for the next three years:

Year	Expected Dividend
1	$1.00
2	2.00
3	2.50

After the third year, the dividend will grow at a constant rate of 5 percent per year. The required return is 10 percent. What is the value of the stock today?

In dealing with nonconstant growth, a time line can be very helpful. Figure 6.2 illustrates one for this problem. The important thing to notice is when constant growth starts. As we've shown, for this problem, constant growth starts at Time 3. This means that we can use our constant growth model to determine the stock price at Time 3, P_3. By far the most common mistake in this situation is to incorrectly identify the start of the constant growth phase and, as a result, calculate the future stock price at the wrong time.

FIGURE 6.2 Time Line

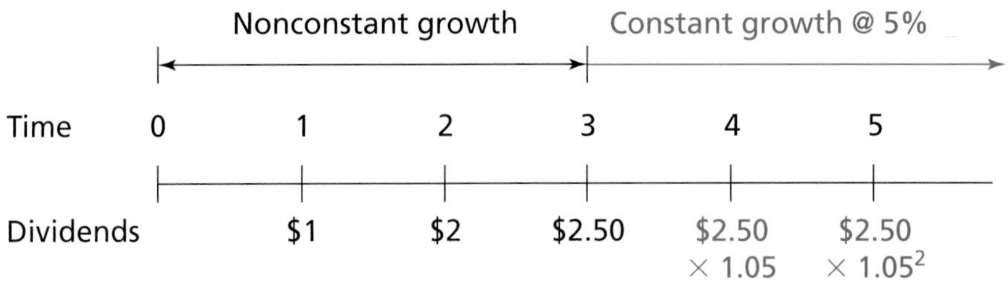

The value of the stock is the present value of all future dividends. To calculate this present value, we first have to compute the present value of the stock price three years down the road, just as we did before. We then have to add in the present value of the dividends that will be paid between now and then. So, the price in three years is:

$$\begin{aligned} P_3 &= D_3 \times (1 + g)/(k - g) \\ &= \$2.50 \times 1.05/(.10 - .05) \\ &= \$52.50 \end{aligned}$$

We can now calculate the total value of the stock as the present value of the first three dividends plus the present value of the price at Time 3, P_3.

$$\begin{aligned} P_0 &= \frac{D_1}{(1 + k)^1} + \frac{D_2}{(1 + k)^2} + \frac{D_3}{(1 + k)^3} + \frac{P_3}{(1 + k)^3} \\ &= \frac{\$1}{1.10} + \frac{2}{1.10^2} + \frac{2.50}{1.10^3} + \frac{52.50}{1.10^3} \\ &= \$.91 + 1.65 + 1.88 + 39.44 \\ &= \$43.88 \end{aligned}$$

The value of the stock today is thus \$43.88.

EXAMPLE 6.12 "Supernormal" Growth

Chain Reaction, Inc., has been growing at a phenomenal rate of 30 percent per year because of its rapid expansion and explosive sales. You believe that this growth rate will last for three more years and that the rate will then drop to 10 percent per year. If the growth rate then remains at 10 percent indefinitely, what is the total value of the stock? Total dividends just paid were \$5 million, and the required return is 20 percent.

Chain Reaction's situation is an example of supernormal growth. It is unlikely that a 30 percent growth rate can be sustained for any extended length of time. To value the equity in this company, we first need to calculate the total dividends over the supernormal growth period:

Year	Total Dividends (in millions)
1	\$5.00 × 1.3 = \$ 6.500
2	6.50 × 1.3 = 8.450
3	8.45 × 1.3 = 10.985

The price at Time 3 can be calculated as:

$$P_3 = D_3 \times (1 + g)/(k - g)$$

where g is the long-run growth rate. So we have:

$$P_3 = \$10.985 \times 1.10/(.20 - .10) = \$120.835 \text{ million}$$

(continued)

To determine the value today, we need the present value of this amount plus the present value of the total dividends:

$$P_0 = \frac{D_1}{(1+k)^1} + \frac{D_2}{(1+k)^2} + \frac{D_3}{(1+k)^3} + \frac{P_3}{(1+k)^3}$$

$$= \frac{\$6.50}{1.20} + \frac{8.45}{1.20^2} + \frac{10.985}{1.20^3} + \frac{120.835}{1.20^3}$$

$$= \$5.42 + 5.87 + 6.36 + 69.93$$

$$= \$87.58$$

The total value of the stock today is thus \$87.58 million. If there were, for example, 20 million shares, then the stock would be worth \$87.58/20 = \$4.38 per share.

DISCOUNT RATES FOR DIVIDEND DISCOUNT MODELS

You may wonder where the discount rates used in the preceding examples come from. The answer is that they come from the *capital asset pricing model* (CAPM). Although a detailed discussion of the CAPM is deferred to a later chapter, we can point out here that, based on the CAPM, the discount rate for a stock can be estimated using this formula:

Discount rate = U.S. T-bill rate + (Stock beta × Stock market risk premium) **(6.16)**

The components of this formula, as we use it here, are defined as follows:

U.S. T-bill rate:	Return on 90-day U.S. T-bills
Stock beta:	Risk relative to an average stock
Stock market risk premium:	Risk premium for an average stock

The basic intuition for this approach can be traced back to Chapter 1. There we saw that the return we expect to earn on a risky asset had two parts, a "wait" component and a "worry" component. We labeled the wait component as the *time value of money,* and we noted that it can be measured as the return we earn from an essentially riskless investment. Here we use the return on a 90-day Treasury bill as the riskless return.

We called the worry component the *risk premium,* and we noted that the greater the risk, the greater the risk premium. Depending on the exact period studied, the risk premium for the market as a whole over the past 80 or so years has averaged about 9.0 percent. This 9.0 percent can be interpreted as the risk premium for bearing an average amount of stock market risk, and we use it as the stock market risk premium.

beta
Measure of a stock's risk relative to the stock market average.

Finally, when we look at a particular stock, we recognize that it may be more or less risky than an average stock. A stock's **beta** is a measure of a single stock's risk relative to an average stock, and we discuss beta at length in a later chapter. For now, it suffices to know that the market average beta is 1.0. A beta of 1.5 indicates that a stock has 50 percent more risk than the average stock, so its risk premium is 50 percent higher. A beta of .50 indicates that a stock is 50 percent less risky than average and has a smaller risk premium.

When this chapter was written, the T-bill rate was about 4.5 percent. Taking the concept of stock beta as given for now, a stock beta of .8 yields an estimated discount rate of 4.5% + (.8 × 9%) = 11.7%. Similarly, a stock beta of 1.2 yields the discount rate of 4.5% + (1.2 × 9%) = 15.3%. For the remainder of this chapter, we will use discount rates calculated according to this CAPM formula.

OBSERVATIONS ON DIVIDEND DISCOUNT MODELS

We have examined three dividend discount models: the constant perpetual growth model, the two-stage dividend growth model, and the nonconstant growth model. Each model has advantages and disadvantages. Certainly, the main advantage of the constant perpetual growth model is that it is simple to compute. However, it has several disadvantages: (1) it is not usable for firms not paying dividends, (2) it is not usable when the growth rate is greater than the discount rate, (3) it is sensitive to the choice of growth rate and discount rate, (4) discount rates and growth rates may be difficult to estimate accurately, and (5) constant perpetual growth is often an unrealistic assumption.

The two-stage dividend growth model offers several improvements: (1) it is more realistic, since it accounts for low, high, or zero growth in the first stage, followed by constant long-term growth in the second stage, and (2) it is usable when the first-stage growth rate is greater than the discount rate. However, the two-stage model is also sensitive to the choice of discount rate and growth rates, and it is not useful for companies that don't pay dividends. The nonconstant growth model is more flexible in this regard, but it still remains sensitive to the discount and growth rates assumed.

Financial analysts readily acknowledge the limitations of dividend discount models. Consequently, they also turn to other valuation methods to expand their analyses. In the next two sections, we discuss some popular stock valuation methods based on the residual income model and based on price ratios.

CHECK THIS

6.3a What are the three parts of a CAPM-determined discount rate?

6.3b Under what circumstances is a two-stage dividend discount model appropriate?

6.4 The Residual Income Model

To this point, we have been valuing only firms that pay dividends. What about the many companies that don't pay dividends? As it turns out, there is an elegant and simple model that we can use.

RESIDUAL INCOME

At the beginning of any period, we can think of the book, or the accounting, equity in a firm as representing the total amount of money that stockholders have tied up in the company. Let B_{t-1} stand for the book equity per share at the beginning of a period that ends at time t. Over the period, the stockholders have a required return on that investment of k. Thus, the required return in dollars, or required earnings per share ($REPS$), during the period that ends at time t is:

$$REPS_t = B_{t-1} \times k$$

The difference between actual earnings, EPS_t, and required earnings, $REPS_t$, during a period is called the *residual income, RI*, and is given by:

$$RI_t = EPS_t - REPS_t = EPS_t - B_{t-1} \times k$$

Economic Value Added (EVA)
A financial performance measure based on the difference between a firm's actual earnings and required earnings.

Residual income is sometimes called **Economic Value Added**, or **EVA** for short. It is also called "abnormal" earnings. Whatever it is called, it is the excess of actual earnings over required earnings. We can also think of it as the value created by a firm in period t.

Next, we can write the value of a share of stock as the sum of two parts. The first part is the current book value of the firm (i.e., what is currently invested). The second part is the present value of all future residual earnings. That is,

$$P_0 = B_0 + \frac{EPS_1 - B_0 \times k}{(1+k)^1} + \frac{EPS_2 - B_1 \times k}{(1+k)^2} + \frac{EPS_3 - B_2 \times k}{(1+k)^3} + \cdots \qquad (6.17)$$

When we developed the constant perpetual growth model for dividend-paying stocks, we made the simplifying assumption that *dividends* grow at a constant rate of g. Here we make the similar assumption that *earnings* grow at a constant rate of g. With this assumption, we can simplify equation (6.17) to:

$$P_0 = B_0 + \frac{EPS_0(1 + g) - B_0 \times k}{k - g} \tag{6.18}$$

residual income model (RIM)
A method for valuing stock in a company that does not pay dividends.

Equation (6.18) is known as the **residual income model**, or **RIM**. If we write both terms in equation (6.18) with a common denominator, we get another way to write the residual income model:

$$P_0 = \frac{EPS_1 - B_0 \times g}{k - g} \tag{6.19}$$

THE RIM VERSUS THE CONSTANT GROWTH DDM

clean surplus relationship (CSR)
An accounting relationship in which earnings minus dividends equals the change in book value per share.

The RIM is closely related to the constant perpetual growth dividend model. To see the connection, assume that the change in book value per share on a stock is equal to earnings per share minus dividends. This is known as the **clean surplus relationship (CSR)**, written as:

$$EPS_1 - D_1 = B_1 - B_0 \quad \text{or} \quad D_1 = EPS_1 + B_0 - B_1$$

Note that in practice the CSR does not exactly hold because various "dirty" surplus changes to book equity are allowed. But it is usually a good approximation, particularly over the long run.

Assuming that earnings and dividends per share grow at rate g, the CSR shows that book value per share must also grow at rate g, so we can write:

$$D_1 = EPS_1 + B_0 - B_1 = EPS_1 + B_0 - B_0(1 + g) = EPS_1 - B_0 \times g \tag{6.20}$$

Plugging the expression for D_1 from equation (6.20) into equation (6.19), we see right away that the residual income model is mathematically the same as the constant perpetual growth model:

$$P_0 = \frac{EPS_1 - B_0 \times g}{k - g} = \frac{D_1}{k - g}$$

So these two approaches are really the same, but the RIM is more flexible because we can apply it to any stock, not just dividend payers.

Although we do not present them, there are other forms of the RIM. For example, a two-stage residual income model incorporates two different periods of growth. Also, the case of nonconstant growth for a number of years followed by constant growth can be handled by another form of the residual income model.

EXAMPLE 6.13 Going Deep

Shares of Superior Offshore International, Inc., trade on the NASDAQ with the ticker symbol DEEP. This company is a provider of subsea construction and commercial diving services. Currently, DEEP pays no dividends. It is July 1, 2007, and DEEP shares are trading at $10.94. We have the following data:

Share Information	July 1, 2007 (Time 0)
EPS_0	\$1.20
Dividends	\$0
Book value per share, B_0	\$5.886

(continued)

Assume g = 9 percent and k = 13 percent. Using the residual income model,

$$P_0 = B_0 + \frac{EPS_0(1 + g) - B_0 \times k}{k - g}$$

$$= \$5.886 + \frac{\$1.20(1.09) - \$5.886 \times .13}{.13 - .09}$$

$$= \$5.886 + \frac{\$1.308 - \$.7652}{.04}$$

$$= \$19.46$$

Verify this price using equation (6.19). Be careful to use g, not $(1 + g)$. Is the market price for DEEP shares too low? If you say yes, what are you assuming about the values for g and k?

EXAMPLE 6.14

Deep Growth

Using the relevant data in Example 6.13 and the residual income model, what growth rate g results in a price of $10.94?

$$P_0 = B_0 + \frac{EPS_0(1 + g) - B_0 \times k}{k - g}$$

$$\$10.94 = 5.886 + \frac{1.20(1 + g) - 5.886 \times .13}{.13 - g}$$

$$\$5.054 \times (.13 - g) = 1.20 + 1.20g - .7652$$

$$\$.6570 - 5.054g = 1.20g + .4348$$

$$.2222 = 6.254g$$

$$g = .0355 \text{ or } 3.55\%$$

CHECK THIS

6.4a What does the residual income model do that the perpetual constant growth model cannot do?

6.4b What is the critical assumption that makes the residual income model mathematically equal to the perpetual constant growth model?

6.5 Price Ratio Analysis

Price ratios are widely used by financial analysts, more so even than dividend discount models. Of course, all valuation methods try to accomplish the same thing, which is to appraise the economic value of a company's stock. However, analysts readily agree that no single method can adequately handle this task on all occasions. In this section, we therefore examine several of the most popular price ratio methods and provide examples of their use in financial analysis.

price-earnings (P/E) ratio
Current stock price divided by annual earnings per share (EPS).

earnings yield (E/P)
Inverse of the P/E ratio: earnings per share divided by price per share.

PRICE-EARNINGS RATIOS

The most popular price ratio used to assess the value of common stock is a company's **price-earnings ratio**, abbreviated as **P/E ratio**. In fact, as we saw in Chapter 3, P/E ratios are reported in the financial press every day. As we discussed, a price-earnings ratio is calculated as the ratio of a firm's current stock price divided by its annual earnings per share (EPS).

The inverse of a P/E ratio is called an **earnings yield**, and it is measured as earnings per share divided by the current stock price (**E/P**). Clearly, an earnings yield and a price-earnings ratio are simply two ways to measure the same thing. In practice, earnings yields are less commonly stated and used than P/E ratios.

Because most companies report earnings each quarter, annual earnings per share can be calculated either as the most recent quarterly earnings per share times four or as the sum of the last four quarterly earnings per share figures. Most analysts prefer the first method of multiplying the latest quarterly earnings per share value times four. However, some published data sources, including *The Wall Street Journal,* report annual earnings per share as the sum of the last four quarters' figures. The difference is usually small, but it can sometimes be a source of confusion.

growth stocks
A term often used to describe high-P/E stocks.

Financial analysts often refer to high-P/E stocks as **growth stocks**. To see why, notice that a P/E ratio is measured as the *current* stock price over *current* earnings per share. Now, consider two companies with the same current earnings per share, where one company is a high-growth company and the other is a low-growth company. Which company do you think should have a higher stock price, the high-growth company or the low-growth company?

WWW

Visit the Starbucks and GM Web sites at www.starbucks.com and www.gm.com

This question is a no-brainer. All else equal, we would be surprised if the high-growth company did not have a higher stock price, and therefore a higher P/E ratio. In general, companies with higher expected earnings growth will have higher P/E ratios, which is why high-P/E stocks are often referred to as growth stocks.

To give an example, Starbucks Corporation is a specialty coffee retailer with a history of aggressive sales growth. Its stock trades on NASDAQ under the ticker symbol SBUX. In mid-2007, SBUX stock traded at \$26.88 with earnings per share (EPS) of \$.87, and so had a P/E ratio of \$26.88/\$.87 = 30.90. This P/E ratio is well above the average P/E ratio of about 16.8 for the S&P 500 (of which SBUX is a member). SBUX has never paid a dividend. Instead, Starbucks reinvests all earnings. So far this strategy has been successful, as the firm has grown at an average rate of 26 percent over the preceding five years.

value stocks
A term often used to describe low-P/E stocks.

The reason high-P/E stocks are called growth stocks seems obvious enough; however, in a seeming defiance of logic, low-P/E stocks are often referred to as **value stocks**. The reason is that low-P/E stocks are often viewed as "cheap" relative to *current* earnings. (Notice again the emphasis on "current.") This suggests that these stocks may represent good investment values, and hence the term value stocks.

In mid-2007, shares of the well-known S&P 500 auto company General Motors (GM) were trading at a price of \$31.08. With earnings per share of EPS = \$3.75, the P/E ratio is \$31.08/\$3.75 = 8.29. This is well below the S&P 500 average, and so General Motors might be considered a value stock.

Having said all this, we want to emphasize that the terms "growth stock" and "value stock" are mostly just commonly used labels. Of course, only time will tell whether a high-P/E stock actually turns out to be a high-growth stock, or whether a low-P/E stock is really a good value. The nearby *Investment Updates* box contains additional discussion of P/E ratios.

PRICE-CASH FLOW RATIOS

price-cash flow (P/CF) ratio
Current stock price divided by current cash flow per share.

Instead of price-earnings (P/E) ratios, many analysts prefer to look at price-cash flow (P/CF) ratios. A **price-cash flow (P/CF) ratio** is measured as a company's current stock price divided by its current annual cash flow per share. Like earnings, cash flow is normally reported quarterly and most analysts multiply the last quarterly cash flow figure by four to obtain annual cash flow. Again, like earnings, many published data sources report annual cash flow as a sum of the latest four quarterly cash flows.

cash flow
In the context of the price-cash flow ratio, usually taken to be net income plus depreciation.

There are a variety of definitions of **cash flow**. In this context, the most common measure is simply calculated as net income plus depreciation, so this is the one we use here. In a later chapter, we examine in detail how cash flow is calculated in a firm's financial statements. Cash flow is usually reported in a firm's financial statements and labeled as cash flow from operations (or operating cash flow).

The difference between earnings and cash flow is often confusing, largely because of the way that standard accounting practice defines net income. Essentially, net income is measured as revenues minus expenses. Obviously, this is logical. However, not all expenses are actually cash expenses. The most important exception is depreciation.

INVESTMENT UPDATES

ONCE A RUST BELT RELIC, U.S. STEEL IS NOW PROFITABLE, EFFICIENT . . . AND UNDERVALUED

Regardless of whether Pittsburgh-based U.S. Steel begins a major buyback program soon, its shares now look attractive, trading around $40. The current price is less than six times projected 2004 profits of $7.35 and six times the Wall Street consensus estimate for 2005 of $6.47 a share.

Bulls note that the 2005 consensus assumes a marked decline in domestic steel prices, which have more than doubled this year to about $650 a ton for benchmark hot-rolled products, up from $300 in late 2003. If steel prices hold around current levels, U.S. Steel could earn $10 or more a share in 2005. That may sound outlandish, but the company netted $2.56 a share from operations in the third quarter and could earn $3 in the current one.

"U.S. Steel is very undervalued," says Alan Fournier, a principal at Pennant Capital Management, a Chatham, N.J., investment firm. "The company is worth 50 percent more than where it's trading."

David Tepper, the head of Appaloosa Management, the company's second-largest shareholder, recently told management on its earnings conference call that U.S. Steel "has the lowest valuation" among the world's major steel makers. The latest publicly disclosed data shows that Tepper's Chatham, N.J.-based firm, a distressed-debt specialist that manages $3 billion, owns 5 percent of the company's 130 million outstanding shares.

Fournier and Tepper want U.S. Steel to buy back stock with its strong earnings and cash flow. Management has resisted those requests, preferring to use free cash to pay down debt, fund pension obligations, and make acquisitions.

Many investors still view U.S. Steel as a rusting relic of a bygone era when steel producers ruled American industry. But the company is now one of the globe's leading steel makers at a time when the industry may be on the brink of years of prosperity. U.S. Steel has world-class mills in the United States and central Europe. It also controls a vast supply of iron ore, a critical steel input in tight supply.

Indeed, U.S. Steel's integrated structure, which made it the industry leader in the early 20th century, is also a major advantage in the early 21st century. "Our position has never been better in my 20-plus years at the company," says John Surma, U.S. Steel's chief executive. "World appetite for steel is strong, and I don't see why that should change. Supply is constrained."

U.S. Steel is the biggest U.S.-based producer, with total expected 2004 production of 22 million tons, but it ranks sixth globally and accounts for just 2 percent of total world production. U.S. Steel generally is viewed as an asset acquirer—last year, it bought a steel outfit in Serbia—but it's conceivable the company could be taken over. One potential buyer is Arcelor, Europe's largest steel manufacturer.

The steel market's strength is being driven by rising demand from China, which now consumes 30 percent of the world's annual output of 1 billion tons. Chinese demand has doubled in the past four years. India, Eastern Europe, and the states of the former Soviet Union are sources of significant steel demand. Domestic steel consumption also has been high. U.S. Steel has a highly profitable steel plant in Slovakia, which is turning into a center of European auto production.

The Street worries that the sharp increase in steel prices will reverse, as it often has in the past. The cycle last turned down—in brutal fashion—in 2001, leading to bankruptcies of nearly half the U.S. steel industry. Given the importance of Chinese demand, steel stocks have been vulnerable to any sign of a slowdown in China's economy. U.S. Steel shares dipped last month when spot prices fell about $100 a ton from their peak summer level of $750.

U.S. Steel stock (with its famed ticker symbol X) rose over $3 last week amid some positive analyst comments. Goldman Sachs' Aldo Mazzaferro raised his rating to Outperform from In-Line, telling clients that the company "appears to be on the verge of a major breakout in earnings power." He lifted his 2005 profit projection to $8.25 a share from $7.90 and boosted his price target to $58 from $49.

Source: Andrew Bary, *Barron's*, November 8, 2004.

When a firm acquires a long-lived asset, such as a new factory, standard accounting practice does not deduct the cost of the factory all at once, even though it is actually paid for all at once. Instead, the cost is deducted over time. These deductions do not represent actual cash payments, however. The actual cash payment occurred when the factory was purchased. At this point you may be a little confused about why the difference is important, but hang in there for a few more paragraphs.

Most analysts agree that in examining a company's financial performance, cash flow can be more informative than net income. To see why, consider the hypothetical example of two identical companies: Twiddle-Dee Co. and Twiddle-Dum Co. Suppose that both companies have the same constant revenues and expenses in each year over a three-year period. These constant revenues and cash expenses (excluding depreciation) yield the same constant annual cash flows, and they are stated as follows:

	Twiddle-Dee	Twiddle-Dum
Revenues	$5,000	$5,000
Cash expenses	−3,000	−3,000
Cash flow	$2,000	$2,000

Thus, both companies have the same $2,000 cash flow in each of the three years of this hypothetical example.

Next, suppose that both companies incur total depreciation of $3,000 spread out over the three-year period. Standard accounting practices sometimes allow a manager to choose among several depreciation schedules. Twiddle-Dee Co. chooses straight-line depreciation, and Twiddle-Dum Co. chooses accelerated depreciation. These two depreciation schedules are tabulated below:

	Twiddle-Dee	Twiddle-Dum
Year 1	$1,000	$1,500
Year 2	1,000	1,000
Year 3	1,000	500
Total	$3,000	$3,000

Note that total depreciation over the three-year period is the same for both companies. However, Twiddle-Dee Co. has the same $1,000 depreciation in each year, while Twiddle-Dum Co. has accelerated depreciation of $1,500 in the first year, $1,000 in the second year, and $500 depreciation in the third year.

Now, let's look at the resulting annual cash flows and net income figures for the two companies, recalling that in each year, Cash flow = Net income + Depreciation:

	Twiddle-Dee		Twiddle-Dum	
	Cash Flow	Net Income	Cash Flow	Net Income
Year 1	$2,000	$1,000	$2,000	$ 500
Year 2	2,000	1,000	2,000	1,000
Year 3	2,000	1,000	2,000	1,500
Total	$6,000	$3,000	$6,000	$3,000

Note that Twiddle-Dum Co.'s net income is lower in the first year and higher in the third year than Twiddle-Dee Co.'s net income. This is purely a result of Twiddle-Dum Co.'s accelerated depreciation schedule, and has nothing to do with Twiddle-Dum Co.'s actual profitability. However, an inexperienced analyst observing Twiddle-Dum Co.'s rapidly rising annual earnings figures might incorrectly label Twiddle-Dum as a growth company. An experienced analyst would observe that there was no cash flow growth to support this naive conclusion.

Financial analysts typically use both price-earnings ratios and price-cash flow ratios. They point out that when a company's earnings per share is not significantly larger than its cash flow per share (CFPS), this is a signal, at least potentially, of good-quality earnings. The term "quality" means that the accounting earnings mostly reflect actual cash flow, not just accounting numbers. When earnings are bigger than cash flow, this may be a signal of poor quality earnings.

Going back to some of our earlier examples, Starbucks Corporation had cash flow per share of CFPS = $1.50, yielding a P/CF ratio of $26.88/$1.50 = 17.92. Notice that cash flow per share was roughly double earnings per share of $.87, suggesting high-quality earnings. GM had cash flow per share of CFPS = $22.75, yielding a P/CF ratio of $31.08/$22.75 = 1.37. GM cash flow per share is an unusually large 6.1 times its earnings per share, perhaps suggesting high-quality earnings.

PRICE-SALES RATIOS

price-sales (P/S) ratio
Current stock price divided by annual sales per share.

An alternative view of a company's performance is provided by its **price-sales (P/S) ratio.** A price-sales ratio is calculated as the current price of a company's stock divided by its current annual sales revenue per share. A price-sales ratio focuses on a company's ability to generate sales growth. Essentially, a high P/S ratio would suggest high sales growth, while a low P/S ratio might indicate sluggish sales growth.

For example, Starbucks Corporation had sales per share of $12.65 to yield a price-sales ratio of P/S = $26.88/$12.65 = 2.12. GM had sales per share of $317.95 for a price-sales ratio of P/S = $31.08/$317.95 = .10. Notice the large variation in price-sales ratios for the two companies. The main reason for this difference is that the two companies are in very different kinds of businesses. Security analysts recognize that price-sales ratios cannot be compared in isolation from other important information.

PRICE-BOOK RATIOS

price-book (P/B) ratio
Market value of a company's common stock divided by its book (or accounting) value of equity.

A very basic price ratio for a company is its **price-book (P/B) ratio**, sometimes called the market-book ratio. A price-book ratio is measured as the market value of a company's outstanding common stock divided by its book value of equity.

Price-book ratios are appealing because book values represent, in principle, historical cost. The stock price is an indicator of current value, so a price-book ratio simply measures what the equity is worth today relative to what it cost. A ratio bigger than 1.0 indicates that the firm has been successful in creating value for its stockholders. A ratio smaller than 1.0 indicates that the company is actually worth less than it cost.

This interpretation of the price-book ratio seems simple enough, but the truth is that because of varied and changing accounting standards, book values are difficult to interpret. For this and other reasons, price-book ratios may not have as much information value as they once did.

APPLICATIONS OF PRICE RATIO ANALYSIS

WWW
Check out the Intel Web site at www.intel.com

Price-earnings ratios, price-cash flow ratios, and price-sales ratios are commonly used to calculate estimates of expected future stock prices. This is done by multiplying a historical average price ratio by an expected future value for the price-ratio denominator variable. For example, Table 6.1 summarizes such a price ratio analysis for Intel Corporation (INTC) based on mid-2007 information.

In Table 6.1, the five-year average ratio row contains five-year average P/E, P/CF, and P/S ratios. The current value row contains values for earnings per share, cash flow per share, and sales per share; and the growth rate row contains five-year projected growth rates for EPS, CFPS, and SPS.

The expected price row contains expected stock prices one year hence. The basic idea is this. Because Intel had an average P/E ratio of 27.30, we will assume that Intel's stock price will be 27.30 times its earnings per share one year from now. To estimate Intel's earnings one year from now, we note that Intel's earnings are projected to grow at a rate of 8.5 percent per year. If earnings continue to grow at this rate, next year's earnings will be equal to this year's earnings times 1.085. Putting it all together, we have

$$\begin{aligned}\text{Expected price} &= \text{Historical P/E ratio} \times \text{Projected EPS}\\ &= \text{Historical P/E ratio} \times \text{Current EPS}\\ &\quad \times (1 + \text{Projected EPS growth rate})\\ &= 27.30 \times \$.86 \times 1.085\\ &= \$25.47\end{aligned}$$

TABLE 6.1 Price Ratio Analysis for Intel Corporation (INTC) Mid-2007 Stock Price: $24.27

	Earnings	Cash Flow	Sales
Five-year average price ratio	27.30 (P/E)	14.04 (P/CF)	4.51 (P/S)
Current value per share	$ .86 (EPS)	$ 1.68 (CFPS)	$ 6.14 (SPS)
Growth rate	8.5%	7.5%	7.0%
Expected stock price	$25.47	$25.36	$29.63

The same procedure is used to calculate an expected price based on cash flow per share:

$$\begin{aligned}\text{Expected price} &= \text{Historical P/CF ratio} \times \text{Projected CFPS}\\ &= \text{Historical P/CF ratio} \times \text{Current CFPS}\\ &\quad \times (1 + \text{Projected CFPS growth rate})\\ &= 14.04 \times \$1.68 \times 1.075\\ &= \$25.36\end{aligned}$$

Finally, an expected price based on sales per share is calculated as

$$\begin{aligned}\text{Expected price} &= \text{Historical P/S ratio} \times \text{Projected SPS}\\ &= \text{Historical P/S ratio} \times \text{Current SPS}\\ &\quad \times (1 + \text{Projected SPS growth rate})\\ &= 4.51 \times \$6.14 \times 1.07\\ &= \$29.63\end{aligned}$$

WWW

See Mickey's Web site at www.disney.go.com

Notice that in the case of Intel, the price ratio methods yield prices ranging from about $25 to about $30. However, when this analysis was made in mid-2007 Intel's stock price was around $24.27. This difference may be explained by the fact that price ratios for Intel have fallen sharply in recent years. For example, Intel's P/E ratio fell from a high of 45.8 in 2002 to just 23.3 in 2006. With such a large price-ratio decline, a historical average price ratio may be inaccurate.

TABLE 6.2 Price Ratio Analysis for Disney Corporation (DIS) Mid-2007 Stock Price: $34.55

	Earnings	Cash Flow	Sales
Five-year average price ratio	24.90 (P/E)	14.70 (P/CF)	1.59 (P/S)
Current value per share	$ 1.61 (EPS)	$ 2.39 (CFPS)	$16.61 (SPS)
Growth rate	14.5%	13%	9%
Expected stock price	$45.90	$39.70	$28.79

EXAMPLE 6.15 **Going to Disneyland**

Table 6.2 contains information about Walt Disney Corporation. Calculate expected share prices using each of the three price ratio approaches we have discussed.

For example, using the P/E approach, we come up with the following estimates of the price of Walt Disney stock in one year:

$$\begin{aligned}\text{Expected price} &= \text{Historical P/E ratio} \times \text{Current EPS}\\ &\quad \times (1 + \text{projected EPS growth})\\ &= 24.90 \times \$1.61 \times 1.145\\ &= \$45.90\end{aligned}$$

CHECK THIS

6.5a Why are high-P/E stocks sometimes called growth stocks?

6.5b Why might an analyst prefer a price-cash flow ratio to a price-earnings ratio?

6.6 An Analysis of the McGraw-Hill Company

Stock market investors have available to them many sources of information about the financial performance of companies with publicly traded stock shares. Indeed, the sheer volume of information available can often be overwhelming. For this reason, several sources publish reference summaries for individual companies.

WWW

Visit the McGraw-Hill Web site at www.mcgraw-hill.com

One well-known example is the *Value Line Investment Survey,* a published reference with frequent updates. *Value Line* provides what many serious investors consider to be the best one-page company summaries available. Current updates to the *Value Line Investment Survey* are available at most stock brokerage offices and many public libraries. In addition, these updates are available (to subscribers) as PDF files on *Value Line*'s Web site. Figure 6.3 presents a one-page summary for the McGraw-Hill Corporation published by *Value Line* in August 2007. We will make frequent reference to information found in the *Value Line* summary in the discussion of McGraw-Hill.

As shown in the title bar of Figure 6.3, McGraw-Hill stock trades on the New York Stock Exchange (NYSE) under the ticker symbol MHP. When this survey went to press in August 2007, McGraw-Hill's stock price was $57.27, with a P/E ratio of 18.8. *Value Line* calculates a P/E ratio as the most recent stock price divided by the latest six months' earnings per share plus earnings per share estimated for the next six months. McGraw-Hill's relative P/E ratio of 1.01 is obtained by dividing its current P/E by the median P/E ratio of all stocks under review by *Value Line*. The dividend yield of 1.4 percent is calculated by dividing estimated dividends for the coming year by the current stock price.

WWW

Check out Value Line's Web site at www.valueline.com

At this point, as you look over *Value Line*'s summary in Figure 6.3, you will realize that *Value Line* has packed a considerable amount of information onto a single page. Because there is so much information on the one-page *Value Line* survey, we can cover only some of the items on the page. Most items are well-explained in Figure 6.4, which contains a complete sample explanation page. However, some items in Figure 6.3 may differ from those in Figure 6.4 reflecting changes made by *Value Line*. In the following discussion, we refer only to information needed to illustrate the analytic methods discussed previously in this chapter.

USING THE DIVIDEND DISCOUNT MODEL

Our first task is to estimate a discount rate for McGraw-Hill. The *Value Line Investment Survey* reports a beta of .90 for McGraw-Hill stock. Using a current Treasury bill rate of 4.5 percent and a historical stock market risk premium of 9 percent, we obtain a CAPM discount rate estimate for McGraw-Hill of $4.5\% + .90 \times 9\% = 12.6\%$.

Our next task is to calculate a sustainable growth rate. *Value Line* reports projected 2008 earnings per share of $3.45 and projected 2008 dividends per share of $.82, implying a retention ratio of $1 - \$.82/\$3.45 = .762$. *Value Line* also reports a projected 2008 return on equity of ROE = 38.5 percent (reported as "Return on Shr. Equity"). Putting these together yields a sustainable growth rate of $.762 \times 38.5\% = 29.34\%$, which may be somewhat high for a mature company like McGraw-Hill.

Finally, with a discount rate and sustainable growth rate we can calculate a share price for McGraw-Hill. Using a constant dividend growth rate model with the 2007 dividend of $D_0 = \$.82$, a discount rate of $k = 12.6$ percent, and a growth rate of 29.34 percent, we get:

$$P_0 = \frac{\$.82 \times 1.2934}{.126 - .2934}$$
$$= \$-6.34$$

which cannot be. The negative price is due to a growth rate greater than the discount rate, indicating we cannot use the constant dividend growth rate model. As a good analyst would, we'll try something else.

USING THE RESIDUAL INCOME MODEL

In reality, a sustainable growth rate of over 29 percent is not feasible. *Value Line* reports that the actual dividend growth rate over the previous five years was 7.5 percent (from the box labeled "Annual Rates"). You can audit this number by calculating a simple or geometric average dividend growth rate using dividends per share from 2002 through 2007. (Which one rounds to 7.5 percent?)

FIGURE 6.3 *Value Line* Analysis Chart

McGRAW-HILL NYSE-MHP

RECENT PRICE **57.27** | P/E RATIO **18.8** (Trailing: 20.1 Median: 22.0) | RELATIVE P/E RATIO **1.01** | DIV'D YLD **1.4%** | VALUE LINE

TIMELINESS 3 Lowered 8/17/07
SAFETY 1 Raised 6/4/93
TECHNICAL 3 Raised 7/6/07
BETA .90 (1.00 = Market)

High:	12.3	18.8	25.8	31.6	33.8	35.4	34.8	35.0	46.1	54.0	69.3	72.5
Low:	9.3	11.2	17.1	23.6	20.9	24.3	25.4	25.9	34.6	40.5	46.4	56.1

Target Price Range
2010 | 2011 | 2012

2010-12 PROJECTIONS

	Price	Gain	Ann'l Total Return
High	105	(+85%)	17%
Low	85	(+50%)	12%

Insider Decisions

	S	O	N	D	J	F	M	A	M
to Buy	0	0	0	0	0	0	0	0	1
Options	0	2	0	2	0	1	0	0	1
to Sell	0	2	0	1	0	0	1	0	0

Institutional Decisions

	3Q2006	4Q2006	1Q2007
to Buy	251	285	263
to Sell	302	310	350
Hld's(000)	276965	279993	275731

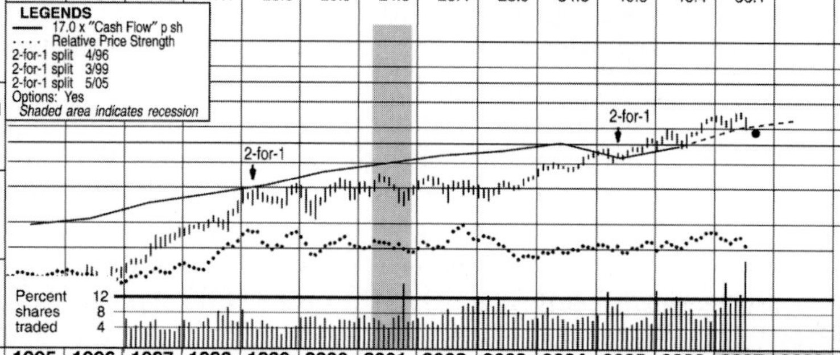

% TOT. RETURN 7/07

	THIS STOCK	VL ARITH. INDEX
1 yr.	8.7	18.6
3 yr.	67.8	50.4
5 yr.	108.3	127.4

1991	1992	1993	1994	1995	1996	1997	1998	1999	2000	2001	2002	2003	2004	2005	2006	2007	2008	© VALUE LINE PUB., INC.	10-12
4.95	5.22	5.55	6.95	7.33	7.72	8.92	9.46	10.20	11.02	12.02	12.48	12.68	13.83	16.35	17.67	***20.25***	***21.60***	Sales per sh A	***25.10***
.50	.52	.57	1.09	1.14	1.23	1.47	1.63	1.81	2.12	2.33	2.57	2.71	2.97	2.52	2.87	***3.55***	***3.90***	"Cash Flow" per sh	***5.05***
.38	.39	.44	.51	.57	.63	.73	.86	1.01	1.18	1.23	1.48	1.64	1.91	2.28	2.56	***3.05***	***3.45***	Earnings per sh B	***4.50***
.28	.28	.29	.29	.30	.33	.36	.39	.43	.47	.49	.51	.54	.60	.66	.73	***.82***	***.82***	Div'ds Decl'd per sh D■	***.88***
.13	.14	.13	.19	.15	.16	.20	.45	.39	.25	.30	.18	.30	.37	.33	.36	***.55***	***.60***	Cap'l Spending per sh	***.70***
2.55	2.31	2.08	2.30	2.58	3.42	3.62	3.94	4.32	4.53	4.80	5.65	6.72	7.86	8.48	7.57	***6.50***	***9.25***	Book Value per sh E	***18.95***
392.37	393.07	395.31	397.38	400.57	398.12	396.41	394.22	391.42	388.57	386.44	383.67	380.79	379.63	367.18	353.96	***338.00***	***338.00***	Common Shs Outst'g C	***338.00***
18.6	19.1	18.2	16.9	16.7	17.7	20.6	23.6	26.8	23.6	24.6	21.1	18.7	20.6	20.4	22.2	*Bold figures are*		Avg Ann'l P/E Ratio	***21.0***
1.19	1.16	1.08	1.11	1.12	1.11	1.19	1.23	1.53	1.53	1.26	1.15	1.07	1.09	1.09	1.20	*Value Line*		Relative P/E Ratio	***1.40***
3.9%	3.7%	3.6%	3.4%	3.2%	3.0%	2.4%	1.9%	1.6%	1.7%	1.6%	1.6%	1.8%	1.5%	1.4%	1.3%	*estimates*		Avg Ann'l Div'd Yield	***1.5%***

CAPITAL STRUCTURE as of 6/30/07
Total Debt $994.5 mill. **Due in 5 Yrs** $994.5 mill.
LT Debt $.3 mill. **LT Interest** Nil
(Less than 1% of Cap'l)
Leases, Uncapitalized Annual rentals $190.5 mill.
Pension Assets-12/06 $1349 mill. **Oblig.** $1205 mill.
Pfd Stock None

Common Stock 338,900,000 shs. as of 7/13/07

MARKET CAP: $19.4 billion (Large Cap)

1997	1998	1999	2000	2001	2002	2003	2004	2005	2006	2007	2008		10-12
3534.1	3729.1	3992.0	4281.0	4645.5	4787.7	4827.9	5250.5	6003.6	6255.1	***6840***	***7300***	Sales ($mill)	***8500***
22.0%	22.8%	24.7%	26.3%	22.5%	27.5%	28.4%	29.9%	25.2%	25.3%	***28.0%***	***29.0%***	Operating Margin	***31.0%***
293.5	299.2	308.4	362.3	420.6	408.8	403.2	392.7	106.8	113.2	***115***	***120***	Depreciation ($mill)	***130***
290.7	341.9	401.6	461.7	480.4	576.8	629.4	736.4	817.5	904.2	***1070***	***1200***	Net Profit ($mill)	***1575***
38.3%	39.0%	39.0%	38.5%	38.5%	36.3%	37.0%	37.0%	39.9%	35.6%	***37.0%***	***37.0%***	Income Tax Rate	***37.0%***
8.2%	9.2%	10.1%	10.8%	10.3%	12.0%	13.0%	14.0%	13.6%	14.5%	***15.6%***	***16.4%***	Net Profit Margin	***18.5%***
258.2	137.3	28.2	20.9	d63.4	d101.0	262.5	479.1	366.1	d210.1	***d370***	***475***	Working Cap'l ($mill)	***1000***
607.0	452.1	354.8	817.5	833.6	458.9	.4	.5	.3	.3	***Nil***	***Nil***	Long-Term Debt ($mill)	***Nil***
1434.7	1551.8	1691.5	1761.0	1853.9	2165.9	2557.1	2984.5	3113.1	2679.6	***2200***	***3125***	Shr. Equity ($mill)	***6400***
15.4%	18.1%	20.6%	18.9%	18.9%	22.4%	24.7%	24.8%	26.3%	34.0%	***48.5%***	***38.5%***	Return on Total Cap'l	***22.5%***
20.3%	22.0%	23.7%	26.2%	25.9%	26.6%	24.6%	24.7%	26.3%	33.7%	***48.5%***	***38.5%***	Return on Shr. Equity	***22.5%***
10.3%	12.1%	13.7%	15.9%	15.7%	17.5%	16.5%	17.0%	18.4%	24.0%	***36.0%***	***29.5%***	Retained to Com Eq	***18.0%***
49%	45%	42%	40%	40%	34%	33%	31%	30%	29%	***26%***	***23%***	All Div'ds to Net Prof	***19%***

CURRENT POSITION ($MILL.)	2005	2006	6/30/07
Cash Assets	748.8	353.5	358.1
Receivables	1114.3	1237.3	1296.2
Inventory (FIFO)	335.3	322.2	430.2
Other	392.5	344.9	361.8
Current Assets	2590.9	2257.9	2446.3
Accts Payable	336.3	372.5	362.4
Debt Due	2.9	2.4	994.2
Other	1885.6	2093.1	2145.5
Current Liab.	2224.8	2468.0	3502.1

ANNUAL RATES of change (per sh)	Past 10 Yrs.	Past 5 Yrs.	Est'd '04-'06 to '10-'12
Sales	8.0%	7.5%	*19.0%*
"Cash Flow"	9.0%	6.0%	*11.5%*
Earnings	14.5%	14.5%	*14.5%*
Dividends	8.0%	7.5%	*4.5%*
Book Value	11.0%	12.0%	*17.0%*

Cal-endar	QUARTERLY SALES ($ mill.)B Mar.31	Jun.30	Sep.30	Dec.31	Full Year
2004	919.9	1245	1722	1361	5250.5
2005	1029	1456	1977	1541	6003.6
2006	1140.7	1527.5	1992.6	1594.3	6255.1
2007	1296.4	1718.2	***2120***	***1705.4***	***6840***
2008	***1390***	***1835***	***2260***	***1815***	***7300***

Cal-endar	EARNINGS PER SHARE B Mar.31	Jun.30	Sep.30	Dec.31	Full Year
2004	.14	.43	.85	.49	1.91
2005	.21	.51	.99	.57	2.28
2006	.24	.63	1.06	.63	2.56
2007	.37	.79	***1.19***	***.70***	***3.05***
2008	***.46***	***.87***	***1.32***	***.80***	***3.45***

Cal-endar	QUARTERLY DIVIDENDS PAID D■ Mar.31	Jun.30	Sep.30	Dec.31	Full Year
2003	.270	.270	.270	.270	1.08
2004	.300	.300	.300	.300	1.20
2005	.165	.165	.165	.165	.66
2006	.18	.18	.18	.18	.72
2007	.205	.205	.205		

BUSINESS: The McGraw-Hill Companies, Inc. is a global information provider serving financial, education, and business information markets through brands such as *Standard & Poors, McGraw-Hill Education, Business Week, Aviation Week, and Platts.* 2006 sales and oper. profit by bus. seg.: Educ., 40%, 20%; Fin'l Svcs., 44%, 76%; Media, 16%, 4%. Has active acquisition program, incl. Macmillan/McGraw-Hill Sch. Pub. joint vent. in '89; purchased remaining 50%, 10/93; divested S&P ComStock, 2/03; Juvenile Retail Publishing, 1/04. Owns 4 TV stations. Has 20,214 emplys. Off./dir. own 2.7% of shrs. (3/07 Proxy). Chrmn., Pres. and CEO: Harold (Terry) McGraw III. Inc.: NY. Addr.: 1221 Ave. of the Americas, NY, NY 10020. Tel.: 212-512-2000. Internet: www.mcgraw-hill.com.

McGraw-Hill subsidiary, Standard & Poor's (S&P), has acquired ClariFI. The company's financial services unit purchased ClariFI, a provider of software and services that focus on quantitative portfolio management research, for an undisclosed amount. This new subsidiary will support S&P's Capital IQ operation and improve the business' efficiency in providing fundamental research solutions. ClariFI will help expand S&P's already elite client base. We view the move as a positive one, as the companies' goals are clearly well-matched.

S&P remains the most notable contributor to gains. The unit continues to benefit from firm demand for its equity and fixed-income information services, both in the U.S. and abroad. In particular, domestic commercial mortgage-backed securities and collateralized debt obligations are doing well despite the contraction in the subprime market. We believe this segment will continue to boost the top and bottom lines.

Meanwhile, the education segment's sales are up and margins have widened considerably. State new-adoption markets have been strong with growth in the double digits. The notable success has been in the areas of math and science from the kindergarten to 12th-grade levels. Also, the education division is enjoying significant adoptions in large urban markets. In all, we expect this segment to continue to thrive from the positive swing in the textbook adoption cycle.

McGraw-Hill's shares are a sound investment choice. Concerns regarding the recent downturn in the corporate lending arena have driven investors to take some profits and caused MHP to lose some ground since our last review. Investors may wish to hold off until the quotation stabilizes. However, we believe the company's business model is solid, and the stock offers worthwhile price appreciation potential out to 2010–2012.

Simon R. Shoucair *August 17, 2007*

Sales (and Operating Margins*) by Business Line

	2005	2006	2007	2008
Education	2672(15.4%)	2524(13.0%)	*2690(13.0%)*	*2800(14.0%)*
Financial Svcs.	2401(37.8%)	2746(43.8%)	*3100(48.0%)*	*3250(49.0%)*
Info./Media Svc.	931(6.5%)	985(5.0%)	*1050(6.0%)*	*1150(6.5%)*
Segment Total	6004(24.8%)	6255(25.3%)	*6840(27.0%)*	*7300(28.0%)*

* After depreciation; before corporate and interest expenses.

(A) Incl. Macmillan/McGraw-Hill Pub. Co. from 10/93. **(B)** Dil. egs., beg. 1997. Excl. nonrecur. gains, (losses): '93, (82¢); '96, $1.23; '98, (5¢); '99, (12¢); '00, 5¢; '01, (53¢); '03, 30¢; '04, 10¢; '05, (7¢); '06, (6¢). Excl. charge for acctg. change: '00, (35¢). Next egs. report due early Oct. **(C)** In millions, adjusted for splits. **(D)** Div. hist. paid in Mar., June, Sept., & Dec. ■ Div. reinv. plan available. **(E)** Incl. intgbls., at 12/31/06: $2,325 million, $15.22/share.

Company's Financial Strength	A+
Stock's Price Stability	90
Price Growth Persistence	100
Earnings Predictability	100

Source: *Value Line* Investment Survey, 2007.

FIGURE 6.4 Value Line Analysis Chart

The Legends box contains the "cash flow" multiple, the amounts and dates of recent stock splits and an indication if options on the stock are traded.

Monthly price ranges of the stock—plotted on a ratio (logarithmic) grid to show percentage changes in true proportion. For example, a ratio chart equalizes the move of a $10 stock that rises to $11 with that of a $100 stock that rises to $110. Both have advanced 10% and over the same space on a ratio grid.

The "cash flow" line—reported earnings plus depreciation ("cash flow") multiplied by a number selected to correlate the stock's 3- to 5-year projected target price, with "cash flow" projected out to 2004.

Recent price—see page 2 of the *Summary & Index* for the date, just under "Index to Stocks."

P/E ratio—the recent price divided by the latest six months' earnings per share plus earnings estimated for the next six months.

Trailing and median P/E—the first is the recent price divided by the sum of reported earnings for the past 4 quarters; the second is an average of the price/earnings ratios over the past 10 years.

Value Line's Ranks—the rank for Timeliness; the rank for Safety; the Technical rank. Beta, the stock's sensitivity to fluctuations of the market as a whole, is included in this box but is not a rank. (*See Glossary for Industry rank.*)

The projected stock price in 2006-08. Also, the total expected % gain/loss before dividends and the Annual Total Return (% including dividends).

The record of insider decisions—the number of times officers and directors bought or sold stock or exercised options during the past nine months.

Stock purchases/sales by institutions—the number of times institutions with more than $100 million of assets under management bought or sold stock during the past three quarters and the total number of shares held by those institutions at the end of each quarter.

Statistical Array—historical financial data appears in regular type.

The capital structure as of the indicated recent date showing, among other things, the $ amount and % of capital in long-term debt and preferred stock. We also show the number of times that interest charges were earned.

Current position—total current assets and total current liabilities, and their detail.

Annual rates of change (on a compound per-share basis). Actual for each of the past 5 and 10 years, estimated for the next 3 to 5 years.

Quarterly sales are shown on a gross basis. Quarterly earnings on a per-share basis (estimates in bold type).

Quarterly dividends paid are actual payments. The total of dividends paid in four quarters may not equal the figure shown in the annual series on dividends declared in the Statistical Array. (Sometimes a dividend declared at the end of the year will be paid in the first quarter of the following year.)

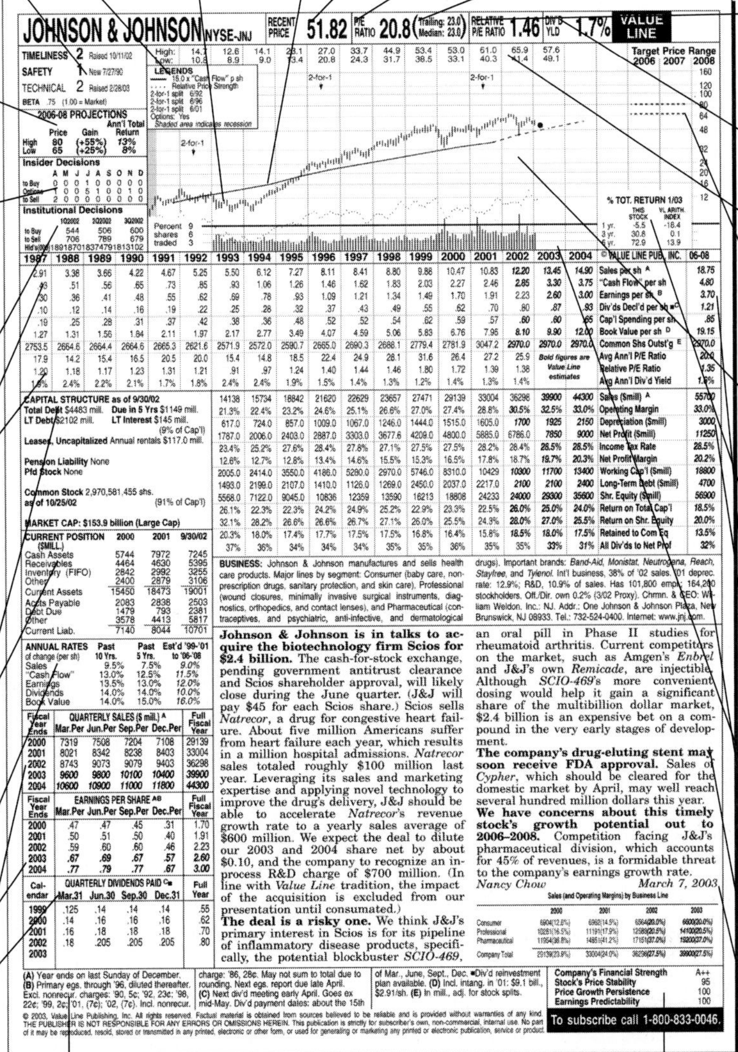

Footnotes explain a number of things, such as the way earnings are reported, whether basic or diluted.

Value Line's Indexes of Financial Strength, Stock's Price Stability, Price Growth Persistence, and Earnings Predictability. (*See Glossary for definitions.*)

Relative P/E ratio—the stock's current P/E divided by the median P/E for all stocks under Value Line review.

Dividend yield—cash dividends estimated to be declared in the next 12 months divided by the recent price.

The stock's highest and lowest price of the year.

Target Price Range—the range in which a stock price is likely to trade in the years 2006-08. Also shown in the "Projections" box on the left.

Relative Price Strength describes the stock's past price performance relative to the Value Line Arithmetic Composite Average of approximately 1,700 stocks. (A rising line indicates the stock price has been rising more than the Value Line universe.)

The % Total Return shows the price appreciation and dividends of a stock and the Value Line Arithmetic Composite Index for the past 1, 3, and 5 years.

Statistical Array—Value Line estimates appearing in the area on the right side are in *bold italics*.

The percent of shares traded monthly—the number of shares traded each month as a % of the total outstanding.

Business Data—a brief description of the company's business and major products along, with other important data.

Analyst's Commentary—an approximately 350-word report on recent developments and prospects—issued every three months on a preset schedule.

The expected date of receipt by subscribers. *The Survey* is mailed on a schedule that aims for delivery to every subscriber on Friday afternoon.

Source: *Value Line,* "How to Invest in Common Stocks: A Guide to Using the Value Line Investment Survey," 2007.

Let's assume that "today" is January 1, 2008. Also, let's keep the 7.5 percent growth rate and 12.6 percent discount rate. From the *Value Line Investment Survey* (VL), we can fill in columns two and three of the table below:

		Forecast	
	End-of-Year 2007 (time 0)	2008 (VL)	2008 (CSR)
Beginning BV per share	NA	$6.50	$6.50
EPS	$3.05	$3.45	$3.2788*
DIV	$ .82	$ .82	$2.7913**
Ending BV per share	$6.50	$9.25	$6.9875*

* 3.05 × 1.075; 6.50 × 1.075.
** 3.2788 − (6.9875 − 6.50).

The fourth column comes from using the clean surplus relationship (CSR). Here, we grow EPS and book value per share using a growth rate of 7.5 percent. Then we calculate the dividend "plug" that makes the change in book value equal to EPS minus dividends.

Now we can estimate two prices for McGraw-Hill shares using the RIM—one from data provided by *Value Line* and one from data using the clean surplus relationship. In addition, we can compare these values using a constant dividend growth rate model that uses a dividend growth rate of 7.5 percent. Using the RIM, we get:

$$P_0 = 6.50 + \frac{3.2788 - 6.50 \times .126}{.126 - .075} = \$54.73 \qquad \text{(CSR)}$$

$$P_0 = 6.50 + \frac{3.45 - (9.25 - 6.50)}{.126 - .075} = \$20.23 \qquad \text{(VL)}$$

Using the DDM, we get:

$$P_0 = \frac{2.7913}{.126 - .075} = \$54.73 \qquad \text{(CSR)}$$

$$P_0 = \frac{.82}{.126 - .075} = \$16.08 \qquad \text{(VL)}$$

The \$.82 used is *Value Line*'s estimate of next year's dividend, D_1, because *Value Line* forecasts no dividend growth between 2007 and 2008. As you would expect, both the RIM and the DDM indicate a price of \$54.73 for McGraw-Hill when we use the CSR. This share value is reasonably close to McGraw-Hill's recently reported stock price of \$57.27. RIM and DDM prices using data from *Value Line* differ, however, because of "dirty surplus."

USING PRICE RATIO ANALYSIS

Value Line reports annual growth rates for sales, cash flow, earnings, dividends, and book values in the box labeled "Annual Rates." These include historical five-year and ten-year growth rates, along with expected growth rates for the next three to five years. We will estimate expected future stock prices using five-year average price ratios that we will calculate along with expected growth rates supplied by *Value Line.*

The *Value Line* survey reports annual average price-earnings ratios, but it does not report average price to cash flow per share ratios, P/CF, or average price to sales per share ratios, P/S. In this case, because all these numbers are on a per-share basis, a quick way to calculate an average P/CF ratio is to multiply an average P/E ratio by the ratio of earnings per share to cash flow per share. That is, P/CFPS = P/E × EPS/CFPS (recall that the "E" in P/E stands for EPS, so they cancel).

For example, McGraw-Hill's 2006 average P/E was 22.20, EPS was \$2.56, CFPS was \$2.87, and SPS was \$17.67. Thus, a quick calculation of McGraw-Hill's 2006 average P/CF ratio is 22.20 × 2.56/2.87 = 19.80. Similarly, the average P/S ratio, (P/EPS) × (EPS/SPS), is

TABLE 6.3 Price Ratio Calculations for McGraw-Hill Co. (MHP)

	2002	2003	2004	2005	2006	Average
P/E	21.10	18.70	20.60	20.40	22.20	20.60
EPS	1.48	1.64	1.91	2.28	2.56	1.97
CFPS	2.57	2.71	2.97	2.52	2.87	2.73
SPS	12.48	12.68	13.83	16.35	17.67	14.60
P/CF	12.15	11.32	13.25	18.46	19.80	14.99
P/S	2.50	2.42	2.84	2.84	3.22	2.77

TABLE 6.4 Price Ratio Analysis for McGraw-Hill Co. (MHP) July 2007 Stock Price: $57.27

	Earnings	Cash Flow	Sales
Five-year average price ratio	20.60 (P/E)	14.99 (P/CF)	2.77 (P/S)
Current value per share, 2006	$ 2.56 (EPS)	$ 2.87 (CFPS)	$17.67 (SPS)
Growth rate	14.5%	11.5%	19.0%
Expected share price	$60.38	$47.97	$58.25

22.20 × $2.56/$17.67 = 3.22. In Table 6.3, we provide average price ratio calculations for P/CF and P/S ratios for the years 2002 through 2006, along with five-year averages for each price ratio.

We use the five-year average price ratios calculated in Table 6.3 in the price ratio analysis presented in Table 6.4. We use the expected growth rates for earnings, cash flow, and sales provided by *Value Line* (from the "Annual Rates" box) to calculate expected share prices for McGraw-Hill *one year from now.* For ease, we restate the three formulas used to calculate expected prices below. As an exercise, you should verify the expected share prices in Table 6.4.

$$\text{Expected share price} = \text{P/E ratio} \times \text{EPS} \times (1 + \text{EPS growth rate})$$

$$\text{Expected share price} = \text{P/CF ratio} \times \text{CFPS} \times (1 + \text{CFPS growth rate})$$

$$\text{Expected share price} = \text{P/S ratio} \times \text{SPS} \times (1 + \text{SPS growth rate})$$

We can now summarize our analysis by listing the stock prices obtained by the different ways we have described in this chapter, along with the model used to derive them.

DDM, with calculated sustainable growth rate:	Not defined
DDM, historical growth rate, *Value Line* input:	$16.08
DDM, historical growth rate, CSR:	$54.73
RIM, historical growth rate, *Value Line* input:	$20.23
RIM, historical growth rate, CSR:	$54.73
Price-earnings model:	$60.38
Price-cash flow model:	$47.97
Price-sales model:	$58.25

Notice the wide range of share values we obtained by our various ways. This is not uncommon in security analysis, and it suggests how daunting a task security analysis sometimes can be. In this case, the price-sales model yields a value closest to the observed stock price of $57.27. However, the goal is not to find a model that yields a value closest to the current price. Rather, the goal is to find a model about which we are confident, For example, if we were confident in the RIM and assumed the clean surplus relationship, then we would conclude that McGraw-Hill stock is fairly priced. But if we use the RIM but did not assume the clean surplus relationship holds, then we would conclude that McGraw-Hill shares are somewhat overpriced.

CHECK THIS

6.6a Locate *Value Line*'s projected growth rate in dividends. How does it compare to the sustainable growth rate we estimated? The historical growth rates? Revalue the stock using the constant perpetual dividend model and this growth rate.

6.6b Assume that the sustainable growth rate we calculated is the growth rate for the next five years only and that dividends will grow thereafter at the rate projected by *Value Line* analysts. Using these growth rates, revalue the stock using the two-stage dividend growth model.

6.7 Summary and Conclusions

In this chapter, we examined several methods of fundamental analysis used by financial analysts to value common stocks. The methods we examined are the learning objectives for the chapter. We illustrated many of these methods with a detailed analysis of the McGraw-Hill Company.

1. The Basic Dividend Discount Model.

A. Dividend discount models value common stock as the sum of all expected future dividend payments, where the dividends are adjusted for risk and the time value of money.

B. The dividend discount model is often simplified by assuming that dividends will grow at a constant growth rate. A particularly simple form of the dividend discount model is the case in which dividends grow at a constant perpetual growth rate. The simplicity of the constant perpetual growth model makes it the most popular dividend discount model. However, it should be applied only to companies with stable earnings and dividend growth.

C. Dividend models require an estimate of future growth. We described the sustainable growth rate, which is measured as a firm's return on equity times its retention ratio, and illustrated its use.

2. The Two-Stage Dividend Growth Model.

A. Companies often experience temporary periods of unusually high or low growth, where growth eventually converges to an industry average. In such cases, analysts frequently use a two-stage dividend growth model.

B. The two-stage growth model can be used with two separate growth rates for two distinct time periods.

C. The two-stage growth model can be used where there is a period with nonconstant dividend growth and a period of constant dividend growth.

3. The Residual Income Model.

A. The difference between actual and required earnings in any period is called residual income. Residual income is sometimes called Economic Value Added.

B. The residual income model is a method that can be used to value a share of stock in a company that does not pay dividends. To derive the residual income model, a series of constant growth assumptions are made for EPS, assets, liabilities, and equity. Together, these growth assumptions result in a sustainable growth rate.

C. The residual income model breaks the value of a share of stock into two parts: the current book value of the firm and the present value of all residual earnings (i.e., income).

D. The clean surplus relationship is an accounting relationship that says earnings minus dividends equals the change in book value per share. The clean surplus relationship might not hold in actual practice. But if the clean surplus relationship is true, then the residual income model is mathematically equivalent to the constant perpetual growth model.

4. **Price Ratio Analysis.**

A. Price ratios are widely used by financial analysts. The most popular price ratio is a company's price-earnings ratio. A P/E ratio is calculated as the ratio of a firm's stock price divided by its earnings per share (EPS).

B. Financial analysts often refer to high-P/E stocks as growth stocks and low-P/E stocks as value stocks. In general, companies with high expected earnings growth will have high P/E ratios, which is why high-P/E stocks are referred to as growth stocks. Low-P/E stocks are referred to as value stocks because they are viewed as cheap relative to current earnings.

C. Instead of price-earnings ratios, many analysts prefer to look at price-cash flow (P/CF) ratios. A price-cash flow ratio is measured as a company's stock price divided by its cash flow per share. Most analysts agree that cash flow can provide more information than net income about a company's financial performance.

D. An alternative view of a company's performance is provided by its price-sales (P/S) ratio. A price-sales ratio is calculated as the price of a company's stock divided by its annual sales revenue per share. A price-sales ratio focuses on a company's ability to generate sales growth. A high P/S ratio suggests high sales growth, while a low P/S ratio suggests low sales growth.

E. A basic price ratio for a company is its price-book (P/B) ratio. A price-book ratio is measured as the market value of a company's outstanding common stock divided by its book value of equity. A high P/B ratio suggests that a company is potentially expensive, while a low P/B value suggests that a company may be cheap.

F. A common procedure using price-earnings ratios, price-cash flow ratios, and price-sales ratios is to calculate estimates of expected future stock prices. However, each price ratio method yields a different expected future stock price. Because each method uses different information, each makes a different prediction.

GET REAL

This chapter introduced you to some of the basics of common stock valuation and fundamental analysis. It focused on three important tools used by stock analysts in the real world to assess whether a particular stock is "rich" or "cheap": dividend discount models, residual income models, and price ratio analysis. How should you, as an investor or investment manager, put this information to use?

The answer is that you need to pick some stocks and get to work! As we discussed in the chapter, experience and judgment are needed to use these models, and the only way to obtain these is through practice. Try to identify a few stocks that look cheap and buy them in a simulated brokerage account such as Stock-Trak. At the same time, find a few that look rich and short them. Start studying P/E ratios. Scan *The Wall Street Journal* (or a similar source of market information) and look at the range of P/Es. What's a low P/E? What's a high one? Do they really correspond to what you would call growth and value stocks?

The Internet is a copious source for information on valuing companies. Try, for example, Stock Sheet (www.stocksheet.com), Market Watch (www.marketwatch.com), Hoovers Online (www.hoovers.com), and Zacks (www.zacks.com). Don't forget to check out the Motley Fool (www.fool.com).

Several trade associations have informative Web sites that can be helpful. For individual investors there is the American Association of Individual Investors (www.aaii.com) and for professional security analysts there is the New York Society of Security Analysts (www.nyssa.org). The Association for Investment Management and Research (www.aimr.com) provides a financial analyst's certification that is highly respected among security analysts.

Key Terms

arithmetic average dividend growth rate 170
beta 180
cash flow 184
clean surplus relationship (CSR) 182
constant perpetual growth model 168
dividend discount model (DDM) 167
earnings yield (E/P) 183
Economic Value Added (EVA) 181
fundamental analysis 167
geometric average dividend growth rate 170
growth stocks 184
payout ratio 172
price-book (P/B) ratio 187
price-cash flow (P/CF) ratio 184
price-earnings (P/E) ratio 183
price-sales (P/S) ratio 187
residual income model (RIM) 182
retained earnings 172
retention ratio 172
sustainable growth rate 172
two-stage dividend growth model 175
value stocks 184

Chapter Review Problems and Self-Test

1. **The Perpetual Growth Model** Suppose dividends for Tony's Pizza Company are projected to grow at 6 percent forever. If the discount rate is 16 percent and the current dividend is \$2, what is the value of the stock?
2. **The Two-Stage Growth Model** Suppose the Titanic Ice Cube Co.'s dividend grows at a 20 percent rate for the next three years. Thereafter, it grows at a 12 percent rate. What value would we place on Titanic assuming a 15 percent discount rate? Titanic's most recent dividend was \$3.
3. **Residual Income Model** Suppose Al's Infrared Sandwich Company has a current book value of \$10.85 per share. The most recent earnings per share were \$2.96 per share, and earnings are expected to grow at 6 percent forever. The appropriate discount rate is 8.2 percent. Assume the clean surplus relationship is true. Assuming the company maintains a constant retention ratio, what is the value of the company according to the residual income model if there are no dividends?
4. **Price Ratio Analysis** The table below contains some information about the Jordan Air Co. Provide expected share prices using each of the three price ratio approaches we have discussed.

PRICE RATIO ANALYSIS FOR JORDAN AIR (CURRENT STOCK PRICE: \$40)

	Earnings	Cash Flow	Sales
Five-year average price ratio	25 (P/E)	7 (P/CF)	1.5 (P/S)
Current value per share	\$2.00 (EPS)	\$6.00 (CFPS)	\$30.00 (SPS)
Growth rate	10%	16%	14%

Answers to Self-Test Problems

1. Plugging the relevant numbers into the constant perpetual growth formula results in:

$$P_0 = \frac{\$2(1.06)}{.16 - .06} = \$21.20$$

As shown, the stock should sell for \$21.20.

2. Plugging all the relevant numbers into the two-stage formula gets us:

$$P_0 = \frac{\$3(1.20)}{.15 - .20}\left[1 - \left(\frac{1.20}{1.15}\right)^3\right] + \left(\frac{1.20}{1.15}\right)^3 \frac{\$3(1.12)}{.15 - .12}$$

$$= \$9.81 + \$127.25$$

$$= \$137.06$$

Thus, the stock should sell for about \$137.

3. Recall the formula for the residual income model when the clean surplus relationship is true:

$$P_0 = B_0 + \frac{EPS_0(1 + g) - B_0 \times k}{k - g}$$

Next, make a table of all the information that you need to put into the formula:

Al's Infrared Sandwich Company	Time 0, i.e., Now
Beginning book value, B_0	\$10.85
Earnings per share, EPS_0	\$ 2.96
Growth rate, g	6%
Discount rate, k	8.2%

We can now solve the problem.

$$P_0 = \$10.85 + \frac{\$2.96(1 + .06) - \$10.85 \times .082}{.082 - .06}$$

$$P_0 = \$113.03$$

4. Using the P/E approach, we come up with the following estimate of the price of Jordan Air in one year:

$$\begin{aligned} \text{Estimated price} &= \text{Average P/E} \times \text{Current EPS} \times (1 + \text{Growth rate}) \\ &= 25 \times \$2 \times 1.10 \\ &= \$55 \end{aligned}$$

Using the P/CF approach, we get:

$$\begin{aligned} \text{Estimated price} &= \text{Average P/CF} \times \text{Current CFPS} \times (1 + \text{Growth rate}) \\ &= 7 \times \$6 \times 1.16 \\ &= \$48.72 \end{aligned}$$

Finally, using the P/S approach, we get:

$$\begin{aligned} \text{Estimated price} &= \text{Average P/S} \times \text{Current SPS} \times (1 + \text{Growth rate}) \\ &= 1.5 \times \$30 \times 1.14 \\ &= \$51.30 \end{aligned}$$

Test Your Investment Quotient

For the remaining questions and problems, the circled numbers in the margin refer to the corresponding learning objective in this chapter.

IQ

1

1. **Sustainable Growth** A company has a return on equity of ROE = 20 percent, and from earnings per share of EPS = \$5, it pays a \$2 dividend. What is the company's sustainable growth rate?

   a. 8 percent
   b. 10 percent
   c. 12 percent
   d. 20 percent

CFA® PROBLEMS

1

2. **Sustainable Growth** If the return on equity for a firm is 15 percent and the retention ratio is 40 percent, the sustainable growth rate of earnings and dividends is which of the following?

   a. 6 percent
   b. 9 percent
   c. 15 percent
   d. 40 percent

CFA® PROBLEMS

① **3. Dividend Discount Model** A common stock pays an annual dividend per share of $2.10. The risk-free rate is 7 percent and the risk premium for this stock is 4 percent. If the annual dividend is expected to remain at $2.10, the value of the stock is closest to:

a. $19.09
b. $30.00
c. $52.50
d. $70.00

CFA® PROBLEMS

① **4. Dividend Discount Model** The constant-growth dividend discount model will not produce a finite value if the dividend growth rate is which of the following?

a. Above its historical average.
b. Above the required rate of return.
c. Below its historical average.
d. Below the required rate of return.

CFA® PROBLEMS

① **5. Dividend Discount Model** In applying the constant-growth dividend discount model, a stock's intrinsic value will do which of the following when the required rate of return is lowered?

a. Decrease.
b. Increase.
c. Remain unchanged.
d. Decrease or increase, depending on other factors.

CFA® PROBLEMS

① **6. Dividend Discount Model** The constant-growth dividend discount model would typically be most appropriate for valuing the stock of which of the following?

a. New venture expected to retain all earnings for several years.
b. Rapidly growing company.
c. Moderate growth, mature company.
d. Company with valuable assets not yet generating profits.

CFA® PROBLEMS

① **7. Dividend Discount Model** A stock has a required return of 15 percent, a constant growth rate of 10 percent, and a dividend payout ratio of 50 percent. What should the stock's P/E ratio be?

a. 3.0
b. 4.5
c. 9.0
d. 11.0

CFA® PROBLEMS

① **8. Dividend Discount Model** Which of the following assumptions does the constant growth dividend discount model require?

I. Dividends grow at a constant rate.
II. The dividend growth rate continues indefinitely.
III. The required rate of return is less than the dividend growth rate.

a. I only
b. III only
c. I and II only
d. I, II, and III

CFA® PROBLEMS

② **9. Dividend Discount Model** A stock will not pay dividends until three years from now. The dividend then will be $2.00 per share, the dividend payout ratio will be 40 percent, and return on equity will be 15 percent. If the required rate of return is 12 percent, which of the following is closest to the value of the stock?

a. $27
b. $33
c. $53
d. $67

CFA® PROBLEMS

① **10. Dividend Discount Model** Assume that at the end of the next year, Company A will pay a $2.00 dividend per share, an increase from the current dividend of $1.50 per share. After that, the dividend is expected to increase at a constant rate of 5 percent. If you require a 12 percent return on the stock, what is the value of the stock?

a. $28.57
b. $28.79
c. $30.00
d. $31.78

CFA® PROBLEMS

1 **11. Dividend Discount Model** A share of stock will pay a dividend of $1.00 one year from now, with dividend growth of 5 percent thereafter. In the context of a dividend discount model, the stock is correctly priced at $10 today. According to the constant dividend growth model, if the required return is 15 percent, what should the value of the stock be two years from now?

a. $11.03
b. $12.10
c. $13.23
d. $14.40

4 **12. Cash Flow** Which of the following implies the highest quality earnings?

a. Cash flow less than earnings.
b. Cash flow greater than depreciation.
c. Cash flow less than earnings minus depreciation.
d. Cash flow greater than earnings.

4 **13. Price Ratios** Two similar companies have the same price-sales and price-earnings ratios. However, company A has a lower price-cash flow ratio than company B. This most likely indicates that

a. A has lower quality earnings than B.
b. A has lower quality cash flow than B.
c. A uses straight-line depreciation, while B uses accelerated depreciation.
d. A uses accelerated depreciation, while B uses straight-line depreciation.

4 **14. Price Ratios** Two similar companies acquire substantial new production facilities, which they both will depreciate over a 10-year period. However, Company A uses accelerated depreciation while Company B uses straight-line depreciation. In the first year that the assets are depreciated, which of the following is most likely to occur?

a. A's P/CF ratio will be higher than B's.
b. A's P/CF ratio will be lower than B's.
c. A's P/E ratio will be higher than B's.
d. A's P/E ratio will be lower than B's.

CFA® PROBLEMS

4 **15. Price Ratios** An analyst estimates the earnings per share and price-to-earnings ratio for a stock market series to be $43.50 and 26 times, respectively. The dividend payout ratio for the series is 65 percent. The value of the stock market series is closest to

a. 396
b. 735
c. 1131
d. 1866

CFA® PROBLEMS

4 **16. P/E Ratio** An analyst gathered the following information about a stock market index:

Required rate of return:	16%
Expected dividend payout ratio:	30%
Expected return on equity investment:	20%

The expected price-earnings (P/E) ratio of the index is closest to

a. 3.5
b. 7.0
c. 15.0
d. 35.00

CFA® PROBLEMS

3 **17. P/E Ratio** A company's return on equity is greater than its required return on equity. The earnings multiplier (P/E) for that company's stock is most likely to be positively related to the

a. Risk-free rate.
b. Market risk premium.
c. Earnings retention ratio.
d. Stock's capital asset pricing model beta.

4 **18. Residual Income Model** The residual income model separates the value of the firm into two basic components. What are these two components?

a. The current book value and the present value of future earnings.
b. The value of earnings per share and the value of cash flow per share.
c. The current value of the firm's shares and the future value of its shares.
d. The time value of money and the value of bearing risk.

(4) **19. Residual Income** Residual income is the difference between

- **a.** Actual earnings less expected earnings.
- **b.** Any increase in the value of the firm.
- **c.** The value of profitable investment projects.
- **d.** The value added by economical use of assets.

(4) **20. Clean Surplus Relation** The clean surplus relation says that

- **a.** Assets minus liabilities minus shareholder's equity equals the change in current assets plus debt payments.
- **b.** The difference between earnings and dividends equals the change in book value.
- **c.** Dividends minus earnings equals one minus the payout ratio.
- **d.** The difference between earnings and dividends equals the change in surplus inventory.

Concept Questions

(1) (2) **1. Dividend Discount Model** What is the basic principle behind dividend discount models?

(4) **2. P/E Ratios** Why do growth stocks tend to have higher P/E ratios than value stocks?

(3) **3. Residual Income Model** What happens in the residual income model when EPS is negative?

(4) **4. Cash Flow** In computing the price-cash flow ratio, how is cash flow per share usually measured?

(1) **5. Stock Valuation** Why does the value of a share of stock depend on dividends?

(1) (2) (3) (4) **6. Stock Valuation** A substantial percentage of the companies listed on the NYSE and the NASDAQ don't pay dividends, but investors are nonetheless willing to buy shares in them. How is this possible given your answer to the previous question?

(1) (2) (3) (4) **7. Dividends** Referring to the previous two questions, under what circumstances might a company choose not to pay dividends?

(1) **8. Constant Perpetual Growth Model** Under what two assumptions can we use the constant perpetual growth model presented in the chapter to determine the value of a share of stock? How reasonable are these assumptions?

(1) **9. Dividend Growth Models** Based on the dividend growth models presented in the chapter, what are the two components of the total return of a share of stock? Which do you think is typically larger?

(1) **10. Constant Perpetual Growth Model** In the context of the constant perpetual growth model, is it true that the growth rate in dividends and the growth rate in the price of the stock are identical?

Questions and Problems

Core Questions

(1) **1. Dividend Valuation** JJ Industries will pay a regular dividend of $4.80 per share for each of the next four years. At the end of the four years, the company will also pay out a $40 per share liquidating dividend, and the company will cease operations. If the discount rate is 12 percent, what is the current value of the company's stock?

(1) **2. Dividend Valuation** In the previous problem, suppose the current share price is $50. If all other information remains the same, what must the liquidating dividend be?

(1) **3. Dividend Discount Model** Trust Bankers just paid an annual dividend of $1.75 per share. The expected dividend growth rate is 5 percent, the discount rate is 10 percent, and the dividends will last for 5 more years. What is the value of the stock? What if the dividends last for 10 more years? 30 years? 100 years?

(1) **4. Dividend Discount Model** China Grove, Inc., will pay dividends for the next 10 years. The expected dividend growth rate for this firm is 6 percent, the discount rate is 13 percent, and

the stock currently sells for $40 per share. How much must the most recent dividend payment have been?

1 **5. Dividend Growth Model** Suppose that McKenzie, Inc., just paid a dividend of $5.00 per share. The company will continue to pay dividends for the next 25 years, and then go out of business. If the discount rate is 11 percent per year, what is the value of the stock for a dividend growth rate of 20 percent? 12 percent? 6 percent? 0 percent? −5 percent?

1 **6. Perpetual Dividend Growth** A company just paid a dividend of $1.95. If the dividends will grow at 5.5 percent per year and you require a return of 11.8 percent, what is the most you should be willing to pay for the stock?

7. Perpetual Dividend Growth Atlantis Seafood Company stock currently sells for $70 per share. The company is expected to pay a dividend of $4.35 per share next year, and analysts project that dividends should increase at 4.5 percent per year for the indefinite future. What must the relevant discount rate be for Atlantis stock?

8. Perpetual Dividend Growth Xytex Products just paid a dividend of $2.90 per share, and the stock currently sells for $53. If the discount rate is 11 percent, what is the dividend growth rate?

9. Perpetual Dividend Growth Star Light & Power increases its dividend 4.5 percent per year every year. This utility is valued using a discount rate of 9 percent, and the stock currently sells for $83 per share. If you buy a share of stock today and hold on to it for at least three years, what do you expect the value of your dividend check to be three years from today?

10. Sustainable Growth Johnson Products earned $3.10 per share last year and paid a $.75 per share dividend. If ROE was 16 percent, what is the sustainable growth rate?

4 **11. Sustainable Growth** Joker stock has a sustainable growth rate of 6 percent, ROE of 17 percent, and dividends per share of $1.65. If the P/E ratio is 19, what is the value of a share of stock?

12. Capital Asset Pricing Model A certain stock has a beta of 1.2. If the risk-free rate of return is 5.1 percent and the market risk premium is 8.5 percent, what is the expected return of the stock? What is the expected return of a stock with a beta of .85?

3 **13. Residual Income Model** Bill's Bakery expects earnings per share of $6.25 next year. Current book value is $4.70 per share. The appropriate discount rate for Bill's Bakery is 12 percent. Calculate the share price for Bill's Bakery if earnings grow at 4 percent forever.

3 **14. Residual Income Model** For Bill's Bakery described in the previous question, suppose instead that current earnings per share are $6.25. Calculate the share price for Bill's Bakery now.

Intermediate Questions

2 **15. Two-Stage Dividend Growth Model** Could I Industries just paid a dividend of $.90 per share. The dividends are expected to grow at a 25 percent rate for the next eight years and then level off to a 7 percent growth rate indefinitely. If the required return is 12 percent, what is the value of the stock today?

2 **16. Two-Stage Dividend Growth Model** The dividend for Should I, Inc., is expected to grow at 21 percent for the next 12 years before leveling off at a 5 percent rate indefinitely. If the firm just paid a dividend of $1.40 and you require a return of 13 percent on the stock, what is the most you should pay per share?

2 **17. Multiple Growth Rates** Netscrape Communications does not currently pay a dividend. You expect the company to begin paying a $6 per share dividend in 10 years, and you expect dividends to grow perpetually at 5.5 percent per year thereafter. If the discount rate is 15 percent, how much is the stock currently worth?

2 **18. Multiple Growth Rates** PerfectlySoft Corp. is experiencing rapid growth. Dividends are expected to grow at 25 percent per year during the next three years, 20 percent over the following year, and then 7 percent per year thereafter indefinitely. The required return on this stock is 14 percent, and the stock currently sells for $75.80 per share. What is the projected dividend for the coming year?

1 **19. Multiple Growth Rates** Leisure Lodge Corporation is expected to pay the following dividends over the next four years: $15.00, $10.00, $5.00, $2.20. Afterwards, the company pledges to maintain a constant 7 percent growth rate in dividends forever. If the required return on the stock is 14 percent, what is the current share price?

1 **20. Multiple Required Returns** Sea Side, Inc., just paid a dividend of $2.75 per share on its stock. The growth rate in dividends is expected to be a constant 5.5 percent per year indefinitely. Investors require an 18 percent return on the stock for the first three years, then a 13 percent return for the next three years, and then an 11 percent return thereafter. What is the current share price?

4 **21. Price Ratio Analysis** Given the information below for Seger Corporation, compute the expected share price at the end of 2008 using price ratio analysis.

Year	2003	2004	2005	2006	2007	2008
Price	$94.50	$100.40	$99.10	$97.90	$121.50	$136.80
EPS	4.34	5.05	5.22	6.06	7.00	8.00
CFPS	7.27	8.24	8.71	10.12	11.80	13.10
SPS	52.60	58.52	57.90	60.69	71.60	78.70

1 **22. Dividend Growth Analysis** In the previous problem, suppose the dividends per share over the same period were $1.00, $1.08, $1.17, $1.25, $1.35, and $1.40, respectively. Compute the expected share price at the end of 2008 using the perpetual growth method. Assume the market risk premium is 8.5 percent, Treasury bills yield 5 percent, and the projected beta of the firm is .90.

4 **23. Price Ratio Analysis for Internet Companies** Given the information below for HooYah! Corporation, compute the expected share price at the end of 2009 using price ratio analysis.

Year	2003	2004	2005	2006	2007	2008
Price	$ 8.00	$ 44.50	$116.00	$193.00	$83.00	$13.50
EPS	−4.00	−3.30	−1.80	−0.55	0.04	0.06
CFPS	−9.00	−6.50	−2.80	−0.25	0.03	0.08
SPS	5.00	13.50	18.10	20.30	23.80	21.95

4 **24. Price Ratio Analysis for Internet Companies** Given the information below for StartUp.Com, compute the expected share price at the end of 2009 using price ratio analysis.

Year	2005	2006	2007	2008
Price	N/A	$ 68.12	$ 95.32	$104.18
EPS	N/A	− 7.55	−4.30	−3.68
CFPS	N/A	−11.05	−8.20	−5.18
SPS	N/A	4.10	6.80	8.13

4 **25. Price Ratio Analysis** The current price of Parador Industries stock is $68 per share. Current earnings per share are $3.80, the earnings growth rate is 7 percent, and Parador does not pay a dividend. The expected return on Parador stock is 13 percent. What one-year ahead P/E ratio is consistent with Parador's expected return and earnings growth rate?

4 **26. Price Ratio Analysis** The current price of Parador Industries stock is $68 per share. Current sales per share are $18.75, the sales growth rate is 9 percent, and Parador does not pay a dividend. The expected return on Parador stock is 13 percent. What one-year ahead P/S ratio is consistent with Parador's expected return and sales growth rate?

Use the following information to answer Problems 27–31.

Abbott Laboratories (ABT) engages in the discovery, development, manufacture, and sale of a line of health care and pharmaceutical products. Below you will find selected information from *Value Line*. Use the *Value Line* estimated 2007 figures as the actual year-end figures for the company. The beta reported was .80 and the risk-free rate was 3.13 percent. Assume a market risk premium of 8 percent.

www.mhhe.com/jm5e

2003	2004	2005	2006	2007	2008	© VALUE LINE PUB., INC.
12.45	12.49	14.51	14.62	***16.65***		Sales per sh
3.01	3.05	3.42	3.51	***4.05***		"Cash Flow" per sh
2.21	2.27	2.50	2.52	***2.83***		Earnings per sh A
.98	1.04	1.10	1.18	***1.30***		Div'ds Decl'd per sh B■
.79	.82	.78	.87	***1.10***		Cap'l Spending per sh
8.27	9.09	9.37	9.14	***10.35***		Book Value per sh C
1580.2	1575.1	1539.2	1537.2	***1535.0***		Common Shs Outst'g D
18.7	18.7	18.1	17.9	***Bold figures are Value Line estimates***		Avg Ann'l P/E Ratio
1.07	.99	.96	.97			Relative P/E Ratio
2.4%	2.5%	2.4%	2.6%			Avg Ann'l Div'd Yield
19681	19678	22336	22476	***25575***		Sales ($mill)
27.0%	28.2%	27.6%	28.2%	***28.3%***		Operating Margin
1274.0	1288.7	1358.9	1558.8	***1825***		Depreciation ($mill)
3479.2	3522.8	3908.5	3841.8	***4405***		Net Profit ($mill)
22.0%	21.4%	24.3%	23.5%	***19.5%***		Income Tax Rate
17.7%	17.9%	17.5%	17.1%	***17.2%***		Net Profit Margin
2650.9	3908.9	3970.5	d669.3	***3785***		Working Cap'l ($mill)
3452.3	4787.9	4571.5	7009.7	***10000***		Long-Term Debt ($mill)
13072	14326	14415	14054	***15865***		Shr. Equity ($mill)
21.5%	18.8%	21.0%	18.8%	***18.0%***		Return on Total Cap'l
26.6%	24.6%	27.1%	27.3%	***28.0%***		Return on Shr. Equity
15.0%	13.4%	15.4%	14.7%	***15.0%***		Retained to Com Eq
44%	45%	43%	46%	***45%***		All Div'ds to Net Prof

The high and low share price each year were:

	2003	2004	2005	2006	2007
High	$47.20	$47.60	$50.00	$49.90	$59.50
Low	33.80	38.30	37.50	39.20	48.80

Avg 40.5 42.95 43.75 44.55 54.15

(1) **27. Constant Perpetual Growth Model** What is the sustainable growth rate and required return for Abbott Laboratories? Using these values, calculate the 2008 share price of Abbott Laboratories Industries stock according to the constant dividend growth model.

(4) **28. Price Ratios** Using the P/E, P/CF, and P/S ratios, estimate the 2008 share price for Abbott Laboratories. Use the average stock price each year to calculate the price ratios.

(3) **29. Residual Income Model** Assume the sustainable growth rate and required return you calculated in Problem 27 are valid. Use the clean surplus relationship to calculate the share price for Abbott Laboratories with the residual income model.

(3) **30. Clean Surplus Dividend** Use the information from the previous problem and calculate the stock price with the clean surplus dividend. Do you get the same stock price as in the previous problem? Why or why not?

(1) (3) (4) **31. Stock Valuation** Given your answers in the previous questions, do you feel Abbott Laboratories is overvalued or undervalued at its current price of around $57? At what price do you feel the stock should sell?

(3) **32. Residual Income Model and Nonconstant Growth** When a stock is going through a period of nonconstant growth for T periods, followed by constant growth forever, the residual income model can be modified as follows:

$$P_0 = \sum_{t=1}^{T} \frac{EPS_t + B_{t-1} - B_t}{(1+k)^t} + \frac{P_T}{(1+k)^T}$$

where

$$P_T = B_T + \frac{EPS_T(1 + g) - B_T \times k}{k - g}$$

Al's Infrared Sandwich Company had a book value of $12.95 at the beginning of the year, and the earnings per share for the past year were $3.41. Molly Miller, a research analyst at Miller, Moore & Associates, estimates that the book value and earnings per share will grow at 12.5 and 11 percent per year for the next four years, respectively. After four years, the growth rate is expected to be 6 percent. Molly believes the required return for the company is 8.2 percent. What is the value per share?

The following questions are from the 2000 Level II CFA® Exam. Use this information to answer Problems 33–38.

The management of Telluride, an international diversified conglomerate based in the United States, believes the recent strong performance of its wholly owned medical supply subsidiary, Sundanci, has gone unnoticed. In order to realize Sundanci's full value, Telluride has announced that it will divest Sundanci in a tax-free spinoff.

Sue Carroll, CFA, is the Director of Research at Kesson and Associates. In developing an investment recommendation for Sundanci, Carroll has directed her analysts to determine a valuation of Sundanci using various disciplines. To assist her analysis, Carroll has gathered the information shown below.

Sundanci Actual 1999 and 2000 Financial Statements for Fiscal Years Ending May 31

($ in millions except per-share data)

Income Statement	**1999**	**2000**
Revenue	$474	$598
Depreciation	20	23
Other operating expenses	368	460
Income before taxes	86	115
Taxes	26	35
Net income	60	80
Dividends	18	24
Earnings per share	$0.714	$0.952
Dividend per share	$0.214	$0.286
Common shares outstanding	84.0	84.0
Balance Sheet		
Current assets	$201	$326
Net property, plant and equipment	474	489
Total assets	675	815
Current liabilities	57	141
Long-term debt	0	0
Total liabilities	57	141
Shareholder equity	618	674
Total liabilities and equity	675	815
Capital expenditures	34	38
Selected Financial Information		
Required rate of return on equity	14%	
Growth rate of industry	13%	
Industry P/E ratio	26	

CFA® PROBLEMS

33. **Sustainable Growth Rate** Calculate the ROE for 2000. What is the sustainable growth rate?

CFA® PROBLEMS

34. **Sustainable Growth Rate** Carroll learns that Sundanci's Board of Directors is considering the following policy changes that will affect Sundanci's sustainable growth rate:

Director A proposes an increase in the quarterly dividend to $.15 per share. This would increase the annual dividend to $.60.

Director B proposes a two-for-one stock split.

Would each of these changes increase, decrease, or not affect Sundanci's sustainable growth rate, given that the other factors remain unchanged? Identify which component of the sustainable growth rate model, if any, is affected by each proposal.

CFA® PROBLEMS

2 35. **Two-Stage Dividend Growth Model** Helen Morgan, CFA, has been asked by Carroll to determine the potential valuation for Sundanci using the dividend discount model. Morgan anticipates that Sundanci's earnings and dividends will grow at 32 percent for two years and 13 percent thereafter. Calculate the current value of a share of Sundanci stock using the two-stage dividend discount model.

CFA® PROBLEMS

4 36. **P/E Ratio Valuation** Christie Johnson, CFA, has been assigned by Carroll to analyze Sundanci using the constant dividend growth price-earnings ratio model. Johnson assumes that Sundanci's earnings and dividends will grow at a constant rate of 13 percent. Note: The constant dividend growth price-earnings ratio using next year's earnings is P/E ratio = Payout ratio/$(k - g)$. Calculate the P/E ratio based on the information given and Johnson's assumptions.

CFA® PROBLEMS

4 37. **P/E Ratio** Identify, within the context of the constant dividend growth model, how each of the following factors will affect the P/E ratio of Sundanci. In other words, will each of the following factors increase, decrease, or possibly increase or decrease the P/E ratio? Assume all other factors remain constant.

a. The beta of Sundanci increases substantially.
b. The estimated growth rate of Sundanci's earnings and dividends increases.
c. The dividend payout ratio of Sundanci increases.
d. The market risk premium increases.

CFA® PROBLEMS

4 38. **Payout Ratio and P/E** Explain why an increase in the dividend payout ratio may not have the effect that the constant dividend growth P/E model suggests.

S&P Problems

www.mhhe.com/edumarketinsight

STANDARD & POOR'S

1. **Constant Perpetual Growth Model** Locate the information for American Electric Power (AEP). If you follow the "Financial Hlts" link you will find the current stock price, most recent dividend, and the five-year growth rate for dividends. Assuming the five-year dividend growth rate is equal to the perpetual growth rate, what is the implied required return for American Electric Power shareholders? Does this number make sense?
2. **Sustainable Growth** What is the sustainable growth rate for AutoZone (AZO)? Under "Excel Analytics" you will find a link for annual ratios. This report shows return on equity and the payout ratio. Calculate the sustainable growth rate for AutoZone each year for the past five years. Is the sustainable growth rate the same every year? Why or why not?
3. **Price Ratio Analysis** Locate the information for Walgreen Co. (WAG). All of the information used in this problem is found under "Excel Analytics." Use the "Mthly. Adj. Prices" link and find the year-end stock price for Walgreen Co. for all available years. Next, find the earnings per share for the last five years using EPS Basic from Operations. Locate the balance sheet for each of the past five years and record the Common Equity and Common Shares Outstanding. Use the Annual Cash Flow Statement to find the Net Cash Flow from Operating Activities. Divide both common equity and cash flow by the shares outstanding each year to find the annual book value per share and cash flow per share. Record these numbers. Calculate the price-earnings ratio, price-cash flow ratio, and price-book value ratio for each year. Using this information, compute the expected share price for Walgreen Co. at the end of the next year using price ratio analysis.

7.1 Introduction to Market Efficiency

efficient markets hypothesis (EMH)
The hypothesis stating that, as a practical matter, investors cannot consistently "beat the market."

WWW

For more on market efficiency, go to http://www.e-m-h.org

Market efficiency is probably the most controversial and intriguing issue in investments. The debate that has raged around market efficiency for decades shows few signs of abating. The central issue in the market efficiency debate is: Can you (or anyone else) consistently "beat the market"?

If the answer to this question is no, then the market is said to be efficient. The **efficient markets hypothesis (EMH)** asserts that, as a practical matter, organized financial markets like the New York Stock Exchange are efficient. The controversy surrounding the EMH centers on this assertion.

In the sections that follow, we discuss many issues surrounding the EMH. You will notice that we focus our discussion on stock markets. The reason is that the debate on the EMH and the associated research have largely centered on these markets. However, the same principles and arguments would also apply to any organized financial market, such as the markets for government bonds, corporate bonds, commodity futures, and options.

CHECK THIS

7.1a What is the central issue in the market efficiency debate?

7.1b How would you state the efficient market hypothesis?

7.2 What Does "Beat the Market" Mean?

excess return
A return in excess of that earned by other investments having the same risk.

Good question. As we discussed in Chapter 1 and elsewhere, there is a risk-return trade-off. On average at least, we expect riskier investments to have larger returns than less risky assets. So the fact that an investment appears to have a high or low return doesn't tell us much. We need to know if the return was high or low relative to the risk involved.

Instead, to determine if an investment is superior to another, we need to compare **excess returns**. The excess return on an investment is the difference between what that investment earned and what other investments with the same risk earned. A positive excess return means that an investment has outperformed other investments of the same risk. Thus, *consistently earning a positive excess return* is what we mean by "beating the market."

CHECK THIS

7.2a What is an excess return?

7.2b What does it mean to "beat the market"?

7.3 Foundations of Market Efficiency

Three economic forces can lead to market efficiency: (1) investor rationality, (2) independent deviations from rationality, and (3) arbitrage. These conditions are so powerful that any one of them can result in market efficiency. We discuss aspects of these conditions in detail throughout this chapter. Given their importance, however, we briefly introduce each of them here. In our discussions, we use the term "rational" to mean only that investors do not systematically overvalue or undervalue financial assets in light of the information that they possess.

FIGURE 7.3 Possible Market Price Reactions to a News Announcement

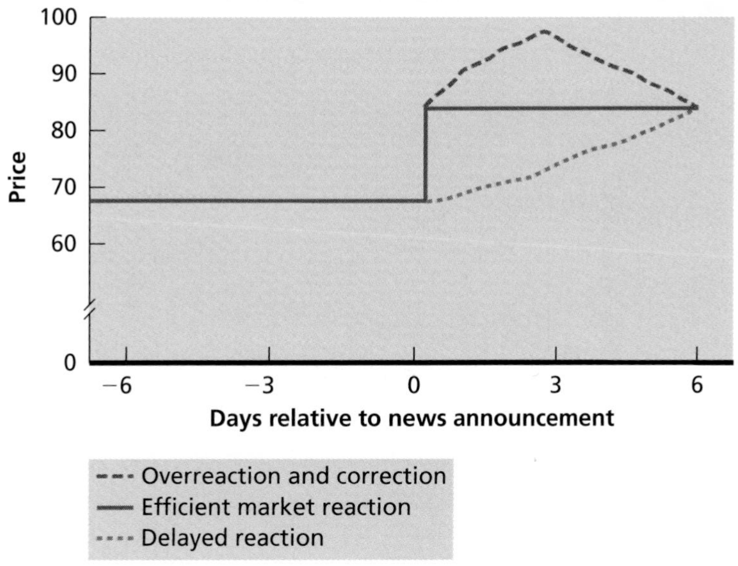

About two out of every million contact lens users in the United States each year are afflicted with AK. Although instances of AK are rare, AK is serious—this infection can lead to vision loss, and sometimes it can lead to the need for a cornea transplant. The CDC determined that the risk of developing AK is about seven times greater for consumers using the Complete Moisture-Plus contact lens solution than for those consumers using other contact lens solutions.

Executives at Advanced Medical Optics chose to recall their product even though they did not find evidence their manufacturing process introduced the parasite that can lead to AK. Further, company officials believed that the occurrences of AK were most likely the result of end users who failed to follow safe procedures when installing contact lenses.

Nevertheless, the recall was announced following the market close on Friday, May 25, 2007. Following the long weekend, EYE shares opened on Tuesday, May 29, 2007, at $34.37, down $5.83 from the Friday close of $40.20. Figure 7.4 is a plot of the price per share of Advanced Medical Optics (EYE) in the days surrounding this news announcement.

event study
A research method designed to help study the effects of news on stock prices.

Researchers use a technique known as an **event study** to test the effects of news announcements on stock prices. When researchers look for effects of news on stock prices, however, they must make sure that overall market news is accounted for in their analysis. The reason is simple. Suppose the whole market had fallen drastically on May 29, 2007. How would researchers be able to separate the overall market decline from the isolated news concerning Advanced Medical Optics?

abnormal returns
The remaining return on a stock after overall market returns have been removed.

To answer this question, researchers calculate **abnormal returns**. The equation to calculate an abnormal return is simply:

$$\text{Abnormal return} = \text{Observed return} - \text{Expected return} \quad (7.1)$$

The expected return can be calculated using a market index (like the NASDAQ 100 Index or the S&P 500 Index) or by using a long-term average return on the stock. Researchers then align the abnormal return on a stock to the days relative to the news announcement. Usually, researchers assign the value of zero to the day a news announcement is made. One day after the news announcement is assigned a value of +1, two days after the news announcement is assigned a value of +2, and so on. Similarly, one day before the news announcement is assigned the value of −1.

According to the efficient market hypothesis, the abnormal return today should relate only to information released on that day. Any previously released information should have no effect on abnormal returns because this information has been available to all traders. Also, the return today cannot be influenced by information that traders do not yet know.

FIGURE 7.4 The Price of Shares for Advanced Medical Optics, May 14, 2007, through June 15, 2007

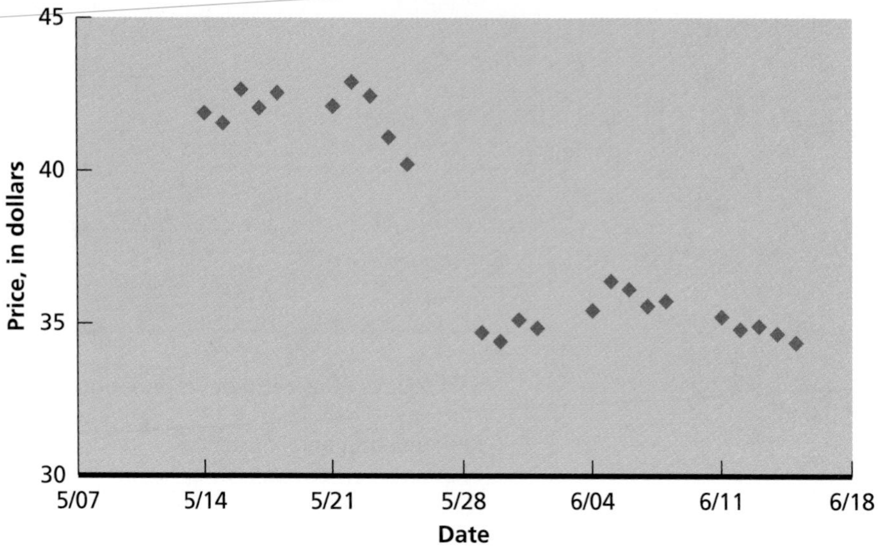

FIGURE 7.5 Cumulative Abnormal Returns for Advanced Medical Optics, March 30, 2007, through July 25, 2007

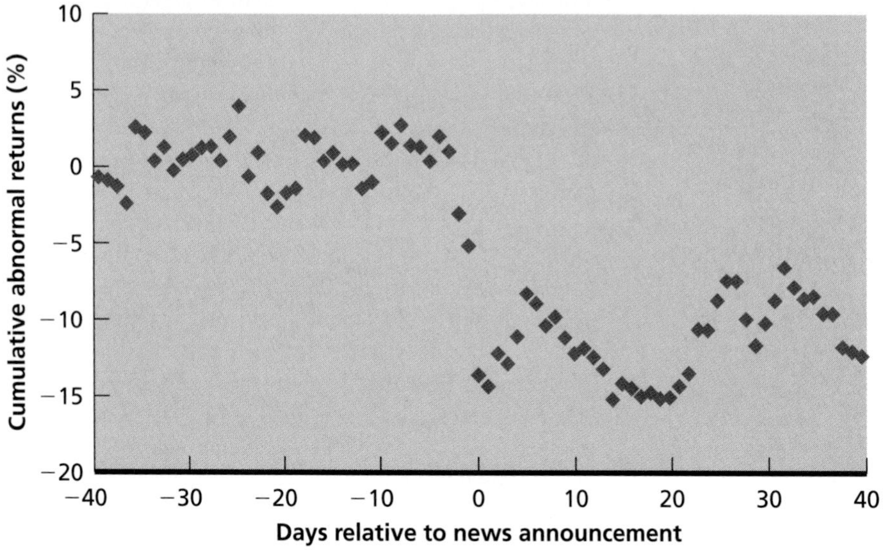

To evaluate abnormal returns, researchers usually accumulate them over some period. Figure 7.5 is a plot of the cumulative abnormal returns for Advanced Medical Optics beginning 40 days before the announcement. The first cumulative abnormal return, or CAR, is just equal to the abnormal return on day −40. The CAR on day −39 is the sum of the first two abnormal returns, the CAR on day −38 is the sum of the first three, and so on. By examining CARs, we can see if there was an over- or underreaction to an announcement.

As you can see in Figure 7.5, Advanced Medical's cumulative abnormal return hovered around zero before the announcement. After the news was released, there was a large, sharp downward movement in the CAR. The stock price gyrated as additional news was released, but the overall pattern of cumulative abnormal returns is essentially what the efficient market hypothesis would predict. That is, there is a band of cumulative abnormal returns, a sharp break in cumulative abnormal returns, and another band of cumulative abnormal returns.

CHECK THIS

7.6a How is a random walk affiliated with the efficient market hypothesis?

7.6b What are the possible market price reactions to a news announcement?

7.6c How do researchers use event studies to examine the effects of news announcements on stock prices?

7.7 Informed Traders and Insider Trading

Recall that if a market is strong-form efficient, no information of any kind, public or private, is useful in beating the market. However, inside information of many types clearly would enable you to earn essentially unlimited returns. This fact generates an interesting question: Should any of us be able to earn returns based on information that is not known to the public?

In the United States (and in many other countries, though not all), making profits on nonpublic information is illegal. This ban is said to be necessary if investors are to have trust in U.S. stock markets. The United States Securities and Exchange Commission (SEC) is charged with enforcing laws concerning illegal trading activities. As a result, it is important for you to be able to distinguish between informed trading, insider trading, and legal insider trading.

INFORMED TRADING

informed trader
An investor who makes a buy or sell decision based on public information and analysis.

When an investor makes a decision to buy or sell a stock based on publicly available information and analysis, this investor is said to be an **informed trader**. The information that an informed trader possesses might come from reading *The Wall Street Journal,* reading quarterly reports issued by a company, gathering financial information from the Internet, talking to other traders, or a host of other sources.

INSIDER TRADING

Some informed traders are also insider traders. When you hear the term *insider trading,* you most likely think that such activity is illegal. However, as you will see at the end of this section, not all insider trading is illegal.

material nonpublic information
Private knowledge that can substantially influence the share price of a stock.

WHO IS AN INSIDER? For the purposes of defining illegal insider trading, an insider is someone who has **material nonpublic information**. Such information is both not known to the public and, if it were known, would impact the stock price. A person can be charged with insider trading when he or she acts on such information in an attempt to make a profit.

Frequently, when an illegal insider trade occurs, there is a *tipper* and a *tippee.* The tipper is the person who has, on purpose, divulged material nonpublic information. The tippee is the person who has knowingly used such information in an attempt to make a profit. For example, a tipper could be a CEO who spills some inside information to a friend who does not work for the company. If the friend then knowingly uses this inside information to make a trade, this tippee is guilty of insider trading.

Proving that a trader is a tippee is difficult for the SEC, because keeping track of insider information flows and subsequent trades is difficult. For example, suppose a person makes a trade based on the advice of a stockbroker. Even if the broker based this advice on material nonpublic information, the trader might not have been aware of the broker's knowledge. The SEC must prove that the trader was, in fact, aware that the broker's information was based on material nonpublic information.

Sometimes, people accused of insider trading claim that they just "overheard" someone talking. Suppose, for example, you are at a restaurant and overhear a conversation between Bill Gates and his CFO concerning some potentially explosive news regarding Microsoft, Inc. If you then go out and make a trade in an attempt to profit from what you overheard, you would be violating the law (even though the information was "innocently obtained"). When you take possession of material nonpublic information, you become an insider and are bound to obey insider trading laws. Note that in this case, Bill Gates and his CFO, although careless, are not necessarily in violation of insider trading laws.

LEGAL INSIDER TRADING A company's corporate insiders can make perfectly legal trades in the stock of their company. To do so, they must comply with the reporting rules made by the U.S. Securities and Exchange Commission. When they make a trade and report it to the SEC, these trades are reported to the public. In addition, corporate insiders must declare that trades that they made were based on public information about the company, rather than "inside" information. Most public companies also have guidelines that must be followed. For example, companies commonly allow insiders to trade only during certain windows throughout the year, often sometime after earnings have been announced.

IT'S NOT A GOOD THING: WHAT DID MARTHA DO? Martha Stewart became one of America's most successful entrepreneurs by telling people how to entertain, cook, and decorate their homes. She built her superhomemaker personality into a far-flung international enterprise. When her company went public in 1999, the initial public offering raised $873 million. Today, Martha Stewart Living Omnimedia, Inc. (MSO), has a market capitalization of around $725 million and employs about 750 people (plus interns). Ms. Stewart controls about 90 percent of the voting power of the shareholders.

Ms. Stewart was in the legal news because the U.S. Securities and Exchange Commission believed that Martha Stewart was told by her friend Sam Waksal, who founded a company called ImClone, that a cancer drug being developed by ImClone had been rejected by the Food and Drug Administration. This development was bad news for ImClone. Martha Stewart sold her 3,928 shares in ImClone on December 27, 2001. On that day, ImClone traded below $60 per share, a level that Stewart claimed triggered an existing stop-loss order. However, the SEC believed that Stewart illegally sold her shares because she had information concerning FDA rejection before it became public.

The FDA rejection was announced after the market closed on Friday, December 28, 2001. This news was a huge blow to ImClone shares, which closed at about $46 per share on the following Monday (the first trading day after the information became public). Shares in ImClone subsequently fell to under $10 per share about six months later, in mid-2002. Ironically, shares of ImClone rallied to sell for more than $80 per share in mid-2004.

In June 2003, Stewart and her stockbroker, Peter Bacanovic, were indicted on nine federal counts. They both pleaded not guilty. Stewart's trial began in January 2004. Just days before the jury began to deliberate, however, Judge Miriam Cedarbaum dismissed the most serious charge—securities fraud. Stewart, however, was convicted on all four counts of obstructing justice and lying to investigators.

Judge Cedarbaum fined Stewart $30,000 and sentenced her to five months in prison, two years of probation, and five months of home confinement after her release. The fine was the maximum allowed under federal rules; the sentence was the minimum the judge could impose. Peter Bacanovic, Stewart's broker, was fined $4,000 and was sentenced to five months in prison and two years of probation.

So, to summarize, Martha Stewart was accused, but not convicted, of insider trading. She was accused, and convicted, of obstructing justice and misleading investigators. Although her conviction bars her from taking on the duties of an executive officer, MSO still paid Martha over $2 million in 2006 (base pay plus perks).

CHECK THIS

7.7a What makes a stock trader an informed trader?

7.7b What traders are considered to be insiders?

7.7c What is the difference between legal insider trading and illegal insider trading?

FIGURE 7.7 Percentage of Managed Equity Funds Beating the Vanguard 500 Index Fund, One-Year Returns

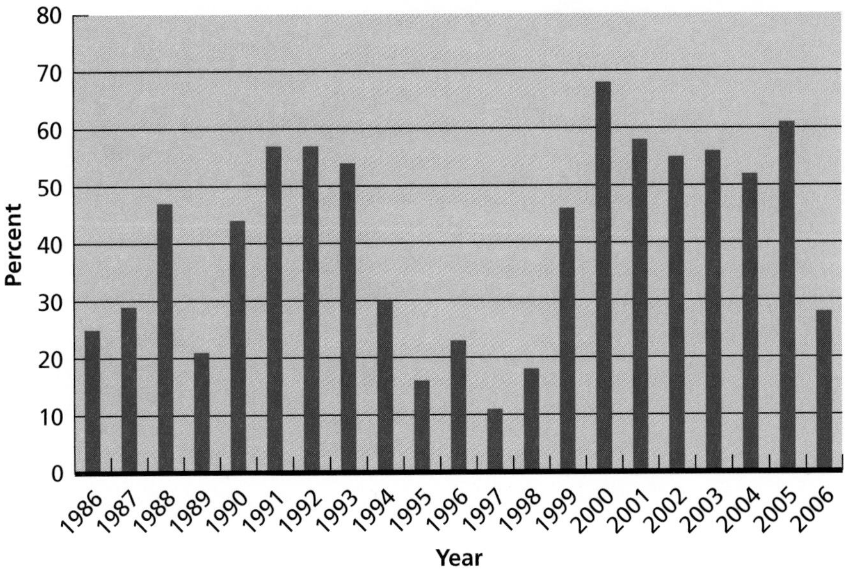

Source: Author calculations.

low level and low variation of the dashed red line means that the percentage of professional money managers who can beat the Vanguard 500 Index Fund over a 10-year investment period is low and stable.

Figures 7.7 and 7.8 are bar charts that show the percentage of managed equity funds that beat the Vanguard 500 Index Fund. Figure 7.7 uses return data for the previous year only, while Figure 7.8 uses return data for the previous 10 years. As you can see from Figure 7.7, in only 9 of the 21 years spanning 1986 through 2006 did more than half the professional money managers beat the Vanguard 500 Index Fund. The performance is worse when it comes to 10-year investment periods (1977–1986 through 1994–2006). As shown in Figure 7.8, in only 2 of these 21 investment periods did more than half the professional money managers beat the Vanguard 500 Index Fund.

Table 7.1 presents more evidence concerning the performance of professional money managers. Using data from 1977 through 2006, we divide this time period into 1-year investment periods, rolling 3-year investment periods, rolling 5-year investment periods, and rolling 10-year investment periods. Then, after we calculate the number of investment periods, we ask two questions: (1) what percentage of the time did half the professionally managed funds beat the Vanguard 500 Index Fund? and (2) what percentage of the time did three-fourths of the professionally managed funds beat the Vanguard 500 Index Fund?

As you see in Table 7.1, the performance of professional money managers is generally quite poor relative to the Vanguard 500 Index Fund. In addition, the performance of professional money managers declines the longer the investment period.

The figures and table in this section raise some difficult and uncomfortable questions for security analysts and other investment professionals. If markets are inefficient, and tools like fundamental analysis are valuable, why don't mutual fund managers do better? Why can't mutual fund managers even beat a broad market index?

The performance of professional money managers is especially troublesome when we consider the enormous resources at their disposal and the substantial survivorship bias that exists. The survivorship bias comes into being because managers and funds that do especially poorly disappear. If beating the market was possible, then this Darwinian process of elimination should lead to a situation in which the survivors, as a group, are capable of doing so. The fact that professional money managers seem to lack the ability to outperform a broad market index is consistent with the notion that, overall, the equity market is efficient.

FIGURE 7.8 Percentage of Managed Equity Funds Beating the Vanguard 500 Index Fund, 10-Year Returns

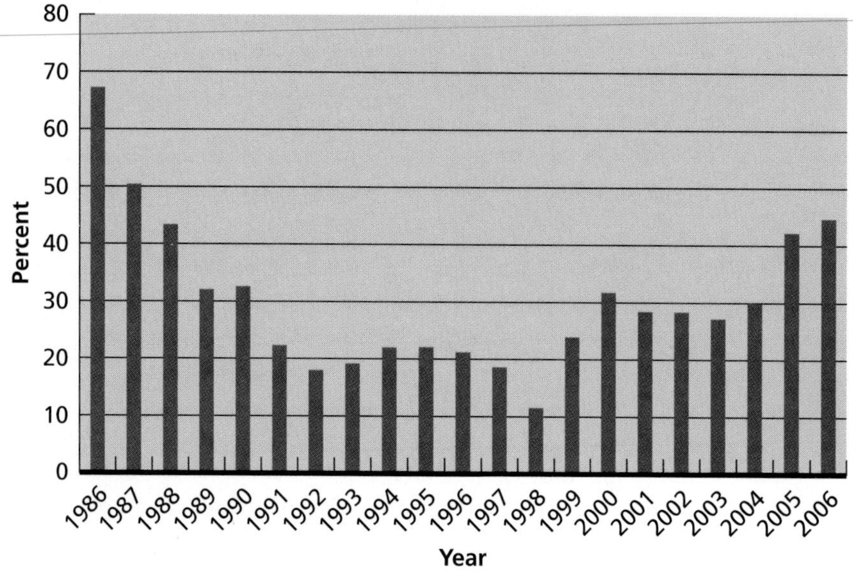

Source: Author calculations.

TABLE 7.1 The Performance of Professional Money Managers versus the Vanguard 500 Index Fund

Length of Each Investment Period (Years)	Span	Number of Investment Periods	Number of Investment Periods Half the Funds Beat Vanguard	Percent	Number of Investment Periods Three-Fourths of the Funds Beat Vanguard	Percent
1	1977–2006	30	14	46.7%	2	6.7%
3	1979–2006	28	13	46.4	2	7.1
5	1981–2006	26	9	34.6	2	7.7
10	1986–2006	21	2	9.5	0	0.0

Source: Author calculations.

So if the market is this efficient, what is the role for portfolio managers? The role of a portfolio manager in an efficient market is to build a portfolio to meet the specific needs of individual investors. You have learned that a basic principle of investing is to hold a well-diversified portfolio. However, exactly which diversified portfolio is optimal varies by investor.

Some factors that influence portfolio choice include the investor's age, tax bracket, risk aversion, and even employer. Employer? Sure, suppose you work for Starbucks and part of your compensation is stock options. Like many companies, Starbucks offers its employees the opportunity to purchase company stock at less than market value. Of course, you would take advantage of this opportunity. You can imagine that you could wind up with a lot of Starbucks stock in your portfolio, which means you are not holding a diversified portfolio. The role of your portfolio manager would be to help you add other assets to your portfolio so that it is once again well diversified.

CHECK THIS

7.9a How well do professional money managers perform, on average, against a broad market index?

7.9b What are the implications of this performance to investors?

7.10 Anomalies

In this section, we discuss some aspects of stock price behavior that are both baffling and potentially hard to reconcile with market efficiency. Researchers call these *market anomalies*. Keep three facts in mind as you read about market anomalies. First, anomalies are generally "small," in that they do not involve many dollars relative to the overall size of the stock market. Second, many anomalies are fleeting and tend to disappear when discovered. Finally, anomalies are not easily used as the basis for a trading strategy, because transaction costs render many of them unprofitable.

THE DAY-OF-THE-WEEK EFFECT

In the stock market, which day of the week has, on average, the biggest return? The question might strike you as silly; after all, what would make one day different from any other on average? On further reflection, though, you might realize that one day is different: Monday.

When we calculate a daily return for the stock market, we take the percentage change in closing prices from one trading day to the next. For every day except Monday this is a 24-hour period. However, because the markets are closed on the weekends, the average return on Monday is based on the percentage change from Friday's close to Monday's close, a 72-hour period. Thus, the average Monday return would be computed over a three-day period, not just a one-day period. Therefore, because of this longer time period, we would predict that Monday should have the highest return; in fact Monday's average return should be three times as large.

Given this reasoning, it may come as a surprise to you to learn that Monday has the lowest average return. In fact, Monday is the only day with a *negative* average return. This is the **day-of-the-week effect**. Table 7.2 shows the average return by day of the week for the S&P 500 for the period January 1950 through December 2006.

day-of-the-week effect
The tendency for Monday to have a negative average return.

In the 57 years spanning 1950 to 2006, the negative return on Monday is significant, both in a statistical sense and in an economic sense. This day-of-the-week effect appears not to be a fluke; it exists in other markets, such as the bond market, and it exists in stock markets outside the United States. It has defied explanation since it was first documented in the early 1980s. As you can see in Table 7.2, the effect is very strong in the 1950–1979 time period. The effect is not apparent in the 1980–2006 time period.

Still, critics of the efficient markets hypothesis point to this strange return behavior as evidence of market inefficiency. While this return behavior is odd, exploiting it presents a problem. That is, how this return behavior can be used to earn a positive excess return is not clear. This is especially true in the 1980–2006 time period (i.e., in the period following the time when the effect was first documented). So whether this strange return behavior points to inefficiency is hard to say.

THE AMAZING JANUARY EFFECT

We saw in Chapter 1 that returns from small-cap common stocks have significantly outdistanced the returns from large-cap common stocks. Beginning in the early 1980s, researchers reported that the difference was too large even to be explained by differences in risk. In other words, small stocks appeared to earn positive excess returns.

TABLE 7.2 Average Daily S&P 500 Returns, by Day of the Week (Dividends Included)

	Weekday				
Time Period	Monday	Tuesday	Wednesday	Thursday	Friday
1950–2006	−0.063%	0.030%	0.096%	0.043%	0.080%
1950–1979	−0.137	0.001	0.094	0.061	0.115
1980–2006	0.020	0.062	0.099	0.024	0.042

Source: Author calculations.

Further research found that, in fact, a substantial percentage of the return on small stocks has historically occurred early in the month of January, particularly in the few days surrounding the turn of the year. Even closer research documents that this peculiar phenomenon is more pronounced for stocks that have experienced significant declines in value, or "losers."

January effect
Tendency for small stocks to have large returns in January.

Thus, we have the famous "small-stock-in-January-especially-around-the-turn-of-the-year-for-losers effect," or SSIJEATTOTYFLE for short. For obvious reasons, this phenomenon is usually just dubbed the **January effect**. To give you an idea of how big this effect is, we first plotted average returns by month going back to 1926 for large stocks in Figure 7.9A. As shown, the average return per month has been just under 1 percent.

In Figure 7.9A, there is nothing remarkable about January; the largest average monthly return for large stocks occurred in July (followed closely by December); the lowest in September. From a statistical standpoint, there is nothing too exceptional about these large stock returns. After all, some month has to be the highest, and some month has to be the lowest.

Figure 7.9B, however, shows average returns by month for small stocks (notice the difference in vertical axis scaling between Figures 7.9A and 7.9B). The month of January definitely jumps out. Over the 81 years covered, small stocks gained, on average, about 6.3 percent in the month of January alone! Comparing Figures 7.9A and 7.9B, we see, outside the month of January, small stocks have not done especially well relative to large stocks. To a lesser extent, we see that small stocks have done better than large stocks in February, but large stocks have done better than small stocks by about the same amount in October.

The January effect appears to exist in many major markets around the world, so it's not unique to the United States (it's actually more pronounced in some other markets). It also exists in some markets other than stock markets. Critics of market efficiency point to enormous gains to be had from simply investing in January and ask: How can an efficient market have such unusual behavior? Why don't investors take advantage of this opportunity and thereby drive it out of existence?

In Table 7.3, you can see that, on average, small stock returns were 4.78 percent higher than large stock returns in the 1926–2006 time period. The next best month in this period (February) is essentially canceled out by the worst month (October). When we break the 1926–2006 time period into smaller time intervals, you can see that the January effect has diminished over time. In fact, in the 1978–2006 time period, the *best* monthly difference of 2.45 percent (January) is essentially canceled out by the worst monthly difference of −2.27 percent (October).

FIGURE 7.9A Large Stocks' Average Monthly Returns, 1926–2006, Dividends Included

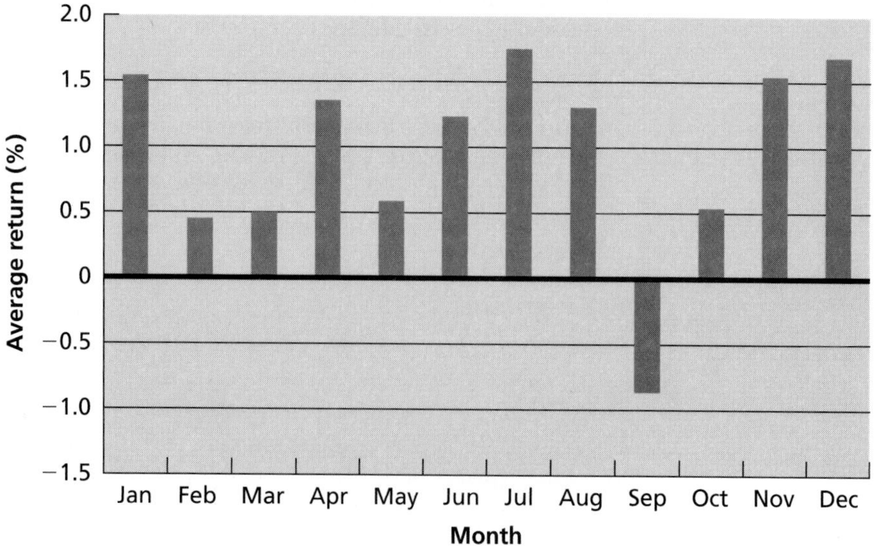

Source: Author calculations.

FIGURE 7.9B Small Stocks' Average Monthly Returns, 1926–2006, Dividends Included

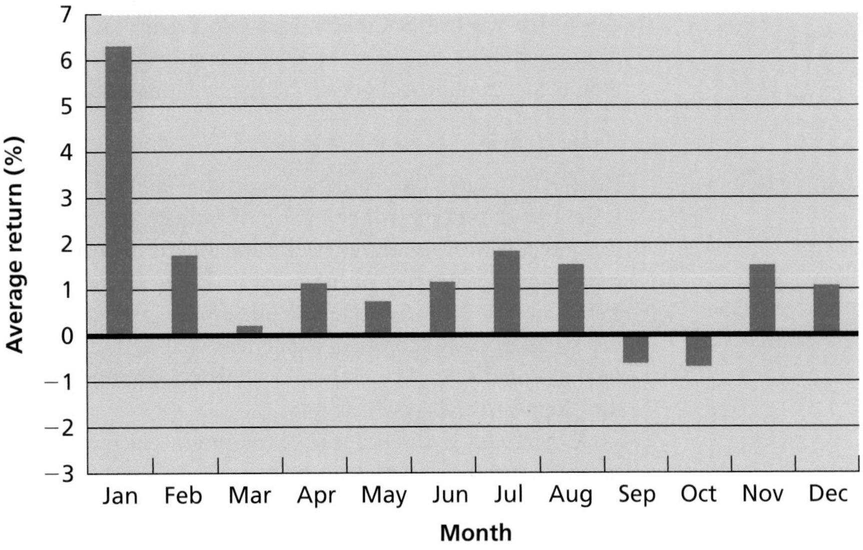

Source: Author calculations.

TABLE 7.3 Monthly Returns of Small Stocks Minus Monthly Returns of Large Stocks, by Various Time Periods, 1926–2006

Time Period	Best Difference (%) Month		Next Best Difference (%) Month		Worst Difference (%) Month	
1926–2006	4.78%	January	1.31%	February	−1.22%	October
1926–1951	6.73	January	1.51	February	−1.64	December
1952–1977	5.42	January	0.87	February	−1.37	October
1978–2006	2.45	January	1.51	February	−2.27	October

Source: Author calculations.

Unlike the day-of-the-week effect, the January effect is at least partially understood. Two factors are thought to be important. The first is tax-loss selling. Investors have a strong tax incentive to sell stocks that have gone down in value to realize the loss for tax purposes. This trading leads to a pattern of selling in these stocks near the end of the year and buying after the turn of the year. In large stocks, this activity wouldn't have much effect, but in the smaller stocks, it could.

The tax-loss selling argument is plausible because researchers have looked to see whether the January effect existed in the United States before there was an income tax—and they found no January effect. However, the January effect has been found in other countries that didn't (or don't) have calendar tax years or didn't (or don't) have capital gains taxes. However, foreign investors in those markets (such as U.S. investors) did (or do). So, debate continues about the tax-loss selling explanation.

The second factor has to do with institutional investors. The argument here has several pieces, but the gist of it is that these large investors compensate portfolio managers based on their performance over the calendar year. Portfolio managers therefore pile into small stocks at the beginning of the year because of their growth potential, bidding up prices. Over the course of the year, they shed the stocks that do poorly because they don't want to be seen as having a bunch of "losers" in their portfolio (this is called "window dressing"). Also, because performance is typically measured relative to the S&P 500, portfolio managers who begin to lag because of losses in small stocks have an incentive to sell them and buy S&P 500 stocks to make sure they don't end up too far behind the S&P 500. Managers who are well ahead late in the year also have an incentive to move into S&P 500 stocks to preserve their leads (this is called "bonus lock-in").

In evaluating the oddity that is known as the January effect, keep in mind that, unlike the day-of-the-week effect, the January effect does not even exist for the market as a whole, so, in big-picture terms, it is not all that important. Also, it doesn't happen every year, so attempts to exploit it will occasionally result in substantial losses.

TURN-OF-THE-YEAR EFFECT

Researchers have delved deeply into the January effect to see whether the effect is due to returns during the whole month of January or to returns bracketing the end of the year. Researchers look at returns over a specific three-week period and compare these returns to the returns for the rest of the year. In Table 7.4, we calculated daily market returns from 1962 through 2006. The specific three-week period we call "Turn-of-the-Year Days" is the last week of daily returns in a calendar year and the first two weeks of daily returns in the next calendar year. Any daily return that does not fall into this three-week period is put into the "Rest-of-the-Days" category.

As you can see in Table 7.4, the returns in the "Turn-of-the-Year Days" category are higher than returns in the "Rest-of-the-Days" category. Further, the difference is apparent in the 1984–2006 period. However, the difference was more than twice as large in the 1962–1983 period.

TURN-OF-THE-MONTH EFFECT

Financial market researchers have also investigated whether a turn-of-the-month effect exists. In Table 7.5, we took daily stock market returns and separated them into two categories. If the daily return is from the last day of any month or the following three days of the following month, it is put into the "Turn-of-the-Month-Days" category. All other daily returns are put into the "Rest-of-the-Days" category.

As you can see in Table 7.5, the returns in the "Turn-of-the-Month" category are higher than the returns in the "Rest-of-the-Days" category. As with the turn-of-the-year anomaly, the turn-of-the-month effect is apparent in each of the three time periods we report. Interestingly, the effect appears to be stronger in the 1984–2006 period than in the 1962–1983 period. Again, the fact that this effect exists is puzzling to proponents of the EMH.

The day-of-the-week, turn-of-the-month, turn-of-the-year, and the January effect are examples of calendar anomalies. There are noncalendar anomalies as well. Two well-known noncalendar anomalies have to do with earnings announcements and price-earnings ratios.

TABLE 7.4 The Turn-of-the-Year Effect

	Market Return on the:		
Time Period	Turn-of-the-Year Days (%)	Rest-of-the-Days (%)	Difference (%)
1962–2006	0.138%	0.039%	0.099%
1962–1983	0.172	0.031	0.141
1984–2006	0.106	0.047	0.059

Source: Author calculations.

TABLE 7.5 The Turn-of-the-Month Effect

	Market Return on the:		
Time Period	Turn-of-the-Month Days (%)	Rest-of-the-Days (%)	Difference (%)
1962–2006	0.135%	0.024%	0.111%
1962–1983	0.126	0.020	0.106
1984–2006	0.143	0.028	0.115

Source: Author calculations.

THE EARNINGS ANNOUNCEMENT PUZZLE

As you saw earlier in this chapter, unexpected news releases can have a dramatic impact on the price of a stock. One news item that is particularly important to investors is an earnings announcement. These announcements contain information about past earnings and future earnings potential.

Researchers have shown that substantial price adjustments do occur in anticipation of the actual earnings. According to the EMH, stock prices should then respond very quickly to unanticipated news, or the earnings "surprise." However, researchers have found that it takes days (or even longer) for the market price to adjust fully. In addition, some researchers have found that buying stocks after positive earnings surprises is a profitable investment strategy.

THE PRICE-EARNINGS (P/E) PUZZLE

As we have discussed elsewhere, the P/E ratio is widely followed by investors and is used in stock valuation. Researchers have found that, on average, stocks with relatively low P/E ratios outperform stocks with relatively high P/E ratios, even after adjusting for other factors, like risk. Because a P/E ratio is publicly available information, according to the EMH, it should already be reflected in stock prices. However, purchasing stocks with relatively low P/E ratios appears to be a potentially profitable investment strategy.

There are many other noncalendar anomalies. For example, the market appears to do worse on cloudy days than sunny days. But rather than continuing with a laundry list of anomalies—however much fun they might provide—we will instead turn to some spectacular events in market history.

CHECK THIS

7.10a What is the day-of-the-week effect?

7.10b What is the amazing January effect?

7.10c What is the turn-of-the-year effect?

7.11 Bubbles and Crashes

As a famous songwriter penned, "History shows again and again, how nature points up the folly of men." Nowhere is this statement seemingly more appropriate in finance than in a discussion of bubbles and crashes.[1]

bubble
A situation where observed prices soar far higher than fundamentals and rational analysis would suggest.

crash
A situation where market prices collapse significantly and suddenly.

A **bubble** occurs when market prices soar far in excess of what normal and rational analysis would suggest. Investment bubbles eventually pop because they are not based on fundamental values. When a bubble does pop, investors find themselves holding assets with plummeting values.

A **crash** is a significant and sudden drop in marketwide values. Crashes are generally associated with a bubble. Typically, a bubble lasts much longer than a crash. A bubble can form over weeks, months, or even years. Crashes, on the other hand, are sudden, generally lasting less than a week. However, the disastrous financial aftermath of a crash can last for years.

THE CRASH OF 1929

During the Roaring Twenties, the stock market was supposed to be the place where everyone could get rich. The market was widely believed to be a no-risk situation. Many people invested their life savings without learning about the potential pitfalls of investing. At the time, investors could purchase stocks by putting up 10 percent of the purchase price and borrowing the remainder from a broker. This level of leverage was one factor that led to the sudden market downdraft in October 1929.

As you can see in Figure 7.10, on Friday, October 25, the Dow Jones Industrial Average closed up about a point, at 301.22. On Monday, October 28, it closed at 260.64, down

[1] Lyrics from "Godzilla," by Donald "Buck Dharma" Roeser (as performed by Blue Oyster Cult).

FIGURE 7.10 Dow Jones Industrial Average, October 21, 1929, to October 31, 1929

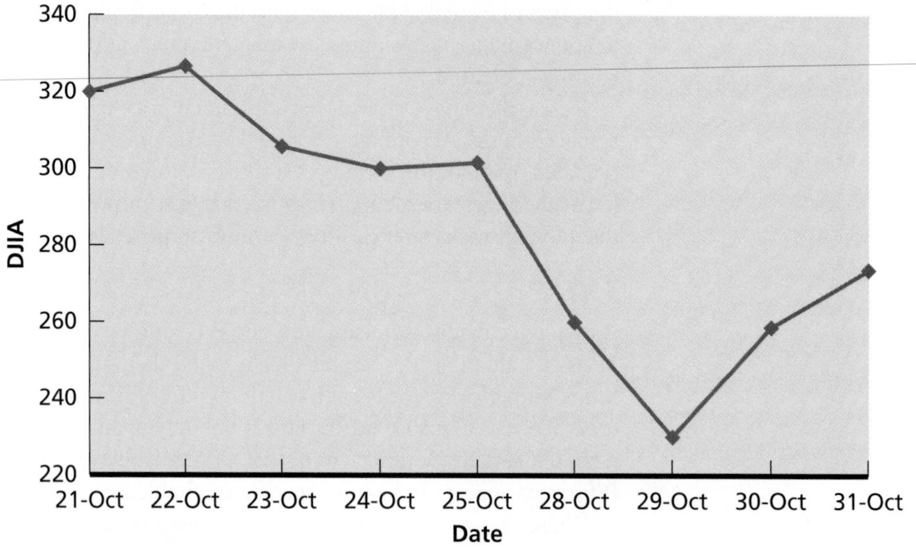

FIGURE 7.11 Dow Jones Industrial Average, October 1928 to October 1932

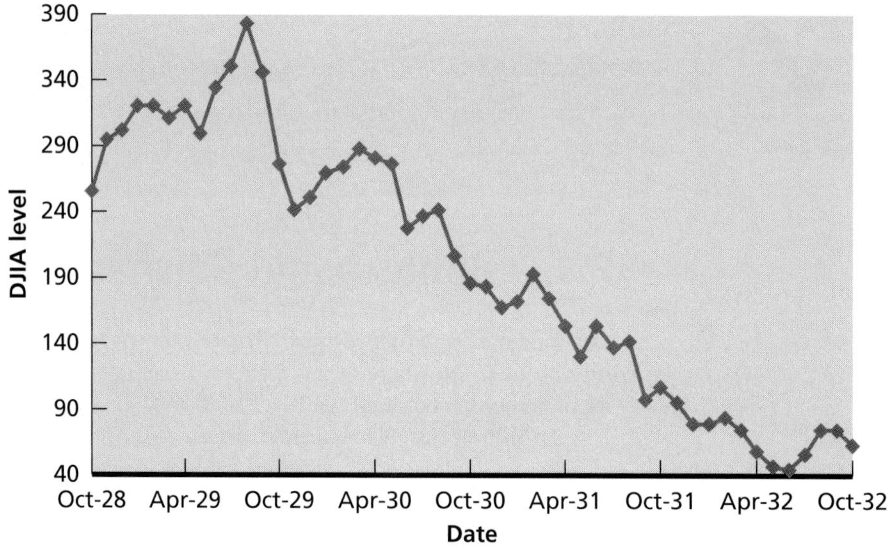

13.5 percent. On Tuesday, October 29, the Dow closed at 230.07, with an interday low of 212.33, which is about 30 percent lower than the closing level on the previous Friday. On this day, known as "Black Tuesday," NYSE volume of 16.4 million shares was more than four times normal levels.

Although the Crash of 1929 was a large decline, it pales with respect to the ensuing bear market. As shown in Figure 7.11, the DJIA rebounded about 20 percent following the October 1929 crash. However, the DJIA then began a protracted fall, reaching the bottom at 40.56 on July 8, 1932. This level represents about a 90 percent decline from the record high level of 386.10 on September 3, 1929. By the way, the DJIA did not surpass its previous high level until November 24, 1954, more than 25 years later.

THE CRASH OF OCTOBER 1987

Once, when we spoke of *the* Crash, we meant October 29, 1929. That was until October 1987. The Crash of 1987 began on Friday, October 16. On huge volume (at the time) of about 338 million shares, the DJIA fell 108 points to close at 2,246.73. It was the first time in history that the DJIA fell by more than 100 points in one day.

FIGURE 7.12 Dow Jones Industrial Average, October 1986 to October 1990

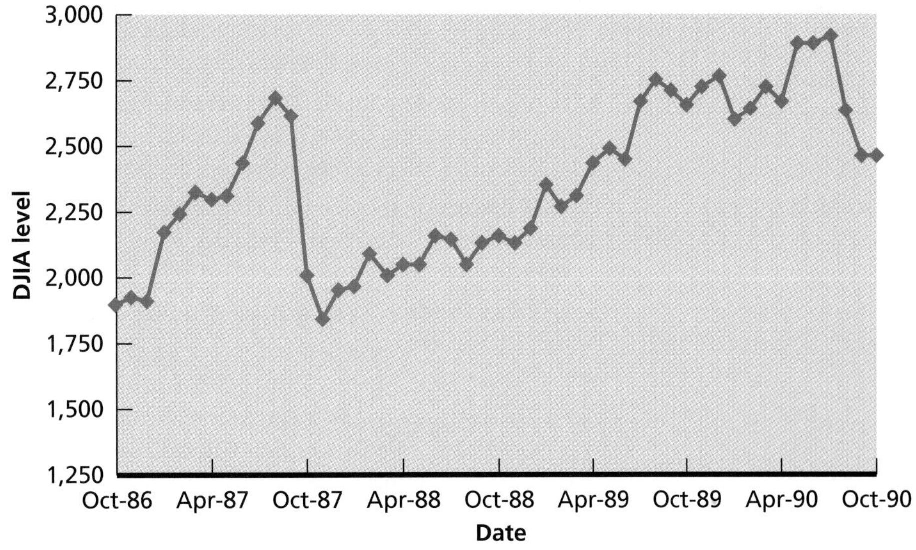

October 19, 1987, now wears the mantle of "Black Monday," and this day was indeed a dark and stormy one on Wall Street; the market lost about 22.6 percent of its value on a new record volume of about 600 million shares traded. The DJIA plummeted 508.32 points to close at 1,738.74.

During the day on Tuesday, October 20, the DJIA continued to plunge in value, reaching an intraday low of 1,616.21. But the market rallied and closed at 1,841.01, up 102 points. From the then market high on August 25, 1987, of 2,746.65 to the intraday low on October 20, 1987, the market had fallen over 40 percent.

After the Crash of 1987, however, there was no protracted depression. In fact, as you can see in Figure 7.12, the DJIA took only two years to surpass its previous market high made in August 1987.

What happened? It's not exactly ancient history, but, here again, debate rages. One faction says that irrational investors had bid up stock prices to ridiculous levels until Black Monday, when the bubble burst, leading to panic selling as investors dumped their stocks. The other faction says that before Black Monday, markets were volatile, volume was heavy, and some ominous signs about the economy were filtering in. From the close on October 13 to the close on October 16, 1987, for example, the market fell by over 10 percent, the largest three-day drop since May 1940 (when German troops broke through French lines near the start of World War II). To top it all off, market values had risen sharply because of a dramatic increase in takeover activity, but Congress was in session and was actively considering antitakeover legislation.

Another factor is that beginning a few years before the Crash of 1987, large investors had developed techniques known as *program trading* designed for very rapid selling of enormous quantities of shares of stock following a market decline. These techniques were still largely untested because the market had been strong for years. However, following the huge sell-off on October 16, 1987, sell orders came pouring in on Monday at a pace never before seen. In fact, these program trades were (and are) blamed by some for much of what happened.

One of the few things we know for certain about the Crash of 1987 is that the stock exchanges suffered a meltdown. The NYSE simply could not handle the volume. Posting of prices was delayed by hours, so investors had no idea what their positions were worth. The specialists couldn't handle the flow of orders, and some specialists actually began selling. NASDAQ went off-line when it became impossible to get through to market makers. It has even been alleged that many stopped answering the phone.

On the two days following the crash, prices *rose* by about 14 percent, one of the biggest short-term gains ever. Prices remained volatile for some time, but as antitakeover talk in Congress died down, the market recovered.

NYSE circuit breakers
Rules that kick in to slow or stop trading when the DJIA declines by more than a preset amount in a trading session.

The Crash of 1987 led to some significant market changes. Upgrades have made it possible to handle much heavier trading volume, for example. One of the most interesting changes was the introduction of **NYSE circuit breakers**. Different circuit breakers are triggered if the DJIA drops by 10, 20, or 30 percent. These 10, 20, and 30 percent decline levels in the DJIA, respectively, will result in the following actions:

1. A 10 percent drop in the DJIA will halt trading for one hour if the decline occurs before 2 P.M.; for one half hour if the decline occurs between 2 and 2:30 P.M.; and it will have no effect if the decline occurs between 2:30 and 4:00 P.M.
2. A 20 percent drop in the DJIA will halt trading for two hours if the decline occurs before 1 P.M.; for one hour if the decline occurs between 1 and 2 P.M.; and for the remainder of the day if it occurs between 2 and 4 P.M.
3. A 30 percent drop will halt trading for the remainder of the day regardless of when the decline occurs.

These specific circuit breaker trigger levels were implemented in 1998. Because circuit breakers are designed to slow a market decline, they are often called "speed bumps." Naturally, how well they work is a matter of debate.

One of the most remarkable things about the crash is how little impact it seems to have had. If you look back at the data in Chapter 1, you will see that the market was actually up slightly in 1987. The postcrash period was one of the better times to be in the market, and the Crash of 1987 increasingly looks like a blip in one of the most spectacular market increases that U.S. investors have ever seen. One thing is clearly true: October is the cruelest month for market investors. Indeed two years after the Crash of 1987, a minicrash occurred on October 13, 1989, as the DJIA fell 190 points in the afternoon (following the collapse of a proposed buyout of United Airlines).

THE ASIAN CRASH

The crash of the Nikkei Index, which began in 1990, lengthened into a particularly long bear market. It is quite like the Crash of 1929 in that respect.

The Asian crash started with a booming bull market in the 1980s. Japan and emerging Asian economies seemed to be forming a powerful economic force. The "Asian economy" became an investor outlet for those wary of the U.S. market after the Crash of 1987.

To give you some idea of the bubble that was forming in Japan between 1955 and 1989, real estate prices in Japan increased by 70 times, and stock prices increased 100 times over. In 1989, price-earnings ratios of Japanese stocks climbed to unheard of levels as the Nikkei Index soared past 39,000. In retrospect, there were numerous warning signals about the Japanese market. At the time, however, optimism about the continued growth in the Japanese market remained high. Crashes never seem to occur when the outlook is poor, so, as with other crashes, many people did not see the impending Nikkei crash.

As you can see in Figure 7.13, in three years from December 1986 to the peak in December 1989, the Nikkei 225 Index rose 115 percent. Over the next three years, the index lost 57 percent of its value. In April 2003, the Nikkei Index stood at a level that was 80 percent off its peak in December 1989.

THE "DOT-COM" BUBBLE AND CRASH

WWW

The growth of the World Wide Web is documented at www.zakon.org/robert/internet/timeline

How many Web sites do you think existed at the end of 1994? Would you believe only about 10,000? By the end of 1999, the number of active Web sites stood at about 9,500,000 and at the end of 2007, there were about 70,000,000 active Web sites.

By the mid-1990s, the rise in Internet use and its international growth potential fueled widespread excitement over the "new economy." Investors did not seem to care about solid business plans—only big ideas. Investor euphoria led to a surge in Internet IPOs, which were commonly referred to as "dot-coms" because so many of their names ended in ".com." Of course, the lack of solid business models doomed many of the newly formed companies. Many of them suffered huge losses and some folded relatively shortly after their IPOs.

The extent of the dot-com bubble and subsequent crash is presented in Table 7.6 and Figure 7.14, which compare the Amex Internet Index and the S&P 500 Index. As shown in

FIGURE 7.13 Nikkei 225 Index, January 1984 to December 2007

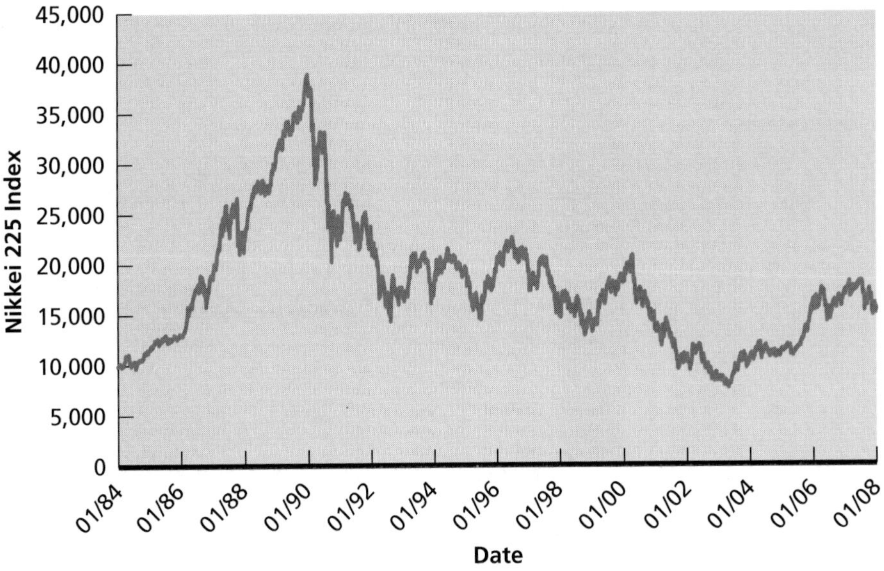

TABLE 7.6 Values of the Amex Internet Index and the S&P 500 Index

Date	Amex Internet Index Value	Gain to Peak from Oct. 1, 1998 (%)	Loss from Peak to Trough (%)	S&P 500 Index Value	Gain to Peak from Oct. 1, 1998 (%)	Loss from Peak to Trough (%)
October 1, 1998	114.68			986.39		
Late March 2000 (peak)	688.52	500%		1,293.72	31%	
Early October 2002 (trough)	58.59		−91%	776.76		−40%

Source: Author calculations.

FIGURE 7.14 Values of the AMEX Internet Index and the S&P 500 Index, October 1995 through December 2007

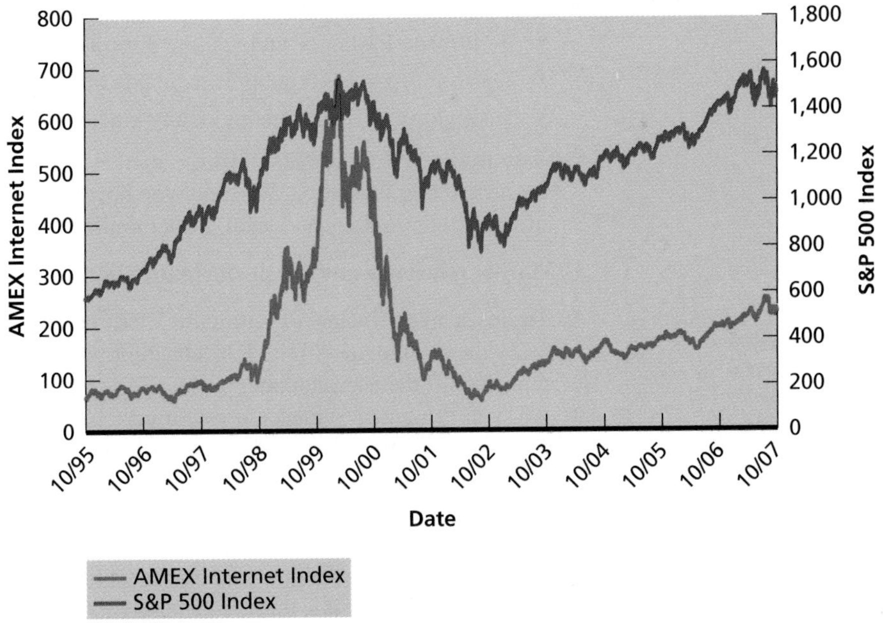

Table 7.6, the Amex Internet Index soared from a level of 114.60 on October 1, 1998, to its peak of 688.52 in late March 2000, an increase of 500 percent. The Amex Internet Index then fell to a level of 58.59 in early October 2002, a drop of 91 percent. By contrast, the S&P 500 Index rallied about 31 percent in the same 1998–2000 time period and fell 40 percent during the 2000–2002 time period.

CHECK THIS

7.11a What is a stock market bubble? A stock market crash?

7.11b What is a major difference between the Crash of October 1929 and the Crash of October 1987?

7.11c What are NYSE circuit breakers? What are they intended to do?

7.12 Summary and Conclusions

In this chapter, we examined market price behavior and market efficiency. Market efficiency is probably the most controversial and intriguing issue in investments. We cover many aspects of market efficiency in this chapter—which we summarize by the chapter's important concepts.

1. The foundations of market efficiency.

A. The efficient markets hypothesis (EMH) asserts that, as a practical matter, organized financial markets like the New York Stock Exchange are efficient.

B. Researchers who study efficient markets often ask whether it is possible to "beat the market." We say that you beat the market if you can consistently earn returns in excess of those earned by other investments having the same risk.

C. If a market is efficient, earning these excess returns is not possible, except by luck. The controversy surrounding the EMH centers on this assertion.

2. The implications of the forms of market efficiency.

A. The EMH states that the market is efficient with respect to some particular information if that information is not useful in earning a positive excess return.

B. The forms of market efficiency and their information sets are:

- *Weak form:* Past price and volume information.
- *Semistrong form:* All publicly available information.
- *Strong form:* All information of any kind, public or private.

C. We discuss how information affects market prices by influencing traders to act on the arrival of information. We show you how to distinguish among informed trading, illegal insider trading, and legal insider trading.

3. Market efficiency and the performance of professional money managers.

A. Testing market efficiency is difficult. We discussed four reasons for this: (1) the risk-adjustment problem, (2) the relevant information problem, (3) the dumb luck problem, and (4) the data snooping problem.

B. We then presented evidence concerning tests of market efficiency. One lesson we demonstrate is that professional money managers have been unable to beat the market consistently—despite their tremendous resources, experience, opportunities, and incentives. Also, this fact is true despite patterns and other oddities that have occurred historically in the stock market.

C. The fact that professional money managers have been unable to beat the market supports the notion that markets are generally rather efficient.

4. **What stock market anomalies, bubbles, and crashes mean for market efficiency.**

A. We discuss some aspects of stock price behavior that are both baffling and hard to reconcile with market efficiency.

B. We discuss the day-of-the-week effect, the amazing January effect, the turn-of-the-year effect, the turn-of-the-month effect, the earnings announcement puzzle, and the price-earnings (P/E) puzzle.

C. We present some market history concerning some famous bubbles and crashes, including the Crash of October 1929, the Crash of October 1987, the Asian crisis, and the dot-com bubble and crash.

GET REAL

This chapter covered market efficiency. In it, we raised a significant question: Can you, or indeed anyone, consistently beat the market? In other words, is the market efficient? This is a question that every investor needs to think about because it has direct, practical implications for investing and portfolio management.

If you think the market is relatively efficient, then your investment strategy should focus on minimizing costs and taxes. Asset allocation is your primary concern, and you will still need to establish the risk level you are comfortable with. But beyond this, you should be a buy-and-hold investor, transacting only when absolutely necessary. Investments such as low-cost, low-turnover mutual funds make a lot of sense. Tools for analyzing the market are irrelevant at best. Thus, in some ways, the appropriate investment strategy is kind of boring, but it's the one that will pay off over the long haul in an efficient market.

In contrast, if you think the market is not particularly efficient, then you've got to be a security picker. You also have to decide what market analyzing tools will be the ones you use. This is also true if you are in the money management business; you have to decide which specific stocks or bonds to hold.

In the end, the only way to find out if you've got what it takes to beat the market is to try, and the best way to try is with a simulated brokerage account such as Stock-Trak. Be honest with yourself: You think you can beat the market; most novice investors do. Some change their minds and some don't. As to which tools to use, you will just have to find out which ones work (or don't work) for you.

Key Terms

abnormal returns 213
bubble 227
crash 227
day-of-the-week effect 223
efficient markets hypothesis (EMH) 208
event study 213
excess return 208
informed trader 215
January effect 224
material nonpublic information 215
NYSE circuit breakers 230
random walk 212

Chapter Review Problems and Self-Test

1. **Market Research** Smolira Investment Trust (SIT) runs a retirement account for college professors, with a current market value of $2 billion. Alchemy, Inc., offers to conduct market research in an attempt to sift through the market data to find a way to increase the return to SIT's portfolio by 30 basis points per year. Alchemy is offering to conduct the research for the sum of $9 million. Is this price too high or too low?

2. **Picking a Money Manager** You are helping your very rich aunt Molly to decide where to invest her portfolio. She is planning to take a 10-year world tour after she invests the bulk of her portfolio. She thinks that picking a money manager is unimportant because she believes any professional money manager must be able to beat the market. She's just planning to pick a professional money manager at random. What do you tell her?

Answers to Self-Test Problems

1. Assuming that Alchemy, Inc., actually can conduct research that allows Smolira Investment Trust (SIT) to increase its portfolio return by 30 basis points, SIT would be willing to pay up to $2,000,000,000 times 0.0030 = $6,000,000 for this research. So the price of $9 million is too high.
2. You could show her Figure 7.8. In this figure, it is clear that picking a professional manager at random gives her about a 25 to 30 percent chance of beating a market fund like the Vanguard 500 Index Fund. If she invests her sizable portfolio in the Vanguard 500 Index Fund, she has about a 70 to 75 percent chance of beating a professional money manager picked at random.

Test Your Investment Quotient

IQ

For the remaining questions and problems, the circled numbers in the margin refer to the corresponding learning objective in this chapter.

(4) 1. **Efficient Markets Hypothesis** A market anomaly refers to

a. An exogenous shock to the market that is sharp but not persistent.
b. A price or volume event that is inconsistent with historical price or volume trends.
c. A trading or pricing structure that interferes with efficient buying or selling of securities.
d. Price behavior that differs from the behavior predicted by the efficient markets hypothesis.

CFA® PROBLEMS

(1) 2. **Efficient Markets Hypothesis** Which of the following assumptions does not imply an informationally efficient market?

a. Security prices adjust rapidly to reflect new information.
b. The timing of one news announcement is independent of other news announcements.
c. The risk-free rate exists, and investors can borrow and lend unlimited amounts at the risk-free rate.
d. Many profit-maximizing participants, each acting independently of the others, analyze and value securities.

CFA® PROBLEMS

(2) 3. **Efficient Markets Hypothesis** After lengthy trial and error, you discover a trading system that would have doubled the value of your investment every six months if applied over the last three years. Which of the following problems makes it difficult to conclude that this is an example of market inefficiency?

a. Risk-adjustment problem
b. Relevant information problem
c. Dumb luck problem
d. Data snooping problem

(2) 4. **Efficient Markets Hypothesis** In discussions of financial market efficiency, which of the following is not one of the stylized forms of market efficiency?

a. Strong form
b. Semistrong form
c. Weak form
d. Economic form

(3) 5. **Beating the Market** Which of the following is not considered a problem when evaluating the ability of a trading system to "beat the market"?

a. Risk-adjustment problem
b. Relevant information problem
c. Data measurement problem
d. Data snooping problem

(4) 6. **Calendar Anomalies** Which month of the year, on average, has had the highest stock market returns as measured by a small-stock portfolio?

a. January
b. March

c. June
d. December

7. **Circuit Breakers** Which of the following intraday changes in the Dow Jones Industrial Average (DJIA) will trigger a circuit breaker halting NYSE trading for one hour?

a. 10 percent drop before 2 P.M.
b. 10 percent drop after 2 P.M.
c. 10 percent rise before 2 P.M.
d. 10 percent rise after 2 P.M.

(2) 8. **Efficient Markets Hypothesis** The SEC has regulations that prohibit trading on inside information. If the market is ______ -form efficient, such regulation is not needed.

a. weak
b. semistrong
c. technical
d. strong

(4) 9. **The January Effect** Which of the following is a possible explanation of the January effect?

I. Institutional window dressing
II. Bonus demand
III. Tax-loss selling

a. I only
b. I and II only
c. I and III only
d. I, II, and III

10. **NYSE Circuit Breakers** Circuit breakers implemented by the NYSE were designed to

a. Reduce the January effect.
b. Reduce the effect of technical trading.
c. Eliminate program trading.
d. Slow a market decline.

(2) 11. **Market Efficiency Implications** Assume the market is semistrong-form efficient. The best investment strategy is to

a. Examine the past prices of a stock to determine the trend.
b. Invest in an actively managed mutual fund whose manager searches for underpriced stocks.
c. Invest in an index fund.
d. Examine the financial statements for a company to find stocks that are not selling at intrinsic value.

(2) 12. **Market Efficiency Implications** Assume the market is weak-form efficient. If this is true, technical analysts ______ earn excess returns and fundamental analysts ______ earn excess returns.

a. could; could
b. could; could not
c. could not; could not
d. could not; could

(1) 13. **Efficient Markets Hypothesis** Which of the following is *not* true concerning the efficient markets hypothesis?

a. Markets that are less organized are not as likely to be efficient.
b. Markets with wide fluctuations in prices cannot be efficient.
c. The efficient markets hypothesis deals only with the stock market.
d. Prices in an efficient market are fair on average.

(2) 14. **Efficient Markets Hypothesis** You purchase a stock that you expect to increase in value over the next year. One year later, after the discovery that the CEO embezzled funds and the company is close to bankruptcy, the stock has fallen in price. Which of the following statements is true?

a. This is a violation of weak-form efficiency.
b. This is a violation of semistrong-form efficiency
c. This is a violation of all forms of market efficiency.
d. This is not a violation of market efficiency.

(2) **15. Efficient Markets Hypothesis** Which of the following statements concerning market efficiency is true?

a. If the market is weak-form efficient, it is also semistrong-form efficient.
b. If the market is semistrong-form efficient, it is also strong-form efficient.
c. If the market is weak-form efficient, it is also strong-form efficient.
d. If the market is semistrong-form efficient, it is also weak-form efficient.

Concept Questions

(2) **1. Efficient Markets** A stock market analyst is able to identify mispriced stocks by comparing the average price for the last 10 days to the average price for the last 60 days. If this is true, what do you know about the market?

(2) **2. Efficient Markets** Critically evaluate the following statement: "Playing the stock market is like gambling. Such speculative investing has no social value, other than the pleasure people get from this form of gambling."

(3) **3. Misconceptions about Efficient Markets** Several celebrated investors and stock pickers have recorded huge returns on their investments over the past two decades. Is the success of these particular investors an invalidation of an efficient stock market? Explain.

(2) **4. Interpreting Efficient Markets** For each of the following scenarios, discuss whether profit opportunities exist from trading in the stock of the firm under the conditions that (1) the market is not weak-form efficient, (2) the market is weak-form but not semistrong-form efficient, (3) the market is semistrong-form but not strong-form efficient, and (4) the market is strong-form efficient.

a. The stock price has risen steadily each day for the past 30 days.
b. The financial statements for a company were released three days ago, and you believe you've uncovered some anomalies in the company's inventory and cost control reporting techniques that are understating the firm's true liquidity strength.
c. You observe that the senior management of a company has been buying a lot of the company's stock on the open market over the past week.
d. Your next-door neighbor, who happens to be a computer analyst at the local steel plant, casually mentions that a German steel conglomerate hinted yesterday that it might try to acquire the local firm in a hostile takeover.

(3) **5. Performance of the Pros** In the mid- to late-1990s, the performance of the pros was unusually poor—on the order of 90 percent of all equity mutual funds underperformed a passively managed index fund. How does this bear on the issue of market efficiency?

(1) **6. Efficient Markets** A hundred years ago or so, companies did not compile annual reports. Even if you owned stock in a particular company, you were unlikely to be allowed to see the balance sheet and income statement for the company. Assuming the market is semistrong-form efficient, what does this say about market efficiency then compared to now?

(2) **7. Efficient Markets Hypothesis** You invest $10,000 in the market at the beginning of the year, and by the end of the year your account is worth $15,000. During the year the market return was 10 percent. Does this mean that the market is inefficient?

(1) **8. Efficient Markets Hypothesis** Which of the following statements are true about the efficient market hypothesis?

a. It implies perfect forecasting ability.
b. It implies that prices reflect all available information.
c. It implies an irrational market.
d. It implies that prices do not fluctuate.
e. It results from keen competition among investors.

(2) **9. Semistrong Efficiency** If a market is semistrong-form efficient, is it also weak-form efficient? Explain.

(2) **10. Efficient Markets Hypothesis** What are the implications of the efficient markets hypothesis for investors who buy and sell stocks in an attempt to "beat the market"?

(2) **11. Efficient Markets Hypothesis** Aerotech, an aerospace technology research firm, announced this morning that it hired the world's most knowledgeable and prolific space researchers. Before

today, Aerotech's stock had been selling for $100. Assume that no other information is received over the next week and the stock market as a whole does not move.

a. What do you expect will happen to Aerotech's stock?
b. Consider the following scenarios:

i. The stock price jumps to $118 on the day of the announcement. In subsequent days it floats up to $123, then falls back to $116.
ii. The stock price jumps to $116 and remains at that level.
iii. The stock price gradually climbs to $116 over the next week.

Which scenario(s) indicate market efficiency? Which do not? Why?

(2) **12. Efficient Markets Hypothesis** When the 56-year-old founder of Gulf & Western, Inc., died of a heart attack, the stock price immediately jumped from $18.00 a share to $20.25, a 12.5 percent increase. This is evidence of market inefficiency, because an efficient stock market would have anticipated his death and adjusted the price beforehand. Assume that no other information is received and the stock market as a whole does not move. Is this statement about market efficiency true or false? Explain.

(2) **13. Efficient Markets Hypothesis** Today, the following announcement was made: "Early today the Justice Department reached a decision in the Universal Product Care (UPC) case. UPC has been found guilty of discriminatory practices in hiring. For the next five years, UPC must pay $2 million each year to a fund representing victims of UPC's policies." Assuming the market is efficient, should investors not buy UPC stock after the announcement because the litigation will cause an abnormally low rate of return? Explain.

(2) **14. Efficient Markets Hypothesis** Newtech Corp. is going to adopt a new chip-testing device that can greatly improve its production efficiency. Do you think the lead engineer can profit from purchasing the firm's stock before the news release on the device? After reading the announcement in *The Wall Street Journal,* should you be able to earn an abnormal return from purchasing the stock if the market is efficient?

(2) **15. Efficient Markets Hypothesis** TransTrust Corp. has changed how it accounts for inventory. Taxes are unaffected, although the resulting earnings report released this quarter is 20 percent higher than what it would have been under the old accounting system. There is no other surprise in the earnings report and the change in the accounting treatment was publicly announced. If the market is efficient, will the stock price be higher when the market learns that the reported earnings are higher?

(3) **16. Efficient Markets Hypothesis** The Durkin Investing Agency has been the best stock picker in the country for the past two years. Before this rise to fame occurred, the Durkin newsletter had 200 subscribers. Those subscribers beat the market consistently, earning substantially higher returns after adjustment for risk and transaction costs. Subscriptions have skyrocketed to 10,000. Now, when the Durkin Investing Agency recommends a stock, the price instantly rises several points. The subscribers currently earn only a normal return when they buy recommended stock because the price rises before anybody can act on the information. Briefly explain this phenomenon. Is Durkin's ability to pick stocks consistent with market efficiency?

(2) **17. Efficient Markets Hypothesis** Your broker commented that well-managed firms are better investments than poorly managed firms. As evidence, your broker cited a recent study examining 100 small manufacturing firms that eight years earlier had been listed in an industry magazine as the best-managed small manufacturers in the country. In the ensuing eight years, the 100 firms listed have not earned more than the normal market return. Your broker continued to say that if the firms were well managed, they should have produced better-than-average returns. If the market is efficient, do you agree with your broker?

(2) **18. Efficient Markets Hypothesis** A famous economist just announced in *The Wall Street Journal* his findings that the recession is over and the economy is again entering an expansion. Assume market efficiency. Can you profit from investing in the stock market after you read this announcement?

(2) **19. Efficient Markets Hypothesis** Suppose the market is semistrong-form efficient. Can you expect to earn excess returns if you make trades based on

a. Your broker's information about record earnings for a stock?
b. Rumors about a merger of a firm?
c. Yesterday's announcement of a successful new product test?

(2) **20. Efficient Markets Hypothesis** The efficient markets hypothesis implies that all mutual funds should obtain the same expected risk-adjusted returns. Therefore, we can simply pick mutual funds at random. Is this statement true or false? Explain.

www.mhhe.com/jm5e

(2) 21. **Efficient Markets Hypothesis** Assume that markets are efficient. During a trading day, American Golf, Inc., announces that it has lost a contract for a large golfing project, which, prior to the news, it was widely believed to have secured. If the market is efficient, how should the stock price react to this information if no additional information is released?

(2) 22. **Efficient Markets Hypothesis** Prospectors, Inc., is a publicly traded gold prospecting company in Alaska. Although the firm's searches for gold usually fail, the prospectors occasionally find a rich vein of ore. What pattern would you expect to observe for Prospectors' cumulative abnormal returns if the market is efficient?

Questions and Problems

Core Questions

(2) 1. **Cumulative Abnormal Returns** On November 14, Thorogood Enterprises announced that the public and acrimonious battle with its current CEO had been resolved. Under the terms of the deal, the CEO would step down from his position immediately. In exchange, he was given a generous severance package. Given the information below, calculate the cumulative abnormal return (CAR) around this announcement. Assume the company has an expected return equal to the market return. Graph and interpret your results. Do your results support market efficiency?

Date	Market Return (%)	Company Return (%)
11/7	0.5	0.4
11/8	0.3	0.4
11/9	−0.2	−0.3
11/10	−0.6	−0.5
11/11	1.3	1.1
11/14	−0.1	1.8
11/15	0.1	0.1
11/16	0.9	0.7
11/17	0.2	0.3
11/18	−0.2	0.0
11/19	0.3	0.2

(2) 2. **Cumulative Abnormal Returns** The following diagram shows the cumulative abnormal returns (CAR) for oil exploration companies announcing oil discoveries over a 30-year period. Month 0 in the diagram is the announcement month. Assume that no other information is received and the stock market as a whole does not move. Is the diagram consistent with market efficiency? Why or why not?

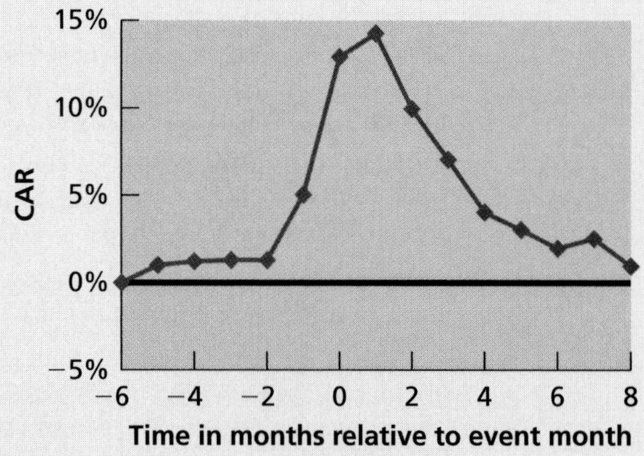

(2) 3. **Cumulative Abnormal Returns** The following figures present the results of four cumulative abnormal returns (CAR) studies. Indicate whether the results of each study support, reject, or

are inconclusive about the semistrong form of the efficient market hypothesis. In each figure, time 0 is the date of an event.

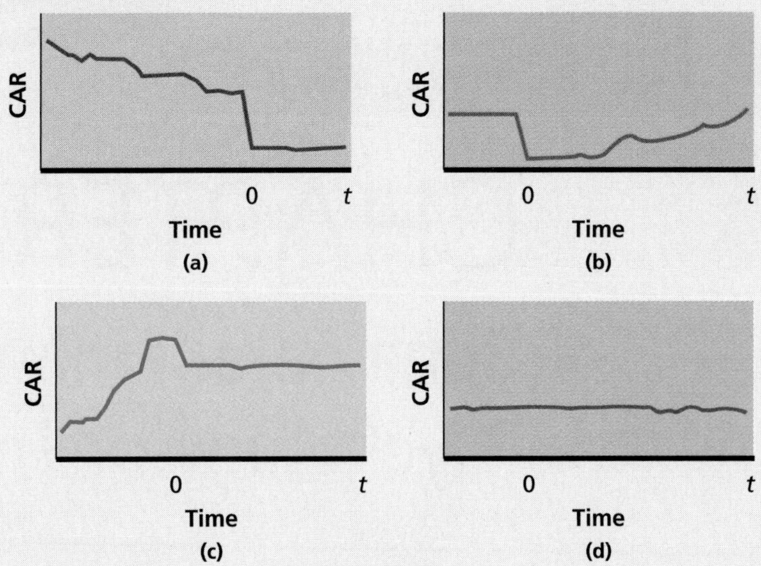

2

4. **Cumulative Abnormal Returns** A study analyzed the behavior of the stock prices of firms that had lost antitrust cases. Included in the diagram are all firms that lost the initial court decision, even if the decision was later overturned on appeal. The event at time 0 is the initial, pre–appeal court decision. Assume no other information was released, aside from that disclosed in the initial trial. The stock prices all have a beta of 1. Is the diagram consistent with market efficiency? Why or why not?

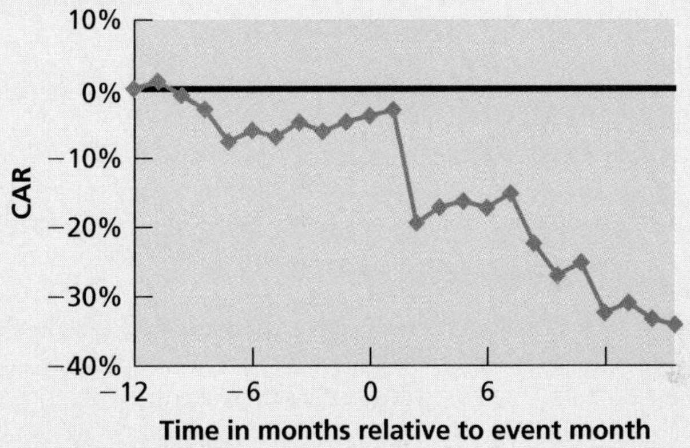

Intermediate Questions

2

5. **Cumulative Abnormal Returns** Ross Co., Westerfield, Inc., and Jordan Company announced a new agreement to market their respective products in China on July 18 (7/18), February 12 (2/12), and October 7 (10/7), respectively. Given the information below, calculate the cumulative abnormal return (CAR) for these stocks as a group. Assume all companies have an expected return equal to the market return. Graph and interpret your results. Do your results support market efficiency?

Ross Co.			Westerfield, Inc.			Jordan Company		
Date	Market Return	Company Return	Date	Market Return	Company Return	Date	Market Return	Company Return
7/12	–0.2	–0.4	2/8	–0.7	–0.9	10/1	0.3	0.5
7/13	0.1	0.3	2/9	–0.8	–0.9	10/2	0.2	0.8
7/16	0.6	0.8	2/10	0.6	0.4	10/3	0.9	1.3
7/17	–0.4	–0.2	2/11	0.8	1.0	10/6	–0.1	–0.5
7/18	–1.9	1.3	2/12	–0.1	0.1	10/7	–2.4	–0.5
7/19	–0.8	–0.6	2/15	1.3	1.4	10/8	0.3	0.3
7/20	–0.9	–1.0	2/16	0.7	0.7	10/9	–0.5	–0.4
7/23	0.6	0.4	2/17	–0.1	0.0	10/10	0.1	–0.1
7/24	0.1	0.0	2/18	0.5	0.4	10/13	–0.2	–0.6

CHAPTER 8

Behavioral Finance and the Psychology of Investing

"The investor's chief problem, and even his worst enemy, is likely to be himself."

–Benjamin Graham

"There are three factors that influence the market: Fear, Greed, and Greed."

–Market folklore

Learning Objectives

Psych yourself up and get a good understanding of:

1. Prospect theory.
2. The implications of investor overconfidence and misperceptions of randomness.
3. Sentiment-based risk and limits to arbitrage.
4. The wide array of technical analysis methods used by investors.

Be honest: Do you think of yourself as a better than average driver? If you do, you are not alone. About 80 percent of the people who are asked this question will say yes. Evidently, we tend to overestimate our abilities behind the wheel. Is the same thing true when it comes to making investment decisions? ■

You will probably not be surprised when we say that human beings sometimes make errors in judgment. How these errors, and other aspects of human behavior, affect investors and asset prices falls under the general heading of "behavioral finance." In the first part of this chapter, our goal is to acquaint you with some common types of mistakes investors make and their financial implications. As you will see, researchers have identified a wide variety of potentially damaging behaviors. In the second part of the chapter, we describe a trading strategy known as "technical analysis." Some investors use technical analysis as a tool to try to exploit patterns in prices. These patterns are thought to exist (by advocates of technical analysis) because of predictable behavior by investors.

8.1 Introduction to Behavioral Finance

Sooner or later, you are going to make an investment decision that winds up costing you a lot of money. Why is this going to happen? You already know the answer. Sometimes you make sound decisions, but you just get unlucky when something happens that you could not have reasonably anticipated. At other times (and painful to admit) you just make a bad decision, one that could have (and should have) been avoided. The beginning of investment wisdom is to recognize the circumstances that lead to poor decisions and thereby cut down on the damage done by investment blunders.

behavioral finance
The area of finance dealing with the implications of investor reasoning errors on investment decisions and market prices.

As we previously noted, the area of research known as **behavioral finance** attempts to understand and explain how reasoning errors influence investor decisions and market prices. Much of the research done in the area of behavioral finance stems from work in the area of cognitive psychology, which is the study of how people, including investors, think, reason, and make decisions. Errors in reasoning are often called *cognitive errors*.

Some proponents of behavioral finance believe that cognitive errors by investors will cause market inefficiencies. Recall that in a previous chapter, we identified three economic conditions that lead to market efficiency: (1) investor rationality, (2) independent deviations from rationality, and (3) arbitrage. For a market to be inefficient, all three of these conditions must be absent. That is, it must be the case that a substantial portion of investors make irrational investment decisions, and the collective irrationality of these investors then must lead to an overly optimistic or pessimistic market situation that cannot be corrected via arbitrage by rational, well-capitalized investors. Whether this actually occurs in financial markets is the subject of a raging debate, and we are not going to take sides. Instead, our goal is to introduce you to the ideas and issues.

CHECK THIS

8.1a What is behavioral finance?

8.1b What three conditions must be absent for a market to be inefficient?

8.2 Prospect Theory

prospect theory
An alternative theory to classical, rational economic decision making, which emphasizes, among other things, that investors tend to behave differently when they face prospective gains and losses.

Prospect theory, developed in the late 1970s, is a collection of ideas that provides an alternative to classical, rational economic decision making. The foundation of prospect theory rests on the idea that investors are much more distressed by prospective losses than they are happy about prospective gains. Researchers have found that a typical investor considers the pain of a \$1 loss to be about twice as great as the pleasure received from the gain of \$1. Also, researchers have found that investors respond in different ways to identical situations. The difference depends on whether the situation is presented in terms of losses or in terms of gains.

Investors seem to be willing to take more risk to avoid the loss of a dollar than they are to make a dollar profit. Also, if an investor has the choice between a sure gain and a gamble that could increase or decrease the sure gain, the investor is likely to choose the sure gain. Choosing a sure gain over a gamble is called *risk-averse behavior.* If the same investor is faced with a sure loss and a gamble that could increase or decrease the sure loss, the investor is likely to take the gamble. Choosing the gamble over the sure loss is called *risk-taking behavior.*

This focus on gains and losses and the tendency of investors to be risk-averse with regard to gains, but risk-taking when it comes to losses, is the essence of prospect theory. In contrast, a fully rational investor (in an economic sense) is presumed to care only about his or her overall wealth, not the gains and losses associated with individual pieces of that wealth.

To give a simple example, suppose you own just two stocks (which is, of course, a bad idea from a diversification standpoint). On a particular day, one stock goes up sharply, but the other goes down so that your total wealth in unchanged. On another day, neither stock changes price at all. In both cases, your total wealth was unaffected, but in the first case you would probably be upset that your big gain was canceled out. If you are, you are focusing on the individual pieces, not the big picture. As we will see in the next few subsections, this kind of thinking can lead to potentially damaging errors in judgment.

FRAME DEPENDENCE

If an investment problem is presented in two different (but really equivalent) ways, investors often make inconsistent choices. That is, how a problem is described, or framed, seems to matter to people. Some people believe that frames are transparent; that is, investors should be able to see through the way the question is asked. Do they? Do you? Try this: Jot down your answers in the following two scenarios.

Scenario One. Suppose we give you $1,000. You have the following choice:

A. You can receive another $500 for sure.

B. You can flip a fair coin. If the coin-flip comes up heads, you get another $1,000, but if it comes up tails, you get nothing.

Scenario Two. Suppose we give you $2,000. You have the following choice:

A. You can lose $500 for sure.

B. You can flip a fair coin. If the coin-flip comes up heads, you lose $1,000, but if it comes up tails, you lose nothing.

What were your answers? Did you choose option A in the first scenario and option B in the second? If that's what you did, you are guilty of just focusing on gains and losses, and not paying attention to what really matters, namely, the impact on your wealth. However, you are not alone. About 85 percent of the people who are presented with the first scenario choose option A, and about 70 percent of the people who are presented with the second scenario choose option B.

If you look closely at the two scenarios, you will see that they are actually identical. You end up with $1,500 for sure if you pick option A, or else you end up with a 50-50 chance of either $1,000 or $2,000 if you pick option B. So you should pick the same option in both scenarios. Which option you prefer is up to you, but the point is that you should never pick option A in one scenario and option B in the other. But people do this because the phrasing, or framing, of the question leads people to answer the questions differently. This phenomenon is known as *frame dependence*.

Our frame dependence example offers several important investment lessons. First, an investor can always frame a decision problem in broad terms (like wealth) or in narrow terms (like gains and losses). Second, broad and narrow frames often lead the investor to make different choices. Although using a narrow frame (like gains and losses) is human nature, doing so can lead to irrational decisions. Therefore, using broad frames, like overall wealth, results in better investment decisions.

MENTAL ACCOUNTS AND LOSS AVERSION

When you add a new stock to your portfolio, it is human nature for you to associate the stock with its purchase price. As the price of the stock changes through time, you will have unrealized gains or losses when you compare the current price to the purchase price. Through time, you will mentally account for these gains and losses, and how you feel about the investment depends on whether you are ahead or behind. This behavior is known as **mental accounting**.

mental accounting
Associating a stock with its purchase price.

When you engage in mental accounting, you unknowingly have a personal relationship with each of your stocks. As a result, selling one of them becomes more difficult. It is as if you have to "break up" with this stock, or "fire" it from your portfolio. As with personal relationships, these "stock relationships" can be complicated and, believe it or not, make selling stocks difficult at times.

In fact, you may have particular difficulty selling a stock at a price lower than your purchase price. If you sell a stock at a loss, you may have a hard time thinking that purchasing the stock in the first place was correct. You may feel this way even if the decision to buy was actually a very good decision. A further complication is that you will also think that if you can just somehow "get even," you will be able to sell the stock without any hard feelings. This phenomenon is known as **loss aversion**, which is the reluctance to sell investments, such as shares of stock, after they have fallen in value. Loss aversion is also called the "break-even" or "disposition effect," and those suffering from it are sometimes said to have "get-evenitis." Legendary investor Warren Buffett offers the following advice: "The stock doesn't know you own it. You have feelings about it, but it has no feelings about you. The stock doesn't know what you paid. People shouldn't get emotionally involved with their stocks."

loss aversion
A reluctance to sell investments after they have fallen in value. Also known as the *break-even or disposition effect.*

To see if you are likely to suffer from loss aversion, consider the following two investments:

Investment One. A year ago, you bought shares in Fama Enterprises for \$40 per share. Today, these shares are worth \$20 each.

Investment Two. A year ago, you bought shares in French Company for \$5 per share. Today, these shares are worth \$20 each.

What will you do? Will you (1) sell one of these stocks; (2) sell both of these stocks; (3) hold one of these stocks; or (4) hold both of these stocks?

Because you are reading about loss aversion, you will undoubtedly recognize that if you choose to keep the shares in Fama Enterprises, you might be suffering from loss aversion. Why do we say might? Well, consider this. Suppose you are considering a new investment in Fama Enterprises. Does your rational analysis say that it is reasonable to purchase shares at \$20? If the rational answer is no, then you should sell. If the rational answer is yes, then you do not suffer from loss aversion. However, if you argued to yourself that if shares in Fama Enterprises were a good buy at \$40, then they must be a steal at \$20, you probably have a raging case of loss aversion. So, to summarize, there are two important lessons from this example:

- **Lesson One**: The market says that shares in Fama Enterprises are worth \$20. The market does not care that you paid \$40 a year ago.
- **Lesson Two**: You should not care about your purchase price of Fama Enterprises either. You must evaluate your shares at their current price.

How about the shares in French Company? Do you sell them and take the profit? Once again, the lessons are the same. The market says that shares in French Company are worth \$20 per share today. The fact that you paid \$5 a year ago is not relevant. Note that selling either of these stocks has tax consequences. Your careful analysis should acknowledge the existence of taxes and transaction fees, and their impact on the net proceeds available to you after you sell a security.

How destructive is loss aversion? Perhaps the most famous case of loss aversion, or "get-evenitis," occurred in 1995, when 28-year-old Nicholas Leeson caused the collapse of his employer, the 233-year-old Barings Bank. At the end of 1992, Leeson had lost about £2 million, which he hid in a secret account. By the end of 1993, his losses were about £23 million, and they mushroomed to £208 million at the end of 1994 (at the time, this was \$512 million). Instead of admitting to these losses, Leeson gambled more of the bank's money in an attempt to "double-up and catch-up." On February 23, 1995, Leeson's losses were about £827 million (\$1.3 billion) and his trading irregularities were uncovered. Although he attempted to flee from prosecution, he was caught, arrested, tried, convicted, and imprisoned. Also, his wife divorced him.

It is unlikely that you will suffer from a case of loss aversion as severe as Nicholas Leeson's, but loss aversion does affect everyday investors. For example, we know that individual investors sell "winners" more frequently than they sell "losers." If a typical individual investor had 100 stocks with unrealized gains, the investor might sell 15 of them and keep 85. If the same investor had 100 stocks with unrealized losses, the investor would tend to sell 10 of them and keep 90. That is, individual investors are typically about 1.5 times more likely to sell a stock that has gone up in price than they are to sell a stock that has fallen in price.

This effect is worse when investors hold mutual funds. With mutual funds, when investors choose to sell, they are more than 2.5 times as likely to sell a winning fund than a losing fund. How about professional money managers who manage the mutual funds? They also suffer from loss aversion.

HOUSE MONEY

Casinos in Las Vegas (and elsewhere) know all about a concept called "playing with house money." The casinos have found that gamblers are far more likely to take big risks with money that they have won from the casino (i.e., the "house money"). Also, casinos have found that gamblers are not as upset about losing house money as they are about losing the money they brought with them to gamble.

It may seem natural for you to feel that some money is precious because you earned it through hard work, sweat, and sacrifice, whereas other money is less precious because it came to you as a windfall. But these feelings are plainly irrational because any dollar you have buys the same amount of goods and services no matter how you obtained that dollar. The lessons are:

- **Lesson One**. There are no "paper profits." Your profits are yours.
- **Lesson Two**. All your money is your money. That is, you should not separate your money into bundles labeled "house money" and "my money."

Let us return to the shares of Fama Enterprises and French Company. Suppose both were to decline to $15. You might feel very differently about the decline depending on which stock you looked at. With Fama Enterprises, the decline makes a bad situation even worse. Now you are down $25 per share on your investment. On the other hand, with French Company, you only "give back" some of your "paper profit." You are still way ahead. This kind of thinking is playing with house money. Whether you lose from your original investment or from your investment gains is irrelevant.

Frame dependence, mental accounting, and the house money effect are all consistent with the predictions of prospect theory. Many other types of judgment errors have been documented. Here are a few examples:

- **Myopic loss aversion**: This behavior is the tendency to focus on avoiding short-term losses, even at the expense of long-term gains. For example, you might fail to invest "retirement" money into stocks because you have a fear of loss in the near term.
- **Regret aversion**: This aversion is the tendency to avoid making a decision because you fear that, in hindsight, the decision would have been less than optimal. Regret aversion relates to myopic loss aversion.
- **Sunk cost fallacy**: This mistake is the tendency to "throw good money after bad." An example is to keep buying a stock or mutual fund in the face of unfavorable developments.
- **Endowment effect**: This effect is the tendency to consider something that you own to be worth more than it would be if you did not own it. Because of the endowment effect, people sometimes demand more money to give up something than they would be willing to pay to acquire it.
- **Money illusion**: If you suffer from a money illusion, you are confused between real buying power and nominal buying power (i.e., you do not account for the effects of inflation).

CHECK THIS

8.2a What is the basic prediction of prospect theory?

8.2b What is frame dependence?

8.2c How are mental accounting and loss aversion related?

8.3 Overconfidence

A serious error in judgment you can make as an investor is to be overconfident. We are all overconfident about our abilities in many areas (recall our question about your driving ability at the beginning of the chapter). Here is another example. Ask yourself: What grade will I receive in this course (in spite of the arbitrary and capricious nature of the professor)? In our experience, almost everyone will either say A or, at worst, B. Sadly, when we ask our students this question, we always feel confident (but not overconfident) that at least some of our students are going to be disappointed.

Concerning investment behavior, overconfidence appears in several ways. The classic example is diversification, or the lack of it. Investors tend to invest too heavily in the company for which they work. When you think about it, this loyalty can be very bad financially. This is because both your earning power (your income) and your retirement nest egg depend on one company.

Other examples of the lack of diversification include investing too heavily in the stocks of local companies. You might also do this because you read about them in the local news or you know someone who works there. That is, you might be unduly confident that you have a high degree of knowledge about local companies versus distant companies.

OVERCONFIDENCE AND TRADING FREQUENCY

If you are overconfident about your investment skill, you are likely to trade too much. You should know that researchers have found that investors who make relatively more trades have lower returns than investors who trade less frequently. Based on brokerage account activity over a particular period, researchers found that the average household earned an annual return of 16.4 percent. However, those households that traded the most earned an annual return of only 11.4 percent. The moral is clear: Excessive trading is hazardous to your wealth.

OVERTRADING AND GENDER: "IT'S (BASICALLY) A GUY THING"

In a study published in 2001, Professors Brad Barber and Terrance Odean examined the effects of overconfidence. Two possible effects of overconfidence are that it leads to more trading and more trading leads to lower returns. If investors could be divided into groups that differed in overconfidence, then these effects could be examined.

Barber and Odean use the fact that psychologists have found that men are more overconfident than women in the area of finance. So, do men trade more than women? Do portfolios of men underperform the portfolios of women? Barber and Odean show that the answer to both questions is yes.

Barber and Odean examined the trading accounts of men and women and find that men trade about 50 percent more than women. They found that both men and women reduce their portfolio returns through excessive trading. However, men did so by 94 basis points more per year than women. The difference is even bigger between single men and single women. Single men traded 67 percent more than single women, and single men reduced their return by 144 basis points compared to single women.

Using four risk measures, and accounting for the effects of marital status, age, and income, Professors Barber and Odean also find that men invested in riskier positions than women. Young and single people held portfolios that displayed more return volatility and contained a higher percentage of stocks in small companies. Investors with higher incomes also accepted more market risk. These results are comforting because it seems to make sense that the relatively young and the relatively wealthy should be willing to take more investment risk, particularly if they do not have dependents.

WHAT IS A DIVERSIFIED PORTFOLIO TO THE EVERYDAY INVESTOR?

It is clear to researchers that most investors have a poor understanding of what constitutes a well-diversified portfolio. Researchers have discovered that the average number of stocks in a household portfolio is about four, and the median is about three.

Ask yourself: What percentage of these households beat the market? If you are like most people, your answer is too low. Researchers have found, however, that even when accounting for trading costs, about 43 percent of the households outperformed the market. Surprised? The lack of diversification is the source of your surprise.

Think about it like this. Suppose all investors held just one stock in their account. If there are many stocks, about half the individual stock returns outperform the market average. Therefore, about half the investors will beat the market. Quickly: Did you think that you would certainly be in that half that would beat the market? If you did, this should show you that you might be prone to overconfidence.

CHECK THIS

8.3a How does overconfidence appear in investment behavior?

8.3b What are the effects of trading frequency on portfolio performance?

8.4 Misperceiving Randomness and Overreacting to Chance Events

representativeness heuristic
Concluding that causal factors are at work behind random sequences.

Cognitive psychologists have discovered that the human mind is a pattern-seeking device. As a result, we can conclude that causal factors or patterns are at work behind sequences of events even when the events are truly random. In behavioral finance, this is known as the **representativeness heuristic**, which says that if something is random, it should look random. But what does random look like?

Suppose we flip a coin 20 times and write down whether we get a head or a tail. Then we do it again. The results of our two sets of 20 flips are:

First 20: T T T H T T T H T T H H H T H H T H H H

Second 20: T H T H H T T H T H T H T T H T H T H H

Do these sequences of heads and tails both look random to you? Most people would say that the first 20 and the second 20 somehow look "different," even though both are random sequences and both have 10 heads and 10 tails.

Let's look at this a bit differently by graphing the results. We'll start at zero. If a head occurs, we will subtract one; if a tail occurs, we will add one. Table 8.1 lists the results. Suppose we graph the two sets of 20 flips in Figure 8.1. Do the two series look different to you? Do you think the line labeled First 20 has a pattern to it, but the line labeled Second 20 appears to be random? If you do, your mind saw a pattern in a random sequence of coin flips, even though both patterns are the result of random coin flips with 10 heads and 10 tails.

THE "HOT-HAND" FALLACY

Basketball fans generally believe that success breeds success. Suppose we look at the recent performance of two basketball players named LeBron and Shaquille. Both of these players make half of their shots. But LeBron just made two shots in a row, while Shaquille just missed two shots in a row. Researchers have found that if they ask 100 basketball fans which player has the better chance of making the next shot, 91 of them will say LeBron, because he has a "hot hand." Further, 84 of these fans believe that it is important for teammates to pass the ball to LeBron after he has made two or three shots in a row.

TABLE 8.1 The Results of Two Sets of 20 Coin Flips

Flip Number	First 20 Flips: Result	+1/−1	Accumulated Sum	Second 20 Flips: Result	+1/−1	Accumulated Sum
			0			0
1	T	1	1	T	1	1
2	T	1	2	H	−1	0
3	T	1	3	T	1	1
4	H	−1	2	H	−1	0
5	T	1	3	H	−1	−1
6	T	1	4	T	1	0
7	T	1	5	T	1	1
8	H	−1	4	H	−1	0
9	T	1	5	T	1	1
10	T	1	6	H	−1	0
11	H	−1	5	T	1	1
12	H	−1	4	H	−1	0
13	H	−1	3	T	1	1
14	T	1	4	T	1	2
15	H	−1	3	H	−1	1
16	H	−1	2	T	1	2
17	T	1	3	H	−1	1
18	H	−1	2	T	1	2
19	H	−1	1	H	−1	1
20	H	−1	0	H	−1	0
Number of heads	10			10		
Number of tails	10			10		

FIGURE 8.1 The Pattern of Two Different Sets of 20 Coin Flips

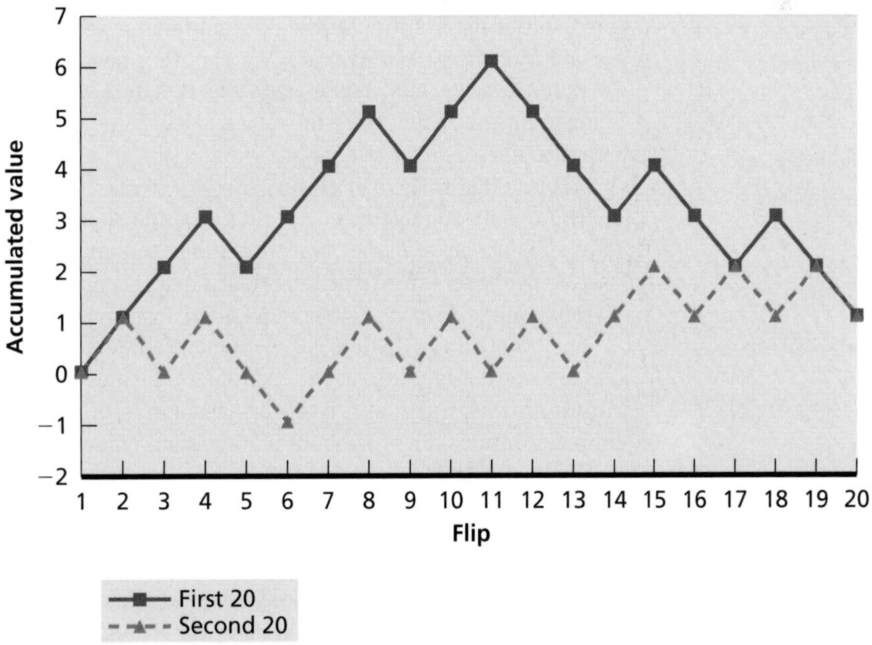

TABLE 8.2 Shooting Percentages and the History of Previous Attempts

Shooting Percentage on Next Shot	History of Previous Attempts
46%	Made 3 in a row
50	Made 2 in a row
51	Made 1
52	First shot of the game
54	Missed 1
53	Missed 2 in a row
56	Missed 3 in a row

But—and the sports fans among you will have a hard time with this—researchers have found that the hot hand is an illusion. That is, players really do not deviate much from their long-run shooting averages, although fans, players, announcers, and coaches think they do. Cognitive psychologists actually studied the shooting percentage of one professional basketball team for a season. The findings are presented in Table 8.2. Detailed analysis of shooting data failed to show that players make or miss shots more or less frequently than what would be expected by chance. That is, statistically speaking, all the shooting percentages in Table 8.2 are the "same."

The shooting percentages in Table 8.2 may suggest that teams will try harder to stop a shooter who has made the last two or three shots. To take this into account, researchers have also studied free throw percentages. Researchers told fans that a certain player was a 70 percent free throw shooter and was about to shoot two foul shots. They asked fans to predict what would happen on the second shot if the player

1. Made the first free throw.
2. Missed the first free throw.

Fans thought that this 70 percent free throw shooter would make 74 percent of the second free throws after making the first free throw, but would only make 66 percent of the second free throws after missing the first free throw. Researchers studied free throw data from a professional basketball team over two seasons. They found that the result of the first free throw does not matter when it comes to making or missing the second free throw. On average, the shooting percentage on the second free throw was 75 percent when the player made the first free throw. On average, the shooting percentage on the second free throw was also 75 percent when the player missed the first free throw.

It is true that basketball players shoot in streaks. But these steaks are within the bounds of long-run shooting percentages. So it is an illusion that players are either "hot" or "cold." If you are a believer in the "hot hand," however, you are likely to reject these facts because you "know better" from watching your favorite teams over the years. You are being fooled by randomness, because randomness often appears in clusters.

clustering illusion
Human belief that random events that occur in clusters are not really random.

The **clustering illusion** is our human belief that random events that occur in clusters are not really random. For example, it strikes most people as very unusual if heads comes up four times in a row during a series of coin flips. However, if a fair coin is flipped 20 times, there is about a 50 percent chance of getting four heads in a row. Ask yourself, if you flip four heads in a row, do you think you have a "hot hand" at coin flipping?

Mutual fund investing is one area where investors seem to fall prey to the clustering illusion. Every year, funds that have had exceptionally good performance receive large inflows of investor money. Despite the universal disclaimer that "past performance is no guarantee of future results," investors nonetheless clearly chase past returns.

FIGURE 8.3 Royal Dutch and Shell 60-40 Price Ratio Deviations, 1962 to 2005

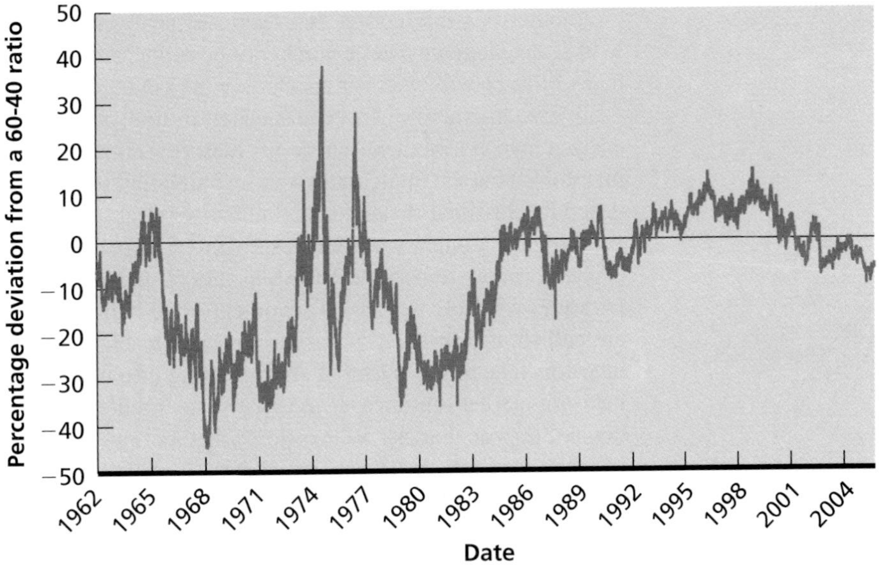

Figure 8.3 plots the daily deviations from the 60-40 ratio of the Royal Dutch price to the Shell price. If the prices of Royal Dutch and Shell are in a 60-40 ratio, there is a zero percentage deviation. If the price of Royal Dutch is too high compared to the Shell price, there is a positive deviation. If the price of Royal Dutch is too low compared to the price of Shell, there is a negative deviation. As you can see in Figure 8.3, there have been large and persistent deviations from the 60-40 ratio. In fact, the ratio was seldom at 60-40 for most of the time from 1962 through mid-2005 (when the companies merged).

CHECK THIS

8.5a What does the term limits to arbitrage mean?

8.5b If there were no limits to arbitrage, what would have been the relationship between 1 share of 3Com and 1.5 shares of Palm?

8.5c If there were no limits to arbitrage, what would have been the relationship between the prices of Royal Dutch and Shell?

8.6 Technical Analysis

technical analysis
Using past price data and other nonfinancial data to identify future trading opportunities.

Many investors try to predict future stock price movements based on investor sentiment, errors in judgment, and/or historical price movements. These investors are using **technical analysis**. Unlike fundamental analysis, technical analysis does not rely on traditional valuation techniques like those presented in our earlier chapters.

WHY DOES TECHNICAL ANALYSIS CONTINUE TO THRIVE?

Proponents of the efficient markets hypothesis do not believe that technical analysis can assist investors in predicting future stock price movements. If that is the case, why is technical analysis still used? In fact, in this Internet and computer age, technical analysis is actually thriving. Why?

One possible reason that technical analysis still exists is that an investor can derive thousands of successful technical analysis systems by using historical security prices. Past movements of security prices are easy to fit into a wide variety of technical analysis systems. As a result, proponents of technical analysis can continuously tinker with their systems and find methods that fit historical prices. This process is known as "backtesting." Alas, successful investment is all about future prices.

Another possible reason that technical analysis still exists is simply that it sometimes works. Again, given a large number of possible technical analysis systems, it is possible that many of them will work (or appear to work) in the short run.

To give an example of a technical analysis tool, or a technical "indicator," consider trying to analyze market sentiment. The term "market sentiment" refers to the prevailing mood among investors about the future outlook of an individual security or the market. Market sentiment is generally classified as optimistic (bullish), neutral (undecided), or pessimistic (bearish).

Market sentiment usually takes time to change. That is, it takes time for, say, 80 percent of the investors to become bullish if only 50 percent of the investors are currently bullish. Investors who rely on market sentiment often believe that once 80 percent of the investors are bullish or bearish, a consensus has been reached. Further, once a consensus is reached, investors take this as a sign of an impending turn in the direction of the market. One way to measure market sentiment is to ask investors whether they think the market is going up or down. Suppose you ask 50 investors whether they are "bullish" or "bearish" on the market over the next month. Twenty say that they are bearish. The market sentiment index (MSI) can then be calculated as:

$$\text{MSI} = \frac{\text{Number of bearish investors}}{\text{Number of bullish investors} + \text{Number of bearish investors}}$$

$$\text{MSI} = \frac{20}{30 + 20} = 0.40$$

The MSI has a maximum value of 1.00, which occurs when every investor you ask is bearish on the market. The MSI has a minimum value of 0.00, which occurs when every investor you ask is bullish on the market. Note that if you are constructing a sentiment index, you will have to decide how many investors to ask, the identity of these investors, and their investment time frame, that is, daily, weekly, monthly, quarterly, or longer. You can construct a sentiment index for any financial asset for any investment time interval you choose.

People who calculate and use sentiment indexes often view them as "contrarian indicators." This means that if most other investors are bearish, perhaps the market is "oversold" and prices are due to rebound. Or if most other investors are bullish, perhaps the market is "overbought" and prices will be heading down.

The following saying is useful when you are trying to remember how to interpret the MSI: "When the MSI is high, it is time to buy; when the MSI is low, it is time to go." Note that there is no theory to guide investors as to what level of the MSI is "high" and what level is "low." This lack of precise guidance is a common problem with a technical indicator like the MSI.

Technical analysis techniques are centuries old, and their number is enormous. Many, many books on the subject have been written. For this reason, we only touch on the subject and introduce some of its key ideas in the next few sections. Although we focus on the use of technical analysis in the stock market, you should be aware that it is very widely used in commodity markets, and most comments herein apply to those markets as well.

Recall that investors with a positive outlook on the market are often called "bulls," and their outlook is characterized as "bullish." A rising market is called a "bull market." In contrast, pessimistic investors are called "bears," and their dismal outlook is characterized as "bearish." A falling market is called a "bear market." Technical analysts essentially search for bullish or bearish signals, meaning positive or negative indicators about stock prices or market direction.

DOW THEORY

Dow theory
A method for predicting market direction that relies on the Dow Industrial and the Dow Transportation averages.

Dow theory is a method of analyzing and interpreting stock market movements that dates back to the turn of the twentieth century. The theory is named after Charles Dow, a cofounder of the Dow Jones Company and an editor of the Dow Jones–owned newspaper, *The Wall Street Journal.*

The essence of Dow theory is that there are, at all times, three forces at work in the stock market: (1) a primary direction or trend, (2) a secondary reaction or trend, and (3) daily fluctuations. According to the theory, the primary direction is either bullish (up) or bearish (down), and it reflects the long-run direction of the market.

WWW

Learn more about Dow theory at www.dowtheory.com and www.thedowtheory.com

However, the market can, for limited periods of time, depart from its primary direction. These departures are called secondary reactions or trends and may last for several weeks or months. These are eliminated by *corrections,* which are reversions to the primary direction. Daily fluctuations are essentially noise and are of no real importance.

The basic purpose of the Dow theory is to signal changes in the primary direction. To do this, two stock market averages, the Dow Jones Industrial Average (DJIA) and the Dow Jones Transportation Average (DJTA), are monitored. If one of these departs from the primary trend, the movement is viewed as secondary. However, if a departure in one is followed by a departure in the other, then this is viewed as a *confirmation* that the primary trend has changed. The Dow theory was, at one time, very well known and widely followed. It is less popular today, but its basic principles underlie more contemporary approaches to technical analysis.

ELLIOTT WAVES

Elliott wave theory
A method for predicting market direction that relies on a series of past market price swings (i.e.,waves).

In the early 1930s, an accountant named Ralph Nelson Elliott developed the **Elliott wave theory**. While recuperating from life-threatening anemia (as well as his disastrous losses in the Crash of October 1929), Elliott read a book on Dow theory and began to study patterns of market price movements. Elliott discovered what he believed to be a persistent and recurring pattern that operated between market tops and bottoms. His theory was that these patterns, which he called "waves," collectively expressed investor sentiment. Through use of sophisticated measurements that he called "wave counting," a wave theorist could forecast market turns with a high degree of accuracy.

In 1935, Elliott published his theory in his book called *The Wave Principle.* His main theory was that there was a repeating eight-wave sequence. The first five waves, which he called "impulsive," were followed by a three-wave "corrective" sequence. Figure 8.4 shows the basic Elliott wave pattern. The impulse waves are labeled numerically, 1 through 5, while the corrective waves are labeled A, B, and C.

WWW

Learn more about the Elliott wave at www.elliottwave.com

The basic Elliott wave theory gets very complicated because, under the theory, each wave can subdivide into finer wave patterns that are classified into a multitude of structures. Notwithstanding the complex nature of the Elliott wave theory, it is still a widely followed indicator.

SUPPORT AND RESISTANCE LEVELS

support level
Price or level below which a stock or the market as a whole is unlikely to fall.

resistance level
Price or level above which a stock or the market as a whole is unlikely to rise.

A key concept in technical analysis is the identification of support and resistance levels. A **support level** is a price or level below which a stock or the market as a whole is unlikely to fall. A **resistance level** is a price or level above which a stock or the market as a whole is unlikely to rise.

The idea behind these levels is straightforward. As a stock's price (or the market as a whole) falls, it reaches a point where investors increasingly believe that it can fall no further—the point at which it "bottoms out." Essentially, purchases by bargain-hungry investors ("bottom

FIGURE 8.4 Basic Elliott Wave Pattern

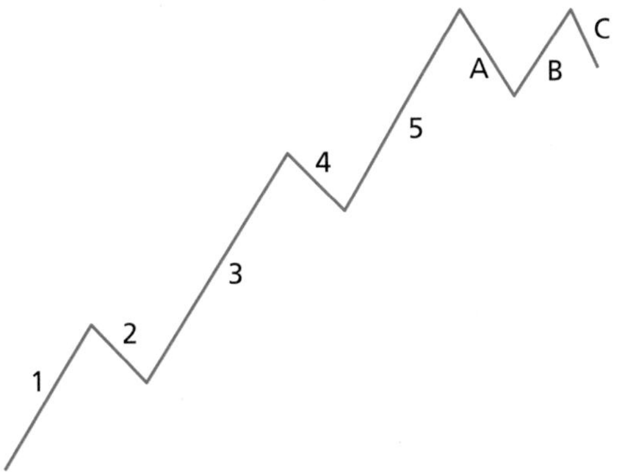

feeders") pick up at that point, thereby "supporting" the price. A resistance level is formed by reverse logic. As a stock's price (or the market as a whole) rises, it reaches a point where investors increasingly believe that it can go no higher—the point at which it "tops out." Once it does, sales by profit-hungry investors ("profit takers") pick up, thereby "resisting" further advances.

Resistance and support areas are usually viewed as psychological barriers. As the DJIA approaches levels with three zeros, such as 11,000, increased talk of "psychologically important" prices appears in the financial press. A "breakout" occurs when a stock (or the market as a whole) closes below a support level or above a resistance level. A breakout is usually interpreted to mean that the price move will continue in that direction.

As this discussion illustrates, much colorful language is used under the heading of technical analysis. We will see many more examples just ahead.

TECHNICAL INDICATORS

WWW

Learn more about charting at www.stockcharts.com Select "Chart School."

WWW

For a trader's glossary, check out www.traders.com/Documentation/RESource_docs/Glossary/glossary.html

Technical analysts rely on a variety of technical indicators to forecast the direction of the market. Every day, *The Wall Street Journal* publishes a variety of such indicators. An excerpt of the "Diaries" section (from www.wsj.com) appears in Figure 8.5.

Much, but not all, of the information presented is self-explanatory. The first item listed in Figure 8.5 is the number of issues traded. This number fluctuates because, on any given day, there may be zero trading volume in some stocks listed on the NYSE. In the rows that follow, we see the number of price advances, the number of price declines, and the number of unchanged prices. The number of stock prices reaching new highs and new lows as of that day is also listed.

One popular technical indicator is called the *advance/decline line*. This indicator shows, for some given period, the cumulative difference between advancing issues and declining issues. For example, Table 8.3 contains advance and decline information for the October 1, 2007, to October 5, 2007, trading week.

In Table 8.3, notice how we take the difference between the number of issues advancing and declining on each day and then cumulate the difference through time. For example, on Monday, 1,702 more issues advanced than declined. On Tuesday, 547 more issues advanced than declined. Over the two days, the cumulative advance/decline is thus 1,702 + 547 = 2,249.

This cumulative advance/decline number, once plotted, is the advance/decline line. A downward-sloping advance/decline line would be considered a bearish signal, whereas an upward-sloping advance/decline line is a bullish signal. The advance/decline line is often used to measure market "breadth." If the market is going up, for example, then technical analysts view it as a good sign if there is market breadth. That is, the signal is more bullish if the advance is accompanied by a steeply upwardly sloping advance/decline line.

The next few rows in Figure 8.5 deal with trading volume. These rows represent trading volume for advancing issues, declining issues, and unchanged issues (which is calculated by subtracting advancing volume and declining volume from volume traded). For a technical analyst, heavy advancing volume is generally viewed as a bullish signal of buyer interest. This is particularly true if more issues are up than down and if a lot of new highs appear as well.

The last three numbers in Figure 8.5, found in the footnotes, are also of interest to technicians. The first, labeled "Closing tick," is the difference between the number of issues that closed on an uptick and those that closed on a downtick. From our discussion of the NYSE short sale rule in a previous chapter, you know that an uptick occurs when the last price

TABLE 8.3 Advance/Decline Line Calculation

Weekday	Issues Advancing	Issues Declining	Difference	Cumulative Difference
Monday	2,511	809	1,702	1,702
Tuesday	1,922	1,375	547	2,249
Wednesday	1,233	2,068	−835	1,414
Thursday	2,023	1,248	775	2,189
Friday	2,505	815	1,690	3,879

FIGURE 8.5 Market Diaries

Markets Diary: Closing Snapshot

DIARIES

GO TO: Volume by Market | Breakdown of Volume | Crossing Session

DOWNLOAD WEEKLY TOTALS (updated Friday)

Monday, October 01, 2007 | Find Historical Data | WHAT'S THIS?

NYSE	Latest close	% Chg from 65-day avg	Previous close	Week ago
Issues traded	3,396	–0.6	3,414	3,411
Advances	2,511	53.5	1,487	1,297
Declines	809	–52.1	1,831	2,029
Unchanged	76	-15.7	96	85
New highs	288	184.8	173	148
New lows	32	–80.7	43	50
Adv. volume*	1,141,184,280	44.2	498,033,600	461,733,310
Decl. volume*	266,575,270	–68.3	786,510,950	870,383,650
Total volume*	1,415,268,850	–14.3	1,306,133,650	1,341,874,770
Closing tick	+817	...	+568	+418
Closing Arms (TRIN)†	0.73	...	1.28	1.20
Block trades*	n.a.	...	4,801	4,433

Nasdaq	Latest close	% Chg from 65-day avg	Previous close	Week ago
Issues traded	3,115	–1.0	3,100	3,133
Advances	2,134	48.9	1,213	1,153
Declines	861	–45.8	1,773	1,855
Unchanged	120	–4.8	114	125
New highs	159	108.7	107	100
New lows	55	–50.9	66	46
Adv. volume*	1,471,349,232	41.6	864,188,885	782,481,288
Decl. volume*	435,168,556	–57.5	973,215,305	1,066,180,664
Total volume*	1,928,225,539	–8.1	1,874,300,769	1,858,170,925
Closing tick	+711	...	+735	+737
Closing Arms (TRIN)†	0.73	...	0.77	0.85
Block trades*	n.a.	...	10,209	8,735

Amex	Latest close	% Chg from 65-day avg	Previous close	Week ago
Issues traded	1,279	1.0	1,300	1,277
Advances	768	30.1	581	504
Declines	434	–26.1	608	669
Unchanged	77	–13.5	111	104
New highs	113	174.2	77	40
New lows	25	–48.2	17	17
Adv. volume*	21,767,100	17.4	14,432,880	11,196,300
Decl. volume*	12,773,590	–32.2	18,053,484	17,848,999
Total volume*	36,395,590	–6.9	38,650,964	30,285,299
Closing tick	+202	...	+74	-23
Closing Arms (TRIN)†	1.04	...	1.20	1.20
Block trades*	n.a.	...	445	279

*Primary market NYSE & Amex only. †Compares the ratio of advancing to declining issues with the ratio of volume of shares rising and falling. Arms Index or TRIN = (advancing issues / declining issues) / (volume of advancing issues / volume of declining issues.) Generally, an Arms of less than 1.00 indicates buying demand; above 1.00 indicates selling pressure.

Source: *The Wall Street Journal,* via www.wsj.com, October 1, 2007.

change was positive; a downtick is just the reverse. The tick gives an indication of where the market was heading as it closed.

The entry labeled "Closing Arms (TRIN)" is the ratio of average trading volume in declining issues to average trading volume in advancing issues. It is calculated as follows:

$$\text{Arms} = \frac{\text{Declining Volume/Declining Issues}}{\text{Advancing Volume/Advancing Issues}} \tag{8.1}$$

The ratio is named after its inventor, Richard Arms; it is often called the "TRIN," which is an acronym for "TR(ading) IN(dex)." Notice that the numerator in this ratio is just the average volume for issues that declined on that day. The denominator is the average volume for advancing issues. Values greater than 1.00 are considered bearish because the indication is that declining shares had heavier volume. Using the number from Figure 8.5 for Monday, we can calculate the Arms value as follows:[2]

$$\text{Arms} = \frac{266{,}575{,}270/809}{1{,}141{,}184{,}280/2{,}511} = \frac{329{,}512}{454{,}474} = 0.73$$

which rounds to the value shown in Figure 8.5. A caveat: Some sources reverse the numerator and the denominator when they calculate this ratio.

The final piece of information in Figure 8.5, "Block trades," refers to trades in excess of 10,000 shares. At one time, these trades were taken to be indicators of buying or selling by large institutional investors. However, today these trades are routine, and it is difficult to see how this information is particularly useful.

RELATIVE STRENGTH CHARTS

relative strength
A measure of the performance of one investment relative to another.

Relative strength charts illustrate the performance of one company, industry, or market relative to another. If you look back at the *Value Line* exhibit in Chapter 6, you will see a plot labeled "relative strength." Very commonly, such plots are created to analyze how a stock has done relative to its industry or the market as a whole.

To illustrate how such plots are constructed, suppose that on some particular day, we invest equal amounts, say $100, in both Ford and GM (the amount does not matter; what matters is that the original investment is the same for both). On every subsequent day, we take the ratio of the value of our Ford investment to the value of our GM investment, and we plot it. A ratio bigger than 1.0 indicates that, on a relative basis, Ford has outperformed GM, and vice versa. Thus, a value of 1.20 indicates that Ford has done 20 percent better than GM over the period studied. Notice that if both stocks are down, a ratio bigger than 1.0 indicates that Ford is down by less than GM.

[2] The footnote in Figure 8.5 contains a mathematically equivalent way to calculate Arms.

EXAMPLE 8.1 Relative Strength

Consider the following series of monthly stock prices for two hypothetical companies:

Month	Susan, Inc.	Carolyn Co.
1	$25	$50
2	24	48
3	22	45
4	22	40
5	20	39
6	19	38

On a relative basis, how has Susan, Inc. done compared to Carolyn Co.?

To answer, suppose we had purchased four shares of Susan, Inc. and two shares of Carolyn Co. for an investment of $100 in each. We can calculate the value of our investment in each month and then take the ratio of Susan, Inc. to Carolyn Co. as follows:

(continued)

Investment Value			
Month	Susan, Inc. (4 shares)	Carolyn Co. (2 shares)	Relative Strength
1	$100	$100	1.00
2	96	96	1.00
3	88	90	0.98
4	88	80	1.10
5	80	78	1.03
6	76	76	1.00

What we see is that over the first four months both stocks were down, but Susan, Inc. outperformed Carolyn Co. by 10 percent. However, after six months the two had done equally well (or equally poorly).

CHARTING

Technical analysts rely heavily on charts showing recent market activity in terms of either prices or, less frequently, volume. In fact, technical analysis is sometimes called "charting," and technical analysts are often called "chartists." There are many types of charts, but the basic idea is that by studying charts of past market prices (or other information), the chartist identifies particular patterns that signal the direction of a stock or the market as a whole. We briefly describe some charting techniques next.

OPEN-HIGH-LOW-CLOSE CHARTS (OHLC) Perhaps the most popular charting method is the bar chart. The most basic bar chart uses the stock's opening, high, low, and closing prices for the period covered by each bar. If the technician is constructing a daily bar chart, the technician will use the daily opening high, daily low, and daily closing prices of the stock. The high and low prices are represented by the top and bottom of the vertical bar and the opening and closing prices are shown by short horizontal lines crossing the vertical bar. The example of a bar chart in Figure 8.6 for Sun Microsystems is from www.stockcharts.com.

PRICE CHANNEL A price channel is a chart pattern using OHLC data that can slope upward, downward, or sideways. Price channels belong to the group of price patterns known as *continuation patterns*. A continuation pattern is a pattern where the price of the stock is expected

FIGURE 8.6 Open-High-Low-Close Bar Chart for Sun Microsystems

FIGURE 8.7 Price Channel Chart for ChevronTexaco

to continue along its main direction. A price channel has two boundaries, an upper trendline and a lower trendline. The upper trendline marks resistance and the lower trendline marks support. If the overall price movement of the stock is downward, the upper trendline is called the main trendline, and the lower trendline is called the channel line. The example of a price channel for ChevronTexaco in Figure 8.7 is from the Web site www.stockcharts.com.

HEAD AND SHOULDERS A head and shoulders chart pattern belongs to a group of price charts known as *reversal patterns.* Reversal pattern charts also use OHLC data. These chart patterns signal that a reversal from the main trendline is possibly going to occur. Because it belongs to the reversal pattern group, a head and shoulders pattern is identified as either a *head and shoulders top* or a *head and shoulders bottom.* The example of a head and shoulders top for CNET Networks in Figure 8.8 is also from the Web site www.stockcharts.com.

FIGURE 8.8 Head and Shoulders Chart for CNET Networks, Inc.

WWW

For an excellent source on Fibonacci numbers and the golden mean, visit www.mcs.surrey.ac.uk/Personal/R.Knott/Fibonacci/fib.html

The ratio converges to 1.618, or ϕ. Market technicians are interested in ϕ because:

$$(\phi - 1)/\phi = 0.618/1.618 = 0.382$$
$$1/\phi = 1.000/1.618 = 0.618 = \phi - 1$$

Market technicians use these numbers to predict support and resistance levels. For example, as a stock increases in value over time, it will occasionally pull back in value. Suppose a stock has increased from \$40 to \$60, and has recently begun to fall a bit in value. Using the $(\phi - 1)/\phi$ ratio, market technicians would predict the primary support area would occur at \$52.36 (\$60 − \$40 = \$20; \$20 × 0.382 = \$7.64; \$60 − \$7.64 = \$52.36). A similar calculation that uses the $1/\phi$ ratio of 0.618 instead of 0.382 results in the secondary support area of \$47.64. If the stock were to pierce this secondary support level and close below it, the rally would be declared over. Market technicians would then begin to look for opportunities to sell the stock short if it subsequently rallied.

Nature provides many instances involving Fibonacci numbers. The number of petals on a flower is often a Fibonacci number. For example, black-eyed susans have 13 petals and ordinary daisies have 34. Also, pinecones and pineapples have spirals containing 8 or 13 scales. There are so many other examples that some observers classify Fibonacci numbers as a "law of nature." Because of this, some market technicians believe that the Fibonacci numbers should also apply to market prices.

OTHER TECHNICAL INDICATORS

We close our discussion of technical analysis by describing a few additional technical indicators. The "odd-lot" indicator looks at whether odd-lot purchases (purchases of fewer than 100 shares) are up or down. One argument is that odd-lot purchases represent the activities of smaller, unsophisticated investors, so when they start buying, it's time to sell. This is a good example of a "contrarian" indicator. In contrast, some argue that because short selling is a fairly sophisticated tactic, increases in short selling are a negative signal.

Some indicators can seem a little silly. For example, there is the "hemline" indicator, which is also known as the "bull markets and bare knees" indicator. Through much of the nineteenth century, long skirts dominated women's fashion and the stock market experienced many bear markets. In the 1920s, flappers revealed their knees and the stock market boomed. Even the stock market crash of October 1987 was predicted by hemlines. During the 1980s, miniskirts flourished, but by October 1987, a fashion shift had women wearing longer skirts.

One of the more famous (or fatuous, depending on how you look at it) indicators is the Super Bowl indicator, which forecasts the direction of the market based on whether the National Football Conference or the American Football Conference wins. A Super Bowl win by a National Football Conference team or an American Football Conference team that used to be in the old National Football League (i.e., Pittsburgh Steelers, Baltimore Colts) is bullish. This probably strikes you as absurd, so you might be surprised to learn that for the period 1967–1988, the Super Bowl indicator forecast the direction of the stock market with more than 90 percent accuracy. A nearby *Investment Updates* box contains more details about this indicator.

CHECK THIS

8.6a What is technical analysis?

8.6b What is the purpose of charting a stock's past price?

8.6c What is the purpose of using technical indicators?

If you want a more recent indicator of stock market performance from the world of sports, consider the Daytona 500 indicator. Winning this race (the "Super Bowl of NASCAR") is an accomplishment for the driver, yet it doesn't seem to carry over to the stock of the winning driver's sponsor. For example, in 2005, Jeff Gordon won the Daytona 500 and stock in his sponsor company, Du Pont, was down 13 percent for the year. Things were even worse for Du Pont stock when Gordon won in 1997; the stock lost 36 percent on the year.

INVESTMENT UPDATES

THE SUPER GUIDE TO INVESTING

Every January, about 90 million people in the United States watch television for a prediction of how well the stock market is going to do in the upcoming year. So you missed it this year? Maybe not. The stock market predictor we are talking about is the Super Bowl!

The Super Bowl indicator has become one of the more famous (or infamous) technical indicators of stock market performance. Here's how it works. In the 1960s, the original National Football League (NFL) and the upstart American Football League (AFL) were fighting for dominance. The Super Bowl indicator says that if a team from the original AFL wins the Super Bowl, the market posts a negative return for the year, and if a team from the original NFL wins, the market will post a gain for the year.

So how has the Super Bowl predictor performed? Take a look at the chart we obtained from www.cnn.com.

For the first 31 Super Bowls, the indicator was correct 28 out of 31 times! The Miami Dolphins are perhaps the best market predictor. When Miami won the Super Bowl in 1973, the market proceeded to drop by 14.7 percent. The next year was an even better indicator. The next year, the Dolphins beat the Minnesota Vikings and the S&P 500 lost 26.5 percent, the worst one-year performance in its history. When the Dolphins lost the Super Bowl in 1972, 1983, and 1985, the S&P 500 posted double-digit gains in each of those years.

So are you ready to bet the ranch on the Super Bowl indicator? It's probably not a good thing. Since 1997 through 2007, the Super Bowl indicator has been unambiguously correct only three times: in 2002, 2005, and 2006. The New England Patriots, an AFL team, won the Super Bowl in 2002 and 2005 and the S&P 500 dropped 30 percent in 2002 (but only .6 percent in 2005). The Pittsburgh Steelers, an original NFL team, won in 2006, and the S&P 500 was up about 14 percent for the year.

Let's look at some other years. The performance in 2001 is not as clear. The Baltimore Ravens won the Super Bowl that year and the market lost 7.6 percent. The Ravens are the descendants of the original Cleveland Browns, a member of the original NFL. In this case, the Super Bowl indicator was incorrect. However, purists (especially in Cleveland) argue that since the Browns have been revived, the Ravens cannot be considered a member of the original NFL. But the Ravens did beat the New York Giants, and old NFL team.

In 2003, the expansion Tampa Bay Buccaneers beat an original AFL team, the Oakland Raiders, and the market went up about 28 percent. In 2007, the Indianapolis Colts won (easily), but it didn't matter. Both the Colts and their opponent, the Chicago Bears, are original NFL teams, so 2007 had to be an up year according to the indicator. It was. The S&P 500 was up about 3.5 percent.

The Predictor (31-7-3)

Bullish years (23)
49ers - '82, '85, '89, '95
Bears- '86
Colts - '71
Cowboys - '72, '93, '94, '96
Giants - '87, '91
Packers, '67, '68, '97
Redskins - '83, '88, '92
Steelers - '75, '76, '79, '80, '06

Bearish years (8)
Dolphins - '73, '74
Jets, '69
Patriots, '02, '05
Raiders - '77, '81, '84

Indicator missed (7)
Broncos - '98, '99
Chiefs - '70
49ers - '90
Cowboys - '78
Rams -'00
Patriots - '04

Inconclusive (3)
Ravens - '01*
Buccaneers - '03**
Colts - '07***

*Created when the old NFL Cleveland Browns moved to Baltimore, the NFL says the Ravens started life as an AFC team in 1996, which would mean the predictor was accurate.
**Expansion team
***A former NFL team beat an original NFL team.

Overall, in the last 15 years before 2005, stock in the sponsor of the winning driver trailed the market by about 20 percent per year. The trend continued in 2006 after Jimmie Johnson won the Daytona 500. The stock of his sponsor, Lowe's, dropped about 6.5 percent during the year, but the S&P 500 increased about 14 percent. However, in 2007, the indicator did not do so well. Kevin Harvick won the race and shares of one of his main sponsors, Shell, outpaced the S&P 500 by about 13 percent.

There are lots of other technical trading rules. How seriously should you take them? That's up to you, but our advice is to keep in mind that life is full of odd coincidences. Just because a bizarre stock market predictor seems to have worked well in the past doesn't mean that it's going to work in the future.

4 **4. Exponential Moving Averages** Using the stock prices in the previous problem, calculate the exponential three-month moving average for both stocks where two-thirds of the average weight is placed on the most recent price.

4 **5. Exponential Moving Averages** Calculate the exponential three-month moving average for Amazon.com and Google where 50 percent of the average weight is placed on the most recent price. How does this exponential moving average compare to your result from the previous problem?

4 **6. Market Sentiment Index** A group of investors was polled each week for the last five weeks about whether they were bullish or bearish concerning the market. Construct the market sentiment index for each week based on these polls. Assuming the market sentiment index is being used as a contrarian indicator, which direction would you say the market is headed?

Week	Bulls	Bears
1	63	58
2	68	53
3	74	47
4	71	50
5	78	43

4 **7. Money Flow** You are given the following information concerning the trades made on a particular stock. Calculate the money flow for the stock based on these trades. Is the money flow a positive or negative signal in this case?

Price	Volume
$70.12	
70.14	3,000
70.13	2,700
70.09	2,100
70.05	1,800
70.07	1,400
70.03	1,900

4 **8. Moving Averages** Suppose you are given the following information on the S&P 500:

Date	Close
12/27/2007	1,476.27
12/28/2007	1,478.49
12/31/2007	1,468.36
1/2/2008	1,447.16
1/3/2008	1,447.16
1/4/2008	1,411.63
1/7/2008	1,416.18
1/8/2008	1,390.19
1/9/2008	1,409.13
1/10/2008	1,420.33

Calculate the simple three-day moving average for the S&P 500 and the exponential three-day moving average where two-thirds of the weight is placed on the most recent close. Why would

www.mhhe.com/jm5e

you want to know the moving average for an index? If the close on January 10, 2008, was above the three-day moving average, would it be a buy or sell signal?

4 **9. Support and Resistance Levels.** Below you will see a stock price chart for Cisco Systems from finance.yahoo.com. Do you see any resistance or support levels? What do support and resistance levels mean for the stock price?

4 **10. Advance/Decline Lines and Arms Ratio** Use the data below to construct the advance/decline line and Arms ratio for the market. Volume is in thousands of shares.

	Advancing	Advancing Volume	Declining	Declining Volume
Monday	757	275,472	2,606	3,876,644
Tuesday	1,876	2,132,903	1,472	2,071,813
Wednesday	1,154	924,308	2,174	3,834,066
Thursday	1,978	3,166,321	1,378	2,155,721
Friday	2,257	3,961,562	1,078	1,176,015

4 **11. Money Flow** A stock had the following trades during a particular period. What was the money flow for the stock? Is the money flow a positive or negative signal in this case?

Price	Volume
$61.85	
61.81	1,600
61.82	1,200
61.85	600
61.84	1,400
61.87	1,100
61.88	800
61.92	1,300
61.91	1,400
61.93	1,000

Intermediate Questions

4

4

12. **Fibonacci Numbers** A stock recently increased in price from \$48 to \$63. Using ϕ, what are the primary and secondary support areas for the stock?

13. **Simple Moving Averages** Below you will find the closing stock prices for eBay over a three-week period. Calculate the simple three-day and five-day moving averages for the stock and graph your results. Are there any technical indications of the future direction of the stock price?

Date	Close
12/19/2007	\$31.67
12/20/2007	33.37
12/21/2007	34.30
12/24/2007	34.17
12/26/2007	34.49
12/27/2007	33.65
12/28/2007	33.78
12/31/2007	33.19
1/2/2008	32.49
1/3/2008	32.84
1/4/2008	31.30
1/7/2008	30.44
1/8/2008	30.01
1/9/2008	29.87
1/10/2008	30.36

4

14. **Exponential Moving Averages** Use the information from the previous problem to calculate the three-day and five-day exponential moving averages for eBay and graph your results. Place two-thirds of the average weight on the most recent stock price. Are there any technical indications of the future direction of the stock price?

4

15. **Put/Call Ratio.** Another technical indicator is the put/call ratio. The put/call ratio is the number of put options traded divided by the number of call options traded. The put/call ratio can be constructed on the market or an individual stock. Below you will find the number of puts and calls traded over a four-week period for all stocks:

Week	Puts	Calls
1	1,631,846	1,874,986
2	1,772,815	1,991,650
3	1,976,277	2,187,450
4	2,182,270	2,392,751

How would you interpret the put/call ratio? Calculate the put/call ratio for each week. From this analysis, does it appear the market is expected to be upward trending or downward trending?

What's on the Web?

1. **Bollinger Bands** You can learn more about Bollinger bands at www.chartsmart.com. What does the site say about using Bollinger bands in technical analysis? Now go to finance.yahoo.com, and enter your favorite stock. Find the technical analysis section and view the Bollinger band for your stock. What does the chart tell you about this stock?

2. **Relative Strength** Relative strength measures the performance of a stock against a "bogey," which is either another stock or suitable index. Pick your favorite stock and go to the technical analysis area of finance.yahoo.com. Compare the relative strength of your stock against a close competitor and the S&P 500 Index. How is this stock performing relative to these bogeys?
3. **Triangles** Go to english.borsanaliz.com. How many different types of triangles are listed on the site? What does each type of triangle mean to a technical analyst?
4. **Market Volume** An important tool for most technical traders is market volume. Go to www.marketvolume.com. Look on the site to find the reasons market volume is considered important.

Stock-Trak Exercises

To access the Stock-Trak Exercise for this chapter, please visit the book Web site at www.mhhe.com/jm5e and choose the corresponding chapter.

Part 3

CHAPTER 9

Interest Rates

"We reckon hours and minutes to be dollars and cents."
–Thomas Chandler Haliburton
(from *The Clockmaker*)

Benjamin Franklin stated a fundamental truth of commerce when he sagely advised young tradesmen to "remember that time is money." In finance, we call this the time value of money. But how much time corresponds to how much money? Interest constitutes a rental payment for money, and an interest rate tells us how much money for how much time. But there are many interest rates, each corresponding to a particular money market. Interest rates state money prices in each of these markets. ■

Learning Objectives

It will be worth your time to increase your rate of interest in these topics:

1. Money market prices and rates.
2. Rates and yields on fixed-income securities.
3. Treasury STRIPS and the term structure of interest rates.
4. Nominal versus real interest rates.

This chapter is the first dealing specifically with interest-bearing assets. As we discussed in a previous chapter, there are two basic types of interest-bearing assets: money market instruments and fixed-income securities. For both types of asset, interest rates are a key determinant of asset values. Furthermore, because trillions of dollars in interest-bearing assets are outstanding, interest rates play a pivotal role in financial markets and the economy.

Because interest rates are one of the most closely watched financial market indicators, we devote this entire chapter to them. We first discuss the many different interest rates that are commonly reported in the financial press, along with some of the different ways interest rates are calculated and quoted. We then go on to describe the basic determinants and separable components of interest rates.

9.1 Interest Rate History and Money Market Rates

Recall from Chapter 3 that money market instruments are debt obligations that have a maturity of less than one year at the time they are originally issued. Each business day, *The Wall Street Journal* publishes a list of current interest rates for several categories of money market securities in its "Money Rates" report. We will discuss each of these interest rates and the securities they represent following a quick look at the history of interest rates.

INTEREST RATE HISTORY

In Chapter 1, we saw how looking back at the history of returns on various types of investments gave us a useful perspective on rates of return. Similar insights are available from interest rate history. For example, in September 2007, short-term interest rates were about 3.8 percent and long-term rates were about 5 percent. We might ask, "Are these rates unusually high or low?" To find out, we examine Figure 9.1, which graphically illustrates 207 years of interest rates in the United States.

Two interest rates are plotted in Figure 9.1, one for bills and one for bonds. Both rates are based on U.S. Treasury securities, or close substitutes. We discuss bills and bonds in detail in this chapter and the next chapter. For now, it is enough to know that bills are short term and bonds are long term, so what is plotted in Figure 9.1 are short- and long-term interest rates.

Probably the most striking feature in Figure 9.1 is the fact that the highest interest rates in U.S. history occurred in the not-too-distant past. Rates began rising sharply in the 1970s and then peaked at extraordinary levels in the early 1980s. They have generally declined since then. The other striking aspect of U.S. interest rate history is the very low short-term interest rates that prevailed from the 1930s to the 1960s. This rate level

FIGURE 9.1 Interest Rate History (U.S. Interest Rates, 1800–2007)

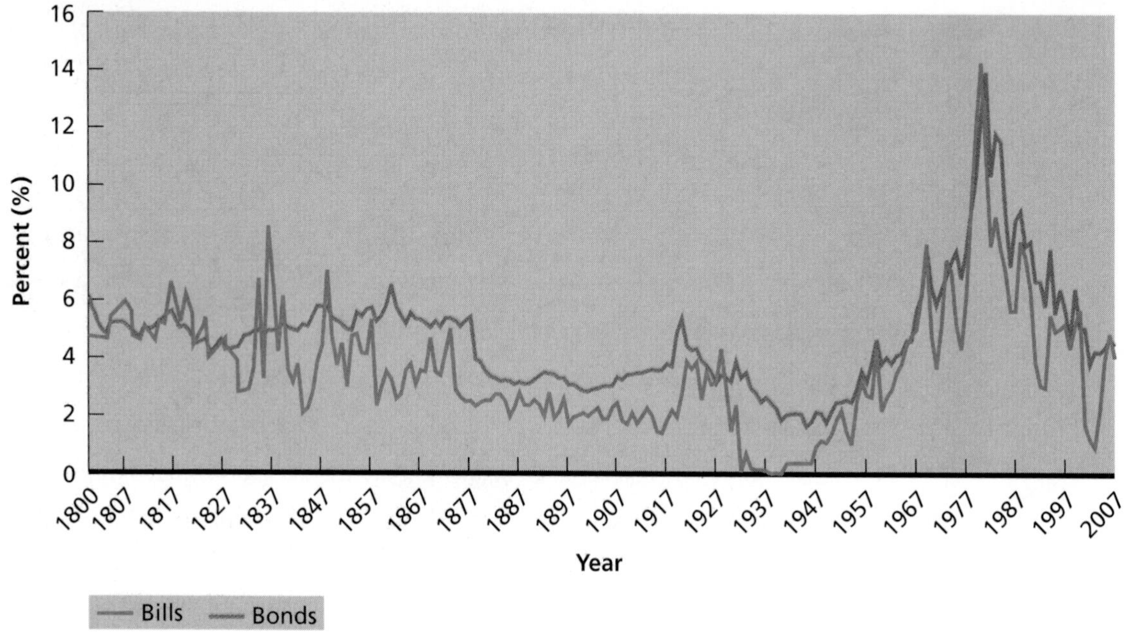

Source: Adapted from Jeremy J. Siegel, *Stocks for the Long Run,* 3rd ed., © McGraw-Hill, 2002; Global Financial Data, and the Federal Reserve Bank of St. Louis.

EXAMPLE 9.1

A Quick Review of the Time Value of Money

Undoubtedly, your instincts tell you that \$1,000 received in three years is not the same as \$1,000 received today. But if you are going to receive \$1,000 today, what is an equivalent amount of money received in three years?

Fortunately, an equation tells us exactly what this is:

$$\text{Future value} = \text{Present value} \times (1 + r)^N \tag{9.1}$$

In this equation, the r represents a periodic interest rate (expressed as a decimal), and the N represents the number of periods (expressed as an integer). Although the periods could be weeks, months, or years, the important thing to remember is that the interest rate must be expressed as an interest rate *per period*.

Suppose you have \$1,000 to invest and you can invest at an annual rate of 3.5 percent per year. In equation (9.1) the per period interest rate enters as 0.035. If you invest for three years ($N = 3$), the amount you will have in three years is:

$$\$1{,}108.718 = \$1{,}000 \times (1 + 0.035)^3 \tag{9.2}$$

which would be rounded to \$1,108.72.

You can also use equation (9.1) to tell you how much a future amount is worth today. If we divide both sides of equation (9.1) by $(1 + r)^N$ and rearrange terms, we get:

$$\text{Present value} = \frac{\text{Future value}}{(1 + r)^N} \tag{9.3}$$

which, by the rules of exponents, can be written as:

$$\text{Present value} = \text{Future value} \times (1 + r)^{-N} \tag{9.4}$$

That is, $(1 + r)^{-N}$ is just another way to write $1/(1 + r)^N$.

If you remember the relationship between equations (9.1) and (9.4), you will soon become very comfortable with *compounding,* which is equation (9.1), and *discounting,* which is equation (9.4).

To continue with our numerical example, first note that $(1 + 0.035)^3 = 1.108718$. Therefore, using equation (9.3),

$$\text{Present value} = \frac{\text{Future value}}{(1 + r)^N}$$

$$\$1{,}000 = \frac{\$1{,}081.718}{1.081718}$$

Suppose you invest \$500 for 4 percent for six years. How much money will you have at the end of six years?

$$\text{Future value} = \text{Present value} \times (1 + r)^N$$

$$\$632.66 = \$500 \times (1.04)^6$$

Now suppose you will be getting \$800 in four years. What is an equivalent amount today if you discount at 3.7 percent?

$$\text{Present value} = \text{Future value} \times (1 + r)^{-N}$$

$$\$691.79 = \$800 \times (1 + 0.037)^{-4}$$

was the result, in large part, of deliberate actions by the Federal Reserve Board to keep short-term rates low—a policy that ultimately proved unsustainable and even disastrous. Much was learned by the experience, however, and now the Fed is more concerned with controlling inflation.

With long-term rates around 5 percent as this chapter was written, many market observers have commented that these interest rate levels are extraordinarily low. Based on the history of interest rates illustrated in Figure 9.1, however, 5 percent may be low relative to the last 30 years, but it is not at all low compared to rates during the 170-year period from 1800 to 1970. Indeed, long-term rates would have to fall well below 4 percent to be considered low by historical standards. Example 9.1 shows how investors use interest rates.

MONEY MARKET RATES

Figure 9.2 reproduces a *Wall Street Journal* "Money Rates" report of interest rates for the most important money market instruments. A commonly quoted interest rate is the **prime rate**. The prime rate is a key short-term interest rate since it is the basis for interest rates that large commercial banks charge on short-term loans (rates are quoted as prime plus or minus a spread). The prime rate is well known as a **bellwether rate** of bank lending to business. Besides a prime rate for the United States, the "Money Rates" report also lists foreign prime rates for Canada, the European Central Bank, Japan, Switzerland, Great Britain, Australia, and Hong Kong.

prime rate
The basic interest rate on short-term loans that the largest commercial banks charge to their most creditworthy corporate customers.

bellwether rate
Interest rate that serves as a leader or as a leading indicator of future trends, e.g., interest rates as a bellwether of inflation.

The **Federal funds rate** (or just "Fed funds") is a fundamental interest rate for commercial bank activity. The Fed funds rate is the interest rate that banks charge each other for overnight loans of $1 million or more. This interbank rate is set by continuous bidding among banks, where banks wishing to lend funds quote "offer rates" (rates at which they are willing to lend), and banks wishing to borrow funds quote "bid rates" (rates they are willing to pay). Notice that four different rates are stated: *high* is the highest rate offered and *low* is the lowest rate bid during a day's trading; *near closing bid* is a bid rate to borrow and *near closing offered* is an offered rate to lend near the end of the day's trading.

Federal funds rate
Interest rate that banks charge each other for overnight loans of $1 million or more.

The Federal Reserve's **discount rate** is another pivotal interest rate for commercial banks. The discount rate is the interest rate that the Fed offers to commercial banks for overnight reserve loans. You might recall from your Money and Banking class that banks are required to maintain reserves equal to some fraction of their deposit liabilities. When a bank cannot supply sufficient reserves from internal sources, it must borrow reserves from other banks through the Federal funds market. Therefore, the Fed discount rate and the Fed funds rate are usually closely linked.

discount rate
The interest rate that the Fed offers to commercial banks for overnight reserve loans.

The Federal Reserve Bank is the central bank of the United States. It is charged with the responsibility of managing interest rates and the money supply to control inflation and promote stable economic growth. The discount rate is a basic tool of monetary policy for the Federal Reserve Bank. An announced change in the discount rate is often interpreted as a signal of the Federal Reserve's intentions regarding future monetary policy. For example, by increasing the discount rate, the Federal Reserve may be signaling that it intends to pursue a tight-money policy, most likely to control budding inflationary pressures. Similarly, by decreasing the discount rate, the Federal Reserve may be signaling an intent to pursue a loose-money policy to stimulate economic activity. Of course, many times a discount rate change is simply a case of the Federal Reserve catching up to financial market conditions rather than leading them. Indeed, the Federal Reserve often acts like the lead goose, who, upon looking back and seeing the flock heading in another direction, quickly flies over to resume its position as "leader" of the flock.

WWW

For the latest on money market rates visit www.money-rates.com

Another important interest rate reported is the **call money rate**, or simply the call rate. "Call money" refers to loans from banks to security brokerage firms, and the call rate is the interest rate that brokerage firms pay on call money loans. As we discussed in Chapter 2, brokers use funds raised through call money loans to make margin loans to customers to finance leveraged stock and bond purchases. The call money rate is the basic rate that brokers use to set interest rates on customer call money loans. Brokers typically charge their customers the call money rate plus a premium, where the broker and the customer may negotiate the premium. For example, a broker may charge a customer the basic call money rate plus 1 percent for a margin loan to purchase common stock.

call money rate
The interest rate brokerage firms pay for call money loans, which are bank loans to brokerage firms. This rate is used as the basis for customer rates on margin loans.

WWW

Visit General Motors Acceptance at www.gmacfs.com
Visit General Electric Capital at www.gecapsol.com

Commercial paper is short-term, unsecured debt issued by the largest corporations. The commercial paper market is dominated by financial corporations, such as banks and insurance companies, or financial subsidiaries of large corporations. A leading commercial

commercial paper
Short-term, unsecured debt issued by the largest corporations.

FIGURE 9.2 Money Market Interest Rates

C6 *Thursday, January 3, 2008*

BORROWING BENCHMARKS

Money Rates

January 2, 2008

Key annual interest rates paid to borrow or lend money in U.S. and international markets. Rates below are a guide to general levels but don't always represent actual transactions.

Inflation

	Nov. index level	CHG FROM (%) Oct. '07	Nov. '06
U.S. consumer price index			
All items	**210.2**	0.6	4.3
Core	**212.4**	0.1	2.3

International rates

	Latest	Week ago	—52-WEEK— High	Low
Prime rates				
U.S.	**7.25**	7.25	8.25	7.25
Canada	**6.00**	6.00	6.25	6.00
Euro zone	**4.00**	4.00	4.00	3.50
Japan	**1.875**	1.875	1.875	1.625
Switzerland	**3.84**	3.86	4.62	2.74
Britain	**5.50**	5.50	5.75	5.00
Australia	**6.75**	6.75	6.75	6.25
Hong Kong	**8.00**	8.00	8.00	8.00
Overnight repurchase				
U.S.	**4.15**	4.15	5.35	1.95
U.K. (BBA)	**5.575**	5.583	6.667	5.030
Euro zone	**3.99**	3.92	4.52	3.52

U.S. government rates

	Latest	Week ago	—52-WEEK— High	Low
Discount	**4.75**	4.75	6.25	4.75
Federal funds				
Effective rate	**4.10**	4.25	5.42	3.20
High	**4.5000**	4.7500	10.0000	4.2000
Low	**3.0000**	1.0000	5.3750	0.2500
Bid	**3.5000**	1.0000	8.0000	0.0100
Offer	**4.5000**	2.5000	10.0000	0.0313
Treasury bill auction				
4 weeks	**3.000**	3.040	5.175	2.750
13 weeks	**3.310**	3.280	5.035	2.850
26 weeks	**3.390**	3.490	4.980	3.190

Secondary market

	Latest	Week ago	—52-WEEK— High	Low
Freddie Mac				
30-year mortgage yields				
30 days	**5.68**	6.05	6.63	5.68
60 days	**5.72**	6.08	6.64	5.69
One-year RNY	**3.375**	3.375	4.460	3.375
Fannie Mae				
30-year mortgage yields				
30 days	**5.896**	6.101	6.727	5.731
60 days	**5.932**	6.127	6.761	5.743
Constant maturity debt index				
Three months	**4.258**	4.397	5.321	4.256
Six months	**4.195**	4.328	5.519	4.171
One year	**3.745**	4.025	5.323	3.745
Bankers acceptances				
30 days	**4.63**	4.93	5.81	4.63

	Latest	Week ago	—52-WEEK— High	Low
60 days	**4.68**	4.94	5.81	4.68
90 days	**4.68**	4.94	5.81	4.68
120 days	**4.68**	4.83	5.73	4.68
150 days	**4.64**	4.82	5.63	4.64
180 days	**4.62**	4.74	5.58	4.62

Other short-term rates

	Latest	Week ago	—52-WEEK— High	Low
Call money	**6.00**	6.00	7.00	6.00
Commercial paper				
30 to 47 days	**4.25**	...	...	...
48 to 59 days	**4.27**	...	...	...
60 to 97 days	**4.29**	...	...	...
98 to 105 days	**4.31**	...	...	...
106 to 120 days	**4.29**	...	...	...
121 to 180 days	**4.24**	...	...	...
181 to 210 days	**4.21**	...	...	...
211 to 240 days	**4.15**	...	...	...
241 to 270 days	**4.11**	...	...	...
Dealer commercial paper				
30 days	**4.60**	4.98	5.78	4.58
60 days	**4.63**	4.95	5.78	4.63
90 days	**4.65**	4.93	5.75	4.65
Euro commercial paper				
30 day	**4.03**	4.02	5.24	3.55
Two month	**4.24**	4.24	5.26	3.60
Three month	**4.30**	4.28	5.23	3.68
Four month	**4.30**	4.30	5.22	3.72
Five month	**4.30**	4.30	5.21	3.76
Six month	**4.28**	4.31	5.16	3.81
London interbank offered rate, or Libor				
One month	**4.57000**	4.85500	5.82375	4.57000
Three month	**4.68063**	4.84250	5.72500	4.68063
Six month	**4.56625**	4.71750	5.59500	4.56625
One year	**4.18750**	4.34375	5.50656	4.18750
Libor Swaps (USD)				
Two year	**3.669**	4.072	5.530	3.669

	Latest	Week ago	—52-WEEK— High	Low
Three year	**3.751**	4.182	5.590	3.751
Five year	**4.031**	4.470	5.710	4.031
Ten year	**4.551**	4.923	5.900	4.550
30 year	**4.912**	5.252	6.070	4.895
Euro Libor				
One month	**4.226**	4.437	4.945	3.607
Three month	**4.663**	4.763	4.953	3.727
Six month	**4.702**	4.774	4.918	3.860
One year	**4.735**	4.774	4.886	3.998
Euro interbank offered rate (Euribor)				
One month	**4.239**	4.459	4.947	3.606
Three month	**4.665**	4.765	4.953	3.726
Six month	**4.703**	4.775	4.917	3.860
One year	**4.733**	4.772	4.885	3.995
Hibor				
One month	**3.053**	3.535	5.704	2.199
Three month	**3.401**	3.680	5.451	3.150
Six month	**3.477**	3.689	5.876	3.459
One year	**3.451**	3.606	5.688	3.451
Asian dollars				
One month	**4.605**	4.861	5.840	4.605
Three month	**4.698**	4.854	5.755	4.698
Six month	**4.594**	4.725	5.600	4.594
One year	**4.253**	4.353	5.936	4.253

	LATEST Offer	Bid	Week ago	52-WEEK High	Low
Eurodollars (mid rates)					
One month	**4.50**	4.62	5.05	5.88	4.56
Two month	**4.55**	4.65	4.98	5.85	4.60
Three month	**4.60**	4.70	4.93	5.83	4.65
Four month	**4.58**	4.68	4.85	5.78	4.63
Five month	**4.55**	4.65	4.80	5.69	4.60
Six month	**4.52**	4.62	4.73	5.60	4.57

Notes on data:
U.S. prime rate and discount rate are effective December 11, 2007. **U.S. prime rate** is the base rate on corporate loans posted by at least 75% of the 30 largest U.S. banks; **Other prime rates** aren't directly comparable; lending practices vary widely by location; **Discount rate** is the charge on loans to depository institutions by the New York Federal Reserve Banks; **Federal-funds rate** is on reserves traded among commercial banks for overnight use in amounts of $1 million or more; **Call money rate** is the charge on loans to brokers on stock-exchange collateral; **Dealer commercial paper rates** are for high-grade unsecured notes sold through dealers by major corporations; **Freddie Mac RNY** is the required net yield for the one-year 2% rate-capped ARM. **Libor** is the British Bankers' Association average of interbank offered rates for dollar deposits in the London market; **Libor Swaps** quoted are mid-market, semi-annual swap rates and pay the floating 3-month Libor rate.

Sources: Merrill Lynch; Bureau of Labor Statistics; Reuters; General Electric Capital Corp.; Garban Intercapital; Tullett Prebon Information, Ltd.

Reuters Group PLC is the primary data provider for several statistical tables in The Wall Street Journal, including foreign stock quotations, futures and foreign exchange tables. Reuters real-time data feeds are used to calculate various Dow Jones Indexes.

Source: *The Wall Street Journal,* January 4, 2008. Reprinted by permission of Dow Jones and Company, Inc., via Copyright Clearance Center, Inc.,

paper rate is the rate that General Electric Capital Corporation (the finance arm of General Electric) pays on short-term debt issues. This commercial paper rate is a benchmark for this market because General Electric Capital is one of the largest single issuers of commercial paper. Most other corporations issuing commercial paper will pay a slightly higher interest rate than this benchmark rate. Commercial paper is a popular investment vehicle for portfolio managers and corporate treasurers with excess funds on hand that they wish to invest on a short-term basis. Euro commercial paper refers to commercial paper denominated in euros rather than dollars.

certificate of deposit (CD)
Large-denomination deposits of $100,000 or more at commercial banks for a specified term.

One important interest rate that is not reported in Figure 9.2 is the rate on **certificates of deposit**, or **CDs**. Certificates of deposit represent large-denomination deposits of $100,000 or more at commercial banks for a specified term. The interest rate paid on CDs usually varies according to the term of the deposit. For example, a one-year CD may pay a higher interest rate than a six-month CD, which in turn may pay a higher interest rate than a three-month CD.

Large-denomination certificates of deposit are generally negotiable instruments, meaning that they can be bought and sold among investors. Consequently, they are often called negotiable certificates of deposit, or negotiable CDs. Negotiable CDs can be bought and sold through a broker. The large-denomination CDs described here should not be confused with the small-denomination CDs that banks offer retail customers. These small-denomination CDs are simply bank time deposits. They normally pay a lower interest rate than large-denomination CDs and are not negotiable instruments.

banker's acceptance
A postdated check on which a bank has guaranteed payment; commonly used to finance international trade transactions.

A **banker's acceptance** is essentially a postdated check upon which a commercial bank has guaranteed payment. Banker's acceptances are normally used to finance international trade transactions. For example, as an importer, you wish to purchase computer components from a company in Singapore and pay for the goods three months after delivery, so you write a postdated check. You and the exporter agree, however, that once the goods are shipped, your bank will guarantee payment on the date specified on the check.

After your goods are shipped, the exporter presents the relevant documentation, and, if all is in order, your bank stamps the word *ACCEPTED* on your check. At this point your bank has created an acceptance, which means it has promised to pay the acceptance's face value (the amount of the check) at maturity (the date on the check). The exporter can then hold on to the acceptance or sell it in the money market. The banker's acceptance rate published in "Money Rates" is the interest rate for acceptances issued by the largest commercial banks.

Eurodollars
U.S. dollar denominated deposits at foreign banks or foreign branches of U.S. banks.

Eurodollars are U.S. dollar denominated deposits at foreign banks or foreign branches of U.S. banks. Eurodollar rates are interest rates paid for large-denomination eurodollar certificates of deposit. Eurodollar CDs are negotiable and are traded in a large, very active Eurodollar money market. The "Money Rates" report lists Eurodollar rates for various maturities obtained from transactions occurring late in the day.

London Interbank Offered Rate (LIBOR)
Interest rate that international banks charge one another for overnight Eurodollar loans.

The **London Interbank Offered Rate (LIBOR)** is the interest rate offered by London commercial banks for dollar deposits from other banks. The LIBOR rate is perhaps the most frequently cited rate used to represent the London money market. Bank lending rates are often stated as LIBOR plus a premium, where the premium is negotiated between the bank and its customer. For example, a corporation may be quoted a loan rate from a London bank at LIBOR plus 2 percent. Euro LIBOR refers to deposits denominated in euros—the common currency of 12 European Union countries. Like LIBOR, the Euro LIBOR rate is calculated by the British Bankers Association (BBA) from quotes provided by London banks. The EURIBOR is an interest rate that also refers to deposits denominated in euros. However, the EURIBOR is based largely on interest rates from banks in the European Union interbank market. HIBOR is an interest rate based on Hong Kong dollars. HIBOR is the interest rate between banks in the Hong Kong interbank market.

U.S. Treasury bill (T-bill)
A short-term U.S. government debt instrument issued by the U.S. Treasury.

U.S. Treasury bills, or just **T-bills**, represent short-term U.S. government debt issued through the U.S. Treasury. The Treasury bill market is the world's largest market for new debt securities with one year or less to maturity. As such, the Treasury bill market leads all other credit markets in determining the general level of short-term interest rates. "Money Rates" reports Treasury bill interest rates set during the most recent weekly Treasury bill auction. Interest rates determined at each Treasury bill auction are closely watched by professional money managers throughout the world. The overnight repurchase, or "repo," rate is essentially the rate charged on overnight loans that are collateralized by U.S. Treasury securities.

WWW

For more on LIBOR, visit www.bba.org.uk

The Federal Home Loan Mortgage Corporation (FHLMC), commonly called "Freddie Mac," and the Federal National Mortgage Association (FNMA), commonly called "Fannie Mae," are government-sponsored agencies that purchase large blocks of home mortgages and combine them into mortgage pools, where each pool may represent several tens of millions of dollars of home mortgages. The interest rates reported in "Money Rates" are an indicator of rates on newly created home mortgages. Because home mortgages are long-term obligations, these are not actually money market rates. However, with several trillion dollars of mortgages outstanding, the mortgage market has a considerable influence on money market activity.

CHECK THIS

9.1a Which money market interest rates are most important to commercial banks?

9.1b Which money market interest rates are most important to nonbank corporations?

9.2 Money Market Prices and Rates

pure discount security
An interest-bearing asset that makes a single payment of face value at maturity with no payments before maturity.

Money market securities typically make a single payment of face value at maturity and make no payments before maturity. Such securities are called **pure discount securities** because they sell at a discount relative to their face value. In this section, we discuss the relationship between the price of a money market instrument and the interest rate quoted on it.

One of the things you will notice in this section is that market participants quote interest rates in several different ways. This inconsistent treatment presents a problem when we wish to compare rates on different investments. Therefore, we must put rates on a common footing before we can compare them.

After going through the various interest rate conventions and conversions needed to compare them, you might wonder why everybody doesn't just agree to compute interest rates and prices in some uniform way. Well perhaps they should, but they definitely do not. As a result, we must review some of the various procedures actually used in money markets. We hope you come to recognize that the calculations are neither mysterious nor even especially difficult, although they are rooted in centuries-old procedures and may sometimes be tedious. However, given the billions of dollars of securities traded every day based on these numbers, it is important to understand them.

One other thing to notice is that the word "yield" appears frequently. For now, you can take it as given that the yield on an interest-bearing asset is simply a measure of the interest rate being offered by the asset. We will discuss the topic of yields in greater detail in the next chapter.

basis point
With regard to interest rates or bond yields, one basis point is 1 percent of 1 percent.

Bond yields and many interest rates are quoted as a percentage with two decimal places, such as 5.82 percent. With this quote, the smallest possible change would be .01 percent, or .0001. This amount, which is 1 percent of 1 percent, is called a **basis point**. So, if an interest rate of 5.82 percent rose to 5.94 percent, we would say this rate rose by 94 − 82 = 12 basis points. The quantity to the left of the decimal point (the "11") is called the "handle." Traders frequently omit the handle when quoting or discussing rates since, presumably, anyone actively trading would know it.

BANK DISCOUNT RATE QUOTES

bank discount basis
A method for quoting interest rates on money market instruments.

Interest rates for some key money market securities, including Treasury bills and banker's acceptances, are quoted on a **bank discount basis**, or simply discount basis. An interest rate quoted on a discount basis is often called a discount yield. If we are given an interest rate quoted on a bank discount basis for a particular money market instrument, then we calculate the price of that instrument as follows:

$$\text{Current price} = \text{Face value} \times \left(1 - \frac{\text{Days to maturity}}{360} \times \text{Discount yield}\right) \quad (9.5)$$

The term "discount yield" here simply refers to the quoted interest rate. It should not be confused with the Federal Reserve's discount rate discussed earlier.

To give an example, suppose a banker's acceptance has a face value of $1 million that will be paid in 90 days. If the interest rate, quoted on a discount basis, is 5 percent, what is the current price of the acceptance?

As the following calculation shows, a discount yield of 5 percent and maturity of 90 days gives a current price of $987,500.

$$\$987{,}500 = \$1{,}000{,}000 \times \left(1 - \frac{90}{360} \times .05\right)$$

The difference between the face value of $1 million and the price of $987,500 is $12,500 and is called the "discount." This discount is the interest earned over the 90-day period until the acceptance matures.

Notice that the formula used to calculate the acceptance price assumes a 360-day business year. This practice dates back to a time when calculations were performed manually. Assuming a 360-day business year, with exactly four 90-day quarters rather than a true 365-day calendar year, made manual discount calculations simpler and less subject to error. Consequently, if $1 million is discounted over a full calendar year of 365 days using a bank discount yield of 5 percent and an assumed 360-day business year, the resulting price of $949,305.56 is calculated as follows:

$$\$949{,}305.56 = \$1{,}000{,}000 \times \left(1 - \frac{365}{360} \times .05\right)$$

EXAMPLE 9.2

Money Market Prices

The rate on a particular money market instrument, quoted on a discount basis, is 4 percent. The instrument has a face value of $100,000 and will mature in 71 days. What is its price? What if it had 51 days to maturity?

Using the bank discount basis formula, we have:

$$\text{Current price} = \text{Face value} \times \left(1 - \frac{\text{Days to maturity}}{360} \times \text{Discount yield}\right)$$

$$\$99{,}211.11 = \$100{,}000 \times \left(1 - \frac{71}{360} \times .04\right)$$

Check for yourself that the price in the second case of a 51-day maturity is $99,433.33.

TREASURY BILL QUOTES

In its online version, *The Wall Street Journal* reports current interest rates on U.S. Treasury bills each business day. Figure 9.3 reproduces a "Treasury Bills" interest rate report. The maturity of each bill issue is stated in year-month-day format, followed by the number of days remaining until the bill matures. The two columns following the days to maturity give the bid and asked discounts for each bill issue. The bid discount is used by Treasury bill dealers to state what they are willing to pay for a Treasury bill, and the asked discount is used to state what price a dealer will accept to sell a Treasury bill. The next column shows the change in the asked discount from the previous day.

WWW

For price and yield data on U.S. Treasury securities visit money.cnn.com and surf to bonds under the "Markets" tab.

For example, consider the bill issue with 83 days to maturity, with a bid discount rate of 3.64 percent and an asked discount rate of 3.63 percent. For a $1 million face value Treasury

FIGURE 9.3 U.S. Treasury Bills

TREASURY BILLS

GO TO: Notes and Bonds

Thursday, September 20, 2007

Quotes are for transactions of $1 million or more. Treasury-bill yields are in 100ths, all yields are to maturity and based on the asked quote. Days to maturity calculated from settlement date. Bid and ask data are discounts from face value.

Maturity	Days to maturity	Bid	Asked	Chg	Asked yield
2007 Sep 27	6	3.43	3.42	−0.11	3.47
2007 Oct 04	13	3.38	3.37	−0.14	3.42
2007 Oct 11	20	3.36	3.35	−0.08	3.40
2007 Oct 18	27	3.37	3.36	−0.13	3.42
2007 Oct 25	34	3.36	3.35	−0.15	3.41
2007 Nov 01	41	3.35	3.34	−0.14	3.40
2007 Nov 08	48	3.44	3.43	−0.21	3.49
2007 Nov 15	55	3.48	3.47	−0.18	3.54
2007 Nov 23	63	3.59	3.58	−0.15	3.65
2007 Nov 29	69	3.62	3.61	−0.14	3.69
2007 Dec 06	76	3.63	3.62	−0.18	3.70
2007 Dec 13	83	3.64	3.63	−0.16	3.71
2007 Dec 20	90	3.68	3.67	−0.16	3.76
2007 Dec 27	97	3.70	3.69	−0.15	3.78
2008 Jan 03	104	3.73	3.72	−0.11	3.81
2008 Jan 10	111	3.73	3.72	−0.11	3.82
2008 Jan 17	118	3.81	3.80	−0.05	3.90
2008 Jan 24	125	3.87	3.86	unch.	3.97
2008 Jan 31	132	3.88	3.87	unch.	3.98
2008 Feb 07	139	3.91	3.90	+0.02	4.01
2008 Feb 14	146	3.90	3.89	+0.03	4.01
2008 Feb 21	153	3.92	3.91	+0.03	4.03
2008 Feb 28	160	3.94	3.93	+0.02	4.06
2008 Mar 06	167	3.96	3.95	+0.02	4.08
2008 Mar 13	174	3.96	3.95	+0.02	4.08

Source: www.wsj.com, September 21, 2007. Reprinted by permission of Dow Jones, Inc. via Copyright Clearance Center, Inc., © 2007 Dow Jones and Company, Inc. All Rights Reserved Worldwide.

bill, the corresponding bid and asked prices can be calculated by using the discounts shown along with our bank discount basis pricing formula. For example, the bid price would be:

$$\text{Bid price} = \$991{,}607.78 = \$1{,}000{,}000 \times \left(1 - \frac{83}{360} \times .0364\right)$$

Check that the ask price would be $991,630.83.

EXAMPLE 9.3

T-Bill Prices

Suppose you wanted to buy a T-bill with 85 days to maturity and a face value of \$5,000,000. How much would you have to pay if the asked discount is 3.41 percent?

Because you are buying, you must pay the asked price. To calculate the asked price, we use the asked discount in the bank discount basis formula:

$$\text{Asked price} = \$4{,}959{,}743.06 = \$5{,}000{,}000 \times \left(1 - \frac{85}{360} \times .0341\right)$$

Calculate a bid price for this T-bill assuming a bid discount of 3.42 percent. Notice that the asked price is higher than the bid price even though the asked discount is lower than the bid discount. The reason is that a bigger discount produces a lower price.

Treasury bill prices may be calculated using a built-in spreadsheet function. An example of how to use an Excel™ spreadsheet to calculate a Treasury bill price is shown in the nearby *Spreadsheet Analysis* box.

The last column in Figure 9.3 lists the asked yield for each Treasury bill issue. It is important to realize that the asked yield is *not* quoted on a discount basis. Instead, it is a "bond equivalent yield." Unlike a discount rate, a bond equivalent yield assumes a 365-day calendar year. Bond equivalent yields are principally used to compare yields on Treasury bills with yields on other money market instruments as well as Treasury bonds and other bonds (we discuss these long-term yields in the next chapter).

BANK DISCOUNT YIELDS VERSUS BOND EQUIVALENT YIELDS

A bank discount yield is converted to a bond equivalent yield using the following formula:

$$\text{Bond equivalent yield} = \frac{365 \times \text{Discount yield}}{360 - \text{Days to maturity} \times \text{Discount yield}} \tag{9.6}$$

This conversion formula is correct for maturities of six months or less. Calculation of bond equivalent yields for maturities greater than six months is a little more complicated, and we will not discuss it here, particularly because T-bills with maturities greater than six months are no longer sold.

For example, suppose the asked discount rate on a T-bill with 170 days to maturity is 3.22 percent. What is the bond equivalent yield? Plugging into the conversion formula, a 3.22 percent discount is converted into a bond equivalent yield as follows:

$$.03315 = \frac{365 \times .0322}{360 - 170 \times .0322}$$

The bond equivalent yield is thus 3.315 percent.

EXAMPLE 9.4

Bond Equivalent Yields

Suppose a T-bill has 45 days to maturity and an asked discount of 5 percent. What is the bond equivalent yield?

Using the bond equivalent yield conversion formulas, we have:

$$.05101 = \frac{365 \times .05}{360 - 45 \times .05}$$

The bond equivalent yield is thus 5.101 percent.

Bond equivalent yields may be calculated using a built-in spreadsheet function. An example of how to use an Excel™ spreadsheet to calculate a bond equivalent yield is shown in the nearby *Spreadsheet Analysis* box.

SPREADSHEET ANALYSIS

	A	B	C	D	E	F	G	H
1								
2		Treasury Bill Price and Yield Calculations						
3								
4	A Treasury bill traded on February 23, 2008 pays $100 on May 15, 2008. Assuming							
5	a discount rate of 4.05 percent, what are its price and bond equivalent yield?							
6	Hint: Use the Excel functions TBILLPRICE and TBILLEQ.							
7								
8		$99.0775	=TBILLPRICE("2/23/2008","5/15/2008",0.0405)					
9								
10		4.144%	=TBILLEQ("2/23/2008","5/15/2008",0.0405)					
11								
12								
13	A credit card charges a nominal annual interest rate of 15 percent. With interest							
14	charged monthly, what is the effective annual rate (EAR) on this credit card?							
15	Hint: Use the Excel function EFFECT.							
16								
17		16.075%	=EFFECT(0.15,12)					

One common cause of confusion about bond equivalent yield calculations is the way that leap years are handled. The rule is that we must use 366 days if February 29 occurs within the next 12 months. For example, 2012 will be a leap year. So, beginning on March 1, 2011, we must use 366 days in the numerator of equation (9.6). Then, beginning on March 1, 2012, we must revert to using 365 days.

EXAMPLE 9.5 Back To The Future: Leap Year Bond Equivalent Yields

Calculate the asked yield (bond equivalent yield) for a T-bill price quoted in December 2011 with 119 days to maturity and an asked discount of 5.41 percent.

Because the 12-month period following the date of the price quote includes February 29, we must use 366 days. Plugging this into the conversion formula, we get:

$$.0560 = \frac{366 \times .0541}{360 - 119 \times .0541}$$

Therefore, 5.60 percent is the ask yield stated as a bond equivalent yield.

We can calculate a Treasury bill asked price using the asked yield, which is a bond equivalent yield, as follows:

$$\text{Bill price} = \frac{\text{Face value}}{1 + \text{Bond equivalent yield} \times \text{Days to maturity}/365} \tag{9.7}$$

For example, just above we calculated the 3.315 percent bond equivalent yield on a T-bill with 170 days to maturity and a 3.22 percent asked discount rate. If we calculate its price using this bond equivalent yield, we get:

$$\$984{,}795 = \frac{\$1{,}000{,}000}{1 + .03315 \times 170/365}$$

Check that, ignoring a small rounding error, you get the same price using the bank discount formula.

BOND EQUIVALENT YIELDS, APRs, AND EARs

Money market rates not quoted on a discount basis are generally quoted on a "simple" interest basis. Simple interest rates are calculated just like the annual percentage rate (APR) on a consumer loan. So, for the most part, money market rates are either bank discount rates or APRs. For example, CD rates are APRs.

In fact, the bond equivalent yield on a T-bill with less than six months to maturity is also an APR. As a result, like any APR, it understates the true interest rate, which is usually called the *effective annual rate,* or EAR. In the context of the money market, EARs are sometimes referred to as effective annual yields, effective yields, or annualized yields. Whatever it is called, to find out what a T-bill, or any other money market instrument, is *really* going to pay you, yet another conversion is needed. We will get to the needed conversion in a moment.

First, however, recall that an APR is equal to the interest rate per period multiplied by the number of periods in a year. For example, if the rate on a car loan is 1 percent per month, then the APR is 1% × 12 = 12%. In general, if we let m be the number of periods in a year, an APR is converted to an EAR as follows:

$$1 + EAR = \left(1 + \frac{APR}{m}\right)^m \qquad (9.8)$$

For example, on our 12 percent APR car loan, the EAR can be determined by:

$$\begin{aligned} 1 + EAR &= \left(1 + \frac{.12}{12}\right)^{12} \\ &= 1.01^{12} \\ &= 1.126825 \\ EAR &= 12.6825\% \end{aligned}$$

Thus, the rate on the car loan is really 12.6825 percent per year.

EXAMPLE 9.6

APRs and EARs

A typical credit card may quote an APR of 18 percent. On closer inspection, you will find that the rate is actually 1.5 percent per month. What annual interest rate are you *really* paying on such a credit card?

With 12 periods in a year, an APR of 18 percent is converted to an EAR as follows:

$$\begin{aligned} 1 + EAR &= \left(1 + \frac{.18}{12}\right)^{12} \\ &= 1.015^{12} \\ &= 1.1956 \\ EAR &= 19.56\% \end{aligned}$$

Thus, the rate on this credit card is really 19.56 percent per year.

Effective annual rates may be calculated using a built-in spreadsheet function. An example of how to use an Excel™ spreadsheet to calculate an effective annual rate is shown in the previous *Spreadsheet Analysis* box.

Now, to see that the bond equivalent yield on a T-bill is just an APR, we can first calculate the price on the bill we considered earlier (3.22 percent asked discount, 170 days to maturity). Using the bank discount formula, the asked price, for $1 million in face value, is:

$$\text{Asked price} = \$984{,}794 = \$1{,}000{,}000 \times \left(1 - \frac{170}{360} \times .0322\right)$$

FIGURE 9.5 Treasury STRIPS (September 2007)

Treasury Bond, Stripped Principal

2017 May 15	63.746	63.766	–0.928	4.72
2017 May 15	62.881	62.901	–0.884	4.86
2017 Aug 15	62.142	62.162	–0.866	4.86
2018 May 15	59.534	59.554	–0.893	4.93
2018 Nov 15	57.813	57.833	–0.908	4.97
2019 Feb 15	56.996	57.016	–0.883	4.99
2019 Aug 15	55.489	55.509	–0.932	5.01
2020 Feb 15	53.932	53.952	–0.911	5.04
2020 May 15	53.100	53.120	–0.948	5.06
2020 Aug 15	52.379	52.399	–0.954	5.07

Stripped Coupon Interest

2009 Feb 15	94.592	94.612	–0.114	4.00
2009 May 15	93.648	93.668	–0.135	4.01
2009 Aug 15	92.616	92.636	–0.193	4.07
2009 Nov 15	91.697	91.717	–0.218	4.06
2010 Feb 15	90.741	90.761	–0.266	4.08
2010 May 15	89.706	89.726	–0.291	4.13
2010 Aug 15	88.825	88.845	–0.316	4.12
2010 Nov 15	87.858	87.878	–0.340	4.14

Treasury Note, Stripped Principal

2009 Feb 15	94.420	94.440	–0.107	4.13
2009 May 15	93.488	93.508	–0.135	4.11
2009 May 15	93.511	93.531	–0.127	4.10
2009 May 15	93.473	93.493	–0.150	4.12
2009 Aug 15	92.604	92.624	–0.132	4.07
2009 Nov 15	91.566	91.586	–0.236	4.13
2009 Nov 15	91.585	91.605	–0.236	4.12
2010 Feb 15	90.614	90.634	–0.230	4.14
2010 Feb 15	90.554	90.574	–0.254	4.17
2010 May 15	89.669	89.689	–0.279	4.15

Source: www.wsj.com, September 20, 2007. Reprinted by permission of Dow Jones and Company, Inc., via Copyright Clearance Center, Inc.

what dealers were willing to pay to buy the STRIPS, and the asked price is a quote of what dealers were willing to accept to sell the STRIPS. The next-to-the-last column in Figure 9.5 reports the change in the asked price quote from the previous day.

The last column in Figure 9.5 lists asked yields, which are yields on the STRIPS based on their asked price quotes. Notice that each maturity has a different asked yield, or interest rate. This shows us that interest rates determined in financial markets generally differ according to the maturity of a security.

STRIPS prices are stated as a price per \$100 of face value. In the very recent past, STRIPS prices were quoted in dollars and thirty-seconds of a dollar. That is, a quote of, say, 74:08 stood for 74 and 8/32 of a dollar, or \$74.25. Today, however, STRIPS prices are quoted to three decimal points. For example, suppose a coupon interest STRIPS has an asked price quote of 93.668. This means that the price per \$100 face value is \$93.668. Thus, the skill of being able to divide by 32 is no longer highly valued, at least in STRIPS trading.

WWW

Read more about STRIPS at www.publicdebt.treas.gov

YIELDS FOR U.S. TREASURY STRIPS

An asked yield for a U.S. Treasury STRIPS is an APR (APRs were discussed earlier in this chapter). It is calculated as two times the true semiannual rate. Calculation of the yield on a STRIPS is a standard time value of money calculation. The price today of the STRIPS is the *present value*; the face value received at maturity is the *future value.* As shown in Example 9.1, the relationship between present value and future value is:

$$\text{Present value} = \frac{\text{Future value}}{(1 + r)^N}$$

In this equation, r is the rate per period and N is the number of periods. Notice that a period is not necessarily one year long.[1] For Treasury STRIPS, the number of periods is two times the number of years to maturity, here denoted by $2M$, and the interest rate is the "yield to maturity" (YTM) divided by 2:

$$\textbf{STRIPS price} = \frac{\textbf{Face value}}{(1 + YTM/2)^{2M}} \qquad \textbf{(9.9)}$$

Consider a STRIPS with an asked price of 55.568, a reported yield of 4.40, and 13.5 years to maturity. The actual semiannual rate is 4.40%/2 = 2.20%. Also, 13.5 years to maturity converts to 2 × 13.5, or 27, semiannual periods. To check that the reported price is correct given the reported yield, we plug in future value, rate per period, and number of periods:

$$\begin{aligned}\text{STRIPS price} &= \frac{\$100}{(1 + .022)^{27}} \\ &= 55.568\end{aligned}$$

If we need to go the other way and calculate the asked yield on a STRIPS given its price, we can rearrange the basic present value equation to solve it for r:

$$r = \left(\frac{\text{Future value}}{\text{Present value}}\right)^{1/N} - 1$$

For STRIPS, $N = 2M$ is the number of semiannual periods, and $r = YTM/2$ is the semiannual interest rate, so the formula is:

$$YTM = 2 \times \left[\left(\frac{\textbf{Face value}}{\textbf{STRIPS price}}\right)^{1/2M} - 1\right] \qquad \textbf{(9.10)}$$

Consider a STRIPS maturing in six years with an asked price of 73.031. Its yield to maturity of 5.3072 percent as calculated immediately below becomes 5.31 percent after rounding to two decimal places.

$$.053072 = 2 \times \left[\left(\frac{100}{73.031}\right)^{1/12} - 1\right]$$

[1] Any financial calculator can perform these calculations, but we will work them the hard way so that you can learn how to do them with any calculator.

As another example, consider a STRIPS maturing in 20 years with an asked price of 26.188. As calculated immediately below, its yield to maturity of 6.8129 percent becomes 6.81 percent after rounding to two decimal places.

$$.068129 = 2 \times \left[\left(\frac{100}{26.188}\right)^{1/40} - 1\right]$$

CHECK THIS

9.4a What is the yield to maturity (YTM) on a STRIPS maturing in five years if its asked price quote is 77.75?

9.4b What is the YTM of a STRIPS maturing in 15 years if its asked price quote is 36.813?

9.4c What is the YTM of a STRIPS maturing in 25 years if its asked price quote is 18.656?

9.5 Nominal versus Real Interest Rates

nominal interest rates
Interest rates as they are normally observed and quoted, with no adjustment for inflation.

There is a fundamental distinction between *nominal* and *real* interest rates. **Nominal interest rates** are interest rates as we ordinarily observe them, for example, as they are reported in *The Wall Street Journal*. Thus, all the money market rates we discussed earlier in this chapter and the STRIPS yields we discussed just above are nominal rates.

REAL INTEREST RATES

real interest rates
Interest rates adjusted for the effect of inflation, calculated as the nominal rate less the rate of inflation.

Real interest rates are nominal rates adjusted for the effects of price inflation. To obtain a real interest rate, simply subtract an inflation rate from a nominal interest rate:

$$\text{Real interest rate} = \text{Nominal interest rate} - \text{Inflation rate} \qquad (9.11)$$

The real interest rate is so-called because it measures the real change in the purchasing power of an investment. For example, if the nominal interest rate for a one-year certificate of deposit is 7 percent, then a one-year deposit of \$100,000 will grow to \$107,000. But if the inflation rate over the same year is 4 percent, you would need \$104,000 after one year passes to buy what cost \$100,000 today. Thus, the real increase in purchasing power for your investment is only \$3,000, and, therefore, the real interest rate is only 3 percent.

Figure 9.6 displays real interest rates based on annual rates of return on U.S. Treasury bills and inflation rates over the 57-year period 1950 through 2007. As shown in Figure 9.6, following a negative spike at the beginning of the Korean War in 1950, real interest rates for Treasury bills were generally positive until the Organization of Petroleum-Exporting Countries' (OPEC) oil embargo in 1973. After this, real rates were generally negative until the Federal Reserve Board initiated a tight-money policy to fight an inflationary spiral in the late 1970s. The tight-money policy caused the 1980s to begin with historically high real interest rates. Throughout the 1980s, real Treasury bill rates were falling as inflation subsided. During this 50-year period the average real Treasury bill interest rate was slightly less than 1 percent.

THE FISHER HYPOTHESIS

Fisher hypothesis
Assertion that the general level of nominal interest rates follows the general level of inflation.

The relationship between nominal interest rates and the rate of inflation is often couched in terms of the *Fisher hypothesis,* which is named for the famous economist Irving Fisher, who formally proposed it in 1930. The **Fisher hypothesis** simply asserts that the general level of nominal interest rates follows the general level of inflation.

According to the Fisher hypothesis, interest rates are on average higher than the rate of inflation. Therefore, it logically follows that short-term interest rates reflect current inflation, while long-term interest rates reflect investor expectations of future inflation. Figure 9.7 graphs nominal interest rates and inflation rates used to create Figure 9.6. Notice that when inflation rates were high, Treasury bill returns tended to be high also, as predicted by the Fisher hypothesis.

FIGURE 9.6 Real T-Bill Rates, 1950 through 2007

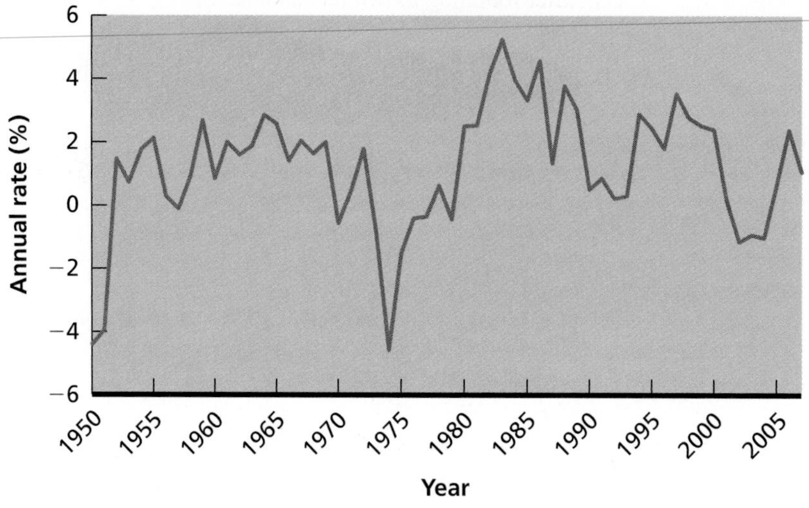

Source: Federal Reserve Board of Governors and Global Financial Data.

FIGURE 9.7 Inflation Rates and T-Bill Rates, 1950 through 2007

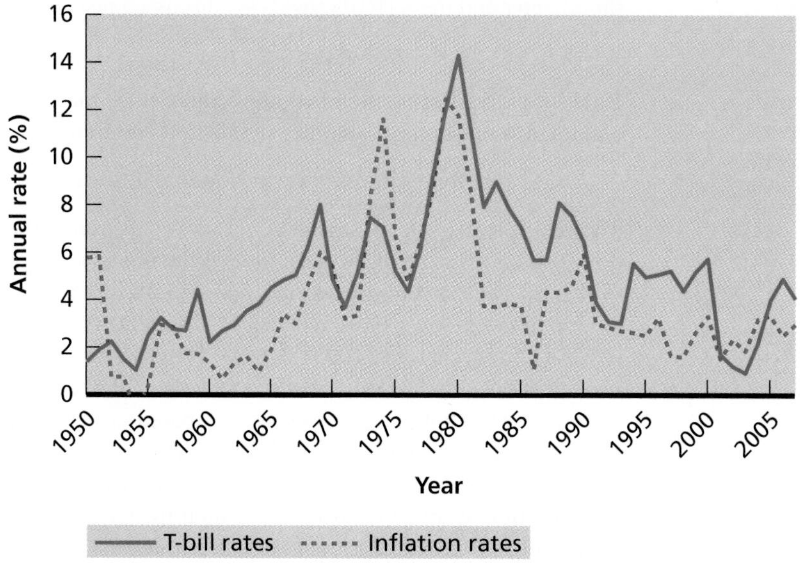

Source: www.wsj.com, September 21, 2007. Reprinted by permission of Dow Jones and Company Inc. via Copyright Clearance Center, Inc., © 2007 Dow Jones and Company Inc. All Rights Reserved Worldwide.

INFLATION-INDEXED TREASURY SECURITIES

In recent years, the U.S. Treasury has issued securities that guarantee a fixed rate of return in excess of realized inflation rates. These inflation-indexed Treasury securities pay a fixed coupon rate on their current principal and adjust their principal semiannually according to the most recent inflation rate. For investors wanting long-term protection against inflation along with the safety of U.S. Treasury bonds, inflation-indexed Treasury securities are perhaps the perfect investment.

For example, suppose an inflation-indexed note is issued with a coupon rate of 3.5 percent and an initial principal of \$1,000. Six months later, the note will pay a coupon of $\$1{,}000 \times 3.5\%/2 =$ \$17.50. Assuming 2 percent inflation over the six months since issuance, the note's principal is then increased to $\$1{,}000 \times 102\% = \$1{,}020$. Six months later, the note pays $\$1{,}020 \times 3.5\%/2 =$ \$17.85, and its principal is again adjusted to compensate for recent inflation.

Price and yield information for inflation-indexed Treasury securities is reported online at www.wsj.com in the same section with other Treasury securities, as shown in Figure 9.8.

expected future interest rates according to expectations theory. But where do expected future interest rates come from? According to the Fisher hypothesis, expectations regarding future interest rates are based on expected future rates of inflation. Thus, expectations theory and the Fisher hypothesis mesh quite nicely.

Furthermore, a basic yield curve determined by inflationary expectations could also accommodate maturity preference theory. All we need to do is add a maturity premium to longer term interest rates. In this view, long-term, default-free interest rates have three components: a real rate, an anticipated future inflation rate, and a maturity premium.

MARKET SEGMENTATION THEORY

market segmentation theory
Debt markets are segmented by maturity, with the result that interest rates for various maturities are determined separately in each segment.

An alternative theory of the term structure of interest rates is the **market segmentation theory**, which asserts that debt markets are segmented according to the various maturities of debt instruments available for investment. By this theory, each maturity represents a separate, distinct market. For example, one group of lenders and borrowers may prefer to lend and borrow using securities with a maturity of 10 years, while another group may prefer to lend and borrow using securities with a maturity of 5 years. Segmentation theory simply states that interest rates corresponding to each maturity are determined separately by supply and demand conditions in each market segment.

Another theory of the term structure, known as the *preferred habitat theory,* is essentially a compromise between market segmentation and maturity preference. In the preferred habitat theory, as in the market segmentation theory, different investors have different preferred maturities. The difference is that they can be induced to move to less preferred maturities by a higher interest rate. In the maturity preference theory, the preferred habitat is always toward shorter maturities rather than longer maturities.

CHECK THIS

9.6a According to the expectations theory, what does an upward-sloping term structure indicate?

9.6b What basic assertion does maturity preference theory make about investor preferences? If this assertion is correct, how does it affect the term structure of interest rates?

9.6c What is a maturity premium?

9.7 Determinants of Nominal Interest Rates: A Modern Perspective

Our understanding of the term structure of interest rates has increased significantly in the last few decades. Also, the evolution of fixed-income markets has shown us that, at least to some extent, traditional theories discussed in our previous section may be inadequate to explain the term structure. We discuss some problems with these theories next and then move on to a modern perspective.

PROBLEMS WITH TRADITIONAL THEORIES

To illustrate some problems with traditional theories, we could examine the behavior of the term structure in the last two decades. What we would find is that the term structure is almost always upward sloping. But contrary to the expectations hypothesis, interest rates have not always risen. Furthermore, as we saw with STRIPS term structure, it is often the case that the term structure turns down at very long maturities. According to the expectations hypothesis, market participants apparently expect rates to rise for 20 or so years and then decline. This seems to be stretching things a bit.

In terms of maturity preference, the world's biggest borrower, the U.S. government, borrows much more heavily short term than long term. Furthermore, many of the biggest buyers of fixed-income securities, such as pension funds, have a strong preference for *long* maturities. It is hard to square these facts with the behavioral assumptions underlying the maturity preference theory.

Finally, in terms of market segmentation, the U.S. government borrows at all maturities. Many institutional investors, such as mutual funds, are more than willing to move among maturities to obtain more favorable rates. At the same time, some bond trading operations do nothing other than buy and sell various maturity issues to exploit even very small perceived premiums. In short, in the modern fixed-income market, market segmentation does not seem to be a powerful force.

MODERN TERM STRUCTURE THEORY

Going back to Chapter 1, we saw that long-term government bonds had higher returns, on average, than short-term T-bills. They had substantially more risk as well. In other words, there appears to be a risk-return trade-off for default-free bonds as well, and long-term bonds appear to have a risk premium.

Notice that this risk premium doesn't result from the possibility of default since it exists on default-free U.S. government debt. Instead, it exists because longer-term bond prices are more volatile than shorter-term prices. As we discuss in detail in the next chapter, the reason is that, for a given change in interest rates, long-term bond prices change more than short-term bonds. Put differently, long-term bond prices are much more sensitive to interest rate changes than short-term bonds. This is called *interest rate risk,* and the risk premium on longer-term bonds is called the *interest rate risk premium.*

The interest rate risk premium carried by long-term bonds leads us to a modern reinterpretation of the maturity preference hypothesis. All else equal, investors do prefer short-term bonds to long-term bonds. The reason is simply that short-term bonds are less risky. As a result, long-term bonds have to offer higher yields to compensate investors for the extra interest rate risk.

Putting it together, the modern view of the term structure suggests that nominal interest rates on default-free securities can be stated as follows:

$$\text{NI} = \text{RI} + \text{IP} + \text{RP} \tag{9.12}$$

where: NI = Nominal interest rate
RI = Real interest rate
IP = Inflation premium
RP = Interest rate risk premium

In equation (9.12), the real rate of interest is assumed to be the same for all securities, and, on average, the real interest rate is positive, as predicted by the Fisher hypothesis.

As we discussed above, the inflation premium (IP) reflects investor expectations of future price inflation. The inflation premium may be different for securities with different maturities because expected inflation may be different over different future horizons. For example, the expected average rate of inflation over the next two years may be different from the expected average rate of inflation over the next five years.

In addition to the real rate and the inflation premium, nominal rates reflect an interest rate risk premium (RP) which increases with the maturity of the security being considered. As a result, if interest rates are expected to remain constant through time, the term structure would have a positive slope. This is consistent with maturity preference theory. Indeed, for zero coupon bonds the interest rate risk premium and the maturity premium are the same thing.

The separate effects of the inflation premium and the interest rate risk premium are difficult to distinguish. For example, the yields for U.S. Treasury STRIPS in Figure 9.5 reveal a substantial yield premium for long-maturity STRIPS over short-term STRIPS. This yield premium for long-maturity STRIPS reflects the combined effects of the inflation premium and the risk premium. However, it is unclear how much of the total premium is caused by an inflation premium and how much is caused by a risk premium. Figure 9.9 shows how nominal interest rates can be separated into the real interest rate, the inflation premium, and the interest rate risk premium.

FIGURE 9.9 The Term Structure of Interest Rates

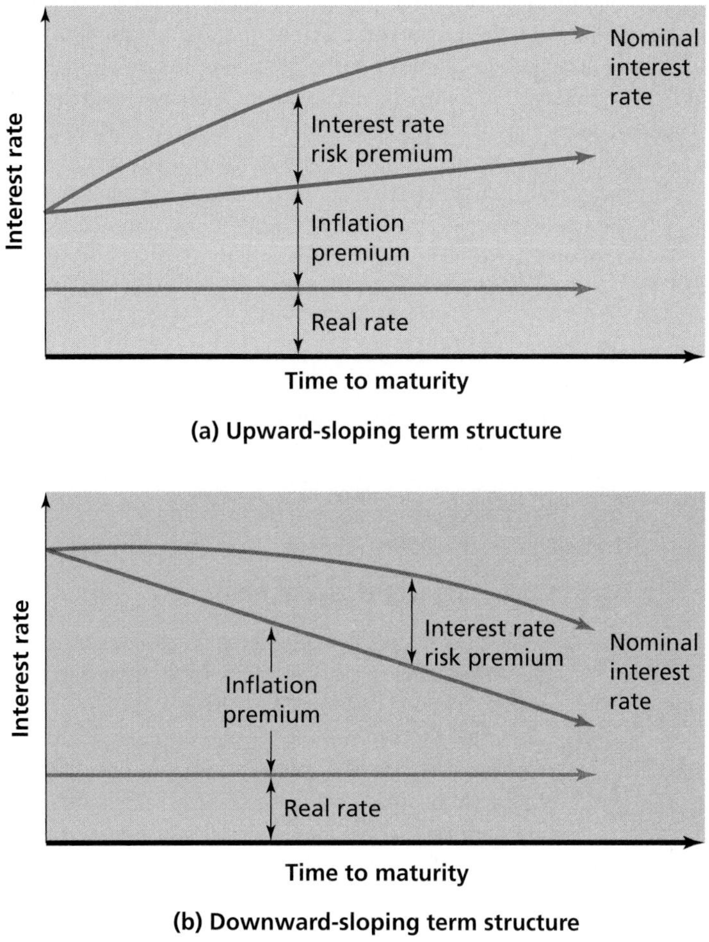

LIQUIDITY AND DEFAULT RISK

Thus far we have examined the components of interest rates on default-free, highly liquid securities such as Treasury STRIPS. We now expand our coverage to securities that are less liquid, not default-free, or both, to present a more detailed decomposition of nominal interest rates. When we are finished, what we will see is that nominal interest rates for individual securities can be decomposed into five basic components as follows:

$$\text{NI} = \text{RI} + \text{IP} + \text{RP} + \text{LP} + \text{DP} \tag{9.13}$$

where: NI = Nominal interest rate
RI = Real interest rate
IP = Inflation premium
RP = Interest rate risk premium
LP = Liquidity premium
DP = Default premium

We have already discussed the first three components of the nominal interest rate. We now consider the two new ones on our list, the default and liquidity premiums.

The *liquidity premium* (LP) is a reflection of the fact that two otherwise identical securities may have very different degrees of liquidity. All else the same, the one with less liquidity would have to offer a higher yield as compensation.

The fifth, and final, component of a nominal interest rate is a *default premium* (DP). Investors demand a default premium to assume the risk of holding a security that might default on its promised payments. Naturally, the greater is the risk of default for a particular bond issue, the larger is the default premium required by investors. The topic of default risk is discussed in detail for corporate bonds and municipal bonds in later chapters.

In addition to the five basic components we have discussed, there is one more important determinant of nominal interest rates, namely, tax status. As we briefly discussed in an earlier chapter, municipal bonds are not taxed at the federal level, but all other bonds are (including Treasury bonds). All else the same, taxable bonds must pay higher rates than nontaxable bonds. As a result, the rate on a high-quality municipal issue will normally be less than the rate on a Treasury issue, even though the Treasury is more liquid and has no default risk.

9.8 Summary and Conclusions

The time value of money is arguably the most important principle of finance. Interest rates are a convenient way to measure and state the time value of money. Furthermore, understanding interest rates is essential for understanding money market and fixed-income securities. This chapter covers many topics relating to interest rates. They are grouped here by the learning objectives of the chapter.

1. Money market prices and rates.

A. Money market is the name of the financial market for short-term borrowing and lending. In the money market, the borrowing and lending period is generally less than a year.

B. Important short-term money market rates include the prime rate, the Federal funds rate, and the Federal Reserve's discount rate. The prime rate is a bellwether of bank lending to business, while the Federal funds rate and the Federal Reserve's discount rate are indicators of the availability of money and credit within the banking system.

2. Rates and yields on fixed-income securities.

A. Fixed-income securities promise a regular payment during the life of the security. In addition, most fixed-income securities also promise a lump sum payment at the end of the life of the security. Generally, when they are issued, fixed-income securities have a life ranging from 2 to 30 years.

B. The Treasury yield curve plots the relationship between yields on U.S. Treasury securities and their maturities. The Treasury yield curve is fundamental to bond market analysis because it represents the interest rates that financial markets are charging to the world's largest debtor with the world's highest credit rating—the U.S. government.

3. Treasury STRIPS and the term structure of interest rates.

A. The term structure of interest rates is the fundamental relationship between time to maturity and interest rates for default-free, pure discount instruments such as U.S. Treasury STRIPS.

B. A number of different theories—including the expectations theory, the maturity preference theory, and the market segmentation theory—have been proposed to explain why the term structure of interest rates and yield curves may be upward sloping at one point in time and then downward sloping or flat at another time. In a modern view of the term structure, yields on default-free, pure discount bonds are determined by the real rate of interest, expectations of future inflation, and an interest rate risk premium.

4. Nominal versus real interest rates.

A. Nominal interest rates are interest rates that we ordinarily observe. Nominal interest rates have five basic components: the real rate, an inflation premium, an interest rate risk premium, a liquidity premium, and a default premium. The real interest rate is the nominal interest rate adjusted for the effects of inflation.

B. U.S. Treasury securities are free of default risk and are generally free from liquidity risk. For other debt issues, however, these two nominal interest rate components are very important.

C. When nominal interest rates change, long-term bond prices change more than short-term bonds. Put differently, long-term bond prices are much more sensitive to interest rate changes than are short-term bonds. This difference in price changes is called interest rate risk.

D. The liquidity premium reflects the fact that two otherwise identical securities could have very different degrees of liquidity. All else the same, the one with less liquidity would have to offer a higher yield as compensation. The fifth component of a nominal interest rate, the default premium, reflects the extra yield that investors demand to assume the risk of holding a security that might default on its promised payments.

GET REAL

This chapter covered the essentials of interest rates. How should you, as an investor or investment manager, put this information to work?

The best thing to do is to buy a variety of instruments discussed in this chapter. STRIPS, in particular, are an important investment vehicle for both institutional and individual investors. To gain some practical experience with the risks and rewards from STRIPS investing, you should invest equal dollar amounts in several different STRIPS with different maturities. Pick short-term (a few years), intermediate-term (10 or so years), and long-term (25 years or longer), for example. Once you make these investments, monitor their yields and prices.

A good place to start with a study of interest rates is to visit some federal government Web sites. Try the U.S. Treasury (www.ustreas.gov), the Bureau of Public Debt (www.publicdebt.treas.gov), the Federal Reserve Board of Governors (www.federalreserve.gov), and the New York (www.ny.frb.org) and St. Louis (www.stls.frb.org) Federal Reserve banks. For the latest money market rates see Money Rates (www.money-rates.com), and for bank lending rates check out Banx (www.banx.com) or Bankrate (www.bankrate.com). Price and yield data for U.S. Treasury securities can be found at CNN (money.cnn.com).

Key Terms

bank discount basis 283
banker's acceptance 282
basis point 283
bellwether rate 280
call money rate 280
certificate of deposit (CD) 282
commercial paper 280
discount rate 280
Eurodollars 282
expectations theory 301
Federal funds rate 280
Fisher hypothesis 297
forward rate 301
London Interbank Offered Rate (LIBOR) 282
market segmentation theory 303
maturity preference theory 302
nominal interest rates 297
prime rate 280
pure discount security 283
real interest rates 297
term structure of interest rates 294
Treasury yield curve 290
U.S. Treasury bill (T-bill) 282
U.S. Treasury STRIPS 294

Chapter Review Problems and Self-Test

1. **Money Market Prices** The rate on a particular money market instrument, quoted on a discount basis, is 5 percent. The instrument has a face value of \$100,000 and will mature in 40 days. What is its price?
2. **Bond Equivalent Yields** Suppose a T-bill has 75 days to maturity and an asked discount of 4 percent. What is the bond equivalent yield?

Answers to Self-Test Problems

1. Using the bank discount basis formula, we have:

$$\text{Current price} = \text{Face value} \times \left(1 - \frac{\text{Days to maturity}}{360} \times \text{Discount yield}\right)$$

$$\$99{,}444.44 = \$100{,}000 \times \left(1 - \frac{40}{360} \times .05\right)$$

You would pay \$99,444.44.

2. Using the bond equivalent yield conversion formula, we have:

$$4.09\% = \frac{365 \times .04}{360 - 75 \times .04}$$

The bond equivalent yield is thus 4.09 percent.

Test Your Investment Quotient

For the remaining questions and problems, the circled numbers in the margin refer to the corresponding learning objective in this chapter.

IQ

(2) 1. **Interest Rates** Which of the following interest rates is a bellwether (leading indicator) rate of bank lending to business?
   - **a.** Unsecured business loan rate.
   - **b.** Prime rate.
   - **c.** Commercial paper rate.
   - **d.** Banker's acceptance rate.

(2) 2. **Interest Rates** Among the following interest rates, which is normally the highest rate?
   - **a.** Commercial paper rate.
   - **b.** U.S. Treasury bill rate.
   - **c.** Federal funds rate.
   - **d.** Federal Reserve discount rate.

(1) 3. **T-Bill Yields** A U.S. Treasury bill with 180 days to maturity has a discount yield of 5 percent and a face value of \$100,000. What is its current price?
   - **a.** \$97,500
   - **b.** \$95,000
   - **c.** \$92,500
   - **d.** \$90,000

(1) 4. **T-Bill Yields** A U.S. Treasury bill with 90 days to maturity has a price of \$95,000. What is its discount yield?
   - **a.** 5 percent
   - **b.** 10 percent
   - **c.** 15 percent
   - **d.** 20 percent

CFA® PROBLEMS

(1) 5. **T-Bill Yields** A 30-day U.S. Treasury bill is selling at a 12 percent yield on a discount basis. Which of the following is the approximate bond equivalent yield?
   - **a.** 6.0 percent
   - **b.** 11.7 percent
   - **c.** 12.0 percent
   - **d.** 12.3 percent

2 **6. Effective Annual Rates** A credit card company states an annual percentage rate (APR) of 12 percent, which is actually a rate of 1 percent per month. What is the EAR?

a. 12 percent
b. 12.68 percent
c. 13.08 percent
d. 13.76 percent

3 **7. STRIPS Yields** A U.S. Treasury STRIPS maturing in 10 years has a current price of $502.57 for $1,000 of face value. What is the yield to maturity of this STRIPS?

a. 7.0 percent
b. 7.12 percent
c. 8.0 percent
d. 8.12 percent

3 **8. STRIPS Yields** A U.S. Treasury STRIPS with $1,000 face value maturing in five years has a yield to maturity of 7 percent. What is the current price of this STRIPS?

a. $930
b. $712.99
c. $708.92
d. $650

CFA® PROBLEMS

2 **9. Bond Yields** An analyst finds that the semiannual interest rate that equates the present value of the bond's cash flow to its current market price is 3.85 percent. Consider the following possible alternatives:

I. The bond equivalent yield on this security is 7.70 percent.
II. The effective annual yield on the bond is 7.85 percent.
III. The bond's yield-to-maturity is 7.70 percent.
IV. The bond's horizon return is 8.35 percent.

Which of these alternatives are true?

a. I and II only
b. II, III, and IV only
c. I, II, and III only
d. III only

CFA® PROBLEMS

3 **10. Forward Rates** An analyst gathered the following spot rates:

Time (years)	Annual Spot Rate
1	15.0%
2	12.5
3	10.0
4	7.5

The one-year forward rate two years from now is closest to

a. −4.91 percent
b. 5.17 percent
c. 10.05 percent
d. 7.5 percent

CFA® PROBLEMS

2 **11. Zeroes** If an investor's required return is 12 percent, the value of a 10-year maturity zero coupon bond with a maturity value of $1,000 is closest to:

a. $312
b. $688
c. $1,000
d. $1,312

4 **12. Fisher Hypothesis** The Fisher hypothesis essentially asserts which of the following?

a. Nominal interest rates follow inflation.
b. Real interest rates follow inflation.
c. Inflation follows real interest rates.
d. Inflation follows nominal interest rates.

CFA® PROBLEMS

(3) **13. Term Structure Theory** Which one of the following statements about the term structure of interest rates is true?

a. The expectations hypothesis indicates a flat yield curve if anticipated future short-term rates exceed current short-term rates.
b. The expectations hypothesis contends that the long-term rate is equal to the anticipated short-term rate.
c. The liquidity premium theory indicates that, all else being equal, longer maturities will have lower yields.
d. The market segmentation theory contends that borrowers and lenders prefer particular segments of the yield curve.

CFA® PROBLEMS

(3) **14. Term Structure Theory** Which one of the following is not an explanation of the relationship between a bond's interest rate and its term to maturity?

a. Default (credit) risk hypothesis
b. Expectations hypothesis
c. Liquidity preference hypothesis
d. Segmentation hypothesis

CFA® PROBLEMS

(3) **15. Term Structure Theory** Which theory explains the shape of the yield curve by considering the relative demands for various maturities?

a. Relative strength theory
b. Segmentation theory
c. Unbiased expectations theory
d. Liquidity premium theory

CFA® PROBLEMS

(3) **16. Term Structure Theory** The concepts of spot and forward rates are most closely associated with which one of the following explanations of the term structure of interest rates?

a. Expectations hypothesis
b. Liquidity premium theory
c. Preferred habitat hypothesis
d. Segmented market theory

(3) **17. Forward Rates** The current one-year interest rate is 6 percent and the current two-year interest rate is 7 percent. What is the implied forward rate for next year's one-year rate?

a. 9 percent
b. 8 percent
c. 7 percent
d. 6 percent

(3) **18. Forward Rates** The current one-year interest rate is 7 percent and the current two-year interest rate is 6 percent. What is the implied forward rate for next year's one-year rate?

a. 7 percent
b. 6 percent
c. 5 percent
d. 4 percent

CFA® PROBLEMS

(3) **19. Forward Rates** The 6-month Treasury bill spot rate is 4 percent, and the 1-year Treasury bill spot rate is 5 percent. The implied 6-month forward rate 6 months from now is which of the following?

a. 3.0 percent
b. 4.5 percent
c. 5.5 percent
d. 5.9 percent

CFA® PROBLEMS

(3) **20. Forward Rates** An analyst gathers the following information:

Years to Maturity	Spot Rate
1	5.00%
2	6.00
3	6.50

Based on the data above, the one-year implied forward rate two years from now is *closest* to:

a. 6.25 percent
b. 7.01 percent
c. 7.26 percent
d. 7.51 percent

Concept Questions

(2) 1. **Interest Rate History** Based on the history of interest rates, what is the range of short-term rates that has occurred in the United States? The range of long-term rates? What is a typical value for each?

(1) 2. **Discount Securities** What are pure discount securities? Give two examples.

(1) 3. **Fed Funds versus the Discount Rate** Compare and contrast the Fed funds rate and the discount rate. Which do you think is more volatile? Which market do you think is more active? Why?

(1) 4. **Commercial Paper** Compare and contrast commercial paper and Treasury bills. Which would typically offer a higher interest rate? Why?

(1) 5. **LIBOR** What is LIBOR? Why is it important?

(1) 6. **Bank Discount Rates** Why do you suppose rates on some money market instruments are quoted on a bank discount basis? (*Hint:* Why use a 360-day year?)

(3) 7. **STRIPS** What are the three different types of Treasury STRIPS that are publicly traded?

(4) 8. **Nominal and Real Rates** When we observe interest rates in the financial press, do we see nominal or real rates? Which are more relevant to investors?

(2) 9. **Munis versus Treasuries** Which would have a higher yield, a municipal bond or a Treasury bond of the same maturity?

CFA® PROBLEMS

(4) 10. **Term Structure** Discuss how each of the following theories for the term structure of interest rates could account for a downward-sloping term structure of interest rates:

a. Pure expectations
b. Liquidity preference
c. Market segmentation

Questions and Problems

Core Questions

1. **STRIPS** What is the price of a Treasury STRIPS with a face value of $100 that matures in 5 years and has a yield to maturity of 4.9 percent?

2. **STRIPS** A Treasury STRIPS matures in 8.5 years and has a yield to maturity of 6.5 percent. If the par value is $100,000, what is the price of the STRIPS? What is the quoted price?

3. **STRIPS** A Treasury STRIPS is quoted at 81.265 and has four years until maturity. What is the yield to maturity?

4. **STRIPS** What is the yield to maturity on a Treasury STRIPS with 12 years to maturity and a quoted price of 50.873?

(4) 5. **Fisher Effect** A stock had a return of 11.7 percent last year. If the inflation rate was 3.4 percent, what was the approximate real return?

(4) 6. **Fisher Effect** Your investments increased in value by 13.4 percent last year but your purchasing power increased by only 9.1 percent. What was the inflation rate?

(1) 7. **Treasury Bill Prices** What is the price of a U.S. Treasury bill with 43 days to maturity quoted at a discount yield of 3.84 percent? Assume a $1 million face value.

(1) 8. **Treasury Bill Prices** In the previous problem, what is the bond-equivalent yield?

(1) 9. **Treasury Bill Prices** How much would you pay for a U.S. Treasury bill with 94 days to maturity quoted at a discount yield of 4.93 percent? Assume a $1 million face value.

(1) 10. **Treasury Bill Prices** In the previous problem, what is the bond-equivalent yield?

Intermediate Questions

11. Treasury Bills A Treasury bill with 41 days to maturity is quoted at 99.515. What is the bank discount yield, the bond equivalent yield, and the effective annual return?

12. Treasury Bills A Treasury bill purchased in December 2011 has 61 days until maturity and a bank discount yield of 4.37 percent. What is the price of the bill as a percentage of face value? What is the bond equivalent yield?

13. Money Market Prices The treasurer of a large corporation wants to invest $20 million in excess short-term cash in a particular money market investment. The prospectus quotes the instrument at a true yield of 5.93 percent; that is, the EAR for this investment is 5.93 percent. However, the treasurer wants to know the money market yield on this instrument to make it comparable to the T-bills and CDs she has already bought. If the term of the instrument is 110 days, what are the bond-equivalent and discount yields on this investment?

Use the following information to answer the next six questions:

U.S. Treasury STRIPS, close of business February 15, 2008:

Maturity	Price	Maturity	Price
Feb 09	97.100	Feb 12	85.184
Feb 10	93.875	Feb 13	80.358
Feb 11	90.123	Feb 14	73.981

3 **14. Treasury STRIPS** Calculate the quoted yield for each of the STRIPS given in the table above. Does the market expect interest rates to go up or down in the future?

3 **15. Treasury STRIPS** What is the yield of the two-year STRIPS expressed as an EAR?

3 **16. Forward Interest Rates** According to the pure expectations theory of interest rates, how much do you expect to pay for a one-year STRIPS on February 15, 2009? What is the corresponding implied forward rate? How does your answer compare to the current yield on a one-year STRIPS? What does this tell you about the relationship between implied forward rates, the shape of the zero coupon yield curve, and market expectations about future spot interest rates?

3 **17. Forward Interest Rates** According to the pure expectations theory of interest rates, how much do you expect to pay for a five-year STRIPS on February 15, 2009? How much do you expect to pay for a two-year STRIPS on February 15, 2011?

3 **18. Forward Interest Rates** This problem is a little harder. Suppose the term structure is set according to pure expectations and the maturity preference theory. To be specific, investors require no compensation for holding investments with a maturity of one year, but they demand a premium of .30 percent for holding investments with a maturity of two years. Given this information, how much would you pay for a one-year STRIPS on February 15, 2009? What is the corresponding implied forward rate? Compare your answer to the solutions you found in Problem 16. What does this tell you about the effect of a maturity premium on implied forward rates?

3 **19. Bond Price Changes** Suppose the (quoted) yield on each of the six STRIPS increases by .25 percent. Calculate the percentage change in price for the one-year, three-year, and six-year STRIPS. Which one has the largest price change? Now suppose that the quoted price on each STRIPS decreases by .500. Calculate the percentage change in (quoted) yield for the one-year, three-year, and six-year STRIPS. Which one has the largest yield change? What do your answers tell you about the relationship between prices, yields, and maturity for discount bonds?

3 **20. Inflation and Returns** You observe that the current interest rate on short-term U.S. Treasury bills is 4.76 percent. You also read in the newspaper that the GDP deflator, which is a common macroeconomic indicator used by market analysts to gauge the inflation rate, currently implies that inflation is 3.3 percent. Given this information, what is the approximate real rate of interest on short-term Treasury bills? Is it likely that your answer would change if you used some alternative measure for the inflation rate, such as the CPI? What does this tell you about the observability and accuracy of real interest rates compared to nominal interest rates?

3 **21. Forward Interest Rates** Consider the following spot interest rates for maturities of one, two, three, and four years.

$r_1 = 5.1\%$ $r_2 = 5.8\%$ $r_3 = 6.3\%$ $r_4 = 7.3\%$

What are the following forward rates, where $f_{1,k}$ refers to a forward rate for the period beginning in one year and extending for k years?

$$f_{1,1} = \qquad ; \; f_{1,2} = \qquad ; \; f_{1,3} =$$

Hint: Use the equation $(1 + r_1)(1 + f_{1,k})^k = (1 + r_{k+1})^{k+1}$ to solve for $f_{1,k}$.

3 **22. Forward Interest Rates** Based on the spot interest rates in the previous question, what are the following forward rates, where $f_{k,1}$ refers to a forward rate beginning in k years and extending for 1 year?

$$f_{2,1} = \qquad ; \; f_{3,1} =$$

Hint: Use the equation $(1 + r_k)^k(1 + f_{k,1}) = (1 + r_{k+1})^{k+1}$ to solve for $f_{k,1}$.

4 **23. Expected Inflation Rates** Based on the spot rates in Question 21, and assuming a constant real interest rate of 2 percent, what are the expected inflation rates for the next four years?

Hint: Use the Fisher hypothesis and the unbiased expectations theory.

Spreadsheet Problems

1 **24. Treasury Bills** A Treasury bill that settles on July 17, 2008, pays \$100,000 on August 21, 2008. Assuming a discount rate of 3.98 percent, what is the price and bond equivalent yield?

2 **25. Effective Annual Rate** You have a car loan with a nominal rate of 6.85 percent. With interest charged monthly, what is the effective annual rate (EAR) on this loan?

What's on the Web?

1. **Yield Curve** What is the shape of the Treasury yield curve today? Go to www.bloomberg.com and find out. Is the yield curve upward sloping or downward sloping? According to the expectations theory, are interest rates in the future expected to be higher or lower than they are today?
2. **STRIPS** Go to www.treasurydirect.gov and search the site for STRIPS to find information on Treasury STRIPS. Answer the following questions: Which Treasury securities are eligible to be stripped? What are minimum par amounts for stripping? How do I buy STRIPS? Why do investors hold STRIPS?
3. **STRIPS** Go to www.bondsonline.com and find the quotes for STRIPS that are offered for sale on the site. How many STRIPS are offered for sale? What is the lowest and highest yield to maturity? Are there STRIPS with the same maturity that have different prices? How could this happen?

CHAPTER 10

Bond Prices and Yields

"More money has been lost reaching for yield than at the point of a gun."

–Raymond Devoe

Learning Objectives

Singing "The Bonds Song"[1] will help you learn:

1. How to calculate bond prices and yields.
2. The importance of yield to maturity.
3. Interest rate risk and Malkiel's theorems.
4. How to measure the impact of interest rate changes on bond prices.

Interest rates go up and bond prices go down. But which bonds go down the most and which go down the least? Interest rates go down and bond prices go up. But which bonds go up the most and which go up the least? For bond portfolio managers, these are important questions about interest rate risk. For anyone managing a bond portfolio, an understanding of interest rate risk rests on an understanding of the relationship between bond prices and yields. ■

In the preceding chapter on interest rates, we introduced the subject of bond yields. As we promised there, we now return to this subject and discuss bond prices and yields in some detail. We first describe how bond yields are determined and how they are interpreted. We then go on to examine what happens to bond prices as yields change. Finally, once we have a good understanding of the relation between bond prices and yields, we examine some of the fundamental tools of bond risk analysis used by fixed-income portfolio managers.

[1] *Lyrics for "The Bonds Song": "BONDS!, bonds, bonds, bonds, BONDS!, bonds, bonds, bonds, etc."*

10.1 Bond Basics

A bond essentially is a security that offers the investor a series of fixed interest payments during its life, along with a fixed payment of principal when it matures. So long as the bond issuer does not default, the schedule of payments does not change. When originally issued, bonds normally have maturities ranging from 2 years to 30 years, but bonds with maturities of 50 or 100 years also exist. Bonds issued with maturities of less than 10 years are usually called notes. A very small number of bond issues have no stated maturity, and these are referred to as perpetuities or consols.

STRAIGHT BONDS

The most common type of bond is the so-called straight bond. By definition, a straight bond is an IOU that obligates the issuer to pay the bondholder a fixed sum of money at the bond's maturity along with constant, periodic interest payments during the life of the bond. The fixed sum paid at maturity is referred to as bond principal, par value, stated value, or face value. The periodic interest payments are called coupons. Perhaps the best example of straight bonds are U.S. Treasury bonds issued by the federal government to finance the national debt. However, corporations and municipal governments also routinely issue debt in the form of straight bonds.

WWW

Check out the fixed income section at www.sifma.org

In addition to a straight bond component, many bonds have additional special features. These features are sometimes designed to enhance a bond's appeal to investors. For example, convertible bonds have a conversion feature that grants bondholders the right to convert their bonds into shares of common stock of the issuing corporation. As another example, "putable" bonds have a put feature that grants bondholders the right to sell their bonds back to the issuer at a special put price.

These and other special features are attached to many bond issues, but we defer discussion of special bond features until later chapters. For now, it is only important to know that when a bond is issued with one or more special features, strictly speaking, it is no longer a straight bond. However, bonds with attached special features will normally have a straight bond component, namely, the periodic coupon payments and fixed principal payment at maturity. For this reason, straight bonds are important as the basic unit of bond analysis.

The prototypical example of a straight bond pays a series of constant semiannual coupons, along with a face value of \$1,000 payable at maturity. This example is used in this chapter because it is common and realistic. For example, most corporate bonds are sold with a face value of \$1,000 per bond, and most bonds (in the United States at least) pay constant semiannual coupons.

COUPON RATE AND CURRENT YIELD

A familiarity with bond yield measures is important for understanding the financial characteristics of bonds. As we briefly discussed in Chapter 3, two basic yield measures for a bond are its coupon rate and current yield.

coupon rate
A bond's annual coupon divided by its par value. Also called *coupon yield* or *nominal yield.*

A bond's **coupon rate** is defined as its annual coupon amount divided by its par value, or, in other words, its annual coupon expressed as a percentage of face value:

$$\text{Coupon rate} = \frac{\text{Annual coupon}}{\text{Par value}} \tag{10.1}$$

For example, suppose a \$1,000 par value bond pays semiannual coupons of \$40. The annual coupon is then \$80, and, stated as a percentage of par value, the bond's coupon rate is \$80/\$1,000 = 8%. A coupon rate is often referred to as the *coupon yield* or the *nominal yield.* Notice that the word "nominal" here has nothing to do with inflation.

current yield
A bond's annual coupon divided by its market price.

A bond's **current yield** is its annual coupon payment divided by its current market price:

$$\text{Current yield} = \frac{\text{Annual coupon}}{\text{Bond price}} \tag{10.2}$$

For example, suppose a \$1,000 par value bond paying an \$80 annual coupon has a price of \$1,032.25. The current yield is \$80/\$1,032.25 = 7.75%. Similarly, a price of \$969.75

implies a current yield of \$80/\$969.75 = 8.25%. Notice that whenever there is a change in the bond's price, the coupon rate remains constant. However, a bond's current yield is inversely related to its price, and it changes whenever the bond's price changes.

CHECK THIS

10.1a What is a straight bond?

10.1b What is a bond's coupon rate? Its current yield?

10.2 Straight Bond Prices and Yield to Maturity

yield to maturity (YTM) The discount rate that equates a bond's price with the present value of its future cash flows. Also called *promised yield* or just *yield*.

The single most important yield measure for a bond is its **yield to maturity**, commonly abbreviated as **YTM**. By definition, a bond's yield to maturity is the discount rate that equates the bond's price with the computed present value of its future cash flows. A bond's yield to maturity is sometimes called its *promised yield*, but, more commonly, the yield to maturity of a bond is simply referred to as its *yield*. In general, if the term "yield" is being used with no qualification, it means yield to maturity.

STRAIGHT BOND PRICES

For straight bonds, the following standard formula is used to calculate a bond's price given its yield:

$$\text{Bond price} = \frac{C/2}{YTM/2}\left[1 - \frac{1}{(1 + YTM/2)^{2M}}\right] + \frac{FV}{(1 + YTM/2)^{2M}}$$

This formula can be simplified just a bit as follows:

$$\text{Bond price} = \frac{C}{YTM}\left[1 - \frac{1}{(1 + YTM/2)^{2M}}\right] + \frac{FV}{(1 + YTM/2)^{2M}} \qquad \textbf{(10.3)}$$

where: C = Annual coupon, the sum of two semiannual coupons
FV = Face Value
M = Maturity in years
YTM = Yield to maturity

In this formula, the coupon used is the annual coupon, which is the sum of the two semiannual coupons. As discussed in our previous chapter for U.S. Treasury STRIPS, the yield on a bond is an annual percentage rate (APR), calculated as twice the true semiannual yield. As a result, the yield on a bond somewhat understates its effective annual rate (EAR).

The straight bond pricing formula has two separate components. The first component is the present value of all the coupon payments. Since the coupons are fixed and paid on a regular basis, you may recognize that they form an ordinary annuity, and the first piece of the bond pricing formula is a standard calculation for the present value of an annuity. The other component represents the present value of the principal payment at maturity, and it is a standard calculation for the present value of a single lump sum.

Calculating bond prices is mostly "plug and chug" with a calculator. In fact, a good financial calculator or spreadsheet should have this formula built into it. In any case, we will work through a few examples the long way just to illustrate the calculations.

Suppose a bond has a \$1,000 face value, 20 years to maturity, an 8 percent coupon rate, and a yield of 9 percent. What's the price? Using the straight bond pricing formula, the price of this bond is calculated as follows:

1. Present value of semiannual coupons:

$$\frac{\$80}{.09}\left[1 - \frac{1}{(1.045)^{40}}\right] = \$736.06337$$

2. Present value of $1,000 principal:

$$\frac{\$1{,}000}{(1.045)^{40}} = \$171.92871$$

The price of the bond is the sum of the present values of coupons and principal:

$$\text{Bond price} = \$736.06 + \$171.93 = \$907.99$$

So, this bond sells for $907.99.

EXAMPLE 10.1

Calculating Straight Bond Prices

Suppose a bond has 20 years to maturity and a coupon rate of 8 percent. The bond's yield to maturity is 7 percent. What's the price?

In this case, the coupon rate is 8 percent and the face value is $1,000, so the annual coupon is $80. The bond's price is calculated as follows:

1. Present value of semiannual coupons:

$$\frac{\$80}{.07}\left[1 - \frac{1}{(1.035)^{40}}\right] = \$854.20289$$

2. Present value of $1,000 principal:

$$\frac{\$1{,}000}{(1.035)^{40}} = \$252.57247$$

The bond's price is the sum of coupon and principal present values:

$$\text{Bond price} = \$854.20 + \$252.57 = \$1{,}106.77$$

This bond sells for $1,106.77.

Straight bond prices may be calculated using a built-in spreadsheet function. An example of how to use an Excel™ spreadsheet to calculate a bond price is shown in the nearby *Spreadsheet Analysis* box.

SPREADSHEET ANALYSIS

	A	B	C	D	E	F	G	H
1								
2		**Calculating the Price of a Coupon Bond**						
3								
4	A Treasury bond traded on March 30, 2008 matures in 20 years on March 30, 2028.							
5	Assuming an 8 percent coupon rate and a 7 percent yield to maturity, what is the							
6	price of this bond?							
7	Hint: Use the Excel function PRICE.							
8								
9		$110.6775	= PRICE("3/30/2008","3/30/2028",0.08,0.07,100,2,3)					
10								
11	For a bond with $1,000 face value, multiply the price by 10 to get $1,106.78.							
12								
13	This function uses the following arguments:							
14								
15		=PRICE("Now","Maturity", Coupon,Yield,100,2,3)						
16								
17	The 100 indicates redemption value as a percent of face value.							
18	The 2 indicates semi-annual coupons.							
19	The 3 specifies an actual day count with 365 days per year.							
20								
21								

PREMIUM AND DISCOUNT BONDS

Bonds are commonly distinguished according to whether they are selling at par value or at a discount or premium relative to par value. These three relative price descriptions—premium, discount, and par bonds—are defined as follows:

1. **Premium bonds:** Bonds with a price greater than par value are said to be selling at a premium. The yield to maturity of a premium bond is less than its coupon rate.
2. **Discount bonds:** Bonds with a price less than par value are said to be selling at a discount. The yield to maturity of a discount bond is greater than its coupon rate.
3. **Par bonds:** Bonds with a price equal to par value are said to be selling at par. The yield to maturity of a par bond is equal to its coupon rate.

The important thing to notice is that whether a bond sells at a premium or discount depends on the relation between its coupon rate and its yield. If the coupon rate exceeds the yield, the bond will sell at a premium. If the coupon is less than the yield, the bond will sell at a discount.

EXAMPLE 10.2 **Premium and Discount Bonds**

Consider two bonds, both with eight years to maturity and a 7 percent coupon. One bond has a yield to maturity of 5 percent while the other has a yield to maturity of 9 percent. Which of these bonds is selling at a premium and which is selling at a discount? Verify your answer by calculating each bond's price.

For the bond with a 9 percent yield to maturity, the coupon rate of 7 percent is less than the yield, indicating a discount bond. The bond's price is calculated as follows:

$$\frac{\$70}{.09}\left[1-\frac{1}{(1.045)^{16}}\right]+\frac{\$1{,}000}{(1.045)^{16}}=\$887.66$$

For the bond with a 5 percent yield to maturity, the coupon rate of 7 percent is greater than the yield, indicating a premium bond. The bond's price is calculated as follows:

$$\frac{\$70}{.05}\left[1-\frac{1}{(1.025)^{16}}\right]+\frac{\$1{,}000}{(1.025)^{16}}=\$1{,}130.55$$

The relationship between bond prices and bond maturities for premium and discount bonds is graphically illustrated in Figure 10.1 for bonds with an 8 percent coupon rate. The vertical axis measures bond prices, and the horizontal axis measures bond maturities.

Figure 10.1 also describes the paths of premium and discount bond prices as their maturities shorten with the passage of time, assuming no changes in yield to maturity. As shown,

FIGURE 10.1 **Premium, Par, and Discount Bond Prices**

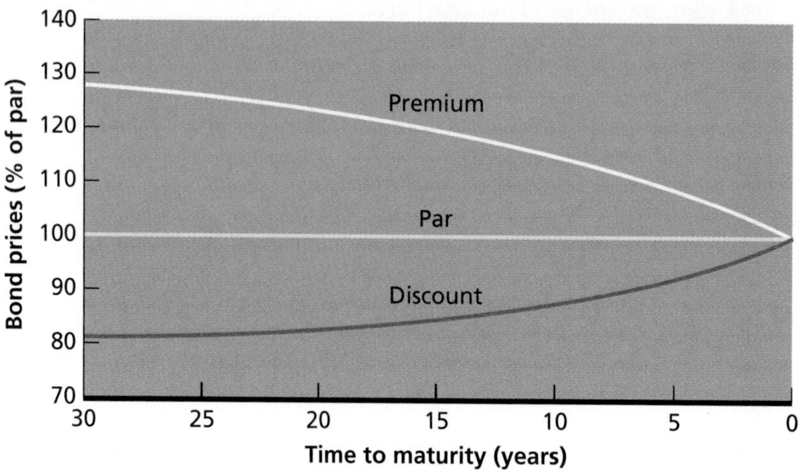

the time paths of premium and discount bond prices follow smooth curves. Over time, the price of a premium bond declines and the price of a discount bond rises. At maturity, the price of each bond converges to its par value.

Figure 10.1 illustrates the general result that, for discount bonds, holding the coupon rate and yield to maturity constant, the longer the term to maturity of the bond the greater is the discount from par value. For premium bonds, holding the coupon rate and yield to maturity constant, the longer the term to maturity of the bond the greater is the premium over par value.

EXAMPLE 10.3

Premium Bonds

Consider two bonds, both with a 9 percent coupon rate and the same yield to maturity of 7 percent, but with different maturities of 5 and 10 years. Which has the higher price? Verify your answer by calculating the prices.

First, because both bonds have a 9 percent coupon and a 7 percent yield, both bonds sell at a premium. Based on what we know, the one with the longer maturity will have a higher price. We can check these conclusions by calculating the prices as follows:

5-year maturity premium bond price:

$$\frac{\$90}{.07}\left[1 - \frac{1}{(1.035)^{10}}\right] + \frac{\$1,000}{(1.035)^{10}} = \$1,083.17$$

10-year maturity premium bond price:

$$\frac{\$90}{.07}\left[1 - \frac{1}{(1.035)^{20}}\right] + \frac{\$1,000}{(1.035)^{20}} = \$1,142.12$$

Notice that the longer maturity premium bond has a higher price, as we predicted.

EXAMPLE 10.4

Discount Bonds

Now consider two bonds, both with a 9 percent coupon rate and the same yield to maturity of 11 percent, but with different maturities of 5 and 10 years. Which has the higher price? Verify your answer by calculating the prices.

These are both discount bonds. (Why?) The one with the shorter maturity will have a higher price. To check, the prices can be calculated as follows:

5-year maturity discount bond price:

$$\frac{\$90}{.11}\left[1 - \frac{1}{(1.055)^{10}}\right] + \frac{\$1,000}{(1.055)^{10}} = \$924.62$$

10-year maturity discount bond price:

$$\frac{\$90}{.11}\left[1 - \frac{1}{(1.055)^{20}}\right] + \frac{\$1,000}{(1.055)^{20}} = \$880.50$$

In this case, the shorter maturity discount bond has the higher price.

RELATIONSHIPS AMONG YIELD MEASURES

We have discussed three different bond rates or yields in this chapter—the coupon rate, the current yield, and the yield to maturity. We've seen the relationship between coupon rates and yields for discount and premium bonds. We can extend this to include current yields by simply noting that the current yield is always between the coupon rate and the yield to maturity (unless the bond is selling at par, in which case all three are equal).

Putting together our observations about yield measures, we have the following:

Premium bonds:	Coupon rate > Current yield > Yield to maturity
Discount bonds:	Coupon rate < Current yield < Yield to maturity
Par value bonds:	Coupon rate = Current yield = Yield to maturity

Thus, when a premium bond and a discount bond both have the same yield to maturity, the premium bond has a higher current yield than the discount bond. However, as shown in Figure 10.1, the advantage of a high current yield for a premium bond is offset by the fact that the price of a premium bond must ultimately fall to its face value when the bond matures. Similarly, the disadvantage of a low current yield for a discount bond is offset by the fact that the price of a discount bond must ultimately rise to its face value at maturity. For these reasons, current yield is not a reliable guide to what an actual yield will be.

If you wish to get current price and yield information for Treasury note and bond issues, try the Internet. The nearby *Work the Web* box displays a typical search query and the search results from a popular Web site.

A NOTE ON BOND PRICE QUOTES

If you buy a bond between coupon payment dates, the price you pay will usually be more than the price you are quoted. The reason is that standard convention in the bond market is to quote prices net of "accrued interest," meaning that accrued interest is deducted to arrive at the quoted price. This quoted price is called the **clean price**. The price you actually pay, however, includes the accrued interest. This price is the **dirty price**, also known as the "full" or "invoice" price.

clean price
The price of a bond net of accrued interest; this is the price that is typically quoted.

dirty price
The price of a bond including accrued interest, also known as the *full* or *invoice price*. This is the price the buyer actually pays.

An example is the easiest way to understand these issues. Suppose you buy a bond with a 12 percent annual coupon, payable semiannually. You actually pay $1,080 for this bond, so $1,080 is the dirty, or invoice, price. Further, on the day you buy it, the next coupon is due in four months, so you are between coupon dates. Notice that the next coupon will be $60.

The accrued interest on a bond is calculated by taking the fraction of the coupon period that has passed, in this case two months out of six, and multiplying this fraction by the next coupon, $60. So, the accrued interest in this example is 2/6 × $60 = $20. The bond's quoted price (i.e., its clean price) would be $1,080 − $20 = $1,060.[2]

Keep in mind that clean prices and accrued interest are purely a quoting convention. The price that matters to you is the invoice price, because that is what you will actually pay for the bond. The only thing that's important about accrued interest on a bond is that it may impact the taxes you owe on the first coupon you receive.

CHECK THIS

10.2a A straight bond's price has two components. What are they?

10.2b What do you call a bond that sells for more than its face value?

10.2c What is the relationship between a bond's price and its term to maturity when the bond's coupon rate is equal to its yield to maturity?

10.2d Does current yield more strongly overstate yield to maturity for long-maturity or short-maturity premium bonds?

[2] The way accrued interest is calculated actually depends on the type of bond being quoted, for example, Treasury or corporate. The difference has to do with exactly how the fractional coupon period is calculated. In our example just above, we implicitly treated the months as having exactly the same length (i.e., 30 days each, 360 days in a year), which is consistent with the way corporate bonds are quoted. In contrast, for Treasury bonds, actual day counts are used. If you look back at our *Spreadsheet Analysis* exhibit, you'll see that we had to specify this treatment to value our Treasury bond.

WORK THE WEB

Current information on Treasury bond prices and yields is available, among other places, at www.zionsbank.com. After you register, you can make an example query like the one shown below:

Set Criteria			
Bond Type:	Treasury		
Limits	**From:**	**To:**	
Maturity:	2013	2019	☐ Exclude
Coupon:	%	%	☐ Exclude
Yield:	%	%	☐ Exclude
Price:			☐ Exclude
Quantity:			☐ Exclude
Posted Since:	mm/yy	hh:mi	
TIPS	○ Only ○ Include ◉ Exclude		
Callable	○ Only ◉ Include ○ Exclude		
Category:	Bonds		

Sort by: Maturity ☐ Descending Then by: (None) ☐ Descending

100 Bonds per page

Search Clear

	Order	Qty(Min)	Issue	Coupon	Maturity	Price	Yield to Worst	Yield to Mat
☐	Buy	980(1)	T Bond Callable 08/08@100	12.000	08/15/2013	106.85937500	4.074(c)	10.407
☐	Buy	1000(1)	T Bond Callable 05/09@100	13.250	05/15/2014	114.17187500	4.214(c)	10.249
☐	Buy	9000(1)	T Bond Callable 08/09@100	12.500	08/15/2014	115.20312500	4.062(c)	9.444
☐	Buy	9000(1)	T Bond Callable 11/09@100	11.750	11/15/2014	115.57812500	4.073(c)	8.764
☐	Buy	9000(1)	T Bond	11.250	02/15/2015	141.83593750	4.526	4.526
☐	Buy	9000(1)	T Bond	10.625	08/15/2015	139.85937500	4.554	4.554
☐	Buy	9000(1)	T Bond	9.875	11/15/2015	135.66406250	4.577	4.577
☐	Buy	9000(1)	T Bond	9.250	02/15/2016	132.22656250	4.58	4.58
☐	Buy	9000(1)	T Bond	7.250	05/15/2016	118.48437500	4.629	4.629
☐	Buy	9000(1)	T Bond	7.500	11/15/2016	120.82812500	4.673	4.673
☐	Buy	9000(1)	T Bond	8.750	05/15/2017	131.07031250	4.703	4.703
☐	Buy	9000(1)	T Bond	8.875	08/15/2017	132.59375000	4.713	4.713
☐	Buy	9000(1)	T Bond	9.125	05/15/2018	136.11718750	4.759	4.759
☐	Buy	9000(1)	T Bond	9.000	11/15/2018	135.99218750	4.792	4.792
☐	Buy	9000(1)	T Bond	8.875	02/15/2019	135.23437500	4.819	4.819
☐	Buy	9000(1)	T Bond	8.125	08/15/2019	129.39062500	4.844	4.844

(n) Floating/Variable rate - (c) Yield to Call - (p) Yield to Par Call - (w) Yield to Middle Call - (u) Yield to Put - (dis) Discount Yield - (r) Pre-Refund - (t) Mandatory Put - (f) Called in Full

37 hits. 16 returned. Page 1

Notice that four of the bonds have a much higher yield to maturity than the rest. The reason is these bonds are callable, as noted in the "Issue" column. We will have more to say about callable bonds in a later chapter.

10.3 More on Yields

In the previous section, we focused on finding a straight bond's price given its yield. In this section, we reverse direction to find a bond's yield given its price. We then discuss the relationship among the various yield measures we have seen. We finish the section with some additional yield calculations.

Before we begin the process of calculating yields, you should be aware of an important assumption made when yield is calculated. This assumption is that an investor will be able to reinvest the coupon interest payments at a rate equal to the yield to maturity of the bond. Therefore, an investor will earn the bond's yield to maturity only if the investor holds the bond to maturity and if all the coupon interest payments received are reinvested at a rate equal to the bond's yield to maturity. The actual rate earned on the bond can be lower or higher than the yield to maturity—it depends on how long the investor holds the bond and the rate at which the coupon payments are reinvested.

CALCULATING YIELDS

To calculate a bond's yield given its price, we use the same straight bond formula used previously. The only way to find the yield is by trial and error. Financial calculators and spreadsheets do it this way at very high speed.

To illustrate, suppose we have a 6 percent bond with 10 years to maturity. Its price is 90, meaning 90 percent of face value. Assuming a \$1,000 face value, the price is \$900 and the coupon is \$60 per year. What's the yield?

To find out, all we can do is try different yields until we come across the one that produces a price of \$900. However, we can speed things up quite a bit by making an educated guess using what we know about bond prices and yields. We know the yield on this bond is greater than its 6 percent coupon rate because it is a discount bond. So let's first try 8 percent in the straight bond pricing formula:

$$\frac{\$60}{.08}\left[1 - \frac{1}{(1.04)^{20}}\right] + \frac{\$1,000}{(1.04)^{20}} = \$864.10$$

SPREADSHEET ANALYSIS

	A	B	C	D	E	F	G	H
1								
2		**Calculating the Yield to Maturity of a Coupon Bond**						
3								
4	A Treasury bond traded on March 30, 2008 matures in 8 years on March 30, 2016.							
5	Assuming an 8 percent coupon rate and a price of 110, what is this bond's yield							
6	to maturity?							
7	Hint: Use the Excel function YIELD.							
8								
9		6.3843%	= YIELD("3/30/2008","3/30/2016",0.08,110,100,2,3)					
10								
11	This function uses the following arguments:							
12								
13		= YIELD("Now","Maturity",Coupon,Price,100,2,3)						
14								
15	Price is entered as a percent of face value.							
16	The 100 indicates redemption value as a percent of face value.							
17	The 2 indicates semi-annual coupons.							
18	The 3 specifies an actual day count with 365 days per year.							
19								
20								

The price with an 8 percent yield is \$864.10, which is somewhat less than the \$900 price, but not too far off.

To finish, we need to ask whether the 8 percent we used was too high or too low. We know that the higher the yield, the lower is the price, thus 8 percent is a little too high. So let's try 7.5 percent:

$$\frac{\$60}{.075}\left[1-\frac{1}{(1.0375)^{20}}\right]+\frac{\$1{,}000}{(1.0375)^{20}}=\$895.78$$

Now we're very close. We're still a little too high on the yield (since the price is a little low). If you try 7.4 percent, you'll see that the resulting price is \$902.29, so the yield is between 7.4 and 7.5 percent (it's actually 7.435 percent).

EXAMPLE 10.5

Calculating YTM

Suppose a bond has eight years to maturity, a price of 110, and a coupon rate of 8 percent. What is its yield?

This is a premium bond, so its yield is less than the 8 percent coupon. If we try 6 percent, we get (check this) \$1,125.61. The yield is therefore a little bigger than 6 percent. If we try 6.5 percent, we get (check this) \$1,092.43, so the answer is slightly less than 6.5 percent. Check that 6.4 percent is almost exact (the exact yield is 6.3843 percent).

Yields to maturity may be calculated using a built-in spreadsheet function. An example of how to use an Excel™ spreadsheet to calculate a yield to maturity is shown in the nearby *Spreadsheet Analysis* box.

YIELD TO CALL

The discussion in this chapter so far has assumed that a bond will have an actual maturity equal to its originally stated maturity. However, this is not always so since most bonds are **callable bonds**. When a bond issue is callable, the issuer can buy back outstanding bonds before the bonds mature. In exchange, bondholders receive a special **call price**, which is often equal to face value, although it may be slightly higher. When a call price is equal to face value, the bond is said to be *callable at par.*

callable bond
A bond is callable if the issuer can buy it back before it matures.

call price
The price the issuer of a callable bond must pay to buy it back.

make-whole call price
The present value of the bond's remaining cash flows.

When a bond is called, the bondholder does not receive any more coupon payments. Therefore, some callable bonds are issued with a provision known as a **make-whole call price**. The make-whole call price is calculated as the present value of the bond's remaining cash flows. The discount rate used to calculate the present value is often the yield of a comparable maturity treasury bond plus a prespecified premium. The first bonds issued to the investment public with a make-whole call provision were the Quaker State Corporation bonds issued in 1995. Since then, callable bonds issues with make-whole call provisions have become common.

Bonds are called at the convenience of the issuer, and a call usually occurs after a fall in market interest rates allows issuers to refinance outstanding debt with new bonds paying lower coupons. However, an issuer's call privilege is often restricted so that outstanding bonds cannot be called until the end of a specified **call protection period**, also termed a *call deferment period.* As a typical example, a bond issued with a 20-year maturity may be sold to investors subject to the restriction that it is callable anytime after an initial five-year call protection period.

call protection period
The period during which a callable bond cannot be called. Also called a *call deferment period.*

If a bond is callable, its yield to maturity may no longer be a useful number. Instead, the **yield to call**, commonly abbreviated **YTC**, may be more meaningful. Yield to call is a yield measure that assumes a bond issue will be called at its earliest possible call date.

yield to call (YTC)
Measure of return that assumes a bond will be redeemed at the earliest call date.

We calculate a bond's yield to call using the straight bond pricing formula we have been using with two changes. First, instead of time to maturity, we use time to the first possible call date. Second, instead of face value, we use the call price. The resulting formula is thus:

$$\text{Callable bond price} = \frac{C}{YTC}\left[1 - \frac{1}{(1 + YTC/2)^{2T}}\right] + \frac{CP}{(1 + YTC/2)^{2T}} \tag{10.4}$$

where: C = Constant annual coupon
CP = Call price of the bond
T = Time in years until earliest possible call date
YTC = Yield to call assuming semiannual coupons

Calculating a yield to call requires the same trial-and-error procedure as calculating a yield to maturity. Most financial calculators either will handle the calculation directly or can be tricked into it by just changing the face value to the call price and the time to maturity to time to call.

To give a trial-and-error example, suppose a 20-year bond has a coupon of 8 percent, a price of 98, and is callable in 10 years. The call price is 105. What are its yield to maturity and yield to call?

Based on our earlier discussion, we know the yield to maturity is slightly bigger than the coupon rate. (Why?) After some calculation, we find it to be 8.2 percent.

To find the bond's yield to call, we pretend it has a face value of 105 instead of 100 ($1,050 versus $1,000) and will mature in 10 years. With these two changes, the procedure is exactly the same. We can try 8.5 percent, for example:

$$\frac{\$80}{.085}\left[1 - \frac{1}{(1.0425)^{20}}\right] + \frac{\$1{,}050}{(1.0425)^{20}} = \$988.51$$

Because $988.51 is a little too high, the yield to call is slightly bigger than 8.5 percent. If we try 8.6, we find that the price is $981.83, so the yield to call is about 8.6 percent (it's 8.6276 percent).

A natural question comes up in this context. Which is bigger, the yield to maturity or the yield to call? The answer depends on the call price. However, if the bond is callable at par (as many are), then, for a premium bond, the yield to maturity is greater. For a discount bond, the reverse is true.

SPREADSHEET ANALYSIS

	A	B	C	D	E	F	G	H
1								
2			Calculating Yield to Call					
3								
4	A bond traded on March 30, 2008 matures in 15 years on March 30, 2023 and may							
5	be called anytime after March 30, 2013 at a call price of 105. The bond pays an							
6	8.5 percent coupon and currently trades at par. What are the yield to maturity							
7	and yield to call for this bond?							
8								
9	Yield to maturity is based on the 2023 maturity and the current price of 100.							
10								
11		8.5000%	= YIELD("3/30/2008","3/30/2023",0.085,100,100,2,3)					
12								
13	Yield to call is based on the 2013 call date and the call price of 105.							
14								
15		9.3080%	= YIELD("3/30/2008","3/30/2013",0.085,100,105,2,3)					
16								
17								

EXAMPLE 10.6 **Yield to Call**

An 8.5 percent coupon bond maturing in 15 years is callable at 105 in 5 years. If the price is 100, which is bigger, the yield to call or the yield to maturity?

Since this is a par bond callable at a premium, the yield to call is bigger. We can verify this by calculating both yields. Check that the yield to maturity is 8.50 percent, whereas the yield to call is 9.308 percent.

Yields to call may be calculated using a built-in spreadsheet function. An example of how to use an Excel™ spreadsheet to calculate a yield to call is shown in the nearby *Spreadsheet Analysis* box.

CHECK THIS

10.3a What does it mean for a bond to be callable?

10.3b What is the difference between yield to maturity and yield to call?

10.3c Yield to call is calculated just like yield to maturity except for two changes. What are the changes?

10.4 Interest Rate Risk and Malkiel's Theorems

interest rate risk
The possibility that changes in interest rates will result in losses in a bond's value.

Bond yields are essentially interest rates, and, like interest rates, they fluctuate through time. When interest rates change, bond prices change. This is called **interest rate risk**. The term "interest rate risk" refers to the possibility of losses on a bond from changes in interest rates.

PROMISED YIELD AND REALIZED YIELD

realized yield
The yield actually earned or "realized" on a bond.

The terms *yield to maturity* and *promised yield* both seem to imply that the yield originally stated when a bond is purchased is what you will actually earn if you hold the bond until it matures. Actually, this is not generally correct. The return or yield you actually earn on a bond is called the **realized yield**, and an originally stated yield to maturity is almost never exactly equal to the realized yield.

The reason a realized yield will almost always differ from a promised yield is that interest rates fluctuate, causing bond prices to rise or fall. One consequence is that if a bond is sold before maturity, its price may be higher or lower than originally anticipated, and, as a result, the actually realized yield will be different from the promised yield.

Another important reason why realized yields generally differ from promised yields relates to the bond's coupons. We will get to this in the next section. For now, you should know that, for the most part, a bond's realized yield will equal its promised yield only if its yield doesn't change at all over the life of the bond, an unlikely event.

INTEREST RATE RISK AND MATURITY

While changing interest rates systematically affect all bond prices, it is important to realize that the impact of changing interest rates is not the same for all bonds. Some bonds are more sensitive to interest rate changes than others. To illustrate, Figure 10.2 shows how two bonds with different maturities can have different price sensitivities to changes in bond yields.

In Figure 10.2, bond prices are measured on the vertical axis, and bond yields are measured on the horizontal axis. Both bonds have the same 8 percent coupon rate, but one bond has a 5-year maturity while the other bond has a 20-year maturity. Both bonds display the inverse relationship between bond prices and bond yields. Since both bonds have the same 8 percent coupon rate, and both sell for par, their yields are 8 percent.

FIGURE 10.2 Bond Prices and Yields

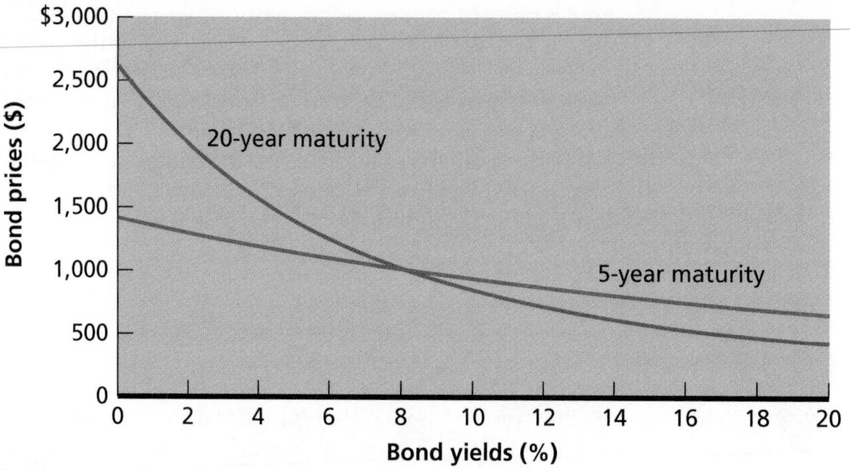

However, when bond yields are greater than 8 percent, the 20-year maturity bond has a lower price than the 5-year maturity bond. In contrast, when bond yields are less than 8 percent, the 20-year maturity bond has a higher price than the 5-year maturity bond. Essentially, falling yields cause both bond prices to rise, but the longer maturity bond experiences a larger price increase than the shorter maturity bond. Similarly, rising yields cause both bond prices to fall, but the price of the longer maturity bond falls by more than the price of the shorter maturity bond.

MALKIEL'S THEOREMS

The effect illustrated in Figure 10.2, along with some other important relationships among bond prices, maturities, coupon rates, and yields, is succinctly described by Burton Malkiel's five bond price theorems.[3] These five theorems are:

1. Bond prices and bond yields move in opposite directions. As a bond's yield increases, its price decreases. Conversely, as a bond's yield decreases, its price increases.
2. For a given change in a bond's yield to maturity, the longer the term to maturity of the bond, the greater will be the magnitude of the change in the bond's price.
3. For a given change in a bond's yield to maturity, the size of the change in the bond's price increases at a diminishing rate as the bond's term to maturity lengthens.
4. For a given change in a bond's yield to maturity, the absolute magnitude of the resulting change in the bond's price is inversely related to the bond's coupon rate.
5. For a given absolute change in a bond's yield to maturity, the magnitude of the price increase caused by a decrease in yield is greater than the price decrease caused by an increase in yield.

The first, second, and fourth of these theorems are the simplest and most important. The first one says that bond prices and yields move in opposite directions. The second one says that longer-term bonds are more sensitive to changes in yields than shorter-term bonds. The fourth one says that lower coupon bonds are more sensitive to changes in yields than higher coupon bonds.

[3] Burton C. Malkiel, "Expectations, Bond Prices, and the Term Structure of Interest Rates," *Quarterly Journal of Economics*, May 1962, pp. 197–218.

TABLE 10.1 Bond Prices and Yields

Yields	Time to Maturity 5 Years	10 Years	20 Years
7%	$1,041.58	$1,071.06	$1,106.78
9%	960.44	934.96	907.99
Price difference	$ 81.14	$ 136.10	$ 198.79

TABLE 10.2 Twenty-Year Bond Prices and Yields

Yields	Coupon Rates 6 Percent	8 Percent	10 Percent
6%	$1,000.00	$1,231.15	$1,462.30
8%	802.07	1,000.00	1,197.93
10%	656.82	828.41	1,000.00

The third theorem says that a bond's sensitivity to interest rate changes increases as its maturity grows, but at a diminishing rate. In other words, a 10-year bond is much more sensitive to changes in yield than a 1-year bond. However, a 30-year bond is only slightly more sensitive than a 20-year bond. Finally, the fifth theorem says essentially that the loss you would suffer from, say, a 1 percent increase in yields is less than the gain you would enjoy from a 1 percent decrease in yields.

Table 10.1 illustrates the first three of these theorems by providing prices for 8 percent coupon bonds with maturities of 5, 10, and 20 years and yields to maturity of 7 percent and 9 percent. Be sure to check these for practice. As the first theorem says, bond prices are lower when yields are higher (9 percent versus 7 percent). As the second theorem indicates, the differences in bond prices between yields of 7 percent and 9 percent are greater for bonds with a longer term to maturity. However, as the third theorem states, the effect increases at a diminishing rate as the maturity lengthens. To see this, notice that $136.10 is 67.7 percent larger than $81.14, while $198.79 is only 46.1 percent larger than $136.10.

To illustrate the last two theorems, we present prices for 20-year maturity bonds with coupon rates and yields to maturity of 6 percent, 8 percent, and 10 percent (again, calculate these for practice) in Table 10.2. To illustrate the fourth theorem, compare the loss on the 6 percent and the 8 percent bonds as yields move from 8 percent to 10 percent. The 6 percent bond loses ($656.82 − $802.07)/$802.07 = −18.1%. The 8 percent bond loses ($828.41 − $1,000)/$1,000 = −17.2%, showing that the bond with the lower coupon is more sensitive to a change in yields. You can (and should) verify that the same is true for a yield increase.

Finally, to illustrate the fifth theorem, take a look at the 8 percent coupon bond in Table 10.2. As yields decrease by 2 percent from 8 percent to 6 percent, its price climbs by $231.15. As yields rise by 2 percent, the bond's price falls by $171.59.

As we have discussed, bond maturity is an important factor determining the sensitivity of a bond's price to changes in interest rates. However, bond maturity is an incomplete measure of bond price sensitivity to yield changes. For example, we have seen that a bond's coupon rate is also important. An improved measure of interest rate risk for bonds that accounts for both differences in maturity and differences in coupon rates is our next subject. A nearby *Investment Updates* box discusses the importance of bonds in an investment portfolio.

INVESTMENT UPDATES

GET A FRESH ANGLE ON YOUR FINANCES

Not sure whether you're saving enough or whether you have the right investment mix? To get a better handle on your portfolio, it sometimes helps to look at your finances from another angle.

1 How Much Do You Need in Conservative Investments to Feel Safe?

Investment advisers and Wall Street firms constantly exhort investors to consider their risk tolerance. For instance, we are often prodded to fill out those irritating questionnaires where we are asked whether our goal is "growth" or "capital preservation."

The answer, of course, is that we want both. Even retirees need growth from their portfolios. Even freshly minted college graduates hanker after some stability.

My advice: Forget risk tolerance. Instead, divide your portfolio into two parts. Designate one portion for "getting rich" and the other for "making sure I'm not poor."

How should you split your savings between the two? That brings us to our first question. Think about how much you need in conservative investments, like high-quality bonds, certificates of deposit, and savings accounts, to cover expected costs, pay for financial emergencies, and have a general sense of financial security.

If you are retired, this stash of safe money might be equal to your living expenses for the next three or five years. If you are still hauling in a paycheck, your conservative investments could amount to just three months' living expenses.

Once you have enough in conservative investments to soothe your fears, that will free you up to be more aggressive with the rest of your portfolio. You might invest your "getting rich" money in a mix of U.S. shares, foreign stocks, real-estate investment trusts, high-yield "junk" bonds and foreign bonds.

What if these investments hit a rough patch? With any luck, you won't be too unnerved, thanks to the financial cushion provided by your safe money.

2 How Much Do You Really Have in Bonds?

When you tote up your holdings of conservative investments, you probably count CDs, Treasury bonds, high-quality corporate bonds, municipals, money-market funds, and savings accounts. But don't stop there.

I would expand the list to include Social Security retirement benefits, pension income, mortgage debt, and any other loans you have. After all, you regularly receive income from Social Security and your pension, just as you would from a bond. Meanwhile, your debts involve making regular payments to other folks.

All these dealings affect your sense of financial security, and they should influence how you structure your portfolio. For instance, if you expect a traditional company pension when you retire, you effectively have a huge position in bonds and thus you might want to load up on stocks in your investment portfolio.

On the other hand, if you have a heap of debts, your financial position is much more precarious and you may want to take less risk with your investments. On that score, consider your mortgage, which probably is your biggest debt. Let's say you have a \$300,000 home and a \$200,000 mortgage. The temptation is to deduct your mortgage from your home's value and declare that your total real-estate investment is \$100,000.

But in truth, your real-estate exposure is equal to your home's full \$300,000 value. Think about it: Whether you are mortgaged to the hilt or you are debt-free, you still benefit from every dollar of home-price appreciation and suffer every dollar of loss.

Meanwhile, I would view your \$200,000 mortgage as a "negative bond" because, instead of earning interest, you are paying it. Suppose you also have \$75,000 in government bonds, which means you have lent money to Uncle Sam. Overall, you owe a lot more money than you are owed—to the tune of \$125,000.

In fact, your financial position may be more perilous than a couple whose portfolio is 100% in stocks but who own their home free and clear. The implication: You may want to tamp down risk, either by buying more bonds or by making extra principal payments on your mortgage.

Source: Jonathan Clements, *The Wall Street Journal*, October 16, 2005.

CHECK THIS

10.4a True or false: A bond price's sensitivity to interest rate changes increases at an increasing rate as maturity lengthens.

10.4b Which is more sensitive to an interest rate shift: a low-coupon bond or a high-coupon bond?

FIGURE 10.3 Bond Duration and Maturity

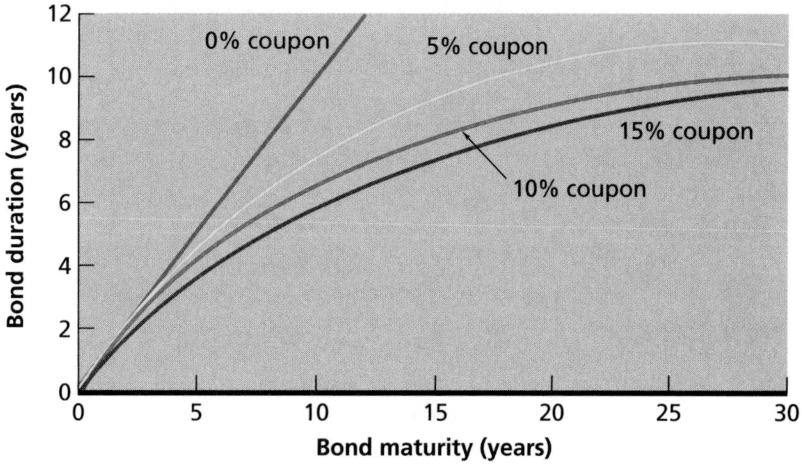

CHECK THIS

10.5a What does duration measure?

10.5b What is the duration of a zero coupon bond?

10.5c What happens to a bond's duration as its maturity grows?

10.6 Bond Risk Measures Based on Duration

In this section, we examine some risk measures that are either based on duration or closely related to it. These measures are commonly used by bond traders and other fixed-income professionals.

DOLLAR VALUE OF AN 01

dollar value of an 01 Change in bond price resulting from a change in yield to maturity of one basis point.

A popular measure of interest rate risk among bond professionals is the **dollar value of an 01** (say "dollar value of an oh-one"), which measures the change in bond price resulting from a one basis point change in yield to maturity, where one basis point is 1 percent of 1 percent, that is, .01 percent, or .0001. The dollar value of an 01 is also known as the *value of a basis point.* The dollar value of an 01 can be stated through the modified duration of a bond as follows:

$$\text{Dollar value of an 01} \approx \text{Modified duration} \times \text{Bond price} \times 0.0001 \qquad (10.10)$$

YIELD VALUE OF A 32nd

yield value of a 32nd Change in yield to maturity that would lead to a 1/32 change in bond price.

When bond prices are quoted in 1/32's of a point, as they are, for example, with U.S. Treasury notes and bonds, the **yield value of a 32nd** is often used by bond professionals as an additional or alternative measure of interest rate risk. The yield value of a 32nd is the change in yield to maturity that would lead to a 1/32 change in bond price. A simple way to obtain the yield value of a 32nd is to multiply the dollar value of an 01 by 32 and then invert the result:

$$\text{Yield value of a 32nd} \approx \frac{1}{32 \times \text{Dollar value of an 01}} \qquad (10.11)$$

EXAMPLE 10.12 **Bond Risk Measures Based on Duration**

The bond in Example 10.11 has a modified duration of 8.27 years. What is its dollar value of an 01? What is its yield value of a 32nd?

We must first calculate the price of this bond using the bond pricing formula provided earlier in this chapter:

$$\text{Bond price} = \frac{6}{.07}\left[1 - \frac{1}{(1 + .035)^{24}}\right] + \frac{100}{(1 + .035)^{24}}$$
$$= \$91.971$$

Then, plugging the modified duration of 8.27 years, and the bond price as a percentage of par value, 91.971, into equation (10.10), we obtain the dollar value of an 01:

$$\text{Dollar value of an 01} \approx 8.27 \times 91.971 \times .0001 = .07606$$

Thus, a one basis point change in yield will change the bond price by about \$0.076, or 7.6 cents (in the opposite direction).

Next we multiply by 32 and invert to obtain the yield value of a 32nd:

$$\text{Yield value of a 32nd} \approx \frac{1}{32 \times .07606} = .41086$$

Now we see that a change in yield of .41 basis point, or .0041 percent, would lead to a change in bond price of about 1/32. As a check, we calculate a bond price obtained by changing the yield from 7 percent to 7.0041 percent:

$$\text{Bond price} = \frac{6}{.070041}\left[1 - \frac{1}{(1 + .03500205)^{24}}\right] + \frac{100}{(1 + .03500205)^{24}}$$
$$= \$91.94$$

The resulting price change is \$0.0314 ≈ \$91.97 − \$91.94. Because 1/32 of a point corresponds to \$0.03125, we see that our computed yield value of a 32nd is quite accurate.

CHECK THIS

10.6a What is the relationship between modified duration and the dollar value of an 01?

10.6b What is the relationship between the dollar value of an 01 and the yield value of a 32nd?

10.7 Dedicated Portfolios and Reinvestment Risk

Duration has another property that makes it a vital tool in bond portfolio management. To explore this subject, we first need to introduce two important concepts, dedicated portfolios and reinvestment risk.

DEDICATED PORTFOLIOS

dedicated portfolio
A bond portfolio created to prepare for a future cash outlay.

A firm can invest in coupon bonds when it is preparing to meet a future liability or other cash outlay. A bond portfolio formed for such a specific purpose is called a **dedicated portfolio**. When the future liability payment of a dedicated portfolio is due on a known date, this date is commonly called the portfolio's *target date*.

Key Terms

callable bond 323
call price 323
call protection period 323
clean price 320
coupon rate 315
current yield 315
dedicated portfolio 334
dirty price 320
dollar value of an 01 333
duration 329
dynamic immunization 339
immunization 337
interest rate risk 325
make-whole call price 323
price risk 337
realized yield 325
reinvestment rate risk 336
yield to call (YTC) 323
yield to maturity (YTM) 316
yield value of a 32nd 333

Chapter Review Problems and Self-Test

1. **Straight Bond Prices** Suppose a bond has 10 years to maturity and a coupon rate of 6 percent. The bond's yield to maturity is 8 percent. What's the price?
2. **Premium Bonds** Suppose we have two bonds, both with a 6 percent coupon rate and the same yield to maturity of 4 percent, but with different maturities of 5 and 15 years. Which has the higher price? Verify your answer by calculating the prices.
3. **Macaulay Duration** A bond has a Macaulay duration of nine years, and its yield increases from 6 percent to 6.25 percent. What will happen to the price of the bond?

Answers to Self-Test Problems

1. Here, the coupon rate is 6 percent and the face value is $1,000, so the annual coupon is $60. The bond's price is calculated as follows:

   Present value of semiannual coupons:

   $$\frac{\$60}{.08}\left[1 - \frac{1}{(1.04)^{20}}\right] = \$407.70979$$

   Present value of $1,000 principal:

   $$\frac{\$1{,}000}{(1.04)^{20}} = \$456.38695$$

   The bond's price is the sum of coupon and principal present values:

   $$\text{Bond price} = \$407.71 + \$456.39 = \$864.10$$

2. Because both bonds have a 6 percent coupon and a 4 percent yield, both bonds sell at a premium, and the one with the longer maturity will have a higher price. We can verify these conclusions by calculating the prices as follows:

   5-year maturity premium bond price:

   $$\frac{\$60}{.04}\left[1 - \frac{1}{(1.02)^{10}}\right] + \frac{\$1{,}000}{(1.02)^{10}} = \$1{,}089.83$$

   15-year maturity premium bond price:

   $$\frac{\$60}{.04}\left[1 - \frac{1}{(1.02)^{30}}\right] + \frac{\$1{,}000}{(1.02)^{30}} = \$1{,}223.96$$

   Notice that the longer maturity premium bond has a higher price, just as we thought.

3. The resulting percentage change in the price of the bond can be calculated as follows:

   $$-9 \times \frac{.0625 - .06}{1.03} = -2.18\%$$

   The bond's price declines by approximately 2.18 percent in response to a 25 basis point increase in yields.

Test Your Investment Quotient

For the remaining questions and problems, the circled numbers in the margin refer to the corresponding learning objective in this chapter.

(2) 1. **Yield to Maturity** The yield to maturity on a bond is

- **a.** Below the coupon rate when the bond sells at a discount and above the coupon rate when the bond sells at a premium.
- **b.** The interest rate that makes the present value of the payments equal to the bond price.
- **c.** Based on the assumption that all future payments received are reinvested at the coupon rate.
- **d.** Based on the assumption that all future payments received are reinvested at future market rates.

(1) 2. **Bond Yields** In which one of the following cases is the bond selling at a discount?

- **a.** Coupon rate is greater than current yield, which is greater than yield to maturity.
- **b.** Coupon rate, current yield, and yield to maturity are all the same.
- **c.** Coupon rate is less than current yield, which is less than yield to maturity.
- **d.** Coupon rate is less than current yield, which is greater than yield to maturity.

(1) 3. **Bond Yields** When are yield to maturity and current yield on a bond equal?

- **a.** When market interest rates begin to level off.
- **b.** If the bond sells at a price in excess of its par value.
- **c.** When the expected holding period is greater than one year.
- **d.** If the coupon and market interest rate are equal.

(1) 4. **Bond Yields** Which of the following states the correct relationship among yield measures for discount bonds?

- **a.** Coupon rate < Current yield < Yield to maturity
- **b.** Current yield < Coupon rate < Yield to maturity
- **c.** Coupon rate < Yield to maturity < Current yield
- **d.** Yield to maturity < Coupon rate < Current yield

(1) 5. **Bond Yields** Which of the following states the correct relationship among yield measures for premium bonds?

- **a.** Coupon rate > Current yield > Yield to maturity
- **b.** Current yield > Coupon rate > Yield to maturity
- **c.** Coupon rate > Yield to maturity > Current yield
- **d.** Yield to maturity > Coupon rate > Current yield

(1) 6. **Bond Prices** Consider a five-year bond with a 10 percent coupon that is presently trading at a yield to maturity of 8 percent. If market interest rates do not change, one year from now the price of this bond

- **a.** Will be higher
- **b.** Will be lower
- **c.** Will be the same
- **d.** Cannot be determined

(1) 7. **Bond Prices** Using semiannual compounding, what would the price of a 15-year, zero coupon bond that has a par value of $1,000 and a required return of 8 percent be?

- **a.** $308
- **b.** $315
- **c.** $464
- **d.** $555

(1) 8. **Bond Prices** If an investor's required return is 12 percent, the value of a 10-year maturity zero coupon bond with a maturity value of $1,000 is *closest* to

- **a.** $312
- **b.** $688
- **c.** $1,000
- **d.** $1,312

CFA® PROBLEMS

(4) 9. **Duration** Another term for bond duration is

a. Actual maturity
b. Effective maturity
c. Calculated maturity
d. Near-term maturity

CFA® PROBLEMS

(4) 10. **Duration** Which of the following is not a property of duration?

a. A longer maturity generally yields a longer duration.
b. Duration generally increases at a decreasing rate as maturity lengthens.
c. A bigger coupon generally yields a longer duration.
d. A higher yield to maturity generally yields a shorter duration.

CFA® PROBLEMS

(4) 11. **Duration** Which statement is true for the Macaulay duration of a zero coupon bond?

a. It is equal to the bond's maturity in years.
b. It is equal to one-half the bond's maturity in years.
c. It is equal to the bond's maturity in years divided by its yield to maturity.
d. It cannot be calculated because of the lack of coupons.

(4) 12. **Duration** Which of the following states the correct relationship between Macaulay duration and modified duration?

a. Modified duration = Macaulay duration/(1 + *YTM*/2)
b. Modified duration = Macaulay duration × (1 + *YTM*/2)
c. Modified duration = Macaulay duration/*YTM*
d. Modified duration = Macaulay duration × *YTM*

CFA® PROBLEMS

(4) 13. **Duration** Which one of the following bonds has the shortest duration?

a. Zero coupon, 10-year maturity
b. Zero coupon, 13-year maturity
c. 8 percent coupon, 10-year maturity
d. 8 percent coupon, 13-year maturity

CFA® PROBLEMS

(4) 14. **Duration** Identify the bond that has the longest duration (no calculations necessary).

a. 20-year maturity with an 8 percent coupon
b. 20-year maturity with a 12 percent coupon
c. 15-year maturity with a 0 percent coupon
d. 10-year maturity with a 15 percent coupon

CFA® PROBLEMS

(4) 15. **Duration** Which bond has the longest duration?

a. 8-year maturity, 6 percent coupon
b. 8-year maturity, 11 percent coupon
c. 15-year maturity, 6 percent coupon
d. 15-year maturity, 11 percent coupon

CFA® PROBLEMS

(4) 16. **Duration** The duration of a bond normally increases with an increase in

a. Term to maturity
b. Yield to maturity
c. Coupon rate
d. All of the above

CFA® PROBLEMS

(4) 17. **Duration** When interest rates decline, what happens to the duration of a 30-year bond selling at a premium?

a. It increases
b. It decreases
c. It remains the same
d. It increases at first, then declines

CFA® PROBLEMS

(4) 18. **Duration** An 8 percent, 20-year corporate bond is priced to yield 9 percent. The Macaulay duration for this bond is 8.85 years. Given this information, how many years is the bond's modified duration?

a. 8.12
b. 8.47
c. 8.51
d. 9.25

CFA® PROBLEMS

(4) **19. Using Duration** A 9-year bond has a yield to maturity of 10 percent and a modified duration of 6.54 years. If the market yield changes by 50 basis points, what is the change in the bond's price?

a. 3.27 percent
b. 3.66 percent
c. 6.54 percent
d. 7.21 percent

CFA® PROBLEMS

(4) **20. Using Duration** A 6 percent coupon bond paying interest semiannually has a modified duration of 10 years, sells for $800, and is priced at a yield to maturity (YTM) of 8 percent. If the YTM increases to 9 percent, the predicted change in price, using the duration concept, is which of the following amounts?

a. $76.56
b. $76.92
c. $77.67
d. $80.00

(4) **21. Immunization** Which of the following strategies is most likely to yield the best interest rate risk immunization results for a bond portfolio?

a. Maturity matching
b. Duration matching
c. Buy and hold
d. Investing in interest rate–sensitive stocks

(4) **22. Immunization** Consider two dedicated bond portfolios both with the same 10-year target dates. One is managed using a buy-and-hold strategy with reinvested coupons. The other is managed using a dynamic immunization strategy. The buy-and-hold portfolio is most likely to outperform the immunized portfolio under what kind of interest rate environment?

a. Steadily rising interest rates.
b. Steadily falling interest rates.
c. Constant interest rates.
d. Performance will be the same under any environment.

(1) **23. Bond Yields** A zero coupon bond paying $100 at maturity 10 years from now has a current price of $50. Its yield to maturity is *closest* to which of the following?

a. 5 percent
b. 6 percent
c. 7 percent
d. 8 percent

CFA® PROBLEMS

(1) **24. Bond Price** A newly issued 10-year option-free bond is valued at par on June 1, 2005. The bond has an annual coupon of 8.0 percent. On June 1, 2008, the bond has a yield to maturity of 7.1 percent. The first coupon is reinvested at 8.0 percent and the second coupon is reinvested at 7.0 percent. The price of the bond on June 1, 2008, is closest to

a. 100.0 percent of par
b. 102.5 percent of par
c. 104.8 percent of par
d. 105.4 percent of par

CFA® PROBLEMS

(3) **25. Interest Rate Risk** The interest rate risk of a noncallable bond is most likely to be positively related to the

a. Risk-free rate
b. Bond's coupon rate
c. Bond's time to maturity
d. Bond's yield to maturity

Concept Questions

(1) **1. Bond Prices** What are premium, discount, and par bonds?

(1) **2. Bond Features** In the United States, what is the normal face value for corporate and U.S. government bonds? How are coupons calculated? How often are coupons paid?

TABLE 11.2

Calculating Expected Returns

		Starcents		Jpod	
(1) State of Economy	(2) Probability of State of Economy	(3) Return If State Occurs	(4) Product (2) × (3)	(5) Return If State Occurs	(6) Product (2) × (5)
Recession	.50	−20%	−10%	30%	15%
Boom	.50	70	35	10	05
	1.00		$E(R_S)$ = 25%		$E(R_J)$ = 20%

In other words, you should expect to earn 20 percent from this stock, on average.

For Starcents, the probabilities are the same, but the possible returns are different. Here we lose 20 percent half the time, and we gain 70 percent the other half. The expected return on Starcents, $E(R_S)$, is thus 25 percent:

$$E(R_S) = .50 \times -20\% + .50 \times 70\% = 25\%$$

Table 11.2 illustrates these calculations.

In Chapter 1, we defined a risk premium as the difference between the returns on a risky investment and a risk-free investment, and we calculated the historical risk premiums on some different investments. Using our projected returns, we can calculate the *projected* or *expected risk premium* as the difference between the expected return on a risky investment and the certain return on a risk-free investment.

For example, suppose risk-free investments are currently offering an 8 percent return. We will say that the risk-free rate, which we label R_f, is 8 percent. Given this, what is the projected risk premium on Jpod? On Starcents? Because the expected return on Jpod, $E(R_J)$, is 20 percent, the projected risk premium is:

$$\begin{aligned} \textbf{Risk premium} &= \textbf{Expected return} - \textbf{Risk-free rate} \\ &= E(R_J) - R_f \\ &= 20\% - 8\% \\ &= 12\% \end{aligned} \tag{11.1}$$

Similarly, the risk premium on Starcents is 25% − 8% = 17%.

In general, the expected return on a security or other asset is simply equal to the sum of the possible returns multiplied by their probabilities. So, if we have 100 possible returns, we would multiply each one by its probability and then add up the results. The sum would be the expected return. The risk premium would then be the difference between this expected return and the risk-free rate.

EXAMPLE 11.1

Unequal Probabilities

Look again at Tables 11.1 and 11.2. Suppose you thought a boom would occur 20 percent of the time instead of 50 percent. What are the expected returns on Starcents and Jpod in this case? If the risk-free rate is 10 percent, what are the risk premiums?

The first thing to notice is that a recession must occur 80 percent of the time (1 − .20 = .80) because there are only two possibilities. With this in mind, Jpod has a 30 percent return in 80 percent of the years and a 10 percent return in 20 percent of the years. To calculate the expected return, we just multiply the possibilities by the probabilities and add up the results:

$$E(R_J) = .80 \times 30\% + .20 \times 10\% = 26\%$$

If the returns are written as decimals:

$$E(R_J) = .80 \times .30 + .20 \times .10 = .26$$

(continued)

TABLE 11.3 Calculating Expected Returns

		Starcents		Jpod	
(1) State of Economy	(2) Probability of State of Economy	(3) Return If State Occurs	(4) Product (2) × (3)	(5) Return If State Occurs	(6) Product (2) × (5)
Recession	.80	−20%	−16%	30%	24%
Boom	.20	70	14	10	2
	1.00		$E(R_S) = -2\%$		$E(R_J) = 26\%$

Table 11.3 summarizes the calculations for both stocks. Notice that the expected return on Starcents is −2 percent.

The risk premium for Jpod is 26% − 10% = 16% in this case. The risk premium for Starcents is negative: −2% − 10% = −12%. This is a little unusual, but, as we will see, it's not impossible.

CALCULATING THE VARIANCE OF EXPECTED RETURNS

WWW

There's more on risk measures at www.investopedia.com and www.teachmefinance.com

To calculate the variances of the expected returns on our two stocks, we first determine the squared deviations from the expected return. We then multiply each possible squared deviation by its probability. Next we add these up, and the result is the variance.

To illustrate, one of our stocks in Table 11.2, Jpod, has an expected return of 20 percent. In a given year, the return will actually be either 30 percent or 10 percent. The possible deviations are thus 30% − 20% = 10% or 10% − 20% = −10%. In this case, the variance is:

$$\text{Variance} = \sigma^2 = .50 \times (10\%)^2 + .50 \times (-10\%)^2$$
$$= .50 \times (.10)^2 + .50 \times (-.10)^2 = .01$$

Notice that we used decimals to calculate the variance. The standard deviation is the square root of the variance:

$$\text{Standard deviation} = \sigma = \sqrt{.01} = .10 = 10\%$$

Table 11.4 contains the expected return and variance for both stocks. Notice that Starcents has a much larger variance. Starcents has the higher expected return, but Jpod has less risk. You could get a 70 percent return on your investment in Starcents, but you could also lose 20 percent. However, an investment in Jpod will always pay at least 10 percent.

Which of these stocks should you buy? We can't really say; it depends on your personal preferences regarding risk and return. We can be reasonably sure, however, that some investors would prefer one and some would prefer the other.

You've probably noticed that the way we calculated expected returns and variances of expected returns here is somewhat different from the way we calculated returns and variances in Chapter 1 (and, probably, different from the way you learned it in your statistics course). The reason is that we were examining historical returns in Chapter 1, so we estimated the average return and the variance based on some actual events. Here, we have projected *future* returns and their associated probabilities. Therefore, we must calculate expected returns and variances of expected returns.

TABLE 11.4 Expected Returns and Variances

	Starcents	Jpod
Expected return, $E(R)$	.25, or 25%	.20, or 20%
Variance of expected return, σ^2	.2025	.0100
Standard deviation of expected return, σ	.45, or 45%	.10, or 10%

EXAMPLE 11.2

More Unequal Probabilities

Going back to Table 11.3 in Example 11.1, what are the variances on our two stocks once we have unequal probabilities? What are the standard deviations?

Converting all returns to decimals, we can summarize the needed calculations as follows:

(1) State of Economy	(2) Probability of State of Economy	(3) Return Deviation from Expected Return	(4) Squared Return Deviation	(5) Product (2) × (4)
Starcents				
Recession	.80	$-.20 - (-.02) = -.18$	.0324	.02592
Boom	.20	$.70 - (-.02) = .72$	.5184	.10368
				$\sigma_S^2 = .12960$
Jpod				
Recession	.80	$.30 - .26 = .04$	.0016	.00128
Boom	.20	$.10 - .26 = -.16$	.0256	.00512
				$\sigma_J^2 = .00640$

Based on these calculations, the standard deviation for Starcents is $\sigma_S = \sqrt{.1296} = 36\%$. The standard deviation for Jpod is much smaller, $\sigma_J = \sqrt{.0064}$, or 8%.

CHECK THIS

11.1a How do we calculate the expected return on a security?

11.1b In words, how do we calculate the variance of an expected return?

11.2 Portfolios

portfolio
Group of assets such as stocks and bonds held by an investor.

Thus far in this chapter, we have concentrated on individual assets considered separately. However, most investors actually hold a **portfolio** of assets. All we mean by this is that investors tend to own more than just a single stock, bond, or other asset. Given that this is so, portfolio return and portfolio risk are of obvious relevance. Accordingly, we now discuss portfolio expected returns and variances.

PORTFOLIO WEIGHTS

There are many equivalent ways of describing a portfolio. The most convenient approach is to list the percentages of the total portfolio's value that are invested in each portfolio asset. We call these percentages the **portfolio weights**.

portfolio weight
Percentage of a portfolio's total value invested in a particular asset.

For example, if we have \$50 in one asset and \$150 in another, then our total portfolio is worth \$200. The percentage of our portfolio in the first asset is \$50/\$200 = .25, or 25%. The percentage of our portfolio in the second asset is \$150/\$200 = .75, or 75%. Notice that the weights sum up to 1.00 (100%) because all of our money is invested somewhere.[1]

PORTFOLIO EXPECTED RETURNS

Let's go back to Starcents and Jpod. You put half your money in each. The portfolio weights are obviously .50 and .50. What is the pattern of returns on this portfolio? The expected return?

[1] Some of it could be in cash, of course, but we would then just consider cash to be another of the portfolio assets.

TABLE 11.5 Expected Portfolio Return

(1) State of Economy	(2) Probability of State of Economy	(3) Portfolio Return If State Occurs	(4) Product (2) × (3)
Recession	.50	$.50 \times -20\% + .50 \times 30\% = 5\%$	2.5
Boom	.50	$.50 \times 70\% + .50 \times 10\% = 40\%$	20.0
			$E(R_P) = 22.5\%$

To answer these questions, suppose the economy actually enters a recession. In this case, half your money (the half in Starcents) loses 20 percent. The other half (the half in Jpod) gains 30 percent. Your portfolio return, R_P, in a recession will thus be:

$$R_P = .50 \times -20\% + .50 \times 30\% = 5\%$$

Table 11.5 summarizes the remaining calculations. Notice that when a boom occurs, your portfolio would return 40 percent:

$$R_P = .50 \times 70\% + .50 \times 10\% = 40\%$$

As indicated in Table 11.5, the expected return on your portfolio, $E(R_P)$, is 22.5 percent.

We can save ourselves some work by calculating the expected return more directly. Given these portfolio weights, we could have reasoned that we expect half our money to earn 25 percent (the half in Starcents) and half of our money to earn 20 percent (the half in Jpod). Our portfolio expected return is thus:

$$\begin{aligned} E(R_P) &= .50 \times E(R_S) + .50 \times E(R_J) \\ &= .50 \times 25\% + .50 \times 20\% \\ &= 22.5\% \end{aligned}$$

This is the same portfolio return that we calculated in Table 11.5.

This method of calculating the expected return on a portfolio works no matter how many assets there are in the portfolio. Suppose we had n assets in our portfolio, where n is any number at all. If we let x_i stand for the percentage of our money in Asset i, then the expected return is:

$$E(R_P) = x_1 \times E(R_1) + x_2 \times E(R_2) + \cdots + x_n \times E(R_n) \qquad \textbf{(11.2)}$$

Equation (11.2) says that the expected return on a portfolio is a straightforward combination of the expected returns on the assets in that portfolio. This result seems somewhat obvious, but, as we will examine next, the obvious approach is not always the right one.

EXAMPLE 11.3 More Unequal Probabilities

Suppose we had the following projections on three stocks:

State of Economy	Probability of State of Economy	Returns		
		Stock A	Stock B	Stock C
Boom	.50	10%	15%	20%
Bust	.50	8	4	0

We want to calculate portfolio expected returns in two cases. First, what would be the expected return on a portfolio with equal amounts invested in each of the three stocks? Second, what would be the expected return if half of the portfolio were in A, with the remainder equally divided between B and C?

(continued)

From our earlier discussion, the expected returns on the individual stocks are:

$$E(R_A) = 9.0\% \quad E(R_B) = 9.5\% \quad E(R_C) = 10.0\%$$

(Check these for practice.) If a portfolio has equal investments in each asset, the portfolio weights are all the same. Such a portfolio is said to be *equally weighted.* Since there are three stocks in this case, the weights are all equal to 1/3. The portfolio expected return is thus:

$$E(R_P) = 1/3 \times 9.0\% + 1/3 \times 9.5\% + 1/3 \times 10.0\% = 9.5\%$$

In the second case, check that the portfolio expected return is 9.375%.

PORTFOLIO VARIANCE OF EXPECTED RETURNS

From the preceding discussion, the expected return on a portfolio that contains equal investments in Starcents and Jpod is 22.5 percent. What is the standard deviation of return on this portfolio? Simple intuition might suggest that half of our money has a standard deviation of 45 percent, and the other half has a standard deviation of 10 percent. So the portfolio's standard deviation might be calculated as follows:

$$\sigma_P = .50 \times 45\% + .50 \times 10\% = 27.5\%$$

Unfortunately, this approach is *completely incorrect!*

Let's see what the standard deviation really is. Table 11.6 summarizes the relevant calculations. As we see, the portfolio's standard deviation is much less than 27.5 percent—it's only 17.5 percent. What is illustrated here is that the variance on a portfolio is *not* generally a simple combination of the variances of the assets in the portfolio.

We can illustrate this point a little more dramatically by considering a slightly different set of portfolio weights. Suppose we put 2/11 (about 18 percent) in Starcents and the other 9/11 (about 82 percent) in Jpod. If a recession occurs, this portfolio will have a return of:

$$R_P = 2/11 \times -20\% + 9/11 \times 30\% = 20.91\%$$

If a boom occurs, this portfolio will have a return of:

$$R_P = 2/11 \times 70\% + 9/11 \times 10\% = 20.91\%$$

Notice that the return is the same no matter what happens. No further calculation is needed: This portfolio has a *zero* variance and no risk!

This portfolio is a nice bit of financial alchemy. We take two quite risky assets and, by mixing them just right, we create a riskless portfolio. It seems very clear that combining assets into portfolios can substantially alter the risks faced by an investor. This observation is crucial. We will begin to explore its implications in the next section.[2]

[2] Earlier, we had a risk-free rate of 8 percent. Now we have, in effect, a 20.91 percent risk-free rate. If this situation actually existed, there would be a very profitable opportunity! In reality, we expect that all riskless investments would have the same return.

TABLE 11.6 Calculating Portfolio Variance and Standard Deviation

(1) State of Economy	(2) Probability of State of Economy	(3) Portfolio Returns If State Occurs	(4) Squared Deviation from Expected Return*	(5) Product (2) × (4)
Recession	.50	5%	$(5 - 22.5)^2 = 306.25$	153.125
Boom	.50	40	$(40 - 22.5)^2 = 306.25$	153.125
			Variance, σ_P^2 =	306.25
			Standard deviation, $\sigma_P = \sqrt{306.25}$ =	17.5%

* Notice that we used percents for all returns. Verify that if we wrote returns as decimals, we would get a variance of .030625 and a standard deviation of .175, or 17.5%.

EXAMPLE 11.4

Portfolio Variance and Standard Deviations

In Example 11.3, what are the standard deviations of the two portfolios?

To answer, we first have to calculate the portfolio returns in the two states. We will work with the second portfolio, which has 50 percent in Stock A and 25 percent in each of stocks B and C. The relevant calculations are summarized as follows:

State of Economy	Probability of State of Economy	Returns			
		Stock A	Stock B	Stock C	Portfolio
Boom	.50	10%	15%	20%	13.75%
Bust	.50	8	4	0	5.00

The portfolio return when the economy booms is calculated as:

$$R_P = .50 \times 10\% + .25 \times 15\% + .25 \times 20\% = 13.75\%$$

The return when the economy goes bust is calculated the same way. Check that it's 5 percent and also check that the expected return on the portfolio is 9.375 percent. Expressing returns in decimals, the variance is thus:

$$\sigma_P^2 = .50 \times (.1375 - .09375)^2 + .50 \times (.05 - .09375)^2 = .0019141$$

The standard deviation is:

$$\sigma_P = \sqrt{.0019141} = .04375, \text{ or } 4.375\%$$

Check: Using equal weights, verify that the portfolio standard deviation is 5.5 percent.

Note: If the standard deviation is 4.375 percent, the variance should be somewhere between 16 and 25 (the squares of 4 and 5, respectively). If we square 4.375, we get 19.141. To express a variance in percentage, we must move the decimal *four* places to the right. That is, we must multiply .0019141 by 10,000—which is the square of 100.

CHECK THIS

11.2a What is a portfolio weight?

11.2b How do we calculate the variance of an expected return?

11.3 Diversification and Portfolio Risk

Our discussion to this point has focused on some hypothetical securities. We've seen that portfolio risks can, in principle, be quite different from the risks of the assets that make up the portfolio. We now look more closely at the risk of an individual asset versus the risk of a portfolio of many different assets. As we did in Chapter 1, we will examine some stock market history to get an idea of what happens with actual investments in U.S. capital markets.

THE EFFECT OF DIVERSIFICATION: ANOTHER LESSON FROM MARKET HISTORY

In Chapter 1, we saw that the standard deviation of the annual return on a portfolio of large-company common stocks was about 20 percent per year. Does this mean that the standard deviation of the annual return on a typical stock in that group is about 20 percent? As you might suspect by now, the answer is no. This observation is extremely important.

To examine the relationship between portfolio size and portfolio risk, Table 11.7 illustrates typical average annual standard deviations for equally weighted portfolios that contain different numbers of randomly selected NYSE securities.

TABLE 11.7 Portfolio Standard Deviations

(1) Number of Stocks in Portfolio	(2) Average Standard Deviation of Annual Portfolio Returns	(3) Ratio of Portfolio Standard Deviation to Standard Deviation of a Single Stock
1	49.24%	1.00
2	37.36	.76
4	29.69	.60
6	26.64	.54
8	24.98	.51
10	23.93	.49
20	21.68	.44
30	20.87	.42
40	20.46	.42
50	20.20	.41
100	19.69	.40
200	19.42	.39
300	19.34	.39
400	19.29	.39
500	19.27	.39
1,000	19.21	.39

Source: These figures are from Table 1 in Meir Statman, "How Many Stocks Make a Diversified Portfolio?" *Journal of Financial and Quantitative Analysis* 22 (September 1987), pp. 353–64. They were derived from E. J. Elton and M. J. Gruber, "Risk Reduction and Portfolio Size: An Analytic Solution," *Journal of Business* 50 (October 1977), pp. 415–37.

In column 2 of Table 11.7, we see that the standard deviation for a "portfolio" of one security is just under 50 percent per year at 49.24 percent. What this means is that if you randomly select a single NYSE stock and put all your money into it, your standard deviation of return would typically have been about 50 percent per year. Obviously, such a strategy has significant risk! If you were to randomly select two NYSE securities and put half your money in each, your average annual standard deviation would have been about 37 percent.

The important thing to notice in Table 11.7 is that the standard deviation declines as the number of securities is increased. By the time we have 100 randomly chosen stocks (and 1 percent invested in each), the portfolio's volatility has declined by 60 percent, from 50 percent per year to 20 percent per year. With 500 securities, the standard deviation is 19.27 percent per year, similar to the 20 percent per year we saw in Chapter 1 for large-company common stocks. The small difference exists because the portfolio securities, portfolio weights, and the time periods covered are not identical. The nearby *Investment Updates* box offers further historical perspective on the need for diversification.

THE PRINCIPLE OF DIVERSIFICATION

Figure 11.1 illustrates the point we've been discussing. What we have plotted is the standard deviation of the return versus the number of stocks in the portfolio. Notice in Figure 11.1 that the benefit in terms of risk reduction from adding securities drops off as we add more and more. By the time we have 10 securities, most of the diversification effect is already realized, and by the time we get to 30 or so, there is very little remaining benefit.

The diversification benefit does depend on the time period over which returns and variances are calculated. For example, the data in Table 11.7 precede 1987. Scholars recently revisited diversification benefits by looking at stock returns and variances from 1986 to 1997 and found that 50 stocks were needed to build a highly diversified portfolio in this time period. The point is that investors should be thinking in terms of 30 to 50 individual stocks when they are building a diversified portfolio.

INVESTMENT UPDATES

WHY A BROAD MIX HELPS IN LONG TERM

Stock-market diversification is sold as a short-term sedative for antsy investors. But it's also your best bet for ensuring decent long-run returns. In recent columns, I've written a lot about diversification. There's a good reason for that: If this 2001 bear market has anything to teach us, it is the value of spreading your stock-market bets widely. Over the past year, the hardest-hit investors have been those who pooh-poohed diversification and loaded up on technology stocks, only to see their portfolios decimated by NASDAQ's implosion. Clearly, these folks would have fared far better with a broader array of stocks. But diversification is more than just a defense against short-run market gyrations. To understand why, consider the performance of large, small, and foreign stocks over the past 30 years.

At first blush, the results seem to encourage investors to shun diversification and instead stick with the big blue-chip stocks they know and love. After all, over the 30 years, large, small, and foreign stocks generated almost exactly the same average annual total return. According to Chicago researchers Ibbotson Associates, Standard & Poor's 500-stock Index of large-company stocks was up an average 13.2% a year, smaller U.S. companies gained 14.7%, and Morgan Stanley's Europe, Australasia, and Far East index climbed 13.1%. In other words, if all you owned was a smattering of blue-chip stocks, you should have done just fine over the past 30 years.

But the raw data don't tell the whole story. Here's why:

Tenacity Tested: Suppose that in 1970 you settled on a portfolio consisting exclusively of large U.S. stocks. Would you have hung onto that portfolio through the entire 30 years? I doubt it. For starters, you had to sit tight through the unnerving stock-market declines of 1973–74, 1976–78, 1980–82, 1987, and 1990. That would have been tough with an all-stock portfolio. But even if you had an unflinching determination to stick with stocks, you would have been constantly second-guessing your commitment to blue-chip companies. For instance, in the 1970s, you would have been tempted to swap into small companies and foreign shares, both of which outpaced U.S. large-company stocks. In the 1980s, foreign markets again outstripped U.S. large companies. Indeed, it was only in the 1990s that these blue-chip stocks reigned supreme.

Out of Time: Planning on sticking with U.S. large-company stocks for the next three decades? Circumstances may intervene. Maybe you will be forced to liquidate your stock portfolio early because you get divorced, lose your job, or get hit with hefty medical bills. Alternatively, maybe your time horizon isn't quite as long as you imagine. For instance, you might be looking at a 30-year retirement. But if you are living off your portfolio, you will probably have to sell many of your stocks before the 30 years are up.

In that case, you will definitely want to be globally diversified, because that will provide vital portfolio protection over this shorter period. For proof, check out the accompanying table. It takes the past 30 years, picks out the roughest 5, 10, 15, and 20-year stretches for large-company stocks, and then shows how other investments fared.

"In each of these bad periods, small stocks and international stocks did better," notes William Reichenstein, an investments professor at Baylor University. "There's a lot to be said for a portfolio that includes a little bit of everything."

FIGURE 11.1 Portfolio Diversification

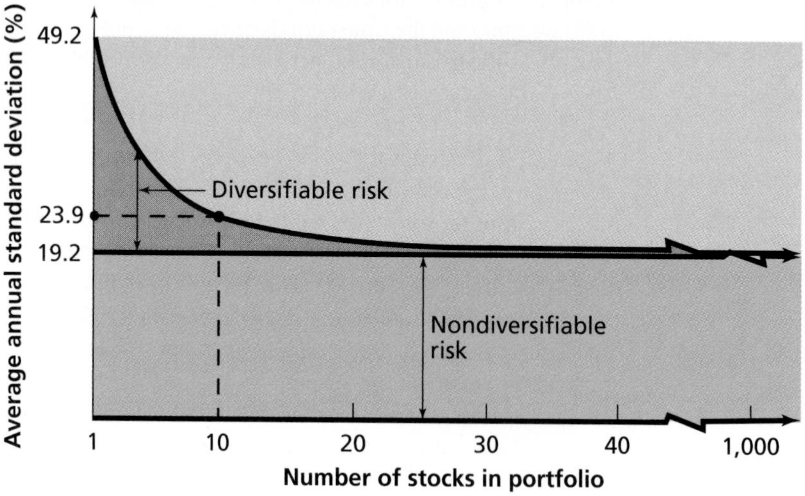

On Target: Diversification won't just limit your losses during rough markets. When it's combined with regular rebalancing, it can also boost returns. When you rebalance, you set targets for what percentage of your portfolio is in different investments. Then, every so often, you re-jigger your portfolio to get back to these targets. If you invest in two market sectors, "a rebalanced portfolio may actually do better than the two assets on their own, because rebalancing forces you to buy low and sell high," says William Bernstein, an investment adviser in North Bend, Ore., and author of "The Intelligent Asset Allocator." "Rebalancing is the only form of market timing that works."

Suppose you held a portfolio that was one-third large stocks, one-third small stocks, and one-third foreign stocks. At the end of each year, you rebalanced to get back to these portfolio targets. Result? According to Ibbotson, over the past 30 years, your portfolio would have gained 14.2% a year before taxes and trading costs, compared with 13.7% if you had never rebalanced. You are most likely to get this performance bonus when you rebalance among different stock-market sectors, which should have roughly comparable long-run returns. But sometimes, you can also bolster returns by rebalancing between stocks and bonds. Consider, for instance, the 10 years through December 1981. Over that stretch, large stocks struggled, climbing just 6.5% a year, but they still outpaced intermediate government bonds, which returned 5.8%. But an annually rebalanced mix of 50% stocks and 50% bonds did even better, gaining 6.6% a year, Mr. Reichenstein calculates.

Source: Jonathan Clements, *The Wall Street Journal*, April 3, 2001.

Hiding Places: How various investments fared during the roughest patches for large-company stocks over the past 30 years

	Worst				30 Years (through Dec. 2000)
	5 Years*	10 Years*	15 Years*	20 Years*	
Large companies	−0.2%	+6.5%	+9.9%	+11.2%	+13.2%
Small companies	+10.8	+17.3	+16.2	+13.3	+14.7
Foreign stocks	+2.6	+10.6	+15.6	+15.4	+13.1
Intermediate bonds	+6.4	+5.8	+9.2	+9.1	+8.5
Inflation	+7.9	+8.6	+6.9	+6.3	+5.0

Note: The results shown are annual averages and include reinvested dividends.

*Through year-end 1977, 1981, 1987, and 1990, respectively.

Source: Jonathan Clements, *The Wall Street Journal*, April 3, 2001.

principle of diversification
Spreading an investment across a number of assets will eliminate some, but not all, of the risk.

Figure 11.1 illustrates two key points. First, some of the riskiness associated with individual assets can be eliminated by forming portfolios. The process of spreading an investment across assets (and thereby forming a portfolio) is called *diversification.* The **principle of diversification** tells us that spreading an investment across many assets will eliminate some of the risk. Not surprisingly, risks that can be eliminated by diversification are called "diversifiable" risks.

The second point is equally important. There is a minimum level of risk that cannot be eliminated by simply diversifying. This minimum level is labeled "nondiversifiable risk" in Figure 11.1. Taken together, these two points are another important lesson from financial market history: Diversification reduces risk, but only up to a point. Put another way, some risk is diversifiable and some is not.

CHECK THIS

11.3a What happens to the standard deviation of return for a portfolio if we increase the number of securities in the portfolio?

11.3b What is the principle of diversification?

11.4 Correlation and Diversification

We've seen that diversification is important. What we haven't discussed is how to get the most out of diversification. For example, in our previous section, we investigated what happens if we simply spread our money evenly across randomly chosen stocks. We saw that significant risk reduction resulted from this strategy, but you might wonder whether even larger gains could be achieved by a more sophisticated approach. As we begin to examine that question here, the answer is yes.

WHY DIVERSIFICATION WORKS

correlation
The tendency of the returns on two assets to move together.

Why diversification reduces portfolio risk as measured by the portfolio standard deviation is important and worth exploring in some detail. The key concept is **correlation**, which is the extent to which the returns on two assets move together. If the returns on two assets tend to move up and down together, we say they are *positively* correlated. If they tend to move in opposite directions, we say they are *negatively* correlated. If there is no particular relationship between the two assets, we say they are *uncorrelated.*

The *correlation coefficient,* which we use to measure correlation, ranges from -1 to $+1$, and we will denote the correlation between the returns on two assets, say A and B, as $\text{Corr}(R_A, R_B)$. The Greek letter ρ (rho) is often used to designate correlation as well. A correlation of $+1$ indicates that the two assets have a *perfect* positive correlation. For example, suppose that whatever return Asset A realizes, either up or down, Asset B does the same thing by exactly twice as much. In this case, they are perfectly correlated because the movement on one is completely predictable from the movement on the other. Notice, however, that perfect correlation does not necessarily mean they move by the same amount.

WWW

Measure portfolio diversification using Instant X-ray at www.morningstar.com (use the search feature)

A zero correlation means that the two assets are uncorrelated. If we know that one asset is up, then we have no idea what the other one is likely to do; there simply is no relation between them. Perfect negative correlation [$\text{Corr}(R_A, R_B) = -1$] indicates that they always move in opposite directions. Figure 11.2 illustrates the three benchmark cases of perfect positive, perfect negative, and zero correlation.

Diversification works because security returns are generally not perfectly correlated. We will be more precise about the impact of correlation on portfolio risk in just a moment. For now, it is useful to simply think about combining two assets into a portfolio. If the two assets

FIGURE 11.2 Correlations

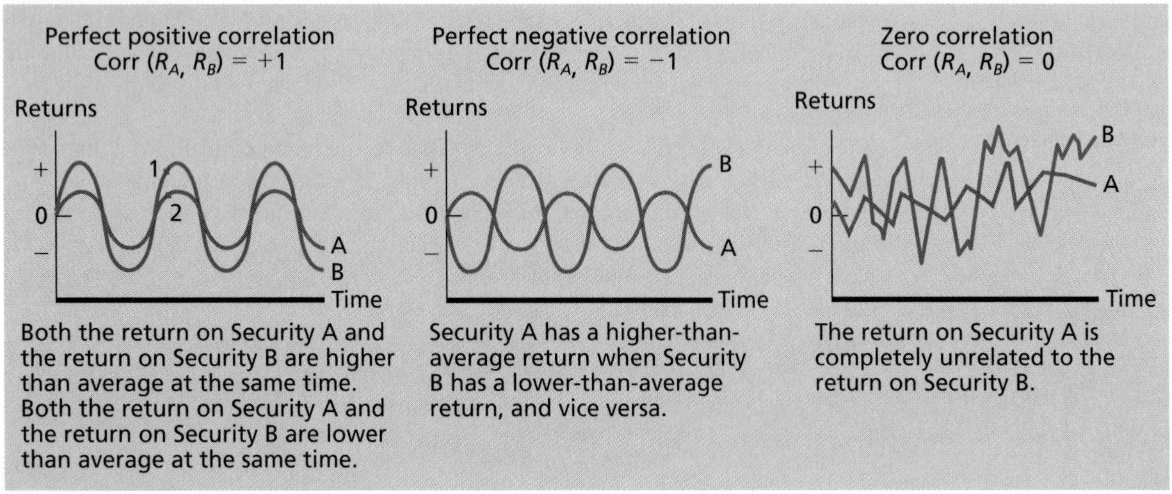

Both the return on Security A and the return on Security B are higher than average at the same time. Both the return on Security A and the return on Security B are lower than average at the same time.

Security A has a higher-than-average return when Security B has a lower-than-average return, and vice versa.

The return on Security A is completely unrelated to the return on Security B.

TABLE 11.8 Annual Returns on Stocks A and B

Year	Stock A	Stock B	Portfolio AB
2003	10%	15%	12.5%
2004	30	−10	10
2005	−10	25	7.5
2006	5	20	12.5
2007	10	15	12.5
Average returns	9	13	11
Standard deviations	14.3	13.5	2.2

are highly positively correlated (the correlation is near +1), then they have a strong tendency to move up and down together. As a result, they offer limited diversification benefit. For example, two stocks from the same industry, say, General Motors and Ford, will tend to be relatively highly correlated because the companies are in essentially the same business, and a portfolio of two such stocks is not likely to be very diversified.

In contrast, if the two assets are negatively correlated, then they tend to move in opposite directions; whenever one zigs, the other tends to zag. In such a case, the diversification benefit will be substantial because variation in the return on one asset tends to be offset by variation in the opposite direction from the other. In fact, if two assets have a perfect negative correlation [$\text{Corr}(R_A, R_B) = -1$], then it is possible to combine them such that all risk is eliminated. Looking back at our example involving Jpod and Starcents in which we were able to eliminate all of the risk, what we now see is that they must be perfectly negatively correlated.

To further illustrate the impact of diversification on portfolio risk, suppose we observed the actual annual returns on two stocks, A and B, for the years 2003–2007. We summarize these returns in Table 11.8. In addition to actual returns on stocks A and B, we also calculated the returns on an equally weighted portfolio of A and B in Table 11.8. We label this portfolio as AB. In 2003, for example, Stock A returned 10 percent and Stock B returned 15 percent. Because Portfolio AB is half invested in each, its return for the year was:

$$1/2 \times 10\% + 1/2 \times 15\% = 12.5\%$$

The returns for the other years are calculated similarly.

At the bottom of Table 11.8, we calculated the average returns and standard deviations on the two stocks and the equally weighted portfolio. These averages and standard deviations are calculated just as they were in Chapter 1 (check a couple just to refresh your memory). The impact of diversification is apparent. The two stocks have standard deviations in the 13 percent to 14 percent per year range, but the portfolio's volatility is only 2.2 percent. In fact, if we compare the portfolio to Stock A, it has a higher return (11 percent vs. 9 percent) and much less risk.

Figure 11.3 illustrates in more detail what is occurring with our example. Here we have three bar graphs showing the year-by-year returns on Stocks A and B and Portfolio AB. Examining the graphs, we see that in 2004, for example, Stock A earned 30 percent while Stock B lost 10 percent. The following year, Stock B earned 25 percent, while A lost 10 percent. These ups and downs tend to cancel out in our portfolio, however, with the result that there is much less variation in return from year to year. In other words, the correlation between the returns on stocks A and B is relatively low.

Calculating the correlation between stocks A and B is not difficult, but it would require us to digress a bit. Instead, we will explain the needed calculation in the next chapter, where we build on the principles developed here.

FIGURE 11.3 Impact of Diversification

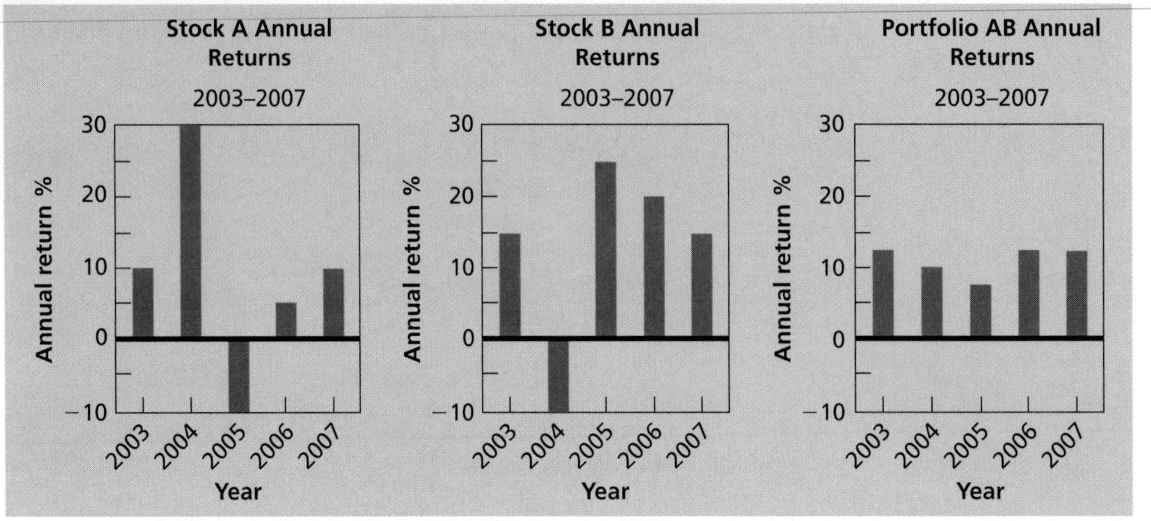

CALCULATING PORTFOLIO RISK

We've seen that correlation is an important determinant of portfolio risk. To further pursue this issue, we need to know how to calculate portfolio variances directly. For a portfolio of two assets, A and B, the variance of the return on the portfolio, σ_P^2, is given by equation (11.3):

$$\sigma_P^2 = x_A^2\sigma_A^2 + x_B^2\sigma_B^2 + 2x_Ax_B\sigma_A\sigma_B\text{Corr}(R_A, R_B) \qquad \textbf{(11.3)}$$

In this equation, x_A and x_B are the percentages invested in assets A and B. Notice that $x_A + x_B = 1$. (Why?)

For a portfolio of three assets, the variance of the return on the portfolio, σ_P^2, is given by equation (11.4):

$$\begin{aligned}\sigma_P^2 = {} & x_A^2\sigma_A^2 + x_B^2\sigma_B^2 + x_C^2\sigma_C^2 + 2x_Ax_B\sigma_A\sigma_B\text{Corr}(R_A, R_B) \\ & + 2x_Ax_C\sigma_A\sigma_C\text{Corr}(R_A, R_C) + 2x_Bx_C\sigma_B\sigma_C\text{Corr}(R_B, R_C)\end{aligned} \qquad \textbf{(11.4)}$$

Note that six terms appear in equation (11.4). There is a term involving the squared weight and the variance of the return for each of the three assets (A, B, and C) as well as a *cross-term* for each pair of assets. The cross-term involves pairs of weights, pairs of standard deviations of returns for each asset, and the correlation between the returns of the asset pair. If you had a portfolio of six assets, you would have an equation with 21 terms. (Can you write this equation?) If you had a portfolio of 50 assets, the equation for the variance of this portfolio would have 1,275 terms! Let's return to equation (11.3).

Equation (11.3) looks a little involved, but its use is straightforward. For example, suppose Stock A has a standard deviation of 40 percent per year and Stock B has a standard deviation of 60 percent per year. The correlation between them is .15. If you put half your money in each, what is your portfolio standard deviation?

To answer, we just plug the numbers into equation (11.3). Note that x_A and x_B are each equal to .50, while σ_A and σ_B are .40 and .60, respectively. Taking $\text{Corr}(R_A, R_B) = .15$, we have:

$$\begin{aligned}\sigma_P^2 &= .50^2 \times .40^2 + .50^2 \times .60^2 + 2 \times .50 \times .50 \times .40 \times .60 \times .15 \\ &= .25 \times .16 + .25 \times .36 + .018 \\ &= .148\end{aligned}$$

Thus, the portfolio variance is .148. As always, variances are not easy to interpret since they are based on squared returns, so we calculate the standard deviation by taking the square root:

$$\sigma_P = \sqrt{.148} = .3847 = 38.47\%$$

Once again, we see the impact of diversification. This portfolio has a standard deviation of 38.47 percent, which is less than either of the standard deviations on the two assets that are in the portfolio.

EXAMPLE 11.5

Portfolio Variance and Standard Deviation

In the example we just examined, Stock A has a standard deviation of 40 percent per year and Stock B has a standard deviation of 60 percent per year. Suppose now that the correlation between them is .35. Also suppose you put one-fourth of your money in Stock A. What is your portfolio standard deviation?

If you put 1/4 (or .25) in Stock A, you must have 3/4 (or .75) in Stock B, so $x_A = .25$ and $x_B = .75$. Making use of our portfolio variance equation (11.3), we have:

$$\begin{aligned}\sigma_P^2 &= .25^2 \times .40^2 + .75^2 \times .60^2 + 2 \times .25 \times .75 \times .40 \times .60 \times .35 \\ &= .0625 \times .16 + .5625 \times .36 + .0315 \\ &= .244\end{aligned}$$

Thus the portfolio variance is .244. Taking the square root, we get:

$$\sigma_P = \sqrt{.244} = .49396 \approx 49\%$$

This portfolio has a standard deviation of 49 percent, which is between the individual standard deviations. This shows that a portfolio's standard deviation isn't necessarily less than the individual standard deviations.

THE IMPORTANCE OF ASSET ALLOCATION, PART 1

asset allocation
How an investor spreads portfolio dollars among assets.

Why are correlation and **asset allocation** important, practical, real-world considerations? Well, suppose that as a very conservative, risk-averse investor, you decide to invest all of your money in a bond mutual fund. Based on your analysis, you think this fund has an expected return of 6 percent with a standard deviation of 10 percent per year. A stock fund is available, however, with an expected return of 12 percent, but the standard deviation of 15 percent is too high for your taste. Also, the correlation between the returns on the two funds is about .10.

Is the decision to invest 100 percent in the bond fund a wise one, even for a very risk-averse investor? The answer is no; in fact, it is a bad decision for any investor. To see why, Table 11.9 shows expected returns and standard deviations available from different combinations of the two mutual funds. In constructing the table, we begin with 100 percent in the stock fund and work our way down to 100 percent in the bond fund by reducing the percentage in the stock fund in increments of .05. These calculations are all done just like our examples just above; you should check some (or all) of them for practice.

Beginning on the first row in Table 11.9, we have 100 percent in the stock fund, so our expected return is 12 percent, and our standard deviation is 15 percent. As we begin to move out of the stock fund and into the bond fund, we are not surprised to see both the expected return and the standard deviation decline. However, what might be surprising to you is the fact that the standard deviation falls only so far and then begins to rise again. In other words, beyond a point, adding more of the lower risk bond fund actually *increases* your risk!

The best way to see what is going on is to plot the various combinations of expected returns and standard deviations calculated in Table 11.9 as we do in Figure 11.4. We simply placed the standard deviations from Table 11.9 on the horizontal axis and the corresponding expected returns on the vertical axis.

investment opportunity set
Collection of possible risk–return combinations available from portfolios of individual assets.

Examining the plot in Figure 11.4, we see that the various combinations of risk and return available all fall on a smooth curve (in fact, for the geometrically inclined, it's a hyperbola). This curve is called an **investment opportunity set** because it shows the possible combinations of risk and return available from portfolios of these two assets. One important thing to notice is that, as we have shown, there is a portfolio that has the smallest standard deviation

TABLE 11.9 Risk and Return with Stocks and Bonds

Portfolio Weights			
Stocks	Bonds	Expected Return	Standard Deviation (Risk)
1.00	.00	12.00%	15.00%
.95	.05	11.70	14.31
.90	.10	11.40	13.64
.85	.15	11.10	12.99
.80	.20	10.80	12.36
.75	.25	10.50	11.77
.70	.30	10.20	11.20
.65	.35	9.90	10.68
.60	.40	9.60	10.21
.55	.45	9.30	9.78
.50	.50	9.00	9.42
.45	.55	8.70	9.12
.40	.60	8.40	8.90
.35	.65	8.10	8.75
.30	.70	7.80	8.69
.25	.75	7.50	8.71
.20	.80	7.20	8.82
.15	.85	6.90	9.01
.10	.90	6.60	9.27
.05	.95	6.30	9.60
.00	1.00	6.00	10.00

FIGURE 11.4 Risk and Return with Stocks and Bonds

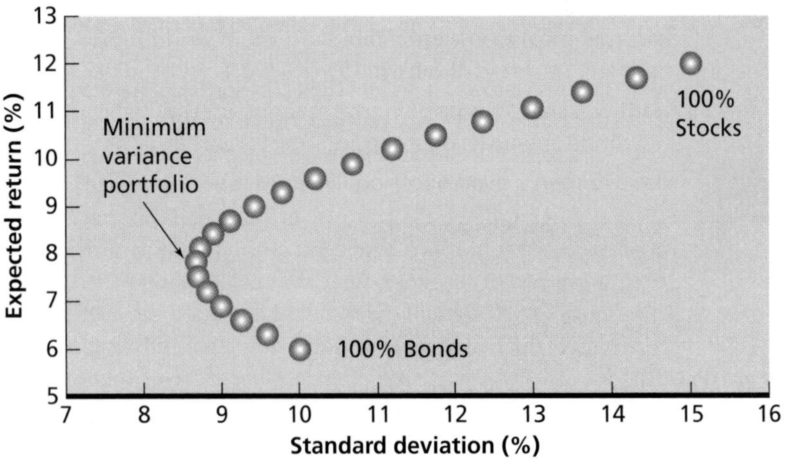

(or variance—same thing) of all. It is labeled "minimum variance portfolio" in Figure 11.4. What are (approximately) its expected return and standard deviation?

WWW

Review modern portfolio theory at www.moneychimp.com

Now we see clearly why a 100 percent bonds strategy is a poor one. With a 10 percent standard deviation, the bond fund offers an expected return of 6 percent. However, Table 11.9 shows us that a combination of about 60 percent stocks and 40 percent bonds has almost the same standard deviation, but a return of about 9.6 percent. Comparing

9.6 percent to 6 percent, we see that this portfolio has a return that is fully 60 percent greater (6% × 1.6 = 9.6%) with the same risk. Our conclusion? Asset allocation matters.

Going back to Figure 11.4, notice that any portfolio that plots below the minimum variance portfolio is a poor choice because, no matter which one you pick, there is another portfolio with the same risk and a much better return. In the jargon of finance, we say that these undesirable portfolios are *dominated* and/or *inefficient*. Either way; we mean that given their level of risk, the expected return is inadequate compared to some other portfolio of equivalent risk. A portfolio that offers the highest return for its level of risk is said to be an **efficient portfolio**. In Figure 11.4, the minimum variance portfolio and all portfolios that plot above it are therefore efficient.

efficient portfolio
A portfolio that offers the highest return for its level of risk.

EXAMPLE 11.6 **More Portfolio Variance and Standard Deviation**

Looking at Table 11.9, suppose you put 57.627 percent in the stock fund. What is your expected return? Your standard deviation? How does this compare with the bond fund?

If you put 57.627 percent in stocks, you must have 42.373 percent in bonds, so x_A = .57627 and x_B = .42373. From Table 11.9, you can see that the standard deviation for stocks and bonds is 15% and 10%, respectively. Also, the correlation between stocks and bonds is .10. Making use of our portfolio variance equation (11.3), we have:

$$\sigma_P^2 = .57627^2 \times .15^2 + .42373^2 \times .10^2 + 2 \times .57627 \times .42373 \times .15 \times .10 \times .10$$
$$= .332 \times .0225 + .180 \times .01 + .0007325$$
$$= .01$$

Thus, the portfolio variance is .01, so the standard deviation is .1, or 10 percent. Check that the expected return is 9.46 percent. Compared to the bond fund, the standard deviation is now identical, but the expected return is almost 350 basis points higher.

MORE ON CORRELATION AND THE RISK-RETURN TRADE-OFF

Given the expected returns and standard deviations on the two assets, the shape of the investment opportunity set in Figure 11.4 depends on the correlation. The lower the correlation, the more bowed to the left the investment opportunity set will be. To illustrate, Figure 11.5 shows the investment opportunity for correlations of −1, 0, and +1 for two stocks, A and B. Notice that Stock A has an expected return of 12 percent and a standard deviation of 15 percent, while Stock B has an expected return of 6 percent and a standard deviation of 10 percent. These are the same expected returns and standard deviations we used to build Figure 11.4, and the calculations are all done the same way; just the correlations are different. Notice also that we use the symbol ρ to stand for the correlation coefficient.

In Figure 11.5, when the correlation is +1, the investment opportunity set is a straight line connecting the two stocks, so, as expected, there is little or no diversification benefit. As the correlation declines to zero, the bend to the left becomes pronounced. For correlations between +1 and zero, there would simply be a less pronounced bend.

Finally, as the correlation becomes negative, the bend becomes quite pronounced, and the investment opportunity set actually becomes two straight-line segments when the correlation hits −1. Notice that the minimum variance portfolio has a *zero* variance in this case.

It is sometimes desirable to be able to calculate the percentage investments needed to create the minimum variance portfolio. For a two-asset portfolio, Equation (11.5) shows the weight in asset A, x_A^*, that achieves the minimum variance.

FIGURE 11.5 Risk and Return with Two Assets

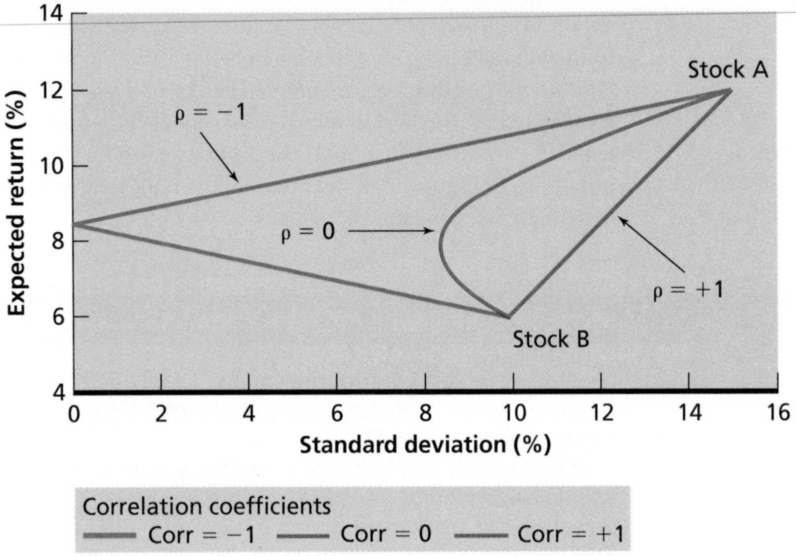

$$x_A^* = \frac{\sigma_B^2 - \sigma_A\sigma_B \text{Corr}(R_A, R_B)}{\sigma_A^2 + \sigma_B^2 - 2\sigma_A\sigma_B \text{Corr}(R_A, R_B)} \tag{11.5}$$

A question at the end of the chapter asks you to prove that Equation (11.5) is correct.

EXAMPLE 11.7 Finding the Minimum Variance Portfolio

Looking back at Table 11.9, what combination of the stock fund and the bond fund has the lowest possible standard deviation? What is the minimum possible standard deviation?

Recalling that the standard deviations for the stock fund and bond fund were .15 and .10, respectively, and noting that the correlation was .1, we have:

$$\begin{aligned} x_A^* &= \frac{.10^2 - .15 \times .10 \times .10}{.15^2 + .10^2 - 2 \times .15 \times .10 \times .10} \\ &= .288136 \\ &\approx 28.8\% \end{aligned}$$

Thus, the minimum variance portfolio has 28.8 percent in stocks and the balance, 71.2 percent, in bonds. Plugging these into our formula for portfolio variance, we have:

$$\begin{aligned} \sigma_P^2 &= .288^2 \times .15^2 + .712^2 \times .10^2 + 2 \times .288 \times .712 \times .15 \times .10 \times .10 \\ &= .007551 \end{aligned}$$

The standard deviation is the square root of .007551, about 8.7 percent. Notice that this is where the minimum occurs in Figure 11.5.

CHECK THIS

11.4a Fundamentally, why does diversification work?

11.4b If two stocks have positive correlation, what does this mean?

11.4c What is an efficient portfolio?

Our discussion of market efficiency in a previous chapter bears on this discussion. We are assuming that relevant information known today is already reflected in the expected return. This assumption is identical to saying that the current price reflects relevant publicly available information. We are thus implicitly assuming that markets are at least reasonably efficient in the semistrong-form sense. Henceforth, when we speak of news, we will mean the surprise part of an announcement and not the portion that the market had expected and therefore already discounted.

EXAMPLE 12.1 **In the News**

Suppose Intel were to announce that earnings for the quarter just ending were up by 40 percent relative to a year ago. Do you expect that the stock price would rise or fall on the announcement?

The answer is that you can't really tell. Suppose the market was expecting a 60 percent increase. In this case, the 40 percent increase would be a negative surprise, and we would expect the stock price to fall. On the other hand, if the market was expecting only a 20 percent increase, there would be a positive surprise, and we would expect the stock to rise on the news.

CHECK THIS

12.1a What are the two basic parts of a return on common stock?

12.1b Under what conditions will an announcement have no effect on common stock prices?

12.2 Risk: Systematic and Unsystematic

It is important to distinguish between expected and unexpected returns because the unanticipated part of the return, that portion resulting from surprises, is the significant risk of any investment. After all, if we always receive exactly what we expect, then the investment is perfectly predictable and, by definition, risk-free. In other words, the risk of owning an asset comes from surprises—unanticipated events.

There are important differences, though, among various sources of risk. Look back at our previous list of news stories. Some of these stories are directed specifically at Flyers, and some are more general. Which of the news items are of specific importance to Flyers?

Announcements about interest rates or GDP are clearly important for nearly all companies, whereas the news about Flyers's president, its research, or its sales is of specific interest to Flyers investors only. We distinguish between these two types of events, because, as we will see, they have very different implications.

SYSTEMATIC AND UNSYSTEMATIC RISK

systematic risk
Risk that influences a large number of assets. Also called *market risk.*

unsystematic risk
Risk that influences a single company or a small group of companies. Also called *unique* or *asset-specific risk.*

The first type of surprise, the one that affects most assets, we label **systematic risk**. A systematic risk is one that influences a large number of assets, each to a greater or lesser extent. Because systematic risks have marketwide effects, they are sometimes called *market risks.*

The second type of surprise we call **unsystematic risk**. An unsystematic risk is one that affects a single asset, or possibly a small group of assets. Because these risks are unique to individual companies or assets, they are sometimes called *unique* or *asset-specific risks.* We use these terms interchangeably.

As we have seen, uncertainties about general economic conditions, such as GDP, interest rates, or inflation, are examples of systematic risks. These conditions affect nearly all companies to some degree. An unanticipated increase, or surprise, in inflation, for example, affects wages and the costs of supplies that companies buy; it affects the value of the assets that companies own; and it affects the prices at which companies sell their products. Forces such as these, to which all companies are susceptible, are the essence of systematic risk.

In contrast, the announcement of an oil strike by a particular company will primarily affect that company and, perhaps, a few others (such as primary competitors and suppliers). It is unlikely to have much of an effect on the world oil market, however, or on the affairs of companies not in the oil business, so this is an unsystematic event.

SYSTEMATIC AND UNSYSTEMATIC COMPONENTS OF RETURN

WWW

Analyze risk at www.portfolioscience.com

The distinction between a systematic risk and an unsystematic risk is never really as exact as we would like it to be. Even the most narrow and peculiar bit of news about a company ripples through the economy. This ripple effect happens because every enterprise, no matter how tiny, is a part of the economy. It's like the proverb about a kingdom that was lost because one horse lost a horseshoe nail. However, not all ripple effects are equal—some risks have a much broader effect than others.

The distinction between the two types of risk allows us to break down the surprise portion, U, of the return on the Flyers stock into two parts. Earlier, we had the actual return broken down into its expected and surprise components: $R - E(R) = U$. We now recognize that the total surprise component for Flyers, U, has a systematic and an unsystematic component, so:

$$R - E(R) = \text{Systematic portion} + \text{Unsystematic portion} \tag{12.3}$$

Because it is traditional, we will use the Greek letter epsilon ϵ to stand for the unsystematic portion. Because systematic risks are often called "market" risks, we use the letter m to stand for the systematic part of the surprise. With these symbols, we can rewrite the formula for the total return:

$$R - E(R) = U = m + \epsilon \tag{12.4}$$

The important thing about the way we have broken down the total surprise, U, is that the unsystematic portion, ϵ, is unique to Flyers. For this reason, it is unrelated to the unsystematic portion of return on most other assets. To see why this is important, we need to return to the subject of portfolio risk.

EXAMPLE 12.2 Systematic versus Unsystematic Events

Suppose Intel were to unexpectedly announce that its latest computer chip contains a significant flaw in its floating point unit that left it unable to handle numbers bigger than a couple of gigatrillion (meaning that, among other things, the chip cannot calculate Intel's quarterly profits). Is this a systematic or unsystematic event?

Obviously, this event is for the most part unsystematic. However, it would also benefit Intel's competitors to some degree and, at least potentially, harm some users of Intel products such as personal computer makers. Thus, as with most unsystematic events, there is some spillover, but the effect is mostly confined to a relatively small number of companies.

CHECK THIS

12.2a What are the two basic types of risk?

12.2b What is the distinction between the two types of risk?

12.3 Diversification, Systematic Risk, and Unsystematic Risk

In the previous chapter, we introduced the principle of diversification. What we saw was that some of the risk associated with individual assets can be diversified away and some cannot. We are left with an obvious question: Why is this so? It turns out that the answer hinges on the distinction between systematic and unsystematic risk.

DIVERSIFICATION AND UNSYSTEMATIC RISK

By definition, an unsystematic risk is one that is particular to a single asset or, at most, a small group of assets. For example, if the asset under consideration is stock in a single company, such things as successful new products and innovative cost savings will tend to increase the value of the stock. Unanticipated lawsuits, industrial accidents, strikes, and similar events will tend to decrease future cash flows and thereby reduce share value.

Here is the important observation: If we hold only a single stock, then the value of our investment will fluctuate because of company-specific events. If we hold a large portfolio, on the other hand, some of the stocks in the portfolio will go up in value because of positive company-specific events, and some will go down in value because of negative events. The net effect on the overall value of the portfolio will be relatively small, however, because these effects will tend to cancel each other out.

Now we see why some of the variability associated with individual assets is eliminated by diversification. When we combine assets into portfolios, the unique, or unsystematic, events—both positive and negative—tend to "wash out" once we have more than just a few assets. This is an important point that bears repeating:

Unsystematic risk is essentially eliminated by diversification, so a portfolio with many assets has almost no unsystematic risk.

In fact, the terms *diversifiable risk* and *unsystematic risk* are often used interchangeably.

DIVERSIFICATION AND SYSTEMATIC RISK

We've seen that unsystematic risk can be eliminated by diversification. What about systematic risk? Can it also be eliminated by diversification? The answer is no because, by definition, a systematic risk affects almost all assets. As a result, no matter how many assets we put into a portfolio, systematic risk doesn't go away. Thus, for obvious reasons, the terms *systematic risk* and *nondiversifiable risk* are used interchangeably.

Because we have introduced so many different terms, it is useful to summarize our discussion before moving on. What we have seen is that the total risk of an investment can be written as:

$$\text{Total risk} = \text{Systematic risk} + \text{Unsystematic risk} \quad (12.5)$$

Systematic risk is also called *nondiversifiable risk* or *market risk*. Unsystematic risk is also called *diversifiable risk, unique risk,* or *asset-specific risk.* Most important, for a well-diversified portfolio, unsystematic risk is negligible. For such a portfolio, essentially all risk is systematic.

CHECK THIS

12.3a Why is some risk diversifiable? Why is some risk not diversifiable?

12.3b Why can't systematic risk be diversified away?

12.4 Systematic Risk and Beta

We now begin to address another question: What determines the size of the risk premium on a risky asset? Put another way, why do some assets have a larger risk premium than other assets? The answer, as we discuss next, is also based on the distinction between systematic and unsystematic risk.

THE SYSTEMATIC RISK PRINCIPLE

Thus far, we've seen that the total risk associated with an asset can be decomposed into two components: systematic and unsystematic risk. We have also seen that unsystematic risk can be essentially eliminated by diversification. The systematic risk present in an asset, on the other hand, cannot be eliminated by diversification.

Based on our study of capital market history in Chapter 1, we know that there is a reward, on average, for bearing risk. However, we now need to be more precise about what we mean by risk. The **systematic risk principle** states that the reward for bearing risk depends only on the systematic risk of an investment.

systematic risk principle
The reward for bearing risk depends only on the systematic risk of an investment.

The underlying rationale for this principle is straightforward: Because unsystematic risk can be eliminated at virtually no cost (by diversifying), there is no reward for bearing it. In other words, the market does not reward risks that are borne unnecessarily.

The systematic risk principle has a remarkable and very important implication:

The expected return on an asset depends only on its systematic risk.

There is an obvious corollary to this principle: No matter how much total risk an asset has, only the systematic portion is relevant in determining the expected return (and the risk premium) on that asset.

MEASURING SYSTEMATIC RISK

Because systematic risk is the crucial determinant of an asset's expected return, we need some way of measuring the level of systematic risk for different investments. The specific measure we will use is called the **beta coefficient**, designated by the Greek letter β. A beta coefficient, or just beta for short, tells us how much systematic risk a particular asset has relative to an average asset. By definition, an average asset has a beta of 1.0 relative to itself. An asset with a beta of .50, therefore, has half as much systematic risk as an average asset. Likewise, an asset with a beta of 2.0 has twice as much systematic risk.

beta coefficient (β)
Measure of the relative systematic risk of an asset. Assets with betas larger (smaller) than 1 have more (less) systematic risk than average.

Table 12.1 presents the estimated beta coefficients for the stocks of some well-known companies. (Note that *Value Line* rounds betas to the nearest .05.) The range of betas in Table 12.1 is typical for stocks of large U.S. corporations. Betas outside this range occur, however, as you can see in our nearby *Work the Web.*

The important thing to remember is that the expected return, and thus the risk premium, on an asset depends only on its systematic risk. Because assets with larger betas have greater systematic risks, they will have greater expected returns. Thus, from Table 12.1, an investor who buys stock in ExxonMobil, with a beta of .90, should expect to earn less and lose less, on average, than an investor who buys stock in General Motors, with a beta of about 1.45.

WWW

Find betas at finance.yahoo.com and www.smartmoney.com

One cautionary note is in order: Not all betas are created equal. For example, in Table 12.1, *Value Line*, a widely used source of betas, reports a beta for IBM of 1.10. At the same time, however, another widely used source, *S&P Stock Reports*, puts IBM's beta at 1.62,

WORK THE WEB

Suppose you want to find the beta for a company like Continental Airlines, Inc. One way is to go to the Web. We went to finance.yahoo.com, looked up Continental Airlines (CAL), and followed the "Key Statistics" link. This is part of what we found:

FINANCIAL HIGHLIGHTS	
Fiscal Year	
Fiscal Year Ends:	31-Dec
Most Recent Quarter (mrq):	30-Jun-07
Profitability	
Profit Margin (ttm):	3.40%
Operating Margin (ttm):	4.29%
Management Effectiveness	
Return on Assets (ttm):	3.05%
Return on Equity (ttm):	60.10%
Income Statement	
Revenue (ttm):	13.56B
Revenue Per Share (ttm):	145.849
Qtrly Revenue Growth (yoy):	5.80%
Gross Profit (ttm):	4.56B
EBITDA (ttm):	980.00M
Net Income Avl to Common (ttm):	461.00M
Diluted EPS (ttm):	4.24
Qtrly Earnings Growth (yoy):	15.20%

TRADING INFORMATION	
Stock Price History	
Beta:	2.74
52-Week Change[3]:	15.95%
S&P500 52-Week Change[3]:	14.38%
52-Week High (17-Jan-07)[3]:	52.40
52-Week Low (15-Aug-07)[3]:	26.21
50-Day Moving Average[3]:	31.70
200-Day Moving Average[3]:	35.68
Share Statistics	
Average Volume (3 month)[3]:	3,955,360
Average Volume (10 day)[3]:	3,102,540
Shares Outstanding[6]:	97.83M
Float:	97.63M
% Held by Insiders[4]:	21.76%
% Held by Institutions[4]:	97.20%
Shares Short (as of 11-Sep-07)[3]:	14.15M
Short Ratio (as of 11-Sep-07)[3]:	3.3
Short % of Float (as of 11-Sep-07)[3]:	14.50%
Shares Short (prior month)[3]:	13.93M

The reported beta for Continental Airlines is 2.74, which means that Continental Airlines has about 2.74 times the systematic risk of a typical stock.

TABLE 12.1 Beta Coefficients

	Beta, β	
Company	**Value Line**	**Standard & Poor's**
ExxonMobil	0.90	0.75
IBM	1.10	1.62
Starbucks	0.80	0.59
Wal-Mart	0.80	0.54
General Motors	1.45	1.21
Microsoft	1.00	0.94
Harley-Davidson	0.90	0.88
eBay	1.15	1.37
Nordstrom	1.25	1.41
Southwest Airlines	1.05	0.98
Yahoo	1.50	1.53

Source: *Value Line* Investment Survey and *S&P Stock Reports.*

substantially larger. The difference results from the different procedures used to calculate beta coefficients. We will have more to say on this subject when we explain how betas are calculated in a later section. Our nearby *Work the Web* box shows one way to find betas online.

EXAMPLE 12.3

Total Risk versus Beta

Consider the following information on two securities. Which has greater total risk? Which has greater systematic risk? Greater unsystematic risk? Which asset will have a higher risk premium?

	Standard Deviation	Beta
Security A	40%	.50
Security B	20	1.50

From our discussion in this section, Security A has greater total risk, but it has substantially less systematic risk. Because total risk is the sum of systematic and unsystematic risk, Security A must have greater unsystematic risk. Finally, from the systematic risk principle, Security B will have a higher risk premium and a greater expected return, despite the fact that it has less total risk.

PORTFOLIO BETAS

Earlier, we saw that the riskiness of a portfolio has no simple relation to the risks of the assets in the portfolio. By contrast, a portfolio beta can be calculated just like a portfolio expected return. For example, looking again at Table 12.1, suppose you put half of your money in Starbucks and half in eBay. Using *Value Line* betas, what would the beta of this combination be? Because Starbucks has a beta of .80 and eBay has a beta of 1.15, the portfolio's beta, β_p would be:

$$\begin{aligned}\beta_p &= .50 \times \beta_{\text{Starbucks}} + .50 \times \beta_{\text{eBay}} \\ &= .50 \times .80 + .50 \times 1.15 \\ &= .975\end{aligned}$$

In general, if we had a large number of assets in a portfolio, we would multiply each asset's beta by its portfolio weight and then add the results to get the portfolio's beta.

EXAMPLE 12.4

Portfolio Betas

Suppose we have the following information

Security	Amount Invested	Expected Return	Beta
Stock A	$1,000	8%	.80
Stock B	2,000	12	.95
Stock C	3,000	15	1.10
Stock D	4,000	18	1.40

What is the expected return on this portfolio? What is the beta of this portfolio? Does this portfolio have more or less systematic risk than an average asset?

To answer, we first have to calculate the portfolio weights. Notice that the total amount invested is $10,000. Of this, $1,000/$10,000 = 10% is invested in Stock A. Similarly, 20 percent is invested in Stock B, 30 percent is invested in Stock C, and 40 percent is invested in Stock D. The expected return, $E(R_p)$, is thus:

$$\begin{aligned}E(R_p) &= .10 \times E(R_A) + .20 \times E(R_B) + .30 \times E(R_C) + .40 \times E(R_D) \\ &= .10 \times 8\% + .20 \times 12\% + .30 \times 15\% + .40 \times 18\% \\ &= 14.9\%\end{aligned}$$

(continued)

Similarly, the portfolio beta, β_P, is:

$$\beta_P = .10 \times \beta_A + .20 \times \beta_B + .30 \times \beta_C + .40 \times \beta_D$$
$$= .10 \times .80 + .20 \times .95 + .30 \times 1.10 + .40 \times 1.40$$
$$= 1.16$$

This portfolio thus has an expected return of 14.9 percent and a beta of 1.16. Because the beta is larger than 1, this portfolio has greater systematic risk than an average asset.

CHECK THIS

12.4a What is the systematic risk principle?

12.4b What does a beta coefficient measure?

12.4c How do you calculate a portfolio beta?

12.4d True or false: The expected return on a risky asset depends on that asset's total risk. Explain.

12.5 The Security Market Line

We're now in a position to see how risk is rewarded in the marketplace. To begin, suppose that Asset A has an expected return of $E(R_A) = 16\%$ and a beta of $\beta_A = 1.6$. Further suppose that the risk-free rate is $R_f = 4\%$. Notice that a risk-free asset, by definition, has no systematic risk (or unsystematic risk), so a risk-free asset has a beta of zero.

BETA AND THE RISK PREMIUM

Consider a portfolio made up of Asset A and a risk-free asset. We can calculate some different possible portfolio expected returns and betas by varying the percentages invested in these two assets. For example, if 25 percent of the portfolio is invested in Asset A, then the expected return is:

$$E(R_p) = .25 \times E(R_A) + (1 - .25) \times R_f$$
$$= .25 \times 16\% + .75 \times 4\%$$
$$= 7\%$$

Similarly, the beta on the portfolio, β_p, would be:

WWW

For more information on risk management visit www.fenews.com

$$\beta_p = .25 \times \beta_A + (1 - .25) \times 0$$
$$= .25 \times 1.6$$
$$= .40$$

Notice that, because the weights have to add up to 1, the percentage invested in the risk-free asset is equal to 1 minus the percentage invested in Asset A.

One thing that you might wonder about is whether the percentage invested in Asset A can exceed 100 percent. The answer is yes. This can happen if the investor borrows at the risk-free rate and invests the proceeds in stocks. For example, suppose an investor has \$100 and borrows an additional \$50 at 4 percent, the risk-free rate. The total investment in Asset A would be \$150, or 150 percent of the investor's wealth. The expected return in this case would be:

$$E(R_p) = 1.50 \times E(R_A) + (1 - 1.50) \times R_f$$
$$= 1.50 \times 16\% - .50 \times 4\%$$
$$= 22\%$$

The beta on the portfolio would be:

$$\begin{aligned}\beta_p &= 1.50 \times \beta_A + (1 - 1.50) \times 0 \\ &= 1.50 \times 1.6 \\ &= 2.4\end{aligned}$$

We can calculate some other possibilities, as follows:

Percentage of Portfolio in Asset A	Portfolio Expected Return	Portfolio Beta
0%	4%	.0
25	7	.4
50	10	.8
75	13	1.2
100	16	1.6
125	19	2.0
150	22	2.4

In Figure 12.1A, we plot these portfolio expected returns against portfolio betas. Notice that all the combinations fall on a straight line.

THE REWARD-TO-RISK RATIO

What is the slope of the straight line in Figure 12.1A? As always, the slope of a straight line is equal to the rise over the run. In this case, as we move out of the risk-free asset into Asset A, the expected return goes from 4 percent to 16 percent, a rise of 12 percent. At the same time, the beta increases from zero to 1.6, a run of 1.6. The slope of the line is thus 12%/1.6 = 7.5%.

Notice that the slope of our line is just the risk premium on Asset A, $E(R_A) - R_f$, divided by Asset A's beta, β_A:

$$\begin{aligned}\text{Slope} &= \frac{E(R_A) - R_f}{\beta_A} \\ &= \frac{16\% - 4\%}{1.6} \\ &= 7.50\%\end{aligned}$$

What this tells us is that Asset A offers a *reward-to-risk* ratio of 7.5 percent.[1] In other words, Asset A has a risk premium of 7.50 percent per "unit" of systematic risk.

THE BASIC ARGUMENT

Now suppose we consider a second asset, Asset B. This asset has a beta of 1.2 and an expected return of 12 percent. Which investment is better, Asset A or Asset B? You might think that we really cannot say—some investors might prefer A; some investors might prefer B. Actually, however, we can say: A is better because, as we will demonstrate, B offers inadequate compensation for its level of systematic risk, at least relative to A.

To begin, we calculate different combinations of expected returns and betas for portfolios of Asset B and a risk-free asset, just as we did for Asset A. For example, if we put 25 percent in Asset B and the remaining 75 percent in the risk-free asset, the portfolio's expected return will be:

$$\begin{aligned}E(R_p) &= .25 \times E(R_B) + (1 - .25) \times R_f \\ &= .25 \times 12\% + .75 \times 4\% \\ &= 6\%\end{aligned}$$

[1] This ratio is sometimes called the *Treynor index*, after one of its originators.

FIGURE 12.1 Betas and Portfolio Returns

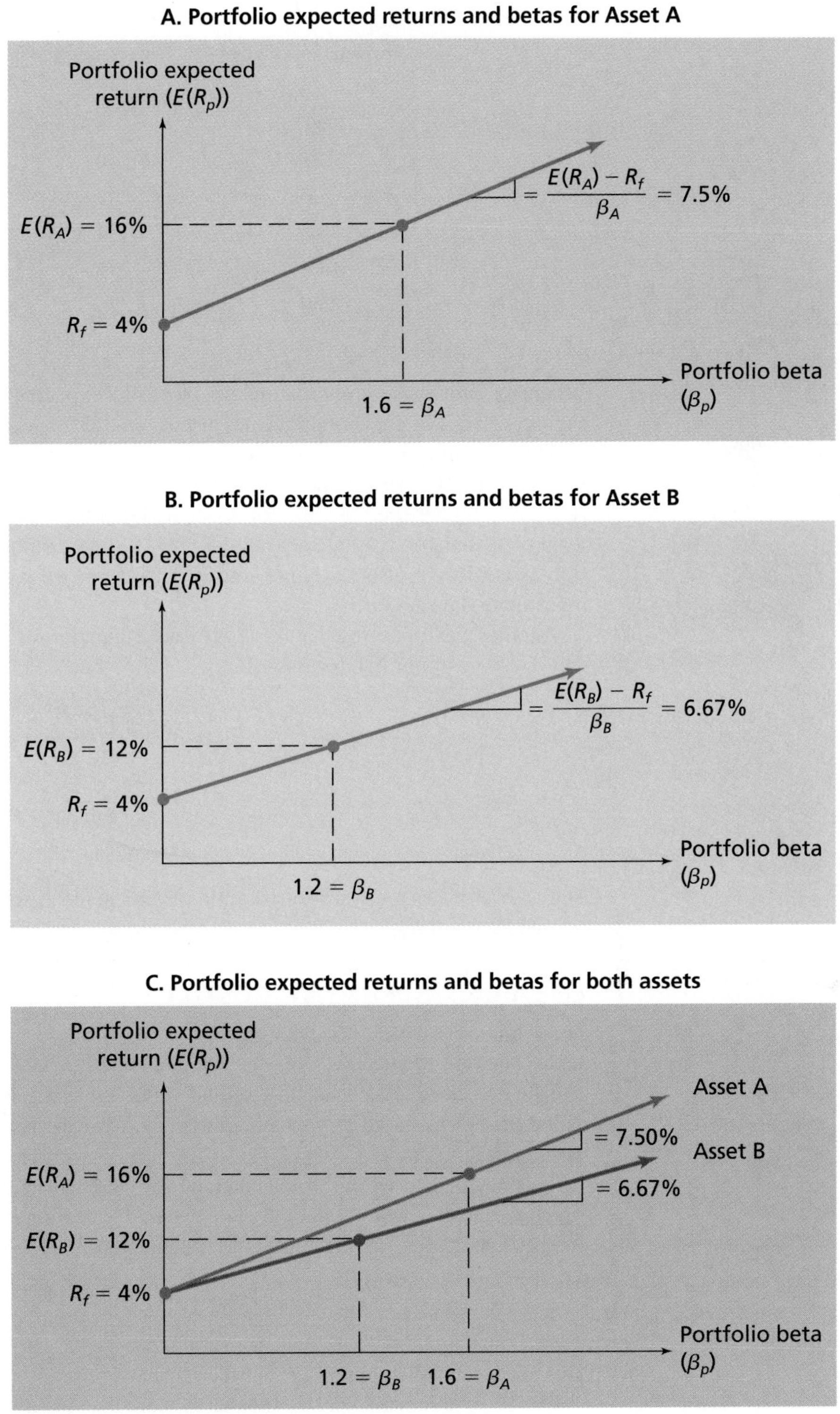

Similarly, the beta on the portfolio, β_p, would be:

$$\begin{aligned}\beta_p &= .25 \times \beta_B + (1 - .25) \times 0 \\ &= .25 \times 1.2 \\ &= .30\end{aligned}$$

Some other possibilities are as follows:

Percentage of Portfolio in Asset B	Portfolio Expected Return	Portfolio Beta
0%	4%	.0
25	6	.3
50	8	.6
75	10	.9
100	12	1.2
125	14	1.5
150	16	1.8

When we plot these combinations of portfolio expected returns and portfolio betas in Figure 12.1B, we get a straight line, just as we did for Asset A.

The key thing to notice is that when we compare the results for Assets A and B, as in Figure 12.1C, the line describing the combinations of expected returns and betas for Asset A is higher than the one for Asset B. What this result tells us is that for any given level of systematic risk (as measured by beta), some combination of Asset A and the risk-free asset always offers a larger return. Therefore, we can state that Asset A is a better investment than Asset B.

Another way of seeing that Asset A offers a superior return for its level of risk is to note that the slope of our line for Asset B is:

$$\begin{aligned} \text{Slope} &= \frac{E(R_B) - R_f}{\beta_B} \\ &= \frac{12\% - 4\%}{1.2} \\ &= 6.67\% \end{aligned}$$

Thus, Asset B has a reward-to-risk ratio of 6.67 percent, which is less than the 7.5 percent offered by Asset A.

THE FUNDAMENTAL RESULT

The situation we described for Assets A and B could not persist in a well-organized, active market because investors would be attracted to Asset A and away from Asset B. As a result, Asset A's price would rise and Asset B's price would fall. Because prices and expected returns move in opposite directions, A's expected return would decline and B's would rise.

This buying and selling would continue until the two assets plot on exactly the same line, which means they would offer the same reward for bearing risk. In other words, in an active, competitive market, we must have the situation that:

$$\frac{E(R_A) - R_f}{\beta_A} = \frac{E(R_B) - R_f}{\beta_B} \tag{12.6}$$

This is the fundamental relation between risk and return.

Our basic argument can be extended to more than just two assets. In fact, no matter how many assets we had, we would always reach the same conclusion:

The reward-to-risk ratio must be the same for all assets in a competitive financial market.

This result is really not too surprising. What it says is that, for example, if one asset has twice as much systematic risk as another asset, its risk premium will simply be twice as large.

returns, such as monthly returns. This argues for using monthly or longer returns. On the other hand, any time we estimate something, we would like to have a large number of recent observations. This argues for using weekly or daily returns. There is no ideal balance; the most common choices are three to five years of monthly data or a single year of weekly data. The betas we get from a year of weekly data are more current in the sense that they reflect only the previous year, but they tend to be less stable than those obtained from longer periods.

Another issue has to do with choice of a market index. All along, we have discussed the return on the "overall market," but we have not been very precise about how to measure this. By far the most common choice is to use the S&P 500 stock market index to measure the overall market, but this is not the only alternative. Different sources use different indexes to capture the overall market, and different indexes will lead to different beta estimates.

You might wonder whether some index is the "correct" one. The answer is yes, but a problem comes up. In principle, in the CAPM, when we speak of the overall market, what we really mean is the market for *every* risky asset of every type. In other words, what we would need is an index that included all the stocks, bonds, real estate, precious metals, and everything else in the entire world (not just the United States). Obviously, no such index exists, so instead we must choose some smaller index to proxy for this much larger one.

Last, a few sources (including *Value Line,* one source for Table 12.1) calculate betas the way we described in Table 12.4, but then they go on to adjust them for statistical reasons. The nature of the adjustment goes beyond our discussion, but such adjustments are another reason why betas differ across sources.

12.7 Extending CAPM

The previous two sections introduced you to the famous capital asset pricing model, or CAPM for short. For investors, the CAPM has a stunning implication: What you earn, through time, on your portfolio depends only on the level of systematic risk you bear. The corollary is equally striking: As a diversified investor, you do not need to be concerned with the total risk or volatility of any individual asset in your portfolio—it is simply irrelevant.

Of course, we should note that the CAPM is a theory, and, as with any theory, whether it is correct is a question for the data. So does the CAPM work or not? Put more directly, does expected return depend on beta, and beta alone, or do other factors come into play? There is no more hotly debated question in all of finance.

In this section, we first present a short history of attempts to test the CAPM. Then we discuss one of the most important extensions of the CAPM, the so-called Fama-French three-factor model.

A (VERY) BRIEF HISTORY OF TESTING CAPM

The CAPM was introduced in the mid-1960s (but, perhaps surprisingly, tests of this model began to appear only in the early 1970s). When researchers test the CAPM, they essentially look to see whether average returns are linearly related to beta. That is, they want to know if asset returns and beta line up as shown in Figure 12.3. The earliest tests of the CAPM suggested that return and risk (as measured by beta) showed a reasonable relationship. However, the relationship was not so strong that financial researchers were content to move on and test other theories.

To summarize years of testing, the relationship between returns and beta appeared to vary depending on the time period that was studied. Over some periods, the relationship was strong. In others, it was apparent but not strong. In others, it was seemingly nonexistent. Over the years, researchers refined their techniques to measure betas. In addition, the question was raised whether researchers could calculate betas at all. The basic argument was that betas could not be calculated relative to the overall market portfolio because we cannot observe the true market portfolio. Nonetheless, despite this insightful critique, researchers continue to test CAPM and debate the findings of CAPM research to this day.

INVESTMENT UPDATE

SMALL CAP VALUE MAY NO LONGER BE A VALUE

Good things come in small packages. Just ask investors in small-cap value stocks.

Value stocks in the Russell 2000 Index, a benchmark for small stocks, have done twice as well as the Standard & Poor's 500 has over the last 24 months.

And over the past decade small-cap value stocks are up an eye-popping 168%, easily outpacing the S&P's 103% advance and the Russell 2000 Growth Index's mere 44% gain.

So, not surprisingly, some small value stocks are starting to look pricey.

The Russell 2000, whose median market cap is about \$576 million, fetches 23.4 times earnings estimates for the next four quarters. That's far richer than the S&P 500's 15.5 times forward earnings, according to Thomson Financial/Baseline.

That's why some money managers advise taking profits in the priciest value small caps and replacing them with shares of larger companies.

"We think it would be a good idea for investors to sell some of their small-cap stocks," says Ned Notzon, chairman of the asset allocation committee at T. Rowe Price Associates.

Small caps (which typically have a market capitalization of \$1 billion or less) can be great long-term-investments, even though their returns can fluctuate much more than shares of large, well-known companies.

For the last 78 years, small caps have generated compound annual returns of 12.7%, compared with 10.4% for large caps, according to Ibbotson Associates. Historically, small-cap value stocks do best—they've risen nearly 15% compared with the 9.6% returns for small-cap growth.

Value stocks typically have stable earnings growth and lower price-to-book and price-to-earnings ratios. Growth stocks tend to have higher growth rates and valuations.

The question is, how long can the current run for small caps last?

Small-cap stocks outperformed others for nearly a decade during the bull market that began in 1974, says Roger Ibbotson, chief executive officer of the Chicago research firm Ibbotson Associates.

But in the fourth year of the two most recent bull markets (which is where we are in the current one), small caps have underperformed big-cap stocks, according to Sam Stovall, chief investment strategist at S&P.

"I would not be optimistic about small caps in 2006," Ibbotson says. "The run has got to be about over, even though momentum is working for the seventh year in a row."

Barry James, a portfolio manager at James Investment Research near Dayton, Ohio, recommends that investors cut their allocations for small caps to 10 to 15% of their portfolios, from 25%.

He's looking for small caps in the technology sector to hold up well, however, and expects smaller energy stocks to resist a broader market decline, even if oil prices drop.

Arthur Nunes, at IMS Capital, says that in the past 20 years, mid-cap stocks—those whose market capitalization is between \$1 billion and \$5 billion—have been silent winners, offering 15.2% returns with a lower risk than small caps.

Ultimately, investors who have profited by thinking small over the last few years may now need to look at the bigger picture.

Source: Dimitra Defotis, October 11, 2005. Reprinted by permission of Dow Jones and Company Inc. via Copyright Clearance Center, Inc.

Despite the debate between CAPM critics and CAPM champions, some important ideas have emerged. Few researchers question these general principles:

- Investing has two dimensions: risk and return.
- It is inappropriate to look at the risk of an individual security. What is appropriate is how the individual security contributes to the risk of a diversified portfolio.
- Risk can be decomposed into systematic risk and nonsystematic risk.
- Investors will be compensated only for taking systematic risk.

THE FAMA-FRENCH THREE-FACTOR MODEL

To illustrate some aspects of the debate surrounding CAPM, we now briefly explore the Fama-French three-factor model, which gets its name from its creators, Gene Fama and Ken French. Table 12.5 illustrates an important finding from years of research into stock market returns. As shown, two groups of stocks have tended to do noticeably better than the market

TABLE 12.5 Average Annual Percentage Returns from 25 Portfolios Formed on Size (Cap) and Book to Market, 1926–2006

	(Lowest B/M) 1	2	3	4	(Highest B/M) 5
1 (smallest cap)	11.68	19.44	21.43	24.86	31.08
2	11.76	17.21	19.45	19.76	20.47
3	12.39	16.04	17.06	17.80	19.64
4	12.36	13.68	15.81	16.95	18.35
5 (largest cap)	11.04	12.59	13.67	14.48	15.31

Source: Author calculations using data from the Web site of Ken French.

as a whole: (1) stocks with a small-market capitalization (small-cap stocks) and (2) stocks that have a higher than average ratio of book (or accounting) value to market value of equity (so-called value stocks).

Table 12.5 is formed as follows. First, for each year of historical data, a large set of stocks are ranked on the basis of their market cap, or size. The smallest 20 percent of the stocks are placed into the market cap quintile number 1, the next smallest 20 percent are placed into market cap quintile number 2, and so on. Then, the same set of stocks are ranked on the basis of their book/market (B/M) ratio. The smallest 20 percent are placed into B/M quintile number 1, the next smallest 20 percent are placed into B/M quintile number 2, and so on.

Let's look at the cell with an average annual return of 11.68 percent. This number is calculated as follows. After the sorting described above, we put stocks into portfolios according to both of their quintile scores, for a total of 25 (= 5 × 5) portfolios. So, for example, the stocks with both the smallest cap and the lowest B/M end up in the quintile 1–1 portfolio. As shown in Table 12.5, over the time period 1926 to 2006, the average annual return for stocks in the quintile 1–1 portfolio is 11.68 percent.

Three things should jump out at you in Table 12.5. Notice that the cell 1–5, which contains stocks with the smallest cap and highest B/M, has had the highest returns. Looking down each column, you can see that in four columns the highest return belongs to the smallest cap quintile (this happens in columns 2, 3, 4, and 5). Looking across each row, you can see that in every row, the highest return belongs to the highest B/M quintile.

WWW

You can download lots of data behind the Fama-French model at http://mba.tuck.dartmouth.edu/pages/faculty/ken.french/

Based on further analysis of these data, Professors Fama and French concluded that differences in beta were not sufficient to explain the differences in returns in Table 12.5. They therefore argue that two additional factors beyond beta must be considered to understand differences in expected returns on stocks, namely, market cap and B/M. Thus, their model of stock returns has a total of three factors. Whether these extra factors are truly sources of systematic risk is a subject of ongoing debate.

12.8 Summary and Conclusions

This chapter covers the essentials of risk and return. Along the way, we introduced a number of definitions and concepts. The most important of these is the security market line, or SML. The SML is important because it tells us the reward offered in financial markets for bearing risk. Because we covered quite a bit of ground, it's useful to summarize the basic economic logic underlying the SML as follows.

1. The difference between expected and unexpected returns.

A. The return on any stock traded in a financial market is composed of two parts. The expected return from the stock is the part of the return that investors predict or expect. This return depends on the information investors have about the stock, and it is based on the market's understanding today of the important factors that will influence the stock in the coming year.

B. The second part of the return on the stock is the uncertain, or risky, part. This is the portion that comes from unexpected information revealed during the year.

2. The difference between systematic risk and unsystematic risk.

A. Based on capital market history, there is a reward for bearing risk. This reward is the risk premium on an asset.

B. The total risk associated with an asset has two parts: systematic risk and unsystematic risk. Unsystematic risk can be freely eliminated by diversification (this is the principle of diversification), so only systematic risk is rewarded. As a result, the risk premium on an asset is determined by its systematic risk. This is the systematic risk principle.

3. The security market line and the capital asset pricing model.

A. An asset's systematic risk, relative to the average, can be measured by its beta coefficient, β_i. The risk premium on an asset is then given by the market risk premium multiplied by the asset's beta coefficient, $[E(R_M) - R_f] \times \beta_i$.

B. The expected return on an asset, $E(R_i)$, is equal to the risk-free rate, R_f, plus the asset's risk premium: $E(R_i) = R_f + [E(R_M) - R_f] \times \beta_i$. This is the equation of the SML, and it is often called the capital asset pricing model (CAPM).

4. The importance of beta.

A. Systematic risk is the crucial determinant of an asset's expected return. Therefore, we need some way of measuring the level of systematic risk for different investments.

B. The specific measure we use is called the beta coefficient, designated by the Greek letter β. A beta coefficient, or just beta for short, tells us how much systematic risk a particular asset has relative to an average asset.

C. By definition, an average asset has a beta of 1.0 relative to itself. An asset with a beta of .50, therefore, has half as much systematic risk as an average asset.

D. Toward the end of the chapter, we showed how betas are calculated and we discussed some of the main reasons different sources report different beta coefficients. We closed the chapter by presenting a discussion of the Fama-French three-factor model, an important extension to the basic CAPM.

GET REAL

An immediate implication of the CAPM is that you, as an investor, need to be aware of the level of systematic risk you are carrying. Look up the betas of the stocks you hold in your simulated brokerage account and compute your portfolio's systematic risk. Is it bigger or smaller than 1.0? More important, is the portfolio's beta consistent with your desired level of portfolio risk?

Betas are particularly useful for understanding mutual fund risk and return. Since most mutual funds are at least somewhat diversified (the exceptions being sector funds and other specialized funds), they have relatively little unsystematic risk, and their betas can be measured with some precision. Look at the funds you own and learn their betas (www.morningstar.com is a good source). Are the risk levels what you intended? As you study mutual fund risk, you will find some other measures exist, most of which are closely related to the measures discussed in this chapter. Take a few minutes to understand these as well.

Does expected return depend on beta, and beta alone, or do other factors come into play? There is no more hotly debated question in all of finance, and the research that exists to date is inconclusive. (Some researchers would dispute this!) At a minimum, beta appears to be a useful measure of market-related volatility, that is, risk. Whether beta is a useful measure of expected return (much less a comprehensive one) awaits more research. Lots more research.

Key Terms

beta coefficient (β) 386
capital asset pricing model (CAPM) 395
covariance 399
market risk premium 394
security market line (SML) 394
systematic risk 383
systematic risk principle 386
unsystematic risk 383

Chapter Review Problems and Self-Test

1. **Risk and Return** Suppose you observe the following situation:

Security	Beta	Expected Return
Sanders	1.8	22.00%
Janicek	1.6	20.44

If the risk-free rate is 7 percent, are these two stocks correctly priced relative to each other? What must the risk-free rate be if they are correctly priced?

2. **CAPM** Suppose the risk-free rate is 8 percent. The expected return on the market is 16 percent. If a particular stock has a beta of .7, what is its expected return based on the CAPM? If another stock has an expected return of 24 percent, what must its beta be?

Answers to Self-Test Problems

1. If we compute the reward-to-risk ratios, we get (22% − 7%)/1.8 = 8.33% for Sanders versus 8.4% for Janicek. Relative to Sanders, Janicek's expected return is too high, so its price is too low.

If they are correctly priced, then they must offer the same reward-to-risk ratio. The risk-free rate would have to be such that:

$$\frac{22\% - R_f}{1.8} = \frac{20.44\% - R_f}{1.6}$$

With a little algebra, we find that the risk-free rate must be 8 percent:

$$22\% - R_f = (20.44\% - R_f)(1.8/1.6)$$
$$22\% - 20.44\% \times 1.125 = R_f - R_f \times 1.125$$
$$R_f = 8\%$$

2. Because the expected return on the market is 16 percent, the market risk premium is 16% − 8% = 8% (the risk-free rate is also 8 percent). The first stock has a beta of .7, so its expected return is 8% + 8% × .7 = 13.6%.

For the second stock, notice that the risk premium is 24% − 8% = 16%. Because this is twice as large as the market risk premium, the beta must be exactly equal to 2. We can verify this using the CAPM:

$$E(R_i) = R_f + [E(R_M) - R_f] \times \beta_i$$
$$24\% = 8\% + (16\% - 8\%) \times \beta_i$$
$$\beta_i = 16\%/8\% = 2.0$$

Test Your Investment Quotient

IQ

For the remaining questions and problems, the circled numbers in the margin refer to the corresponding learning objective in this chapter.

CFA® PROBLEMS

(3) 1. **Portfolio Return** According to the CAPM, what is the rate of return of a portfolio with a beta of 1?

a. Between R_M and R_f
b. The risk-free rate, R_f
c. Beta × $(R_M - R_f)$
d. The return on the market, R_M

www.mhhe.com/jm5e

(1) **2. Stock Return** The return on a stock is said to have which two of the following basic parts?

a. An expected return and an unexpected return.
b. A measurable return and an unmeasurable return.
c. A predicted return and a forecast return.
d. A total return and a partial return.

(1) **3. News Components** A news announcement about a stock is said to have which two of the following parts?

a. An expected part and a surprise.
b. Public information and private information.
c. Financial information and product information.
d. A good part and a bad part.

(1) **4. News Effects** A company announces that its earnings have increased 50 percent over the previous year, which matches analysts' expectations. What is the likely effect on the stock price?

a. The stock price will increase.
b. The stock price will decrease.
c. The stock price will rise and then fall after an overreaction.
d. The stock price will not be affected.

(1) **5. News Effects** A company announces that its earnings have decreased 25 percent from the previous year, but analysts expected a small increase. What is the likely effect on the stock price?

a. The stock price will increase.
b. The stock price will decrease.
c. The stock price will rise and then fall after an overreaction.
d. The stock price will not be affected.

(1) **6. News Effects** A company announces that its earnings have increased 25 percent from the previous year, but analysts actually expected a 50 percent increase. What is the likely effect on the stock price?

a. The stock price will increase.
b. The stock price will decrease.
c. The stock price will rise and then fall after an overreaction.
d. The stock price will not be affected.

(1) **7. News Effects** A company announces that its earnings have decreased 50 percent from the previous year, but analysts only expected a 25 percent decrease. What is the likely effect on the stock price?

a. The stock price will increase.
b. The stock price will decrease.
c. The stock price will rise and then fall after an overreaction.
d. The stock price will not be affected.

(2) **8. Security Risk** The systematic risk of a security is also called its

a. Perceived risk
b. Unique or asset-specific risk
c. Market risk
d. Fundamental risk

(2) **9. Security Risk** Which type of risk is essentially eliminated by diversification?

a. Perceived risk
b. Market risk
c. Systematic risk
d. Unsystematic risk

(2) **10. Security Risk** The systematic risk principle states that

a. Systematic risk doesn't matter to investors.
b. Systematic risk can be essentially eliminated by diversification.
c. The reward for bearing risk is independent of the systematic risk of an investment.
d. The reward for bearing risk depends only on the systematic risk of an investment.

(2) **11. Security Risk** The systematic risk principle has an important implication, which is

a. Systematic risk is preferred to unsystematic risk.
b. Systematic risk is the only risk that can be reduced by diversification.
c. The expected return on an asset is independent of its systematic risk.
d. The expected return on an asset depends only on its systematic risk.

3 **12. CAPM** A financial market's security market line (SML) describes

- **a.** The relationship between systematic risk and expected returns.
- **b.** The relationship between unsystematic risk and expected returns.
- **c.** The relationship between systematic risk and unexpected returns.
- **d.** The relationship between unsystematic risk and unexpected returns.

CFA® PROBLEMS

3 **13. Risk Aversion** Which of the following is not an implication of risk aversion for the investment process?

- **a.** The security market line is upward sloping.
- **b.** The promised yield on AAA-rated bonds is higher than on A-rated bonds.
- **c.** Investors expect a positive relationship between expected return and risk.
- **d.** Investors prefer portfolios that lie on the efficient frontier to other portfolios with equal rates of return.

CFA® PROBLEMS

2 **14. Unsystematic Risk** In the context of capital market theory, unsystematic risk

- **a.** Is described as unique risk.
- **b.** Refers to nondiversifiable risk.
- **c.** Remains in the market portfolio.
- **d.** Refers to the variability in all risk assets caused by macroeconomic factors and other aggregate market-related variables.

CFA® PROBLEMS

3 **15. Security Market Line** Which of the following statements about the security market line (SML) is false?

- **a.** Properly valued assets plot exactly on the SML.
- **b.** The SML leads all investors to invest in the same portfolio of risky assets.
- **c.** The SML provides a benchmark for evaluating expected investment performance.
- **d.** The SML is a graphic representation of the relationship between expected return and beta.

Concept Questions

2 **1. Diversifiable Risk** In broad terms, why is some risk diversifiable? Why are some risks nondiversifiable? Does it follow that an investor can control the level of unsystematic risk in a portfolio, but not the level of systematic risk?

1 **2. Announcements and Prices** Suppose the government announces that, based on a just-completed survey, the growth rate in the economy is likely to be 2 percent in the coming year, compared to 5 percent for the year just completed. Will security prices increase, decrease, or stay the same following this announcement? Does it make any difference whether the 2 percent figure was anticipated by the market? Explain.

2 **3. Announcements and Risk** Classify the following events as mostly systematic or mostly unsystematic. Is the distinction clear in every case?

- **a.** Short-term interest rates increase unexpectedly.
- **b.** The interest rate a company pays on its short-term debt borrowing is increased by its bank.
- **c.** Oil prices unexpectedly decline.
- **d.** An oil tanker ruptures, creating a large oil spill.
- **e.** A manufacturer loses a multi-million-dollar product liability suit.
- **f.** A Supreme Court decision substantially broadens producer liability for injuries suffered by product users.

2 **4. Announcements and Risk** Indicate whether the following events might cause stocks in general to change price, and whether they might cause Big Widget Corp.'s stock to change price.

- **a.** The government announces that inflation unexpectedly jumped by 2 percent last month.
- **b.** Big Widget's quarterly earnings report, just issued, generally fell in line with analysts' expectations.
- **c.** The government reports that economic growth last year was at 3 percent, which generally agreed with most economists' forecasts.
- **d.** The directors of Big Widget die in a plane crash.
- **e.** Congress approves changes to the tax code that will increase the top marginal corporate tax rate. The legislation had been debated for the previous six months.

www.mhhe.com/jm5e

② **5. Diversification and Risk** True or false: The most important characteristic in determining the expected return of a well-diversified portfolio is the variances of the individual assets in the portfolio. Explain.

① **6. Announcements** As indicated by examples in this chapter, earnings announcements by companies are closely followed by, and frequently result in, share price revisions. Two issues should come to mind. First, earnings announcements concern past periods. If the market values stocks based on expectations of the future, why are numbers summarizing past performance relevant? Second, these announcements concern accounting earnings. Such earnings may have little to do with cash flow, so, again, why are they relevant?

④ **7. Beta** Is it possible that a risky asset could have a beta of zero? Explain. Based on the CAPM, what is the expected return on such an asset? Is it possible that a risky asset could have a negative beta? What does the CAPM predict about the expected return on such an asset? Can you give an explanation for your answer?

③ **8. Relative Valuation** Suppose you identify a situation in which one security is overvalued relative to another. How would you go about exploiting this opportunity? Does it matter if the two securities are both overvalued relative to some third security? Are your profits certain in this case?

③ **9. Reward-to-Risk Ratio** Explain what it means for all assets to have the same reward-to-risk ratio. How can you increase your return if this holds true? Why would we expect that all assets have the same reward-to-risk ratio in liquid, well-functioning markets?

CFA® PROBLEMS

② **10. Systematic versus Firm-Specific Risk** Dudley Trudy, CFA, recently met with one of his clients. Trudy typically invests in a master list of 30 securities drawn from several industries. After the meeting concluded, the client made the following statement: "I trust your stock-picking ability and believe that you should invest my funds in your five best ideas. Why invest in 30 companies when you obviously have stronger opinions on a few of them?" Trudy plans to respond to his client within the context of Modern Portfolio Theory.

a. Contrast the concept of systematic and firm-specific risk and give one example of each.

b. Critique the client's suggestion. Discuss the impact of the systematic risk and firm-specific risk on portfolio risk as the number of securities in a portfolio is increased.

Questions and Problems

Core Questions

③ **1. Stock Betas** A stock has an expected return of 14.4 percent, the risk-free rate is 4.5 percent, and the market risk premium is 7.5 percent. What must the beta of this stock be?

③ **2. Market Returns** A stock has an expected return of 10.5 percent, its beta is .75, and the risk-free rate is 5 percent. What must the expected return on the market be?

③ **3. Risk-Free Rates** A stock has an expected return of 16 percent, a beta of 1.35, and the expected return on the market is 13 percent. What must the risk-free rate be?

③ **4. Market Risk Premium** A stock has a beta of .8 and an expected return of 11 percent. If the risk-free rate is 5.5 percent, what is the market risk premium?

④ **5. Portfolio Betas** You own a stock portfolio invested 20 percent in Stock Q, 15 percent in Stock R, 40 percent in Stock S, and 25 percent in Stock T. The betas for these four stocks are 1.2, .6, 1.5, and .9, respectively. What is the portfolio beta?

④ **6. Portfolio Betas** You own 400 shares of Stock A at a price of $60 per share, 500 shares of Stock B at $85 per share, and 900 shares of Stock C at $25 per share. The betas for the stocks are 1.2, .9, and 1.6, respectively. What is the beta of your portfolio?

④ **7. Stock Betas** You own a portfolio equally invested in a risk-free asset and two stocks. If one of the stocks has a beta of 1.05, and the total portfolio is exactly as risky as the market, what must the beta be for the other stock in your portfolio?

③ **8. Expected Returns** A stock has a beta of .85, the expected return on the market is 13 percent, and the risk-free rate is 5.8 percent. What must the expected return on this stock be?

③ **9. CAPM and Stock Price** A share of stock sells for $53 today. The beta of the stock is 1.2, and the expected return on the market is 12 percent. The stock is expected to pay a dividend of $1.10 in one year. If the risk-free rate is 5.5 percent, what will the share price be in one year?

(4) **10. Portfolio Weights** A stock has a beta of 1.2 and an expected return of 14 percent. A risk-free asset currently earns 5 percent.

a. What is the expected return on a portfolio that is equally invested in the two assets?
b. If a portfolio of the two assets has a beta of .5, what are the portfolio weights?
c. If a portfolio of the two assets has an expected return of 12 percent, what is its beta?
d. If a portfolio of the two assets has a beta of 1.80, what are the portfolio weights? How do you interpret the weights for the two assets in this case? Explain.

Intermediate Questions

(3) **11. Portfolio Risk and Return** Asset W has an expected return of 10.5 percent and a beta of .9. If the risk-free rate is 6 percent, complete the following table for portfolios of Asset W and a risk-free asset. Illustrate the relationship between portfolio expected return and portfolio beta by plotting the expected returns against the betas. What is the slope of the line that results?

Percentage of Portfolio in Asset W	Portfolio Expected Return	Portfolio Beta
0%		
25		
50		
75		
100		
125		
150		

(3) **12. Relative Valuation** Stock Y has a beta of 1.25 and an expected return of 14 percent. Stock Z has a beta of .70 and an expected return of 9 percent. If the risk-free rate is 6 percent and the market risk premium is 7 percent, are these stocks correctly priced?

(3) **13. Relative Valuation** In the previous problem, what would the risk-free rate have to be for the two stocks to be correctly priced relative to each other?

(3) **14. CAPM** Using the CAPM, show that the ratio of the risk premiums on two assets is equal to the ratio of their betas.

(3) **15. Relative Valuation** Suppose you observe the following situation:

Security	Beta	Expected Return
Oxy Co.	1.15	13.4
More-On Co.	.80	11

Assume these securities are correctly priced. Based on the CAPM, what is the expected return on the market? What is the risk-free rate?

(3) **16. Calculating Beta** Show that another way to calculate beta is to take the covariance between the security and the market and divide by the variance of the market's return.

(4) **17. Calculating Beta** Fill in the following table, supplying all the missing information. Use this information to calculate the security's beta.

	Returns		Return Deviations		Squared Deviations		Product of
Year	Security	Market	Security	Market	Security	Market	Deviations
2003	14	10					
2004	−8	−4					
2005	21	15					
2006	38	21					
2007	16	7					

(4) **18. Analyzing a Portfolio** You have $100,000 to invest in a portfolio containing Stock X, Stock Y, and a risk-free asset. You must invest all of your money. Your goal is to create a portfolio that has an expected return of 13 percent and that has only 70 percent of the risk of the overall market. If X has an expected return of 31 percent and a beta of 1.8, Y has an expected return of 20 percent and a beta of 1.3, and the risk-free rate is 7 percent, how much money will you invest in Stock Y? How do you interpret your answer?

www.mhhe.com/jm5e

investment benchmark. The need for this form of scrutiny arises in a number of situations, including:

- An investor planning to choose a mutual fund wants to first compare the investment performance of several dozen candidate funds.
- A pension fund administrator wants to select a money manager and thus needs to compare the investment performance of a group of money managers.
- An employer wants to compare the performance of several investment companies before selecting one for inclusion in her company-sponsored 401(k) retirement plan.

In the first section of this chapter, we examine several useful evaluation measures of portfolio performance and discuss how they might be applied to these and similar situations.

In the second part of the chapter, we discuss the important problem of risk management from the perspective of an investor or money manager concerned with the possibility of a large loss. Specifically, we examine methods to assess the probabilities and magnitudes of losses we might expect to experience during a set future time period. These risk assessment techniques are commonly employed in a number of situations, including:

- A New York Stock Exchange specialist wants to know how much of a loss is possible with a 5 percent probability during the coming day's trading from the specialist firm's inventory.
- The foreign currency manager of a commercial bank wants to know how much of a loss is possible with a 2 percent probability on the bank's foreign currency portfolio during the coming week.
- A futures exchange clearinghouse wants to know how much margin funds should be deposited by exchange members to cover extreme losses that might occur with a "once in a century" probability.

Methods used to assess risk in these and similar scenarios fall into the category commonly referred to as "Value-at-Risk." Value-at-Risk techniques are widely applied by commercial banks, securities firms, and other financial institutions to assess and understand the risk exposure of portfolios under their management.

13.1 Performance Evaluation

performance evaluation
The assessment of how well a money manager achieves a balance between high returns and acceptable risks.

Investors have a natural (and very rational) interest in how well particular investments have done. This is true whether the investor manages his or her own portfolio or has money managed by a professional. Concern with investment performance motivates the topic of **performance evaluation**. In general terms, performance evaluation focuses on assessing how well a money manager achieves high returns balanced with acceptable risks.

Going back to our discussion of efficient markets in an earlier chapter, we raised the question of risk-adjusted performance and whether anyone can consistently earn an "excess" return, thereby "beating the market." The standard example is an evaluation of investment performance achieved by the manager of a mutual fund. Such a performance evaluation is more than an academic exercise, because its purpose is to help investors decide whether they would entrust investment funds with the fund manager. Our goal here is to introduce you to the primary tools used to make this assessment.

PERFORMANCE EVALUATION MEASURES

raw return
States the total percentage return on an investment with no adjustment for risk or comparison to any benchmark.

A variety of measures are used to evaluate investment performance. Here, we examine three of the best-known and most popular measures: the Sharpe ratio, the Treynor ratio, and Jensen's alpha. But before we do so, let us first briefly discuss a naive measure of performance evaluation—the **raw return** on a portfolio.

The raw return on an investment portfolio, here denoted by R_p, is simply the total percentage return on the portfolio with no adjustment for risk or comparison to any benchmark. Calculating percentage returns was discussed in Chapter 1. The fact that a raw portfolio return

WORK THE WEB

The various performance measures we have discussed are frequently used to evaluate mutual funds, or, more accurately, mutual fund managers. For example, the information below concerns the Fidelity Low-Priced Stock Fund, which is a small-cap value fund. We obtained the numbers from www.morningstar.com by entering the fund's ticker symbol (FLPSX) and following the "Risk Measures" link. By the way, you will see the abbreviation "MPT" in this context quite a bit. MPT is an acronym for "modern portfolio theory," which is the general label for things related to Markowitz-type portfolio analysis and the CAPM.

For this fund, the beta is 1.25, so the degree of market risk is above average. The fund's alpha is 1.95 percent, which could indicate superior past performance. The fund's standard deviation is 10.66 percent. The mean reported, 16.90 percent, is the geometric return of the fund over the past three years. The Sharpe ratio for the fund is 1.08. Of course, we cannot judge this value in isolation, but at least we know it is positive. Other measures of risk are reported here, but they are specific to Morningstar. To learn more, visit Morningstar's Web site.

Fidelity Low-Priced Stock FLPSX See Fund Family Data ▸▸ **Finance**

Volatility Measurements	Trailing 3-Yr through 08-31-07	*Trailing 5-Yr through 08-31-07	
Standard Deviation	10.66	Sharpe Ratio	1.08
Mean	16.90	Bear Market Decile Rank*	5

Modern Portfolio Theory Statistics	Trailing 3-Yr through 08-31-07	
	Standard Index S&P 500 TR	**Best Fit Index** Morningstar Mid Cap TR
R-Squared	74	90
Beta	1.25	0.99
Alpha	1.95	-0.82

CHECK THIS

13.2a Explain the difference between systematic risk measured by beta and total risk measured by standard deviation. When are they essentially the same?

13.2b Alter the returns data in Table 13.1 so that portfolios *A*, *B*, and *C* all have a raw return of 15 percent. Which among these three portfolios then have a Treynor ratio or Jensen's alpha greater than that of the market portfolio *M*?

SHARPE-OPTIMAL PORTFOLIOS

In this section, we show how to obtain a funds allocation with the highest possible Sharpe ratio. Such a portfolio is said to be "Sharpe optimal." The method is closely related to the procedure of obtaining a Markowitz efficient frontier discussed in a previous chapter. This fact is no surprise because both methods are used to achieve an optimal balance of risk and return for investment portfolios.

To illustrate the connection, have a look at Figure 13.2. This figure shows the investment opportunity set of risk-return possibilities for a portfolio of two assets, a stock fund and a bond fund. Now the question is: "Of all of these possible portfolios, which one is Sharpe optimal?" To find out, consider the portfolio labeled *A* in the figure. Notice that we have drawn a straight line from the risk-free rate running through this point.

FIGURE 13.2 The Sharpe-Optimal Portfolio

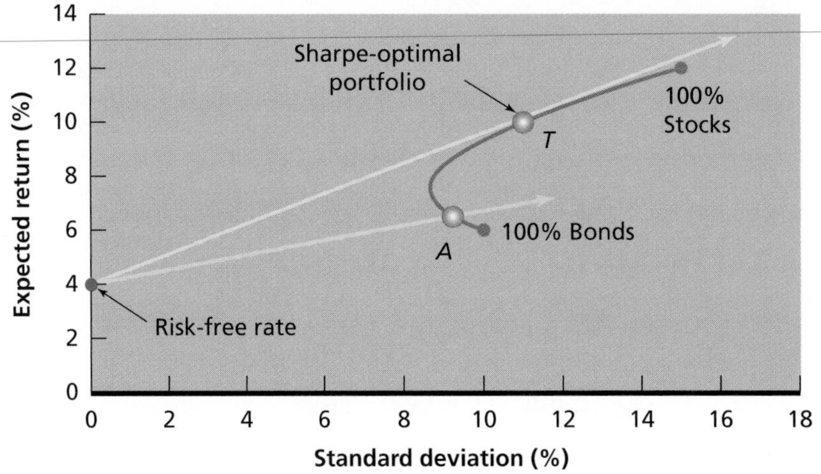

Portfolio *T* has the highest Sharpe ratio of any possible combination of these two assets, so it is Sharpe optimal.

What is the slope of this straight line? As always, the slope of a straight line is the "rise over the run." In this case, the return rises from the risk-free rate, R_f, to the expected return on portfolio *A*, so the rise is $E(R_A) - R_f$. At the same time, risk moves from zero for a risk-free asset up to the standard deviation on portfolio *A*, so the run is $\sigma_A - 0 = \sigma_A$. Thus, the slope is $[E(R_A) - R_f]/\sigma_A$, which is just the Sharpe ratio for portfolio *A*.

So, the slope of a straight line drawn from the risk-free rate to a portfolio in Figure 13.2 tells us the Sharpe ratio for that portfolio. This is always the case, even if there are many assets, not just two. The problem of finding the Sharpe-optimal portfolio thus boils down to finding the line with the steepest slope. Looking again at Figure 13.2, we quickly figure out that the line with the steepest slope is always going to be the one that just touches (i.e., is tangent to) the investment opportunity set. We have labeled this portfolio *T* (for tangent).

We now have an interesting and important result. The Markowitz efficient frontier tells us which portfolios are efficient, but it does not tell us which of the efficient portfolios is the best. What Figure 13.2 shows is that, of those efficient portfolios, one is the very best, at least in the sense of being Sharpe optimal.

To illustrate how to find the Sharpe optimal portfolio, recall from Chapter 11 that the returns of the stock and bond funds are 12 percent and 6 percent. The standard deviations are 15 percent and 10 percent, respectively, and the correlation is .10. From our discussion in Chapter 11, we know that the expected return on a portfolio of two assets is given by:

$$E(R_p) = x_S E(R_S) + x_B E(R_B)$$

where x_S and x_B are the percentages invested in the stock and bond fund, respectively. Also from Chapter 11, the variance on a portfolio of these two assets is:

$$\sigma_P^2 = x_S^2\sigma_S^2 + x_B^2\sigma_B^2 + 2x_S x_B \sigma_S \sigma_B \text{Corr}(R_S, R_B)$$

Putting it all together, the Sharpe ratio for our two-asset portfolio looks like this:

$$\frac{E(R_p) - R_f}{\sigma_p} = \frac{x_S E(R_S) + x_B E(R_B) - R_f}{\sqrt{x_S^2\sigma_S^2 + x_B^2\sigma_B^2 + 2x_S x_B \sigma_S \sigma_B \text{Corr}(R_S, R_B)}} \quad (13.5)$$

Our task is to find the values of x_S and x_B that make this ratio as large as possible. This looks like a tough job, but, as our nearby *Spreadsheet Analysis* box shows, it can be done relatively easily. As shown there, assuming a risk-free interest rate of 4 percent, the highest possible Sharpe ratio is .553 based on a 70–30 mix between stocks and bonds.

SPREADSHEET ANALYSIS

	A	B	C	D	E	F	G	H
1								
2		Optimal Sharpe Ratio with Two Risky Assets, Stocks and Bonds						
3								
4	Expected Returns:							
5		Stocks =	0.12					
6		Bonds =	0.06				Portfolio Return, E(Rp) =	0.102
7								
8		Risk-Free Rate =	0.04				Portfolio Standard Deviation, SD(Rp) =	0.112
9								
10	Standard Deviations:						Sharpe Ratio =	0.553
11		Stocks =	0.15					
12		Bonds =	0.10					
13				Portfolio Weights to Maximize Sharpe Ratio:				
14	Correlation between						Stocks =	0.7000
15		Stocks and Bonds =	0.10				Bonds =	0.3000
16							(= 1 – H14)	
17								
18	Formulas for Portfolio Return, Portfolio Standard Deviation, and Sharpe Ratio:							
19								
20	E(Rp) =	H14*C5+H15*C6						
21								
22	SD(Rp) =	SQRT(H14*H14*C11*C11+H15*H15*C12*C12+2*H14*H15*C15*C11*C12)						
23								
24	Sharpe Ratio = (E(Rp) - RF) / SD(Rp) = (H6-C8)/H8							
25								
26	Using SOLVER® to compute portfolio weights that maximize the Sharpe Ratio:							
27								
28								
29								
30								
31								
32								
33								
34								
35								
36								
37								
38								
39								
40								
41								
42								
43								
44								
45								
46								

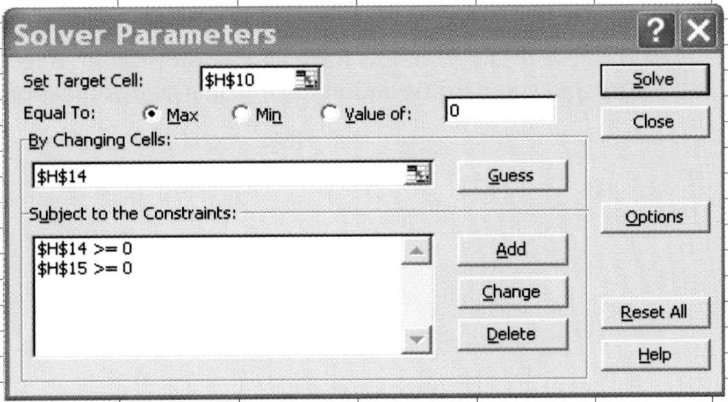

You can use the Solver tool to solve for the weights that maximize the Sharpe ratio. In the nearby *Spreadsheet Analysis,* we did just that. Once the formulas are entered for the portfolio return, standard deviation, and Sharpe ratio, we can solve for the portfolio weights that give us the highest possible Sharpe ratio. We do not have to worry about the weight in bonds because the weight in bonds is simply equal to one minus the weight in stocks.

You can see in the *Spreadsheet Analysis* that we ask Solver to change the portfolio weight in stocks so that the maximum Sharpe ratio is obtained. Note that we also required that the weights in stocks and bonds both be equal to or greater than zero. If any of the returns, standard deviations, or correlations are changed, the Solver tool must be rerun. Build this spreadsheet yourself and see if you get the same answer we did. Then, change the correlation between stocks and bonds to .20. Does the Sharpe ratio increase or decrease? What happens to the weights?

EXAMPLE 13.6 Sharpe-Optimal Portfolio Calculations

Suppose you have the following expected return and risk information for stocks and bonds that will be used to form a Sharpe-optimal portfolio.

$$E(R_S) = .12 \quad \sigma_S = .15 \quad E(R_B) = .06 \quad \sigma_B = .10 \quad \text{Corr}(R_S, R_B) = .10 \quad R_F = .04$$

In the case of just two risky assets, stocks and bonds, the formulas for the portfolio weights for the optimal Sharpe portfolio are:

$$x_S = \frac{\sigma_B^2 \times [E(R_S) - R_F] - \text{Corr}(R_S, R_B) \times \sigma_S \times \sigma_B \times [E(R_B) - R_F]}{\sigma_B^2 \times [E(R_S) - R_F] + \sigma_S^2 \times [E(R_B) - R_F] - [E(R_S) + E(R_B) - 2 \times R_F] \times \text{Corr}(R_S, R_B) \times \sigma_S \times \sigma_B}$$

and

$$x_B = 1 - x_S$$

Calculate the Sharpe-optimal portfolio weights and the expected return and standard deviation for the Sharpe-optimal portfolio.

Inserting the expected return and risk information into these formulas yields these optimal Sharpe portfolio weights for stocks and bonds:

$$x_S = \frac{.10^2 \times [.12 - .04] - .10 \times .15 \times .10 \times [.06 - .04]}{.10^2 \times [.12 - .04] + .15^2 \times [.06 - .04] - [.12 + .06 - 2 \times .04] \times .10 \times .15 \times .10}$$
$$= .70$$

and

$$x_B = 1 - x_S = 1 - .70 = .30$$

With these results, we now have all the information needed to calculate the expected return and standard deviation for the Sharpe-optimal portfolio:

$$E(R_P) = x_S E(R_S) + x_B E(R_B)$$
$$= .70 \times .12 + .30 \times .06$$
$$= .102, \text{ or } 10.2\%$$

$$\sigma_P = \sqrt{x_S^2 \sigma_S^2 + x_B^2 \sigma_B^2 + 2 x_S x_B \sigma_S \sigma_B \text{Corr}(R_S, R_B)}$$
$$= \sqrt{.70^2 \times .15^2 + .30^2 \times .10^2 + 2 \times .70 \times .30 \times .15 \times .10 \times .10}$$
$$= .112, \text{ or } 11.2\%$$

CHECK THIS

13.2c What is a Sharpe-optimal portfolio?

13.2d Among the many Markowitz efficient portfolios, which one is Sharpe optimal?

13.3 Investment Risk Management

investment risk management
Concerns a money manager's control over investment risks, usually with respect to potential short-run losses.

In the first part of this chapter, we discussed performance evaluation within a framework of optimizing the trade-off between risk and return for an investment portfolio. In the remainder of this chapter, we examine **investment risk management** within the framework of a

INVESTMENT UPDATES

SHARPE POINT: RISK GAUGE IS MISUSED

William F. Sharpe was probably the biggest expert in the room when economists from around the world gathered in Sonoma, Calif., to hash out a pressing problem in July: How to gauge hedge-fund risk.

About 40 years ago, Dr. Sharpe, now a retired professor from Stanford University, created a simple calculation for measuring the return that investors should expect for the level of volatility they are accepting. The so-called Sharpe Ratio became a cornerstone of modern finance, as investors used it to help select money managers and mutual funds. But at the Sonoma meeting, the use of the ratio was criticized by many prominent academics—including Dr. Sharpe himself.

The ratio is commonly used—"misused," Dr. Sharpe says—for promotional purposes by hedge funds. "That is very disturbing," says the 71-year-old Dr. Sharpe. Hedge funds often use complex strategies that are vulnerable to surprise events and elude any simple formula for measuring risk. "Past average experience may be a terrible predictor of future performance," Dr. Sharpe says.

"This is becoming more of a problem because there is a movement to offer retail versions of hedge funds," says Andrew Lo, a Massachusetts Institute of Technology finance professor and a partner in the AlphaSimplex Group, a hedge fund that manages $350 million. "The typical retail investor might very well be misled by amazing looking Sharpe Ratios."

"Hedge funds can manipulate the ratio to misrepresent their performance," adds Dr. Sharpe, a founder of Financial Engines, a Palo Alto, Calif., investment adviser and manager. In a recent study, Dr. Lo found that the annual Sharpe Ratio for hedge funds can be overstated by as much as 65%. "You can legitimately generate very attractive Sharpe Ratios and still, in time, lose money," he says. "People should not take the Sharpe Ratio at face value."

Even if it isn't manipulated, Dr. Sharpe says, it doesn't foreshadow hedge-fund woes because "no number can." The formula can't predict such troubles as the inability to sell off investments quickly if they start to head south, nor can it account for extreme unexpected events. Long-Term Capital Management, a huge hedge fund in Connecticut, had a glowing Sharpe Ratio before it abruptly collapsed in 1998 when Russia devalued its currency and defaulted on debt.

In Hong Kong, the government bars hedge funds from opening unless they can prove they aren't going to fail—and yet there is no adequate measure, says Sally Wong, executive director of the Hong Kong Investment Funds Association. Her problem with the Sharpe Ratio is that it assumes that a fund's returns will remain even over time. "Many hedge-fund strategies have greater downside events," Ms. Wong says. She favors another measure, the Sortino Ratio. That is similar to the Sharpe Ratio, but instead of using the standard deviation as the denominator, it uses downside deviation—the amount a portfolio strays from its average downturns—to distinguish between "good" and "bad" volatility.

But even the namesake of that ratio is troubled by its use for evaluating hedge funds. "I think it's used too much because it makes hedge funds look good," says Frank Sortino, who developed the ratio 20 years ago and is director of the Pension Research Institute in San Francisco. "It's misleading to say the least," he adds. "I hate that they're using my name."

Dr. Sharpe feels similarly. "I never named it the Sharpe Ratio," he says of his formula. "I called it the Reward-to-Variability ratio."

Source: Ianthe Jeanne Dugan, *The Wall Street Journal*, August 31, 2005.

money manager's concern over potential losses for an investment portfolio within a specific time horizon. We focus on what is known as the Value-at-Risk approach. However, risk can be viewed in many different ways, and, for some alternative viewpoints, we suggest reading the nearby *Investment Updates* box.

Value-at-Risk (VaR)
Assesses risk by stating the probability of a loss a portfolio might experience within a fixed time horizon with a specified probability.

VALUE-AT-RISK

An important goal of this chapter is to learn how to assess portfolio risk using **Value-at-Risk**. In essence, the Value-at-Risk (usually abbreviated VaR) method involves evaluating the probability of a significant loss. The basic approach we describe here is widely used by many different financial institutions.

EXAMPLE 13.7 **VaR Risk Statistic**

You agree with J. P. Morgan that the stock market will fluctuate and have become concerned with how these fluctuations might affect your stock portfolio. Having read about the VaR method for measuring investment risk, you decide to apply it to your portfolio.

Suppose you believe that there is a 5 percent chance of a return of −18 percent or worse in the coming week. Mathematically, this risk assessment can be stated as:

$$\text{Prob}\ (R_p \leq -18\%) = 5\%$$

Taken together, this −18 percent or worse expected loss and 5 percent probability form a VaR "statistic" for your stock portfolio.

normal distribution
A statistical model for assessing probabilities related to many phenomena, including security returns.

The VaR measure of investment risk is closely related to something we discussed way back in Chapter 1. There we said that if the returns on an investment follow a **normal distribution**, then we can state the probability that a portfolio's return will be within a certain range. Since a normal distribution is completely specified by its mean and standard deviation, these are all that we need to state this probability.

For example, suppose you own an S&P 500 Index fund. What is the probability of a return of −7 percent or worse in a particular year? As we saw in Chapter 1, since 1925, the return on the S&P 500 Index has averaged 13 percent per year with a standard deviation of about 20 percent per year. A return of −7 percent is exactly one standard deviation below the average (.13 − .20 = −.07). We know from Chapter 1 (and basic statistics) that the odds of being within one standard deviation are about 2/3, or .67. Being *within* one standard deviation of the mean of .13 means being *between* .13 plus .20 and .13 minus .20, i.e., between −.07 and +.33.

If the odds of being within this range are 2/3, then the odds of being *outside* this range are about 1/3. Finally, if we are outside this range, then half of the time we'll be above this range and half of the time we'll be below. Half of 1/3 is 1/6, so we'll experience a return of −.07 or worse 1/6, or about 17 percent, of the time.

WWW

Learn all about VaR at www.gloriamundi.org

Putting it together, if you own an S&P 500 Index fund, this risk assessment can be stated:

$$\text{Prob}(R_p \leq -.07) = 17\%$$

Your VaR statistic is thus a return of –.07 or worse with a probability of 17 percent. By the way, here is an important note: When we say a loss of –.07 or worse, we mean that, *one year from now*, your portfolio value is down by 7 percent or more.

CHECK THIS

13.3a What is the probability of realizing a portfolio return one or more standard deviations below the expected mean return?

13.3b What is the probability of realizing a portfolio return two or more standard deviations below the expected mean return?

13.3c Your portfolio has a mean return of 15 percent and a return standard deviation of 25 percent. What portfolio return is two standard deviations below the mean?

INVESTMENT UPDATES

HOW TO PLAY THE GAME OF RISK WHEN INVESTING YOUR MONEY

If we want our portfolios to go up, we need to spend a little time looking down. Take too much risk with our investments, and we could end up selling in a panic at the worst possible time. Take too little risk, and we will likely clock unnecessarily low returns. So how do we settle on the right amount of risk? Here are some thoughts on this messy notion:

Looking for Danger

High risk is meant to lead to high returns. But what do we mean by "high risk"? If we bet all our money on a couple of hot stocks, we are undoubtedly taking a ton of risk. But there is every chance we will lose our shirts. Instead, when academics talk about risk getting rewarded, they are referring to market risk. When investing in stocks, we can eliminate the risk of owning any one stock by spreading our money across a fistful of different companies. But even if we do that, we will still take a hit if the broad market declines. This market risk, which we can't diversify away, is the risk we get rewarded for taking.

What does this mean for our portfolios? If we want higher long-run returns, we need to take more market risk, by keeping less in conservative investments and more in stocks. But to be confident of getting our reward, we need to ensure that our stock portfolios are well diversified. This diversification has the added advantage of bolstering our tenacity. Have shares just tumbled 20%? If all we own are a couple of stocks, we will no doubt fret over whether our shares will ever bounce back. But if we own a broadly diversified portfolio, we will have greater confidence that our stocks should eventually generate decent gains.

Looking Up

To gauge risk, investment experts have traditionally looked at an investment's volatility, as reflected in statistical measures such as standard deviation and beta. Standard deviation is a gauge of how far an investment's results have strayed from its average performance, while beta measures an investment's price gyrations relative to a broad market index.

But investors often dismiss such statistical measures, complaining that they aren't bothered when volatility works to their advantage and generates big gains. Instead, what they care about is losses, and it is these losses that risk measures should seek to capture. But in fact, upside volatility is a great measure of downside risk. Consider technology stocks. Their dismal performance in the recent bear market was foretold by their equally astonishing rise during the late 1990s bull market.

Looking Out

When measuring risk, some experts don't just look at volatility. They also consider longer-run performance. For instance, if we hold stocks for 20 years, we are unlikely to lose money and we will almost certainly outpace bonds. That has led some commentators to argue that stocks are less risky than bonds. But this is nonsense. If we look out far enough, the highest-returning investments will always appear to be the least risky. Indeed, I fear such foolishness could lead folks to bet far too much on stocks.

"Over a long enough period, risk and return become the same thing," says William Bernstein, author of "The Intelligent Asset Allocator" and an investment adviser in North Bend, Ore. "The reason stocks have seemed so low risk is because the returns have been so high. But the high returns may not be true going forward." Moreover, not everybody has a 20-year time horizon, and not many investors can ignore short-term market turmoil. "People feel risk in their gut in the short term and in their brain in the long term," Mr. Bernstein says. "Unfortunately, they react to their gut."

Looking Pale

How much risk can each of us stomach? Mutual-fund companies and investment advisers have questionnaires that try to help folks figure out whether they are aggressive or conservative investors. But often, people later discover that their risk tolerance is far higher or lower. What to do? Eleanor Blayney, a financial planner in McLean, Va., says investors should spend time studying their own investment history. "The best indicator of risk tolerance is past behavior," she argues. In particular, Ms. Blayney likes to ask clients what they believe their best and worst investment decisions were. She says aggressive investors tend to fret about missing out on gains, while conservative investors tend to dwell on their losses.

Looking for Safety

Even if we set out to take a lot of risk, we often gravitate toward investments we perceive to be safe. For instance, we may choose to invest a hefty amount in the stock market. But when it comes to picking individual stocks, we often select companies we view as safe. Indeed, if we didn't think a stock was a pretty safe bet, we probably wouldn't have the courage to buy.

Result? We tend to invest in widely admired corporations or those shares that have lately performed well. Meanwhile, we shy away from companies that have had financial problems or have suffered steep share-price declines, even though studies suggest that these tarnished companies often generate market-beating gains. "People will accept that risk gets rewarded if they are forced to listen to the finance-professor spiel," says Hersh Shefrin, a finance professor at Santa Clara University in California. "They will accept the notion intellectually. But emotionally, they associate good stocks with safe stocks."

Source: Jonathan Clements, *The Wall Street Journal*, February 2, 2002.

13.4 More on Computing Value-at-Risk

In this section we extend our discussion of computing VaR. Our goal is mainly to examine how to evaluate horizons that are shorter or longer than one year. The easiest way to do this is to take our earlier example concerning the S&P 500 and extend it a bit.

Once again, suppose you own an S&P 500 Index fund. What is the probability of a loss of 30 percent or more over the next *two* years? To answer, we need to know the average two-year return and the average two-year return standard deviation. Getting the average two-year return is easy enough; we just have to double the one-year average. So, the two-year average return is $2 \times .13 = .26$, or 26 percent.

WWW

Learn about the risk management profession at www.garp.com

The two-year standard deviation is a little trickier. The two-year *variance* is just double the one-year variance. In our case, the one-year variance is $.20^2 = .04$, and the two-year variance is thus .08. As always, to get the two-year standard deviation, we take the square root of this, which is .28, or 28 percent. The main thing to notice is that the two-year standard deviation is not just double the one-year number. In fact, if you look at it, the two-year number is equal to the one-year number multiplied by the square root of 2, or 1.414.

Now we can answer our question. A two-year loss of 30 percent is equal to the two-year average return of 26 percent less two standard deviations: $.26 - 2 \times .28 = -.30$. From Chapter 1, we know that the odds of being within two standard deviations are 95 percent, so the odds of being outside this range are 5 percent. The odds of being on the bad side (the loss side) are half that, namely, 2.5 percent.

EXAMPLE 13.8 VaR Risk Statistic

The Ned Kelley Hedge Fund focuses on investing in bank and transportation companies in Australia with above-average risk. The average annual return is 15 percent with an annual return standard deviation of 50 percent. What loss level can we expect over a two-year investment horizon with a probability of .17?

We assume a two-year expected return of 30 percent. The one-year variance is $.50^2 = .25$, so the two-year variance is .50. Taking the square root, we get a two-year standard deviation of .7071, or 70.71 percent. A loss probability of .17 corresponds to one standard deviation below the mean, so the answer to our question is $.30 - .7071 = -.4071$, a substantial loss. We can write this succinctly as:

$$\text{Prob}(R_p \leq -40.71\%) = 17\%$$

Notice that there is a 17 percent chance of a 40.71 percent loss or worse over the next two years.

EXAMPLE 13.9 VaR Risk Statistic

Going back to the Ned Kelley Hedge Fund in our previous example, what loss level might we expect over six months with a probability of .17?

The six-month expected return is half of 15 percent, or 7.5 percent. The six-month standard deviation is $.5 \times \sqrt{1/2} = .3536$. So the answer to our question is $.075 - .3536 = -.2786$. Again, we can write this succinctly as:

$$\text{Prob}(R_p \leq -27.86\%) = 17\%$$

Thus there is a 17 percent chance of a 27.86 percent loss or worse over the next six months.

EXAMPLE 13.10

A One-in-Twenty Loss

For the Ned Kelley Hedge Fund specified in our previous examples, what is the expected loss for the coming year with a probability of 5 percent?

In this case, with an annual return mean of 15 percent and an annual return standard deviation of 50 percent, set $T = 1$ for a one year time horizon and calculate this VaR statistic:

$$\text{Prob}[R_{p,1} \leq E(R_p) \times 1 - 1.645\sigma_p \times \sqrt{1}] = \text{Prob}(R_{p,1} \leq 15\% - 1.645 \times 50\%)$$
$$= \text{Prob}(R_{p,1} \leq -67.25\%) = 5\%$$

Thus we can expect a loss of 67.25 percent or worse over the next year with a 5 percent probability.

EXAMPLE 13.11

A One-in-a-Hundred Loss

For the Ned Kelley Hedge Fund specified in our previous examples, what is the expected loss for the coming month with a 1 percent probability?

Setting $T = 1/12$ for a one-month time horizon, we calculate this VaR statistic:

$$\text{Prob}[R_{p,T} \leq E(R_p) \times 1/12 - 2.326\sigma_p \times \sqrt{1/12}]$$
$$= \text{Prob}(R_{p,T} \leq 1.25\% - 2.326 \times 50\% \times .2887)$$
$$= \text{Prob}(R_{p,T} \leq -32.32\%) = 1\%$$

Thus we can expect a loss of 32.32 percent or more with a 1 percent probability over the next month.

In general, if we let T stand for the number of years, then the expected return on a portfolio over T years, $E(R_{p,T})$ can be written as:

$$E(R_{p,T}) = E(R_p) \times T \quad (13.6)$$

Similarly, the standard deviation can be written as:

$$\sigma_{p,T} = \sigma_p \times \sqrt{T} \quad (13.7)$$

If the time period is less than a year, the T is just a fraction of a year.

WWW

Check out risk grades at www.riskmetrics.com

When you do a VaR analysis, you have to pick the time horizon and loss level probability. You can pick any probability you want, of course, but the most common are 1, 2.5, and 5 percent. We know that 2.5 percent, which is half of 5 percent, corresponds to two standard deviations (actually 1.96 to be more precise) below the expected return. To get the 1 percent and 5 percent numbers, you would need to find an ordinary "z" table to tell you the number of standard deviations. We'll save you the trouble. The 1 percent level is 2.326 standard deviations below the average, and the 5 percent level is 1.645 "sigmas" below.

Wrapping up our discussion, the VaR statistics for these three levels can be summarized as follows:

$$\text{Prob}[R_{p,T} \leq E(R_p) \times T - 2.326 \times \sigma_p\sqrt{T}] = 1\% \quad (13.8)$$
$$\text{Prob}[R_{p,T} \leq E(R_p) \times T - 1.96 \times \sigma_p\sqrt{T}] = 2.5\%$$
$$\text{Prob}[R_{p,T} \leq E(R_p) \times T - 1.645 \times \sigma_p\sqrt{T}] = 5\%$$

Notice that if T, the number of years, is equal to 1, the 1 percent level corresponds to once in a century. Similarly, 5 percent is once every 20 years, and 2.5 percent is once every 40 years.

As an application of Value-at-Risk, consider the problem of determining VaR statistics for a Sharpe-optimal stock and bond portfolio. As with any VaR problem for a portfolio, remember that the key to the problem is to first determine the expected return and standard deviation for the portfolio. From our discussion in Chapter 11 and earlier in this chapter, we know that the expected return and standard deviation of a stock and bond portfolio are specified by these two equations:

$$E(R_P) = x_S\, E(R_S) + x_B E(R_B)$$

$$\sigma_P = \sqrt{x_S^2 \sigma_S^2 + x_B^2 \sigma_B^2 + 2 x_S x_B \sigma_S \sigma_B \text{Corr}(R_S, R_B)}$$

Thus the problem of calculating VaR statistics for a Sharpe-optimal portfolio is the same for any portfolio once the appropriate portfolio weights are determined.

CHECK THIS

13.4a Your portfolio allocates 40 percent of funds to ABC stock and 60 percent to XYZ stock. ABC has a return mean and standard deviation of 15 percent and 20 percent, respectively. XYZ stock has a return mean and standard deviation of 25 percent and 30 percent, respectively. What is the portfolio return standard deviation if the return correlation between ABC and XYZ stocks is zero?

13.4b Based on your answer to the previous question, what is the smallest expected loss for your portfolio in the coming year with a probability of 1 percent? What is the smallest expected loss for your portfolio in the coming month with a probability of 5 percent?

13.5 Summary and Conclusions

In this chapter, we covered the related topics of performance measurement and risk management.

1. How to calculate the three best-known portfolio evaluation measures.

A. Our goal with performance measurement is essentially to rank investments based on their risk-adjusted returns. We introduced and discussed the three most frequently used tools to do this: the Sharpe ratio, the Treynor ratio, and Jensen's alpha.

B. As we saw, each has a somewhat different interpretation. Also, which one is the most suitable depends on the specific question to be answered.

2. The strengths and weaknesses of these three portfolio evaluation measures.

A. Sharpe ratio. *Strength:* No beta estimate is necessary, and standard deviations can be calculated unambiguously. *Weakness:* Total risk is frequently not what really matters. However, for a relatively well-diversified portfolio, most of the risk is systematic, so there's not much difference between total risk and systematic risk.

B. Treynor ratio. *Strength:* The Treynor ratio standardizes everything, including any excess return, relative to beta. *Weakness:* The Treynor measure requires a beta estimate.

C. Jensen's alpha. *Strength:* Jensen's alpha is easy to interpret. *Weakness:* The Jensen measure requires a beta estimate. Betas from different sources can differ substantially, and, as a result, what appears to be a positive alpha might just be due to a mismeasured beta.

3. How to calculate a Sharpe-optimal portfolio.

A. The slope of a straight line drawn from the risk-free rate to a portfolio on a return–standard deviation graph tells us the Sharpe ratio for that portfolio. This is always the case, even if with many assets, not just two. The portfolio with the highest slope is called Sharpe-optimal.

B. The problem of finding the Sharpe-optimal portfolio boils down to finding the portfolio with the steepest slope. The line with the steepest slope is always going to be the one that just touches (i.e., is tangent to) the investment opportunity set. That portfolio is sometimes labeled portfolio *T* (for tangent).

C. The Markowitz efficient frontier tells us which portfolios are efficient. The Markowitz efficient frontier does not tell us which one of the efficient portfolios is the best. Given a risk-free rate, the Sharpe-optimal portfolio is the best portfolio, at least as measured by the Sharpe ratio.

4. How to calculate and interpret Value-at-Risk.

A. We introduce the popular and widely used method to assess portfolio risk called "Value-at-Risk," or VaR. Here the goal is usually to assess the probability of a large loss within a fixed time frame.

B. Investors use this tool both to better understand the risks of their existing portfolios and to assess the risks of potential investments. The VaR measure is closely related to something we discussed way back in Chapter 1.

C. If the returns on an investment follow a normal distribution, then we can state the probability that a portfolio's return will be within a certain range. Because a normal distribution is completely specified by its mean and standard deviation, these two statistics are all that we need to state the probability of a loss of a certain size.

GET REAL

This chapter covered the essentials of performance evaluation and investment risk management. With thousands of mutual funds and investment companies competing for performance while trying to control risk, these topics are especially important. If you wish to learn more about these subjects, a good place to start is the Internet.

Some useful and informative Web sites on investment performance analysis are Performance Analysis (www.andreassteiner.net/performanceanalysis), an informative Web site on investment performance analysis; Professor William F. Sharpe (www. stanford.edu/~wfsharpe), Web site of the Nobel laureate who created the Sharpe ratio; and FinPlan (www.finplan.com), a financial planning Web site with a useful section on investment performance analysis. You can also consult www.garp .com, which is the Web site of the Global Association of Risk Professionals (GARP), an independent organization of financial risk management practitioners and researchers.

Because financial institutions generally prefer that their risk profiles be kept private, a large part of the world of financial risk management is hidden from public view. Nevertheless, the field of risk management is large and growing. If you want to know more about this fascinating subject, some interesting Web sites that provide a wealth of information are Gloria Mundi (www.gloriamundi.org), a site that tells you all about Value-at-Risk; Risk Metrics (www.riskmetrics.com), a leading risk management consultancy group; Margrabe (www.margrabe.com), the Web site of a professional risk management consultant; and E-Risks (www.erisks.com), a general resource site for risk management.

Key Terms

investment risk management 422
Jensen's alpha 416
normal distribution 424
performance evaluation 414
raw return 414
Sharpe ratio 415
Treynor ratio 415
Value-at-Risk (VaR) 423

Chapter Review Problems and Self-Test

1. **Performance Measures** Compute Sharpe ratios, Treynor ratios, and Jensen's alphas for portfolios *A*, *B*, and *C* based on the following returns data, where *M* and *F* stand for the market portfolio and risk-free rate, respectively:

Portfolio	R_p	σ_p	β_p
A	10%	30%	0.75
B	15%	25%	1.00
C	20%	40%	1.50
M	15%	15%	1.00
F	5%	0%	0.00

2. **Value-at-Risk (VaR)** A portfolio manager believes her $100 million stock portfolio will have a 10 percent return standard deviation during the coming week and that her portfolio's returns are normally distributed. What is the probability of her losing $10 million or more? What is the dollar loss expected with a 5 percent probability? What is the dollar loss expected with a 1 percent probability?

Answers to Self-Test Problems

1. Using equations (13.1), (13.2), and (13.4) yields these performance measurement values:

Portfolio	Sharpe Ratio	Treynor Ratio	Jensen's Alpha
A	.167	.0667	−2.5%
B	.400	.10	0%
C	.375	.10	0%
M	.667	.10	0%

2. Because a mean is not given but the time horizon is only one week, we can simply assume a mean of zero. Thus the probability of a $10 million or greater loss is the probability of a loss of one or more return standard deviations, which for a normal distribution is 15.87 percent. For a normal distribution, a realization 1.645 or more standard deviations below the mean occurs with a 5 percent probability, yielding a potential loss of at least 1.645 × $10 million = $16.45 million. For a normal distribution, a realization 2.326 or more standard deviations below the mean occurs with a 1 percent probability, yielding a potential loss of at least 2.326 × $10 million = $23.26 million.

Test Your Investment Quotient

For the remaining questions and problems, the circled numbers in the margin refer to the corresponding learning objective in this chapter.

IQ

(2)

1. **Beta and Standard Deviation** Beta and standard deviation differ as risk measures in that beta measures
   - **a.** Only unsystematic risk, whereas standard deviation measures total risk.
   - **b.** Only systematic risk, whereas standard deviation measures total risk.

CFA® PROBLEMS

c. Both systematic and unsystematic risk, whereas standard deviation measures only unsystematic risk.
d. Both systematic and unsystematic risk, whereas standard deviation measures only systematic risk.

Answer Questions 2 through 8 based on the following information.

Risk and Return Data			
Portfolio	Average Return	Standard Deviation	Beta
P	17%	20%	1.1
Q	24%	18%	2.1
R	11%	10%	0.5
S	16%	14%	1.5
S&P 500	14%	12%	1.0

A pension fund administrator wants to evaluate the performance of four portfolio managers. Each manager invests only in U.S. common stocks. During the most recent five-year period, the average annual total return on the S&P 500 was 14 percent, and the average annual rate on Treasury bills was 8 percent. The table above shows risk and return measures for each portfolio.

CFA® PROBLEMS

1 **2. Treynor Ratio** The Treynor portfolio performance measure for Portfolio *P* is
a. 8.18
b. 7.62
c. 6.00
d. 5.33

CFA® PROBLEMS

1 **3. Sharpe Ratio** The Sharpe portfolio performance measure for Portfolio *Q* is
a. .45
b. .89
c. .30
d. .57

1 **4. Jensen's Alpha** The Jensen's alpha portfolio performance measure for Portfolio *R* is
a. 2.4 percent
b. 3.4 percent
c. 0 percent
d. –1 percent

1 **5. Treynor Ratio** Which portfolio has the highest Treynor ratio?
a. *P*
b. *Q*
c. *R*
d. *S*

1 **6. Sharpe Ratio** Which portfolio has the highest Sharpe ratio?
a. *P*
b. *Q*
c. *R*
d. *S*

1 **7. Jensen's Alpha** Which portfolio has the highest Jensen's alpha?
a. *P*
b. *Q*
c. *R*
d. *S*

1 **8. Sharpe Ratio** Assuming uncorrelated returns, the Sharpe ratio for a master portfolio with equal allocations to Portfolio *S* and Portfolio *Q* is
a. .71
b. 1.4
c. .95
d. 1.05

CFA® PROBLEMS

9. **Normal Distribution** Given a data series that is normally distributed with a mean of 100 and a standard deviation of 10, about 95 percent of the numbers in the series will fall within

    a. 60 to 140
    b. 70 to 130
    c. 80 to 120
    d. 90 to 110

10. **Normal Distribution** Given a data series that is normally distributed with a mean of 100 and a standard deviation of 10, about 99 percent of the numbers in the series will fall within

    a. 60 to 140
    b. 80 to 120
    c. 70 to 130
    d. 90 to 110

11. **Normal Distribution** A normal distribution is completely specified by its

    a. Mean and correlation
    b. Variance and correlation
    c. Variance and standard deviation
    d. Mean and standard deviation

12. **Standard Normal Distribution** A normal random variable is transformed into a standard normal random variable by

    a. Subtracting its mean and dividing by its standard deviation.
    b. Adding its mean and dividing by its standard deviation.
    c. Subtracting its mean and dividing by its variance.
    d. Adding its mean and multiplying by its standard deviation.

13. **Standard Normal Distribution** The probability that a standard normal random variable is either less than −1 or greater than +1 is

    a. 2 percent
    b. 5 percent
    c. 10 percent
    d. 31.74 percent

14. **Standard Normal Distribution** The probability that a standard normal random variable is either less than −1.96 or greater than +1.96 is approximately

    a. 2 percent
    b. 5 percent
    c. 10 percent
    d. 31.74 percent

(4) 15. **Value-at-Risk (VaR)** The Value-at-Risk statistic for an investment portfolio states

    a. The probability of an investment loss.
    b. The value of the risky portion of an investment portfolio.
    c. The smallest investment loss expected with a specified probability.
    d. The largest investment loss expected with a specified probability.

Concept Questions

(2) 1. **Performance Evaluation Ratios** Explain the difference between the Sharpe ratio and the Treynor ratio.

(2) 2. **Performance Evaluation Measures** What is a common weakness of Jensen's alpha and the Treynor ratio?

(2) 3. **Jensen's Alpha** Explain the relationship between Jensen's alpha and the security market line (SML) of the capital asset pricing model (CAPM).

(2) 4. **Sharpe Ratio** What is one advantage and one disadvantage of the Sharpe ratio?

5. **Normal Distribution** Which two parameters completely specify a normal distribution?

(3) 6. **Optimal Sharpe Ratio** What is meant by a Sharpe-optimal portfolio?

In this section of the *Journal*, the information is divided into sections according to categories of the underlying commodities or financial instruments. For example, the section "Agricultural Futures" lists futures price information for wheat, oats, soybeans, live cattle, (live) lean hogs, coffee, sugar and cocoa, among others. The section "Metal & Petroleum Futures" reports price information for copper, gold, and petroleum products. Separate sections report financial futures, which include "Interest Rate," "Currency," and "Index" categories.

Each section states the contract name, futures exchange, and contract size, along with price information for various contract maturities. For example, under "Metal & Petroleum Futures" we find the Copper contract traded at the Commodities Exchange (CMX), i.e., the COMEX (which is a division of the New York Mercantile Exchange). The standard contract size for copper is 25,000 pounds per contract. The futures price is quoted in cents per pound.

EXAMPLE 14.1

Futures Quotes

In Figure 14.1, locate the gold and wheat contracts. Where are they traded? What are the contract sizes for the gold and wheat contracts and how are their futures prices specified?

The gold contract trades on the CMX, the COMEX Division of the New York Mercantile Exchange. One gold contract calls for delivery of 100 troy ounces. The gold futures price is quoted in dollars per ounce.

Wheat contracts are traded on the Chicago Board of Trade (CBT), the Kansas City Board of Trade (KC), and the Minneapolis Grain Exchange (MPLS). One wheat contract calls for delivery of 5,000 bushels of wheat, and wheat futures prices are quoted in cents per bushel. Why do you think there are different wheat prices at these exchanges? Isn't wheat wheat?

WWW

For futures prices and price charts, visit these Web sites:
futures.tradingcharts.com
www.barchart.com

The reporting format for each futures contract is similar. For example, the first column of a price listing gives the contract delivery/maturity month. For each maturity month, the next six columns report futures prices observed during the previous day at the opening of trading ("Open"), the highest intraday price ("High"), an area to signal a life of contract high or low, the lowest intraday price ("Low"), the price at close of trading ("Settle"), and the change in the settle price from the previous day ("Chg"). The last column reports open interest for each contract maturity, which is the number of contracts outstanding at the end of that day's trading.

By now, we see that four of the contract terms for futures contracts are stated in the futures prices listing. These are:

1. The identity of the underlying commodity or financial instrument.
2. The futures contract size.
3. The futures maturity date.
4. The futures price.

Exact contract terms for the delivery process are available from the appropriate futures exchange on request.

EXAMPLE 14.2

Futures Prices

In Figure 14.1, locate the soybean contract with the greatest open interest. Explain the information provided.

The soybean (or just "bean") contract with the greatest open interest is specified by the contract maturity with the greatest number of contracts outstanding, so the November 2007 contract is the one we seek. One contract calls for delivery of 5,000 bushels of beans (a bushel, of course, is four pecks and weighs about 60 pounds). The closing price for delivery at maturity is quoted in cents per bushel. Because there are 5,000 bushels in a single contract, the total contract value is the quoted price per bushel of 847.00 cents times 5,000, or $42,350 for the November contract.

INVESTMENT UPDATES

GARISH JACKETS ADD TO CLAMOR OF CHICAGO PITS

For the inhabitants of Chicago's futures and options trading pits, dressing for success means throwing good taste to the wind.

Take James Oliff, a trader in the Chicago Mercantile Exchange's newly opened Mexican peso futures pit. Daily, he dons a multicolored jacket bedecked with cacti and sombreros, in keeping, he says, with the "theme" of the product he trades.

Twisting and turning to display his gaudy garb, the veteran currency options trader explains: "I wanted a jacket that would be easy to pick out in the crowd. Runners get orders to me more quickly, and clerks find me faster when I'm trying to do trades."

It's important to have what veterans of the mayhem describe as "pit presence" to make money in the crowded and noisy trading pits of the Merc and the Chicago Board of Trade. That elusive quality, they say, involves such stratagems as finding the best spot in the pit from which to communicate with clerks and other traders, maintaining good posture and using a loud, well-projected voice and forceful hand signals to attract attention.

Increasingly, in places such as the CBOT's bond pit, where hundreds of people cram into a space only slightly larger than a tennis court, garb is being used to grab attention. Hence the insatiable demand for magenta, lime-green, and silver-lamé jackets, featuring designs that run the gamut from the Mighty Morphin Power Rangers to bucolic farmhouses and sunflowers.

"I'd come in buck naked if I could," says Thomas Burke, a trader in the CBOT's overpopulated bond-futures pit. "As it is, the more obnoxious the jacket, the better. The louder it is, the more I can rest my voice and let my jacket draw the attention."

Chicago's exchanges quietly tolerate the proliferation of the garish trading jackets. Dress codes ban jeans and still require members to wear shirts with collars and don ties (although some of these may be little more than strings, having been worn daily for more than a decade). The rules also say that trading jackets must have sleeves that come below the elbow and contain pockets into which the traders stuff their trading cards and other documents. But during the past decade, traders say, exchange efforts to regulate the color and design of the jackets, or gently encourage their wearers to opt for something in quiet good taste, have been dropped as an exercise in futility.

Robert Pierce, who trades corn options at the CBOT, says the old brown jackets made him look like a UPS delivery man. "When someone gave me a UPS cap on the floor one day as a joke, I decided it was time for a change of style," he says. The switch, to a comparatively tasteful multicolored geometric pattern, has the added advantage of disguising pen and pencil marks, adds his wife, Cathy.

Dawn Guera, a former clerk at the CBOT, has spun the traders' need to stand out in the crowd into a four-year-old business designing and manufacturing custom trading jackets. Traders wander into her storefront operation next door to the CBOT to choose from dozens of fabrics with designs ranging from a subdued Harvard University crest on a crimson background to a slinky leopard skin pattern or turquoise frogs cavorting on a neon-pink background.

"Everyone has their own hobbies and interests and wants the jackets to reflect that," she explains, pointing to fabrics with designs of dice and cards aimed at traders willing to acknowledge their addiction to gambling in the markets. "It's like a vanity license plate."

And, at $50 a pop, traders are willing, even eager, to order multiple jackets, Ms. Guera says, especially since many believe that washing or dry cleaning a "lucky" jacket will launder out the luck in it. Some, like the CBOT's Gilbert Leistner, take a seasonal approach to jackets: in summer and fall he wears a brightly colored turquoise and aquamarine jacket decorated with tropical fish, but switches to a Southwestern theme come Thanksgiving.

"It's my version of going south for the winter," he says, adding he's contemplating donning something in gold lamé for New Year's celebrations.

Ms. Guera, a former sportswear designer in New York, says traders have a long way to go before they'll pull themselves off the worst-dressed lists. To be sure, some of the early emphasis on flashiness is easing a bit, she says, and demands for fluorescent geometric patterns are giving way to a new trend favoring subtler paisley-type patterns with lapels, cuffs, and pockets in a contrasting, solid color.

"I think it would be great if we could really push the fashion envelope here and remove the collar and cuffs from the jackets, or even persuade the exchanges to let traders wear vests instead," she says. "I'm looking for a way of making this whole trading process more artistic and creative."

Source: Suzanne McGee, *The Wall Street Journal*, July 31, 1995.

To get an idea of the magnitude of financial futures trading, take a look at the second entry under "Interest Rate Futures" in Figure 14.1, the CBT Treasury note contract. One contract calls for the delivery of $100,000 in par value notes. The total open interest in these contracts often exceeds 2 million contracts. Thus, the total face value represented by these contracts is close to 2 *trillion* dollars.

Who does all this trading? The orders originate from money managers around the world and are sent to the various exchanges' trading floors and electronic systems for execution. On the floor, the orders are executed by professional traders who are quite aggressive at getting the best prices. On the floor, futures traders can be recognized by their colorful jackets. As *The Wall Street Journal* article in the nearby *Investment Updates* box reports, these garish jackets add a touch of color to the clamor of the pits. Of course, garish jackets are not required for electronic trading. (Who knows what these traders are wearing!) In the next section, we will discuss how and why futures contracts are used for speculation and hedging.

CHECK THIS

14.1a What is a forward contract?

14.1b What is a futures contract, and why is it different from a forward contract?

14.1c What is a futures price?

14.2 Why Futures?

The major economic purpose of futures contracts is to allow hedgers to transfer risk to speculators. Therefore, a viable futures market cannot exist without participation by both hedgers and speculators. We begin to help you understand the use of futures markets by describing how speculators use futures markets.

SPECULATING WITH FUTURES

WWW

To learn more about futures, visit www.usafutures.com

Suppose you are thinking about speculating on commodity prices because you believe that you can accurately forecast future prices. The most convenient way to speculate is to use futures contracts. If you believe that gold prices will increase, then you can speculate on this belief by buying gold futures. Alternatively, if you think gold prices will decrease, you can speculate by selling gold futures.

long position
A market position where the holder benefits from price increases and loses from price decreases.

short position
A market position where the holder benefits from price decreases and loses from price increases.

speculator
A person or firm that takes the risk of loss for the chance for profit.

Buying a futures contract is often referred to as "going long," or establishing a **long position**. Selling a futures contract is often called "going short," or establishing a **short position**. A **speculator** accepts price risk in an attempt to profit on the direction of prices. Speculators can go long or short futures contracts. A speculator who is long benefits from price increases and loses from price decreases. The opposite is true for a speculator who is short.

To illustrate the basics of speculating, suppose you believe the price of gold will go up. In particular, suppose the current price for delivery in three months is \$800 per ounce (this \$800 is called the "futures" price). You think that gold will be selling for much more than \$800 three months from now, so you go long 100 gold contracts that expire in three months. When you do, you are obligated to take delivery of gold and pay the agreed-upon price, \$800 per ounce. Each gold contract represents 100 troy ounces, so 100 contracts represents 10,000 ounces of gold with a total contract value of 10,000 × \$800 = \$8,000,000. In futures jargon, you have an \$8 million long gold position.

Suppose your belief turns out to be correct, and three months later, the market price of gold is \$820 per ounce. Your three-month futures contracts have just expired. So, to fulfill the terms of your long futures position, you accept delivery of 10,000 troy ounces of gold, pay \$800 per ounce, and immediately sell the gold at the market price of \$820 per ounce. Your profit is \$20 per ounce, or 10,000 × \$20 = \$200,000. Of course, you will pay some brokerage commissions and taxes out of this profit.

Suppose your belief turns out to be incorrect and gold prices fall. You will lose money in this case because you are obligated to buy the 10,000 troy ounces at the agreed-upon price of \$800 per ounce. If gold prices fell to, say, \$775 per ounce, you would lose \$25 per ounce, or 10,000 × \$25 = \$250,000. In addition, you will pay some brokerage commissions.

As this gold example shows, futures speculation can lead to substantial gains and losses. An important point is that your gains from futures speculation depend on accurate forecasts of the direction of future prices. You must ask yourself: Is it easy to forecast price changes?

Consider another example of commodity speculation. Suppose you analyze weather patterns and you are convinced that the coming winter months will be colder than usual. You believe that this will cause heating oil prices to rise. You can speculate on this belief by going long heating oil futures.

The standard contract size for heating oil is 42,000 gallons. Suppose you go long 10 contracts at a futures price of \$1.90 per gallon. This represents a long position with a total contract value of $10 \times 42,000 \times \$1.90 = \$798,000$.

If the price of heating oil at contract maturity is, say, \$1.50 per gallon, your loss before commissions would be 40 cents per gallon, or $10 \times 42,000 \times \$.40 = \$168,000$. Of course, if heating oil prices rose by 40 cents per gallon, you would gain \$168,000 (less applicable commissions) instead.

Once again, futures speculation can lead to substantial gains and losses. The important point from this example is that your gains from futures speculation depend on you making more accurate weather forecasts than other traders. So ask yourself: How easy is it to outforecast other traders?

EXAMPLE 14.3

What Would Juan Valdez Do?

After an extensive analysis of political currents in Central and South America, you conclude that future coffee prices will be lower than currently indicated by futures prices. Would you go long or short? Analyze the impact of a swing in coffee prices of 20 cents per pound in either direction if you have a 10-contract position, where each contract calls for delivery of 37,500 pounds of coffee.

You would go short because you expect prices to decline. Because you are short 10 contracts, you must deliver $10 \times 37,500 = 375,000$ pounds of coffee to fulfill your contract. If coffee prices fall to 20 cents below your originally contracted futures price, then you make 20 cents per pound, or $\$.20 \times 375,000 = \$75,000$. Of course, if you are wrong and the political situation destabilizes, the resulting \$.20 increase in coffee prices would generate a \$75,000 loss in your short futures position.

HEDGING WITH FUTURES

PRICE RISK Many businesses face price risk when their activities require them to hold a working inventory. By a working inventory, we mean that firms purchase and store goods for later resale at market prices. Price risk is the risk that the firm will not be able to sell its goods at a price sufficiently higher than the acquisition cost.

For example, suppose you own a regional heating oil distributorship and must keep a large pre–heating season inventory of heating oil of, say, 2.1 million gallons. In futures market jargon, this heating oil inventory represents a long position in the underlying commodity. If heating oil prices go up, the value of the heating oil you have in inventory goes up in value, but if heating oil prices fall, the value of the heating oil you have to sell goes down. Your risk is not trivial, because even a 15-cent per gallon fluctuation in the price of heating oil will cause your inventory to change in value by \$315,000. Because you are in the business of distributing heating oil, and not in the business of speculating on heating oil prices, you decide to remove this price risk from your business operations.

hedger
Trader who seeks to transfer price risk by taking a futures position opposite to an existing position in the underlying asset.

underlying asset
The commodity or financial instrument on which the futures contract is based.

THE MECHANICS OF SHIFTING PRICE RISK An important function of futures markets is that they allow firms that have price risk to shift it to others who want price risk. A person or company that wants to shift price risk to others is called a **hedger**. Hedgers transfer price risk by taking a futures market position that is the opposite of their existing position in the **underlying asset**. You can think about this using a portfolio approach. Hedgers look to add a futures market position to their position in the underlying asset that will provide cash to the hedgers when their position in the underlying asset declines in value. However, the cost of adding a futures position is that the futures position draws down cash when the position in the underlying asset generates value.

In the case of your heating oil enterprise, the heating oil you have in inventory represents a long position in the underlying asset. Therefore, the value of this heating oil inventory can be protected by taking a short position in heating oil futures contracts. Hedgers often say they are "selling" futures contracts when they are initiating a short position. Because you are using this short position for hedging purposes, you have created a **short hedge**.

short hedge
Adding a short futures position to a long position in the underlying asset.

With a short hedge in place, changes in the value of your long position in the underlying asset are offset by an approximately equal, but opposite, change in value of your short futures position.

AN EXAMPLE OF A SHORT HEDGE One of the first questions a hedger has to answer is how many futures contracts are needed to shift risk. This question has many answers, and most can be found in a course devoted to futures contracts and other derivatives. However, a reasonable hedging strategy is known as a **full hedge**. When a hedger has an equal, but opposite, futures position to the position in the underlying asset, the hedger is said to have a full hedge.

full hedge
A futures position that is equal, but opposite, the position in the underlying asset.

Heating oil futures contracts are traded on the New York Mercantile Exchange (NYM), and the standard contract size for heating oil futures is 42,000 gallons per contract. Because you wish to full hedge 2.1 million gallons, you need to sell 2,100,000/42,000 = 50 heating oil contracts.

Suppose the average acquisition price of your 2.1 million gallons of heating oil is \$1.30 per gallon, and that today's futures price for delivery during your heating season is \$1.90. In the past, market conditions in your distribution area were such that you could sell your heating oil to your customers at a price 20 cents higher than the prevailing futures price. To help finance your inventory purchases, you borrowed money. During the heating season, you have to make a debt payment of \$500,000.

Given these numbers, you can forecast your pretax profit per gallon of heating oil. Revenues are 2,100,000 × \$2.10 = \$4,410,000. The cost of the heating oil is 2,100,000 × \$1.30 = \$2,730,000. Subtracting this cost and the debt payment of \$500,000 from revenue results in a pretax profit of \$1,180,000, or \$1,180,000/2,100,000 = \$.56 per gallon.

However, if heating oil prices decrease by \$.40, your pretax profit per gallon of heating oil will only be \$.16. You view this risk as unacceptable and decide to hedge by selling 50 heating oil futures contracts at a price of \$1.90 per gallon. Table 14.1 summarizes three possible outcomes: heating oil prices remain steady, they increase by \$.40, and they decrease by \$.40.

As you can see in Table 14.1, your pretax profit will be \$.56 in all three cases. To see this, suppose heating oil prices fall by \$.40. In this case, revenues are 2,100,000 × \$1.70 = \$3,570,000. The cost of the heating oil is 2,100,000 × \$1.30 = \$2,730,000. Subtracting this cost and the debt payment of \$500,000 from revenues results in an unhedged pretax profit of \$340,000, or \$340,000/2,100,000 = \$.16 per gallon. However, if you had a short hedge in place, your pretax futures profit is \$840,000 because (\$1.90 – \$1.50) × 42,000 × 50 = \$840,000. Adding \$840,000 to the unhedged pretax profit of \$340,000 results in a hedged pretax profit of \$1,180,000, which is \$1,180,000/2,100,000 = \$.56 per gallon.

In fact, your pretax profit will remain steady for a wide range of prices. We illustrate this result in Figure 14.2. In Figure 14.2, the blue line represents your pretax profit per gallon of heating oil for a wide range of possible heating oil selling prices. The red line represents your futures market gains or losses. Note that heating oil futures prices and futures contract gains (losses) appear across the top and on the right side of the graph. If futures prices remain unchanged at \$1.90, you have no futures gain or loss. If futures prices fall to \$1.50, your futures gain is \$.40.

In Figure 14.2, the purple line remains steady at a value of \$.56. This means that for a wide range of heating oil selling prices, your pretax profit remains unchanged if you employ the short hedge.

Your business activities may also include distributing other petroleum products like gasoline and natural gas. Futures contracts are also available for gasoline and natural gas, and therefore they may be used for hedging purposes. In fact, your business activities might dictate you use another common hedge, known as a **long hedge**.

long hedge
Adding a long futures position to a short position in the underlying asset.

TABLE 14.1 Hedging Heating Oil Inventory during the Heating Season

	Base Case: No Change in Heating Oil Price	Heating Oil Price Decrease	Heating Oil Price Increase
Heating oil inventory (gal.)	2,100,000	2,100,000	2,100,000
Selling, price, per gallon	$2.10	$1.70	$2.50
Average purchase price, per gallon	$1.30	$1.30	$1.30
Futures price	$1.90	$1.50	$2.30
Without a Hedge			
Revenue	$4,410,000	$3,570,000	$5,250,000
Cost of inventory sold	$2,730,000	$2,730,000	$2,730,000
Interest expense	$ 500,000	$ 500,000	$ 500,000
Pretax profit	$1,180,000	$ 340,000	$2,020,000
Pretax profit, per gallon	$ 0.56	$ 0.16	$ 0.96
With Short Hedge (short futures at $1.90):			
Revenue	$4,410,000	$3,570,000	$5,250,000
Cost of inventory sold	$2,730,000	$2,730,000	$2,730,000
Interest expense	$ 500,000	$ 500,000	$ 500,000
Futures gain (loss)	$ 0	$ 840,000	($ 840,000)
Pretax profit	$1,180,000	$1,180,000	$1,180,000
Hedge effect (constant pretax profit)	$ 0.56	$ 0.56	$ 0.56
Futures gain (loss), per gallon	$ 0.00	$ 0.40	($ 0.40)

FIGURE 14.2 Heating Oil Selling Prices, Pretax Profits, and Futures Profits

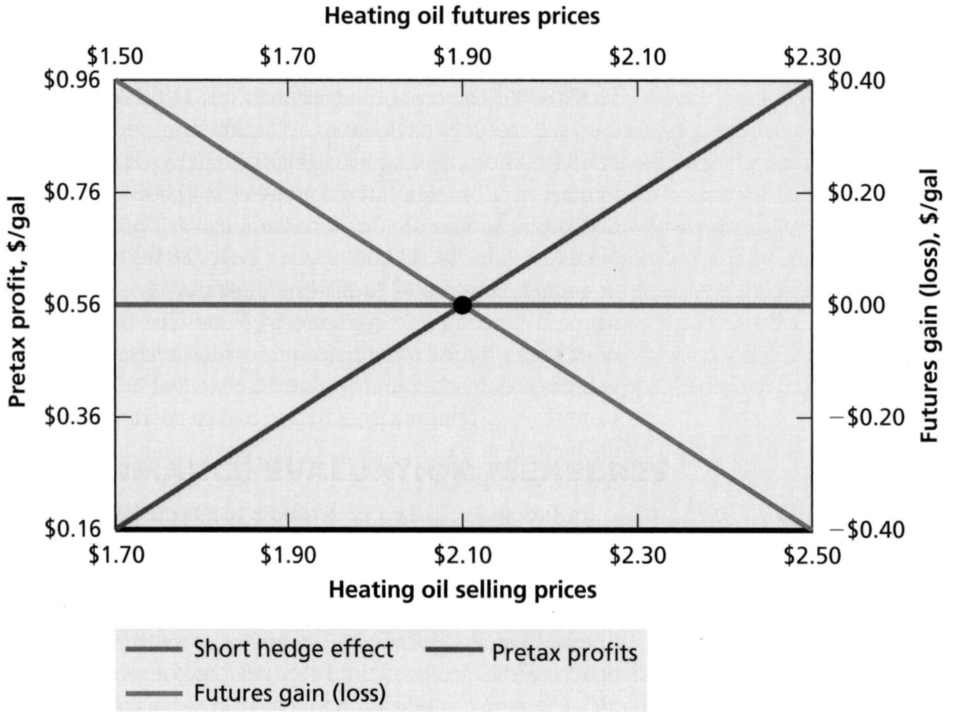

Firms that use a long hedge do not currently own the underlying asset, but plan to acquire it in the future. In this case, it is as if the firm is "short" the underlying asset because if the price increases between now and the time at which the firm actually purchases the underlying asset, the firm will pay more than it thought. Note that the firm does not go into the market and establish a short position in the underlying asset. That would be speculating. Rather, its planned business activities create situations where the firm is exposed to price increases in the underlying asset. This exposure is what gives rise to the saying that the firm is effectively "short the underlying."

FINAL THOUGHTS ABOUT HEDGING In real hedging applications, many factors influence the exact profit recognized. But this example provides you with an overview of how hedging works. The important thing to remember is this: *If you want to shed risk, do not take risk.* That is, if you are long the underlying asset, do not buy futures too!

There is an easy way to remember which position to take in the futures market. In the heating oil example above, pretax profits per gallon change penny by penny with heating oil price changes. That is, the slope of the blue line in Figure 14.2 is one. To eliminate price risk, the hedger needs to add a futures position to the underlying position that results in a slope of zero. What number do we have to add to one to get zero? Obviously, the answer is negative one, which is the slope of the red line in Figure 14.2.

Figure 14.2 is sometimes called "the X" or "the cross" in that it shows how the risk of the futures position offsets the risk of the underlying position. If you can remember Figure 14.2, you will remember which futures position to take when you want to hedge.

Hedging greatly reduces and, in some cases, eliminates the possibility of a loss from a decline in the price of the underlying asset. However, by hedging with futures, the firm also eliminates the possibility of a gain from a price increase in the underlying asset. This is an important point. If the price of the underlying asset rises, you will incur a loss on your futures position.

However, forgone opportunities for increases in the value of the underlying asset represent the bulk of hedging costs. Failure to shift price risk through hedging means that the firm is actually holding price risk. Some people think that holding price risk that could be shifted is the same as taking price risk. The owners of the firm must decide whether they are price risk shifters or price risk holders.

EXAMPLE 14.4

Short Hedging

Suppose you have an inventory of 1.8 million pounds of soybean oil. Describe how you would hedge this position.

Because you are long in the underlying commodity, soybean oil, you need to go short in futures (i.e., sell). A single bean oil contract calls for delivery of 60,000 pounds of bean oil. To hedge your position, you need to sell 1.8 million/60,000 = 30 futures contracts.

EXAMPLE 14.5

More Hedging

You need to buy 360,000 pounds of orange juice concentrate in three months. How can you hedge the price risk associated with this planned purchase? One orange juice contract calls for delivery of 15,000 pounds of orange juice concentrate.

In this example, if the price of concentrate increases between now and when you actually purchase the orange juice concentrate, you will pay more than you thought. So, effectively, you have a "short" position in the underlying asset because you do not currently own it (but you do plan to buy it later). To offset the risk of higher orange juice concentrate prices when you actually buy, you need to establish a long futures position today (this hedge is known as a long hedge). You should buy 360,000/15,000 = 24 contracts.

EXAMPLE 14.6 **Even More Hedging**

Suppose your company will receive payment of £15 million in three months, at which time your company will convert the British pounds to U.S. dollars. What is the standard futures contract size for British pounds? Describe how you could use futures contracts to lock in an exchange rate from British pounds to U.S. dollars for your planned receipt of £15 million, including how many contracts are required.

Your company will be receiving £15 million, so you are effectively long British pounds. Think of your British pound exposure like this. Suppose in the extreme case that the value of these British pounds is zero when you try to exchange them for U.S. dollars. So, if the British pound per U.S. dollar exchange rate falls, the British pound you will receive will decline in value.

To hedge these British pounds, you can use a short hedge. That is, you short (or sell) British pound futures contracts today. As with any short position, your short position in British pound futures obligates you to deliver the underlying asset. In this case, you are obligated to deliver British pounds and receive U.S. dollars at the prevailing British pound per U.S. dollar exchange rate when the futures contract expires. One British pound contract calls for delivery of £62,500. You will therefore sell £15 million/£62,500 = 240 contracts.

CHECK THIS

14.2a Explain what is meant by a long position in futures and what is meant by a short position in futures.

14.2b Suppose a hedger employs a futures hedge that is two-thirds the size of the underlying position. Why do you think this is called a "partial" hedge?

14.2c You have a short position in the underlying asset. How would you modify Figure 14.2 in this case?

14.2d Suppose a firm has a long position in the underlying asset. What happens if this firm buys futures contracts instead of selling futures contracts? Create an example like the one shown in Table 14.1 to help explain the consequences. (By the way, this activity is jokingly referred to as a "Texas hedge.")

14.3 Futures Trading Accounts

A futures exchange, like a stock exchange, allows only exchange members to trade on the exchange. Exchange members may be firms or individuals trading for their own accounts, or they may be brokerage firms handling trades for customers. Some firms conduct both trading and brokerage operations on the exchange. In this section, we discuss the mechanics of a futures trading account as it pertains to a customer with a trading account at a brokerage firm.

> **WWW**
> For a list of online futures brokers visit the Commodities & Futures section of Investor Links at www.investorlinks.com

The biggest customer trading accounts are those of corporations that use futures to manage their business risks and money managers who hedge or speculate with clients' funds. Many individual investors also have futures trading accounts of their own, although speculation by individual investors is not recommended without a full understanding of all risks involved. Whether a futures trading account is large or small, the mechanics of account trading are essentially the same.

> **futures margin**
> Deposit of funds in a futures trading account dedicated to covering potential losses from an outstanding futures position.

There are several essential things to know about futures trading accounts. The first thing is that margin is required. In this way, futures accounts resemble the stock margin accounts we discussed in a previous chapter; however, the specifics are quite different. **Futures margin** is a deposit of funds in a futures trading account dedicated to covering potential losses from

initial margin
Amount required when a futures contract is first bought or sold. Initial margin varies with the type and size of a contract, but it is the same for long and short futures positions.

marking-to-market
In futures trading accounts, the process whereby gains and losses on outstanding futures positions are recognized on a daily basis.

maintenance margin
The minimum margin level required in a futures trading account at all times.

margin call
Notification to increase the margin level in a trading account.

reverse trade
A trade that closes out a previously established futures position by taking the opposite position.

an outstanding futures position. An **initial margin** is required when a futures position is first established. The amount varies according to contract type and size, but margin requirements for futures contracts usually range between 2 percent and 5 percent of total contract value. Initial margin is the same for both long and short futures positions.

The second thing to know about a futures trading account is that contract values in outstanding futures positions are marked to market on a daily basis. **Marking-to-market** is a process whereby gains and losses on outstanding futures positions are recognized at the end of each trading day.

For example, suppose one morning you call your broker and instruct her to go long five U.S. Treasury bond contracts for your account. A few minutes later, she calls back to confirm order execution at a futures price of 110. Because the Treasury bond contract size is \$100,000 par value, contract value is 110% $\times$ \$100,000 = \$110,000 per contract. Thus, the total position value for your order is \$550,000, for which your broker requires \$25,000 initial margin. In addition, your broker requires that at least \$20,000 in **maintenance margin** be present at all times. The necessary margin funds are immediately wired from a bank account to your futures account.

Now, at the end of trading that day Treasury bond futures close at a price of 108. Overnight, all accounts are marked to market. Your Treasury bond futures position is marked to \$108,000 per contract, or \$540,000 total position value, representing a loss of \$10,000. This loss is deducted from your initial margin to leave only \$15,000 of margin funds in your account.

Because the maintenance margin level on your account is \$20,000, your broker will issue a **margin call** on your account. Essentially, your broker will notify you that you must immediately restore your margin level to the initial margin level of \$25,000, or else she will close out your Treasury bond futures position at whatever trading price is available at the exchange.

This example illustrates what happens when a futures trading account is marked to market and the resulting margin funds fall below the maintenance margin level. The alternative, and more pleasant, experience occurs when a futures price moves in your favor, and the marking-to-market process adds funds to your account. In this case, marking-to-market gains can be withdrawn from your account so long as remaining margin funds are not less than the initial margin level.

The third thing to know about a futures trading account is that a futures position can be closed out at any time; you do not have to hold a contract until maturity. A futures position is closed out by simply instructing your broker to close out your position. To actually close out a position, your broker will enter a **reverse trade** for your account.

A reverse trade works like this: Suppose you are currently short five Treasury bond contracts, and you instruct your broker to close out the position. Your broker responds by going long five Treasury bond contracts for your account. In this case, going long five contracts is a reverse trade because it cancels exactly your previous five-contract short position. At the end of the day in which you make your reverse trade, your account will be marked to market at the futures price realized by the reverse trade. From then on, your position is closed out, and no more gains or losses will be realized.

This example illustrates that closing out a futures position is no more difficult than initially entering into a position. There are two basic reasons to close out a futures position before contract maturity. The first is to capture a current gain or loss, without realizing further price risk. The second is to avoid the delivery requirement that comes from holding a futures contract until it matures. In fact, over 98 percent of all futures contracts are closed out before contract maturity, which indicates that less than 2 percent of all futures contracts result in delivery of the underlying commodity or financial instrument.

Before closing this section, let's briefly list the three essential things to know about a futures trading account as discussed above:

1. Margin is required.
2. Futures accounts are marked to market daily.
3. A futures position can be closed out any time by a reverse trade.

Understanding the items in this list is important to anyone planning to use a futures trading account.

CHECK THIS

14.3a What are the three essential things you should know about a futures trading account?

14.3b What is meant by initial margin for a futures position? What is meant by maintenance margin for a futures position?

14.3c Explain the process of marking-to-market a futures trading account. What is a margin call, and when is one issued?

14.3d How is a futures position closed out by a reverse trade? What proportion of all futures positions are closed out by reverse trades rather than by delivery at contract maturity?

14.4 Cash Prices versus Futures Prices

We now turn to the relationship between today's price of some commodity or financial instrument and its futures price. We begin by examining current cash prices.

CASH PRICES

cash price
Price of a commodity or financial instrument for current delivery. Also called the *spot price.*

cash market
Market in which commodities or financial instruments are traded for immediate delivery. Also called the *spot market.*

The **cash price** of a commodity or financial instrument is the price quoted for current delivery. The cash price is also called the *spot price*, as in "on the spot." In futures jargon, terms like "spot gold" or "cash wheat" are used to refer to commodities being sold for current delivery in what is called the **cash market** or the *spot market.*

Figure 14.3 reproduces the "Cash Prices" column of *The Wall Street Journal*, published the same day as the "Futures Prices" column seen in Figure 14.1. The column is divided into sections according to commodity categories. For example, the section "Grains and Feeds" lists spot price information for wheat, corn, soybeans, and similar crops. Other commodity sections include "Food," "Fats and Oils," "Energy," and "Metals." Each section gives commodity names along with cash market prices for the day of trading and one year earlier.

CASH-FUTURES ARBITRAGE

Intuitively, you might think that the cash price of a commodity is closely related to its futures price. If you do, then your intuition is quite correct. In fact, your intuition is backed up by strong economic argument and more than a century of experience observing the simultaneous operation of cash and futures markets.

As a routine matter, cash and futures prices are closely watched by market professionals. To understand why, suppose you notice that spot gold is trading for $730 per ounce while the two-month futures price is $780 per ounce. Do you see a profit opportunity?

You should, because buying spot gold today at $730 per ounce while simultaneously selling gold futures at $780 per ounce locks in a $50 per ounce profit. True, gold has storage costs (you have to put it somewhere), and a spot gold purchase ties up capital that could be earning interest. However, these costs are small relative to the $50 per ounce gross profit, which is $50 / $730 = 6.8% per two months, or about 49 percent per year (with compounding). Furthermore, this profit is risk-free! Alas, in reality, such easy profit opportunities are the stuff of dreams.

cash-futures arbitrage
Strategy for earning risk-free profits from an unusual difference between cash and futures prices.

basis
The difference between the cash price and the futures price for a commodity, i.e., basis = cash price − futures price.

Earning risk-free profits from an unusual difference between cash and futures prices is called **cash-futures arbitrage**. In a competitive market, cash-futures arbitrage has very slim profit margins. In fact, the profit margins are almost imperceptible when they exist at all.

Comparing cash prices for commodities in Figure 14.3 with their corresponding futures prices reported in Figure 14.1, you will find that cash prices and futures prices are seldom equal. In futures jargon, the difference between a cash price and a futures price is called **basis.**[1]

[1] The official Commodity Trading Manual of the Chicago Board of Trade defines basis as the difference between the cash and the futures price, i.e., basis = cash price − futures price. We will be consistent with the CBOT definition. For nonagricultural futures, however, the basis is nearly always defined as the futures price minus the cash price.

FIGURE 14.3 Commodity Cash Prices

Cash Prices

Wednesday, August 22,2007

These prices reflect buying and selling of a variety of actual or "physical" commodities in the marketplace--separate from the futures price on an exchange, which reflects what the commodity might be worth in future months.

	Wednesday	Year ago
Energy		
European crude oil spot prices, 11 a.m. ET,		
Northwestern Europe		
Forties	66.56	71.50
Brent	67.53	70.90
Bonny light	70.58	72.20
Urals-Mediterranean	65.28	66.20
Domestic crude oil spot prices, 4 p.m. ET		
West Texas intmdt, Cushing	69.32	71.42
West Texas sour, Midlands	63.57	66.17
Louisiana sweet, St. James	69.82	71.42
Alaska North Slope, Pac delivery	70.71	70.06
Refined products		
Fuel oil, No. 2 NY	1.9283	1.9501
Diesel,500ppm low sulfur NY	2.0008	2.2026
Diesel,15ppm ultra-low sulf NY	2.0633	n.a.
Gasoline,conv prem NY	2.0990	2.2044
Gasoline,RBOB prem NY	2.1465	n.a.
Gasoline,conv reg NY	1.8990	1.8444
Gasoline,RBOB reg NY	1.9190	n.a.
Gasoline,CARBOB,reg LA-m	1.9250	2.1350
Propane,nontet,Mont Belvieu-g	1.1675	1.1238
Butane,normal,Mont Belvieu-g	1.3875	1.3150
Natural gas Henry Hub	5.8050	7.1700
Metals		
Gold, per troy oz		
Engelhard industrial	661.27	629.82
Engelhard fabricated	710.86	677.05
Handy & Harman base	659.50	628.10
Handy & Harman fabricated	712.26	678.35
London a.m. fixing	657.15	623.50
London p.m. fixing	659.50	628.10
Krugerrand,wholesale	665.50	629.50
Maple Leaf	692.48	649.48
American Eagle	692.48	649.48

	Wednesday	Year ago
Mexican peso	803.16	756.96
Austria crown	649.44	615.13
Austria phil	692.48	649.48
Silver, troy oz.		
Engelhard industrial	11.7600	12.5400
Engelhard fabricated	14.1120	15.0480
Handy & Harman base	11.7000	12.5000
Handy & Harman fabricated	14.0400	15.0000
London fixing,spot price	£5.8723	£6.5645
(U.S.$ equivalent)	11.6800	12.4200
Coins,wholesale $1,000 face-a	8211	8835
Other metals		
Platinum,free market	1240.0	1231.0
Platinum,Engelhard industrial	1244.0	1233.0
Platinum,Engelhard fabricated	1344.0	1333.0
Palladium,Engelhard industrial	322.0	345.0
Palladium,Engelhard fabricated	422.0	445.0
Aluminum,Comex spot	1.0655	1.1250
Antimony-d	2.6250	2.6250
Copper,Comex spot	3.2270	3.4730
Lead,NA solder-d	176.307	78.949
Stainless steel scrap,US-d	4030	2158
Tin,NA solder-d	907.662	552.733
Zinc,NA-d	148.618	163.773
Fibers and Textiles		
Burlap,10-oz,40-inch NY yd-n,w	0.4475	0.4050
Cotton,1 1/16 std lw-mdMphs	0.5220	0.4930
Hides,hvy native steers fob-u	86.375	87.500
Wool,64s,staple,Terr del-u,w	2.70	1.65
Grains and Feeds		
Barley,top-quality Mnnpls-u	4.30	3.15
Bran,wheat middlings, KC-u	57	59
Corn,No. 2 yellow,Cent IL-bp,u	3.2800	2.0450
Corn gluten feed,Midwest-u,w	78.85	54.27
Cottonseed meal-u,w	152	135
Hominy feed,Cent IL-u,w	97	58
Meat-bonemeal,50% pro IL-u,w	238	158

	Wednesday	Year ago
Oats,No.2 milling,Mnnpls-u	2.6250	2.0250
Sorghum,(Milo) No.2 Gulf-u	7.7150	5.0000
SoybeanMeal,Cent IL,rail,ton48%-u	219.20	161.70
Soybeans,No.1 yllw IL-bp,u	7.7150	5.2100
Wheat,Spring14%-pro Mnpls-u	6.8950	4.7975
Wheat,No.2 soft red,St.Louis-bp,u	6.3250	3.1550
Wheat,hard,KC	6.7650	4.8825
Wheat,No.1soft white,Portld,OR-u	7.0000	3.9400
Food		
Beef,carcass equiv. index		
choice 1-3,600-900 lbs.-u	134.13	135.37
select 1-3,600-900 lbs.-u	127.76	123.86
Broilers,dressed 'A'	0.8150	0.7075
Broilers,12-city comp wghtd	0.7997	0.7138
Butter,AA Chicago	1.4050	1.3150
Cheddar cheese,bbl,Chicago	193.75	124.50
Cheddar cheese,blk,Chicago	196.75	123.50
Milk,Nonfat dry,Chicago	193	90
Cocoa,Ivory Coast	2112	1812
Coffee,Brazilian,Comp	1.1148	1.0367
Coffee,Colombian, NY	1.2414	1.1719
Eggs,large white,Chicago	0.9350	0.5750
Flour,hard winter KC	17.25	12.85
Hams,17-20 lbs,Mid-US fob	n.a.	n.a.
Hogs,Iowa-So. Minnesota	66.33	72.14
Hogs,Sioux Falls,SD	48.00	56.00
Pork bellies,12-14 lb MidUS	0.9100	n.a.
Pork loins,13-19 lb MidUS	1.0950	n.a.
Steers,Tex.-Okla. Choice	n.a.	n.a.
Steers,feeder,Okla. City	122.88	126.25
Sugar,cane,raw,world,fob	11.42	13.09
Fats and Oils		
Corn oil,crude wet/dry mill	40.00	25.00
Grease,choice white,Chicago-u,s	n.2650	0.1675
Lard,Chicago	0.3550	n.a.
Soybean oil,crude;Centl IL-u	0.3382	0.2469
Tallow,bleach;Chicago-u	0.2700	0.1725
Tallow,edible,Chicago	0.3200	n.a.

KEY TO CODES: a=ask; b=bid; bp=country elevator bids to producers; c=corrected; d=Ryan's Notes; e=Manfra,Tordella & Brooks; g=ICE; m=midday; n=nominal; n.a.=not quoted or not available;u=USDA; w=weekly

Source: WSJ Market Data Group

Source: Reprinted by permission of *The Wall Street Journal*, August 23, 2007.

carrying-charge market
The case where the futures price is greater than the cash price; i.e., the basis is negative.

inverted market
The case where the futures price is less than the cash price; i.e., the basis is positive.

For commodities with storage costs, the cash price is usually less than the futures price. This is referred to as a **carrying-charge market**. Sometimes, however, the cash price is greater than the futures price, and this is referred to as an **inverted market**. We can summarize this discussion of carrying-charge markets, inverted markets, and basis as follows:

$$\text{Carrying-charge market: Basis} = \text{Cash price} - \text{Futures price} < 0 \quad (14.1)$$
$$\text{Inverted market: Basis} = \text{Cash price} - \text{Futures price} > 0$$

A variety of factors can lead to an economically justifiable difference between a commodity's cash price and its futures price, including availability of storage facilities, transportation costs, and seasonal price fluctuations. However, the primary determinants of the cash-futures basis are storage costs and interest costs. Storage cost is the cost of holding the commodity in a storage facility, and interest cost refers to interest income forgone on funds used to buy and hold the commodity.

If a futures price rises far enough above a cash price to more than cover storage costs and interest expense, commodity traders will undertake cash-futures arbitrage by buying in the cash market and selling in the futures market. This drives down the futures price and drives up the cash price until the basis is restored to an economically justifiable level.

Similarly, if a futures price falls far enough relative to a cash price, traders will undertake cash-futures arbitrage by short selling in the cash market and buying in the futures market. This drives down the cash price and drives up the futures price until an economically justifiable basis is restored. In both cases, arbitrage ensures that the basis is kept at an economically appropriate level.

SPOT-FUTURES PARITY

We can be slightly more precise in illustrating the relationship between spot and futures prices for financial futures. Consider the example of futures contracts for shares of stock in a single company. One place such futures contracts are traded in the United States is OneChicago, a joint venture of the major Chicago exchanges. Single-stock futures contracts have a standard contract size of 100 shares of the underlying stock, but futures prices are quoted on a per-share basis.

WWW

For more information on single-stock futures trading visit www.onechicago.com and the Futures Source Web site at www.futuresource.com

Suppose we are examining a particular single-stock futures contract that calls for delivery of 100 shares of stock in one year. The current (i.e., cash or spot) stock price is \$50 per share, and the stock does not pay dividends. Also, 12-month T-bills are yielding 6 percent. What should the futures price be? To answer, notice that you can buy 100 shares of stock for \$50 per share, or \$5,000 total. You can eliminate all of the risk associated with this purchase by selling one futures contract. The net effect of this transaction is that you have created a risk-free asset. Because the risk-free rate is 6 percent, your investment must have a future value of $\$5{,}000 \times 1.06 = \$5{,}300$. In other words, the futures price should be \$53 per share.

Suppose the futures price is, in fact, \$52 per share. What would you do? To make money, you would short 100 shares of stock at \$50 per share and invest the \$5,000 proceeds at 6 percent.[2] Simultaneously, you would buy one futures contract.

At the end of the year, you would have \$5,300. You would use \$5,200 to buy the stock to fulfill your obligation on the futures contract and then return the stock to close out the short position. You pocket \$100. This is just another example of cash-futures arbitrage.

More generally, if we let F be the futures price, S be the spot price, and r be the risk-free rate, then our example illustrates that:

$$F = S(1 + r) \tag{14.2}$$

spot-futures parity The relationship between spot prices and futures prices that holds in the absence of arbitrage opportunities.

In other words, the futures price is simply the future value of the spot price, calculated at the risk-free rate. This is the famous **spot-futures parity** condition. This condition must hold in the absence of cash-futures arbitrage opportunities.

More generally, if r is the risk-free rate per period, and the futures contract matures in T periods, then the spot-futures parity condition is:

$$F_T = S(1 + r)^T \tag{14.3}$$

Notice that T could be a fraction of one period. For example, if we have the risk-free rate per year, but the futures contract matures in six months, T would be 1/2.

EXAMPLE 14.7 Parity Check

A non–dividend-paying stock has a current price of \$12 per share. The risk-free rate is 4 percent per year. If a futures contract on the stock matures in three months, what should the futures price be?

From our spot-futures parity condition, we have:

$$\begin{aligned} F_T &= S(1 + r)^T \\ &= \$12(1.04)^{1/4} \\ &= \$12.12 \end{aligned}$$

The futures price should be \$12.12. Notice that r and T are expressed in years for this example. Therefore, we set $r = .04$ and $T = 1/4$.

[2] For the sake of simplicity, we ignore the fact that individual investors do not earn interest on the proceeds from a short sale, and we assume the stock does not pay dividends.

MORE ON SPOT-FUTURES PARITY

In our spot-futures parity example just above, we assumed that the underlying financial instrument (the stock) had no cash flows (no dividends). If there are dividends (for a stock future) or coupon payments (for a bond future), then we need to modify our spot-futures parity condition.

For a stock, we let D stand for the dividend, and we assume that the dividend is paid in one period, at or near the end of the futures contract's life. In this case, the spot-futures parity condition becomes:

$$F = S(1 + r) - D \tag{14.4}$$

Notice that we have simply subtracted the amount of the dividend from the future value of the stock price. The reason is that if you buy the futures contract, you will not receive the dividend, but the dividend payment will reduce the stock price.

An alternative, and very useful, way of writing the dividend-adjusted spot-futures parity result in equation (14.4) is to define d as the dividend yield on the stock. Recall that the dividend yield is just the upcoming dividend divided by the current price. In our current notation, this is just $d = D/S$. With this in mind, we can write the dividend-adjusted parity result as:

$$\begin{aligned} F &= S(1 + r) - D(S/S) \qquad (14.5)\\ &= S(1 + r) - S(D/S) \\ &= S(1 + r) - Sd \\ &= S(1 + r - d) \end{aligned}$$

Finally, as above, if there is something other than a single period involved, we would write:

$$F_T = S(1 + r - d)^T \tag{14.6}$$

where T is the number of periods (or fraction of a period), and r is the interest rate per period.

For example, suppose there is a futures contract on a stock with a current price of \$80. The futures contract matures in six months. The risk-free rate is 7 percent per year, and the stock has an annual dividend yield of 3 percent. What should the futures price be?

Plugging in the values to our dividend-adjusted parity equation, we have:

$$\begin{aligned} F_T &= S(1 + r - d)^T \\ &= \$80(1 + .07 - .03)^{1/2} \\ &= \$81.58 \end{aligned}$$

Notice that we set T equal to 1/2 because the contract matures in six months.

CHECK THIS

14.4a What is the spot price for a commodity?

14.4b With regard to futures contracts, what is the basis?

14.4c What is an inverted market?

14.4d What is the spot-futures parity condition?

14.5 Stock Index Futures

There are a number of futures contracts on stock market indexes. Because these contracts are particularly important, we devote this entire section to them. We first describe the contracts and then discuss some trading and hedging strategies involving their use.

BASICS OF STOCK INDEX FUTURES

Locate the section labeled "Index Futures" in Figure 14.1. Here we see various stock index futures contracts. The third contract listed, on the S&P 500 Index, is the most important. With this contract, actual delivery would be very difficult or impossible because the seller

WWW

For information on stock index futures visit the Web site at CME group's www.cmegroup.com

of the contract would have to buy all 500 stocks in exactly the right proportions to deliver. Clearly, this is not practical, so this contract features cash settlement.

To understand how stock index futures work, suppose you bought one S&P 500 contract at a futures price of 1,540. The contract size is $250 times the level of the index. What this means is that, at maturity, the buyer of the contract will pay the seller $250 times the difference between the futures price of 1,540 and the level of the S&P 500 Index at contract maturity.

For example, suppose that at maturity the S&P had actually fallen to 1,510. In this case, the buyer of the contract must pay $250 × (1,540 − 1,510) = $7,500 to the seller of the contract. In effect, the buyer of the contract has agreed to purchase 250 "units" of the index at a price of $1,540 per unit. If the index is below 1,540, the buyer will lose money. If the index is above that, then the seller will lose money.

EXAMPLE 14.8 **Index Futures**

Suppose you are convinced that the Dow stocks are going to skyrocket in value. Consequently, you buy 20 DJIA futures contracts maturing in six months at a price of 13,900. Suppose that the Dow Jones Index is at 14,320 when the contracts mature. How much will you make or lose?

The futures price is 13,900, and the contract size is $10 times the level of the index. At maturity, if the index is at 14,320, you make $10 × (14,320 − 13,900) = $4,200 per contract. With 20 contracts, your total profit is $84,000.

INDEX ARBITRAGE

index arbitrage
Strategy of monitoring the futures price on a stock index and the level of the underlying index to exploit deviations from parity.

The spot-futures parity relation we developed above is the basis for a common trading strategy known as **index arbitrage**. Index arbitrage refers to monitoring the futures price on a stock index along with the level of the underlying index. The trader looks for violations of parity and trades as appropriate.

For example, suppose the S&P 500 futures price for delivery in one year is 1,540. The current level is 1,500. The dividend yield on the S&P is projected to be 3 percent per year, and the risk-free rate is 5 percent. Is there a trading opportunity here?

From our dividend-adjusted parity equation (14.6), the futures price should be:

$$\begin{aligned} F_T &= S(1 + r - d)^T \\ &= 1{,}500(1 + .05 - .03)^1 \\ &= 1{,}530 \end{aligned}$$

Thus, based on our parity calculation, the futures price is too high. We want to buy low, sell high, so we buy the index and simultaneously sell the futures contract.

program trading
Computer-assisted monitoring of relative prices of financial assets; it sometimes includes computer submission of buy and sell orders to exploit perceived arbitrage opportunities.

Index arbitrage is often implemented as a **program trading** strategy. While this term covers a lot of ground, it generally refers to the monitoring of relative prices by computer to more quickly spot opportunities. In some cases it includes submitting the needed buy and sell orders using a computer to speed up the process.

Whether a computer is used in program trading is not really the issue; instead, a program trading strategy is any coordinated, systematic procedure for exploiting (or trying to exploit) violations of parity or other arbitrage opportunities. Such a procedure is a trading "program" in the sense that whenever certain conditions exist, certain trades are made. Thus, the process is sufficiently mechanical that it can be automated, at least in principle.

Technically, the NYSE defines program trading as the simultaneous purchase or sale of at least 15 different stocks with a total value of $1 million or more. Program trading can account for up to half the total trading volume on the NYSE, but not all program trading involves stock-index arbitrage.

Another phenomenon was often associated with index arbitrage and, more generally, futures and options trading. S&P 500 futures contracts have four expiration months per year, and they expire on the third Friday of those months. On these same four Fridays, options on the S&P Index and various individual stock options also expired. These Fridays were dubbed the "triple witching hour" because all three types of contracts expired, sometimes leading to unusual price behavior.

In particular, on triple witching hour Fridays, all positions must be liquidated, or "unwound." To the extent that large-scale index arbitrage and other program trading has taken place, enormous buying or selling sometimes occurs late in the day on such Fridays, as positions are closed out. Large price swings and, more generally, increased volatility are often seen. To curtail this problem, the exchanges have adopted rules regarding the size of a position that can be carried to expiration. In addition, options on the S&P 500 Index now expire on Friday morning.

WWW

For information on program trading, visit www.programtrading.com

For information on stock-index arbitrage, visit www.indexarb.com

HEDGING STOCK MARKET RISK WITH FUTURES

We earlier discussed hedging using futures contracts in the context of a business protecting the value of its inventory. We now discuss some hedging strategies available to portfolio managers based on financial futures. Essentially, an investment portfolio is an inventory of securities, and financial futures can be used to reduce the risk of holding a securities portfolio.

We consider the specific problem of an equity portfolio manager wishing to protect the value of a stock portfolio from the risk of an adverse movement of the overall stock market. Here, the portfolio manager wishes to establish a short hedge position to reduce risk and must determine the number of futures contracts required to properly hedge a portfolio.

In this hedging example, you are responsible for managing a broadly diversified stock portfolio with a current value of $185 million. Analysis of market conditions leads you to believe that the stock market is unusually susceptible to a price decline during the next few months. Of course, nothing is certain regarding stock market fluctuations, but still you are sufficiently concerned to believe that action is required.

A fundamental problem exists for you, however, in that no futures contract exactly matches your particular portfolio. As a result, you decide to protect your stock portfolio from a fall in value caused by a falling stock market using stock index futures. This is an example of a **cross-hedge**, where a futures contract on a related, but not identical, commodity or financial instrument is used to hedge a particular spot position.

cross-hedge
Hedging a particular spot position with futures contracts on a related, but not identical, commodity or financial instrument.

Thus, to hedge your portfolio, you wish to establish a short hedge using stock index futures. To do this, you need to know how many index futures contracts are required to form an effective hedge. Three basic inputs are needed to calculate the number of stock index futures contracts required to hedge a stock portfolio:

1. The current value of your stock portfolio.
2. The beta of your stock portfolio.
3. The contract value of the index futures contract used for hedging.

Based on previous chapters, you are familiar with the concept of beta as a measure of market risk for a stock portfolio. Essentially, beta measures portfolio risk relative to the overall stock market. We will assume that you have maintained a beta of 1.25 for your $185 million stock portfolio.

You believe that the market (and your portfolio) will fall in value over the next three months and you decide to eliminate market risk from your portfolio. That is, you would like to convert your risky portfolio with a beta of 1.25 to a riskless portfolio with a beta of zero. Because you hold a stock portfolio, you know that you will need to establish a short hedge using futures contracts. You decide to use futures contracts on the S&P 500 Index, because this is the index you used to calculate the beta for your portfolio.

From *The Wall Street Journal,* you find that the S&P 500 futures price for contracts that mature in three months is currently 1,480. Because the contract size for the S&P 500 futures is 250 times the index level, the current value of a single S&P 500 Index futures contract is $\$250 \times 1{,}480 = \$370{,}000$.

You now have all the information you need to calculate the number of S&P 500 Index futures contracts needed to hedge your $185 million stock portfolio. The number of stock index futures contracts needed to convert the beta of your portfolio from 1.25 to zero is determined by the following formula:

$$\text{Number of contracts} = (\beta_D - \beta_P) \times \frac{V_P}{V_F} \qquad (14.7)$$

where: β_D = Desired beta of the stock portfolio
β_P = Current beta of the stock portfolio
V_P = Value of the stock portfolio
V_F = Value of one stock index futures contract

For your particular hedging problem, $\beta_D = 0$, $\beta_P = 1.25$, V_P = \$185 million, and V_F = \$370,000, thereby yielding this calculation:

$$\text{Number of contracts} = (0 - 1.25) \times \frac{\$185{,}000{,}000}{\$370{,}000} = -625$$

Thus, you can establish an effective short hedge by going short 625 S&P 500 Index futures contracts. This short hedge will protect your stock portfolio against the risk of a general fall in the stock market during the remaining three-month life of the futures contract.

Equation (14.7) reinforces the notion that you want to go short futures contracts to lower the beta of your portfolio. The negative number of contracts is a reminder that you are trying to shed risk, which calls for a short position in the S&P 500 Index futures market.

You can see that equation (14.7) can also be used to change the beta of your portfolio to any level you want. However, any level other than zero is not considered a hedge, because your portfolio will still retain some systematic risk.

EXAMPLE 14.9

Hedging with Stock Index Futures

How many stock index futures contracts are required to hedge a \$250 million stock portfolio, assuming a portfolio beta of .75 and an S&P 500 Index futures level of 1,500?

Using equation (14.7) and the knowledge that a true hedge reduces the portfolio beta to zero, we have:

$$\text{Number of contracts} = (0 - .75) \times \frac{250{,}000{,}000}{375{,}000} = -500$$

Therefore, you need to short 500 stock index futures contracts to hedge this \$250 million portfolio. In this example, note that the value of one futures contract is given by \$250 × 1,500 = \$375,000.

HEDGING INTEREST RATE RISK WITH FUTURES

Having discussed hedging a stock portfolio, we now turn to hedging a bond portfolio. As we will see, the bond portfolio hedging problem is similar to the stock portfolio hedging problem. Once again, we will be cross-hedging, but this time using futures contracts on U.S. Treasury notes. Here, our goal is to protect the bond portfolio against changing interest rates.

In this example, you are responsible for managing a bond portfolio with a current value of \$100 million. Recently, rising interest rates have caused your portfolio to fall in value slightly, and you are concerned that interest rates may continue to trend upward for the next several months. You decide to establish a short hedge based on 10-year Treasury note futures.

The formula for the number of U.S. Treasury note futures contracts needed to hedge a bond portfolio is:

$$\text{Number of contracts} = \frac{D_P \times V_P}{D_F \times V_F} \quad (14.8)$$

where: D_P = Duration of the bond portfolio
V_P = Value of the bond portfolio
D_F = Duration of the futures contract
V_F = Value of a single futures contract

We already know the value of the bond portfolio, which is \$100 million. Also, suppose that the duration of the portfolio is given as eight years. Next, we must calculate the duration of the futures contract and the value of the futures contract.

As a useful rule of thumb, the duration of an interest rate futures contract is equal to the duration of the underlying instrument plus the time remaining until contract maturity:

$$D_F = D_U + M_F \tag{14.9}$$

where: D_F = Duration of the futures contract
D_U = Duration of the underlying instrument
M_F = Time remaining until contract maturity

For simplicity, let us suppose that the duration of the underlying U.S. Treasury note is 6 1/2 years and the futures contract has a maturity of 1/2 year, yielding a futures contract duration of 7 years.

The value of a single futures contract is the current futures price times the futures contract size. The standard contract size for U.S. Treasury note futures contracts is \$100,000 par value. Now suppose that the futures price is 110, or 110 percent of par value. This yields a futures contract value of \$100,000 × 110 = \$110,000.

You now have all inputs required to calculate the number of futures contracts needed to hedge your bond portfolio. The number of U.S. Treasury note futures contracts needed to hedge the bond portfolio is calculated as follows:

$$\text{Number of contracts} = \frac{8 \times \$100{,}000{,}000}{7 \times \$110{,}000} = 1{,}038.96$$

Thus, you can establish an effective short hedge by going short 1,039 futures contracts for 10-year U.S. Treasury notes. This short hedge will protect your bond portfolio against the risk of a general rise in interest rates during the life of the futures contracts.

EXAMPLE 14.10 Hedging with U.S. Treasury Note Futures

How many futures contracts are required to hedge a \$250 million bond portfolio with a portfolio duration of 5 years using 10-year U.S. Treasury note futures with a duration of 7.5 years and a futures price of 105?

Using the formula for the number of contracts, we have:

$$\text{Number of contracts} = \frac{5 \times \$250{,}000{,}000}{7.5 \times \$105{,}000} = 1{,}587$$

You therefore need to sell 1,587 contracts to hedge this \$250 million portfolio.

FUTURES CONTRACT DELIVERY OPTIONS

cheapest-to-deliver option
Seller's option to deliver the cheapest instrument when a futures contract allows several instruments for delivery. For example, U.S. Treasury note futures allow delivery of any Treasury note with a maturity between 6 1/2 and 10 years.

Many futures contracts have a delivery option, whereby the seller can choose among several different "grades" of the underlying commodity or instrument when fulfilling delivery requirements. Naturally, we expect the seller to deliver the cheapest among available options. In futures jargon, this is called the **cheapest-to-deliver option**. The cheapest-to-deliver option is an example of a broader feature of many futures contracts, known as a "quality" option. Of course, futures buyers know about the delivery option, and therefore the futures prices reflect the value of the cheapest-to-deliver instrument.

As a specific example of a cheapest-to-deliver option, the 10-year Treasury note contract allows delivery of *any* Treasury note with a maturity between 6 1/2 and 10 years. This complicates the bond portfolio hedging problem. For the portfolio manager trying to hedge a bond portfolio with U.S. Treasury note futures, the cheapest-to-deliver feature means that a note can be hedged only based on an assumption about which note will actually be delivered. Furthermore, through time the cheapest-to-deliver note may vary, and, consequently, the hedge will have to be monitored regularly to make sure that it correctly reflects the note issue that is most likely to be delivered. Fortunately, because this is a common problem, many commercial advisory services provide this information to portfolio managers and other investors.

CHECK THIS

14.5a What is a cross-hedge?

14.5b What are the three basic inputs required to calculate the number of stock index futures contracts needed to hedge an equity portfolio?

14.5c What are the basic inputs required to calculate the number of U.S. Treasury note futures contracts needed to hedge a bond portfolio?

14.5d What is the cheapest-to-deliver option?

14.6 Summary and Conclusions

The topic of this chapter is futures markets. In this chapter, we surveyed the basics of futures markets and contracts—which we summarize by the chapter's important concepts.

1. The basics of futures markets and how to obtain price quotes for futures contracts.

A. A futures contract is an agreement between a buyer and a seller for a future transaction at a price set today. Futures contracts are managed through organized futures exchanges. The existence of a futures exchange virtually eliminates default risk. Four major terms for standardized futures contracts are: (1) the identity of the underlying commodity or financial instrument; (2) the futures contract size; (3) the futures maturity date, and (4) the future price at which the contract will be fulfilled.

B. Most commodity futures contracts call for delivery of a physical commodity. Financial futures require delivery of a financial instrument or, in many cases, cash. Futures contracts are a type of derivative security, because the value of the contract is derived from the value of an underlying instrument.

C. Quotes for futures prices are available through the financial press. These days, however, delayed intradaily quotes for futures prices are available at the Web site of many futures exchanges.

2. The risks involved in futures market speculation.

A. Speculators accept price risk in an attempt to profit on the direction of prices. Speculators can go long or short futures contracts. Speculators buy futures contracts if they think prices are going to go higher. Buying futures is often referred to as "going long," or establishing a long position. Speculators sell futures contracts if they think prices are going lower. Selling futures is often called "going short," or establishing a short position.

B. Futures speculation can lead to substantial gains and losses. An important point is that your gains from futures speculation depend on accurate forecasts of the direction of future prices.

You must ask yourself: Is it easy to forecast price changes?

C. You can sustain losses in futures markets far in excess of your original margin deposit. As futures market prices move against your position, you could be asked to deposit more money into your futures trading account.

3. How cash prices and futures prices are linked.

A. The cash price of a commodity or financial instrument is the price quoted for current delivery. The cash price is also called the spot price.

B. The futures price is simply the future value of the spot price, calculated at the risk-free rate. This statement is the famous spot-futures parity condition. This condition must hold in the absence of cash-futures arbitrage opportunities.

4. How futures contracts can be used to transfer price risk.

A. Hedging is the major economic reason for the existence of futures markets. However, a viable futures market requires participation by both hedgers and speculators.

B. Hedgers transfer price risk to speculators, and speculators absorb price risk. Therefore, hedging and speculating are complementary activities.

C. Hedgers transfer price risk by taking a futures position opposite to their position in the spot market. For example, if the hedger has an inventory of some commodity, the hedger is said to be long in the spot market. Therefore, the hedger will offset price risk in the spot market by taking a short position in the futures market.

GET REAL

This chapter covered the essentials of what many consider to be a complex subject, futures contracts. We hope you realize that futures contracts per se are not complicated at all; in fact, they are, for the most part, quite simple. This doesn't mean that they're for everybody, of course. Because of the tremendous leverage possible, very large gains and losses can (and do) occur with great speed.

To experience some of the gains and losses from outright speculation, you should buy and sell a variety of contracts in a simulated brokerage account such as Stock-Trak. Be sure to go both long and short and pick a few of each major type of contract.

The Internet offers a rich source for more information on trading futures. Probably the best place to begin is by visiting the Web sites of the major futures exchanges: the CME Group (www.cmegroup.com), the IntercontinentalExchange (www.theice.com), the New York Mercantile Exchange (www.nymex.com), and the Kansas City Board of Trade (www.kcbt.com). You might also visit the Web sites of some major international futures exchanges. The reference section of Numa's Web site (www.numa.com/ref/exchange) maintains an extensive list of the world's futures exchanges. Bear in mind that the list changes frequently due to mergers.

For information on futures markets regulation, the federal agency charged with regulating U.S. futures markets is the Commodities Futures Trading Commission (www.cftc.gov). The professional organization charged with self-regulation is the National Futures Association (www.nfa.futures.org). General information on futures markets and trading can be found at the Futures Industry Association (www.futuresindustry.org).

Useful Web sites on trading futures are Futures Trading (www.futures-trading.org), Commodity Traders Club (www.ctcn.com), Daily Futures (www.dailyfutures.com), and Trading Markets (www.tradingmarkets.com). For a very large list of links to anything and everything related to futures, visit the commodities and futures section of Investor Links (www.investorlinks.com).

Key Terms

basis 450
carrying-charge market 451
cash-futures arbitrage 450
cash market 450
cash price 450
cheapest-to-deliver option 457
cross-hedge 455
forward contract 437
full hedge 445
futures contract 437
futures margin 448
futures price 437
hedger 444
index arbitrage 454
initial margin 449
inverted market 451
long hedge 445
long position 443
maintenance margin 449
margin call 449
marking-to-market 449
program trading 454
reverse trade 449
short hedge 445
short position 443
speculator 443
spot-futures parity 452
underlying asset 444

Chapter Review Problems and Self-Test

1. **Futures Gains and Losses** Suppose you purchase 10 orange juice contracts today at the settle price of \$1 per pound. How much do these 10 contracts cost you? If the settle price is lower tomorrow by 2 cents per pound, how much do you make or lose? The contract size is 15,000 pounds.
2. **Spot-Futures Parity** There is a futures contract on a stock, which is currently selling at \$200 per share. The contract matures in two months; the risk-free rate is 5 percent annually. The current dividend yield on the stock is 0 percent. What does the parity relationship imply the futures price should be?

Answers to Self-Test Problems

1. If you go long (purchase) 10 contracts, you pay nothing today (you will be required to post margin, but a futures contract is an agreement to exchange cash for goods later, not today). If the settle price drops by 2 cents per pound, you lose 15,000 pounds (the contract size) × \$.02 = \$300 per contract. With 10 contracts, you lose \$3,000.
2. The spot-futures parity condition is:

$$F_T = S(1 + r - d)^T$$

where S is the spot price, r is the risk-free rate, d is the dividend yield, F is the futures price, and T is the time to expiration measured in years.

Plugging in the numbers we have, with zero for the dividend yield and 1/6 for the number of years (2 months out of 12), gets us:

$$F_{1/6} = \$200(1 + .05)^{1/6} = \$201.63$$

Test Your Investment Quotient

IQ

For the remaining questions and problems, the circled numbers in the margin refer to the corresponding learning objective in this chapter.

(1) 1. **Futures Exchanges** Which of the following futures exchange in the United States was the first to be founded?

- **a.** Kansas City Board of Trade (KBOT)
- **b.** Chicago Mercantile Exchange (CME)
- **c.** New York Mercantile Exchange (NYMX)
- **d.** Chicago Board of Trade (CBOT)

(1) 2. **Futures Exchanges** The first financial futures contracts, introduced in 1972, were

- **a.** Currency futures at the CME
- **b.** Interest rate futures at the CBOT
- **c.** Stock index futures at the KBOT
- **d.** Wheat futures at the CBOT

(1) 3. **Futures Exchanges** Which of the following futures exchanges trades futures contracts on common stocks?

- **a.** OneBoston
- **b.** OneChicago
- **c.** FutureRama
- **d.** Niffe-Quorum

(1) 4. **Futures versus Forward Contracts** Which of the following statements is true regarding the distinction between futures contracts and forward contracts?

- **a.** Futures contracts are exchange-traded, whereas forward contracts are OTC-traded.
- **b.** All else equal, forward prices are higher than futures prices.
- **c.** Forward contracts are created from baskets of futures contracts.
- **d.** Futures contracts are cash-settled at maturity, whereas forward contracts result in delivery.

CFA® PROBLEMS

(1) **5. Futures versus Forward Contracts** In which of the following ways do futures contracts differ from forward contracts?

I. Futures contracts are standardized.
II. For futures, performance of each party is guaranteed by a clearinghouse.
III. Futures contracts require a daily settling of any gains or losses.

a. I and II only
b. I and III only
c. II and III only
d. I, II, and III

CFA® PROBLEMS

(1) **6. Futures Contracts** The open interest on a futures contract at any given time is the total number of outstanding

a. Contracts
b. Unhedged positions
c. Clearinghouse positions
d. Long and short positions

(2) **7. Futures Margin** Initial margin for a futures contract is usually

a. Regulated by the Federal Reserve.
b. Less than 2 percent of contract value.
c. In the range between 2 percent and 5 percent of contract value.
d. In the range between 5 percent and 15 percent of contract value.

CFA® PROBLEMS

(2) **8. Futures Margin** In futures trading, the minimum level to which an equity position may fall before requiring additional margin is *most accurately* termed the

a. Initial margin
b. Variation margin
c. Cash flow margin
d. Maintenance margin

CFA® PROBLEMS

(2) **9. Futures Margin** A silver futures contract requires the seller to deliver 5,000 troy ounces of silver. An investor sells one July silver futures contract at a price of $8 per ounce, posting a $2,025 initial margin. If the required maintenance margin is $1,500, the price per ounce at which the investor would first receive a maintenance margin call is closest to

a. $5.92
b. $7.89
c. $8.11
d. $10.80

(2) **10. Futures Margin** Which of the following statements is false about futures account margin?

a. Initial margin is higher than maintenance margin.
b. A margin call results when account margin falls below maintenance margin.
c. Marking-to-market of account margin occurs daily.
d. A margin call results when account margin falls below initial margin.

(1) **11. Futures Contracts** Which of the following contract terms changes daily during the life of a futures contract?

a. Futures price
b. Futures contract size
c. Futures maturity date
d. Underlying commodity

(1) **12. Futures Trading Accounts** Which of the following is perhaps the least essential thing to know about a futures trading account?

a. Margin is required.
b. Futures accounts are marked-to-market daily.
c. A futures position can be closed by a reverse trade.
d. A commission is charged for each trade.

CFA® PROBLEMS

(1) **13. Futures Delivery** On the maturity date, stock index futures contracts require delivery of

a. Common stock
b. Common stock plus accrued dividends
c. Treasury bills
d. Cash

www.mhhe.com/jm5e

(1) **14. Futures Delivery** On the maturity date, Treasury note futures contracts require delivery of

a. Treasury notes plus accrued coupons over the life of the futures contract
b. Treasury notes
c. Treasury bills
d. Cash

(3) **15. Spot-Futures Parity** A Treasury bond futures contract has a quoted price of 100. The underlying bond has a coupon rate of 7 percent, and the current market interest rate is 7 percent. Spot-futures parity then implies a cash bond price of

a. 93
b. 100
c. 107
d. 114

(3) **16. Spot-Futures Parity** A stock index futures contract maturing in one year has a currently traded price of $1,000. The cash index has a dividend yield of 2 percent, and the interest rate is 5 percent. Spot-futures parity then implies a cash index level of

a. $933.33
b. $970.87
c. $1,071
d. $1,029

(3) **17. Spot-Futures Parity** A stock index futures contract matures in one year. The cash index currently has a level of $1,000 with a dividend yield of 2 percent. If the interest rate is 5 percent, then spot-futures parity implies a futures price of

a. $943.40
b. $970.87
c. $1,060
d. $1,030

(3) **18. Futures Hedging** You manage a $100 million stock portfolio with a beta of .8. Given a contract size of $100,000 for a stock index futures contract, how many contracts are needed to hedge your portfolio?

a. 8
b. 80
c. 800
d. 8,000

(4) **19. Futures Hedging** You manage a $100 million bond portfolio with a duration of 9 years. You wish to hedge this portfolio against interest rate risk using T-bond futures with a contract size of $100,000 and a duration of 12 years. How many contracts are required?

a. 750
b. 1,000
c. 133
d. 1,333

(4) **20. Futures Hedging** Which of the following is not an input needed to calculate the number of stock index futures contracts required to hedge a stock portfolio?

a. The value of the stock portfolio.
b. The beta of the stock portfolio.
c. The contract value of the index futures contract.
d. The initial margin required for each futures contract.

Concept Questions

(1) **1. Understanding Futures Quotations** Using Figure 14.1, answer the following questions:

a. How many exchanges trade wheat futures contracts?
b. If you have a position in 10 gold futures, what quantity of gold underlies your position?
c. If you are short 20 oat futures contracts and you opt to make delivery, what quantity of oats must you supply?
d. Which maturity of the unleaded gasoline contract has the largest open interest? Which one has the smallest open interest?

(4) 2. **Hedging with Futures** Kellogg's uses large quantities of corn in its breakfast cereal operations. Suppose the near-term weather forecast for the corn-producing states is droughtlike conditions, so corn prices are expected to rise. To hedge its costs, Kellogg's decides to use the Chicago Board of Trade corn futures contracts. Should the company be a short hedger or a long hedger in corn futures?

(4) 3. **Hedging with Futures** Suppose one of Fidelity's mutual funds closely mimics the S&P 500 Index. The fund has done very well during the year, and, in November, the fund manager wants to lock in the gains he has made using stock index futures. Should he take a long or short position in S&P 500 Index futures?

(4) 4. **Hedging with Futures** A mutual fund that predominantly holds long-term Treasury bonds plans on liquidating the portfolio in three months. However, the fund manager is concerned that interest rates may rise from current levels and wants to hedge the price risk of the portfolio. Should she buy or sell Treasury bond futures contracts?

(4) 5. **Hedging with Futures** An American electronics firm imports its completed circuit boards from Japan. The company signed a contract today to pay for the boards in Japanese yen upon delivery in four months; the price per board in yen was fixed in the contract. Should the importer buy or sell Japanese yen futures contracts?

(4) 6. **Hedging with Futures** Jed Clampett just dug another oil well, and, as usual, it's a gusher. Jed estimates that, in two months, he'll have 2 million barrels of crude oil to bring to market. However, Jed would like to lock in the value of this oil at today's prices, since the oil market has been skyrocketing recently. Should Jed buy or sell crude oil futures contracts?

(4) 7. **Hedging with Futures** The town of South Park is planning a bond issue in six months and Kenny, the town treasurer, is worried that interest rates may rise, thereby reducing the value of the bond issue. Should Kenny buy or sell Treasury bond futures contracts to hedge the impending bond issue?

(1) 8. **Futures Markets** Is it true that a futures contract represents a zero-sum game, meaning that the only way for a buyer to win is for a seller to lose, and vice versa?

(1) 9. **Program Trading** Program traders closely monitor relative futures and cash market prices, but program trades are not actually made on a fully mechanical basis. What are some of the complications that might make program trading using, for example, the S&P 500 contract more difficult than the spot-futures parity formula indicates?

(1) 10. **Short Selling** What are the similarities and differences in short selling a futures contract and short selling a stock? How do the cash flows differ?

Questions and Problems

Core Questions

(1) (2) 1. **Understanding Futures Quotations** Using Figure 14.1, answer the following questions:

a. What was the settle price for December 2007 coffee futures on this date? What is the total dollar value of this contract at the close of trading for the day?

b. What was the settle price for September 2007 gasoline futures on this date? If you held 10 contracts, what is the total dollar value of your futures position?

c. Suppose you held an open position of 25 December 2007 Industrial Average futures on this day. What is the change in the total dollar value of your position for this day's trading? If you held a long position, would this represent a profit or a loss to you?

d. Suppose you are short 10 December 2007 soybean oil futures contracts. Would you have made a profit or a loss on this day?

(2) 2. **Futures Profits and Losses** You are long 20 November 2007 soybean futures contracts. Calculate your dollar profit or loss from this trading day using Figure 14.1.

(2) 3. **Futures Profits and Losses** You are short 15 December 2007 corn futures contracts. Calculate your dollar profit or loss from this trading day using Figure 14.1.

(2) 4. **Futures Profits and Losses** You are short 30 September 2007 five-year Treasury note futures contracts. Calculate your profit or loss from this trading day using Figure 14.1.

(1) 5. **Open Interest** Referring to Figure 14.1, what is the total open interest on the December 2007 Japanese yen contract? Does it represent long positions, short positions, or both? Based on the settle price on the contract, what is the dollar value of the open interest?

(3) 6. **Spot-Futures Parity** A non-dividend-paying stock is currently priced at $71.18. The risk-free rate is 5 percent, and a futures contract on the stock matures in four months. What price should the futures be?

(3) 7. **Spot-Futures Parity** A non-dividend-paying stock has a futures contract with a price of $49.09 and a maturity of three months. If the risk-free rate is 4.5 percent, what is the price of the stock?

(3) 8. **Spot-Futures Parity** A non-dividend-paying stock has a current share price of $58.13 and a futures price of $59.92. If the maturity of the futures contract is eight months, what is the risk-free rate?

(3) 9. **Spot-Futures Parity** A stock has a current share price of $94.17 and a dividend yield of 1.5 percent. If the risk-free rate is 5.4 percent, what is the futures price if the maturity is four months?

(3) 10. **Spot-Futures Parity** A stock futures contract is priced at $81.27. The stock has a dividend yield of 1.25 percent, and the risk-free rate is 6.1 percent. If the futures contract matures in six months, what is the current stock price?

Intermediate Questions

(2) 11. **Margin Call** Suppose the initial margin on heating oil futures is $6,750, the maintenance margin is $5,000 per contract, and you establish a long position of 10 contracts today, where each contract represents 42,000 gallons. Tomorrow, the contract settles down $.03 from the previous day's price. Are you subject to a margin call? What is the maximum price decline on the contract that you can sustain without getting a margin call?

(2) 12. **Marking-to-Market** You are long 10 gold futures contracts, established at an initial settle price of $785 per ounce, where each contract represents 100 ounces. Your initial margin to establish the position is $2,025 per contract, and the maintenance margin is $1,700 per contract. Over the subsequent four trading days, gold settles at $779, $776, $781, and $787, respectively. Compute the balance in your margin account at the end of each of the four trading days, and compute your total profit or loss at the end of the trading period. Assume that a margin call requires you to fund your account back to the initial margin requirement.

(2) 13. **Marking-to-Market** You are short 25 gasoline futures contracts, established at an initial settle price of $2.085 per gallon, where each contract represents 42,000 gallons. Your initial margin to establish the position is $7,425 per contract, and the maintenance margin is $6,500 per contract. Over the subsequent four trading days, oil settles at $2.071, $2.099, $2.118, and $2.146, respectively. Compute the balance in your margin account at the end of each of the four trading days, and compute your total profit or loss at the end of the trading period. Assume that a margin call requires you to fund your account back to the initial margin requirement.

(2) 14. **Futures Profits** You went long 20 December 2008 crude oil futures contracts at a price of $72.18. Looking back at Figure 14.1, if you closed your position at the settle price on this day, what was your profit?

(2) 15. **Futures Profits** You shorted 15 December 2007 British pound futures contracts at the high price for the day. Looking back at Figure 14.1, if you closed your position at the settle price on this day, what was your profit?

(3) 16. **Index Arbitrage** Suppose the CAC-40 Index (a widely followed index of French stock prices) is currently at 5,092, the expected dividend yield on the index is 2 percent per year, and the risk-free rate in France is 7 percent annually. If CAC-40 futures contracts that expire in six months are currently trading at 5,241, what program trading strategy would you recommend?

(4) 17. **Cross-Hedging** You have been assigned to implement a three-month hedge for a stock mutual fund portfolio that primarily invests in medium-sized companies. The mutual fund has a beta of 1.15 measured relative to the S&P Midcap 400, and the net asset value of the fund is $280 million. Should you be long or short in the Midcap 400 futures contracts? Assuming the Midcap 400 Index is at 756 and its futures contract size is 500 times the index, determine the appropriate number of contracts to use in designing your cross-hedge strategy.

(3) 18. **Spot-Futures Parity** Suppose the 180-day S&P 500 futures price is 1,349.32, while the cash price is 1,325.19. What is the *implied difference* between the risk-free interest rate and the dividend yield on the S&P 500?

(3) 19. **Spot-Futures Parity** Suppose the 180-day S&P 500 futures price is 1,407.11, while the cash price is 1,370.48. What is the *implied dividend yield* on the S&P 500 if the risk-free interest rate is 7 percent?

WWW

Visit these option exchanges:
www.cboe.com
www.amex.com
www.phlx.com
www.nyse.com
www.pacificex.com

traded. For example, there are organized options exchanges, and there are over-the-counter (OTC) options markets. The largest volume of stock options trading in the United States takes place at the Chicago Board Options Exchange (CBOE). However, stock options are also actively traded at the Philadelphia Stock Exchange (PHLX), the American Stock Exchange (AMEX), the Boston Stock Exchange (BSE), the International Securities Exchange (launched in late 2006), and the New York Stock Exchange Archipelago (NYSE)[1].

OPTION PRICE QUOTES

Closing prices for stock options traded at the major options exchanges are reported each day in the free online version of *The Wall Street Journal,* www.wsj.com. Figure 15.1 reproduces a page from the "Listed Options" report available in the Markets Data Center section of the Web site.

For the Intel options listed in Figure 15.1, the first and second columns state expiration months and strike prices for the various options shown. By convention, standardized stock

[1] The NYSE Archipelago acquired the parent company of the Pacific Stock Exchange (PSE) in 2005.

FIGURE 15.1 Listed Options Quotations

Prices at close October 05, 2007

Intel (INTC) — Underlying stock price*: 25.54

Expiration	Strike	Call Last	Call Volume	Call Open Interest	Put Last	Put Volume	Put Open Interest
Oct	10.00	15.80	15	518	...	...	2000
Apr	12.50	13.45	128	102	...	...	...
Oct	15.00	10.82	39	2171	...	...	3046
Jan	15.00	10.62	59	30897	...	...	47468
Oct	17.50	8.00	10	3456	...	...	14920
Jan	17.50	8.30	11	65590	0.07	11	143609
Oct	20.00	5.72	31	24735	0.01	4	34676
Nov	20.00	5.80	5	33	...	...	100
Jan	20.00	5.90	216	140687	0.17	26	147441
Apr	20.00	6.30	7	1235	0.39	7	2481
Oct	22.50	3.15	391	60332	0.04	224	40056
Nov	22.50	3.30	48	942	0.16	5	720
Jan	22.50	3.70	633	178985	0.47	271	128675
Apr	22.50	4.30	260	3863	0.82	158	3980
Oct	25.00	0.96	11361	118639	0.35	7211	95545
Nov	25.00	1.27	5325	8259	0.70	832	10573
Jan	25.00	1.95	3772	189129	1.18	146	84228
Apr	25.00	2.63	171	10283	1.70	485	7093
Oct	27.50	0.08	11897	90427	2.00	736	11785
Nov	27.50	0.30	1105	18329	2.23	530	12144
Jan	27.50	0.83	1866	143546	2.59	531	13354
Apr	27.50	1.45	162	17976	2.99	213	10070
Oct	30.00	0.02	23	15174	4.26	4	96
Nov	30.00	0.06	84	669	4.35	264	1327
Jan	30.00	0.30	600	181333	4.55	2	7003
Apr	30.00	0.72	1060	17814	...	...	2369
Jan	32.50	0.13	13	29771	...	...	324
Apr	32.50	...	...	17411	7.10	20	719
Jan	35.00	0.04	144	23534	...	...	...
Apr	35.00	...	...	6944	9.45	5	80
Oct	37.50	...	...	84	11.70	15	...

**Underlying stock price* represents listed exchange price only. It may not match the composite closing price.

Source: www.wsj.com. Reprinted by permission of *The Wall Street Journal*, October 5, 2007.

WORK THE WEB

Here is a stock quote and an option chain for Starbucks Corp. (SBUX) from Yahoo! Finance (finance.yahoo.com).

STARBUCKS CP (NasdaqGS:SBUX) Edit

Last Trade:	**26.45**	Day's Range:	26.43 - 26.75
Trade Time:	12:05PM ET	52wk Range:	25.22 - 40.01
Change:	↓ 0.39 (1.45%)	Volume:	3,054,091
Prev Close:	26.84	Avg Vol (3m):	12,407,200
Open:	26.68	Market Cap:	19.74B
Bid:	26.45 x 15400	P/E (ttm):	32.53
Ask:	26.46 x 12600	EPS (ttm):	0.81
1y Target Est:	34.82	Div & Yield:	N/A (N/A)

New! Try our new Charts in Beta

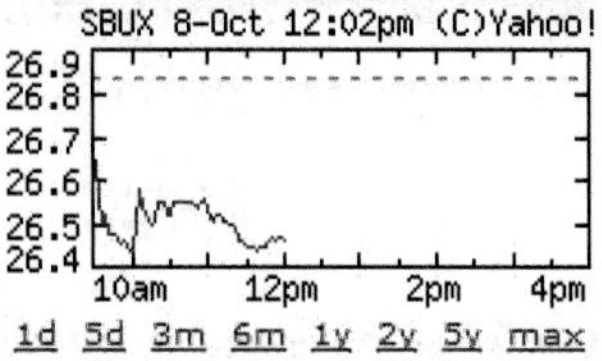

1d 5d 3m 6m 1y 2y 5y max

Market Updates Hourly from Fox Business Now. Watch.

NEW Add Quotes to Your Web Site   Add SBUX to Portfolio   Set Alert   Download Data

Quotes delayed, except where indicated otherwise. For consolidated real-time quotes (including real-time pre/post market data), sign up for a free trial of Real-time Quotes.

View By Expiration: **Oct 07** | Nov 07 | Jan 08 | Apr 08 | Jan 09 | Jan 10

CALL OPTIONS Expire at close Fri, Oct 19, 2007

Strike	Symbol	Last	Chg	Bid	Ask	Vol	Open Int
15.00	SQXJC.X	**12.30**	**0.00**	11.40	11.60	50	73
17.50	SQXJW.X	**9.20**	**0.00**	8.90	9.10	50	87
22.50	SQXJX.X	**4.10**	↓ 0.30	3.90	4.10	1	719
25.00	SQXJE.X	**1.50**	↓ 0.45	1.55	1.60	78	8,642
27.50	SQXJY.X	**0.15**	↓ 0.04	0.10	0.15	44	32,043
30.00	SQXJF.X	**0.05**	**0.00**	N/A	0.05	2	22,625
32.50	SQXJZ.X	**0.05**	**0.00**	N/A	0.05	9	12,699
35.00	SQXJG.X	**0.02**	**0.00**	N/A	0.05	3	7,180
37.50	SQXJU.X	**0.01**	**0.00**	N/A	0.05	4	2,133
40.00	SQXJH.X	**0.05**	**0.00**	N/A	0.05	100	734
42.50	SQXJV.X	**0.05**	**0.00**	N/A	0.05	0	273

PUT OPTIONS Expire at close Fri, Oct 19, 2007

Strike	Symbol	Last	Chg	Bid	Ask	Vol	Open Int
17.50	SQXVW.X	**0.05**	**0.00**	N/A	0.05	0	30
22.50	SQXVX.X	**0.03**	**0.00**	N/A	0.05	5	3,790
25.00	SQXVE.X	**0.10**	**0.00**	0.05	0.10	42	23,717
27.50	SQXVY.X	**1.10**	↑ 0.30	1.10	1.15	46	31,422
30.00	SQXVF.X	**3.50**	↑ 0.30	3.50	3.60	10	6,854
32.50	SQXVZ.X	**5.80**	**0.00**	6.00	6.10	10	3,200
35.00	SQXVG.X	**8.35**	**0.00**	8.40	8.60	31	100

Highlighted options are in-the-money.

options expire on the Saturday following the third Friday of their expiration month. Because of this convention, the exact date on which an option expires can be known exactly by referring to a calendar to identify the third Friday of its expiration month.

These first three contract terms—the identity of the underlying stock, the strike price, and the expiration month—will not change during the life of the option. However, because the price of a stock option depends in part on the price of the underlying stock, the price of an option changes as the stock price changes.

Option prices are reported in columns 3 and 6 of Figure 15.1. Column 3 gives call option prices, and column 6 gives put option prices. Option prices are stated on a per-share basis, but the actual price of an option contract is 100 times the per-share price. This is because each option contract represents an option on 100 shares of stock. Fractional contracts for, say, 50 shares, are not normally available.

In Figure 15.1, trading volume for each contract is reported in columns 4 and 7. Column 4 states the number of call option contracts traded for each available strike-maturity combination, while column 7 states the number of put option contracts traded for each strike-maturity combination. Columns 5 and 8 show open interest for each call and put option contract.

Useful online sources for option prices include the Chicago Board Options Exchange (quote.cboe.com) and Yahoo! Finance (finance.yahoo.com). The nearby *Work the Web* box

option chain
A list of available option contracts and their prices for a particular security arrayed by strike price and maturity.

contains an **option chain** for Starbucks Corp. (SBUX) stock options. The small box reports the time and price for the last trade in Starbucks stock, along with the change in price from the previous day and the trading volume for the current day. The large box contains the Starbucks option chain, with separate sections for call options and put options and with a strike price column dividing the two sections.

The second column of each section (labeled "Symbol") lists ticker symbols for specific option contracts. The tickers for Starbucks options have five letters identifying the contract. The sixth letter (X) is just used by Yahoo! to indicate an option ticker. The first three letters are SQX, which is a modified ticker symbol for Starbucks stock. For the next two letters, the first letter specifies the expiration month and whether the option is a call or a put, while the second letter identifies the strike price. Option tickers are discussed in more detail below.

The third column ("Last") reports the option price for the last trade. The fourth column ("Chg") states the change in price from the previous day's last trade, where a zero indicates either no change in price or no trade that day. The next two columns ("Bid" and "Ask") contain representative bid and ask price quotes from dealers. Finally, the seventh column ("Vol") reports trading volume as the number of contracts traded that day, and the eighth column ("Open Int") states open interest as the total number of contracts outstanding.

CHECK THIS

15.1a What is a call option? What is a put option?

15.1b What are the six basic contract terms that an options contract must specify?

15.1c What is an option chain?

STOCK OPTION TICKER SYMBOLS

To trade stock options, it is useful to know something about option ticker symbols. The ticker symbol for a stock option identifies not only the underlying stock, but also the option type, the expiration date, and the strike price. A stock option ticker symbol has two parts. The first part contains a three-letter symbol for the underlying stock. The second part contains a two-letter symbol specifying the option type—put or call, the expiration month, and the strike price. For example, consider Coca-Cola call options with a $50 strike price with a March expiration. The ticker symbol is KO-CJ. The first part is KO, the ticker symbol for Coca-Cola stock. The second part is CJ, where C indicates a March call option and J indicates a $50 strike price. As another example, consider Disney put options with a $35 strike price and a September expiration. The ticker symbol is DIS-UG. The first part is DIS, the ticker symbol for Disney stock. The second part is UG, where U indicates a September put option and G indicates a $35 strike price.

Table 15.1 specifies the letters used to indicate option type, expiration month, and strike price. Notice that the 12 letters A–L denote the 12 expiration months January through December for call options. Similarly, the 12 letters M–X represent the 12 expiration months for put options. The 20 letters A–T represent strike prices from 5 through 100 in five-dollar increments. The six letters U–Z are reserved for the six strikes, 7.5, 12.5, 17.5, 22.5, 27.5, and 32.5, respectively. For strikes greater than 100, the letters repeat themselves. For example, the letter A represents strikes of 5, 105, 205, and so on.

Options exchanges use special option ticker symbols for NASDAQ stocks, which have four or more letters in their stock ticker symbols. For example, the ticker symbol for Starbucks stock is SBUX, which becomes SQX for Starbucks stock options. So a Starbucks October call option with a $25 strike price has the ticker symbol SQX-JE. Similarly, the ticker symbol for Sun Microsystems is SUNW, which becomes SUQ for Sun stock options and a November put option with a $5 strike price has the ticker symbol SUQ-WA. Many brokers insulate their customers from this inconvenience and accept full NASDAQ

WWW

For information on option ticker symbols, see
www.cboe.com
www.schaeffersresearch.com
www.optionsxpress.com

TABLE 15.1 Stock Option Ticker Symbol and Strike Price Codes

Expiration Month	Calls	Puts
January	A	M
February	B	N
March	C	O
April	D	P
May	E	Q
June	F	R
July	G	S
August	H	T
September	I	U
October	J	V
November	K	W
December	L	X

Strike		Strike	
5	A	70	N
10	B	75	O
15	C	80	P
20	D	85	Q
25	E	90	R
30	F	95	S
35	G	100	T
40	H	7.5	U
45	I	12.5	V
50	J	17.5	W
55	K	22.5	X
60	L	27.5	Y
65	M	32.5	Z

stock tickers for option orders. So, for example, an order to buy SQX-JE options would be accepted as SBUX-JE by most brokers. Also, options for many securities have more complicated option ticker symbols for which it is necessary to refer to an official list of ticker symbols maintained by the options exchanges. If you are interested in seeing such a complete list, go to the CBOE Web site (www.cboe.com).

CHECK THIS

15.1d What are the option types, expiration months, and strike prices for the following Alcoa (AA) options: AA-FF, AA-RF, AA-HK, and AA-TL?

15.1e What are the two-letter extensions for the following options: January 80 calls, July 25 puts, April 12.5 calls, and October 27.5 puts?

15.2 The Options Clearing Corporation

WWW

Visit the OCC at www.optionsclearing.com

Suppose that you order a new car through a local dealer and pay a $2,000 deposit. Further suppose that, two weeks later, you receive a letter informing you that your dealer had entered bankruptcy. No doubt, you would be quite upset at the prospect of losing your $2,000 deposit.

Now consider a similar situation where you pay $2,000 for several call options through a broker. On the day before expiration, you tell your broker to exercise the options, because they would produce, say, a $5,000 payoff. Then, a few days later, your broker tells you that the call writer entered bankruptcy proceedings and that your $2,000 call premium and $5,000 payoff were lost. No doubt, this default would upset you. However, this situation cannot occur if your option trade was made on a registered options exchange.

Options Clearing Corporation (OCC) Private agency that guarantees that the terms of an option contract will be fulfilled if the option is exercised; issues and clears all option contracts trading on U.S. exchanges.

Option traders who transact on option exchanges have an important ally. The **Options Clearing Corporation (OCC)**, founded in 1973, is the clearing agency for these options exchanges: the American Stock Exchange, the Chicago Board Options Exchange, the International Securities Exchange, NYSE Arca, Philadelphia Stock Exchange, and the Boston Stock Exchange.

Once an option trade is made on an options exchange, the Options Clearing Corporation steps in and becomes a party to both sides of the trade. In other words, the option buyer effectively purchases the option from the OCC, and the seller effectively sells the option to the OCC. In this way, each investor is free from the worry that the other party will default. Each option investor simply looks to the OCC.

Most options investors are unaware of the OCC because only member firms of an options exchange deal directly with it. However, in fact, all option contracts traded on U.S. options exchanges are originally issued, guaranteed, and cleared by the OCC. Brokerage firms merely act as intermediaries between investors and the OCC.

The OCC is an agency consisting of brokerage firms that are called "clearing members." The OCC's clearing members represent more than 100 of the largest U.S. broker-dealers, futures commission merchants, and non-U.S. securities firms. To guarantee the performance of all trades, the OCC has capital contributed by clearing members. If existing capital were to prove insufficient, the OCC could draw additional funds from its members. This structure ensures the integrity of the options markets.

The OCC began life as the clearinghouse for listed equity options. Today, however, the OCC clears many products. The OCC is regulated by both the Securities and Exchange Commission (SEC) and the Commodities Futures Trading Commission (CFTC). Under the watchful eye of the SEC, the OCC clears trades for put and call options on common stocks, stock indexes, foreign currencies, and single-stock futures. With CFTC oversight, the OCC clears and settles trades in futures contracts and options on futures contracts.

WWW

Visit the OIC at www.optionseducation.org

The OCC also sponsors the Options Industry Council (OIC). Founded in 1992, the OIC was created to educate investors about the benefits and risks of exchange-traded equity options. Today, each year the OIC conducts hundreds of seminars and webcasts, and it distributes thousands of interactive CDs and brochures. In addition, the OIC has an extensive Web site and there is even a "Help Desk" tab that focuses on options education.

CHECK THIS

15.2a Who makes up the OCC? Who regulates the OCC?

15.2b How does the OCC protect option traders?

15.2c What is the OIC and what does it do?

15.3 Why Options?

As a stock market investor, a basic question you might ask is: "Why buy stock options instead of shares of stock directly?" Good question! To answer it properly, we need to compare the possible outcomes from two investment strategies. The first investment strategy entails simply buying stock. The second strategy involves buying a call option that allows the holder to buy stock any time before option expiration.

For example, suppose you buy 100 shares of IBM stock at a price of \$90 per share, representing an investment of \$9,000. Afterwards, three things could happen: the stock price could go up, go down, or remain the same. If the stock price goes up, you make money; if it goes down, you lose money. Of course, if the stock price remains the same, you break even.

WWW

To learn more about options, see www.cboe.com/LearnCenter/

Now, consider the alternative strategy of buying a call option with a strike price of \$90 expiring in three months at a per-share price of \$5. This corresponds to a contract price of \$500 since the standard option contract size is 100 shares. The first thing to notice about this strategy is that you have invested only \$500, and therefore the most that you can lose is only \$500.

To compare the two investment strategies just described, let's examine three possible cases for IBM's stock price at the close of trading on the third Friday of the option's expiration month. In case 1, the stock price goes up to \$100. In case 2, the stock price goes down to \$80. In case 3, the stock price remains the same at \$90.

> **Case 1:** If the stock price goes up to \$100, and you originally bought 100 shares at \$90 per share, then your profit is 100 × (\$100 − \$90) = \$1,000. As a percentage of your original investment amount of \$9,000, this represents a return on investment of \$1,000/\$9,000 = 11.11%.

Alternatively, if you originally bought the call option, you can exercise the option and buy 100 shares at the strike price of \$90 and sell the stock at the \$100 market price. After accounting for the original cost of the option contract, your profit is 100 × (\$100 − \$90) − \$500 = \$500. As a percentage of your original investment of \$500, this represents a return on investment of \$500/\$500 = 100%.

Case 2: If the stock price goes down to \$80, and you originally bought 100 shares at \$90 per share, then your loss is 100 × (\$80 − \$90) = −\$1,000. As a percentage of your original investment, this represents a return of −\$1,000/\$9,000 = −11.11%.

If instead you originally bought the call option, exercising the option would not pay, and it would expire worthless. You would then realize a total loss of your \$500 investment, and your return is −100 percent.

Case 3: If the stock price remains the same at \$90, and you bought 100 shares, you break even, and your return is zero percent.

However, if you bought the call option, exercising the option would not pay, and it would expire worthless. Once again, you would lose your entire \$500 investment.

As these three cases illustrate, the outcomes of the two investment strategies differ significantly, depending on subsequent stock price changes. Whether one strategy is preferred over another is a matter for each individual investor to decide. What is important is the fact that options offer an alternative means of formulating investment strategies.

EXAMPLE 15.1

Stock Returns

Suppose you bought 100 shares of stock at \$50 per share. If the stock price goes up to \$60 per share, what is the percentage return on your investment? If, instead, the stock price falls to \$40 per share, what is the percentage return on your investment?

If the stock goes to \$60 per share, you make \$10/\$50 = 20%. If it falls to \$40, you lose \$10/\$50 = 20%.

EXAMPLE 15.2

Call Option Returns

In Example 15.1, suppose that you bought one call option contract for \$200. The strike price is \$50. If the stock price is \$60 just before the option expires, should you exercise the option? If you exercise the option, what is the percentage return on your investment? If you don't exercise the option, what is the percentage return on your investment?

If the stock price is \$60, you should definitely exercise. If you do, you will make \$10 per share, or \$1,000, from exercising. Once we deduct the \$200 original cost of the option, your net profit is \$800. Your percentage return is \$800/\$200 = 400%. If you don't exercise, you lose your entire \$200 investment, so your loss is 100 percent.

EXAMPLE 15.3

More Call Option Returns

In Example 15.2, if the stock price is \$40 just before the option expires, should you exercise the option? If you exercise the option, what is the percentage return on your investment? If you don't exercise the option, what is the percentage return on your investment?

If the stock price is \$40, you shouldn't exercise since, by exercising, you will be paying \$50 per share. If you did exercise, you would lose \$10 per share, or \$1,000, plus the \$200 cost of the option, or \$1,200 total. This would amount to a \$1,200/\$200 = 600% loss! If you don't exercise, you lose the \$200 you invested, for a loss of 100 percent.

Of course, we can also calculate percentage gains and losses from a put option purchase. Here we make money if the stock price declines. So, suppose you buy a put option with a strike price of \$20 for \$.50. If you exercise your put when the stock price is \$18, what is your percentage gain?

You make \$2 per share since you are selling at \$20 when the stock is worth \$18. Your put contract cost \$50, so your net profit is \$200 − \$50 = \$150. As a percentage of your original \$50 investment, you made \$150/\$50 = 300%.

CHECK THIS

15.3a If you buy 100 shares of stock at \$10 and sell out at \$12, what is your percentage return?

15.3b If you buy one call contract with a strike of \$10 for \$100 and exercise it when the stock is selling for \$12, what is your percentage return?

15.4 Stock Index Options

Following the tremendous success of stock options trading on the Chicago Board Options Exchange, the exchange looked for other new financial products to offer to investors and portfolio managers. In 1982, the CBOE created stock index options, which, at the time, represented a new type of option contract.

INDEX OPTIONS: FEATURES AND SETTLEMENT

stock index option
An option on a stock market index. The most popular stock index options are options on the S&P 100 Index, S&P 500 Index, and Dow Jones Industrials Index.

A **stock index option** is an option on a stock market index. The first stock index options were contracts on the Standard & Poor's Index of 100 large companies representative of American industry. This index is often simply called the "S&P 100." S&P 100 Index options trade under the ticker symbol OEX, and S&P 100 Index options are referred to as "OEX options." The second stock index options introduced by the CBOE were contracts on the Standard & Poor's index of 500 companies, the "S&P 500." S&P 500 Index options trade under the ticker symbol SPX and are referred to as "SPX options." In 1997, the CBOE introduced options on the Dow Jones Industrial Average (DJIA), which trade under the ticker symbol DJX.

Besides the different underlying indexes, the major difference between SPX, DJX, and OEX contracts is that OEX options are American style, whereas SPX and DJX options are European style. The CBOE also lists the "XEO option," which is based on the S&P 100 Index. The XEO option has European-style exercise. As we noted earlier, American-style options can be exercised any time before expiration, whereas European-style options can be exercised only on the last day before option expiration.

WWW
Learn more about trading index options at www.cboe.com

cash-settled option
An option contract settled by a cash payment from the option writer to the option holder when the option is exercised.

Before stock index options could be introduced, one very important detail that had to be worked out was what to do when an index option is exercised. Exchange officials saw that settlement by delivery was obviously impractical because of the number of stocks comprising an index. Instead, a cash settlement procedure was adopted for index options. For this reason, all stock index options are **cash-settled options**. With cash settlement, when a stock index option is exercised, the option writer pays a cash amount to the option buyer based on the difference between the exercise date index level and the option's strike price. For example, suppose you had purchased an SPX call option with a strike price of \$1,520, and the S&P 500 Index was \$1,540 on the day of exercise. The difference between the index level and the strike price is \$1,540 − \$1,520 = \$20. Because the contract size for SPX options is 100 times the S&P 500 Index, the option writer must pay 100 × \$20 = \$2,000 to the option holder exercising the option.

In the example above, the contract size for SPX options was stated to be 100 times the S&P 500 Index. In fact, the contract size for almost all standardized stock index options is 100 times the underlying index. Thus, the actual price of a stock index option is 100 times the price stated on an index level basis. There are only a few exceptions to this rule. For example, the CBOE offers so-called Reduced Value index options with a contract size that is one-tenth the size of standard index options. Reduced Value index options are appealing to some individual investors, but they represent only a minuscule share of all index options trading.

INDEX OPTION PRICE QUOTES

Options now are available for a wide variety of stock market indexes. Each business day, the online version of *The Wall Street Journal* provides a summary of the previous day's activity in stock index options. Figure 15.2, "Index Options Trading," contains some information that can be found in the Markets Data Center at www.wsj.com.

Part One of Figure 15.2, "Ranges for Underlying Indexes," contains information on the major stock market indexes for which index options are now available. In the first column of this box, the name of each index and (in parentheses) its ticker symbol are listed. Columns 2, 3, 4, and 5 report the corresponding high, low, close, and net change values, respectively, for each stock market index from the previous day's trading. For each stock index, the columns

FIGURE 15.2 Index Options Trading, Part One

Ranges for Underlying Indexes
Prices at close Tuesday, November 20, 2007

	High	Low	Close	Net Change	From Dec. 31	%Change
AM-Mexico (MXY)	255.68	248.52	250.17	0.67	12.19	5.12
Bank (BKX)	93.01	88.30	90.82	-0.38	-26.70	-22.72
Biotechnology (BTK)	807.64	788.21	801.90	1.27	47.65	6.32
CB Tech (TXX)	731.28	706.75	720.02	0.39	56.47	8.51
DJ Industrials (DJX)	131.07	128.40	130.10	0.52	5.47	4.39
DJ Transportation (DTX)	451.59	435.92	442.55	-3.25	-13.47	-2.95
DJ Utilities (DUX)	529.75	520.16	527.94	7.49	71.17	15.58
Eurotop 100 (EUR)	311.96	308.02	311.41	3.31	2.13	0.69
Gold/Silver (XAU)	171.95	164.34	171.95	7.67	29.70	20.88
HK Fltg (HKO)	531.15	531.15	531.15	5.37	146.01	37.91
Institutional -A.M. (XII)	697.45	682.45	691.65	4.02	10.01	1.47
IW Internet (IIX)	231.23	221.95	226.49	-0.45	26.14	13.05
Leaps S&P 100 (OAX)	135.88	132.99	134.80	0.97	2.72	2.06
Leaps S&P 500 (LSY)	145.26	141.93	143.97	0.64	2.14	1.51
Major Market (XMI)	1360.00	1332.67	1350.84	11.59	104.84	8.41
MS Consumer (CMR)	744.09	731.92	739.71	5.68	44.21	6.36
MS Cyclical (CYC)	960.05	935.28	947.93	2.19	54.49	6.10
MS High Tech (MSH)	618.50	594.58	605.35	-3.73	37.15	6.54
MS Internet (MOX)	21.74	21.10	21.46	0.08	5.09	31.09
MS Multi National (NFT)	801.23	787.01	796.26	6.28	23.57	3.05
Nasdaq 100 (NDX)	2064.08	1990.12	2029.94	8.80	273.04	15.54
Oil Services(OSX)	284.89	273.62	282.88	9.25	82.98	41.51
Pharmaceutical (DRG)	342.47	337.53	340.33	0.75	-4.73	-1.37
PSE Technology (PSE)	948.59	922.91	935.46	-1.43	59.95	6.85
Russell 2000 (RUT)	757.28	736.52	749.33	-1.00	-38.33	-4.87
S&P Midcap (MID)	844.39	823.78	834.66	-1.12	30.29	3.77
S&P100 (OEX)	679.38	664.97	674.01	4.84	13.60	2.06
S&P500-A.M. (SPX)	1452.64	1419.28	1439.70	6.43	21.40	1.51
Semiconductor (SOX)	421.79	405.44	413.02	-4.53	-54.90	-11.73
Street.Com (DOT)	283.58	275.15	280.00	1.12	32.71	13.23
Utility (UTY)	568.87	558.26	567.19	8.56	73.82	14.96
Value Line (VLE)	2226.39	2168.74	2201.21	-3.46	-15.53	-0.70
Volatility (VIX)	27.35	23.62	24.88	-1.13	13.32	115.22

Source: www.wsj.com. Reprinted by permission of *The Wall Street Journal*, November 20, 2007, © 2007 Dow Jones & Company, Inc. All Rights Reserved Worldwide.

FIGURE 15.2 Index Options Trading, Part Two

Prices at close November 20, 2007

S&P500-A.M. (SPX)						Chicago Exchange
Underlying Index	High	Low	Close	Net Change	From Dec.31	%Change
S&P500-A.M.	1452.64	1419.28	1439.70	6.43	21.40	1.51
		Strike	Volume	Last	Net Change	Open Interest
Jan		1350.00 put	15,125	32.00	+0.80	34,799
Jan		1375.00 put	9,597	31.40	-5.60	36,743
Jan		1400.00 put	3,067	37.80	-4.40	46,018
Jan		1400.00 call	184	85.60	+2.60	69
Jan		1425.00 put	4,367	45.50	-3.00	22,304
Jan		1425.00 call	3	71.00	+5.70	1,315
Jan		1430.00 call	22	65.40	...	...
Jan		1435.00 call	2	64.90	+4.90	2
Jan		1450.00 call	4,262	52.20	+0.20	11,675
Jan		1450.00 put	12,379	55.60	-5.40	24,154
Jan		1455.00 put	2	65.50	+2.50	1,871
Jan		1475.00 call	5,627	35.50	-3.00	19,382
Jan		1475.00 put	504	66.50	-5.00	16,855
Jan		1500.00 call	4,581	26.40	-1.80	34,324
Jan		1500.00 put	105	79.40	-5.60	27,488
Jan		1510.00 call	207	24.00	+2.00	2,200
Jan		1520.00 put	4	91.50	-8.50	18
Jan		1525.00 call	5,257	18.60	+1.60	30,724
Jan		1525.00 put	8	89.50	-2.50	8,673
Jan		1530.00 call	150	16.80	...	511
Jan		1540.00 call	2	11.00	-3.00	2,491
Jan		1550.00 call	4,418	10.70	+0.30	25,522
Call Vol.		283,030	Open Int.			3,561,760
Put Vol.		510,069	Open Int.			6,217,501

Volume figures are unofficial. Open interest reflects previous trading day.

Source: www.wsj.com. Reprinted by permission of *The Wall Street Journal*, November 20, 2007, © 2007 Dow Jones & Company, Inc. All Rights Reserved Worldwide.

labeled "From Dec. 31" and "% Change" report the index level value change and percentage value change, respectively, since the beginning of the current year.

The majority of trading in stock index options is conducted on the Chicago Board Options Exchange, which lists OEX and SPX options (among others). Part Two of Figure 15.2 is a partial listing of the options trading data for options on the S&P 500 Index (SPX). You might notice that the name of this option is "S&P 500-A.M." The name indicates that this option expires on the morning of the third Friday of the month (other options expire at the close of trading on the third Friday of the month).

Part Two of Figure 15.2 reports some options that expire in January 2008. The first column of data shows that these options all expire in January. The second column reports the strike and whether the option is a call or a put. The third column reports trading volume measured as the number of contracts traded during the previous day's trading. The fourth column, labeled "Last," reports the contract price for the last trade of the previous day, and the fifth column, labeled "Net Change," reports the price change from the last price on the previous day. Finally, the sixth column, labeled "Open Interest," lists the total number of contracts outstanding.

At the bottom of Part Two of Figure 15.2, you can see total volume and open interest for calls and puts. As noted, the unofficial trading volume is measured by the estimated number of contracts traded on a given day. Open interest is measured by the total number of contracts outstanding on the previous trading day.

EXAMPLE 15.4

Index Options

Suppose you bought 10 July 1290 SPX call contracts at a quoted price of $5. How much did you pay in total? At option expiration, suppose the S&P 500 is at 1300. What would you receive? What is your profit, if any?

The price per SPX contract is 100 times the quoted price. Because you bought 10 contracts, you paid a total of $5 × 100 × 10 = $5,000. If, at expiration, the S&P 500 is at 1300, you would receive $100 × (1300 − 1290) = $1,000 per contract, or $10,000 in all. This $10,000 would be paid to you in cash, because index options feature cash settlement. Your profit is $5,000.

CHECK THIS

15.4a In addition to the underlying asset, what is the major difference between an ordinary stock option and a stock index option?

15.4b In addition to the underlying index, what is the major difference between the OEX and SPX option contracts?

15.5 Option "Moneyness"

in-the-money option An option that would yield a positive payoff if exercised.

To understand option payoffs and profits, we need to know two important terms related to option value: **in-the-money options** and **out-of-the-money options**. Essentially, an in-the-money option is one that would yield a positive payoff if exercised immediately and an out-of-the-money option is one that would not yield a positive payoff if exercised.

EXAMPLE 15.5

In-the-Money Call Option

IBM stock is currently $55 per share. Let's look at a call option to buy IBM stock at $50 ($50 is the strike price). The stock price is greater than the strike price. If the call option were exercised immediately, there would be a positive payoff of $5 = $55 − $50. Because the option has a positive payoff if it is exercised immediately, this option is known as an in-the-money option.

EXAMPLE 15.6

Out-of-the-Money Call Option

IBM stock is currently $55 per share. Let's look at a call option to buy IBM stock at $60 ($60 is the strike price). Because the stock price is less than the strike price, immediate exercise would not benefit the option holder. Because option exercise would not yield a positive payoff, this option is called an out-of-the-money option.

EXAMPLE 15.7

In-the-Money Put Option

GE stock is selling at $33. Let's look at a put option to sell GE at a price of $40 per share ($40 is the strike price). Notice that the stock price is less than the strike price. If the put option were exercised immediately, it would yield a payoff of $7 = $40 − $33. Because the option has a positive payoff if exercised immediately, it is known as an in-the-money option.

EXAMPLE 15.8 Out-of-the-Money Put Option

GE stock is selling at $33. Let's look at a put option to sell GE at a price of $30 per share ($30 is the strike price). Because the stock price is greater than the strike price, immediate exercise would not benefit the option holder. Because option exercise would not yield a positive payoff, this option is called an out-of-the-money option.

out-of-the-money option
An option that would not yield a positive payoff if exercised.

If this all seems a little complicated, simply remember that if the stock price, S, is greater than the strike price, K, a call option is said to be "in the money" and a put option is said to be "out of the money." Likewise, if the current stock price is less than the strike price, a call option is "out of the money" and a put option is "in the money." The chart immediately below summarizes the relationship between the stock price and the strike price for in-the-money and out-of-the-money options.

	In the Money	Out of the Money
Call option	$S > K$	$S < K$
Put option	$S < K$	$S > K$

CHECK THIS

15.5a All else equal, would an in-the-money option or an out-of-the-money option have a higher price? Why?

15.5b Does an out-of-the-money option ever have value? Why?

15.6 Option Payoffs and Profits

Options are appealing because they offer investors a wide variety of investment strategies. In fact, there is essentially no limit to the number of different investment strategies available using options. However, fortunately for us, only a small number of basic strategies are available, and more complicated strategies are built from these. We discuss the payoffs from these basic strategies here and in the next section.

OPTION WRITING

option writing
Taking the seller's side of an option contract.

Thus far, we have discussed options from the standpoint of the buyer only. However, options are contracts, and every contract must link at least two parties. The two parties to an option contract are the buyer and the seller. The seller of an option is called the "writer," and the act of selling an option is referred to as **option writing**.

By buying an option you buy the right, but not the obligation, to exercise the option before the option's expiration date. By selling or writing an option, you take the seller's side of the option contract. As a result, option writing involves receiving the option price and, in exchange, assuming the obligation to satisfy the buyer's exercise rights if the option is exercised.

call writer
One who has the obligation to sell stock at the option's strike price if the option is exercised.

put writer
One who has the obligation to buy stock at the option's strike price if the option is exercised.

For example, a **call writer** is obligated to sell stock at the option's strike price if the buyer decides to exercise the call option. Similarly, a **put writer** is obligated to buy stock at the option's strike price if the buyer decides to exercise the put option.

OPTION PAYOFFS

It is useful to think about option investment strategies in terms of their initial cash flows and terminal cash flows. The initial cash flow of an option is the price of the option, also called the option *premium*. To the option buyer, the option price (or premium) is a cash outflow. To the option writer, the option price (or premium) is a cash inflow. The terminal cash flow of an option is the option's payoff that could be realized from the exercise privilege. To the option buyer, a payoff entails a cash inflow. To the writer, a payoff entails a cash outflow.

WWW

To learn more on options, see
www.numa.com
www.optionscentral.com
www.optionsxpress.com

For example, suppose the current price of IBM stock is \$80 per share. You buy a call option on IBM with a strike price of \$80. The premium is \$4 per share. Thus, the initial cash flow is −\$400 for you and +\$400 for the option writer. What are the terminal cash flows for you and the option writer if IBM has a price of \$90 when the option expires? What are the terminal cash flows if IBM has a price of \$70 when the option expires?

If IBM is at \$90, then you experience a cash inflow of \$10 per share, whereas the writer experiences an outflow of \$10 per share. If IBM is at \$70, you both have a zero cash flow when the option expires because it is worthless. Notice that in both cases the buyer and the seller have the same cash flows, just with opposite signs. This shows that options are a "zero-sum game," meaning that any gains to the buyer must come at the expense of the seller and vice versa.

OPTION PAYOFF DIAGRAMS

When investors buy options, the price that they are willing to pay depends on their assessment of the likely payoffs (cash inflows) from the exercise privilege. Likewise, when investors write options, an acceptable selling price depends on their assessment of the likely payoffs (cash outflows) resulting from the buyers' exercise privilege. Given this, a general understanding of option payoffs is critical for understanding how option prices are determined.

A payoff diagram is a very useful graphical device for understanding option payoffs. The payoffs from buying a call option and the payoffs from selling (or writing) a call option are seen in the payoff diagram in Figure 15.3. The vertical axis of Figure 15.3 measures option payoffs, and the horizontal axis measures the possible stock prices on the option expiration date. These examples assume that the call option has a strike price of \$50 and that the option will be exercised only on its expiration date.

In Figure 15.3, notice that the call option payoffs are zero for all stock prices below the \$50 strike price. This is because the call option holder will not exercise the option to buy stock at the \$50 strike price when the stock is available in the stock market at a lower price. In this case, the option expires worthless.

FIGURE 15.3 Call Option Payoffs

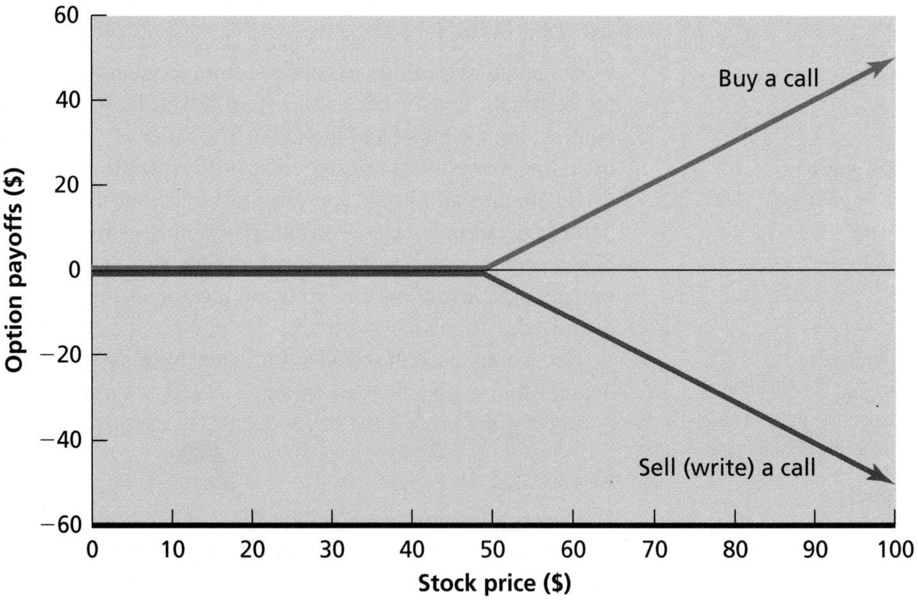

FIGURE 15.4 Put Option Payoffs

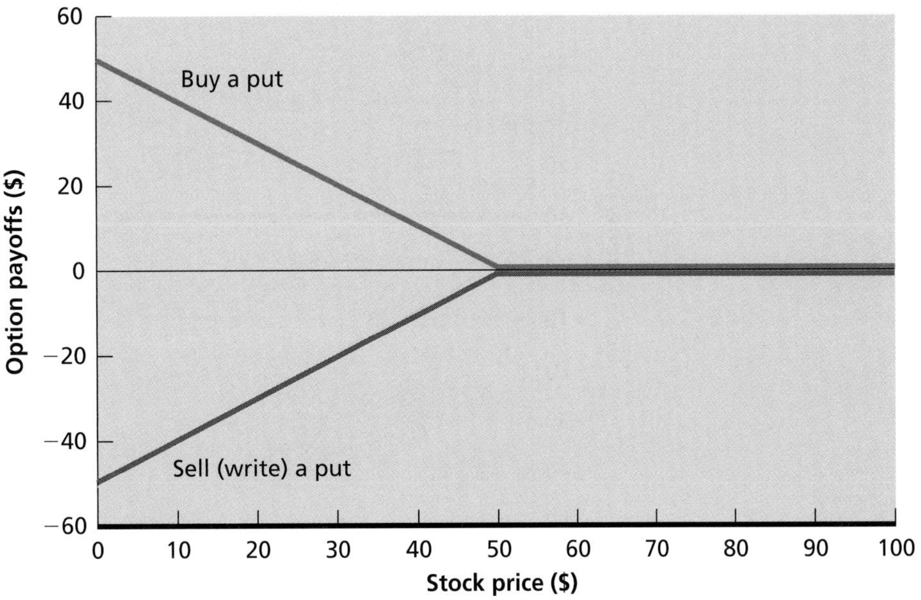

In contrast, if the stock price is higher than the $50 strike price, the call option payoff is equal to the difference between the market price of the stock and the strike price of the option. For example, if the stock price is $60, the call option payoff is equal to $10, which is the difference between the $60 stock price and the $50 strike price. This payoff is a cash inflow to the buyer, because the option buyer can buy the stock at the $50 strike price and sell the stock at the $60 market price. However, this payoff is a cash outflow to the writer, because the option writer must sell the stock at the $50 strike price when the stock's market price is $60.

Putting it all together, the distinctive "hockey-stick" shape of the call option payoffs shows that the payoff is zero if the stock price is below the strike price. Above the strike price, however, the buyer of the call option gains $1 for every $1 increase in the stock price. Of course, as shown, the call option writer loses $1 for every $1 increase in the stock price above the strike price.

Figure 15.4 is an example of a payoff diagram illustrating the payoffs from buying a put option and from selling (or writing) a put option. As with our call option payoffs, the vertical axis measures option payoffs, and the horizontal axis measures the possible stock prices on the option expiration date. Once again, these examples assume that the put has a strike price of $50, and that the option will be exercised only on its expiration date.

In Figure 15.4, the put option payoffs are zero for all stock prices above the $50 strike price. This is because a put option holder will not exercise the option to sell stock at the $50 strike price when the stock can be sold in the stock market at a higher price. In this case, the option expires worthless.

In contrast, if the stock price is lower than the $50 strike price, the put option payoff is equal to the difference between the market price of the stock and the strike price of the option. For example, if the stock price is $40, the put option payoff is equal to $10, which is the difference between the $40 stock price and the $50 strike price. This payoff is a cash inflow to the buyer, because the option buyer can buy the stock at the $40 market price and sell the stock at the $50 strike price. However, this payoff is a cash outflow to the writer, because the option writer must buy the stock at the $50 strike price when the stock's market price is $40.

Our payoff diagrams illustrate an important difference between the maximum possible gains and losses for puts and calls. Notice that if you buy a call option, there is no upper limit

FIGURE 15.5 Call Option Profits

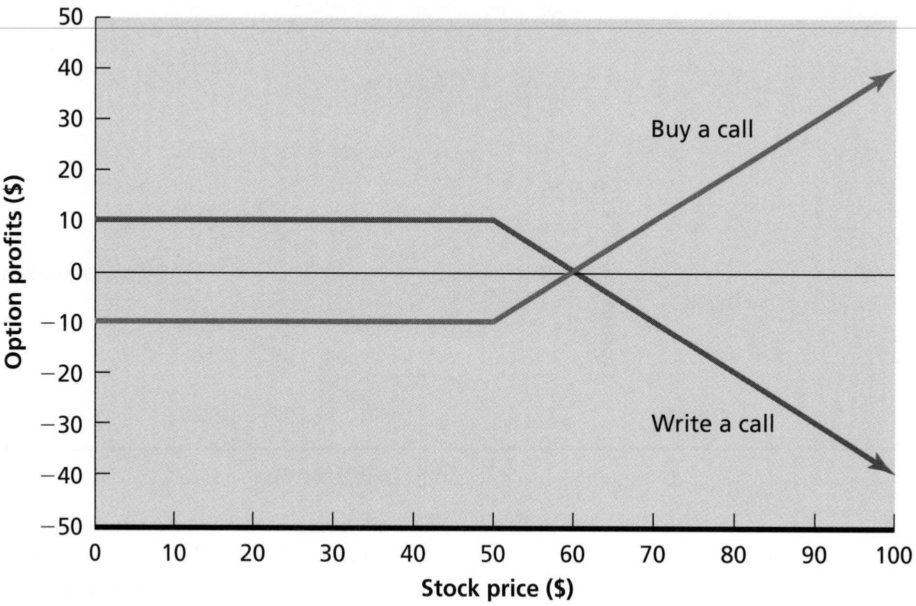

to your potential profit because there is no upper limit to the stock price. However, with a put option, the most you can make is the strike price. In other words, the best thing that can happen to you if you buy a put is for the stock price to go to zero. Of course, whether you buy a put or a call, your potential loss is limited to the option premium you pay.

Similarly, as shown in Figure 15.3, if you write a call, there is no limit to your possible loss, but your potential gain is limited to the option premium you receive. As shown in Figure 15.4, if you write a put, both your gain and loss are limited, although the potential loss could be substantial.

OPTION PROFIT DIAGRAMS

WWW

For even more on options, see www.investorlinks.com

Between them, Figures 15.3 and 15.4 tell us essentially everything we need to know about the payoffs from the four basic strategies involving options, buying and writing puts and calls. However, these figures give the payoffs at expiration only and so do not consider the original cash inflow or outflow. Option profit diagrams are an extension of payoff diagrams that do take into account the initial cash flow.

As we have seen, the profit from an option strategy is the difference between the option's terminal cash flow (the option payoff) and the option's initial cash flow (the option price, or premium). An option profit diagram simply adjusts option payoffs for the original price of the option. This means that the option premium is subtracted from the payoffs from buying options and added to payoffs from writing options.

To illustrate, Figures 15.5 and 15.6 are profit diagrams corresponding to the four basic investment strategies for options. In each diagram, the vertical axis measures option profits, and the horizontal axis measures possible stock prices. Each profit diagram assumes that the option's strike price is $50 and that the put and call option prices are both $10. Notice that in each case the characteristic hockey-stick shape is maintained; the "stick" is just shifted up or down.

CHECK THIS

15.6a What is option writing?

15.6b What are the payoffs from writing call options?

15.6c What are the payoffs from writing put options?

FIGURE 15.6 Put Option Profits

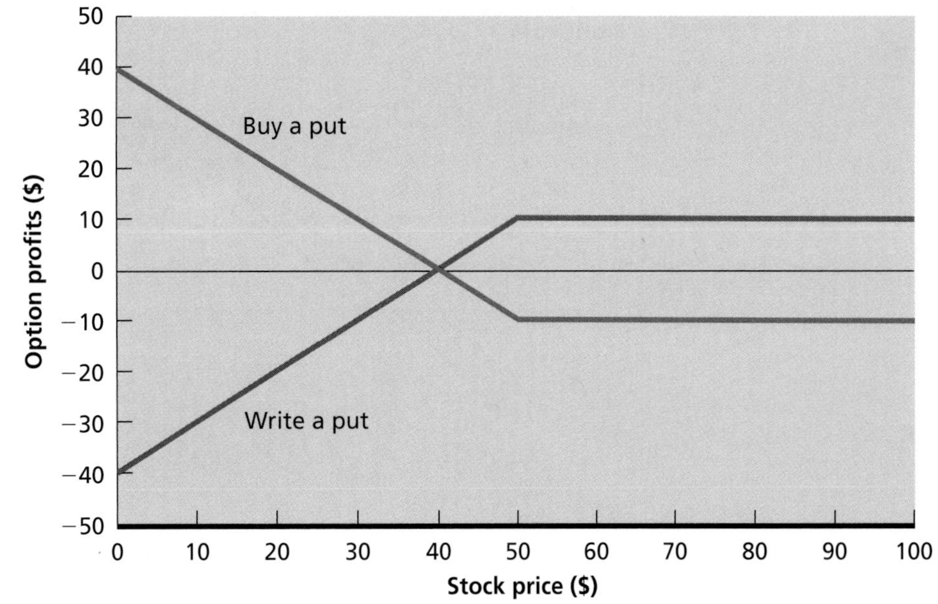

15.7 Using Options to Manage Risk

Thus far, we have considered the payoffs and profits from buying and writing individual calls and puts. In this section, we consider what happens when we start to combine puts, calls, and shares of stock. We could examine any of numerous combinations, but we will stick to just a few of the most basic and important strategies. Note that in the following discussion, the diagrams represent pretax outcomes.

THE PROTECTIVE PUT STRATEGY

Suppose you own a share of Emerson Electric Co. (EMR) stock, currently worth \$45. Suppose you also purchase a put option with a strike price of \$45 for \$2. What is the net effect of this purchase?

To answer, we can compare what happens if Emerson stock stays at or above \$45 to what happens if it drops below \$45. If Emerson stock stays at or above \$45, your put will expire worthless, because you would choose not to exercise it. You would lose the \$2 you paid for the put option. However, if Emerson stock falls below \$45, you would exercise your put, and the put writer would pay you \$45 for your stock. No matter how far below \$45 the price falls, you have guaranteed that you will receive \$45 for your Emerson share of stock.

protective put
Strategy of buying a put option on a stock already owned. This strategy protects against a decline in value.

Thus, by purchasing a put option, you have protected yourself against a price decline. In the jargon of Wall Street, you have paid \$2 to eliminate the "downside risk." For this reason, the strategy of buying a put option on a stock you already own is called a **protective put** strategy. Figure 15.7 shows the net effect of the protective put strategy. Notice that the net effect resembles the profit diagram of a long call. That is, when an investor, who owns stock, buys a put, the profit diagram of this new portfolio resembles the profit diagram of a long call.

The protective put strategy reduces the overall risk faced by an investor, so it is a conservative strategy. This fact is a good example of how options, or any derivative asset, can be used to decrease risk rather than increase it. Stated differently, options can be used to hedge as well as speculate, so they do not inherently increase risk.

Buying a put option on an asset you own is just like buying insurance. When you buy car insurance, for example, you are effectively buying a put option on your car. If, because of an accident or theft, your car's value declines, you "exercise" your option, and the insurance company helps pay for the decline in the value of your car.

FIGURE 15.7 Protective Put on a Share of Emerson Stock

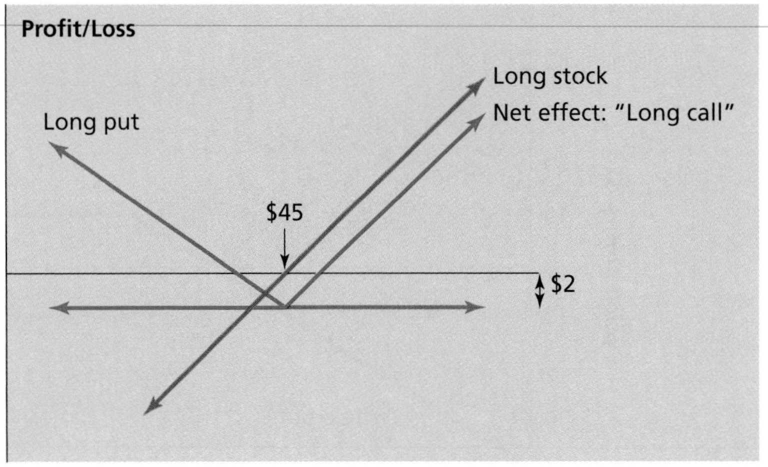

THE PROTECTIVE PUT STRATEGY AND CORPORATE RISK MANAGEMENT

Suppose you own and operate a gold mine. Your revenue stream is risky because it will change as world gold prices change. However, your costs, which mostly consist of moving around tons of dirt and boulders, do not change as world gold prices change. Therefore, your profits change as world gold prices change.

This "underlying risk exposure" is the blue line in Figure 15.8. Suppose you decide to protect your operation from the possibility of low gold prices with the purchase of a put option. The put option profit is the red line in Figure 15.8. Your "net exposure" is the green line in Figure 15.8.

To construct your net exposure, you simply combine the blue line and the red line. Once you do, you see that to the left of the vertical axis, the result is that if gold prices fall, the decrease in profits reflects only the cost of purchasing the put option; decreases in the price of gold will not adversely affect your profits.

To the right of the vertical axis, if gold prices increase, your profits will increase too. However, they will be smaller than if you had not purchased the put option.

FIGURE 15.8 Using Puts to Manage Risk

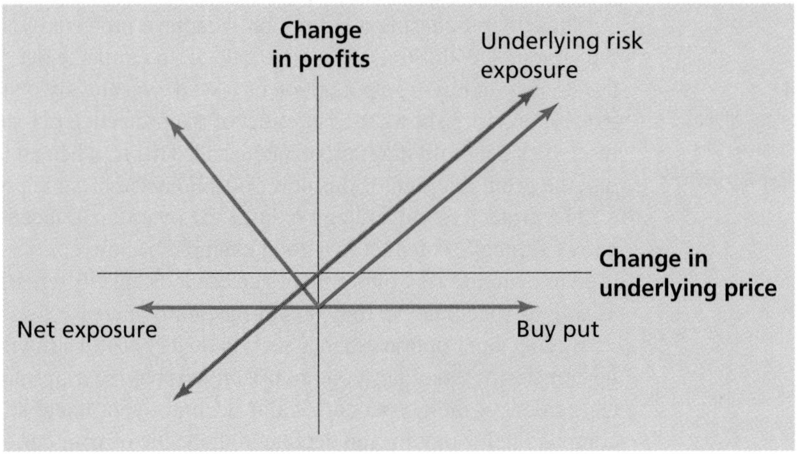

FIGURE 15.9 Using Calls to Manage Risk

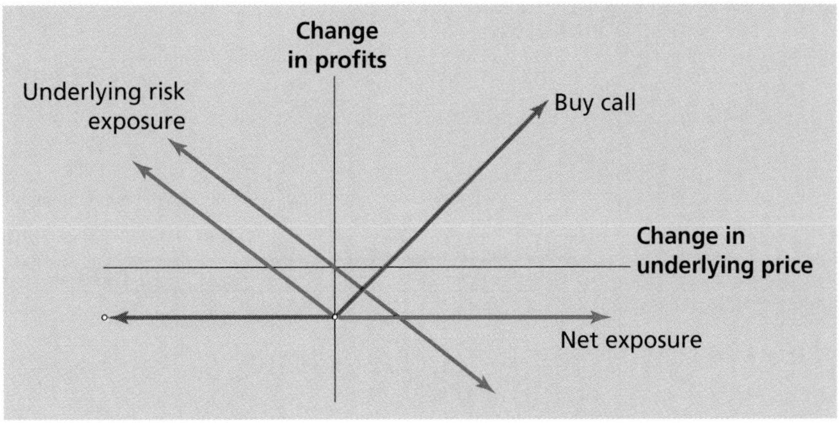

USING CALL OPTIONS IN CORPORATE RISK MANAGEMENT

Suppose you own and operate an airline that uses jet aircraft. Assume that you and your employees are skilled at competitively pricing seats on your flights. This skill results in a relatively stable revenue stream. However, your operating costs will vary with world prices for jet fuel because, after labor, jet fuel is the second largest operating expense for an airline.

The competitive nature of the airline industry means that you cannot easily pass higher fuel prices on to passengers by raising fares. Changes in jet fuel prices thus could affect your profits. Fortunately, you can protect your profits using call options.

The red line in Figure 15.9 represents your underlying exposure to increases in jet fuel prices. Suppose you decide to protect your profits from the possibility of high jet fuel prices with the purchase of a call option. The call option profit is the blue line in Figure 15.9. Your net exposure is the green line in Figure 15.9.

To construct your net exposure, you simply combine the blue line and the red line. Once you do, you see that to the left of the vertical axis, the result is that if jet fuel prices fall, your profits will increase. However, because you purchased call options, your profits will decrease by the amount of the cost of purchasing the call options. Decreases in the price of jet fuel thus will increase your profits.

To the right of the vertical axis, if the price of jet fuel increases, the decrease in your profits reflects only the cost of purchasing the call option. That is, the increase in jet fuel prices will not adversely affect your profits.

CHECK THIS

15.7a What is a protective put strategy, and how does it work?

15.7b Explain how a company can use options today to protect itself from higher future input prices.

15.8 Option Trading Strategies

WWW

For ideas on option trading strategies, see www.commodityworld.com

In this section, we present three types of option trading strategies. In the first type, traders add an option position to their stock position. Strategies in this category help traders modify their stock risk. The second type of option trading strategy is called a spread. A spread strategy involves taking a position on two or more options of the same type at the same time. By same type, we mean call options only or put options only. The third type of option trading strategy is called a combination. In a combination, the trader takes a position in a mixture of

FIGURE 15.10 Covered Call Option on Emerson Stock

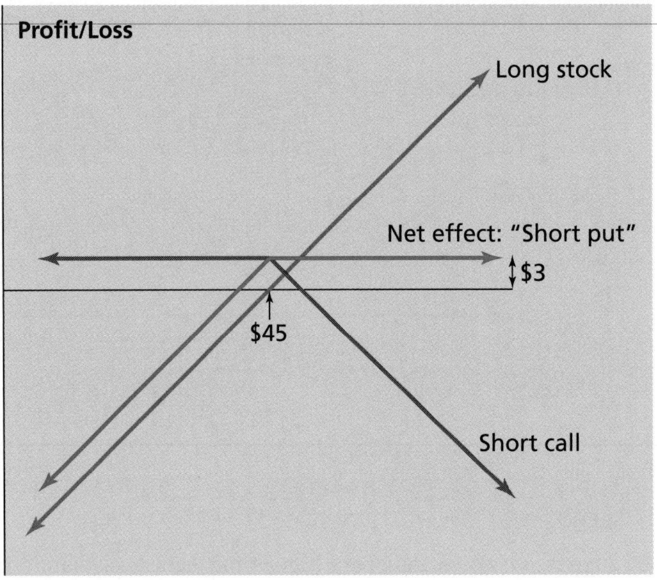

call and put options. Note that the effects of these strategies are pretax effects. Nonetheless, learning about these pretax effects is important for option traders.

THE COVERED CALL STRATEGY

Suppose you own a share of Emerson Electric Co. (EMR) stock, which is currently worth $45. Now, instead of buying a put, consider selling a call option for, say, $3, with an exercise price of $45. What is the net effect of this strategy?

To answer, we can compare what happens if Emerson stock stays below $45 (the exercise price on the option you sold) to what happens if Emerson stock price rises above $45. If Emerson stock stays below $45, the option will expire worthless, and you pocket the $3 premium you received from selling the call option. If Emerson stock rises above $45, the call option holder will exercise the call option against you, and you must deliver the Emerson stock in exchange for $45.

WWW

For more on covered calls, see www.writecall.com

Thus, when you sell a call option on stock you already own, you keep the option premium no matter what. The worst thing that can happen to you is that you will have to sell your stock at the exercise price. Because you already own the stock, you are said to be "covered," and this is why the strategy is known as the **covered call** strategy.

covered call
Strategy of selling a call option on stock already owned.

Let's examine your covered call strategy further. Emerson stock is currently selling for $45. Because the strike price on the call option is $45, the net effect of this strategy is to give up the possibility of profits on the stock in exchange for the certain option premium of $3. Figure 15.10 shows the covered call option position on Emerson stock. Notice that the net effect resembles the profit diagram of a short put. That is, when an investor, who owns stock, sells a call, the profit diagram of this new portfolio resembles the profit diagram of a short put.

In the jargon of Wall Street, a covered call exchanges uncertain future "upside" potential for certain cash today, thereby reducing risk and potential reward. In contrast, a strategy of selling call options on stock you do not own is known as a "naked" call strategy and, as we saw earlier, has unlimited potential losses. Thus, selling call options is either highly risky or else acts to reduce risk, depending on whether you are covered or naked. This distinction is important to understand.

SPREADS

spread
An option trading strategy involving two or more call options or two or more put options.

A **spread** strategy involves taking a position on two or more options of the same type. By same type, we mean call options only or put options only.

AMERICAN PUTS A similar arbitrage argument applies to American put options. For example, suppose a current stock price is $S = \$40$, and a put option with a strike price of $K = \$50$ has a price of $P = \$5$. This \$5 put price is less than the option's intrinsic value of $K - S = \$10$. To exploit this profit opportunity, you first buy the put option at is price of $P = \$5$, and then buy the stock at its current price of $S = \$40$. At this point, you have acquired the stock for \$45, which is the sum of the put price plus the stock price.

Now you immediately exercise the put option, thereby selling the stock to the option writer at the strike price of $S = \$50$. Because you acquired the stock for \$45 and sold the stock for \$50, you have earned an arbitrage profit of \$5. Again, you would not realistically expect such an easy arbitrage opportunity to exist. Therefore, we conclude that the price of an American put option price is never less than its intrinsic value:

$$\text{American put option price} \geq \text{MAX}[K - S, 0] \tag{15.4}$$

EUROPEAN CALLS Because European options cannot be exercised before expiration, we cannot use the arbitrage strategies that we used to set lower bounds for American options. We must use a different approach (which can be found in many textbooks that focus on options). It turns out that the lower bound for a European call option is greater than its intrinsic value.

$$\text{European call option price} \geq \text{MAX}[S - K/(1 + r)^T, 0] \tag{15.5}$$

EUROPEAN PUTS The lower bound for a European put option price is less than its intrinsic value. In fact, in-the-money European puts will frequently sell for less than their intrinsic value. How much less? Using an arbitrage strategy that accounts for the fact that European put options cannot be exercised before expiration, the lower bound for a European put option is:

$$\text{European put option price} \geq \text{MAX}[K/(1 + r)^T - S, 0] \tag{15.6}$$

To give you some intuition, let's look at an extreme case. Suppose the stock price falls to zero before expiration and there is absolutely no chance that the stock price will recover before expiration. American put holders would immediately exercise their puts because it is impossible for the puts to get further into the money. European put holders also would like to exercise their puts immediately for the same reason. However, they cannot. In this example, you can see that European put holders have a riskless asset that will be worth \$$K$ at expiration. Therefore, it is worth the present value of \$$K$. Looking at Equation (5.6), you can see that the lower bound increases as the option get closer to expiration.

A STRONGER BOUND When no dividends are paid, Equation (15.5) also becomes the lower bound for American call option prices. Equation (15.5) is a "stronger" lower bound than Equation (15.3). To illustrate why Equation (15.5) is stronger, consider an example where $S = \$44$, $K = \$40$, $r = 10$ percent, and $T = 1$ year. Equation (15.5) says that for American (or European) call option on a non-dividend paying stock: $C \geq S - K/(1 + r)^T$, i.e., $C \geq \$44 - \$40/(1.1) = \$7.64$. Equation (15.3), however, says that, for American (not European) calls: $C \geq S - K$, or $C \geq \$44 - \$40 = \$4$. So, Equation (15.5) is a stronger (i.e., higher) lower bound than Equation (15.3). That is, stating that the American call price must exceed \$7.64 is stronger than saying the American call price must exceed \$4.

CHECK THIS

15.10a What is the most a European call option could be worth? How about an American call option?

15.10b What is the most a European put option could be worth? How about an American put option?

Chapter Review Problems and Self-Test

1. **Call Option Payoffs** You purchase 25 call option contracts on Blue Ox stock. The strike price is $22, and the premium is $1. If the stock is selling for $24 per share at expiration, what are your call options worth? What is your net profit? What if the stock were selling for $23? $22?

2. **Stock versus Options** Stock in Bunyan Brewery is currently priced at $20 per share. A call option with a $20 strike and 60 days to maturity is quoted at $2. Compare the percentage gains and losses from a $2,000 investment in the stock versus the option in 60 days for stock prices of $26, $20, and $18.

3. **Put-Call Parity** A call option sells for $8. It has a strike price of $80 and six months until expiration. If the underlying stock sells for $60 per share, what is the price of a put option with an $80 strike price and six months until expiration? The risk-free interest rate is 6 percent per year.

Answers to Self-Test Problems

1. Blue Ox stock is selling for $24. You own 25 contracts, each of which gives you the right to buy 100 shares at $22. Your options are thus worth $2 per share on 2,500 shares, or $5,000. The option premium was $1, so you paid $100 per contract, or $2,500 total. Your net profit is $2,500. If the stock is selling for $23, your options are worth $2,500, so your net profit is exactly zero. If the stock is selling for $22, your options are worthless, and you lose the entire $2,500 you paid.

2. Bunyan stock costs $20 per share, so if you invest $2,000, you'll get 100 shares. The option premium is $2, so an option contract costs $200. If you invest $2,000, you'll get $2,000/$200 = 10 contracts. If the stock is selling for $26 in 60 days, your profit on the stock is $6 per share, or $600 total. The percentage gain is $600/$2,000 = 30%.

   In this case, your options are worth $6 per share, or $600 per contract. You have 10 contracts, so your options are worth $6,000 in all. Since you paid $2,000 for the 10 contracts, your profit is $4,000. Your percentage gain is a whopping $4,000/$2,000 = 200%.

   If the stock is selling for $20, your profit is $0 on the stock, so your percentage return is 0 percent. Your options are worthless (why?), so the percentage loss is −100 percent. If the stock is selling for $18, verify that your percentage loss on the stock is −10 percent and your loss on the options is again −100 percent.

3. Using the put-call parity formula, we have:

$$C - P = S - K/(1 + r)^T$$

Rearranging to solve for P, the put price, and plugging in the other numbers gets us:

$$\begin{aligned} P &= C - S + K/(1 + r)^T \\ &= \$8 - \$60 + 80/(1.06)^{1/2} \\ &= 25.70 \end{aligned}$$

Test Your Investment Quotient

For the remaining questions and problems, the circled numbers in the margin refer to the corresponding learning objective in this chapter.

IQ

(1) 1. **Option Contracts** Which of the following is not specified by a stock option contract?
   a. The underlying stock's price.
   b. The size of the contract.
   c. Exercise style—European or American.
   d. Contract settlement procedure—cash or delivery.

1 2. **Option Contracts** A July 50 call option contract for SOS stock is identified by which ticker symbol?

a. SOS-JG
b. SOS-JS
c. SOS-GJ
d. SOS-SJ

1 3. **Option Contracts** An April 40 put option contract for SOS stock is identified by which ticker symbol?

a. SOS-HD
b. SOS-HP
c. SOS-DH
d. SOS-PH

CFA® PROBLEMS

2 4. **Option Payoffs** All of the following statements about the value of a call option at expiration are true, except that the:

a. Short position in the same call option can result in a loss if the stock price exceeds the exercise price.
b. Value of the long position equals zero or the stock price minus the exercise price, whichever is higher.
c. Value of the long position equals zero or the exercise price minus the stock price, whichever is higher.
d. Short position in the same call option has a zero value for all stock prices equal to or less than the exercise price.

3 5. **Option Strategies** Which of the following stock option strategies has the greatest potential for large losses?

a. Writing a covered call
b. Writing a covered put
c. Writing a naked call
d. Writing a naked put

CFA® PROBLEMS

3 6. **Option Strategies** Which statement does not describe an at-the-money protective put position (comprised of owning the stock and the put)?

a. Protects against loss at any stock price below the strike price of the put.
b. Has limited profit potential when the stock price rises.
c. Returns any increase in the stock's value, dollar for dollar, less the cost of the put.
d. Provides a pattern of returns similar to a stop-loss order at the current stock price.

4 7. **Put-Call Parity** Which of the following is not included in the put-call parity condition?

a. Price of the underlying stock.
b. Strike price of the underlying call and put option contracts.
c. Expiration dates of the underlying call and put option contracts.
d. Volatility of the underlying stock.

4 8. **Put-Call Parity** According to the put-call parity condition, a risk-free portfolio can be created by buying 100 shares of stock and

a. Writing one call option contract and buying one put option contract.
b. Buying one call option contract and writing one put option contract.
c. Buying one call option contract and buying one put option contract.
d. Writing one call option contract and writing one put option contract.

CFA® PROBLEMS

3 9. **Option Strategies** Investor A uses options for defensive and income reasons. Investor B uses options as an aggressive investment strategy. What is an appropriate use of options for Investors A and B, respectively?

a. Writing covered calls / buying puts on stock not owned.
b. Buying out-of-the-money calls / buying puts on stock owned.
c. Writing naked calls / buying in-the-money calls.
d. Selling puts on stock owned / buying puts on stock not owned.

CFA® PROBLEMS

3 10. **Option Strategies** Which one of the following option combinations best describes a straddle? Buy both a call and a put on the same stock with

a. Different exercise prices and the same expiration date.
b. The same exercise price and different expiration dates.

c. The same exercise price and the same expiration date.
d. Different exercise prices and different expiration dates.

3

11. Option Strategies Which of the following strategies is the riskiest options transaction if the underlying stock price is expected to increase substantially?

a. Writing a naked call option.
b. Writing a naked put option.
c. Buying a call option.
d. Buying a put option.

CFA® PROBLEMS

2

12. Option Gains and Losses You create a "strap" by buying two calls and one put on ABC stock, all with a strike price of $45. The calls cost $5 each, and the put costs $4. If you close your position when ABC stock is priced at $55, what is your per-share gain or loss?

a. $4 loss
b. $6 gain
c. $10 gain
d. $20 gain

CFA® PROBLEMS

2

13. Option Gains and Losses A put on XYZ stock with a strike price of $40 is priced at $2.00 per share, while a call with a strike price of $40 is priced at $3.50. What is the maximum per-share loss to the writer of the uncovered put and the maximum per-share gain to the writer of the uncovered call?

	Maximum Loss to Put Writer	Maximum Gain to Call Writer
a.	$38.00	$ 3.50
b.	$38.00	$36.50
c.	$40.00	$ 3.50
d.	$40.00	$40.00

CFA® PROBLEMS

2

14. Option Pricing If a stock is selling for $25, the exercise price of a put option on that stock is $20, and the time to expiration of the option is 90 days, what are the minimum and maximum prices for the put today?

a. $0 and $5
b. $0 and $20
c. $5 and $20
d. $5 and $25

3

15. Option Strategies Which of the following strategies is most suitable for an investor wishing to eliminate "downside" risk from a long position in stock?

a. A long straddle position.
b. A short straddle position.
c. Writing a covered call option.
d. Buying a protective put option.

CFA® PROBLEMS

3

16. Covered Calls The current price of an asset is $75. A three-month, at-the-money American call option on the asset has a current value of $5. At what value of the asset will a covered call writer break even at expiration?

a. $70
b. $75
c. $80
d. $85

CFA® PROBLEMS

3

17. Option Strategies The current price of an asset is $100. An out-of-the-money American put option with an exercise price of $90 is purchased along with the asset. If the break-even point for this hedge is at an asset price of $114 at expiration, then the value of the American put at the time of purchase must have been

a. $0
b. $4
c. $10
d. $14

CFA® PROBLEMS

3 **18. Option Strategies** The following diagram shows the value of a put option at expiration:

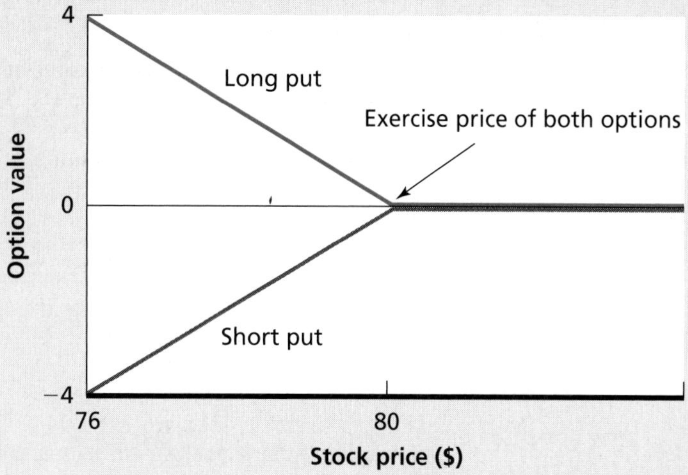

Ignoring transaction costs, which of the following statements about the value of the put option at expiration is true?

a. The value of the short position in the put is $4 if the stock price is $76.
b. The value of the long position in the put is −$4 if the stock price is $76.
c. The long put has value when the stock price is below the $80 exercise price.
d. The value of the short position in the put is zero for stock prices equaling or exceeding $76.

1 **19. Options Tickers** A letter indicating an exchange is sometimes added to an options ticker. Which of the following correctly matches these letters with their exchanges?

a. X–PSX, A–AMEX, C–CBOE, P–PHLX
b. X–NYSE, A–AMEX, C–CBOT, P–PSE
c. X–PSX, A–AMEX, C–CBOT, P–PHLX
d. X–PHLX, A–AMEX, C–CBOE, P–PSE

1 **20. Options Tickers** Which of the following is not a legitimate option ticker?

a. DIS-JF
b. DIS-VL
c. DIS-ZG
d. DIS-PH

Concept Questions

1 **1. Basic Properties of Options** What is a call option? A put option? Under what circumstances might you want to buy each? Which one has greater potential profit? Why?

1 **2. Calls versus Puts** Complete the following sentence for each of these investors:

a. A buyer of call options
b. A buyer of put options
c. A seller (writer) of call options
d. A seller (writer) of put options

The (buyer/seller) of a (put/call) option (pays/receives) money for the (right/obligation) to (buy/sell) a specified asset at a fixed price for a fixed length of time.

2 **3. Option Break-even** In general, if you buy a call option, what stock price is needed for you to break even on the transaction ignoring taxes and commissions? If you buy a put option?

3 **4. Protective Puts** Buying a put option on a stock you own is sometimes called "stock price insurance." Why?

2 **5. Defining Intrinsic Value** What is the intrinsic value of a call option? How do we interpret this value?

2 **6. Defining Intrinsic Value** What is the intrinsic value of a put option? How do we interpret this value?

(2) 7. **Arbitrage and Options** You notice that shares of stock in the Patel Corporation are going for $50 per share. Call options with an exercise price of $35 per share are selling for $10. What's wrong here? Describe how you could take advantage of this mispricing if the option expires today.

Use the following options quotations to answer questions 8 through 11:

Option & N. Y. Close	Strike Price	Expiration	Calls		Puts	
			Vol.	Last	Vol.	Last
Milson						
59	55	Mar	98	3.50	66	1.06
59	55	Apr	54	6.25	40	1.94
59	55	Jul	25	8.63	17	3.63
59	55	Oct	10	10.25	5	3.25

(1) 8. **Interpreting Options Quotes** How many options contracts on Milson stock were traded with an expiration date of July? How many underlying shares of stock do these options contracts represent?

(1) (2) 9. **Interpreting Options Quotes** Are the call options in the money? What is the intrinsic value of a Milson Corp. call option?

(1) (2) 10. **Interpreting Options Quotes** Are the put options in the money? What is the intrinsic value of a Milson Corp. put option?

(1) (2) 11. **Interpreting Options Quotes** Two of the options are clearly mispriced. Which ones? At a minimum, what should the mispriced options sell for? Explain how you could profit from the mispricing in each case.

(3) 12. **Option Strategies** Recall the options strategies of a protective put and covered call discussed in the text. Suppose you have sold short some shares of stock. Discuss analogous option strategies and how you would implement them. (*Hint:* They're called protective calls and covered puts.)

(4) 13. **Put-Call Parity** A put and a call option have the same maturity and strike price. If both are at the money, which is worth more? Prove your answer and then provide an intuitive explanation.

(4) 14. **Put-Call Parity** A put and a call option have the same maturity and strike price. If they also have the same price, which one is in the money?

(4) 15. **Put-Call Parity** One thing the put-call parity equation tells us is that given any three of a stock, a call, a put, and a T-bill, the fourth can be synthesized or replicated using the other three. For example, how can we replicate a share of stock using a put, a call, and a T-bill?

Questions and Problems

Core Questions

(2) 1. **Call Option Payoffs** Suppose you purchase eight call contracts on Macron Technology stock. The strike price is $70, and the premium is $4. If, at expiration, the stock is selling for $76 per share, what are your call options worth? What is your net profit?

(2) 2. **Put Option Payoffs** Suppose you purchase five put contracts on Testaburger Co. The strike price is $45, and the premium is $3. If, at expiration, the stock is selling for $37 per share, what are your put options worth? What is your net profit?

(2) 3. **Stock versus Options** Stock in Cheezy-Poofs Manufacturing is currently priced at $65 per share. A call option with a $65 strike and 90 days to maturity is quoted at $3.25. Compare the percentage gains and losses from a $13,000 investment in the stock versus the option in 90 days for stock prices of $60, $65, and $70.

Use the following options quotations to answer questions 4 through 7:

Close	Strike Price	Expiration	Calls		Puts	
			Vol.	Last	Vol.	Last
Hendreeks						
103	100	Feb	72	5.20	50	2.40
103	100	Mar	41	8.40	29	4.90
103	100	Apr	16	10.68	10	6.60
103	100	Jul	8	14.30	2	10.10

1 **4. Option Quotes** Suppose you buy 50 March 100 call option contracts. How much will you pay, ignoring commissions?

2 **5. Calculating Option Payoffs** In Problem 4, suppose that Hendreeks stock is selling for $107.50 per share on the expiration date. How much is your options investment worth? What if the stock price is $102.40 on the expiration date?

2 **6. Calculating Option Payoffs** Suppose you buy 30 April 100 put option contracts. What is your maximum gain? On the expiration date, Hendreeks is selling for $84.60 per share. How much is your options investment worth? What is your net gain?

2 **7. Calculating Option Payoffs** Suppose you write 30 of the February 100 put contracts. What is your net gain or loss if Hendreeks is selling for $90 at expiration? For $110? What is the break-even price, that is, the terminal stock price that results in a zero profit?

4 **8. Put-Call Parity** A call option is currently selling for $5. It has a strike price of $70 and six months to maturity. What is the price of a put option with a $70 strike price and six months to maturity? The current stock price is $67, and the risk-free interest rate is 5 percent.

4 **9. Put-Call Parity** A call option currently sells for $9. It has a strike price of $80 and five months to maturity. A put with the same strike and expiration date sells for $5. If the risk-free interest rate is 4 percent, what is the current stock price?

4 **10. Put-Call Parity** A put option with a strike price of $90 sells for $7.40. The option expires in two months, and the current stock price is $92. If the risk-free interest rate is 5 percent, what is the price of a call option with the same strike price?

Intermediate Questions

4 **11. Put-Call Parity** A call option is currently selling for $7.20. It has a strike price of $55 and five months to maturity. The current stock price is $58, and the risk-free rate is 5.3 percent. The stock has a dividend yield of 1.2 percent. What is the price of a put option with the same exercise price?

4 **12. Put-Call Parity** A call option is currently selling for $4.60. It has a strike price of $70 and three months to maturity. A put option with the same strike price sells for $8.30. The risk-free rate is 6 percent, and the stock has a dividend yield of 1.8 percent. What is the current stock price?

4 **13. Put-Call Parity** A put option is currently selling for $8.30. It has a strike price of $80 and seven months to maturity. The current stock price is $83. The risk-free rate is 5 percent, and the stock has a dividend yield of .9 percent. What is the price of a call option with the same strike price?

2 **14. Call Option Writing** Suppose you write 20 call option contracts with a $50 strike. The premium is $4.20. Evaluate your potential gains and losses at option expiration for stock prices of $40, $50, and $60.

15. Put Option Writing Suppose you write 15 put option contracts with a $45 strike. The premium is $3.80. Evaluate your potential gains and losses at option expiration for stock prices of $35, $45, and $55.

16. Index Options Suppose you buy one SPX call option contract with a strike of 1400. At maturity, the S&P 500 Index is at 1432. What is your net gain or loss if the premium you paid was $23?

17. Option Strategies You write a put with a strike price of $60 on stock that you have shorted at $60 (this is a "covered put"). What are the expiration date profits to this position for stock prices of $50, $55, $60, $65, and $70 if the put premium is $3.90?

18. Option Strategies You buy a call with a strike price of $70 on stock that you have shorted at $70 (this is a "protective call"). What are the expiration date profits to this position for stock prices of $60, $65, $70, $75, and $80 if the call premium is $4.90?

3 **19. Option Strategies** You simultaneously write a covered put and buy a protective call, both with strike prices of $80, on stock that you have shorted at $80. What are the expiration date payoffs to this position for stock prices of $70, $75, $80, $85, and $90?

3 **20. Option Strategies** You simultaneously write a put and buy a call, both with strike prices of $80, naked, i.e., without any position in the underlying stock. What are the expiration date payoffs to this position for stock prices of $70, $75, $80, $85, and $90?

3 **21. Option Strategies** You buy a straddle, which means you purchase a put and a call with the same strike price. The put price is $3.80 and the call price is $5.20. Assume the strike price is $75. What are the expiration date profits to this position for stock prices of $65, $70, $75, $80,

www.mhhe.com/jm5e

16.2 The One-Period Binomial Option Pricing Model

In the previous section, we made good use of the fact that the call option would always expire in the money. Suppose we want to allow the call option to expire in the money or out of the money.[3] How do we proceed in this case? Well, we need a different option pricing model. We will start our tour of option pricing models by looking at the one-period binomial option pricing model (BOPM).

THE ONE-PERIOD BINOMIAL OPTION PRICING MODEL—THE ASSUMPTIONS

Suppose the stock price today is S, and the stock pays no dividends. We will assume that the stock price in one period is either $S \times u$ or $S \times d$, where u (for "up" factor) is bigger than 1 and d (for "down" factor) is less than 1.[4] For example, suppose the stock price today is \$100, and u and d are 1.10 and .95, respectively. With these numbers, the stock price in one period will either be $\$100 \times 1.10 = \$110$ or $\$100 \times .95 = \$95$.

THE ONE-PERIOD BINOMIAL OPTION PRICING MODEL—THE SETUP

Suppose we start with the values given in Table 16.1. To begin to calculate the call price today, suppose an investor

- Buys one share of stock, and
- Sells one call option.

TABLE 16.1 Inputs for the One-Period BOPM

S	=	\$100 (current stock price)
u	=	1.10 (up factor)
d	=	.95 (down factor)
r	=	3% (riskless interest rate per period)
K	=	\$100 (strike price)
T	=	1 period (time to option expiration)

A key question to ask is: What is the value of this portfolio today and in one period when the option expires? To answer this question, we first write down all the prices that we know today and all the prices we know at expiration. We show these prices on two "trees" in Figure 16.1. In the world of option pricing models, a collection of stock or option prices is known as a tree.

As shown in Figure 16.1, we know the stock price today (\$100) but we do not know the call price today (we are trying to calculate this). In one period when the option expires, we know that the stock price will either increase to \$110 (which is $S \times u = \$100 \times 1.10$) or decrease to \$95 (which is $S \times d = \$100 \times .95$).

At expiration, we know that the call option is worth its intrinsic value. If the stock price increases to \$110, the intrinsic value of the call option, C_u, is MAX[110 − 100,0], or \$10. Similarly, if the stock price decreases to \$95, the call option intrinsic value, C_d, is MAX[95 − 100, 0], or \$0.

What is the value of the portfolio of one share of stock and short one call option? If the stock price increases to \$110, the call finishes in the money—with an intrinsic value equal to \$10.

[3] We limit our discussion here to call options. Of course, we can make parallel statements for put options.

[4] Note that we are assuming that d is less than 1.0, but d does not necessarily have to be less than 1.0.

FIGURE 16.1 Stock Price Tree and Option Price Tree

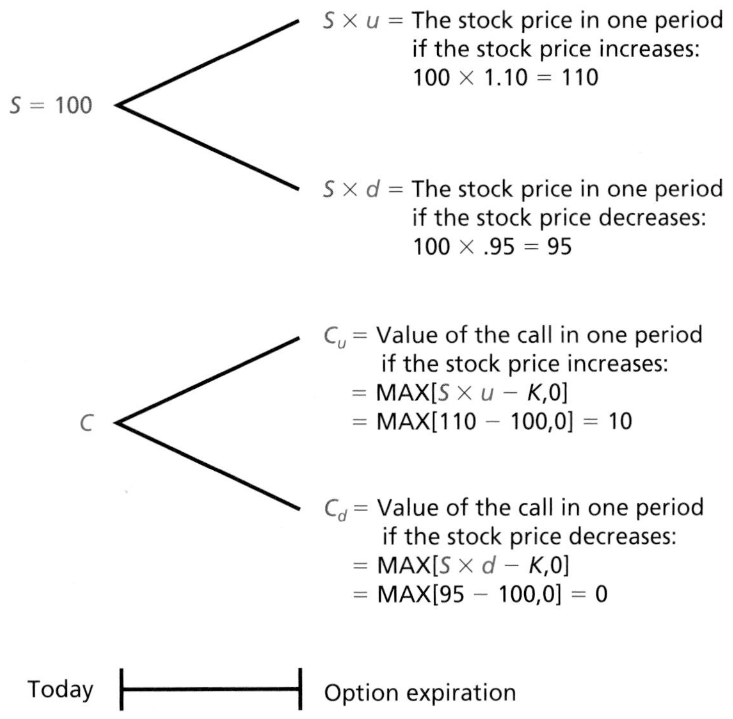

Because the investor sold the call option, the investor owes the intrinsic value. Therefore, the portfolio value is \$110 − \$10, or \$100. If the stock price decreases to \$95, the call finishes out of the money, so it has an intrinsic value equal to \$0. Therefore, the portfolio value is \$95 + \$0 = \$95.

THE ONE-PERIOD BINOMIAL OPTION PRICING MODEL—THE FORMULA

Is there a way to form a portfolio of stock and options that is worth the same amount regardless of the price of the stock in one period? It turns out that there is, and this way is a truly brilliant insight. Instead of buying one share, suppose the investor buys a "fractional" share of stock (which we will represent by the Greek letter delta, Δ). What happens in this case?

In Figure 16.2, we know all values at expiration except Δ. The key to the solution hinges on the fact that the investor can choose the size of the fractional share, Δ. That is, the investor can choose a value for Δ where the portfolio has the same value at expiration for both stock prices. In other words, the investor can choose Δ so that $\Delta S \times u - C_u = \Delta S \times d - C_d$.

FIGURE 16.2 Introducing a Fractional Share, Δ, into the Portfolio Tree

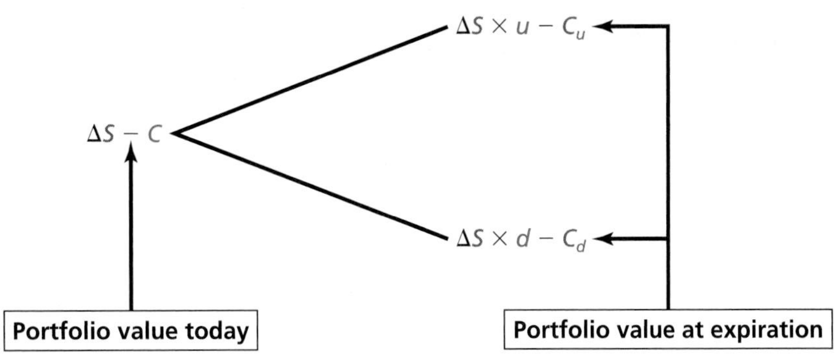

For simplicity, we will drop the multiplication sign when we calculate Δ as follows:

$$\Delta Su - \Delta Sd = C_u - C_d$$
$$\Delta(Su - Sd) = C_u - C_d$$
$$\Delta = \frac{C_u - C_d}{Su - Sd}$$

Using the numbers in our example:

$$\Delta = \frac{C_u - C_d}{Su - Sd} = \frac{10 - 0}{110 - 95} = \frac{10}{15} = \frac{2}{3}$$

Have we succeeded in making the portfolio riskless? Yes:

$$(\Delta S \times u) - C_u = (\Delta S \times d) - C_d$$
$$(2/3)(100)(1.10) - 10 = (2/3)(100)(.95) - 0$$
$$73.33 - 10 = 63.33$$

We now have what we need to calculate the call price today, C. We choose Δ so that the portfolio has the same value for both possible stock prices. That is, the portfolio of long Δ shares and short one call option is riskless (for the right value of Δ). Therefore, a riskless portfolio today should be worth $(\Delta S - C)(1 + r)$ in one period. So,

$$(\Delta S - C)(1 + r) = \Delta S \times u - C_u \tag{16.1}$$

The only unknown value in equation (16.1) is C. Rearranging the values in equation (16.1) results in:

$$C = \frac{\Delta S(1 + r - u) + C_u}{1 + r} \tag{16.2}$$

We can calculate the call price today using equation (16.2):

$$C = \frac{\Delta S(1 + r - u) + C_u}{1 + r}$$
$$= \frac{(2/3)(100)(1 + .03 - 1.10) + 10}{1.03}$$
$$= \frac{(200/3)(-0.07) + 10}{1.03}$$
$$= \frac{5.33}{1.03} = \$5.18$$

Equation (16.2) is one way to write the formula for the one-period binomial option pricing model. Now that we know the price of the call, we can use put-call parity to calculate the price of a put with a strike of $100:

$$P + S = C + K/(1 + r_f)$$
$$P + 100 = 5.18 + 100/(1.03)$$
$$P = 5.18 + 100/(1.03) - 100$$
$$= \$2.27$$

EXAMPLE 16.1 Using the One-Period Binomial Option Pricing Model

A stock is currently selling for $25 per share. In one period, it will be worth either $20 or $30. The riskless interest rate is 5 percent per period. There are no dividends. What is today's price of a call option with a strike price of $27?

To answer this question, we can use the one-period binomial option pricing model:

$$C = \frac{\Delta S(1 + r - u) + C_u}{1 + r}$$

(continued)

To calculate Δ:

$$\Delta = \frac{C_u - C_d}{Su - Sd} = \frac{3 - 0}{30 - 20} = \frac{3}{10}$$

We also have to calculate u, which is \$30/\$25 = 1.20. We can now calculate the price of the call option:

$$C = \frac{\Delta S(1 + r - u) + C_u}{1 + r}$$

$$= \frac{(3/10)(\$25)(1 + .05 - 1.20) + \$3}{1.05}$$

$$= \frac{(\$75/10)(-.15) + \$3}{1.05}$$

$$= \frac{\$1.875}{1.05} = \$1.79$$

WHAT IS DELTA?

Delta, Δ, is an important proportion. We will use delta later in the chapter when we are talking about hedging the risk of adverse stock price movements using options.

An easy way to think about delta is to recall that delta is a proportion of shares to calls that is needed to form a risk-free portfolio. That is, a portfolio of shares and calls that does not change in value when the stock price changes. Remember, the investor can choose many values for delta. However, there is only one delta that helps the investor form a risk-free portfolio.

Therefore, a delta of 2/3 means that we need two shares and three calls to form a risk-free portfolio. The portfolio is risk-free because losses (gains) in the call options are offset by gains (losses) in the stock. So you can think of delta as the fractional share amount needed to offset, or hedge, changes in the price of one call.

In our detailed example, we calculated a delta of 2/3, or .67. This means that the number of shares to hedge one call is .67. Similarly, the number of calls to hedge one share is 1/Δ, or 3/2. That is, we need 3 call options to hedge 2 shares.

CHECK THIS

16.2a Suppose the stock price today is \$95, not \$100 as shown in Figure 16.1. Nothing else changes in the detailed example that follows Figure 16.1. Does delta still equal .67? What is the call price?

16.2b You calculate a delta of .8. How many shares and calls are needed to form a risk-free portfolio? What positions (i.e., long or short) does the investor have in shares and calls?

16.3 The Two-Period Binomial Option Pricing Model

In the previous section, we could price an option one period before it expires. Suppose there are two periods to expiration. What do we do in this case? It turns out that we repeat much of the process we used in the previous section.

In this section, we calculate the price of a European call option. However, we can use this method to calculate the price of a European put option, too. Using a slight modification to allow for early exercise, this technique can also be used to calculate prices for American calls and puts. In fact, this basic technique is so powerful that, with the right modifications, it can be used to price an exotic array of options.

TABLE 16.2 Inputs for the Two-Period BOPM

S_0	=	50	Stock price today
u	=	1.20	Up amount ($u > 1$) per period
d	=	.85	Down amount ($d < 1$) per period
r_f	=	8%	Risk-free interest rate per period
K	=	55	Strike price
T	=	2	Time to option expiration

The best way to learn this technique is to work a detailed example. Suppose we have the set of inputs given in Table 16.2.

We need to point out one more important assumption. That is, in our detailed example, we assume that u, d, and r_f do not change in the two periods until option expiration. With this additional assumption and the inputs in Table 16.2, we will show that the call option is worth \$6.29 today.

STEP 1: BUILD A PRICE TREE FOR STOCK PRICES THROUGH TIME

The upper part of Figure 16.3 shows the stock prices through time. Because there are more than two dates, we denote the stock price today as S_0. Starting at S_0 = \$50, S_1 (the stock price at time 1) is:

$$S_0 \times u = \$50 \times 1.20 = \$60 \quad \text{if the stock price increases}$$
$$S_0 \times d = \$50 \times 0.85 = \$42.50 \quad \text{if the stock price decreases}$$

Next, if the stock price in one period is \$60, then the price in two periods will be either \$60 × 1.20 = \$72 or \$60 × .85 = \$51. Similarly, if the price in one period is \$42.50, then the price in two periods will be either \$42.50 × 1.20 = \$51 or \$42.50 × .85 = \$36.13.

Thus, there are three stock price in two periods, corresponding to a sequence of (1) two up moves, (2) two down moves, or (3) one up move and one down move. Notice that it doesn't matter if we go up, then down or down, then up. We end up at \$51 either way. In symbols, the three possible S_2 stock prices are:

1. $S_2 = S_{uu} = S_0 \times u \times u = S_0 \times u^2$ (two up moves).
2. $S_2 = S_{dd} = S_0 \times d \times d = S_0 \times d^2$ (two down moves).
3. $S_2 = S_{ud} = S_0 \times u \times d = S_0 \times d \times u$ (one up move and one down move).

STEP 2: USE THE INTRINSIC VALUE FORMULA TO CALCULATE THE POSSIBLE OPTION PRICES AT EXPIRATION

As we calculated, the three possible stock prices at expiration are \$72, \$51, and \$36.13. We plug each of these stock prices into the intrinsic value formula. Because the strike price is K = \$55, the possible values for the call option at expiration are:

$$\text{MAX}[S_T - K{,}0] = \text{MAX}[\$72 - \$55{,}0] = \$17$$
$$\text{MAX}[S_T - K{,}0] = \text{MAX}[\$51 - \$55{,}0] = \$0$$
$$\text{MAX}[S_T - K{,}0] = \text{MAX}[\$36.13 - \$55{,}0] = \$0$$

Notice that in two of the possible cases, the call has zero value at expiration.

FIGURE 16.3 Stock Price Tree, Call Price Tree, and Delta Values—Two-Period Binomial Option Pricing Model

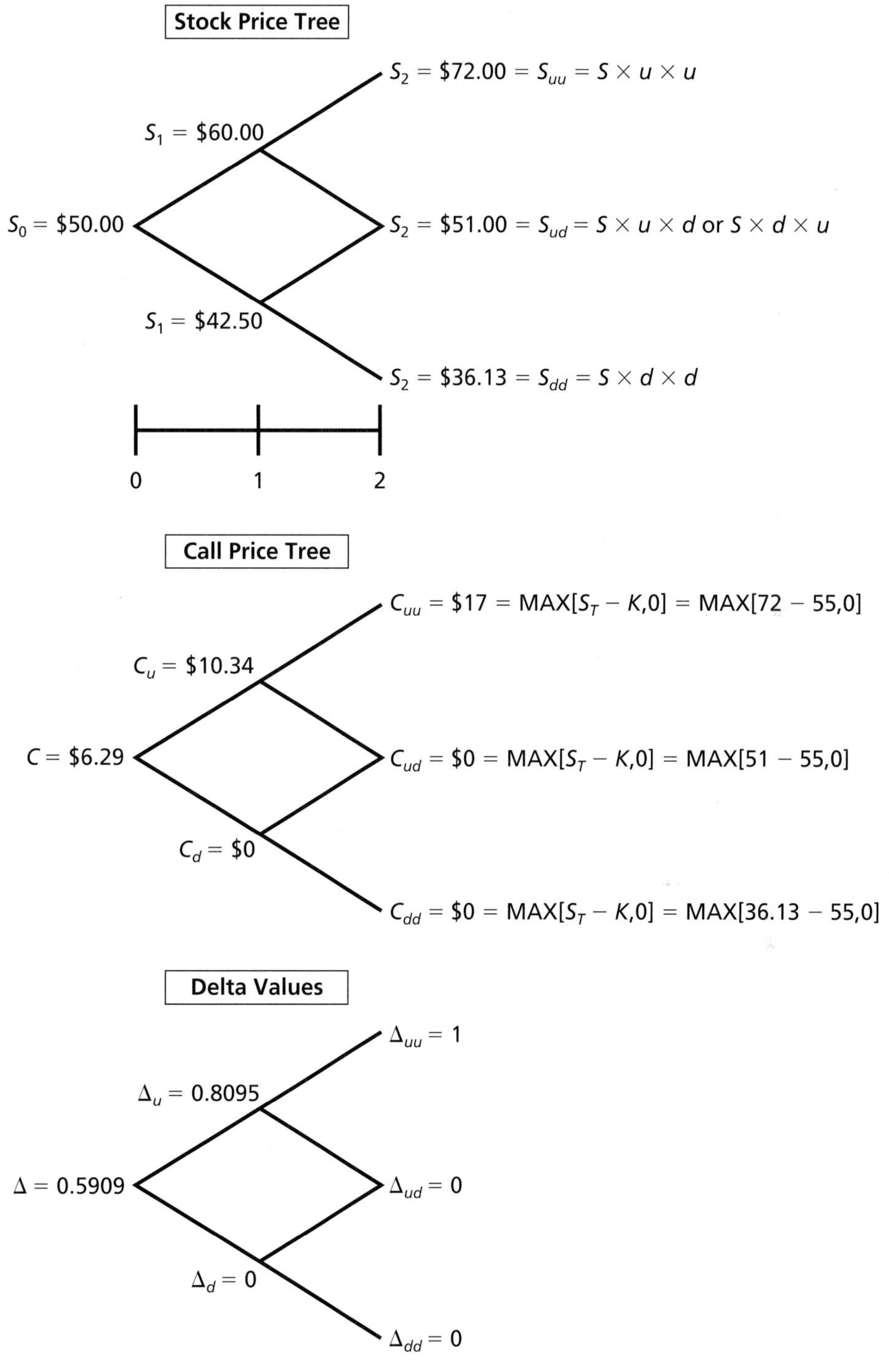

STEP 3: CALCULATE THE FRACTIONAL SHARE NEEDED TO FORM EACH RISK-FREE PORTFOLIO AT THE NEXT-TO-LAST DATE

To form the risk-free portfolios, we need to calculate the possible values for Δ in the next-to-last period. Recall that the portfolio is risk-free when the investor sells one call and buys a fraction, Δ, of one share.

Let us begin by looking at the point where the stock price is \$60. You can see that the two possible stock prices from that point are \$72 and \$51. In addition, because the strike price is \$55, two call option values, \$17 and \$0, are possible. You can see that it is as if we have an option with one period to expiration. Therefore, we can use the notation from the one-period binomial option pricing model to calculate Δ:

$$\Delta = \frac{C_u - C_d}{Su - Sd} = \frac{17 - 0}{72 - 51} = \frac{17}{21} = .8095$$

Likewise, from the point where the stock price is \$42.50, the two possible stock prices are \$51 and \$36.13. Note, however, that because the strike price is \$55, the option is worth \$0 regardless of the stock price in one period. In this case, the Δ is:

$$\Delta = \frac{C_u - C_d}{Su - Sd} = \frac{0 - 0}{51 - 36.13} = \frac{0}{14.87} = 0$$

STEP 4: CALCULATE ALL POSSIBLE OPTION PRICES AT THE NEXT-TO-LAST DATE

We can now use these values for Δ to calculate the call prices when the stock price is \$60 or when it is \$42.50. When the stock price is \$60, we use $\Delta = .8095$, $C_u = \$17$, $r = 8\%$, and $u = 1.20$ to calculate the call price:

$$C = \frac{\Delta S(1 + r - u) + C_u}{(1 + r)} = \frac{(.8095 \times 60)(1 + .08 - 1.20) + 17}{(1.08)} = \$10.34$$

When the stock price is \$42.50, we use $\Delta = 0$, $C_u = \$0$, $r = 8\%$, and $u = 1.20$ to calculate the call price:

$$C = \frac{\Delta S(1 + r - u) + C_u}{(1 + r)} = \frac{(0 \times 42.50)(1 + .08 - 1.20) + 0}{(1.08)} = \$0$$

The intuition for a call with zero value is simple. Ask yourself: What price am I willing to pay today for a call option that will always have a value of zero in one period? Or think of it like this: This call option gives you the right to buy shares for \$55 next period. However, the stock price will always be lower than \$55 next period. How much are you willing to pay today for this call option? We are sure that you said zero (aren't we?).

STEP 5: REPEAT THIS PROCESS BY WORKING BACK TO TODAY

From the point where the stock price is \$50, there are two possible stock prices, \$60 and \$42.50. If the stock price is \$60, we know the call option is worth \$10.34. When the stock price is \$42.50, we know that the call option is worth \$0. In this case, Δ is:

$$\Delta = \frac{C_u - C_d}{Su - Sd} = \frac{10.34 - 0}{60 - 42.50} = \frac{10.34}{17.50} = .5909$$

Using $\Delta = .5909$, $C_u = \$10.34$, $r = 8\%$, and $u = 1.20$, we calculate the call price as:

$$C = \frac{\Delta S(1 + r - u) + C_u}{(1 + \mathrm{r})} = \frac{(.5909 \times 50)(1 + .08 - 1.20) + 10.34}{(1.08)} = \$6.29$$

Using put-call parity, the price of the put with a \$55 strike is:

$$P = C - S + \frac{K}{(1 + r)} = 6.29 - 50 + \frac{55}{1.08} = \$7.22$$

We summarize these calculations in Figure 16.3. Note that, over time, as S increases, so do Δ and C.

CHECK THIS

16.3a Look at Table 16.2. Suppose that $K = \$45$ and all other inputs remain the same. What is the price of a call option? What is the price of a put option?

16.3b Look at Table 16.2. Suppose that $u = 1.30$ and all other inputs remain the same. What is the price of a call option? What is the price of a put option?

16.4 The Binomial Option Pricing Model with Many Periods

When we have more than two periods, nothing really changes. We still work backwards one period at a time. Figure 16.4 shows a binomial tree with five periods to option expiration. Now there are six option values at expiration. To calculate today's option price, you would have to calculate 14 intermediate option prices, which would be fairly tedious and explains why computers come in handy to calculate option prices.

Looking at Figure 16.4, note the various paths that the stock can follow after the stock has increased or decreased in price. There are five ways that the stock could wind up at the black dot. For example, from the diamond marked *U* the stock could follow the blue or red path to the black dot at the end of the tree. The collection of possible stock price paths is also called the "lattice."

As another example, from the diamond marked *D* the stock could follow the orange or green path to the yellow dot at the end of the tree. The stock price today can wind up at the yellow dot following ten paths. In Figure 16.4, we show the number of ways that the stock can

FIGURE 16.4 A Five-Period Stock Price Tree

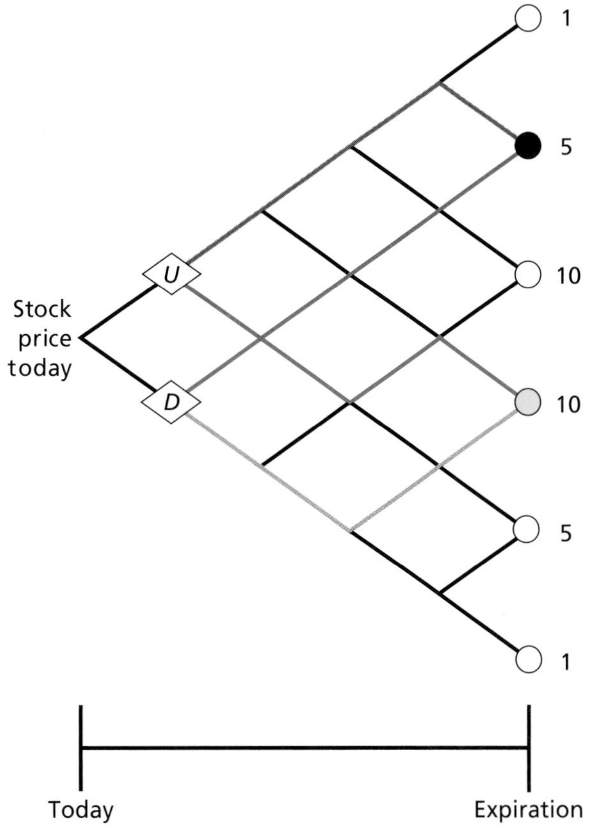

FIGURE 16.5 An 18-Period Stock Price Tree

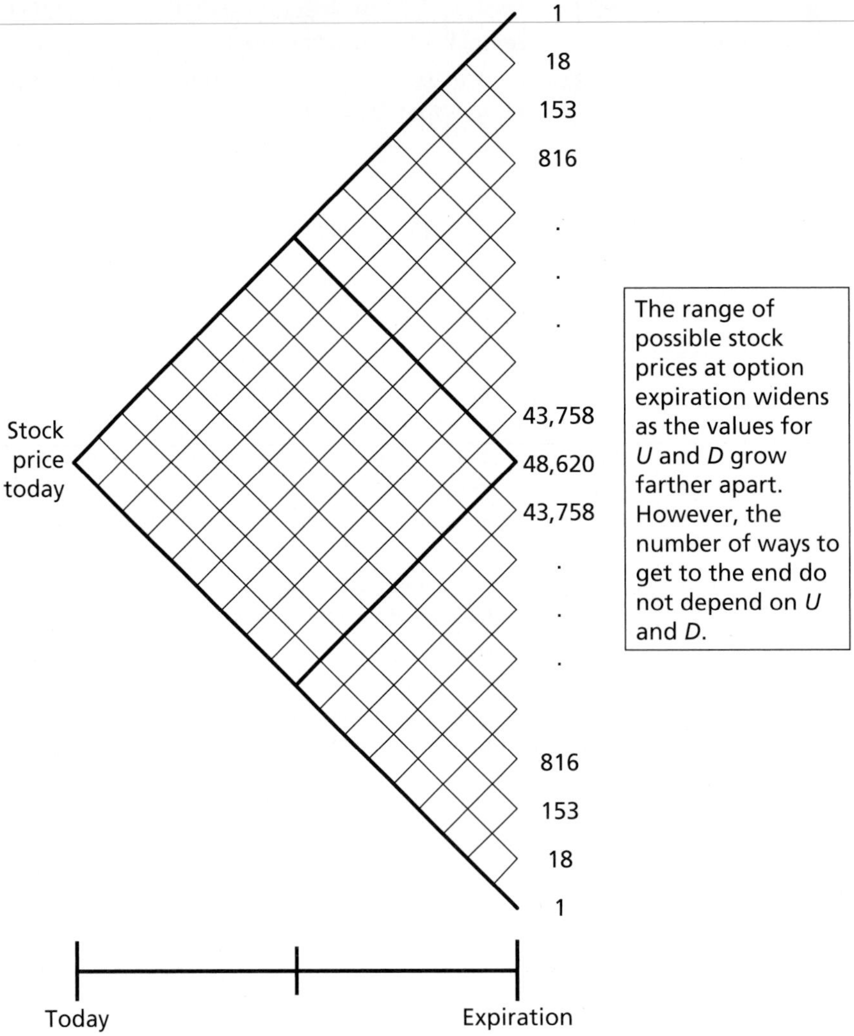

follow to the end points of the tree. As you can see, the stock can follow only one path to reach the highest and lowest possible prices. Also, you will notice that the way the numbers increase from 1 to 10 and then decrease back to 1 is symmetric.

Let's get crazy. Figure 16.5 shows a lattice with 18 periods to expiration. We have superimposed a two-period binomial option pricing lattice over it. In this way, you can see that two periods can be subdivided into many periods.

There are many possible stock paths in Figure 16.5. In fact, there are 2^{18} (or 262,144) of them! Yikes! We have written down the possible ways that the stock price can wander to its ending prices at the option expiration date. As before, there is only one way to get to the highest possible stock price. However, there are 18 paths to the next highest stock price. You can see a symmetry to the way the paths increase in number from 1 to 48,620 and then decrease back to 1.

If you wanted to calculate today's option price, you don't have to worry about the number of paths. However, you do have to worry about the number of intersections at which the stock price can increase or decrease. With 18 periods to expiration, you would need to calculate 19 expiration day stock prices and 170 intermediate option prices (that should seem like a lot to you).

What happens when the number of periods gets *really* big? The answer is that we could always use a computer to handle the calculations, but we can use a more elegant method. As it happens, when the number of periods gets huge, the price calculated using our binomial approach converges to the price from the famous Black-Scholes option pricing model, which we study in the next section.

CHECK THIS

16.4a Why is it that nothing really changes when there are more than two periods to expiration?

16.4b Why don't you have to worry about the number of paths the stock price can take before expiration? What do you have to worry about?

16.5 The Black-Scholes Option Pricing Model

Option pricing theory made a great leap forward in the early 1970s with the development of the Black-Scholes option pricing model by Fischer Black and Myron Scholes. Recognizing the important theoretical contributions by Robert Merton, many finance professionals knowledgeable in the history of option pricing theory refer to an extended version of the Black-Scholes model as the Black-Scholes-Merton option pricing model. In 1997, Myron Scholes and Robert Merton were awarded the Nobel Prize in Economics for their pioneering work in option pricing theory. Unfortunately, Fischer Black had died two years earlier and so did not share the Nobel Prize, which cannot be awarded posthumously. The nearby *Investment Updates* box presents *The Wall Street Journal* story of the Nobel Prize award.

Our focus is on the basic Black-Scholes model. The Black-Scholes option pricing model states the value of a European option on a non-dividend-paying stock as a function of these five input factors:

1. The current price of the underlying stock.
2. The strike price specified in the option contract.
3. The risk-free interest rate over the life of the option contract.
4. The time remaining until the option contract expires, sometimes called **expiry**.
5. The price volatility of the underlying stock (i.e., the distribution of possible stock prices at expiration).

expiry
A shortened way of saying "time to maturity."

In the model, the five inputs are defined as follows:

S = Current stock price

K = Option strike price

r = Risk-free interest rate

T = Time remaining until option expiration

σ = Sigma, representing stock price volatility

WWW

The CBOE has a free options calculator that will do most of the calculations in this chapter at www.cboe.com

In terms of these five inputs, the Black-Scholes formula for the price of a European call option on a single share of common stock is:

$$C = SN(d_1) - Ke^{-rT}N(d_2) \qquad (16.3)$$

The Black-Scholes formula for the price of a European put option on a share of common stock is:

$$P = Ke^{-rT}N(-d_2) - SN(-d_1) \qquad (16.4)$$

In these call and put option formulas, the numbers d_1 and d_2 are calculated as:

$$d_1 = \frac{\ln(S/K) + (r + \sigma^2/2)T}{\sigma\sqrt{T}} \quad \text{and} \quad d_2 = d_1 - \sigma\sqrt{T}$$

INVESTMENT UPDATES

TWO U.S. ECONOMISTS WIN THE NOBEL PRIZE FOR WORK ON OPTIONS

Two economists with close ties to Wall Street, Robert C. Merton and Myron S. Scholes, won the Nobel Memorial Prize in Economic Science for path-breaking work that helped spawn the $148 billion stock-options industry.

The Nobel economics prize is given to innovators whose work breaks new ground and sires whole bodies of economic research. But this year, the prize committee chose laureates not only with distinguished academic records, but also with especially pragmatic bents, to split the $1 million award. Prof. Merton, 53 years old, teaches at Harvard Business School, while Prof. Scholes, 56, has emeritus status from the Stanford Graduate School of Business.

In the early 1970s, Prof. Scholes, with the late mathematician Fischer Black, invented an insightful method of pricing options and warrants at a time when most investors and traders still relied on educated guesses to determine the value of various stock-market products. Prof. Merton later demonstrated the broad applicability of the Black-Scholes options-pricing formula, paving the way for the incredible growth of markets in options and other derivatives.

"Thousands of traders and investors now use this formula every day to value stock options in markets throughout the world," the Royal Swedish Academy of Sciences said yesterday.

The Black-Scholes Formula

In their paper, Black and Scholes obtained exact formulas for pricing options.

$$C = SN(d) - Ke^{-rT}N(d - \sigma\sqrt{T})$$

According to the formula, the value of the call option C is given by the difference between the expected share value (the first term on the right-hand-side of the equation) and the expected cost (the second term) if the option is exercised at maturity.

The Black-Scholes option-pricing model "is really the classic example of an academic innovation that has been adopted widely in practice," said Gregg Jarrell, professor of economics at the University of Rochester's William E. Simon Business School and former chief economist at the Securities and Exchange Commission. "It is one of the most elegant and precise models that any of us has ever seen."

Options allow investors to trade the future rights to buy or sell assets—such as stocks—at a set price. An investor who holds 100 shares of International Business Machines Corp. stock today, for example, might buy an option that grants the right to sell 100 IBM shares at a fixed price in three months' time. The investor is therefore partially protected against a fall in the stock price during the life of the option.

Until the Black-Scholes model gained acceptance, the great minds of economics and finance were unable to develop a method of putting an accurate price on those options. The problem was how to evaluate the risk associated with options, when the underlying stock price changes from moment to moment. The risk of an option depends on the price of the stock underlying the option.

That breakthrough allowed the economists to create a pricing formula that included the stock price, the agreed sale or "strike" price of the option, the stock's volatility, the risk-free interest rate offered with a secure bond, and the time until the option's expiration. They published their work in 1973, the same year the Chicago Board Options Exchange turned the scattered world of options trading into a more formal market.

Prof. Merton himself forged a formal theoretical framework for the Black-Scholes formula, and extended the analysis to other derivative products—financial instruments in which the value of the security depends on the value of another indicator, such as mortgage, interest, or exchange rates. More broadly, his work allowed economists and financial professionals to view a wide variety of commonly traded financial instruments—such as corporate bonds—as derivatives and to price them using the ideas first expounded by Dr. Black and Prof. Scholes. "For the most part, the thing was conceived entirely in theory," said Prof. Merton.

The practical implications soon became apparent, however, as market participants flocked to the Black-Scholes-Merton approach to determine how much options are worth. "It's just a terrific yardstick for investors to help make that judgment," said Bill Kehoe, vice president and manager of the options marketing group at Merrill Lynch & Co., and an options trader since 1961.

Options markets have grown astronomically in the quarter century since the formula reached trading floors around the country. The value of U.S. exchange-traded options in 1995 was $118 billion. Last year, it surged to $148 billion, and in the first nine months of 1997, the figure hit $155 billion. More than 100,000 options series are now available. "Even now, we calculate the value of options world-wide using the Black-Scholes formula," said Yair Orgler, chairman of the Tel Aviv Stock Exchange.

Source: Michael M. Phillips, *The Wall Street Journal*, October 15, 1997.

WWW

For many links to option-related topics, see www.numa.com

In the formulas above, call and put option prices are algebraically represented by C and P, respectively. In addition to the five input factors S, K, r, T, and σ, the following three mathematical functions are used in the call and put option pricing formulas:

1. e^x, or $exp(x)$, denoting the natural exponent of the value of x.
2. $ln(x)$, denoting the natural logarithm of the value of x.
3. $N(x)$, denoting the standard normal probability of the value of x.

EXAMPLE 16.2 Computing Black-Scholes Option Prices

Calculate call and put option prices, given the following inputs to the Black-Scholes option pricing formula.

Stock price	S = \$50
Strike price	K = \$45
Time to maturity	T = 3 months
Stock volatility	σ = 25%
Interest rate	r = 6%

Referring to equations (16.3) and (16.4), first we compute values for d_1 and d_2:

$$\begin{aligned} d_1 &= \frac{\ln(50/45) + (.06 + .25^2/2)\,.25}{.25\sqrt{.25}} \\ &= \frac{.10536 + .09125 \times .25}{.125} \\ &= 1.02538 \\ d_2 &= d_1 - .25\sqrt{.25} \\ &= .90038 \end{aligned}$$

The following standard normal probabilities are provided:

$$N(d_1) = N(1.02538) = .84741 \qquad N(-d_1) = 1 - N(d_1) = .15259$$
$$N(d_2) = N(.90038) = .81604 \qquad N(-d_2) = 1 - N(d_2) = .18396$$

We can now calculate the price of the call option as:

$$\begin{aligned} C &= \$50 \times .84741 - \$45 \times e^{-.06 \times .25} \times .81604 \\ &= \$50 \times .84741 - \$45 \times .98511 \times .81604 \\ &= \$6.195 \end{aligned}$$

and the price of the put option as:

$$\begin{aligned} P &= \$45 \times e^{-.06 \times .25} \times .18396 - \$50 \times .15259 \\ &= \$45 \times .98511 \times .18396 - \$50 \times .15259 \\ &= \$.525 \end{aligned}$$

Exact standard normal probabilities provided in this example are obtained from Excel using the function NORMSDIST(x). A detailed example of how to use an Excel spreadsheet to calculate Black-Scholes option prices is shown in a *Spreadsheet Analysis* box later in this chapter.

EXAMPLE 16.3 Using a Web-Based Option Calculator

The purpose of Example 16.2 was to show you that the Black-Scholes formula is not hard to use—even if at first it looks imposing. If you are in a hurry to price an option or if you simply want to verify the price of an option that you have calculated, a number of option calculators are available on the Web. Let's check our previous answers by using the option calculator we found at www.numa.com.

(continued)

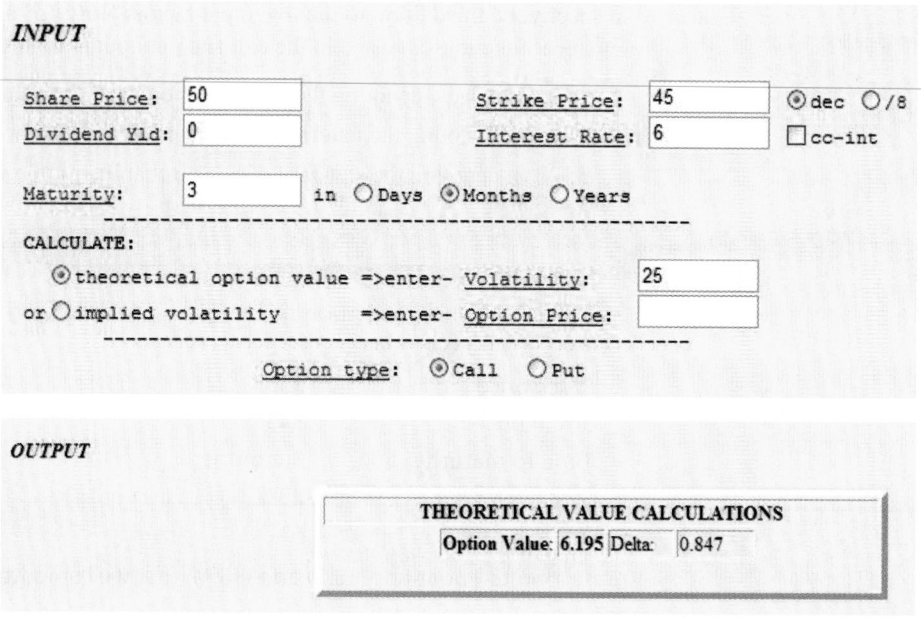

As you can see, our answers in Example 16.2 check out. You might be wondering what delta is. We discuss delta later in the chapter.

CHECK THIS

16.5a Consider the following inputs to the Black-Scholes option pricing model.

$S = \$65$ $\quad r = 5\%$

$K = \$60$ $\quad \sigma = 25\%$

$T = .25$ years

These input values yield a call option price of \$6.78 and a put option price of \$1.03.

Verify these prices from your own calculations.

16.6 Varying the Option Price Input Values

An important goal of this chapter is to provide an understanding of how option prices change as a result of varying each of the five input values. Table 16.3 summarizes the sign effects of the five inputs on call and put option prices. A plus sign indicates a positive effect, and a minus sign indicates a negative effect.

TABLE 16.3 Five Inputs Affecting Option Prices

	Sign of Input Effect	
Input	**Call**	**Put**
Underlying stock price (S)	+	−
Strike price of the option contract (K)	−	+
Time remaining until option expiration (T)	+	+
Volatility of the underlying stock price (σ)	+	+
Risk-free interest rate (r)	+	−

FIGURE 16.6 Put and Call Option Prices

Input values:
$K = \$100$
$T = 1/4$ year
$r = 5\%$
$\sigma = 25\%$

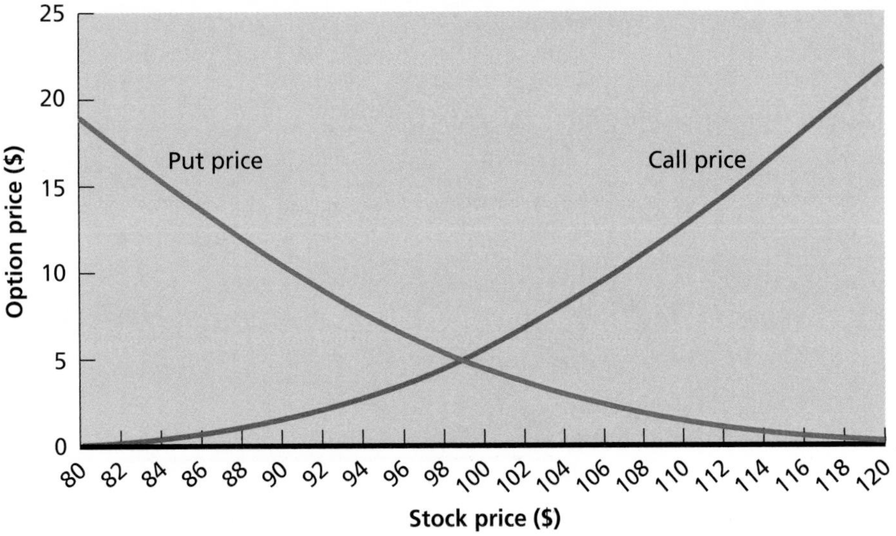

The two most important inputs determining stock option prices are the stock price and the strike price. However, the other input factors are also important determinants of option value. We next discuss each input factor separately.

VARYING THE UNDERLYING STOCK PRICE

Certainly, the price of the underlying stock is one of the most important determinants of the price of a stock option. As the stock price increases, the call option price increases and the put option price decreases. This is not surprising, because a call option grants the right to buy stock shares and a put option grants the right to sell stock shares at a fixed strike price. Consequently, a higher stock price at option expiration increases the payoff of a call option. Likewise, a lower stock price at option expiration increases the payoff of a put option.

For a given set of input values, the relationship between call and put option prices and an underlying stock price is illustrated in Figure 16.6. In Figure 16.6, stock prices are measured on the horizontal axis and option prices are measured on the vertical axis. Notice that the graph lines describing relationships between call and put option prices and the underlying stock price have a convex (bowed) shape. Convexity is a fundamental characteristic of the relationship between option prices and stock prices.

VARYING THE OPTION'S STRIKE PRICE

As the strike price increases, the call price decreases and the put price increases. This is reasonable, since a higher strike price means that we must pay a higher price when we exercise a call option to buy the underlying stock, thereby reducing the call option's value. Similarly, a higher strike price means that we will receive a higher price when we exercise a put option to sell the underlying stock, thereby increasing the put option's value. Of course, this logic works in reverse also; as the strike price decreases, the call price increases and the put price decreases.

VARYING THE TIME REMAINING UNTIL OPTION EXPIRATION

Time remaining until option expiration is an important determinant of option value. As time remaining until option expiration lengthens, both call and put option prices normally increase. This is expected, since a longer time remaining until option expiration allows more time for the stock price to move away from a strike price and increase the option's payoff, thereby making the option more valuable. The relationship between call and put option prices and time remaining until option expiration is illustrated in Figure 16.7, where time remaining until option expiration is measured on the horizontal axis and option prices are measured on the vertical axis.

FIGURE 16.7 Option Prices and Time to Expiration

Input values:
S = \$100
K = \$100
r = 5%
σ = 25%

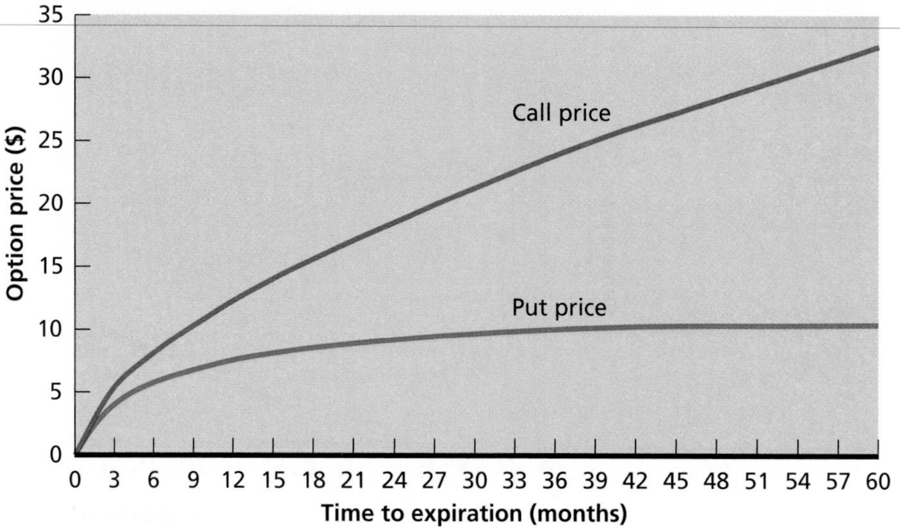

FIGURE 16.8 Option Prices and Sigma

Input values:
S = \$100
K = \$100
T = ¼ year
r = 5%

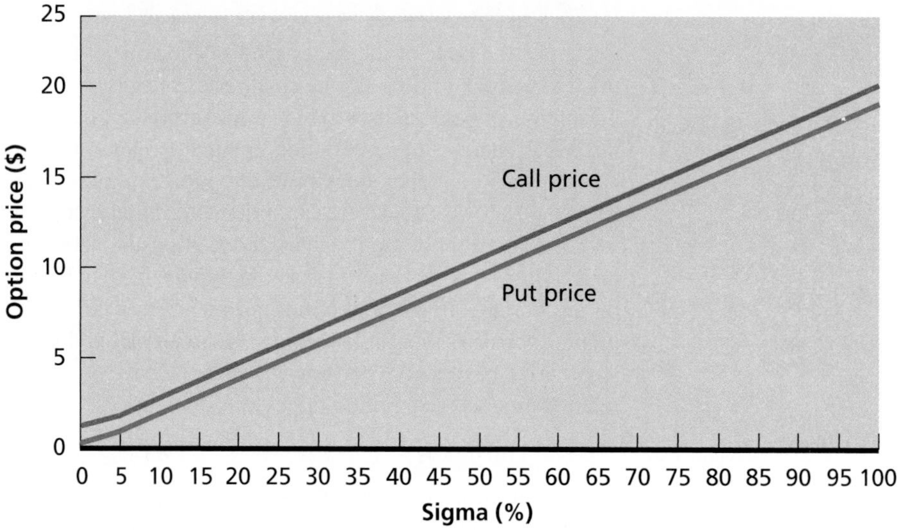

VARYING THE VOLATILITY OF THE STOCK PRICE

Stock price volatility (sigma, σ) plays an important role in determining option value. As stock price volatility increases, both call and put option prices increase. This is as expected, since the more volatile the stock price, the greater is the likelihood that the stock price will move farther away from a strike price and increase the option's payoff, thereby making the option more valuable. The relationship between call and put option prices and stock price volatility is graphed in Figure 16.8, where volatility is measured on the horizontal axis and option prices are measured on the vertical axis.

VARYING THE INTEREST RATE

Although seemingly not as important as the other inputs, the interest rate still noticeably affects option values. As the interest rate increases, the call price increases and the put price decreases. This is explained by the time value of money. A higher interest rate implies a

FIGURE 16.9 Option Prices and Interest Rates

Input values:
$S = \$100$
$K = \$100$
$T = 1/4$ year
$\sigma = 25\%$

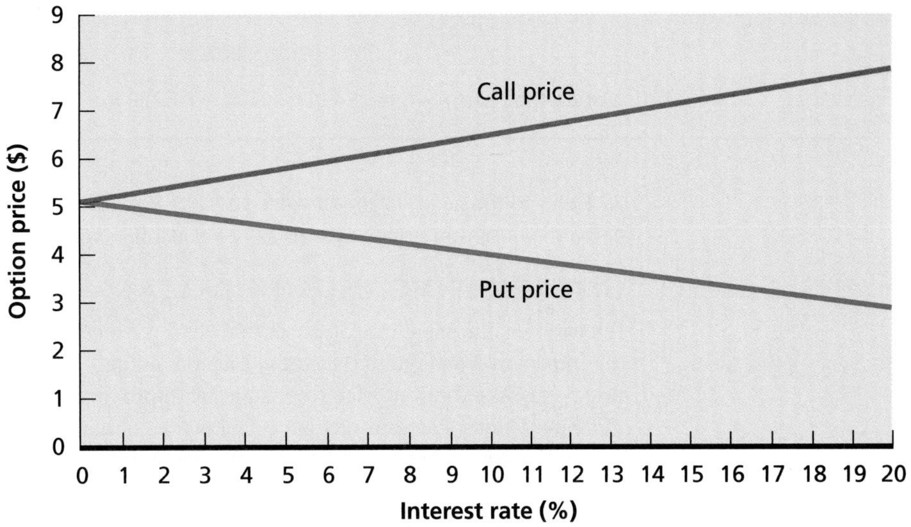

greater discount, which lowers the present value of the strike price that we pay when we exercise a call option or receive when we exercise a put option. Figure 16.9 graphs the relationship between call and put option prices and interest rates, where the interest rate is measured on the horizontal axis and option prices are measured on the vertical axis.

16.7 Measuring the Impact of Stock Price Changes on Option Prices

Investment professionals using options in their investment strategies have standard methods to state the impact of changes in input values on option prices. The two inputs that most affect stock option prices over a short period, say, a few days, are the stock price and the stock price volatility. The approximate impact of a stock price change on an option price is stated by the option's **delta**. In the Black-Scholes option pricing model, expressions for call and put option deltas are stated as follows, where the mathematical function and $N(x)$ were previously defined:

delta
Measure of the dollar impact of a change in the underlying stock price on the value of a stock option. Delta is positive for a call option and negative for a put option.

$$\textit{Call option delta} = N(d_1) > 0$$
$$\textit{Put option delta} = -N(-d_1) < 0$$

As shown above, a call option delta is always positive and a put option delta is always negative. This can be seen in Table 16.3, where + indicates a positive effect for a call option and − indicates a negative effect for a put option resulting from an increase in the underlying stock price.

EXAMPLE 16.4 Computing Call and Put Option Deltas

Given the inputs to the Black-Scholes option pricing formula provided in Example 16.2, calculate call and put option deltas. The necessary values for d_1, $N(d_1)$, and $N(-d_1)$ were provided in Example 16.2.

$$N(d_1) = N(1.02538) = .84741 \quad N(-d_1) = 1 - N(d_1) = .15259$$

(continued)

Therefore:

$$\textit{Call option delta} = N(d_1) = .84741$$

$$\textit{Put option delta} = -N(-d_1) = -.15259$$

Notice that $N(d_1) - 1 = .84741 - 1 = -.15259 = -N(-d_1)$.

Refer to the nearby *Spreadsheet Analysis* box for examples of calculating Black-Scholes call and put option prices as well as deltas using a spreadsheet.

INTERPRETING OPTION DELTAS

Interpreting the meaning of an option delta is relatively straightforward. Delta measures the impact of a change in the stock price on an option price, where a $1 change in the stock price causes an option price to change by approximately delta dollars. For example, using the input values stated immediately below, we obtain a call option price (rounded) of $6.20 and a put option price (rounded) of $.52. These input values yield a call option delta of +.85 and a put option delta of −.15.

$S = \$50 \qquad r = 6\%$

$K = \$45 \qquad \sigma = 25\%$

$T = .25$

If we change the stock price from $50 to $51, we get a call option price of $7.06 and a put option price of $.39. Thus, a +$1 stock price change increased the call option price by $.86

SPREADSHEET ANALYSIS

	A	B	C	D	E	F	G
1							
2		Calculating Black-Scholes Option Prices					
3							
4	XYZ stock has a price of $50 and an annual return volatility of 25 percent. The riskless						
5	interest rate is 6 percent. Calculate call and put option prices with a strike price of $45						
6	and a 3-month time to expiration (0.25 years).						
7							
8	Stock =	50		d1 =	1.0254	N(d1) =	0.84741
9	Strike =	45				N(-d1) =	0.15259
10	Volatility =	0.25		d2 =	0.9004	N(d2) =	0.81604
11	Time =	0.25				N(-d2) =	0.18396
12	Rate =	0.06					
13					exp(-Rate x Time) =		0.98511
14							
15	Call Price =	Stock x N(d1) -Strike x exp(-Rate x Time) x N(d2) =					6.195
16	Put Price =	Strike x exp(-Rate x Time) x N(-d2) - Stock x N(-d1) =					0.525
17							
18							
19	Formula entered in E8 is =(LN(B8/B9)+(B12+0.5*B10^2)*B11)/(B10*SQRT(B11))						
20	Formula entered in E10 is =E8-B10*SQRT(B11)						
21	Formulas entered in G8 and G9 are =NORMSDIST(E8) and =NORMSDIST(-E8)						
22	Formulas entered in G10 and G11 are =NORMSDIST(E10) and =NORMSDIST(-E10)						
23							
24							
25		Calculating Black-Scholes Deltas					
26							
27	Call Delta =	N(d1) =					0.84741
28	Put Delta =	N(d1) - 1 = -N(-d1) =					-0.15259
29							

and decreased the put option price by \$.13. These price changes are close to, but not exactly equal to, the call option delta value of +.85 and put option delta value of −.15.

CHECK THIS

16.7a Why do investors care about option deltas?

16.7b Why do you think deltas for call options are positive but deltas for put options are negative?

16.8 Hedging Stock with Stock Options

Now that we know how to calculate option prices and option deltas, we turn our attention to an important way investors use options. Options provide investors with the opportunity to protect themselves against losses. Taking advantage of this opportunity is known as hedging.

Suppose you own 1,000 shares of XYZ stock, the stock we analyzed in the *Spreadsheet Analysis* earlier in the chapter. From the assumptions used in the *Spreadsheet Analysis,* we calculated prices and deltas for call and put options. If we had used all the same assumptions but used a stock price of \$49 instead of \$50, we would get a different set of prices and deltas for call and put options. Table 16.4 provides a convenient summary (notice we have rounded the option prices to two decimal places). In Table 16.4, all option prices use these inputs: a strike of \$45, volatility of 25%, risk-free rate of 6%, and three months to maturity.

Further suppose that you want to protect yourself against declines in XYZ stock price. That is, you want to hedge: You want to have a portfolio that does not change in value if the stock price changes. Thus, you want changes in your portfolio value from stock price changes to be equal to changes in the value of your portfolio due to options.

Change in stock price × Shares = Change in option price × Number of options (16.5)

From earlier in the chapter, we know that the delta of an option is a prediction of how the option price will change when the stock price changes. So we can rewrite equation (16.5) as:

Change in stock price × Shares = Option delta × Number of options (16.6)

HEDGING USING CALL OPTIONS—THE PREDICTION

As shown in Table 16.3, stock prices and call option prices are directly related. When the stock price increases, so do prices of call options on these shares. From Table 16.4, the call option delta is .8474 when XYZ stock price is \$50. The call option delta is a prediction that the call option price will increase (decrease) by about \$.85 if the stock price increases (decreases) by \$1.00.

So, to hedge declines in XYZ share prices using call options, you need to write, or sell, call options to protect against a price decline. But notice that if the price of XYZ stock fell by \$1.00 and you had 1,000 options, you would gain only \$847.40. This would partially, but

TABLE 16.4 Using the Black-Scholes Option Model for Hedging

XYZ Stock Price	Call Price	Call Delta	Put Price	Put Delta
\$50	\$6.195	0.8474	\$0.525	−0.1526
\$49	\$5.368	0.8061	\$0.698	−0.1939
Change in option price:	\$−0.83		\$0.17	

not fully, offset your loss of \$1,000. You can do better by writing more options. Fortunately, you can use equation (16.6) to tell you how many call options to write:

$$\text{Change in stock price} \times \text{Shares} = \text{Option delta} \times \text{Number of options}$$
$$-1 \times 1{,}000 = .8474 \times \text{Number of options}$$
$$\text{Number of options} = -1{,}000/.8474 = -1{,}180.08$$

The minus sign confirms that you should write, or sell, call options. Because traded call options have 100 options per contract, you would need to write:

$$-1{,}180.08/100 \approx -12$$

call option contracts to create a hedge using call options with a strike of \$45.

HEDGING USING CALL OPTIONS—THE RESULTS

Suppose you write 12 call option contracts at a price of \$6.20 (rounded) per option, or \$620 per contract. Further, just as you feared, XYZ stock fell in value by \$1.00, so you suffered a \$1,000 loss in the value of your shares. But what happened to the value of the call options you wrote? At the new XYZ stock price of \$49, each call option is now worth \$5.37 (rounded), a decrease of \$.83 for each call, or \$83 per contract. Because you wrote 12 call option contracts, your call option gain was \$996.

Your gain in the call options nearly offsets your loss of \$1,000 in XYZ shares. Why isn't it exact? You can see from Table 16.4 that delta also fell when the stock price fell. This means that you did not sell quite enough options. But because options contracts consist of 100 shares, you really did about as well as you could with this simple hedge.

HEDGING USING PUT OPTIONS—THE PREDICTION

As shown in Table 16.3, stock prices and put option prices are inversely related. When the stock price increases, put option prices on these shares decrease. From Table 16.4, the put option delta is −.1526 when the stock price is \$50. The put option delta is a prediction that the put option price will decrease (increase) by about \$.15 if the stock price increases (decreases) by \$1.00.

Therefore, you want to purchase put options to profit from their price increase if the stock price decreases. But notice that if the price of XYZ stock fell by \$1.00 and if you had 1,000 put options, you would gain only \$152.60. This is insignificant when compared to your \$1,000 loss in XYZ shares. You will have to purchase more put options if you are going to have a better hedge. Fortunately, equation (16.6) also tells you how many put options to purchase:

$$\text{Change in stock price} \times \text{Shares} = \text{Option delta} \times \text{Number of options}$$
$$-1 \times 1{,}000 = -.1526 \times \text{Number of options}$$
$$\text{Number of options} = -1{,}000/-.1526 = 6{,}553.08$$

Because this number is positive, this confirms that you want to purchase put options. Because traded put options have 100 options per contract, you would need to purchase:

$$6{,}553.08/100 \approx 66$$

put option contracts to create a hedge using put options with a strike of \$45.

HEDGING USING PUT OPTIONS—THE RESULTS

Suppose you purchase 66 put option contracts at a price of \$.53 (rounded) per option, or \$53 per contract. Again, as you feared, XYZ stock fell in value by \$1.00, so you suffered a \$1,000 loss in the value of your shares. But what happened to the value of the put options? At the new XYZ stock price of \$49, each put option is now worth \$.70, an increase of \$.17 for each put option, or \$17 per contract. Because you purchased 66 put option contracts, your put option gain was \$1,122.

Your gain in the put options more than offsets your loss of \$1,000 in XYZ shares. Why isn't it exact? You can see from Table 16.4 that the put delta also fell when the stock price fell (but it increased in absolute value). This means that you purchased too many put options. If you had purchased 59 put option contracts, you would have offset your share loss more closely. How would you have known that 59 put options make a better hedge than 66 options?

By constructing a table similar to Table 16.4 in advance, you would know that these put options increase in value by $.17 when the stock falls in value by $1. Therefore, each put option contract increases by about $17. Dividing $1,000 by $17 yields 58.82, telling us that 59 put contracts will provide a good hedge.

CHECK THIS

16.8a What happens to call and put prices when the price of the underlying stock changes?

16.8b What is the goal of a hedger who uses options?

16.9 Hedging a Stock Portfolio with Stock Index Options

Portfolio managers can hedge their entire equity portfolio by using stock index options. In this section, we examine how an equity portfolio manager might hedge a diversified stock portfolio using stock index options.

To begin, suppose that you manage a $10 million diversified portfolio of large-company stocks and that you maintain a portfolio beta of 1.00 for this portfolio. With a beta of 1.00, changes in the value of your portfolio closely follow changes in the Standard & Poor's 500 Index. Therefore, you decide to use options on the S&P 500 Index as a hedging vehicle. S&P 500 Index options trade on the Chicago Board Options Exchange (CBOE) under the ticker symbol SPX. SPX option prices are reported daily in the "Market Data Center" section at www.wsj.com. Each SPX option has a contract value of 100 times the current level of the S&P 500 Index.

SPX options are a convenient hedging vehicle for an equity portfolio manager because they are European style and because they settle in cash at expiration. For example, suppose you hold one SPX call option with a strike price of 1500 and at option expiration, the S&P 500 Index stands at 1507. In this case, your cash payoff is 100 times the difference between the index level and the strike price, or 100 × ($1507 − 1500) = $700. Of course, if the expiration date index level falls below the strike price, your SPX call option expires worthless.

Hedging a stock portfolio with index options requires first calculating the number of option contracts needed to form an effective hedge. While you can use either put options or call options to construct an effective hedge, we assume that you decide to use call options to hedge your $10 million equity portfolio. Using stock index call options to hedge an equity portfolio involves writing a certain number of option contracts. In general, the number of stock index option contracts needed to hedge an equity portfolio is stated by the equation:

$$\text{Number of option contracts} = \frac{\text{Portfolio beta} \times \text{Portfolio value}}{\text{Option delta} \times \text{Option contract value}} \tag{16.7}$$

In your particular case, you have a portfolio beta of 1.00 and a portfolio value of $10 million. You now need to calculate an option delta and option contract value.

The option contract value for an SPX option is simply 100 times the current level of the S&P 500 Index. Checking the CBOE Web site, you see that the S&P 500 Index has a value of 1508, which means that each SPX option has a current contract value of $150,800.

To calculate an option delta, you must decide which particular contract to use. You decide to use options with an October expiration and a strike price of 1500, that is, the October 1500

TABLE 16.5 Coca-Cola Employee Stock Options

Inputs	Input Value Assumptions	
Stock price	$44.55	$44.55
Exercise price	$44.655	$44.655
Time horizon	15 years	6 years
Volatility	25.53%	30.20%
Risk-free interest rate	5.65%	3.40%
Dividend yield	1.59%	1.70%
Black-Scholes-Merton option value	$19.92	$13.06

employee stock options representing more than half a million shares of Coke stock. The options had a stated term of 15 years, but, to allow for the fact that employee stock options are often exercised before maturity, Coca-Cola used two time horizon assumptions to value the options: the longest possible term of 15 years and an expected term of 6 years. The company then adjusted the interest rate, dividend yield, and volatility assumptions to each of these terms.

WWW

Visit the Coca-Cola Web site at www.coca-cola.com for more investor information

The different input values assumed and the resulting Black-Scholes option values are summarized in Table 16.5. Notice that Coca-Cola assumed a higher volatility and dividend yield, but a lower riskless interest rate for the six-year time horizon assumption. This seems reasonable given that stock market volatility was high and interest rates were low in 2002 compared to recent experience. A *Wall Street Journal* article discussing the valuation of these Coke options is contained in the nearby *Investment Updates* box.

16.12 Summary and Conclusions

In this chapter, we examined stock option prices. Many important concepts and details of option pricing were covered. We summarize some of these aspects by the learning objectives of the chapter below. However, be warned. The following summary does not include important details of how to calculate option prices. You will need to study the body of the chapter to become proficient in these important details.

1. How to price options using the one-period and two-period binomial models.

A. We show the details for a method to price European call options using the one-period and two-period binomial models. With a slight modification to allow for early exercise, this technique can also be used to calculate prices for American calls and puts. In fact, this basic technique is so powerful that, with the right modifications, it can be used to price an exotic array of options.

B. The details of this method are:

- *Step 1:* Build a price tree for stock prices through time.
- *Step 2:* Use the intrinsic value formula to calculate the possible option prices at expiration.
- *Step 3:* Calculate the fractional share needed to form each risk-free portfolio at the next-to-last date.
- *Step 4:* Calculate all the possible option prices at the next-to-last date.
- *Step 5:* Repeat this process by working back to today.

2 10. **Hedging with Options** Suppose you have a stock market portfolio with a beta of .95 that is currently worth \$300 million. You wish to hedge against a decline using index options. Describe how you might do so with puts and calls. Suppose you decide to use SPX calls. Calculate the number of contracts needed if the contract you pick has a delta of .50, and the S&P 500 Index is at 1340.

1 11. **One-Period Binomial Option Pricing** A stock is currently selling for \$52. In one period, the stock will move up by 1.15 or down by .87. A call option with a strike price of \$50 is available. If the risk-free rate of interest is 2.5 percent per period, what is the value of the call option?

1 12. **One-Period Binomial Option Pricing** A stock is currently priced at \$74 and will move up by a factor or 1.12 or down by a factor of .94 over the next period. The risk-free rate of interest is 3.50 percent. What is the value of a call option with a strike price of \$75?

1 13. **One-Period Binomial Option Pricing** A stock with a current price \$58 has a put option available with a strike price of \$60. The stock will move up 1.13 or down .88 over the next period and the risk-free rate is 3 percent. What is the price of the put option?

Intermediate Questions

2 14. **Black-Scholes Model** A call option matures in six months. The underlying stock price is \$85, and the stock's return has a standard deviation of 20 percent per year. The risk-free rate is 4 percent per year, compounded continuously. If the exercise price is \$0, what is the price of the call option?

2 15. **Black-Scholes Model** A call option has an exercise price of \$65 and matures in six months. The current stock price is \$73, and the risk-free rate is 5 percent per year, compounded continuously. What is the price of the call if the standard deviation of the stock is 0 percent per year?

2 16. **Black-Scholes Model** A stock is currently priced at \$55. A call option with an expiration of one year has an exercise price of \$60. The risk-free rate is 12 percent per year, compounded continuously, and the standard deviation of the stock's return is infinitely large. What is the price of the call option?

4 17. **Employee Stock Options** In its 10-Q dated November 2, 2007, Dell, Inc., had outstanding employee stock options representing over 272 million shares of its stock. Dell accountants estimated the value of these options using the Black-Scholes-Merton formula and the following assumptions:

S = current stock price = \$30.05
K = option strike price = \$32.16
r = risk-free interest rate = .043
σ = stock volatility = .29
T = time to expiration = 3.5 years

What was the estimated value of these employee stock options per share of stock? *Note:* Dell pays no dividends.

4 18. **Employee Stock Options** Suppose you hold Dell employee stock options representing options to buy 10,000 shares of Dell stock. You wish to hedge your position by buying put options with three-month expirations and a \$35 strike price. How many put option contracts are required? Use the same assumptions specified in the previous problem. (Note that such a trade may not be permitted by the covenants of many ESO plans. Even if the trade were permitted, it could be considered unethical.)

4 19. **Employee Stock Options** Immediately after establishing your put options hedge, volatility for Dell stock suddenly jumps to 45 percent. This changes the number of put options required to hedge your Dell employee stock options. How many put option contracts are now required? (Except for the new volatility, use the same assumptions specified in the previous problem.)

20. **Two-Period Binomial Option Pricing** A stock is currently selling for \$59. Over the next two periods, the stock will move up by a factor of 1.15 or down by a factor of .87 each period. A call option with a strike price of \$60 is available. If the risk-free rate of interest is 2.5 percent per period, what is the value of the call option?

21. **Two-Period Binomial Option Pricing** A stock is currently priced at \$64 and will move up by a factor or 1.18 or down by a factor of .85 each period over each of the next two periods. The risk-free rate of interest is 3 percent. What is the value of a put option with a strike price of \$70?

22. **Two-Period Binomial Option Pricing** A stock with a current price \$82 has a call option available with a strike price of \$80. The stock will move up by a factor of 1.14 or down by a factor of .88 each period for the next two periods and the risk-free rate is 3.5 percent. What is the price of the call option today?

www.mhhe.com/jm5e

Use the following information for the next three problems: Donna Donie, CFA, has a client who believes the common stock price of TRT Materials (currently $58 per share) could move substantially in either direction in reaction to an expected court decision involving the company. The client currently owns no TRT shares, but asks Donie for advice about implementing a strangle strategy to capitalize on the possible stock price movement. Donie gathers the TRT option pricing data shown below. *Note*: A long strangle is similar to a long straddle but involves purchasing a put option at K_1 and purchasing a call option at K_2 where $K_1 < K_2$.

	Call Option	Put Option
Price	$ 5	$ 4
Strike price	$60	$55
Time to expiration	90 days	90 days

CFA® PROBLEMS

23. **Strangles** Should Donie choose a long strangle strategy or a short strangle strategy to achieve the client's objective? Justify your recommendation with one reason.

CFA® PROBLEMS

24. **Strangle Payoff** For the appropriate strategy in the previous problem, calculate at expiration the maximum possible loss per share, the maximum possible gain per share, and the break-even stock price(s).

CFA® PROBLEMS

(2)

25. **Delta** The delta of the call option in the previous problems is .625, and TRT stock does not pay any dividends. Calculate the approximate change in price for the call option if TRT's stock price immediately increases to $59.

(2)

Spreadsheet Question

26. **Black-Scholes Model** A stock has a price of $78 and an annual return volatility of 55 percent. The risk-free rate is 3.8 percent. Using a computer spreadsheet program, calculate the call and put option prices with a strike price of $75 and a 57-day expiration. Also calculate the deltas of the call and put.

What's on the Web?

1. **Black-Scholes Model** Go to www.numa.com and find the options pricing calculator. There is a call and a put option on a stock that expire in 30 days. The strike price is $55 and the current stock price is $58.70. The standard deviation of the stock is 45 percent per year, and the risk-free rate is 4.8 percent per year, compounded continuously. What is the price of the call and the put? What are the deltas for the call and the put?
2. **Black-Scholes Model** Go to www.cboe.com and find the options pricing calculator. A stock is currently priced at $98 per share and has a standard deviation of 58 percent per year. Options are available with an exercise price of $95, and the risk-free rate of interest is 5.2 percent per year, compounded continuously. What is the price of the call and the put that expire next month? What are the deltas of the call and the put? How do you interpret these numbers? How do your answers change for an exercise price of $100?
3. **Implied Standard Deviation** Go to www.numa.com and find the options pricing calculator. You purchased a call option for $11.50 that matures in 55 days. The strike price is $95 and the underlying stock has a price of $99.50. If the risk-free rate is 5.4 percent, compounded continuously, what is the implied standard deviation of the stock? Using this implied standard deviation, what is the price of a put option with the same characteristics?
4. **Black-Scholes-Merton Model** Recalculate the first two problems assuming a dividend yield of 2 percent per year. How does this change your answers?

CHAPTER 17

Projecting Cash Flow and Earnings

"Financial statements are like fine perfume; to be sniffed, but never swallowed."

–Abraham Briloff

Cash flow is a company's lifeblood, and, for a healthy company, the primary source of cash flow is earnings. Security analysts strive to make accurate predictions about future cash flow and earnings because an analyst who predicts these well has a head start in forecasting future stock performance. ■

Learning Objectives

Help yourself grow as a stock analyst by knowing:

1. How to obtain financial information about companies.
2. How to read basic financial statements.
3. How to use performance and price ratios.
4. How to use the percentage of sales method in financial forecasting.

Like any security analyst, we must examine financial statements to make cash flow and earnings projections. The quality of our financial statement analysis depends on accurate and timely financial statements. Generally, firms issue financial statements that provide a fair and accurate summary of the firm's financial health. You should know, however, that firms do have some discretion in reporting financial information. In rare cases, firms issue inaccurate, or even fraudulent, financial statements. Therefore, Abraham Briloff offers sound advice when he advocates a careful viewing of financial statements.

In a previous chapter, we examined some important concepts of stock analysis and valuation. Many of these concepts depend on either cash flow or earnings forecasts. In this chapter, we probe more deeply into the topic of stock valuation through an analysis of financial statements. In particular, we focus on cash flow and earnings forecasting. In this chapter, you will become acquainted with the financial accounting concepts necessary to understand basic financial statements and to make forecasts of cash flow and earnings. You may not become an expert analyst—this requires experience. But you will have a solid grasp of the fundamentals, which is a really good start.

Most investors have a difficult time reading the financial statements that are directly issued by firms. These investors rely on secondary sources of financial information. Bear in mind, however, that no one is paid well just for reading secondary sources of financial information.

By studying this chapter, you are taking an important step toward becoming "financial-statement literate" (a good course in financial accounting is also very helpful). Ultimately, you learn how to read financial statements by reading financial statements! You know that your golf or tennis game improves with practice. Your financial statement reading skills also improve with practice. If you have an aptitude for it, financial statement analysis is a skill worth mastering. Good analysts are paid well because they provide good analyses. Who knows? Perhaps you, too, will become a financial analyst.

17.1 Sources of Financial Information

WWW

Review Regulation FD at the SEC Web site www.sec.gov

Good financial analysis begins with good financial information. An excellent primary source of financial information about any company is its annual report to stockholders. Most companies expend considerable resources preparing and distributing annual reports. In addition to their stockholders, companies also make annual reports available to anyone requesting a copy. A convenient way to request copies of annual reports from several companies simultaneously is to use the annual reports service provided by *The Wall Street Journal*. Just visit www.wsj.com and enter a stock symbol in the appropriate box. A company research page appears and you can click on "Annual Reports." *The Wall Street Journal* maintains a free annual reports service where you can select documents for participating companies.

The Internet is a convenient source of financial information about many companies. For example, the New York Stock Exchange Web site (www.nyse.com) provides a directory of Web sites for companies whose stock trades on the exchange. The content of company Web sites varies greatly, but many provide recent quarterly or annual financial reports—just surf to the investor relations section of their site.

EDGAR
Electronic archive of company filings with the SEC.

10K
Annual company report filed with the SEC.

10Q
Quarterly updates of 10K reports filed with the SEC.

Regulation FD (Fair Disclosure)
Requires companies making a public disclosure of material non-public information to do so fairly without preferential recipients.

material nonpublic information
Any information that could reasonably be expected to affect the price of a security.

In addition to company annual reports, a wealth of primary financial information is available to investors through the Securities and Exchange Commission. The SEC requires corporations with publicly traded securities to prepare and submit financial statements on a regular basis. When received, these documents are made available for immediate public access through the SEC's Electronic Data Gathering and Retrieval (EDGAR) archives. The **EDGAR** archives are accessible free of charge through the Internet (www.sec.gov) and are an excellent source of timely financial information.

The most important EDGAR document is the annual **10K** report, often simply called the "10K." Companies are required to submit an EDGAR-compatible 10K file to the SEC at the end of each fiscal year. They are also required to file quarterly updates, called 10Qs. The **10Q** is a mini-10K filed each quarter, except when the 10K is filed. Every 10K and 10Q report contains three important financial statements: a balance sheet, an income statement, and a cash flow statement. You must be familiar with these three financial statements to analyze company earnings and cash flow.

The Securities and Exchange Commission's **Regulation FD (Fair Disclosure)** stipulates that when a company discloses **material nonpublic information** to security analysts and stockholders who may trade on the basis of the information, it must also make a simultaneous disclosure of that information to the general public. Most companies satisfy Regulation FD by distributing important announcements via e-mail alerts. To receive these e-mail alerts automatically, you can simply register for the service at the company's Web site. You can usually find the registration page in the investor relations section of the company's Web site.

17.2 Financial Statements

Financial statements reveal the hard facts about a company's operating and financial performance. This is why the SEC requires timely dissemination of financial statements to the public. It's also why security analysts spend considerable time poring over a firm's financial statements before making an investment recommendation. A firm's balance sheet, income statement, and cash flow statement are essential reading for security analysts. Each of these interrelated statements offers a distinct perspective. The **balance sheet** provides a snapshot view of a company's assets and liabilities on a particular date. The **income statement** measures operating performance over an accounting period, usually a quarter or a year, and summarizes company revenues and expenses. The **cash flow statement** reports how cash was generated and where it was used over the accounting period. Understanding the format and contents of these three financial statements is a prerequisite for understanding earnings and cash flow analysis.

balance sheet
Accounting statement that provides a snapshot view of a company's assets and liabilities on a particular date.

income statement
Summary statement of a firm's revenues and expenses over a specific accounting period, usually a quarter or a year.

cash flow statement
Analysis of a firm's sources and uses of cash over the accounting period, summarizing operating, investing, and financing cash flows.

We begin by considering the basic structure and general format of financial statements through a descriptive analysis of the balance sheet, income statement, and cash flow statement of a hypothetical intergalactic company—the Borg Corporation.

THE BALANCE SHEET

Table 17.1 presents year-end 2535 and 2536 balance sheets for Borg Corporation. The format of these balance sheets is typical of those contained in company annual reports distributed to stockholders and company 10K filings with the SEC. You will see quickly the accounting practice of specifying subtraction with parentheses and calculating subtotals with underlines. For example, Borg's 2536 fixed assets section is reproduced below, with the left numerical column following standard accounting notation and the right numerical column following standard arithmetic notation:

Fixed Assets	Accounting Style	Numeric Style
Plant facilities	$35,000	$35,000
Production equipment	20,000	+20,000
Administrative facilities	15,000	+15,000
Distribution facilities	10,000	+10,000
Accumulated depreciation	(20,000)	−20,000
Total fixed assets	$60,000	= $60,000

WWW

Look at the Research/ Tools section at www.thestreet.com

In the accounting style column, locate the row labeled "Total fixed assets." The single underline indicates this number will be used in another sum. Referring to Table 17.1, notice that total fixed assets is a subtotal used to calculate total assets, which is indicated by a double underline. With these conventions in mind, let us look over these sample balance sheets and try to become familiar with their format and contents.

asset
Anything a company owns that has value.

The Borg Corporation balance sheet has four major **asset** categories: current assets, fixed assets, goodwill, and other assets. Current assets are cash or items that will be converted to cash or be used within a year. For example, inventory will be sold, accounts receivable will be collected, and materials and supplies will be used within a year. Cash is, of course, the quintessential current asset. Fixed assets have an expected life longer than one year and are used in normal business operations. Fixed assets may be tangible or intangible. Property, plant, and equipment are the most common tangible fixed assets. The Borg Corporation has no intangible fixed assets. However, rights, patents, and licenses are examples of intangible assets. Except for land, all fixed assets normally depreciate in value over time. Goodwill measures the premium paid over market value to acquire an asset. Other assets include miscellaneous items not readily fitting into any of the other asset categories.

liability
A firm's financial obligation.

The Borg balance sheet has three major **liability** categories: current liabilities, long-term debt, and other liabilities. Current liabilities normally require payment or other action within a one-year period. These include accounts payable and short-term debt. Long-term debt includes notes, bonds, or other loans with a maturity longer than one year. Other liabilities include miscellaneous items not belonging to any other liability category.

equity
An ownership interest in the company.

Shareholder **equity** is the difference between total assets and total liabilities. It includes paid-in capital, which is the amount received by the company from issuing common stock, and retained earnings, which represents accumulated income not paid out as dividends but instead used to finance company growth.

TABLE 17.1	Borg Corporation Balance Sheets, 2536 and 2535	
	Year 2536	Year 2535
Current assets		
Cash	$ 2,000	$ 1,480
Accounts receivable	6,200	6,200
Prepaid expenses	1,500	1,500
Materials and supplies	1,300	1,300
Inventory	9,000	9,000
Total current assets	$20,000	$19,480
Fixed assets		
Plant facilities	$35,000	$35,000
Production equipment	20,000	20,000
Administrative facilities	15,000	15,000
Distribution facilities	10,000	
Accumulated depreciation	(20,000)	(17,000)
Total fixed assets	$60,000	$53,000
Goodwill	$ 5,000	
Other assets	3,000	3,000
Total assets	$88,000	$75,480
Current liabilities		
Short-term debt	$10,000	$10,000
Accounts payable	5,000	5,000
Total current liabilities	$15,000	$15,000
Long-term debt	$30,000	$20,000
Other liabilities	3,000	3,000
Total liabilities	$48,000	$38,000
Shareholder equity		
Paid-in capital	$10,000	$10,000
Retained earnings	30,000	27,480
Total shareholder equity	$40,000	$37,480
Total liabilities and equity	$88,000	$75,480
Shares outstanding	2,000	2,000
Year-end stock price	$40	$36

The fundamental accounting equation for balance sheets states that assets are equal to liabilities plus equity:

$$\text{Assets} = \text{Liabilities} + \text{Equity} \tag{17.1}$$

This equation says that the balance sheet must always "balance" because the left side must always equal the right side. If an imbalance occurs when a balance sheet is created, then an accounting error has been made and needs to be corrected.

Financial analysts often find it useful to condense a balance sheet down to its principal categories. This has the desirable effect of simplifying further analysis while still revealing the basic structure of the company's assets and liabilities. How much a balance sheet can be condensed and still be useful is a subjective judgment of the analyst. When making this decision, recall Albert Einstein's famous dictum: "Simplify as much as possible, but no more."

TABLE 17.2

Borg Corporation Condensed 2536 Balance Sheet

Cash	$ 2,000	Current liabilities	$15,000
Operating assets	18,000	Long-term debt	30,000
Fixed assets	60,000	Other liabilities	3,000
Goodwill and Other assets	8,000	Shareholder equity	40,000
Total assets	$88,000	Total liabilities and equity	$88,000

Table 17.2 is a condensed version of Borg's 2536 balance sheet that still preserves its basic structure. Notice that the current assets rows are reduced to two components, cash and operating assets. We separate cash from operating assets for a good reason.

Later, we show that the net cash increase from the cash flow statement is used to adjust cash on the balance sheet. This adjustment is more clearly illustrated by first separating current assets into cash and operating assets.

CHECK THIS

17.2a What are some examples of current assets?

17.2b What are some examples of fixed assets?

17.2c What are some examples of current liabilities?

17.2d Which accounts in Table 17.1 show changes between 2535 and 2536 balance sheets?

THE INCOME STATEMENT

Table 17.3 is a condensed income statement for Borg Corporation. This income statement reports revenues and expenses for the corporation over a one-year accounting period. Examine it carefully and be sure you are familiar with its top-down structure.

income
The difference between a company's revenues and expenses, used to pay dividends to stockholders or kept as retained earnings within the company to finance future growth.

The income statement begins with net sales, from which cost of goods sold (COGS) is subtracted to yield gross profit. Cost of goods sold represents direct costs of production and sales, that is, costs that vary directly with the level of production and sales. Next, depreciation and operating expenses are subtracted from gross profit to yield operating **income**. Operating expenses are indirect costs of administration and marketing. That is, these costs do not vary directly with production and sales. Subtracting interest expense on debt from operating income yields pretax income. Finally, subtracting income taxes from pretax income

TABLE 17.3

Borg Corporation Income Statement, Year 2536

	Year 2536
Net sales	$110,000
Cost of goods sold	(89,000)
Gross profit	$21,000
Depreciation	(3,000)
Other operating expenses	(10,000)
Operating income	$ 8,000
Interest expense	(2,000)
Pretax income	$ 6,000
Income taxes	(2,400)
Net income	$ 3,600
Dividends	(1,080)
Retained earnings	$ 2,520

yields net income. Net income is often referred to as the "bottom line" because it is normally the last line of the income statement. In this example, however, we have added dividends and retained earnings information (items that often appear in a separate financial statement). To avoid a separate statement, we show here that Borg Corporation paid dividends during the year. The sum of dividends and retained earnings is equal to net income:

$$\text{Net income} = \text{Dividends} + \text{Retained earnings} \tag{17.2}$$

In Table 17.3, note that we assume a 40 percent tax rate.

CHECK THIS

17.2e What is cost of goods sold (COGS)?

17.2f What is the difference between gross profit and operating income?

17.2g What is the difference between net income and pretax income?

17.2h What is meant by retained earnings?

THE CASH FLOW STATEMENT

The cash flow statement reports where a company generated cash and where cash was used over a specific accounting period. The cash flow statement assigns all cash flows to one of three categories: operating cash flows, investment cash flows, or financing cash flows.

Table 17.4 is a condensed cash flow statement for Borg Corporation. The cash flow statement begins with net income, which is the principal accounting measure of earnings for a corporation. However, net income and **cash flow** are not the same and often deviate greatly from each other. A primary reason why net income differs from cash flow is that net income contains **noncash items**. For example, depreciation is a noncash expense that must be added to net income when calculating cash flow. Adjusting net income for noncash items yields **operating cash flow**.

cash flow
Income realized in cash form.

noncash items
Income and expense items not realized in cash form.

operating cash flow
Cash generated by a firm's normal business operations.

investment cash flow
Cash flow resulting from purchases and sales of fixed assets and investments.

financing cash flow
Cash flow originating from the issuance or repurchase of securities and the payment of dividends.

Operating cash flow is the first of three cash flow categories reported in the cash flow statement. The second and third categories are investment cash flow and financing cash flow. **Investment cash flow** (or "investing" cash flow) includes any purchases or sales of fixed assets and investments. For example, Borg's purchase of Klingon Enterprises distribution facilities reported in footnote "a" is an investment cash flow. **Financing cash flow** includes any funds raised by issuing securities or expended by a repurchase of outstanding securities. In this example, Borg's $10,000 debt issue and $1,080 dividend payout reported in footnote "b" are examples of financing cash flows.

Standard accounting practice specifies that dividend payments to stockholders are financing cash flows, whereas interest payments to bondholders are operating cash flows. One reason is that dividend payments are discretionary, while interest payments are mandatory. Also, dividend payouts are not tax deductible, but interest payments are.

TABLE 17.4 **Borg Corporation** Condensed 2536 Cash Flow Statement

	Year 2536
Net income	$ 3,600
Depreciation	3,000
Operating cash flow	$ 6,600
Investment cash flow[a]	(15,000)
Financing cash flow[b]	8,920
Net cash increase	$520

[a] December 31, 2536, purchase of distribution facilities from Klingon Enterprises for $15,000 (including $5,000 goodwill).

[b] Issue of $10,000 par value 5 percent coupon bonds, less a $1,080 dividend payout.

The sum of operating cash flow, investment cash flow, and financing cash flow yields the net change in the firm's cash. This change is the "bottom line" of the cash flow statement and reveals how much cash flowed into or out of the company's cash account during an accounting period. In this case, $520 of cash flowed into Borg Corporation (you can also see this change in cash by comparing the cash columns in Table 17.1).

CHECK THIS

17.2i What is the difference between net income and operating cash flow?

17.2j What are some noncash items used to calculate operating cash flow?

17.2k What is the difference between an investment cash flow and a financing cash flow?

17.2l What is meant by net increase in cash?

17.2m Can you explain why a cash item like interest expense does not appear on the cash flow statement?

PERFORMANCE RATIOS AND PRICE RATIOS

Annual reports and 10Ks normally contain various items of supplemental information about the company. For example, certain profitability ratios may be reported to assist interpretation of the company's operating efficiency. For Borg Corporation, some standard profitability ratios for 2536 are calculated immediately below:

Ratio	Formula	Calculation
Gross margin	$\frac{\text{Gross profit}}{\text{Net sales}}$	$\frac{\$21{,}000}{\$110{,}000} = 19.09\%$
Operating margin	$\frac{\text{Operating income}}{\text{Net sales}}$	$\frac{\$8{,}000}{\$110{,}000} = 7.27\%$
Return on assets (ROA)	$\frac{\text{Net income}}{\text{Total assets}}$	$\frac{\$3{,}600}{\$88{,}000} = 4.09\%$
Return on equity (ROE)	$\frac{\text{Net income}}{\text{Shareholder equity}}$	$\frac{\$3{,}600}{\$40{,}000} = 9.00\%$

return on assets (ROA) Net income stated as a percentage of total assets.

return on equity (ROE) Net income stated as a percentage of shareholder equity.

Notice that **return on assets (ROA)** and **return on equity (ROE)** are calculated using current year-end values for total assets and shareholder equity. It could be argued that prior-year values should be used for these calculations. However, the use of current year-end values is more common.

Annual reports and 10Ks may also report per-share calculations of book value, earnings, and operating cash flow, respectively. Per-share calculations require the number of common stock shares outstanding. Borg's balance sheet reports 2,000 shares of common stock outstanding. Thus, for Borg Corporation, these per-share values are calculated as follows:

Ratio	Formula	Calculation
Book value per share (BVPS)	$\frac{\text{Shareholder equity}}{\text{Shares outstanding}}$	$\frac{\$40{,}000}{2{,}000} = \$20.00$
Earnings per share (EPS)	$\frac{\text{Net income}}{\text{Shares outstanding}}$	$\frac{\$3{,}600}{2{,}000} = \$1.80$
Cash flow per share (CFPS)	$\frac{\text{Operating cash flow}}{\text{Shares outstanding}}$	$\frac{\$6{,}600}{2{,}000} = \$3.30$

WWW

Check out the security analysis sections at www.uoutperform.com

Notice that cash flow per share (CFPS) is calculated using operating cash flow—*not* the bottom line on the cash flow statement (see Table 17.4). Most of the time when you hear the term "cash flow," it refers to operating cash flow.

WORK THE WEB

One of the more frequent uses of financial ratios is in stock screening. Stock screening is the process of selecting stocks based on specific criteria. A popular method used by the legendary investor Warren Buffett, among others, is searching for value stocks that have high growth potential. A value stock has relatively low price-earnings ratios. However, low price-earnings ratios can be an indication of low future growth potential, so we also want to determine if these stocks have future growth possibilities.

We went to www.cnbc.com, clicked on the "Investing" tab, and then the "Stock Screener" tab. You can see that there are some preset screens, like "Solid Stocks Solid Companies" and "Small Cap Value." However, we created our own screen looking for stocks that are large, growing, and cheap. That is, our screen looks for stocks with a market cap greater than $5 billion; P/E less than 20; estimated EPS growth greater than 20 percent; and P/S less than 1.3. Here is what we found:

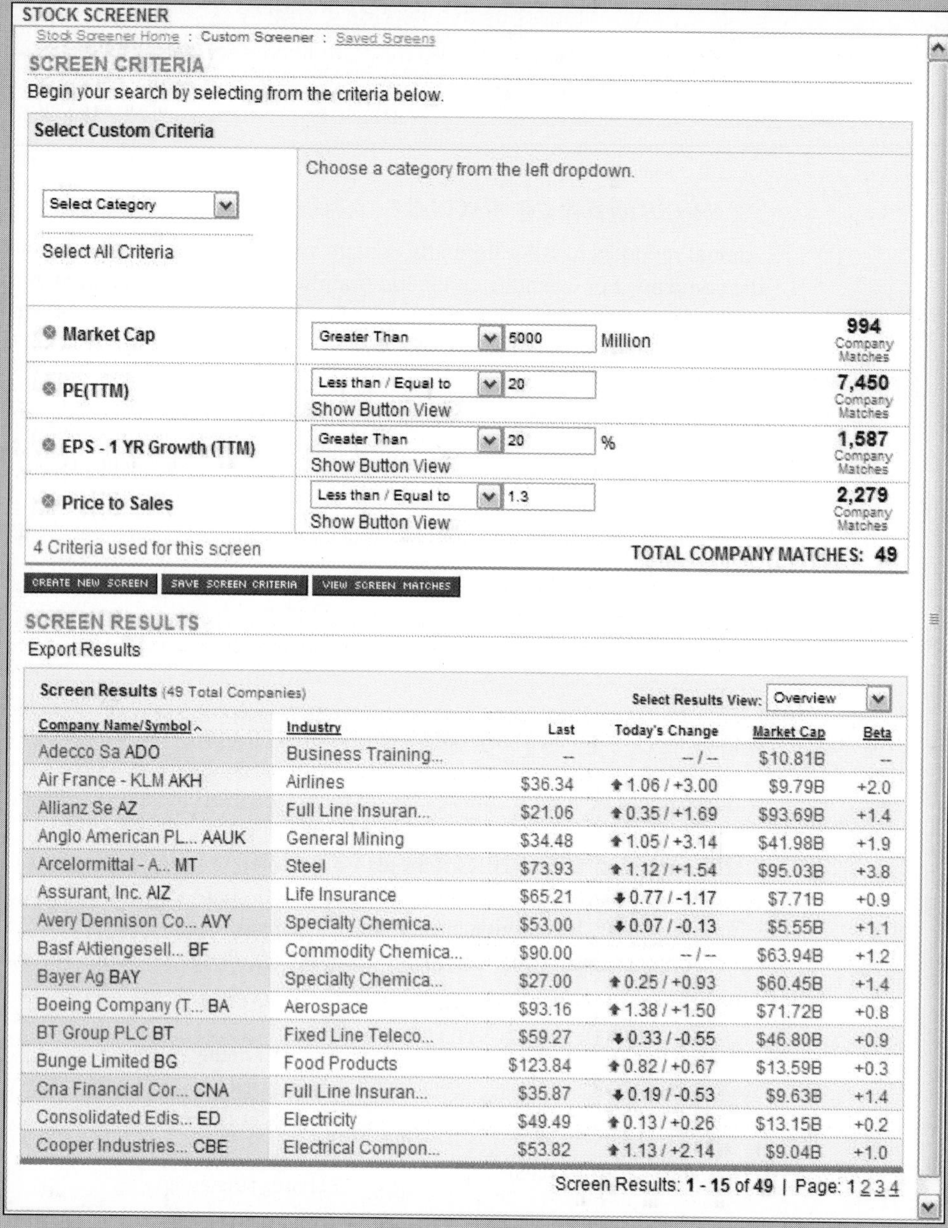
STOCK SCREENER

Stock Screener Home : Custom Screener : Saved Screens

SCREEN CRITERIA

Begin your search by selecting from the criteria below.

Select Custom Criteria

Select Category

Select All Criteria

Choose a category from the left dropdown.

Criterion	Setting	Company Matches
Market Cap	Greater Than 5000 Million	994
PE(TTM)	Less than / Equal to 20	7,450
EPS - 1 YR Growth (TTM)	Greater Than 20 %	1,587
Price to Sales	Less than / Equal to 1.3	2,279

4 Criteria used for this screen — TOTAL COMPANY MATCHES: 49

CREATE NEW SCREEN | SAVE SCREEN CRITERIA | VIEW SCREEN MATCHES

SCREEN RESULTS

Export Results

Screen Results (49 Total Companies) — Select Results View: Overview

Company Name/Symbol	Industry	Last	Today's Change	Market Cap	Beta
Adecco Sa ADO	Business Training...	--	-- / --	$10.81B	--
Air France - KLM AKH	Airlines	$36.34	↑1.06 / +3.00	$9.79B	+2.0
Allianz Se AZ	Full Line Insuran...	$21.06	↑0.35 / +1.69	$93.69B	+1.4
Anglo American PL... AAUK	General Mining	$34.48	↑1.05 / +3.14	$41.98B	+1.9
Arcelormittal - A... MT	Steel	$73.93	↑1.12 / +1.54	$95.03B	+3.8
Assurant, Inc. AIZ	Life Insurance	$65.21	↓0.77 / -1.17	$7.71B	+0.9
Avery Dennison Co... AVY	Specialty Chemica...	$53.00	↓0.07 / -0.13	$5.55B	+1.1
Basf Aktiengesell... BF	Commodity Chemica...	$90.00	-- / --	$63.94B	+1.2
Bayer Ag BAY	Specialty Chemica...	$27.00	↑0.25 / +0.93	$60.45B	+1.4
Boeing Company (T... BA	Aerospace	$93.16	↑1.38 / +1.50	$71.72B	+0.8
BT Group PLC BT	Fixed Line Teleco...	$59.27	↓0.33 / -0.55	$46.80B	+0.9
Bunge Limited BG	Food Products	$123.84	↑0.82 / +0.67	$13.59B	+0.3
Cna Financial Cor... CNA	Full Line Insuran...	$35.87	↓0.19 / -0.53	$9.63B	+1.4
Consolidated Edis... ED	Electricity	$49.49	↑0.13 / +0.26	$13.15B	+0.2
Cooper Industries... CBE	Electrical Compon...	$53.82	↑1.13 / +2.14	$9.04B	+1.0

Screen Results: 1 - 15 of 49 | Page: 1 2 3 4

Using stock screening as an investment tool is not really this simple. What we have done here is narrowed the universe of stocks to a few stocks that meet our criteria. It is now up to us to further examine the companies to determine if they are actually good investments. In other words, stock screening is not the end of the investment process—it simply narrows the field.

Recall that in a previous chapter, we made extensive use of price ratios to analyze stock values. Using per-share values calculated immediately above, and Borg's year-end stock price of $40 per share, we get the following price ratios:

Ratio	Formula	Calculation
Price-book (P/B)	$\frac{\text{Stock price}}{\text{BVPS}}$	$\frac{\$40}{\$20} = 2.00$
Price-earnings (P/E)	$\frac{\text{Stock price}}{\text{EPS}}$	$\frac{\$40}{\$1.80} = 22.22$
Price-cash flow (P/CF)	$\frac{\text{Stock price}}{\text{CFPS}}$	$\frac{\$40}{\$3.30} = 12.12$

We use these price ratios later when assessing the potential impact of a sales campaign on Borg Corporation's future stock price. Our nearby *Work the Web* box shows another use for price ratios.

CHECK THIS

17.2n What is the difference between gross margin and operating margin?

17.2o What is the difference between return on assets and return on equity?

17.2p What is the difference between earnings per share and cash flow per share?

17.2q How is cash flow per share calculated?

17.3 Financial Statement Forecasting

In December 2536, Borg publicly announces the completion of an acquisition of some distribution outlets from Klingon Enterprises, LLC. The stated purpose of the acquisition was to expand sales. Complementing the acquisition, Borg also announces plans for a marketing campaign to increase next year's net sales to a targeted $137,500.

As a Borg analyst, you must examine the potential impact of these actions. You immediately contact Borg management to inquire about the details of the acquisition and the marketing campaign. Armed with this additional information, you decide to construct **pro forma financial statements** for Borg Corporation for the year 2537.

pro forma financial statements
Statements prepared using certain assumptions about future income, cash flow, and other items. Pro forma literally means according to prescribed form.

THE PERCENTAGE OF SALES APPROACH

A simple model to construct pro forma financial statements is one in which every item increases at the same rate as sales. This may be a reasonable assumption for some financial statement items. For others, such as long-term debt, it probably is not, because the amount of long-term debt is something set by company management. Therefore, long-term debt levels do not necessarily relate directly to the level of sales.

A more sophisticated model builds on the basic idea of separating the income statement and balance sheet items into two groups: those that do vary directly with sales and those that do not. Given a sales forecast, calculating how much financing the firm will need to support the predicted sales level is easy. This quick and practical model is known as the **percentage of sales approach**. You have decided to use this approach to generate pro forma financial statements for Borg Corporation for the year 2537.

percentage of sales approach
A financial planning method in which some accounts vary with the level of predicted sales.

THE PRO FORMA INCOME STATEMENT

The Borg Corporation announced projected sales for the year 2537 of $137,500—an increase of 25 percent over 2536. We use the 2536 Borg Corporation income statement and several assumptions to generate the pro forma income statement. From Table 17.3, we see

TABLE 17.5 **Borg Corporation** Pro Forma Income Statement, Year 2537

	Year 2536	Year 2537
Net sales	$110,000	$137,500
Cost of goods sold	(89,000)	(111,250)
Gross profit	$ 21,000	$ 26,250
Depreciation	(3,000)	(3,750)
Other operating expenses	(10,000)	(12,500)
Operating income	$ 8,000	$ 10,000
Interest expense	(2,000)	(2,500)
Pretax income	$ 6,000	$ 7,500
Income taxes	(2,400)	(3,000)
Net income	$ 3,600	$ 4,500
Dividends	(1,080)	(1,350)
Retained earnings	$ 2,520	$ 3,150
Profit margin	3.27%	3.27%
Total costs/Net sales	94.55%	94.55%

that in the year 2536, the ratio of total costs to net sales was about 94.55 percent (actually 94.5454 percent). We assume the ratio of total costs to sales will be 94.55 percent in the year 2537 also.

Table 17.5 is our pro forma income statement for the Borg Corporation for 2537. To generate Table 17.5, we assume that the ratio of cost of goods sold to net sales will be the same in 2537 as it was in 2536 (80.91 percent).

We see in Table 17.4 that depreciation in the year 2536 was \$3,000. Accountants grapple with various methods to produce depreciation schedules. Here, as a practical matter, we simply apply the percentage of sales approach. Depreciation expense as a percentage of sales in 2536 was \$3,000/\$110,000 $\approx$ 2.7272 percent. For the year 2537, we estimate depreciation expense to be (\$3,000/\$110,000) $\times$ \$137,500 = \$3,750. (Note that we multiplied the actual ratio in 2536 to estimated sales in the year 2537.)

The Borg Corporation financed the purchase of the distribution outlets with 5 percent coupon bonds, which represent long-term debt. To estimate the 2537 interest expense, we assume that the Borg Corporation pays 4 percent simple interest on its short-term debt and 8 percent on its existing long-term debt. Given these assumptions, the 2536 interest expense of \$2,000 was split \$400 (\$10,000 $\times$ .04) for short-term debt and \$1,600 (\$20,000 $\times$ .08) for long-term debt. Therefore, the additional \$10,000 in long-term debt added at the end of 2536 will increase interest expense on long-term debt to \$2,100 (\$20,000 $\times$ .08 + \$10,000 $\times$ .05). Adding an assumed \$400 for interest on short-term debt, the total interest expense in the year 2537 will be \$2,500.

Finally, recall that we assume that the ratio of total costs to net sales will be the same in 2537 as it was in 2536 (about 94.55 percent). To achieve this, we assume that the other operating expenses account is our "plug" and if we set this account to \$12,500, we maintain the desired ratio of 94.55 percent.

The effect of assuming that total costs are a constant percentage of sales is to assume that the profit margin (net income/net sales) is constant. To check this, notice that in Table 17.5 Borg Corporation's profit margin was \$3,600/\$110,000 = 3.27 percent in 2536 and \$4,500/\$137,500 = 3.27 percent projected for 2537. In this calculation, a tax rate of 40 percent is assumed for both years.

Next, we need to project the dividend payment. The decision of how much of net income will be paid in dividends is a decision that rests with the management of the Borg Corporation. However, two dividend payment schemes are reasonable: one where the *dollar* payout is the same from year to year, and one where the *percentage* payout is the same from year to year.

We will assume that Borg management has a policy of paying a dividend that is a constant percentage of net income. For 2536, the dividend payout ratio was $1,080/$3,600 = 30 percent. We can also calculate the ratio of the addition to retained earnings to net income, which is $2,520/$3,600 = 70 percent for 2536. This ratio is called the *retention ratio* or *plowback ratio,* and it is equal to one minus the dividend payout ratio. The term "plowback ratio" is logical because if net income is not paid out to the shareholders, it must be retained by the company. Assuming the payout ratio is constant, the projected dividends are $4,500 × .30 = $1,350. Thus, the addition to retained earnings is $3,150.

THE PRO FORMA BALANCE SHEET

To generate a pro forma balance sheet, we start with the balance sheet for 2536 shown in Table 17.1. On this balance sheet, we assume that some of the items vary directly with sales and others do not. For the items that do vary with sales, we express each as a percentage of sales for the year just completed, year 2536. When an item does not vary directly with sales, we write "n/a" for "not applicable." For example, on the asset side, inventory is equal to about 8.2 percent of sales in 2536. We assume that this percentage also applies to 2537, so for each $1 increase in sales, inventory will increase by $.082.

capital intensity ratio
A firm's total assets divided by its sales, or the amount of assets needed to generate $1 in sales.

The ratio of total assets to sales for 2536 is $88,000/$110,000 = .80, or 80 percent. The ratio of total assets to sales is sometimes called the **capital intensity ratio**. This ratio tells us the amount of assets needed to generate $1 in sales. So the higher this ratio, the more capital intensive is the firm. For the Borg Corporation, $.80 in assets was needed to generate $1 in sales in 2536. If we assume that capital intensity ratio is constant, total assets of $110,000 will be needed to generate sales of $137,500 in 2537.

On the liability side of the balance sheet, we have assumed that only accounts payable vary with sales. The reason is that we expect Borg to place more orders with its suppliers as sales increase, so payables will change directly with sales. Short-term debt, on the other hand, represents bank borrowing. This account is not likely to vary directly with sales. Therefore, we write n/a in the "Percent of Sales" column for short-term debt in Table 17.6. Similarly, we write n/a for long-term debt because long-term debt will not vary directly with sales. The same is true for other liabilities and the paid-in capital account.

Retained earnings, however, will change with an increase in sales, but the increase in retained earnings will not be a simple percentage of sales. Instead, we must calculate the change in retained earnings based on our projected net income and dividends, which come from our pro forma income statement.

We can now construct a partial pro forma balance sheet for the Borg Corporation, as shown in Table 17.6. We construct the column labeled 2537 by using the percentage of sales wherever possible to calculate projected amounts. For example, inventory in 2537 is projected to be ($9,000/$110,000) × $137,500 = $11,250. More generally, the ratio of total fixed assets to sales was about 54.5 percent in 2536. For 2537 total fixed assets is projected to be ($60,000/$110,000) × $137,500 = $75,000. This amount represents an increase of $15,000 from the total fixed assets in 2536.

For the items that do not vary directly with sales, note that we initially assume no change and simply write in the existing amounts. You can see the application of this method in the column labeled 2537 in Table 17.6. Notice that the change in retained earnings is projected to be $3,150—which is the amount shown in Table 17.5.

Inspecting the partial pro forma balance sheet for the Borg Corporation, we see that total assets are projected to increase by $22,000 in 2537. However, without additional financing, liabilities and equity will increase by only $4,400, leaving a shortfall, or imbalance, of $22,000 − $4,400 = $17,600. In Table 17.6, to be safe, we have calculated this $17,600 shortfall in two ways: as the difference between total assets ($110,000) and total liabilities

TABLE 17.6 Borg Corporation Partial Pro Forma Balance Sheet, Year 2537

	2536	Approximate Percent of Sales	2537	Change
Current assets				
Cash	$ 2,000	1.8%	$ 2,500	$ 500
Accounts receivable	6,200	5.6	7,750	1,550
Prepaid expenses	1,500	1.4	1,875	375
Materials and supplies	1,300	1.2	1,625	325
Inventory	9,000	8.2	11,250	2,250
Total current assets	$20,000	18.2	$ 25,000	$ 5,000
Total fixed assets	$60,000	54.5	$ 75,000	$15,000
Other assets	$8,000	7.3	$ 10,000	$ 2,000
Total assets	$88,000	80.0	$110,000	$22,000
Current liabilities				
Short-term debt	$10,000	n/a	$ 10,000	$ 0
Accounts payable	5,000	4.5	6,250	1,250
Total current liabilities	$15,000		$ 16,250	$ 1,250
Long-term debt	$30,000	n/a	$ 30,000	$ 0
Other liabilities	3,000	n/a	3,000	0
Total liabilities	$48,000		$ 49,250	$ 1,250
Shareholder equity				
Paid-in capital	$10,000	n/a	$ 10,000	$ 0
Retained earnings	30,000	n/a	33,150	3,150
Total shareholder equity	$40,000		$ 43,150	$ 3,150
Total liabilities and equity	$88,000		$ 92,400	$ 4,400
External financing needed:			$ 17,600	$17,600
Through short-term debt:				$ 2,500
Through long-term debt:				$15,100

and equity ($92,400) and as the difference between the change in total assets ($22,000) and the change in total assets and liabilities ($4,400). We have labeled the shortfall amount as *external financing needed (EFN).*

SCENARIO ONE

The creation of a pro forma income statement and a pro forma balance sheet points out a potentially serious problem with Borg Corporation's projected sales increase of 25 percent—it isn't going to happen unless Borg Corporation can somehow raise $17,600 in new financing. For analysts working for the Borg Corporation, this is a good example of how the planning process can point out problems and potential conflicts. For example, if the Borg Corporation had a goal of not raising new financing, then an increase in sales of 25 percent is not possible.

If we take the need for $17,600 in new financing as given, we know that the Borg Corporation has three possible sources: short-term debt, long-term debt, and new equity. The choice of the exact combination of the three sources of financing is a decision that the management of the Borg Corporation must make. For illustration, however, we will choose one of the many possible combinations.

Suppose the Borg Corporation decides to borrow the needed funds, some via short-term debt and some via long-term debt. In Table 17.6, you can see that current assets increased by \$5,000, but current liabilities increased only by \$1,250 (the increase in accounts payable). If the Borg Corporation wanted to keep the ratio between current assets and current liabilities constant, it should borrow \$2,500 in short-term debt. In 2536, the ratio between total current assets and total current liabilities was 4 to 3, or 1.3333 (\$20,000/\$15,000). In 2537, total current assets are \$25,000, which means total current liabilities should be \$18,750, or \$2,500 more than the amount shown in Table 17.6.

If Borg borrows \$2,500 in short-term debt, this leaves \$15,100 to be raised by issuing additional long-term debt. These financing amounts are shown at the bottom of Table 17.6. Table 17.7 shows a completed pro forma balance sheet given this assumed financing decision.

We have used a combination of short-term debt and long-term debt to solve the financing problem for the Borg Corporation. It is extremely important for us to emphasize that this is only one possible strategy—and it might not even be the best strategy for the Borg Corporation. As analysts, we could (and should) investigate many other scenarios. For example, we would have to ask how the increased debt load would affect future earnings of the company.

TABLE 17.7 **Borg Corporation** Pro Forma Balance Sheet, Year 2537

	2536	Approximate Percent of Sales	2537	Change
Current assets				
Cash	\$ 2,000	1.8%	\$ 2,500	\$ 500
Accounts receivable	6,200	5.6	7,750	1,550
Prepaid expenses	1,500	1.4	1,875	375
Materials and supplies	1,300	1.2	1,625	325
Inventory	9,000	8.2	11,250	2,250
Total current assets	\$20,000	18.2	\$ 25,000	\$ 5,000
Total fixed assets	\$60,000	54.5	\$ 75,000	\$15,000
Other assets	\$ 8,000	7.3	\$ 10,000	\$ 2,000
Total assets	\$88,000	80.0	\$110,000	\$22,000
Current liabilities				
Short-term debt	\$10,000	n/a	\$ 12,500	\$ 2,500
Accounts payable	5,000	4.5	6,250	1,250
Total current liabilities	\$15,000		\$ 18,750	\$ 3,750
Long-term debt	\$30,000	n/a	\$ 45,100	\$15,100
Other liabilities	3,000	n/a	3,000	0
Total liabilities	\$48,000	n/a	\$ 66,850	\$18,850
Shareholder equity				
Paid-in capital	\$10,000	n/a	\$ 10,000	\$ 0
Retained earnings	30,000	n/a	33,150	3,150
Total shareholder equity	\$40,000		\$ 43,150	\$ 3,150
Total liabilities and equity	\$88,000		\$110,000	\$22,000
External financing needed (EFN):			\$ 0	\$ 0

SCENARIO TWO

The assumption that assets are a fixed percentage of sales is convenient, but it may not be suitable in many cases. In particular, we made a hidden assumption when we constructed pro forma financial statements for the Borg Corporation: We assumed that the Borg Corporation was using its fixed assets at 100 percent of capacity, because any increase in sales led to an increase in fixed assets. For most businesses, there would be some slack, or excess capacity, and production could be increased by, perhaps, running an extra shift or utilizing spare equipment.

If we assume that the Borg Corporation is running at 75 percent of capacity, then the need for external funds will be quite different. When we say "75 percent of capacity," we mean that the current sales level is 75 percent of the full-capacity sales level:

$$\text{Current sales} = \$110{,}000 = .75 \times \text{Full-capacity sales}$$
$$\text{Full-capacity sales} = \$110{,}000/.75 = \$146{,}667$$

This calculation tells us that sales could increase by one-third, from \$110,000 to \$146,667, before any new fixed assets would be needed.

In Scenario One, we assumed that adding \$15,000 in net fixed assets would be necessary. In our current scenario, no spending on fixed assets is needed, because sales are projected to rise only to \$137,500, which is substantially less than the \$146,667 full-capacity sales level. As a result, our Scenario One estimate of \$17,600 in external funds needed is too high. In fact, an argument could be made in Scenario Two that the level of external funds needed is \$2,600.

To begin, you can see in Table 17.8 that we have now written n/a next to the total fixed assets account and we have written in a value of \$60,000 (the same as for the year 2536). When

TABLE 17.8 **Borg Corporation** Pro Forma Balance Sheet, Year 2537

	2536	Percent of Sales	2537	Change
Current assets				
Cash	\$ 2,000	1.8%	\$ 2,500	\$ 500
Accounts receivable	6,200	5.6	7,750	1,550
Prepaid expenses	1,500	1.4	1,875	375
Materials and supplies	1,300	1.2	1,625	325
Inventory	9,000	8.2	11,250	2,250
Total current assets	\$20,000	18.2	\$25,000	\$5,000
Total fixed assets	\$60,000	n/a	\$60,000	\$ 0
Other assets	\$ 8,000	7.3	\$10,000	\$2,000
Total assets	\$88,000		\$95,000	\$7,000
Current liabilities				
Short-term debt	\$10,000	n/a	\$12,600	\$2,600
Accounts payable	5,000	4.5	6,250	1,250
Total current liabilities	\$15,000		\$18,850	\$3,850
Long-term debt	\$30,000	n/a	\$30,000	\$ 0
Other liabilities	3,000	n/a	3,000	0
Total liabilities	\$48,000	n/a	\$51,850	\$3,850
Shareholder equity				
Paid-in capital	\$10,000	n/a	\$10,000	\$ 0
Retained earnings	30,000	n/a	33,150	3,150
Total shareholder equity	\$40,000		\$43,150	\$3,150
Total liabilities and equity	\$88,000		\$95,000	\$7,000

there is no change assumed for the total fixed assets account, the total assets account increases by $7,000. On the liability side of the balance sheet as shown in Table 17.5, a sales level of $137,500 generates an increase of $3,150 in retained earnings. In addition, this sales level means that the accounts payable account will increase by $1,250. The difference between the increase in total assets and the increase in total liabilities and equity would be $2,600 without any external financing ($7,000 − $3,150 − $1,250). In Table 17.8, a completed year 2537 pro forma balance sheet, we see that this is the amount that the short-term debt account has increased. That is, we have assumed that the Borg Corporation will use only short-term debt as its EFN source. You will note, however, that this assumption means that the ratio between total current assets and total current liabilities will decrease (slightly).

EXAMPLE 17.1

EFN and Capacity Usage

Suppose the Borg Corporation was operating at 88 percent of capacity. What would sales be at full capacity? What is the EFN in this case? What is the capital intensity ratio at full capacity?

Full-capacity sales would be $110,000/.88 = $125,000. From Table 17.1, we know that fixed assets are $60,000. At full capacity, the ratio of fixed assets to sales is $60,000/$125,000 = .48. This tells us that the Borg Corporation needs $.48 in fixed assets for every $1 in sales once the Borg Corporation reaches full capacity. At the projected sales level of $137,500, the Borg Corporation needs $137,500 × .48 = $66,000 in fixed assets. This is $9,000 less than the year 2537 value of $75,000 shown in Table 17.6. Therefore, EFN is $17,600 − $9,000 = $8,600. Current assets and other assets would still be $25,000 and $10,000, respectively, so total assets would be $101,000. The capital intensity ratio would then be $101,000/$137,500 = .7345.

CHECK THIS

17.3a What is the basic idea behind the percentage of sales approach?

17.3b Unless it is modified, what does the percentage of sales approach assume about fixed asset capacity usage?

PROJECTED PROFITABILITY AND PRICE RATIOS

In addition to preparing pro forma financial statements, you also decide to calculate projected profitability ratios and per-share values under the new sales forecast. These are reported immediately below and compared with their original year-end values.

	Year 2536	Year 2537
Gross margin	19.09%	19.09%
Operating margin	7.27%	7.27%
Return on assets (ROA)	4.09%	4.09%/4.74%
Return on equity (ROE)	9.00%	10.43%
Book value per share (BVPS)	$20	$21.57
Earnings per share (EPS)	$ 1.80	$ 2.25
Cash flow per share (CFPS)	$ 3.30	$ 4.25

Note that two ROA numbers are provided for 2537. The first is from Scenario One, where we assume Borg is already running at 100 percent capacity. The second is from Scenario Two, where we assume Borg is running at 75 percent capacity.

One common method of analysis is to calculate projected stock prices under the new sales scenario using prior-period price ratios and projected per-share values from pro forma financial statements. For Borg Corporation, you decide to take your previously calculated year-end 2536 price ratios and multiply each ratio by its corresponding pro forma per-share value. The results of these projected stock price calculations (rounded) are shown immediately below.

$$P/B \times BVPS = 2 \times \$21.57 = \$43.14$$
$$P/E \times EPS = 22.22 \times \$2.25 = \$50.00$$
$$P/CF \times CFPS = 12.12 \times \$4.25 = \$51.51$$

Which projected stock price is correct? Well, it clearly depends on which sales level is realized and which price ratio the financial markets will actually use to value Borg Corporation's stock. This is where experience and breadth of knowledge count immensely. Of course, no one can make perfectly accurate predictions, but the analyst's job is to expertly assess the situation and make an investment recommendation supported by reasonable facts and investigation. But some analysts are better than others. Like professional baseball players, professional stock analysts with better batting averages can do very well financially.

17.4 Starbucks Corporation Case Study

After carefully reading the analysis of Borg Corporation, you should have a reasonably clear picture of how to do an earnings and cash flow analysis using pro forma financial statements. In this section, we present an analysis based on the 2007 financial statements for Starbucks Corporation. As you will see, using data for a real company is challenging.

WWW

Visit Starbucks Web site at www.starbucks.com

This section begins with a review of the 2007 financial statements for Starbucks. We then proceed to analyze the effects on earnings and cash flow that might result from two sales projection scenarios. The analysis is similar to that for Borg Corporation, with a few important differences. Note that amounts shown are in thousands of dollars (except earnings per share).

Table 17.9 is the 2007 condensed balance sheet for Starbucks. This balance sheet shows that at fiscal year-end 2007 (September 28, 2007), Starbucks had \$5,344 million of total assets and \$2,284 million of shareholder equity. In Table 17.10, which is the 2007 condensed income statement for Starbucks, the bottom line reveals that Starbucks earned \$672.6 million in net income from \$9,411 million in net revenues.

From these values, we calculate Starbucks return on assets (ROA) as 12.6 percent and return on equity (ROE) as 29.4 percent. As of its fiscal year-end date, Starbucks Corporation had 770.1 million shares outstanding. Therefore, earnings per share in 2007 were \$.87, and book value per share was \$2.97. Based on a fiscal year-end 2007 stock price of \$26.20, the price-book ratio for Starbucks was 8.82, and the price-earnings ratio was 30.11.

Starbucks stock price gradually decreased in value before the company filed its annual financial information with the SEC on November 29, 2007. At the close of trading on December 14, 2007, Starbucks stock price closed at \$21.25. At this time, the price-book ratio for Starbucks was 7.15, and the price-earnings ratio was 24.43.

PRO FORMA INCOME STATEMENT

To construct a 2008 pro forma income statement for Starbucks, we use forecasted sales and the percentage of sales approach, just as we did for the Borg Corporation. As shown in the nearby *Work the Web* box, we visited finance.yahoo.com and entered the ticker symbol for Starbucks, SBUX.

Clicking on the "Analyst Estimates" link, we saw that the highest estimate for Starbucks's 2008 revenue was \$11.20 billion, or an increase of about 19 percent from Starbucks's 2007 revenue level of \$9.41 billion. However, finding ourselves in a frothy

TABLE 17.13 Starbucks Corporation Pro Forma Balance Sheet, 2008 ($ in 000's)

	2007	Percent of Sales	2008 (High)	Change	2008 (Low)	Change
Current assets						
Cash and cash equivalents	$ 281,261	3.0%	$ 351,000	$ 69,739	$ 460,119	$ 178,858
Short-term investments	157,433	1.7	198,900	41,467	187,000	29,567
Accounts receivable	287,925	3.1	362,700	74,775	341,000	53,075
Inventory	691,658	7.3	854,100	162,442	803,000	111,342
Prepaid expenses	148,757	1.6	187,200	38,443	176,000	27,243
Deferred income taxes	129,453	1.4	163,800	34,347	154,000	24,547
Total current assets	$1,696,487		$2,117,700	$421,213	$2,121,119	$ 424,632
Fixed assets						
Long-term investments	$ 279,868	3.0%	$ 351,000	$ 71,132	$ 330,000	$ 50,132
Property, plant, and equipment, net	2,890,433	30.7	3,591,900	701,467	3,377,000	486,567
Other assets	219,422	2.3	269,100	49,678	253,000	33,578
Total fixed assets	$3,389,723	36.0%	$4,212,000	$ 822,277	$3,960,000	$ 570,277
Goodwill	$ 215,625	2.3%	$ 269,100	$ 53,475	$ 253,000	$ 37,375
Other intangible assets	42,043	0.4	46,800	4,757	44,000	1,957
Total assets	$5,343,878	56.8%	$6,645,600	$1,301,722	$6,378,119	$1,034,241
Current liabilities						
Accounts payable	$ 390,836	4.2%	$ 491,400	$ 100,564	$ 462,000	$ 71,164
Accrued expenses	1,053,707	11.2	1,310,400	256,693	1,232,000	178,293
Short-term debt	711,023	n/a	711,023	0	711,023	0
Total current liabilities	$2,155,566		$2,512,823	$ 357,257	$2,405,023	$ 249,457
Long-term debt	$ 550,121	n/a	$ 659,861	$ 109,740	$ 550,121	0
Other long-term liabilities	354,074	n/a	354,074	0	354,074	0
Total liabilities	$3,059,761		$3,526,758	$ 466,997	$3,309,218	$ 249,457
Shareholder equity						
Paid-in capital & other equity	$ 94,751	n/a	$ 94,751	$ 0	$ 94,751	$ 0
Retained earnings	2,189,366	n/a	3,024,091	834,725	2,974,150	784,784
Total stockholder equity	$2,284,117		$3,118,842	$ 834,725	$3,068,901	$ 784,784
Total liabilities and equity	$5,343,878		$6,645,600	$1,301,722	$6,378,119	$1,034,241
External financing needed:			$ 0	$ 0	$ 0	$ 0

Starbucks simply issues long-term debt for their external financing requirement. Using the low sales forecast, we assume that management puts the excess cash generated into the cash and cash equivalent accounts. Notice that the cash account balance would be $330,000 using the percentage of sales approach. The balance of $460,119 reflects the percentage of sales level plus $130,119. Table 17.13 presents these pro forma balance sheets.

CHECK THIS

17.4a Use the high sales estimate and data in Table 17.12 to determine the level of external financing needed if short-term and long-term investments were held at their 2007 levels.

17.4b Using the high sales estimate and data in Table 17.12, do you think it is more likely that Starbucks will use short-term or long-term debt if external financing needed was $109,740,000? What financial data support your answer?

VALUING STARBUCKS USING RATIO ANALYSIS

We now turn our attention to valuing Starbucks using ratio analysis and the pro forma income statement and balance sheets that we generated. Immediately below, we report actual and projected profitability and per-share values for 2007 and 2008.

	2007	2008 (High Sales Forecast)	2008 (Low Sales Forecast)
Gross margin	57.5%	57.5%	57.5%
Operating margin	10.1%	10.0%	10.0%
Return on assets (ROA)	12.6%	12.6%	12.3%
Return on equity (ROE)	29.4%	26.8%	25.6%
Earnings per share (EPS)	$0.87	$1.08	$1.02
Book value per share (BVPS)	$2.97	$4.05	$3.99

For Starbucks, taking the 2007 price ratios and multiplying each ratio by its corresponding projected 2008 per-share value results in the following stock price calculations:

Using Fiscal Year-End Stock Price of $26.20			2008 (High Sales Forecast)	2008 (Low Sales Forecast)
P/E ratio	30.11	P/E × EPS	$32.52	$30.71
P/B ratio	8.82	P/B × BVPS	$35.72	$35.19
Using SEC Reporting Date Stock Price of $21.25			**2006 (High Sales Forecast)**	**2006 (Low Sales Forecast)**
P/E ratio	24.43	P/E × EPS	$26.38	$24.92
P/B ratio	7.15	P/B × BVPS	$28.96	$28.53

Using ratio analysis, we generate Starbucks's prices that range from $24.92 to $35.72. Our estimated price range for Starbucks covers most of the price range ($23–$37) forecast by actual analysts (see the preceding *Work the Web* box).

Looking across sales forecasts, you can see that the prices we generate for Starbucks do not differ greatly. In fact, our projected Starbucks's stock prices are more sensitive to the values picked for the price-earnings (P/E) ratio and price-book (P/B) ratio than they are to the value of the sales forecast picked.

VALUING STARBUCKS USING A TWO-STAGE RESIDUAL INCOME MODEL

In a previous chapter, we introduced the residual income model (RIM), which is an appropriate valuation model to use when you are trying to value the shares of a company, like Starbucks, that does not pay dividends. The version of RIM that we introduced earlier in the text incorporated the assumption that earnings would grow at a constant rate forever. However, for a fast-growing company like Starbucks, this is not really a reasonable assumption. Eventually, the growth rate in earnings for Starbucks must decrease.

Fortunately for us, the RIM can be modified to reflect the assumption that earnings grow at rate g_1 for T periods and then grow at rate g_2 forever thereafter. The RIM in this case is:

$$P_0 = BVPS_0 + \frac{EPS_0(1 + g_1) - BVPS_0 \times k}{k - g_1}\left[1 - \left(\frac{1 + g_1}{1 + k}\right)^T\right] + \frac{EPS_0\,(1 + g_1)^T\,(1 + g_2) - BVPS_0(1 + k)^T k}{(k - g_2)/(1 + k)^T} \quad (17.3)$$

In equation (17.3) we need values for earnings per share, EPS_0, and book value per share, $BVPS_0$, as of time 0 (2007 in this case). We can pluck these values, \$.87 and \$2.97, respectively, from data provided above. However, we need earnings growth rates for the two periods, and an appropriate discount rate.

From the preceding *Work the Web* box, we can see that analysts collectively think that Starbucks will be able to grow earnings at 21 percent for the next five years. After that, we will assume that Starbucks will be able to grow earnings *forever* at 5 percent. Even though this is a significant dropoff from 21 percent, it is still quite a bit higher than the long-term real growth rate of the U.S. economy, which is 3 percent. Therefore, in equation (17.3), $g_1 = .21$ and $g_2 = .05$.

We calculate an initial discount rate using the capital asset pricing model (CAPM). If we use a risk-free rate of 3.1 percent, a market risk premium of 9 percent, and a Starbucks beta of .80 (from *Value Line*), the discount rate, k, is $3.1 + .80 \times 9.0 = 10.3\%$.

Using these inputs into equation (17.3), we obtain this value for Starbucks:

$$P_0 = 2.97 + \frac{.87 \times 1.21 - 2.97 \times .103}{.103 - .21}\left[1 - \left(\frac{1.21}{1.103}\right)^5\right] + \frac{.87 \times (1.21)^5 \times 1.05 - 2.97 \times (1.103)^5 \times .103}{(.103 - .05)/(1.103)^5}$$

$$= 2.97 + 4.11 + 57.60 = \$64.68$$

This estimate is about 200 percent higher than the Starbucks stock price of \$21.25, which was observed at the time Starbucks filed its financial information with the SEC. Like any good analyst would, we now vary our inputs to see how sensitive the estimated price is to changes in these inputs. Even though we could change the growth rates, we will not. Instead, we will vary the discount rate and the length of time that Starbucks will exhibit an earnings growth rate of 21 percent.

We generate a set of additional discount rates by varying the beta for Starbucks. Beginning with the value of .80, we selected four other beta values, while keeping the risk-free rate and the market risk premium the same as before. We suspect that the length of time that Starbucks will grow earnings at the robust rate of 21 percent could be too long. But we cannot be sure, so we vary this length of time from three to five years. We then recalculate a Starbucks price for each of these combinations. The results appear immediately below.

		Length of Time Starbucks Grows Earnings at 21%		
Beta	**Discount Rate**	**3 Years**	**4 Years**	**5 Years**
0.70	9.4	42.60	57.01	76.14
0.80	10.3	**35.79**	48.14	64.68
0.90	11.2	**30.84**	41.67	56.30
1.00	12.1	**27.04**	**36.69**	49.81
1.10	13.0	**24.01**	**32.67**	44.55

From this sensitivity analysis, it appears that both the discount rate and the length of time that Starbucks grows its earnings by 21 percent are important in estimating a value for Starbucks. We highlighted six values that are in line with the Starbucks prices we generated with our ratio analysis and observed in our nearby *Work the Web* box. For an analyst, performing various "what-if" scenarios concerning input values that are used in valuation formulas is good practice.

VALUING STARBUCKS: WHAT DOES THE MARKET SAY?

As with many publicly traded companies, analysts frequently offer conflicting opinions concerning the future growth prospects of Starbucks and its current value. You can read an opinion about Starbucks in our nearby *Investment Updates* box. If you are a believer in the efficient markets hypothesis, the easiest way to value Starbucks is to look at what its shares are selling for in the open market. After all, the market price for Starbucks shares is the result of the collective assessment from thousands of analysts and investors. If, however, you believe that you are an above-average prognosticator for future sales and earnings growth for Starbucks, you can use the methods in this chapter to assist you in your personal investing decisions concerning Starbucks and other companies.

The methods presented in this chapter are intended to help you become a better financial analyst. Calibrating these methods to a publicly traded company is a useful way to get familiar with how inputs and assumptions affect the resulting valuation. These methods could be valuable to you if you are an internal analyst. For example, suppose you are asked to calculate whether the company you work for needs more financing to meet its expected sales growth levels. You can use the percentage of sales approach when you perform this task.

The methods in this chapter are especially useful if you are trying to value a nontraded company after you are given its financial data. Someday, you might find yourself working on calculating a per-share tender offer in a hostile takeover attempt. In any case, we are confident that this chapter will help you become more "financial-statement literate" and help you develop as a financial analyst.

17.5 Summary and Conclusions

In this chapter, we focus on earnings and cash flow analysis using financial statement information. Several important aspects of financial statements and their use were covered. We summarize these points by the important concepts of the chapter.

1. Obtaining financial information about companies.

A. Good financial analysis begins with good financial information. A primary source of financial information is a company's annual report. In addition, the annual 10K report and the quarterly 10Q updates filed with the SEC are available from the EDGAR archives.

B. The Internet is a convenient source of financial information about many companies. For example, the New York Stock Exchange Web site (www.nyse.com) provides a directory of Web sites for companies whose stock trades on the exchange.

2. Reading basic financial statements.

A. Three financial statements are essential reading for securities analysts: the balance sheet, the income statement, and the cash flow statement. The balance sheet has three sections: assets, liabilities, and equity. A fundamental accounting identity for balance sheets states that assets equal liabilities plus equity.

B. The income statement reports revenues and expenses. Companies use their net income to pay dividends or to finance future growth. Net income is the "bottom line" for a company.

C. The cash flow statement reports how cash was generated and where it was used. The cash flow statement assigns all cash flows to one of three categories: operating cash flow, investment cash flow, or financing cash flow.

3. Using performance and price ratios.

A. Profitability ratios based on financial statement information are often reported to help investors interpret a company's operating efficiency. Standard profitability ratios include gross margin, operating margin, return on assets (ROA), and return on equity (ROE).

B. Annual reports, 10Ks, and 10Qs also report per-share calculations of book value, earnings, and operating cash flow, respectively. If we divide the stock price by these per-share values, we get three important ratios: the price to book ratio (P/B), the price-earnings ratio (P/E), and the cash flow per share (CFPS).

4. Using the percentage of sales method in financial forecasting.

A. Financial analysts often make projections about sales growth, futures costs, and net income. These forecasts can be used to construct a forecasted, or pro forma, set of financial statements.

B. The percentage of sales approach is a method analysts can use to construct pro forma financial statements. This approach is based on the basic idea of separating the income statement and balance sheet items into two groups: those that do vary directly with sales and those that do not. Given a sales forecast, analysts can use the percentage of sales approach to calculate how much financing the firm will need to support the predicted sales level.

GET REAL

This chapter delves deeper into earnings and cash flow concepts, which are two of the most important tools of fundamental analysis. It focuses on using financial statement information to develop pro forma numbers to use in stock valuation. How should you, as an investor or investment manager, get started putting this information to work? The answer is that you need to get your fingers dirty! Dig into the financial statements of a few companies and develop your own pro forma financial statements.

Excellent sources for financial statement information are the SEC Edgar data base (www.sec.gov) and Free EDGAR (www.freeedgar.com). Other useful online sources are Report Gallery (www.reportgallery.com), Annual Report Service (www.annualreportservice.com), and Free Annual Reports (www.prars.com). Other useful Internet sites for company analysis are Global Reports (www.global-reports.com) and Corporate Information (www.corporateinformation.com).

A good place to start is to download the most recent financial reports for Starbucks from SEC Edgar (www.sec.gov) or the Starbucks company Web site (www.starbucks.com). Then try your hand at developing pro forma financial statements for Starbucks similar to the ones developed in this chapter.

A next step is to pick a company you are interested in and examine its financial statements. As you read a company's financial statements, an important exercise is to try to understand what each number really represents. Why is it there? Is it a cash or market value? Or is it just an accounting number (like depreciation)? Once you are familiar with a company's current financial statements, try to develop pro forma statements for various sales scenarios as was done in this chapter. You really can learn a lot by doing this.

Key Terms

10K 546
10Q 546
asset 547
balance sheet 547
capital intensity ratio 555
cash flow 550
cash flow statement 547
EDGAR 546
equity 547
financing cash flow 550
income 549
income statement 547
investment cash flow 550
liability 547
material nonpublic information 546
noncash items 550
operating cash flow 550
percentage of sales approach 553
pro forma financial statements 553
Regulation FD 546
return on assets (ROA) 551
return on equity (ROE) 551

Chapter Review Problems and Self-Test

1. **Margin Calculations** Use the following income statement for Paul Bunyan Lumber Co. to calculate gross and operating margins.

Paul Bunyan Lumber 2008 Income Statement	
Net sales	$8,000
Cost of goods sold	(6,400)
Gross profit	$1,600
Operating expenses	(400)
Operating income	$1,200
Other income	80
Net interest expense	(120)
Pretax income	$1,160
Income tax	(464)
Net income	$ 696
Earnings per share	$ 3.48
Recent share price	$76.56

2. **Return Calculations** Use the following balance sheet for Paul Bunyan Lumber Co. along with the income statement in the previous question to calculate return on assets and return on equity.

Paul Bunyan Lumber 2008 Balance Sheet	
Cash and cash equivalents	$ 400
Operating assets	400
Property, plant, and equipment	3,160
Other assets	216
Total assets	$4,176
Current liabilities	$ 720
Long-term debt	612
Other liabilities	60
Total liabilities	$1,392
Paid-in capital	$ 600
Retained earnings	2,184
Total shareholder equity	$2,784
Total liabilities and equity	$4,176

3. **Pro Forma Income Statements** Prepare a pro forma income statement for Paul Bunyan Lumber Co. assuming a 5 percent increase in sales. Based only on the pro forma income statement, what is the projected stock price? (*Hint:* What is the price-earnings ratio?)

Answers to Self-Test Problems

1. Gross margin is $1,600/$8,000 = 20%
   Operating margin is $1,200/$8,000 = 15%
2. Return on assets is $696/$4,176 = 16.67%
   Return on equity is $696/$2,784 = 25%
3. With 5 percent sales growth, sales will rise to $8,400 from $8,000. The pro forma income statement follows. A constant gross margin is assumed, implying that cost of goods sold will also rise by 5 percent. A constant tax rate of 40 percent is used.

Paul Bunyan Lumber Pro Forma 2009 Income Statement	
Net sales	$8,400
Cost of goods sold	(6,720)
Gross profit	$1,680
Operating expenses	(400)
Operating income	$1,280
Other income	80
Net interest expense	(120)
Pretax income	$1,240
Income tax	(496)
Net income	$ 744
Earnings per share	$3.72

To get a projected stock price, notice that the 2008 price-earnings ratio was $76.56/$3.48 = 22. Using this ratio as a benchmark, the pro forma earnings of $3.72 imply a stock price of 22 × $3.72 = $81.84.

Test Your Investment Quotient

For the remaining questions and problems, the circled numbers in the margin refer to the corresponding learning objective in this chapter.

IQ

CFA® PROBLEMS

(2) 1. **Balance Sheet Assets** White Company assets as of December 31, 2007:

Cash and cash equivalents	$ 150
Operating assets	$1,190
Property, plant, and equipment	$1,460
Total assets	$2,800

White Co. experienced the following events in 2008:

Old equipment that cost $120 and that was fully depreciated was scrapped

Depreciation expense was $125

Cash payments for new equipment were $200

Based on the information above, what was White Co.'s net amount of property, plant, and equipment at the end of 2008?

a. $1,415
b. $1,535
c. $1,655
d. $1,660

(2) 2. **Cash Flow** Cash flow per share is calculated as

a. Net cash flow/Shares outstanding.
b. Operating cash flow/Shares outstanding.
c. Investing cash flow/Shares outstanding.
d. Financing cash flow/Shares outstanding.

(2) 3. **Cash Flow** Which of the following is not an adjustment to net income used to obtain operating cash flow?

a. Changes in operating assets
b. Changes in current liabilities
c. Loss on sale of assets
d. Dividends paid

2 **4. Cash Flow** The difference between net income and operating cash flow is at least partially accounted for by which of the following items?

a. Retained earnings
b. Cash and cash equivalents
c. Depreciation
d. Dividends paid

3 **5. Financial Ratios** Which of the following profitability ratios is incorrect?

a. Gross margin = Gross profit/Cost of goods sold
b. Operating margin = Operating income/Net sales
c. Return on assets = Net income/Total assets
d. Return on equity = Net income/Shareholder equity

3 **6. Financial Ratios** Which of the following per-share ratios is incorrect?

a. Book value per share = Total assets/Shares outstanding
b. Earnings per share = Net income/Shares outstanding
c. Cash flow per share = Operating cash flow/Shares outstanding
d. Dividends per share = Dividends paid/Shares outstanding

2 **7. Dividend Payment** A dividend payment has which of the following effects on the balance sheet?

a. An increase in shares outstanding
b. A decrease in shareholder equity
c. A decrease in paid-in capital
d. An increase in retained earnings

4 **8. Sales Growth** A particular firm is operating at less than full capacity. If sales are expected to grow at only a modest rate next year, which of the following is true?

a. Assets will likely increase faster than sales in the short-term future.
b. Dividends should be reduced to conserve cash.
c. No further financial planning should be performed until the sales growth rate increases.
d. External financing will likely not be needed next year.

4 **9. Capacity Usage** Which of the following is true regarding the full-capacity sales level of a firm?

a. A firm that is operating at less than full capacity will never need external financing.
b. For a firm that is operating at less than full capacity, fixed assets will typically increase at the same rate as sales.
c. A firm with excess capacity has the room to expand without increasing its investment in fixed assets.
d. Only firms operating at full capacity can grow rapidly.

Use the following raw data to answer the next four questions:

Net income:	$16
Depreciation/amortization:	$4
Repurchase of outstanding common stock:	$10
Issuance of new debt:	$18
Sale of property:	$12
Purchase of equipment:	$14
Dividend payments:	$4

2 **10. Cash Flow Analysis** Operating cash flow is

a. $20
b. $16
c. $12
d. $30

2 **11. Cash Flow Analysis** Investing cash flow is

a. $2
b. $(2)
c. $12
d. $(12)

2 **12. Cash Flow Analysis** Financing cash flow is

a. $8
b. $(8)

c. $4
d. $(4)

(2) **13. Cash Flow Analysis** Net cash increase is

a. $18
b. $20
c. $22
d. $24

Use the following financial data to answer the next three questions:

Cash payments for interest:	$ (12)
Retirement of common stock:	$ (32)
Cash payments to merchandise suppliers:	$ (85)
Purchase of land:	$ (8)
Sale of equipment:	$30
Payments of dividends:	$ (37)
Cash payment for salaries:	$ (35)
Cash collection from customers:	$260
Purchase of equipment:	$(40)

CFA® PROBLEMS

(2) **14. Cash Flow Analysis** Cash flows from operating activities are

a. $91
b. $128
c. $140
d. $175

CFA® PROBLEMS

(2) **15. Cash Flow Analysis** Cash flows from investing activities are

a. $(67)
b. $(48)
c. $(18)
d. $(10)

CFA® PROBLEMS

(2) **16. Cash Flow Analysis** Cash flows from financing activities are

a. $(81)
b. $(69)
c. $(49)
d. $(37)

CFA® PROBLEMS

(2) **17. Cash Flow Analysis** A firm has net sales of $3,000, cash expenses (including taxes) of $1,400, and depreciation of $500. If accounts receivable increase over the period by $400, cash flow from operations equals

a. $1,200
b. $1,600
c. $1,700
d. $2,100

CFA® PROBLEMS

(2) **18. Cash Flow Analysis** A firm using straight-line depreciation reports gross investment in fixed assets of $80 million, accumulated depreciation of $45 million, and annual depreciation expense of $5 million. The approximate average age of fixed assets is

a. 7 years
b. 9 years
c. 15 years
d. 16 years

(2) **19. Preferred Dividends** What proportion of preferred stock dividends received by a corporation is normally exempt from federal income taxation?

a. 25–35 percent
b. 50–60 percent
c. 70–80 percent
d. 90–100 percent

(3) **20. Price Ratios** All else the same, which of the following ratios is unaffected by an increase in depreciation?

a. Price-earnings (P/E)
b. Price-book (P/B)
c. Price-cash flow (P/CF)
d. Price-sales (P/S)

Concept Questions

1 1. **10K and 10Q** What are the 10K and 10Q reports? Who are they filed by? What do they contain? Who are they filed with? What is the easiest way to retrieve one?

4 2. **Sales Forecast** Why do you think most long-term financial planning begins with sales forecasts? Put differently, why are future sales the key input?

2 3. **Current Events** What makes current assets and liabilities "current"? Are operating assets "current"?

2 4. **Income and EPS** What is the relationship between net income and earnings per share (EPS)?

2 5. **Noncash Items** Why do we say depreciation is a "noncash item"?

2 6. **Cash Flow** What are the three sections on a standard cash flow statement?

2 7. **Operating Cash Flow** In the context of the standard cash flow statement, what is operating cash flow?

3 8. **Comparing ROE and ROA** Both ROA and ROE measure profitability. Which one is more useful for comparing two companies? Why?

2 9. **Retained Earnings** What is the difference between the "retained earnings" number on the income statement and the balance sheet?

3 10. **Gross!** What is the difference between gross margin and operating margin? What do they tell us? Generally speaking, are larger or smaller values better?

3 11. **More Gross** Which is larger, gross margin or operating margin? Can either be negative? Can both?

2 12. **Dividends and Taxes** Are dividends paid a tax-deductible expense to the paying company? Suppose a company receives dividends from another. How are these taxed?

2 13. **Cash Flow** The bottom line on a standard cash flow statement is calculated how? What exactly does it represent?

2 14. **Retained Earnings** Take a look at the balance sheet for Starbucks (Table 17.12). On it, retained earnings are about \$2.2 billion. How do you interpret this amount? Does it mean that Starbucks has \$2.2 billion in cash available to spend?

CFA® PROBLEMS

3 15. **Price Ratios** Peninsular Research has a client who has inquired about the valuation method best suited for comparison of companies in an industry that has the following characteristics:

Principal competitors within the industry are located in the United States, France, Japan, and Brazil.
The industry is currently operating at a cyclical low, with many firms reporting losses.
The industry is subject to rapid technological change.

John Jones, CFA, recommends that the client consider the price-earnings ratio, price-book value ratio, and price-sales ratio. Determine which one of the three valuation ratios is most appropriate for comparing companies in this industry. Support your answer with two reasons that make that ratio superior to either of the other two ratios.

Questions and Problems

Core Questions

2 1. **Income Statements** Given the following information for Smashville, Inc., construct an income statement for the year:

Cost of goods sold:	\$149,000
Investment income:	\$1,900
Net sales:	\$294,000
Operating expense:	\$62,000
Interest expense:	\$6,200
Dividends:	\$4,300
Tax rate:	35%

What are retained earnings for the year?

TABLE 18.1 Jack Russell Corp. Five-Year Note Issue

Issue amount	$20 million	Note issue total face value is $20 million
Issue date	12/15/2007	Notes offered to the public in December 2007
Maturity date	12/31/2012	Remaining principal due December 31, 2012
Face value	$1,000	Face value denomination is $1,000 per note
Coupon interest	$100 per annum	Annual coupons are $100 per note
Coupon dates	6/30, 12/31	Coupons are paid semiannually
Offering price	100	Offer price is 100 percent of face value
Yield to maturity	10%	Based on stated offer price
Call provision	Not callable	Notes may not be paid off before maturity
Security	None	Notes are unsecured
Rating	Not rated	Privately placed note issue

means 100 percent of the $1,000 face value, the notes have a yield to maturity of 10 percent. The notes are not callable, which means that the debt may not be paid off before maturity.

unsecured debt
Bonds, notes, or other debt issued with no specific collateral pledged as security for the bond issue.

The Jack Russell Corp. notes are **unsecured debt**, which means that no specific collateral has been pledged as security for the notes. In the event that the issuer defaults on its promised payments, the noteholders may take legal action to acquire sufficient assets of the company to settle their claims as creditors.

When issued, the Jack Russell Corp. notes were not reviewed by a rating agency like Moody's or Standard & Poor's. Thus, the notes are unrated. If the notes were to be assigned a credit rating, they would probably be rated as "junk grade." The term "junk," commonly used for high-risk debt issues, is unduly pejorative. After all, the company must repay the debt. However, if the company is in a high-risk industry such as software, the probability that the company may have difficulty paying off the debt in a timely manner is high.

Reflecting their below-average credit quality, the Jack Russell Corp. notes were not issued to the general public. Instead, the notes were privately placed with two insurance companies. Such private placements are common among relatively small debt issues. Private placements will be discussed in greater detail later in this chapter.

18.2 Types of Corporate Bonds

debentures
Unsecured bonds issued by a corporation.

Debentures are the most frequently issued type of corporate bond. Debenture bonds represent an unsecured debt of a corporation. Debenture bondholders have a legal claim as general creditors of the corporation. In the event of a default by the issuing corporation, the bondholders' claim extends to all corporate assets. However, they may have to share this claim with other creditors who have an equal legal claim or yield to creditors with a higher legal claim.

mortgage bond
Debt secured with a property lien.

In addition to debentures, there are three other basic types of corporate bonds: mortgage bonds, collateral trust bonds, and equipment trust certificates. **Mortgage bonds** represent debt issued with a lien on specific property, usually real estate, pledged as security for the bonds. A mortgage lien gives bondholders the legal right to foreclose on property pledged by the issuer to satisfy an unpaid debt obligation. However, in actual practice, foreclosure and sale of mortgaged property following a default may not be the most desirable strategy for bondholders. Instead, it is common for a corporation in financial distress to reorganize itself and negotiate a new debt contract with bondholders. In these negotiations, a mortgage lien can be an important bargaining tool for the trustee representing the bondholders.

collateral trust bond
Debt secured with financial collateral.

Collateral trust bonds are characterized by a pledge of financial assets as security for the bond issue. Collateral trust bonds are commonly issued by holding companies, which may pledge the stocks, bonds, or other securities issued by their subsidiaries as collateral for their own bond issue. The legal arrangement for pledging collateral securities is similar to that for a mortgage lien. In the event of an issuer's default on contractual obligations to bondholders, the bondholders have a legal right to foreclose on collateralized securities in the amount necessary to settle an outstanding debt obligation.

equipment trust certificate
Shares in a trust with income from a lease contract.

Equipment trust certificates represent debt issued by a trustee to purchase heavy industrial equipment that is leased and used by railroads, airlines, and other companies with a demand for heavy equipment. Under this financial arrangement, investors purchase equipment trust certificates, and the proceeds from this sale are used to purchase equipment. Formal ownership of the equipment remains with a trustee appointed to represent the certificate holders.

The trustee then leases the equipment to a company. In return, the company promises to make a series of scheduled lease payments over a specified leasing period. The trustee collects the lease payments and distributes all revenues, less expenses, as dividends to the certificate holders. These distributions are conventionally called dividends because they are generated as income from a trust. The lease arrangement usually ends after a specified number of years when the leasing company makes a final lease payment and may take possession of the used equipment.

From the certificate holders' point of view, this financial arrangement is superior to a mortgage lien since they actually own the equipment during the leasing period. Thus, if the leasing corporation defaults, the equipment can be sold without the effort and expense of a formal foreclosure process. Because the underlying equipment for this type of financing is typically built according to an industry standard, the equipment can usually be quickly sold or leased to another company in the same line of business.

WWW

Visit the Northwest Airlines Web site at www.nwa.com

Figure 18.1 is a *Wall Street Journal* bond announcement for an aircraft equipment trust for Northwest Airlines. Notice that the $243 million issue is split into two parts: $177 million of senior notes paying 8.26 percent interest and $66 million of subordinated notes paying 9.36 percent interest. The senior notes have a first claim on the aircraft in the event of a default by the airline, while the subordinated notes have a secondary claim. In the event of a default, investment losses for the trust will primarily be absorbed by the subordinated noteholders. For this reason, the subordinated notes are riskier and, therefore, pay a higher interest rate. Of course, if no default actually occurs, the subordinated notes would turn out to actually be a better investment. However, there is no way of knowing this in advance.

CHECK THIS

18.2a Given that a bond issue is one of the four basic types discussed in this section, how would the specific bond type affect the credit quality of the bond?

18.2b Why might some bond types be more or less risky with respect to the risk of default?

18.2c Given that a default has occurred, why might the trustee's job of representing the financial interests of the bondholders be easier for some bond types than for others?

18.3 Bond Indentures

indenture summary
Description of the contractual terms of a new bond issue included in a bond's prospectus.

prospectus
Document prepared as part of a security offering detailing information about a company's financial position, its operations, and investment plans.

A bond indenture is a formal written agreement between the corporation and the bondholders. It is an important legal document that spells out in detail the mutual rights and obligations of the corporation and the bondholders with respect to the bond issue. Indenture contracts are often quite long, sometimes several hundred pages, and make for very tedious reading. In fact, very few bond investors ever read the original indenture, but instead might refer to an **indenture summary** provided in the **prospectus** that was circulated when the

FIGURE 18.1 Equipment Trust Notes Issue

These securities have not been registered under the Securities Act of 1933 and may not be offered or sold in the United States or to U.S. persons except in accordance with the resale restrictions applicable thereto. These securities having been previously sold, this announcement appears as a matter of record only.

$243,000,000

NWA Trust No. 1

$177,000,000 8.26% Class A Senior Aircraft Notes

$66,000,000 9.36% Class B Subordinated Aircraft Notes

NORTHWEST AIRLINES

The 8.26% Class A Senior Aircraft Notes and the 9.36% Class B Subordinated Aircraft Notes are secured by, among other things, a security interest in certain aircraft sold by Northwest Airlines, Inc. ("Northwest") to an owner trust for a purchase price of $443 million and the lease relating to such Aircraft, including the right to receive amounts payable by Northwest under such lease. The Noteholders also have the benefit of a liquidity facility, initially provided by General Electric Capital Corporation, to support certain payments of interest on the Notes.

Lehman Brothers | **BT Securities Corporation**

Source: Reprinted by permission of Dow Jones & Company, Inc., via Copyright Clearance Center, Inc., © 1994 Dow Jones & Company, Inc. All Rights Reserved Worldwide.

bond issue was originally sold to the public. Alternatively, a summary of the most important features of an indenture is published by debt rating agencies.

The Trust Indenture Act of 1939 requires that any bond issue subject to regulation by the Securities and Exchange Commission (SEC), which includes most corporate bond and note issues sold to the general public, must have a trustee appointed to represent the interests of the bondholders. Also, all responsibilities of a duly appointed trustee must be specified in detail in the indenture. Some corporations maintain a blanket or open-ended indenture that applies to all currently outstanding bonds and any new bonds that are issued, while other corporations write a new indenture contract for each new bond issue sold to the public.

Descriptions of the most important provisions frequently specified in a bond indenture agreement are presented next.

BOND SENIORITY PROVISIONS

WWW

The Trust Indenture Act of 1939 is available at the SEC Web site www.sec.gov

A corporation may have several different bond issues outstanding; these issues normally can be differentiated according to the seniority of their claims on the firm's assets. Seniority usually is specified in the indenture contract.

Consider a corporation with two outstanding bond issues: (1) a mortgage bond issue with certain real estate assets pledged as security and (2) a debenture bond issue with no specific assets pledged as security. In this case, the mortgage bond issue has a senior claim on the pledged assets but no specific claim on other corporate assets. The debenture bond has a claim on all corporate assets not specifically pledged as security for the mortgage bond, but it would have only a residual claim on assets pledged as security for the mortgage bond issue. This residual claim would apply only after all obligations to the mortgage bondholders have been satisfied.

As another example, suppose a corporation has two outstanding debenture issues. In this case, seniority is normally assigned to the bonds first issued by the corporation. The bonds issued earliest have a senior claim on the pledged assets and are called **senior debentures**. The bonds issued later have a junior or subordinate claim and are called **subordinated debentures**.

senior debentures
Bonds that have a higher claim on the firm's assets than other bonds.

subordinated debentures
Bonds that have a claim on the firm's assets after those with a higher claim have been satisfied.

negative pledge clause
Bond indenture provision that prohibits new debt from being issued with seniority over an existing issue.

The seniority of an existing debt issue is usually protected by a **negative pledge clause** in the bond indenture. A negative pledge clause prohibits a new issue of debt with seniority over a currently outstanding issue. However, it may allow a new debt issue to share equally in the seniority of an existing issue. A negative pledge clause is part of the indenture agreement of most senior debenture bonds.

CALL PROVISIONS

Most corporate bond issues have a call provision allowing the issuer to buy back all or part of its outstanding bonds at a specified call price sometime before the bonds mature. The most frequent motive for a corporation to call outstanding bonds is to take advantage of a general fall in market interest rates. Lower interest rates allow the corporation to replace currently outstanding high-coupon bonds with a new issue of bonds paying lower coupons. Replacing existing bonds with new bonds is called **bond refunding**.

bond refunding
Process of calling an outstanding bond issue and refinancing it with a new bond issue.

TRADITIONAL FIXED-PRICE CALL PROVISIONS There are two major types of call provisions, *traditional fixed-price* and *make-whole*. From an investor's point of view, a fixed-price call provision has a distinct disadvantage. For example, suppose an investor is currently holding bonds paying 10 percent coupons. Further suppose that, after a fall in market interest rates, the corporation is able to issue new bonds that only pay 8 percent coupons. By calling existing 10 percent coupon bonds, the issuer forces bondholders to surrender their bonds in exchange for the fixed call price. But this happens at a time when the bondholders can reinvest funds only at lower interest rates. If instead the bonds were noncallable, the bondholders would continue to receive the original 10 percent coupons.

For this reason, callable bonds are less attractive to investors than noncallable bonds. Consequently, a callable bond will sell at a lower price than a comparable noncallable bond. Despite their lower prices, corporations generally prefer to issue fixed-price callable bonds. However, to reduce the price gap between callable and noncallable bonds, issuers typically allow the indenture contract to specify certain restrictions on their ability to call an outstanding bond issue. Three features are commonly used to restrict an issuer's call privilege:

1. Callable bonds usually have a *deferred call provision* which provides a *call protection period* during which a bond issue cannot be called. For example, a bond may be call-protected for a period of five years after its issue date.

FIGURE 18.2 Noncallable Bonds and Fixed-Price Callable Bonds

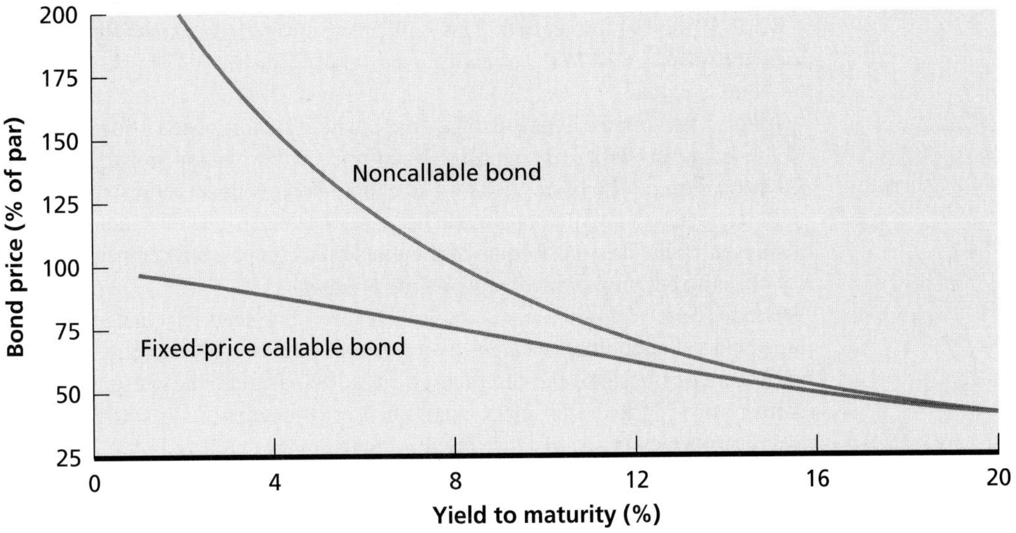

2. A call price often includes a *call premium* over par value. A standard arrangement stipulates a call premium equal to one-year's coupon payments for a call occurring at the earliest possible call date. Over time, the call premium is gradually reduced until it is eliminated entirely. After some future date, the bonds become callable at par value.
3. Some indentures specifically prohibit an issuer from calling outstanding bonds for the purpose of refunding at a lower coupon rate but still allow a call for other reasons. This *refunding provision* prevents the corporation from calling an outstanding bond issue solely as a response to falling market interest rates. However, the corporation can still pay off its bond debt ahead of schedule by using funds acquired from, say, earnings, or funds obtained from the sale of newly issued common stock.

After a bond's call protection period has elapsed, a rational investor would be unwilling to pay much more than the call price for the bond since the issuer might call the bond at any time and pay only the call price for the bond. Consequently, a bond's call price serves as an effective ceiling on its market price. It is important for bond investors to understand how the existence of a price ceiling for callable bonds alters the standard price-yield relationship for bonds.

The relationship between interest rates and prices for comparable callable and noncallable bonds is illustrated in Figure 18.2. In this example, the vertical axis measures bond prices, and the horizontal axis measures bond yields. In this two-bond example, both bonds pay an 8 percent coupon and are alike in all respects except that one of the bonds is callable any time at par value.

As shown in Figure 18.2, the noncallable bond has the standard *convex price-yield relationship,* where the price-yield curve is bowed toward the origin. When the price-yield curve is bowed to the origin this is called *positive convexity.* In contrast, the fixed-price callable bond has a convex or bowed price-yield relationship in the region of high yields, but is bowed away from the origin in the region of low yields. This is called *negative convexity.* The important lesson here is that no matter how low market interest rates might fall, the maximum price of an unprotected fixed-price callable bond is generally bounded above by its call price.

CHECK THIS

18.3a After a call protection period has elapsed, why is the call price an effective ceiling on the market price of a callable bond with a fixed-price call provision?

MAKE-WHOLE CALL PROVISION In just the last few years, a new type of call provision, a "make-whole" call, has become common in the corporate bond market. If a callable bond has a make-whole call provision, bondholders receive approximately what the bond is worth if the bond is called. This call provision gets its name because the bondholder does not suffer a loss in the event of a call; that is, the bondholder is "made whole" when the bond is called.

Like a fixed-price call provision, a make-whole call provision allows the borrower to pay off the remaining debt early. Unlike a fixed-price call provision, however, a make-whole call provision requires the borrower to make a lump-sum payment representing the present value of all payments that will not be made because of the call. The discount rate used to calculate the present value is usually equal to the yield on a comparable maturity U.S. Treasury security plus a fixed, prespecified *make-whole premium.*

Because the yield of a comparable U.S. Treasury security changes over time, the call price paid to bondholders changes over time. As interest rates decrease, the make-whole call price increases because the discount rate used to calculate the present value decreases. As interest rates increase, the make-whole call price decreases. In addition, make-whole call provisions typically specify that the minimum amount received by a bondholder is the par value of the bond.

As interest rates decline, even in the region of low yields, the price of bonds with a make-whole call provision will increase. That is, these bonds exhibit the standard *convex price-yield relationship* in all yield regions. In contrast, recall that bond prices with a fixed-price call provision exhibit *negative convexity* in the region of low yields.

EXAMPLE 18.1 **Calculating the Make-Whole Call Premium**

As reported on www.reuters.com, on July 12, 2007, XTO Energy Inc. sold a total of $1.25 billion worth of notes and bonds. The first tranche issue of $300 million in notes has the following terms:

Settlement date:	7/16/2007 (assumed)
First payment:	2/1/2008
Maturity:	8/1/2012
Coupon:	5.90%
Price:	99.864
Yield:	5.931%
Spread:	90 basis points above U.S. Treasury notes
Make-whole call:	15 basis points above U.S. Treasury notes
Ratings:	Baa2 (Moody's); BBB (S&P)

If these notes were called immediately, what price would XTO Energy have to pay to these note holders? To calculate the make-whole call premium of these notes, we need to add 15 basis points to the yield of comparable-maturity U.S. Treasury notes.

We find the yield of comparable-maturity U.S. Treasury notes by subtracting the 90 basis point spread from the yield of the XTO notes, 5.931% − .90% = 5.031%. Then we add the 15 basis point make-whole premium: 5.031% + .15% = 5.181%. Discounting the remaining cash flows of the note at 5.181 percent, we get a make-whole call price of about $103.13—which is about $3.27 more than the current price of the notes ($99.864). You must remember to use the standard bond pricing formula to discount these cash flows.

You can verify this price using Excel. Using the information above, enter =PRICE("7/16/2007","8/1/2012",0.059,0.05181,100,2) into an Excel cell and you will get a price of $103.15.

CHECK THIS

18.3b Suppose you hold a bond with a make-whole call provision. The coupon rate on this bond is 5.90 percent. At what yield to maturity will this bond sell for par?

PUT PROVISIONS

put bonds
Bonds that can be sold back to the issuer at a prespecified price on any of a sequence of prespecified dates. Also called *extendible bonds.*

A bond issue with a put provision grants bondholders the right to sell their bonds back to the issuer at a special *put price,* normally set at par value. These so-called **put bonds** are "putable" on each of a series of designated *put dates.* These are often scheduled to occur annually but sometimes occur at more frequent intervals. At each put date, the bondholder decides whether to sell the bond back to the issuer or continue to hold the bond until the next put date. For this reason, put bonds are often called *extendible bonds* because the bondholder has the option of extending the maturity of the bond at each put date.

Notice that by granting bondholders an option to sell their bonds back to the corporation at par value, the put feature provides an effective floor on the market price of the bond. Thus, the put feature offers protection to bondholders from rising interest rates and the associated fall in bond prices.

A put feature also helps protect bondholders from acts of the corporation that might cause a deterioration of the bond's credit quality. However, this protection is not granted without a cost to bond investors, because a putable bond will command a higher market price than a comparable nonputable bond.

CHECK THIS

18.3c Using Figure 18.2 as a guide, what would the price-yield relationship look like for a noncallable bond putable at par value?

18.3d Under what conditions would a put feature not yield an effective floor for the market price of a put bond? (*Hint*: Think about default risk.)

BOND-TO-STOCK CONVERSION PROVISIONS

convertible bonds
Bonds that holders can exchange for common stock according to a prespecified conversion ratio.

Some bonds have a valuable bond-to-stock conversion feature. These bonds are called convertible bonds. **Convertible bonds** grant bondholders the right to exchange each bond for a designated number of common stock shares of the issuing firm. To avoid confusion in a discussion of convertible bonds, it is important to understand some basic terminology.

1. The number of common stock shares acquired in exchange for each converted bond is called the *conversion ratio*:

$$\text{Conversion ratio} = \text{Number of stock shares acquired by conversion}$$

2. The par value of a convertible bond divided by its conversion ratio is called the bond's *conversion price*:

$$\text{Conversion price} = \frac{\text{Bond par value}}{\text{Conversion ratio}}$$

3. The market price per share of common stock acquired by conversion times the bond's conversion ratio is called the bond's *conversion value*:

$$\text{Conversion value} = \text{Price per share of stock} \times \text{Conversion ratio}$$

For example, suppose a convertible bond with a par value of $1,000 can be converted into 20 shares of the issuing firm's common stock. In this case, the conversion price is

WWW

There is a convertible bond calculator at: www.numa.com

$1,000/20 = $50. Continuing this example, suppose the firm's common stock has a market price of $40 per share; then the conversion value of a single bond is 20 × $40 = $800.

Figure 18.3 is *The Wall Street Journal* announcement of an issue of convertible subordinated notes by Advanced Micro Devices (AMD). The notes pay a 6 percent coupon rate and mature in 2005. The conversion price for this note issue is $37 per share, which

FIGURE 18.3 Convertible Notes Issue

This announcement is neither an offer to sell, nor a solicitation of an offer to buy, any of these securities. The offer is made only by the Prospectus and related Prospectus Supplement.

$517,500,000

AMD

Advanced Micro Devices, Inc.

6% Convertible Subordinated Notes due 2005

The 6% Convertible Subordinated Notes due 2005 (the "Notes") will be convertible at the option of the holder into shares of common stock, par value $.01 per share (the "Common Stock"), of Advanced Micro Devices, Inc. (the "Company") at any time at or prior to maturity, unless previously redeemed or repurchased, at a conversion price of $37.00 per share (equivalent to a conversion rate of 27.027 shares per $1,000 principal amount of Notes), subject to adjustment in certain events.

Price 100%

Copies of the Prospectus and related Prospectus Supplement may be obtained in any State from such of the undersigned as may legally offer these securities in compliance with the securities laws of such State.

Donaldson, Lufkin & Jenrette
Securities Corporation

Salomon Smith Barney

Source: Reprinted with permission from Dow Jones & Company, Inc., © 1998 Dow Jones & Company, Inc. All Rights Reserved Worldwide.

implies a conversion ratio of 27.027 shares of common stock for each $1,000 face value note.

From an investor's perspective, the conversion privilege of convertible bonds has the distinct advantage that bondholders can receive a share of any increase in common stock value. However, the conversion option has a price. A corporation can sell convertible bonds at par value with a coupon rate substantially less than the coupon rate of comparable nonconvertible bonds. This forgone coupon interest represents the price of the bond's conversion option.

When convertible bonds are originally issued, their conversion ratio is customarily set to yield a conversion value of 10 percent to 20 percent less than par value. For example, suppose the common stock of a company has a price of $30 per share and the company issues convertible bonds with a par value of $1,000 per bond. To set the original conversion value at $900 per bond, the company would set a conversion ratio of 30 stock shares per bond. Thereafter, the conversion ratio is fixed, but each bond's conversion value becomes linked to the firm's stock price, which may rise or fall in value. The price of a convertible bond reflects the conversion value of the bond. In general, the higher the conversion value the higher the bond price, and vice versa.

WWW

Visit the AMD Web site at www.amd.com

Investing in convertible bonds is more complicated than owning nonconvertible bonds, because the conversion privilege presents convertible bondholders with an important timing decision. When is the best time to exercise a bond's conversion option and exchange the bond for shares of common stock? The answer is that investors should normally postpone conversion as long as possible, because while they hold the bonds they continue to receive coupon payments. After converting to common stock, they lose all subsequent coupons. In general, unless the total dividend payments on stock acquired by conversion are somewhat greater than the forgone bond coupon payments, investors should hold on to their convertible bonds to continue to receive coupon payments.

The rational decision of convertible bondholders to postpone conversion as long as possible is limited, however, since convertible bonds are almost always callable. Firms customarily call outstanding convertible bonds when their conversion value has risen by 10 percent to 15 percent above bond par value, although there are many exceptions to this rule. When a convertible bond issue is called by the issuer, bondholders are forced to make an immediate decision whether to convert to common stock shares or accept a cash payment of the call price. Fortunately, the decision is simple—convertible bondholders should choose whichever is more valuable, the call price or the conversion value.

CHECK THIS

18.3e Describe the conversion decision that convertible bondholders must make when the bonds mature.

GRAPHICAL ANALYSIS OF CONVERTIBLE BOND PRICES

The price of a convertible bond is closely linked to the value of the underlying common stock shares that can be acquired by conversion. A higher stock price implies a higher bond price, and, conversely, a lower stock price yields a lower bond price.

The relationship between the price of a convertible bond and the price of the firm's common stock is depicted in Figure 18.4. In this example, the convertible bond's price is measured on the vertical axis, and the stock price is measured along the horizontal axis. The straight, upward-sloping line is the bond's conversion value; the slope of the line is the conversion ratio. The horizontal line represents the price of a comparable nonconvertible bond with the same coupon rate, maturity, and credit quality.

in-the-money bond
A convertible bond whose conversion value is greater than its call price.

A convertible bond is said to be an **in-the-money bond** when its conversion value is greater than its call price. If an in-the-money convertible bond is called, rational bondholders will convert their bonds into common stock. When the conversion value is less

FIGURE 18.4 Convertible Bond Prices

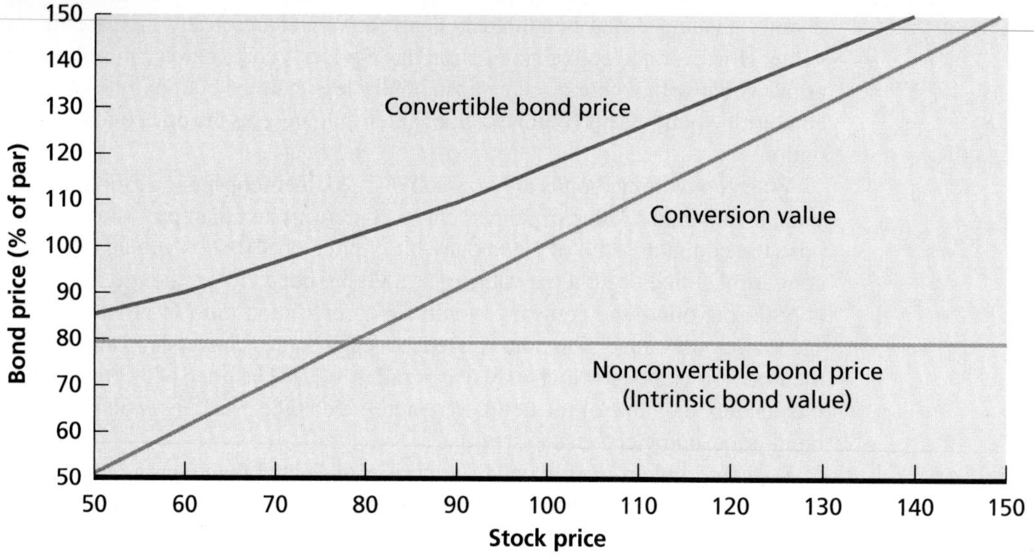

than the call price, a convertible bond is said to be *out of the money.* If an out-of-the-money bond is called, rational bondholders will accept the call price and forgo the conversion option. In practice, however, convertible bonds are seldom called when they are out of the money.

The curved line in Figure 18.4 shows the relationship between a convertible bond's price and the underlying stock price. As shown, there are two lower bounds on the value of a convertible bond. First, a convertible bond's price can never fall below its **intrinsic bond value**, also commonly called its *investment value* or *straight bond value.* This value is what the bond would be worth if it were not convertible, but otherwise identical in terms of coupon, maturity, and credit quality. Second, a convertible bond can never sell for less than its *conversion value* because, if it did, investors could simply buy the bond and convert, thereby realizing an immediate, riskless profit.

intrinsic bond value
The price below which a convertible bond cannot fall, equal to the value of a comparable nonconvertible bond. Also called *investment value.*

Thus, the *floor value* of a convertible bond is its intrinsic bond value or its conversion value, whichever is larger. As shown in Figure 18.4, however, a convertible bond will generally sell for more than this floor value. This extra is the amount that investors are willing to pay for the right, but not the obligation, to convert the bond at a future date at a potentially much higher stock price.

An interesting variation of a bond-to-stock conversion feature occurs when the company issuing the bonds is different from the company whose stock is acquired by the conversion. In this case, the bonds are called **exchangeable bonds**. Figure 18.5 presents a *Wall Street Journal* announcement of an issue of exchangeable subordinated debentures by the McKesson Corporation. These debentures are exchangeable for common stock shares of Armor All Products Corporation. McKesson is a retail distributor, and Armor All markets consumer chemical products. Exchangeable bonds, while not unusual, are less common than convertible bonds.

exchangeable bonds
Bonds that can be converted into common stock shares of a company other than the issuer's.

CHECK THIS

18.3f For nonconvertible bonds, the call price is a ceiling on the market price of the bond. Why might the call price not be an effective ceiling on the price of a convertible bond?

FIGURE 18.5 Exchangeable Debentures Issue

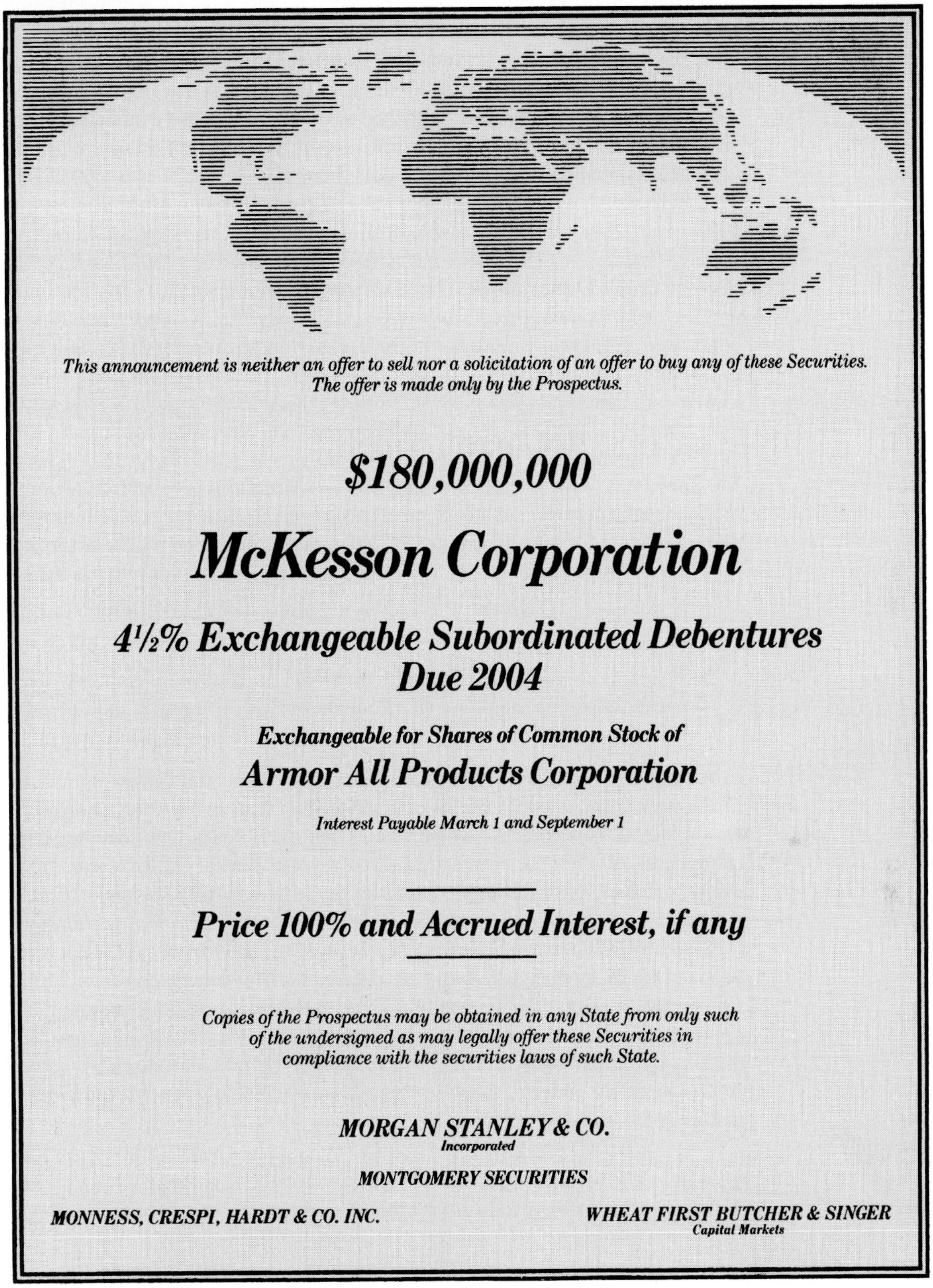

Source: Reprinted with permission from Dow Jones & Company, Inc., © 1994 by Dow Jones & Company, Inc. All Rights Reserved Worldwide.

BOND MATURITY AND PRINCIPAL PAYMENT PROVISIONS

term bonds
Bonds issued with a single maturity date.

Term bonds represent the most common corporate bond maturity structure. A term bond issue has a single maturity date. On this date, all outstanding bond principal must be paid off. The indenture contract for a term bond issue normally stipulates the creation of a *sinking fund,* that is, an account established to repay bondholders through a series of fractional redemptions before the bond reaches maturity. Thus, at maturity, only a fraction of the original bond issue will still be outstanding. Sinking fund provisions are discussed in more detail later.

serial bonds
Bonds issued with a regular sequence of maturity dates.

An alternative maturity structure is provided by **serial bonds**, where a fraction of an entire bond issue is scheduled to mature in each year over a specified period. Essentially, a serial bond issue represents a collection of subissues with sequential maturities. As an example, a serial bond issue may stipulate that one-tenth of an entire bond issue must be redeemed in each year over a 10-year period, with the last fraction redeemed at maturity. Serial bonds generally do not have a call provision, whereas term bonds usually do have a call provision.

When originally issued, most corporate bonds have maturities of 30 years or less. However, in recent years some companies have issued bonds with 40- and 50-year maturities. In 1993, Walt Disney Company made headlines in the financial press when it sold 100-year maturity bonds. This bond issue became popularly known as the "Sleeping Beauty" bonds, after the classic Disney movie. However, the prince might arrive early for these bonds since they are callable after 30 years. Nevertheless, this was the first time since 1954 that 100-year bonds were sold by any borrower in the United States. Only days later, however, Coca-Cola issued $150 million of 100-year maturity bonds. Both the Disney and Coke bond issues locked in the unusually low interest rates prevailing in 1993.

SINKING FUND PROVISIONS

sinking fund
An account used to provide for scheduled redemptions of outstanding bonds.

The indentures of most term bonds include a **sinking fund** provision that requires the corporation to make periodic payments into a trustee-managed account. Account reserves are then used to provide for scheduled redemptions of outstanding bonds. The existence of a sinking fund is an important consideration for bond investors mainly for two reasons:

1. A sinking fund provides a degree of security to bondholders, since payments into the sinking fund can be used only to pay outstanding obligations to bondholders.
2. A sinking fund provision requires fractional bond issue redemptions according to a preset schedule. Therefore, some bondholders will be repaid their invested principal before the stated maturity for their bonds whether they want repayment or not.

As part of a *scheduled sinking fund redemption,* some bondholders may be forced to surrender their bonds in exchange for cash payment of a special *sinking fund call price.* For this reason, not all bondholders may be able to hold their bonds until maturity, even though the entire bond issue has not been called according to a general call provision. For example, the indenture for a 25-year maturity bond issue may require that one-twentieth of the bond issue be retired annually, beginning immediately after an initial 5-year call protection period.

Typically, when a redemption is due, the sinking fund trustee will select bonds by lottery. Selected bonds are then called, and the affected bondholders receive the call price, which for sinking fund redemptions is usually par value. However, the issuer normally has a valuable option to buy back the required number of bonds in the open market and deliver them to the sinking fund trustee instead of delivering the cash required for a par value redemption. Issuers naturally prefer to exercise this option when bonds can be repurchased in the open market at less than par value.

CHECK THIS

18.3g For bond investors, what are some of the advantages and disadvantages of a sinking fund provision?

COUPON PAYMENT PROVISIONS

Coupon rates are stated on an annual basis. For example, an 8 percent coupon rate indicates that the issuer promises to pay 8 percent of a bond's face value to the bondholder each year. However, splitting an annual coupon into two semiannual payments is an almost universal practice in the United States. An exact schedule of coupon payment dates is specified in the bond indenture when the bonds are originally issued.

INVESTMENT UPDATES

KATRINA CLAIMS COULD LEAVE HOLDERS OF A "CAT BOND" WITH MAJOR LOSSES

As Hurricane Katrina approached the Gulf Coast, those anxiously following the storm included big investors around the globe. They are owners of $5.3 billion of "catastrophe bonds" that insurers issued in recent years to help pay claims from natural disasters.

Now, it appears holders of one such "cat bond" may be out of pocket by almost $200 million, while most of the other investors have avoided such losses.

The bond in question: a special-purpose vehicle called Kamp Re. Under the terms of the $190 million bond, issued in August, investors lose their money if Zurich Financial Services, the big Swiss insurance company, pays insurance claims of more than $1 billion on any hurricane or earthquake in the United States within five years. Zurich's total losses from Katrina, which hit New Orleans and the Gulf Coast on Aug. 29, are estimated at almost $2 billion, according to the company.

Several people in the market said the Kamp Re bonds are being quoted at zero value in anticipation that investors have been wiped out. The bonds were sold in a private placement to institutional investors, like most cat bonds. If the Kamp Re bondholders lose all of their investment, it would be the first cat-bond issue to totally call in investors' funds, though some have cost investors modest chunks of their principal in past years. The event could lead investors to demand more protection, such as higher trigger points and interest payments, some market participants said.

Catastrophe bonds, or "cat bonds" for short, were launched in the 1990s by financial wizards on Wall Street and elsewhere to provide insurance companies an alternative to steeply priced reinsurance. In short, reinsurance is coverage insurers buy to spread the risk of losses from policies they sell to individuals and companies.

Here is how cat bonds generally work: Insurance companies sell bonds to investors and agree to pay them an annual interest rate, typically three to five percentage points above the benchmark London interbank offered rate, or Libor. At current rates, the cost would be about 7% to 9%. The money raised is placed in a trust fund.

If a natural catastrophe strikes of sufficient magnitude—measured by wind speed, earthquake force, or, as in the Kamp Re instance, insured losses—the issuer gets to keep the cash to help pay its policyholders' claims. The bonds typically have a three-year maturity but often are rolled over.

Buyers of cat bonds are mostly sophisticated investors like hedge funds, pension funds, and banks, which see them as an opportunity to diversify their investment portfolios. Since they first appeared, the global insurance industry has issued $13.41 billion of natural-catastrophe bonds. The largest single issuer is Swiss Re, also based in Zurich, which has more than $1 billion in catastrophe bonds outstanding.

Katrina, to be sure, was a big deal: U.S. risk-management firm ISO estimated Tuesday that total private-sector insurance claims would amount to $34.4 billion, making it the costliest natural disaster in history.

Source: Charles Fleming, *The Wall Street Journal*, October 6, 2005.

If a company suspends payment of coupon interest, it is said to be in default. Default is a serious matter. In general, bondholders have an unconditional right to the timely payment of interest and principal. They also have a right to bring legal action to enforce such payments. Upon suspension of coupon payments, the bondholders could, for example, demand an acceleration of principal repayment along with all past-due interest. However, a corporation in financial distress has a right to seek protection in bankruptcy court from inflexible demands by bondholders. As a practical matter, it is often in the best interests of both the bondholders and the corporation to negotiate a new debt contract. Indeed, bankruptcy courts normally encourage a settlement that minimizes any intervention on their part.

18.4 Protective Covenants

protective covenants
Restrictions in a bond indenture designed to protect bondholders.

In addition to the provisions already discussed, a bond indenture is likely to contain a number of **protective covenants**. These agreements are designed to protect bondholders by restricting the actions of a corporation that might cause a deterioration in the credit quality of a bond issue. Protective covenants can be classified into two types: negative covenants and positive, or affirmative, covenants.

A *negative covenant* is a "thou shalt not" for the corporation. Here are some examples of negative covenants that might be found in an indenture agreement:

1. The firm cannot pay dividends to stockholders in excess of what is allowed by a formula based on the firm's earnings.
2. The firm cannot issue new bonds that are senior to currently outstanding bonds. Also, the amount of a new bond issue cannot exceed an amount specified by a formula based on the firm's net worth.
3. The firm cannot refund an existing bond issue with new bonds paying a lower coupon rate than the currently outstanding bond issue it would replace.
4. The firm cannot buy bonds issued by other companies, nor can it guarantee the debt of any other company.

A *positive covenant* is a "thou shalt." It specifies things that a corporation must do, or conditions that it must abide by. Here are some common examples of positive covenants:

1. Proceeds from the sale of assets must be used either to acquire other assets of equal value or to redeem outstanding bonds.
2. In the event of a merger, acquisition, or spinoff, the firm must give bondholders the right to redeem their bonds at par value.
3. The firm must maintain the good condition of all assets pledged as security for an outstanding bond issue.
4. The firm must periodically supply audited financial information to bondholders.

CHECK THIS

18.4a Why would a corporation voluntarily include protective covenants in its bond indenture contract?

18.5 Event Risk

event risk
The possibility that the issuing corporation will experience a significant change in its bond credit quality.

Protective covenants in a bond indenture help shield bondholders from event risk. **Event risk** is broadly defined as the possibility that some structural or financial change to the corporation will cause a significant deterioration in the credit quality of a bond issue, thereby causing the affected bonds to lose substantial market value.

A classic example of event risk, and what could happen to bondholders without adequate covenant protection, is provided by an incident involving Marriott Corporation, best known for its chain of hotels and resorts. In October 1992, Marriott announced its intention to spin off part of the company. The spinoff, called Host Marriott, would acquire most of the parent company's debt and its poorly performing real estate holdings. The parent, Marriott International, would be left relatively debt-free with possession of most of the better performing properties, including its hotel management division.

On the announcement date, the affected Marriott bonds fell in value by about 30 percent, reflecting severe concern about the impact of the spinoff on the credit quality of the bonds. On the same day, Marriott stock rose in value by about 30 percent, reflecting a large wealth transfer from bondholders to stockholders. A subsequent bondholder legal challenge was unsuccessful. Standard & Poor's later announced that it was formally revising its credit

INVESTMENT UPDATES

MARRIOTT TO SPLIT, MAKING 2 FIRMS

Marriott Corp. shareholders approved a plan to split the company into a real-estate concern, with most of Marriott's debt, and a high-growth hotel-management company.

The split, approved by 85% of the shares voted, was the main issue at Marriott's annual meeting Friday. Under the plan, which is expected to take effect in September, stockholders will receive a share of Marriott International, Inc., the hotel-management operation, for each Marriott share they own. Then Marriott Corp. will be renamed Host Marriott Corp., an entity that will operate the real-estate side of the business.

The plan stunned bondholders when it was announced in October. They argued that the financial support of their debt was being undermined, and a suit by some of the bondholders is still pending.

Marriott shares have risen 60% since the plan's announcement. In New York Stock Exchange trading Friday, Marriott closed at $27.785, up 12.5 cents. The stock has traded as low as $15.50 in the past year.

The Marriott family controls more than 25% of the 100.8 million shares outstanding as of Jan. 1.

Marriott's directors set a distribution date for the split dividend of Sept. 10 for shares of record Sept. 1.

J. W. Marriott, 61 years old and currently chairman and president of the company, will be chairman, president, and chief executive officer of Marriott International, while his brother, Richard E. Marriott, 54, will be chairman of Host Marriott. Richard Marriott is currently vice chairman and executive vice president of the company.

In addition to the bondholders' lawsuit seeking to block the reorganization, Marriott had faced a suit by holders of preferred stock. Marriott said that the holders have agreed to dismiss their case and convert their preferred shares into common stock.

The suit by the group of bondholders, representing about a dozen institutional investors, is still pending, however. Under the reorganization plan, holders of about $1.5 billion in Marriott bonds would have the option to swap their notes for new notes of a unit of the new real-estate entity. The company will retain $2.1 billion of Marriott's $3 billion long-term debt and will own 139 hotels and other real-estate assets.

Larry Kill, attorney for the bondholders, said the suit would proceed despite the shareholder vote. "This was a very unfair transaction," he said.

As a separate company, Host Marriott would have had about $1.2 billion in sales in 1992, according to the company's estimates. Marriott International, Inc., the new hotel concern, will operate more than 760 hotels through Marriott's four hotel-management units and related management services. Marriott International would have had $7.8 billion in sales last year, the company estimates.

In 1992, Marriott had net income of $85 million, or 64 cents a share, on sales of $8.72 billion. It had about $3 billion in long-term debt as of Jan. 1.

Moody's Investors Service, Inc., downgraded its ratings on the senior unsecured debt of Marriott Corp., affecting about $2.3 billion in debt, to Ba-2 from single-B-2. Moody's said the bond-exchange plan will leave a Host Marriott unit highly leveraged "with modest debt protection." Moody's said it expects only gradual improvement in operating earnings, given the sluggish economy and glut of hotel rooms. Moody's said, however, that the Host Marriott unit will be well-positioned for increased earnings when the recovery hits full speed.

Source: Jyoti Thottam, *The Wall Street Journal*, July 26, 1993. Reprinted by permission of Dow Jones & Company, Inc.,

WWW

Visit Marriott and Host Marriott Web sites at www.marriott.com and www.hostmarriott.com

ratings on Marriott bonds to recognize the impact of the spinoff. (Credit ratings are discussed in detail in a later section.) Debt remaining with Marriott International would have an investment-grade rating, while bonds assigned to Host Marriott would have junk bond status. *The Wall Street Journal* report covering the story is reproduced in the nearby *Investment Updates* box.

CHECK THIS

18.5a What are some possible protective covenants that would have protected Marriott bondholders from the adverse impact of the spinoff described here?

18.6 Bonds without Indentures

private placement
A new bond issue sold to one or more parties in private transactions not available to the public.

The Trust Indenture Act of 1939 does not require an indenture when a bond issue is not sold to the general public. For example, the bonds may be sold only to one or more financial institutions in what is called a **private placement**. Private placements are exempt from registration requirements with the SEC. Nevertheless, even privately placed debt issues often have a formal indenture contract.

When a corporation issues debt without an indenture, it makes an unconditional promise to pay interest and principal according to a simple debt contract. Debt issued without an indenture is basically a simple IOU of the corporation. Bond analysts sometimes reserve the designation "bonds" to mean corporate debt subject to an indenture and refer to corporate debt not subject to an indenture as "notes." However, bonds and notes are more commonly distinguished on the basis of maturity, where bonds designate relatively long maturities, say, 10 years or longer, and notes designate maturities less than 10 years. Both definitions overlap since most long-term debt is issued subject to an indenture, and most privately placed short-term debt is issued as a simple IOU. In between, however, privately placed intermediate-maturity debt may or may not be issued subject to an indenture and therefore might be referred to as either a bond or a note regardless of the existence of an indenture. As in any profession, the jargon of investments is sometimes ambiguous.

18.7 Preferred Stock

preferred stock
A security with a claim to dividend payments that is senior to common stock.

Preferred stock has some of the features of both bonds and common stock. Preferred stockholders have a claim to dividend payments that is senior to the claim of common stockholders—hence the term "preferred stock." However, their claim is subordinate to the claims of bondholders and other creditors. A typical preferred stock issue has the following basic characteristics:

1. Preferred stockholders do not normally participate with common stockholders in the election of a board of directors. However, a few preferred stock issues do grant voting rights to their holders.
2. Preferred stockholders are promised a stream of fixed dividend payments. Thus, preferred dividends resemble bond coupons.
3. Preferred stock normally has no specified maturity, but it is often callable by the issuer.
4. Management can suspend payment of preferred dividends without setting off a bankruptcy process, but only after suspending payment of all common stock dividends.
5. If preferred dividends have been suspended, all unpaid preferred dividends normally become a cumulative debt that must be paid in full before the corporation can resume any payment of common stock dividends. Preferred stock with this feature is termed *cumulative preferred.*
6. Some preferred stock issues have a conversion feature similar to convertible bonds. These are called *convertible preferred stock.*

All else equal, preferred stock normally pays a lower interest rate to investors than do corporate bonds. This is because, when most investors buy preferred stock, the dividends received are taxed at the same rate as bond interest payments. However, if a business corporation buys preferred stock, it can usually exclude at least 70 percent of the preferred dividends from income taxation. As a result, most preferred stock is owned by corporations that can take advantage of the preferential tax treatment of preferred dividends. However, companies that issue ordinary preferred stock must treat preferred dividends the same as common stock dividends for tax purposes and, therefore, cannot deduct preferred dividends from their taxable income.

CHECK THIS

18.7a From the perspective of common stockholders and management, what are some of the advantages of issuing preferred stock instead of bonds or new shares of common stock?

18.8 Adjustable-Rate Bonds

adjustable-rate bonds
Securities that pay coupons that change according to a prespecified rule. Also called *floating-rate bonds* or simply *floaters*.

Many bond, note, and preferred stock issues allow the issuer to adjust the annual coupon according to a rule or formula based on current market interest rates. These securities are called **adjustable-rate bonds**; they are also sometimes called *floating-rate bonds* or *floaters*.

For example, a typical adjustment rule might specify that the coupon rate be reset annually to be equal to the current rate on 180-day maturity U.S. Treasury bills plus 2 percent. Alternatively, a more flexible rule might specify that the coupon rate on a bond issue cannot be set below 105 percent of the yield to maturity of newly issued five-year Treasury notes. Thus, if five-year Treasury notes have recently been sold to yield 6 percent, the minimum allowable coupon rate is $1.05 \times 6\% = 6.3\%$.

Adjustable-rate bonds and notes are often putable at par value. For this reason, an issuer may set a coupon rate above an allowable minimum to discourage bondholders from selling their bonds back to the corporation.

CHECK THIS

18.8a How does an adjustable coupon rate feature affect the interest rate risk of a bond?

18.8b How might bondholders respond if the coupon rate on an adjustable-rate putable bond was set below market interest rates?

18.9 Corporate Bond Credit Ratings

credit rating
An assessment of the credit quality of a bond issue based on the issuer's financial condition.

WWW

Visit these rating agency Web sites: Duff & Phelps at www.dufflic.com
Fitch at www.fitchibca.com
Moody's at www.moodys.com
S&P at www.standardandpoors.com

When a corporation sells a new bond issue to investors, it usually subscribes to several bond rating agencies for a credit evaluation of the bond issue. Each contracted rating agency then provides a **credit rating**—an assessment of the credit quality of the bond issue based on the issuer's financial condition. Rating agencies charge a fee for this service. As part of the contractual arrangement between the bond issuer and the rating agency, the issuer agrees to allow a continuing review of its credit rating even if the rating deteriorates. Without a credit rating a new bond issue would be very difficult to sell to the public, which is why almost all bond issues originally sold to the general public have a credit rating assigned at the time of issuance. Also, most public bond issues have ratings assigned by several rating agencies.

Established rating agencies in the United States include Duff & Phelps, Inc. (D&P); Fitch Investors Service (Fitch); McCarthy, Crisanti and Maffei (MCM); Moody's Investors Service (Moody's); and Standard & Poor's Corporation (S&P). Of these, the two best known rating agencies are Moody's and Standard & Poor's. These companies publish regularly updated credit ratings for thousands of domestic and international bond issues.

TABLE 18.2 Corporate Bond Credit Rating Symbols

Rating Agency			
Moody's	**Duff & Phelps**	**Standard & Poor's**	**Credit Rating Description**
		Investment-Grade Bond Ratings	
Aaa	1	AAA	Highest credit rating, maximum safety
Aa1	2	AA+	
Aa2	3	AA	High credit quality, investment-grade bonds
Aa3	4	AA−	
A1	5	A+	
A2	6	A	Upper-medium quality, investment-grade bonds
A3	7	A−	
Baa1	8	BBB+	
Baa2	9	BBB	Lower-medium quality, investment-grade bonds
Baa3	10	BBB−	
		Speculative-Grade Bond Ratings	
Ba1	11	BB+	Low credit quality, speculative-grade bonds
Ba2	12	BB	
Ba3	13	BB−	
B1	14	B+	Very low credit quality, speculative-grade bonds
B2	15	B	
B3	16	B−	
		Extremely Speculative-Grade Bond Ratings	
Caa	17	CCC+	Extremely low credit standing, high-risk bonds
		CCC	
		CCC−	
Ca		CC	Extremely speculative
C		C	
		D	Bonds in default

It is important to realize that corporate bond ratings are assigned to particular bond issues and not to the issuer of those bonds. For example, a senior bond issue is likely to have a higher credit rating than a subordinated issue even if both are issued by the same corporation. Similarly, a corporation with two bond issues outstanding may have a higher credit rating assigned to one issue because that issue has stronger covenant protection specified in the bond's indenture contract.

Seniority and covenant protection are not the only things affecting bond ratings. Bond rating agencies consider a number of factors before assigning a credit rating, including an appraisal of the financial strength of the issuer, the caliber of the issuer's management, and the issuer's position in an industry as well as the industry's position in the economy. In general, a bond rating is intended to be a comparative indicator of overall credit quality for a particular bond issue. However, the rating in itself is not a recommendation to buy or sell a bond.

Table 18.2 summarizes corporate bond rating symbols and definitions used by Moody's (first column), Duff & Phelps (second column), and Standard & Poor's (third column). As shown, bond credit ratings fall into three broad categories: investment-grade, speculative-grade, and extremely speculative-grade.

18.12 Summary and Conclusions

In this chapter, we cover the important topic of corporate bonds. Bonds are a major source of capital used by corporations. This chapter covers many aspects of this market, including the following items—grouped by the chapter's important concepts.

1. Corporate bond basics.

A. A corporate bond represents a corporation's promise to pay bondholders a fixed sum of money at maturity, along with periodic payments of interest. The sum paid at maturity is the bond's principal, and the periodic interest payments are coupons. Most bonds pay fixed coupons, but some pay floating coupon rates adjusted regularly according to prevailing market interest rates.

B. The largest category of corporate bond investors is life insurance companies, which own about a third of all outstanding corporate bonds. Remaining ownership shares are roughly equally distributed among individual investors, pension funds, banks, and foreign investors.

C. The existence of an active secondary market for corporate bonds is important to most bond investors. The greatest total volume of bond trading occurs in the OTC market.

2. Callable bonds.

A. Corporate bonds are usually callable, which means that the issuer has the right to buy back outstanding bonds before maturity. When a bond issue is called, bondholders surrender their bonds in exchange for a prespecified call price.

B. Make-whole call provisions have become common in the corporate bond market. If a callable bond is called and has a make-whole call provision, bondholders receive the approximate value of what the bond is worth. This call provision gets its name because the bondholder does not suffer a loss if the bond is called.

3. The different types of corporate bonds.

A. Debentures are the most common type of corporate bond. Debenture bonds represent the unsecured debt of a corporation. Mortgage bonds represent debt issued with a lien on specific property pledged as security for the bonds. Collateral trust bonds are characterized by a pledge of financial assets as security for a bond issue. Equipment trust certificates are issued according to a lease form of financing, where investors purchase equipment trust certificates and the proceeds from this sale are used to purchase equipment that is leased to a corporation.

B. A bond indenture is a formal agreement between the corporation and bondholders that spells out the legal rights and obligations of both parties with respect to a bond issue. An indenture typically specifies the seniority of a bond issue, along with any call provisions, put provisions, bond-to-stock conversion provisions, and sinking fund provisions.

4. The basics of bond ratings.

A. When a corporation sells a new bond issue to the public, it usually has a credit rating assigned by several independent bond rating agencies. Without a credit rating, a new bond issue would be difficult to sell, which is why almost all bond issues sold to the public have credit ratings assigned.

B. Bonds with a speculative or lower grade rating, commonly called high-yield bonds, or junk bonds, represent corporate debt with higher than average credit risk. Credit ratings for junk bonds are frequently revised to reflect changing financial conditions.

GET REAL

This chapter explored the world of corporate bonds, an important category of investments for institutions, such as pension funds and life insurance companies, and also for individuals. This category also includes convertible bonds and preferred stock. How should you put this information to work?

Now that you understand the most important features of corporate bonds, you need to buy several different issues to experience the real-world gains and losses that come with managing a bond portfolio. So, with a simulated brokerage account (such as Stock-Trak), try putting roughly equal dollar amounts into three or four different corporate bond issues. Be sure to include some junk bonds in your selections. Check the credit ratings of the bond issues you have selected at a site such as Bonds Online (www.bondsonline.com).

You can find out more information about corporate bonds at the many Web sites now specializing in bonds, including Investing In Bonds (www.investinginbonds.com) and Bond Markets (www.sifma.org). The Web sites of bond rating agencies such as Moody's (www.moodys.com), Standard & Poor's (www.standardandpoors.com), Duff & Phelps (www.duffllc.com), and Fitch (www.fitchibca.com) are also quite informative.

As you monitor the prices of your bonds, notice how interest rates influence their prices. You may also notice that for bonds with lower credit ratings, the stock price of the issuing company is an important influence. Why do you think this is so?

Of course, with the convertible issues the bond price will definitely be influenced by the underlying stock value, but the impact depends on the specific conversion features of the bond, including whether the bond is in the money or not.

Key Terms

Chapter Review Problems and Self-Test

1. **Callable Bonds** A particular bond matures in 30 years. It is callable in 10 years at 110. The call price is then cut by 1 percent of par each year until the call price reaches par. If the bond is called in 12 years, how much will you receive? Assume a $1,000 face value.
2. **Convertible Bonds** A convertible bond features a conversion ratio of 50. What is the conversion price? If the stock sells for $30 per share, what is the conversion value?

3. **Convertible Bonds** A convertible bond has an 8 percent coupon, paid semiannually, and will mature in 15 years. If the bond were not convertible, it would be priced to yield 9 percent. The conversion ratio on the bond is 40, and the stock is currently selling for $24 per share. What is the minimum value of this bond?

Answers to Self-Test Problems

1. The call price will be 110% − 2 × 1% = 108% of face value, or $1,080.
2. The conversion price is face value divided by the conversion ratio, $1,000/50 = $20. The conversion value is what the bond is worth on a converted basis, 50 × $30 = $1,500.
3. The minimum value is the larger of the conversion value and the intrinsic bond value. The conversion value is 40 × $24 = $960. To calculate the intrinsic bond value, note that we have a face value of $1,000 (by assumption), a semiannual coupon of $40, an annual yield of 9 percent (4.5 percent per half-year), and 15 years to maturity (30 half-years). Using the standard bond pricing formula from an earlier chapter, the bond's price (be sure to verify this) if it were not convertible is $918.56. This convertible bond thus will sell for more than $960.

Test Your Investment Quotient

For the remaining questions and problems, the circled numbers in the margin refer to the corresponding learning objective in this chapter.

IQ

(1) 1. **Trust Certificates** An airline elects to finance the purchase of some new airplanes using equipment trust certificates. Under the legal arrangement associated with such certificates, the airplanes are pledged as collateral, but which other factor applies?

CFA® PROBLEMS

- **a.** The airline still has legal title to the planes.
- **b.** Legal title to the planes resides with the manufacturer.
- **c.** The airline does not get legal title to the planes until the manufacturer is paid off.
- **d.** Legal title to the planes resides with a third party who then leases the planes to the airline.

(2) 2. **Callable Bonds** What does the call feature of a bond mean?

CFA® PROBLEMS

- **a.** Investor can call for payment on demand.
- **b.** Investor can only call if the firm defaults on an interest payment.
- **c.** Issuer can call the bond issue prior to the maturity date.
- **d.** Issuer can call the issue during the first three years.

(2) 3. **Callable Bonds** Who benefits from a call provision on a corporate bond?

CFA® PROBLEMS

- **a.** The issuer
- **b.** The bondholders
- **c.** The trustee
- **d.** The government regulators

(2) 4. **Callable Bonds** Which of the following describes a bond with a call feature?

CFA® PROBLEMS

- **a.** It is attractive, because the immediate receipt of principal plus premium produces a high return.
- **b.** It is more likely to be called when interest rates are high, because the interest savings will be greater.
- **c.** It would usually have a higher yield than a similar noncallable bond.
- **d.** It generally has a higher credit rating than a similar noncallable bond.

(2) 5. **Callable Bonds** Which of the following is not a component of call risk for a bond investor?

CFA® PROBLEMS

- **a.** The cash flow pattern for the bond is not known with certainty.
- **b.** When the issuer calls a bond, the investor is exposed to reinvestment risk.
- **c.** The value of a callable bond drops when expected interest rate volatility decreases.
- **d.** The capital appreciation potential of a callable bond is lower than a noncallable bond.

(2) 6. **Callable Bonds** Two bonds are identical, except one is callable and the other is noncallable. Compared to the noncallable bond, the callable bond has

- **a.** Negative convexity and a lower price.
- **b.** Negative convexity and a higher price.
- **c.** Positive convexity and a lower price.
- **d.** Positive convexity and a higher price.

www.mhhe.com/jm5e

CFA® PROBLEMS

7. **Convexity** What does positive convexity on a bond imply?

   a. The direction of change in yield is directly related to the change in price.
   b. Prices increase at a faster rate as yields drop than they decrease as yields rise.
   c. Price changes are the same for both increases and decreases in yields.
   d. Prices increase and decrease at a faster rate than the change in yield.

8. **Convexity** A bond with negative convexity is best described as having a price-yield relationship displaying

   a. Positive convexity at high yields and negative convexity at low yields.
   b. Negative convexity at high yields and positive convexity at low yields.
   c. Negative convexity at low and high yields and positive at medium yields.
   d. Positive convexity at low and high yields and negative at medium yields.

CFA® PROBLEMS

9. **Convexity and Duration** Which of the following *most accurately* measures interest rate sensitivity for bonds with embedded options?

   a. Convexity
   b. Effective duration
   c. Modified duration
   d. Macaulay duration

10. **Convexity and Duration** Which of the following most accurately measures interest rate sensitivity for bonds *without* embedded options?

   a. Convexity
   b. Effective duration
   c. Modified duration
   d. Macaulay duration

CFA® PROBLEMS

11. **Indentures** Which of the following is not a responsibility of a corporate trustee with regard to a bond's trust indenture?

   a. Checking compliance
   b. Authenticating the bonds issued
   c. Negotiating the terms
   d. Declaring defaults

CFA® PROBLEMS

12. **Refundings** The refunding provision of an indenture allows bonds to be retired unless

   a. They are replaced with a new issue having a lower interest cost.
   b. The remaining time to maturity is less than five years.
   c. The stated time period in the indenture has not passed.
   d. The stated time period in the indenture has passed.

CFA® PROBLEMS

13. **Debentures** Holders of unsecured debentures with a negative pledge clause can claim which of the following assurances?

   a. No additional secured debt will be issued in the future.
   b. If any secured debt is issued in the future, the unsecured debentures must be redeemed at par.
   c. The debentures will be secured, but to a lesser degree than any secured debt issued in the future.
   d. The debentures will be secured at least equally with any secured debt issued in the future.

14. **Credit Risk** An "original issue junk" bond is *best* described as a bond issued

   a. Below investment grade.
   b. At an original issue discount.
   c. As investment grade, but declined to speculative grade.
   d. As below investment grade, but upgraded to speculative grade.

CFA® PROBLEMS

15. **Credit Risk** A "fallen angel" bond is *best* described as a bond issued

   a. Below investment grade.
   b. At an original issue discount.
   c. As investment grade, but declined to speculative grade.
   d. As a secured bond, but the collateral value declined below par value.

CFA® PROBLEMS

16. **Preferred Stock** Nonconvertible preferred stock has which of the following in comparison to common stock?

   a. Preferential claim on a company's earnings.
   b. A predetermined dividend rate.

WORK THE WEB

As we mentioned earlier in this chapter, municipal bonds are less liquid than Treasury securities and often have higher bid-ask spreads. So how high can the spreads go? We went to www.municipalbonds.com to find out. Below you see part of what we found for the second quarter of 2007.

All Information for Trade Date: **06/13/2007**.

Worst Ten Spreads Between Lowest BID and Highest OFFER

CUSIP	Municipal Bond Name / Description	Coupon	Maturity	Bid Side Customer Sold to Dealer (Lowest / Highest)	Offer Side Customer Purchase from Dealer (Lowest / Highest)	Spread	# of Trades	Volume (000)
59465E-FC-2	MICHIGAN ST HOSP FIN AUTH REV HOSP-ST JOHN HOSP & MED CTR-A	5.250	05/15/2026	4.950 / 4.950	104.500 / 104.500	99.550	2	190
89602N-KY-9	TRIBOROUGH BRDG & TUNL AUTH N Y REVS GEN-SER A	5.000	11/15/2037	4.803 / 4.803	102.441 / 102.441	97.638	6	+6
626853-BX-2	MURRAY CITY UTAH HOSP REV REF-IHC HEALTH SVCS INC	4.750	05/15/2020	4.690 / 4.690	99.850 / 99.850	95.160	5	1120
358802-N5-1	FRISCO TEX INDPT SCH DIST SCH BLDG	2.750	08/15/2039	63.728 / 100.272	64.173 / 100.000	36.272	4	+4
05922K-FF-1	BALTIMORE MD PROJ REV REF-WTR PROJS-SER A	5.125	07/01/2042	95.940 / 98.550	99.948 / 105.050	9.110	9	70

This table shows some alarming news for municipal bond investors. As you can see, the biggest bid-ask spread in the table is for a hospital bond in Michigan. Assuming trades occurred at the bid and ask (offer) prices posted, the lowest price received by a customer on this day was 4.95 and the highest price paid by a customer was 104.50. Assuming a $5,000 par value, this means one customer sold this bond for $247.50 and another paid about $5,225 for the same bond. These prices represent a whopping difference of about $4,977. In addition, look at the difference between the lowest (63.728) and highest (100.272) bids for the fourth bond listed. If these prices are posted simultaneously, they represent about a $1,827 difference in the price that an investor can sell this bond, assuming a $5,000 par value.

serial bonds
Bonds issued with maturity dates scheduled at intervals, so that a fraction of the bond issue matures in each year of a multiple-year period.

Municipal bonds are commonly issued with a serial maturity structure, hence the term **serial bonds**. In a serial bond issue, a fraction of the total issue amount is scheduled to mature in each year over a multiple-year period. As an example, a serial bond issue may contain bonds that mature in each year over a 5-year period, with the first group maturing 11 years after the original issue date and the last group maturing 15 years after issuance. The

FIGURE 19.6 Municipal Securities

Tax Exempt Bonds

Thursday, June 14, 2007

Issue	Coupon	Maturity	Price	Change	Bid Yield
Anaheim CA Pub Fin Auth	4.750	09-01-33	99.399	.147	4.79
CA Ed Facs Ath rev bds	4.500	10-01-33	94.540	.425	4.87
CA Ed Facs Ath rev bds	4.750	10-01-37	100.074	...	4.74
CA gen oblig ref bds	4.500	08-01-30	92.926	.181	5.01
CA gen oblig ref bds	4.250	08-01-33	90.337	.136	4.90
CA State var purp gen	4.250	12-01-35	89.569	...	4.93
DallasFtWorthTX JointRv0	5.000	11-01-32	100.428	...	4.92
DC general obligation	4.750	06-01-36	97.993	-.305	4.88
DC general obligation	4.750	06-01-33	98.530	-.146	4.85
DC Wtr & Swr Auth publ	5.000	10-01-38	102.010	-.001	4.75
Houston TX Hghr Ed Fin Cp	4.500	11-15-37	93.108	...	4.94
Houston TX Hghr Ed Fin Cp	5.000	05-15-47	101.639	.055	4.79
Hudson Yrds Infrastrctr NY	4.500	02-15-47	92.666	-.164	4.92
Judson Ind Sch Dist TX	4.500	02-01-35	93.258	...	4.95
Long Island Pwr Auth NY	4.250	05-01-33	91.121	-.137	4.85
MA Sch Bldg Auth dedicated	4.750	08-15-32	99.412	...	4.79
MA Sch Bldg Auth dedicated	4.500	08-15-35	93.918	...	4.90
Mass Wtr Res Auth	4.500	08-01-46	91.283	.048	5.01
Miami-Dade FL avi rev Ser	5.000	10-01-39	100.352	...	4.96
Miami-Dade FL avi rev Ser	5.000	10-01-40	100.120	...	4.98
Miss. Hlth & Ed Facs Auth	4.500	01-15-41	92.511	.154	4.96

Source: Reprinted with permission from *The Wall Street Journal*, June 14, 2007, © 2007 Dow Jones & Company, Inc. All Rights Reserved Worldwide.

purpose of a serial maturity structure is to spread out the principal repayment, thereby avoiding a lump-sum repayment at a single maturity date.

term bonds
Bonds from an issue with a single maturity date.

When an entire bond issue matures on a single date, the bonds are called **term bonds**. Term bonds normally have a sinking fund provision. A sinking fund is a trustee-managed account to which the issuer makes regular payments. Account reserves are dedicated to redeeming a fraction of the bond issue on each of a series of scheduled redemption dates. Each redemption usually proceeds by lottery, where randomly selected bonds are called and the affected bondholders receive the sinking fund call price. Alternatively, scheduled redemptions can be implemented by purchasing bonds from investors at current market prices. This latter option is usually selected by the issuer when the bonds are selling at a discount from par value. The motive for a sinking fund provision is similar to that for a serial maturity structure; it provides a means for the issuer to avoid a lump-sum principal repayment at a single maturity date.

put bonds
Bonds that can be sold back to the issuer.

Some municipal bonds are putable, and these are called **put bonds**. The holder of a put bond, also called a *tender offer bond,* has the option of selling the bond back to the issuer, normally at par value. Some put bonds can be tendered any time, whereas others can be tendered only on regularly scheduled dates. Weekly, monthly, quarterly, semiannual, and annual put date schedules are all used. Notice that with a put bond, maturity is effectively the choice of the bondholder. This feature protects bondholders from rising interest rates and the associated fall in bond prices. However, a putable bond will have a higher price than a comparable nonputable bond. The price differential simply reflects the value of the put option to sell back the bonds.

variable-rate notes
Securities that pay an interest rate that changes according to market conditions. Also called *floaters.*

While most municipal bonds maintain a constant coupon rate (hence the term fixed-rate bonds), interest rate risk has induced many municipalities to issue **variable-rate notes**, often called *floaters.* For these debt issues, the coupon rate is adjusted periodically according to an index-based rule. For example, at each adjustment the coupon rate may be set at 60 percent of the prevailing rate on 91-day maturity U.S. Treasury bills. A variable-rate note may also be putable, in which case it is called a *variable-rate demand obligation,* often abbreviated to VRDO. A stipulation attached to most VRDOs allows the issuer to convert an entire variable-rate issue to a fixed-rate issue following a specified conversion procedure. Essentially, the issuer notifies each VRDO holder of the intent to convert the outstanding VRDO issue to a fixed-rate issue on a specific future date. In response, VRDO holders have the option of tendering their VRDOs for cash, or they can accept conversion of their VRDOs into fixed-rate bonds.

TYPES OF MUNICIPAL BONDS

There are two basic types of municipal bonds: revenue bonds and general obligation bonds, often referred to as GOs. General obligation bonds are issued by all levels of municipal governments, including states, counties, cities, towns, school districts, and water districts. They are secured by the general taxing powers of the municipalities issuing the bonds. For state governments and large city governments, tax revenue is collected from a diverse base of income taxes on corporations and individuals, sales taxes, and property taxes. In contrast, tax revenues for smaller municipalities are largely derived from property taxes, although sales taxes have become increasingly important. Because of their large, diverse tax bases, general obligation bonds issued by states and large cities are often called *unlimited tax bonds* or *full faith and credit bonds.*

However, some general obligation bonds are called *limited tax bonds.* The distinction between limited and unlimited tax bonds arises when a constitutional limit or other statutory limit is placed on the power of a municipality to assess taxes. For example, an amendment to the California state constitution, popularly known as Proposition 13 when it was enacted, placed rigid limits on the ability of California municipalities to assess taxes on real estate.

revenue bonds
Municipal bonds secured by revenues collected from a specific project or projects.

Revenue bonds constitute the bulk of all outstanding municipal bonds. **Revenue bonds** are bonds secured by proceeds collected from the projects they finance. Thus, the credit quality of a revenue bond issue is largely determined by the ability of a project to generate where 10 percent or more of the issue finances facilities used by private entities and is secured by payments from private entities.

Interest on private activity bonds is tax-exempt only if the bond issue falls into a so-called qualified category. Qualified private activity bonds that still enjoy a tax-exempt interest privilege include public airport bonds, multifamily housing bonds, nonvehicular mass commuting bonds, and various other project bonds. The major types of private activity bonds that do not qualify for tax-exempt interest are those used to finance sports stadiums, convention facilities, parking facilities, and industrial parks. However, these taxable private activity bonds may still enjoy exemption from state and local income tax. In any case, as a result of the 1986 act and the continuing need to finance private activity projects, new issues of taxable municipal revenue bonds are frequently sold with yields similar to corporate bond yields.

19.9 Summary and Conclusions

The topic of this chapter is government bonds. The government bonds covered in this chapter include U.S. Treasury bonds, notes, and bills, as well as state, city, county, and local municipal bonds. In this chapter, we cover many aspects of these investments—which we summarize by the chapter's important concepts.

1. The basics of U.S. Treasury securities and how they are sold.

A. The U.S. federal government is the largest single borrower in the world, with about $5 trillion of publicly held debt. Responsibility for managing this debt belongs to the U.S. Treasury, which issues Treasury bills, notes, and bonds at regular auctions to finance government debt.

B. Treasury bills are short-term obligations that are sold on a discount basis. Treasury notes are medium-term obligations that pay fixed semiannual coupons as well as payment of face value at maturity. Treasury bonds are long-term obligations that pay their face value at maturity and pay fixed semiannual coupons.

2. The workings of the STRIPS program and pricing treasury bonds.

A. The U.S. Treasury sponsors the STRIPS program, where Treasury bonds and notes are broken down into principal strips, which represent face-value payments, and coupon strips, which represent individual coupon payments. Because each strip created under the STRIPS program represents a single future payment, strips effectively become zero coupon bonds.

B. Treasury bond and note price quotes are stated on a percentage of par basis: a price of 102 equals par value plus 2 percent. Fractions of a percent are stated in thirty-seconds. Thus, a price stated as 102:28 is actually equal to 102 + 28/32, or 102.875. Because Treasury bonds and notes pay semiannual coupons, bond yields are stated on a semiannual basis.

C. The U.S. Treasury also issues securities that guarantee a fixed rate of return in excess of realized inflation rates. These inflation-indexed Treasury securities are commonly called TIPS. TIPS pay a fixed coupon rate on their current principal and adjust their principal semiannually according to the most recent inflation rate.

3. How federal agencies borrow money.

A. Several federal agencies are authorized to issue securities directly to the public. Bonds issued by U.S. government agencies have a credit quality almost identical to U.S. Treasury issues, but agency notes and bonds are attractive to many investors because they offer higher yields than comparable U.S. Treasury securities. However, the market for agency debt is less active than the market for U.S. Treasury debt and investors are potentially subject to state income taxes on agency debt interest, while U.S. Treasury debt interest is not subject to state taxes.

B. Another large market for government debt is the market for municipal government debt. Total municipal debt outstanding currently exceeds $2 trillion, divided among most of the more than 85,000 state and local governments in the United States. Individual investors hold about half this debt, while the remainder is roughly split equally between holdings of property and casualty insurance companies and commercial banks.

4. How municipalities borrow money.

A. Municipal notes and bonds are intermediate- to long-term interest-bearing obligations of state and local governments or agencies of those governments. Municipal debt is commonly called the tax-exempt market because the coupon interest is usually exempt from federal income tax, which makes municipal bonds attractive to investors in the highest income tax brackets. However, yields on municipal debt are less than yields on corporate debt with similar features and credit quality, thus eliminating much of the advantage of the tax exemption.

B. Most municipal bonds pay a constant coupon rate, but some municipal notes pay variable coupon rates that change according to prevailing market interest rates. Also, a call provision is a standard feature of most municipal bond issues. A call provision allows an issuer to retire outstanding bonds before they mature.

C. There are two basic types of municipal bonds: revenue bonds and general obligation bonds. Revenue bonds, which constitute the bulk of all outstanding municipal bonds, are secured by proceeds collected from the projects they finance. General obligation bonds, which are issued by all levels of municipal governments, are secured by the general taxing powers of the municipalities issuing the bonds.

D. As part of the process for issuing municipal bonds to the public, a rating agency is paid a fee to assign a credit rating to a new bond issue. In the last two decades, municipalities have increasingly been obtaining bond insurance for new bond issues through an insurance policy written by a commercial insurance company. With bond insurance, the credit quality of the bond issue is determined by the financial strength of the insurance company, not the municipality alone.

GET REAL

This chapter covered government bonds, a large and important securities market. How should you put your knowledge to work? Begin by purchasing (in a simulated brokerage account like Stock-Trak) the various types of government securities that are available for trading out there. Observe how their prices and yields change over time.

You should also learn more about buying Treasury securities. A great place to start is www.treasurydirect.gov. There you can examine and download the forms needed to bid in the regular auctions. You can also obtain current Treasury auction information, including forthcoming auctions and the results of previous auctions. You can also read about the *Treasury Direct* program, which is probably the best way of purchasing Treasury issues for individual investors. But if you prefer U.S. Savings Bonds, you can check out the section of the Web site that tells you all you need to know about them.

You will probably find that you cannot trade municipal bonds through a simulated brokerage account. The reason is that the market for municipals is so thin that getting timely price information for a particular issue isn't possible. In practice, municipal bonds are best suited for buy-and-hold investors who buy the bonds when originally issued and hold them until maturity. You can now buy municipal bonds online through a number of brokers. Try, for example, First Miami (www.firstmiami.com) or Lebenthal Investments (www.lebenthal.com). Also take a look at Muni Auction (www.muniauction.com).

Key Terms

bid-ask spread 619
call provision 628
default risk 626
discount basis 614
face value 614
general obligation bonds (GOs) 626
hybrid bonds 631
imputed interest 614
insured municipal bonds 632
private activity bonds 634
put bonds 630
revenue bonds 630
serial bonds 629
stop-out bid 622
STRIPS 615
term bonds 630
variable-rate notes 630
yield to call (YTC) 618
zero coupon bond 615

Chapter Review Problems and Self-Test

1. **Treasury Yields** A callable Treasury bond's price is 140:25. It has a coupon rate of 10 percent, makes semiannual payments, and matures in 21 years. What yield would be reported in the financial press?
2. **Equivalent Yields** A particular investor faces a 40 percent tax rate. If a AA-rated municipal bond yields 4 percent, what must a similar taxable issue yield for the investor to be impartial to them?

Answers to Self-Test Problems

1. First, note that this is a callable issue selling above par, so the yield to call will be reported. All callable Treasury bonds are callable at face value five years before they mature. Thus, to calculate the yield to call, all we have to do is pretend that the bond has 16 years to maturity instead of 21. We therefore have a bond with a price of 140.78125 (after converting from thirty-seconds), a coupon of 10 percent paid semiannually, and a maturity of 16 years (or 32 periods). Verify, using the standard bond formula from an earlier chapter, that the semiannual yield to call is 3 percent, so the reported yield would be 6 percent.
2. The equivalent taxable yield is the municipal yield "grossed up" by one minus the tax rate:

$$\frac{4\%}{1 - .40} = 6.67\%$$

Test Your Investment Quotient

For the remaining questions and problems, the circled numbers in the margin refer to the corresponding learning objective in this chapter.

(2) 1. **Zero Coupon Bonds** What is the yield to maturity (YTM) on a zero coupon bond?

   a. The interest rate realized if the bond is held to maturity.
   b. The interest rate realized when the bond is sold.
   c. The coupon yield for an equivalent coupon bond.
   d. A fixed rate when the bond is issued.

(1) 2. **Treasury Notes** The coupon rate for a Treasury note is set

   a. The same for all Treasury note issues.
   b. By a formula based on the size of the Treasury note issue.
   c. According to prevailing interest rates at time of issuance.
   d. According to the supply and demand for money.

(1) 3. **Treasury Notes and Bonds** U.S. Treasury notes and bonds have face value denominations as small as

   a. $1,000
   b. $5,000
   c. $10,000
   d. $25,000

CFA® PROBLEMS

1 **4. Treasury Bonds** What is the dollar value of a U.S. Treasury bond quoted at 92:24?

a. $922.75
b. $922.40
c. $927.50
d. Indeterminable

CFA® PROBLEMS

1 **5. Treasury Bonds** The following are quotes for a U.S. Treasury bond:

Bid	Asked
102:02	102:05

1 If the face value of the bond is $1,000, the price an investor should pay for the bond is *closest* to

a. $1,020.63
b. $1,021.56
c. $1,025.00
d. $1,026.25

1 **6. Treasury Bonds** A trader purchases $5 million face value of Treasury bonds at 95:16 and then later sells the bonds at 95:24. What is the round-trip gain on these transactions?

a. $1,250
b. $12,500
c. $4,000
d. $40,000

2 **7. Treasury STRIPS** When originally issued, a 10-year maturity Treasury note can be stripped into how many separate components?

a. 10
b. 11
c. 20
d. 21

1 **8. Treasury Bills** Treasury bills are sold on a discount basis, meaning that the difference between their issued price and their redemption value is

a. The same for all T-bill issues.
b. The imputed interest on the T-bill.
c. Never less than the issued price.
d. The bond equivalent yield for the T-bill.

1 **9. Treasury Auctions** Which of the following statements about single-price Treasury auctions is false?

a. Competitive bidders pay the stop-out bid.
b. Noncompetitive bidders pay the stop-out bid plus a small premium.
c. Noncompetitive bidders pay the stop-out bid.
d. All of the above are true.

1 **10. Treasury Dealers** When trading U.S. Treasury securities, Treasury dealers

a. Buy at the bid price and sell at the asked price.
b. Sell at the bid price and buy at the asked price.
c. Buy at the stop-out bid price and sell at the market price.
d. Sell at the stop-out bid price and buy at the market price.

1 **11. Savings Bonds** A Series EE Savings Bond with a face value of $1,000 is originally sold for

a. $1,000.
b. $500.
c. A price based on the recent inflation rate.
d. 90 percent of the price of a recently issued five-year T-note.

1 **12. Savings Bonds** Series EE savings bonds are guaranteed to double in price if they are held for

a. 10 years
b. 5 years
c. 15 years
d. 20 years

(1) **13. Savings Bonds** A Series I savings bond with a face value of $1,000 is originally sold at a price of

a. $1,000.
b. $500.
c. A price based on the recent inflation rate.
d. 90 percent of the price of a recently issued five-year T-note.

(1) **14. Savings Bonds** The interest rate on Series I savings bonds is reset every six months as

a. 90 percent of the rate on newly issued five-year T-notes.
b. 90 percent of the rate on newly issued five-year T-notes plus the recent inflation rate.
c. A fixed rate plus the recent inflation rate.
d. An adjustable rate plus the recent inflation rate.

CFA® PROBLEMS

(3) **15. Agency Bonds** Which statement applies to a bond issued by an agency of the U.S. government?

a. It is exempt from the federal income tax on interest.
b. It becomes a direct obligation of the U.S. Treasury in case of default.
c. It is secured by assets held by the agency.
d. None of the above.

CFA® PROBLEMS

(3) **16. Agency Bonds** Which is true for bonds issued by all agencies of the U.S. government?

a. They become direct obligations of the U.S. Treasury.
b. They are secured bonds backed by government holdings.
c. They are exempt from federal income tax.
d. None of the above.

(3) **17. Agency Bonds** Which of the following investors is most likely to invest in agency bonds?

a. High-income individual with a need for liquidity.
b. High-income individual living in a triple income tax municipality.
c. Commercial bank.
d. Life insurance company.

(4) **18. Municipal Bonds** Which of the following constitutes the bulk of all outstanding municipal bonds?

a. Revenue bonds
b. General obligation bonds
c. Moral obligation bonds
d. Private activity bonds

(4) **19. Municipal Bonds** Which of the following investors is most likely to invest in locally issued municipal bonds?

a. High-income individual with a need for liquidity.
b. High-income individual living in a triple income tax municipality.
c. Commercial bank.
d. Life insurance company.

CFA® PROBLEMS

(4) **20. Revenue Bonds** A revenue bond is distinguished from a general obligation bond in that revenue bonds have which of the following characteristics?

a. They are issued by counties, special districts, cities, towns, and state-controlled authorities, whereas general obligation bonds are issued only by the states themselves.
b. They are typically secured by limited taxing power, whereas general obligation bonds are secured by unlimited taxing power.
c. They are issued to finance specific projects and are secured by the revenues of the project being financed.
d. They have first claim to any revenue increase of the issuing tax authority.

(4) **21. Insured Municipal Bonds** Which of the following is not a method used by municipal bond insurers to manage default risk?

a. Only insure bonds from municipalities with a good credit rating.
b. Diversify default risk by writing insurance policies for municipalities spread across a wide geographic area.
c. Maintain substantial investment portfolios as a source of financial reserves.
d. All of the above are used to manage default risk.

CFA® PROBLEMS

4 **22. Insured Municipal Bonds** Which one of the following generally is not true of an insured municipal bond?

a. The price on an insured bond is higher than that on an otherwise identical uninsured bond.
b. The insurance can be canceled in the event the issuer fails to maintain predetermined quality standards.
c. The insurance premium is a one-time payment made at the time of issuance.
d. The insurance company is obligated to make all defaulted principal and/or interest payments in a prompt and timely fashion.

CFA® PROBLEMS

4 **23. Taxable Equivalent Yield** A municipal bond carries a coupon of 6 3/4 percent and is trading at par. To a taxpayer in the 34 percent tax bracket, what would the taxable equivalent yield of this bond be?

a. 4.5 percent
b. 10.2 percent
c. 13.4 percent
d. 19.9 percent

CFA® PROBLEMS

4 **24. Taxable Equivalent Yield** A 20-year municipal bond is currently priced at par to yield 5.53-percent. For a taxpayer in the 33 percent tax bracket, what equivalent taxable yield would this bond offer?

a. 8.25 percent
b. 10.75 percent
c. 11.40 percent
d. None of the above

CFA® PROBLEMS

4 **25. Taxable Equivalent Yield** The coupon rate on a tax-exempt bond is 5.6 percent, and the coupon rate on a taxable bond is 8 percent. Both bonds sell at par. At what tax bracket (marginal tax rate) would an investor show no preference between the two bonds?

a. 30.0 percent
b. 39.6 percent
c. 41.7 percent
d. 42.9 percent

Concept Questions

1 **1. Bills versus Bonds** What are the key differences between T-bills and T-bonds?

1 **2. Notes versus Bonds** What are the key differences between T-notes and T-bonds?

1 **3. Zeroes** What two Treasury securities are zeroes?

1 **4. Spreads** What are typical spreads for T-notes and T-bonds? Why do you think they differ from issue to issue?

1 3 **5. Agencies versus Treasuries** From an investor's standpoint, what are the key differences between Treasury and agency issues?

1 4 **6. Municipals versus Treasuries** From an investor's standpoint, what are the main differences between Treasury and municipal issues?

4 **7. Serial Bonds** What are serial bonds? What purpose does this structure serve?

4 **8. VRNs** In the context of the muni market, what are variable-rate notes? What is likely true about their risks compared to those of ordinary issues?

4 **9. Revenues versus General Obligation Munis** What is the difference between a revenue bond and a general obligation bond?

4 **10. Private Activity Munis** What is a private activity muni? What type of investor would be interested in it?

1 4 **11. Treasury versus Municipal Bonds** Treasury and municipal yields are often compared to calculate critical tax rates. What concerns might you have about such a comparison? What do you think is true about the calculated tax rate?

1 **12. Callable Treasury Bonds** For a callable Treasury bond selling above par, is it necessarily true that the yield to call will be less than the yield to maturity? Why or why not?

3 **13. Callable Agency Issues** For a callable agency bond selling above par, is it necessarily true that the yield to call will be less than the yield to maturity? Why or why not?

(1) (4) **14. Treasury versus Municipal Bonds** Why might the yield to maturity on, say, a BBB-rated municipal bond with moderate default risk actually be less than that of a U.S. Treasury bond with no default risk?

(1) (4) **15. Treasury versus Municipal Bonds** In a recent issue of *The Wall Street Journal*, compare the yields on U.S. Treasury bonds with the yields on municipal bonds. Why might these yield spreads depend on the state of the economy?

Questions and Problems

Core Questions

(2) **1. STRIPS Price** What is the price of a STRIPS with a maturity of 18 years, a face value of $10,000, and a yield to maturity of 6.7 percent?

(2) **2. STRIPS YTM** A STRIPS with 13 years until maturity and a face value of $10,000 is trading for $4,131. What is the yield to maturity?

(1) **3. Treasury Auctions** The Federal Reserve announces an offering of Treasury bills with a face value of $50 billion. Noncompetitive bids are made for $9 billion, along with the following competitive bids:

Bidder	Price Bid	Quantity Bid
A	$9,400	$15 billion
B	9,405	14 billion
C	9,410	11 billion
D	9,415	8 billion
E	9,425	10 billion
F	9,430	9 billion

In a single-price auction, which bids are accepted and what prices are paid by each bidder? How much money is raised by the entire offering?

(4) **4. Municipal Bonds** A municipal bond with a coupon rate of 3.8 percent has a yield to maturity of 4.3 percent. If the bond has 10 years to maturity, what is the price of the bond?

(4) **5. Yield to Maturity** A municipal bond with a coupon rate of 4.9 percent sells for $4,750 and has seven years until maturity. What is the yield to maturity of the bond?

(4) **6. Yield to Maturity** A municipal bond has 24 years until maturity and sells for $5,820. If the coupon rate on the bond is 5.70 percent, what is the yield to maturity?

(4) **7. Yield to Call** Assume the bond in the previous problem can be called in 10 years. What is the yield to call if the call price is 110 percent of par?

(4) **8. Aftertax Yield** A municipal bond has a yield to maturity of 4.9 percent. What corporate bond yield would make an investor in the 38 percent tax bracket indifferent between the two bonds, all else the same?

(4) **9. Tax Equivalent Yields** A taxable corporate issue yields 7.4 percent. For an investor in a 31 percent tax bracket, what is the equivalent aftertax yield?

(4) **10. Tax Rates** A taxable issue yields 6.9 percent, and a similar municipal issue yields 4.3 percent. What is the critical marginal tax rate?

Intermediate Questions

(1) **11. Treasury Prices** A Treasury bill has a bid yield of 4.23 and an asked yield of 4.21. The bill matures in 140 days. What is the least you could pay to acquire a bill? (Note: You may need to review material from an earlier chapter for the relevant formula.)

(1) **12. Treasury Prices** At what price could you sell the Treasury bill referred to in the previous question? What is the dollar spread for this bill? (Note: You may need to review material from an earlier chapter for the relevant formula.)

(1) **13. Treasury Prices** A Treasury issue is quoted at 107:13 bid and 107:15 ask. What is the least you could pay to acquire a bond?

(1) **14. Treasury Prices** A noncallable Treasury bond has a quoted yield of 6.89 percent. It has a 7.5 percent coupon and 12 years to maturity. What is its dollar price assuming a $1,000 par value? What is its quoted price?

1 **15. Treasury Yields** A Treasury bond with the longest maturity (30 years) has an asked price quoted at 97:09. The coupon rate is 5.7 percent, paid semiannually. What is the yield to maturity of this bond?

1 **16. Treasury Yields** In a recent *Wall Street Journal*, locate the Treasury bond with the longest maturity (the so-called bellwether bond). Verify that, given the ask price, the reported yield is correct.

1 **17. Yield to Call** A Treasury bond maturing in November 2014 and callable in November 2009 has a quoted price of 107:06 and a coupon rate of 11.75 percent. Assuming the bond matures in exactly 6 years, what is the yield to call?

1 **18. Callable Treasury Bonds** In a recent *Wall Street Journal*, examine the yields on Treasury bonds maturing in 2014 and 2015. Why do you think the yields for the issues maturing in 2014 are so different?

Spreadsheet Problems

2 **19. STRIPS Price** A STRIPS traded on May 1, 2008, matures in 13 years on May 1, 2021. Assuming a 5.9 percent yield to maturity, what is the STRIPS price?

2 **20. STRIPS YTM** A STRIPS traded on July 1, 2008, matures in 19 years on July 1, 2027. The quoted STRIPS price is 38.50. What is its yield to maturity?

What's on the Web?

1. **Treasury Auctions** Go to www.treasurydirect.gov and find the next Treasury auctions scheduled. When are the auctions scheduled? What instruments will be offered at these auctions?
2. **Treasury Auctions** Go to www.treasurydirect.gov and find the recently completed Treasury auctions for bills and notes. When did the auctions occur? What were the yields for each bill and note sold at these auctions?
3. **Municipal Bond Spreads** Go to www.municipalbonds.com. What was the highest bid-side spread for the most recent quarter? What was the highest offer-side spread over this same period? What were the dollar amounts of these spreads?
4. **Municipal Bond Prices** Go to www.municipalbonds.com and find the municipal bonds traded yesterday for your state. What was the most active bond in terms of the number of trades? Which bond traded the highest dollar amount? How many bonds had a spread of more than one point in trading yesterday?
5. **Savings Bonds** In this chapter, we discussed U.S. Series EE savings bonds. There are also Series HH savings bonds. These two bonds are different in several respects. Go to www.treasurydirect.gov and find out how the Series HH bonds work. What are the differences in these two types of savings bonds?

Stock-Trak Exercises

STOCK | TRAK
GLOBAL PORTFOLIO SIMULATIONS

To access the Stock-Trak Exercise for this chapter, please visit the book Web site at www.mhhe.com/jm5e and choose the corresponding chapter.

Appendix A

Answers to Test Your Investment Quotient Questions

Chapter 1

1-1 b (*Source:* 1994 Level I CFA Study Guide © 1994)
1-2 b (*Source:* 2001 Level I CFA Practice Exam © 2001)
1-3 c (*Source:* 2001 Level I CFA Practice Exam © 2001)
1-4 b (*Source:* 2001 Level I CFA Practice Exam © 2001)
1-5 b (*Source:* 2003 Level I CFA Practice Exam © 2003)
1-6 c (*Source:* 1994 Level I CFA Study Guide © 1994)
1-7 d
1-8 a
1-9 a
1-10 d
1-11 d
1-12 d
1-13 d
1-14 a (*Source:* 2003 Level I CFA Practice Exam © 2003)
1-15 b (*Source:* 2001 Level I CFA Practice Exam © 2001)

Chapter 2

2-1 a (*Source:* 2003 Level I CFA Practice Exam © 2003)
2-2 c (*Source:* 2003 Level I CFA Practice Exam © 2003)
2-3 c
2-4 c
2-5 b
2-6 b
2-7 b
2-8 a
2-9 c
2-10 b
2-11 a
2-12 a
2-13 c
2-14 c
2-15 d

Chapter 3

3-1 d
3-2 a
3-3 c
3-4 a
3-5 c
3-6 b
3-7 c
3-8 c
3-9 c
3-10 c (*Source:* 2003 Level I CFA Practice Exam © 2003)

Chapter 4

4-1 c (*Source:* 2001 Level I CFA Practice Exam © 2001)
4-2 b
4-3 d
4-4 d
4-5 d
4-6 d
4-7 a
4-8 b
4-9 a
4-10 c
4-11 b
4-12 d
4-13 a
4-14 a
4-15 d

Chapter 5

5-1 c
5-2 b
5-3 c
5-4 c (*Source:* 2003 Level I CFA Practice Exam © 2003)
5-5 a (*Source:* 2003 Level I CFA Practice Exam © 2003)
5-6 b (*Source:* 1991 Level I CFA Study Guide © 1991)
5-7 c (*Source:* 1991 Level I CFA Study Guide © 1991)
5-8 a (*Source:* 1991 Level I CFA Study Guide © 1991)
5-9 a (*Source:* 1991 Level I CFA Study Guide © 1991)
5-10 b (*Source:* 1990 Level I CFA Study Guide © 1990)
5-11 c (*Source:* 1990 Level I CFA Study Guide © 1990)
5-12 b
5-13 c
5-14 b
5-15 c

Chapter 6

6-1 c
6-2 a (*Source:* 1994 Level I CFA Study Guide © 1994)
6-3 a (*Source:* 1998 Level I CFA Practice Exam © 1998)
6-4 b (*Source:* 1994 Level I CFA Study Guide © 1994)
6-5 b (*Source:* 1994 Level I CFA Study Guide © 1994)
6-6 c (*Source:* 1994 Level I CFA Study Guide © 1994)
6-7 d (*Source:* 1994 Level I CFA Study Guide © 1994)
6-8 c (*Source:* 1998 Level I CFA Study Guide © 1998)
6-9 c (*Source:* 1994 Level I CFA Study Guide © 1994)
6-10 a (*Source:* 1991 Level I CFA Study Guide © 1991)

6-11 a (*Source:* 1994 Level I CFA Study Guide © 1994)
6-12 d
6-13 d
6-14 c
6-15 c (*Source:* 1998 Level I CFA Study Guide © 1998)
6-16 c (*Source:* 2001 Level I CFA Practice Exam © 2001)
6-17 c (*Source:* 2001 Level I CFA Practice Exam © 2001)
6-18 a
6-19 a
6-20 b

Chapter 7

7-1 d (*Source:* 2003 Level I CFA Practice Exam © 2003)
7-2 c (*Source:* 2001 Level I CFA Practice Exam © 2001)
7-3 d
7-4 d
7-5 c
7-6 a
7-7 a
7-8 d
7-9 c
7-10 d
7-11 c
7-12 d
7-13 b
7-14 d
7-15 d

Chapter 8

8-1 d (*Source:* 1994 Level I CFA Practice Exam © 1994)
8-2 c
8-3 d
8-4 b
8-5 a
8-6 b
8-7 c
8-8 a
8-9 d
8-10 b
8-11 c
8-12 b
8-13 c
8-14 b
8-15 d

Chapter 9

9-1 b
9-2 a
9-3 a
9-4 d
9-5 d (*Source:* 1988 Level I CFA Study Guide © 1988)
9-6 b
9-7 a
9-8 c
9-9 c (*Source:* 1991 Level I CFA Study Guide © 1991)
9-10 b (*Source:* 2001 Level I CFA Practice Exam © 2001)
9-11 a (*Source:* 2001 Level I CFA Practice Exam © 2001)
9-12 a
9-13 d (*Source:* 1993 Level I CFA Study Guide © 1993)
9-14 a (*Source:* 1988 Level I CFA Study Guide © 1988)
9-15 b (*Source:* 1989 Level I CFA Study Guide © 1989)
9-16 a (*Source:* 1992 Level I CFA Study Guide © 1992)
9-17 b
9-18 c
9-19 d (*Source:* 1994 Level I CFA Study Guide © 1994)
9-20 d (*Source:* 1998 Level I CFA Practice Exam © 1998)

Chapter 10

10-1 b (*Source:* 1993 Level I CFA Study Guide © 1993)
10-2 c (*Source:* 1989 Level I CFA Study Guide © 1989)
10-3 d (*Source:* 1992 Level I CFA Study Guide © 1992)
10-4 a
10-5 a
10-6 b (*Source:* 1991 Level I CFA Study Guide © 1991)
10-7 a (*Source:* 1991 Level I CFA Study Guide © 1991)
10-8 a (*Source:* 1998 Level I CFA Practice Exam © 1998)
10-9 b (*Source:* 1992 Level I CFA Study Guide © 1992)
10-10 c (*Source:* 1992 Level I CFA Study Guide © 1992)
10-11 a (*Source:* 1994 Level I CFA Study Guide © 1994)
10-12 a
10-13 c (*Source:* 1988 Level I CFA Study Guide © 1988)
10-14 c (*Source:* 1990 Level I CFA Study Guide © 1990)
10-15 c (*Source:* 1992 Level I CFA Study Guide © 1992)
10-16 a (*Source:* 1991 Level I CFA Study Guide © 1991)
10-17 a (*Source:* 1992 Level I CFA Study Guide © 1992)
10-18 b (*Source:* 1992 Level I CFA Study Guide © 1992)
10-19 a (*Source:* 1992 Level I CFA Study Guide © 1992)
10-20 d (*Source:* 2003 Level I CFA Practice Exam © 2003)
10-21 b
10-22 a
10-23 c
10-24 c (*Source:* 2003 Level I CFA Practice Exam © 2003)
10-25 c (*Source:* 2003 Level I CFA Practice Exam © 2003)

Chapter 11

11-1 d
11-2 c
11-3 c
11-4 b (*Source:* 1994 Level I CFA Study Guide © 1994)
11-5 c (*Source:* 2003 Level I CFA Practice Exam © 2003)
11-6 a (*Source:* 2003 Level I CFA Practice Exam © 2003)
11-7 a (*Source:* 2003 Level I CFA Practice Exam © 2003)
11-8 b
11-9 b
11-10 a
11-11 d
11-12 b
11-13 d
11-14 c (*Source:* 1994 Level I CFA Study Guide © 1994)
11-15 a (*Source:* 1994 Level I CFA Study Guide © 1994)

Chapter 12

12-1 d (*Source:* 1994 Level I CFA Study Guide © 1994)
12-2 a
12-3 a
12-4 d
12-5 b
12-6 b
12-7 b
12-8 c
12-9 d
12-10 d
12-11 d
12-12 a
12-13 b (*Source:* 2003 Level I CFA Practice Exam © 2003)
12-14 a (*Source:* 2003 Level I CFA Practice Exam © 2003)
12-15 b (*Source:* 2003 Level I CFA Practice Exam © 2003)

Chapter 13

13-1 b (*Source:* 1994 Level I CFA Study Guide © 1994)
13-2 a (*Source:* 1994 Level I CFA Study Guide © 1994)
13-3 b (*Source:* 1994 Level I CFA Study Guide © 1994)

13-4 c
13-5 a
13-6 b
13-7 b
13-8 d
13-9 c (*Source:* 1994 Level I CFA Study Guide © 1994)
13-10 c
13-11 d
13-12 a
13-13 d
13-14 b
13-15 c

Chapter 14

14-1 d
14-2 a
14-3 b
14-4 a
14-5 d (*Source:* 1993 Level I CFA Study Guide © 1993)
14-6 a (*Source:* 1999 Level I CFA Practice Exam © 1999)
14-7 c
14-8 d (*Source:* 2003 Level I CFA Practice Exam © 2003)
14-9 c (*Source:* 2003 Level I CFA Practice Exam © 2003)
14-10 d
14-11 a
14-12 d
14-13 d (*Source:* 1993 Level I CFA Study Guide © 1993)
14-14 b
14-15 b
14-16 b
14-17 d
14-18 c
14-19 a
14-20 d

Chapter 15

15-1 a
15-2 c
15-3 d
15-4 c (*Source:* 2003 Level I CFA Practice Exam © 2003)
15-5 c
15-6 b (*Source:* 1992 Level I CFA Study Guide © 1992)
15-7 d
15-8 a
15-9 a (*Source:* 1990 Level I CFA Study Guide © 1990)
15-10 c (*Source:* 1994 Level I CFA Study Guide © 1994)
15-11 a
15-12 b (*Source:* 1993 Level I CFA Study Guide © 1993)
15-13 a (*Source:* 1993 Level I CFA Study Guide © 1993)
15-14 b (*Source:* 1991 Level I CFA Study Guide © 1991)
15-15 d
15-16 a (*Source:* 2003 Level I CFA Practice Exam © 2003)
15-17 d (*Source:* 2003 Level I CFA Practice Exam © 2003)
15-18 c (*Source:* 2003 Level I CFA Practice Exam © 2003)
15-19 d
15-20 c

Chapter 16

16-1 a
16-2 d
16-3 c
16-4 a (*Source:* 1992 Level I CFA Study Guide © 1992)
16-5 d (*Source:* 1990 Level I CFA Study Guide © 1990)
16-6 a (*Source:* 1989 Level I CFA Study Guide © 1989)
16-7 a (*Source:* 1993 Level I CFA Study Guide © 1993)
16-8 b (*Source:* 1998 Level I CFA Study Guide © 1998)
16-9 d
16-10 a
16-11 c
16-12 d
16-13 a
16-14 b
16-15 b
16-16 d
16-17 a
16-18 c
16-19 c
16-20 d

Chapter 17

17-1 b (*Source:* 1999 Level I CFA Practice Exam © 1999)
17-2 b
17-3 d
17-4 c
17-5 a
17-6 a
17-7 b
17-8 d
17-9 c
17-10 a
17-11 b
17-12 c
17-13 c
17-14 b (*Source:* 1994 Level I CFA Study Guide © 1994)
17-15 c (*Source:* 1994 Level I CFA Study Guide © 1994)
17-16 b (*Source:* 1994 Level I CFA Study Guide © 1994)
17-17 a (*Source:* 1994 Level I CFA Study Guide © 1994)
17-18 b (*Source:* 1994 Level I CFA Study Guide © 1994)
17-19 c
17-20 d

Chapter 18

18-1 d (*Source:* 1990 Level I CFA Study Guide © 1990)
18-2 c (*Source:* 1988 Level I CFA Study Guide © 1988)
18-3 a (*Source:* 1989 Level I CFA Study Guide © 1989)
18-4 c (*Source:* 1990 Level I CFA Study Guide © 1990)
18-5 c (*Source:* 1998 Level I CFA Practice Exam © 1998)
18-6 a
18-7 b (*Source:* 1991 Level I CFA Study Guide © 1991)
18-8 a
18-9 b (*Source:* 2003 Level I CFA Practice Exam © 2003)
18-10 b
18-11 c (*Source:* 1992 Level I CFA Study Guide © 1992)
18-12 a (*Source:* 1989 Level I CFA Study Guide © 1989)
18-13 d (*Source:* 1990 Level I CFA Study Guide © 1990)
18-14 a
18-15 c (*Source:* 1998 Level I CFA Practice Exam © 1998)
18-16 b (*Source:* 1990 Level I CFA Study Guide © 1990)
18-17 b (*Source:* 1988 Level I CFA Study Guide © 1988)
18-18 d (*Source:* 1994 Level I CFA Study Guide © 1994)
18-19 b (*Source:* 1991 Level I CFA Study Guide © 1991)
18-20 c (*Source:* 1993 Level I CFA Study Guide © 1993)
18-21 c (*Source:* 1991 Level I CFA Study Guide © 1991)
18-22 d (*Source:* 1994 Level I CFA Study Guide © 1994)
18-23 d
18-24 b
18-25 a (*Source:* 2003 Level I CFA Practice Exam © 2003)

Chapter 19

19-1 a
19-2 c
19-3 a

19-4 c (*Source:* 1990 Level I CFA Study Guide © 1990)
19-5 b (*Source:* 1998 Level I CFA Practice Exam © 1998)
19-6 b
19-7 d
19-8 b
19-9 b
19-10 a
19-11 b
19-12 a
19-13 a
19-14 c
19-15 d (*Source:* 1992 Level I CFA Study Guide © 1992)
19-16 d (*Source:* 1989 Level I CFA Study Guide © 1989)
19-17 d
19-18 a
19-19 b
19-20 c (*Source:* 1990 Level I CFA Study Guide © 1990)
19-21 d
19-22 b (*Source:* 1991 Level I CFA Study Guide © 1991)
19-23 b (*Source:* 1992 Level I CFA Study Guide © 1992)
19-24 a (*Source:* 1991 Level I CFA Study Guide © 1991)
19-25 a (*Source:* 1994 Level I CFA Study Guide © 1994)

Chapter 20 (Web site only)

20-1 d
20-2 a
20-3 c
20-4 c
20-5 a
20-6 c
20-7 b
20-8 c
20-9 b
20-10 c (*Source:* 1988 Level I CFA Study Guide © 1988)
20-11 b (*Source:* 1988 Level I CFA Study Guide © 1988)
20-12 a (*Source:* 1989 Level I CFA Study Guide © 1989)
20-13 d (*Source:* 1991 Level I CFA Study Guide © 1991)
20-14 a (*Source:* 1991 Level I CFA Study Guide © 1991)
20-15 b (*Source:* 1990 Level I CFA Study Guide © 1990)
20-16 a (*Source:* 1989 Level I CFA Study Guide © 1989)
20-17 c (*Source:* 1991 Level I CFA Study Guide © 1991)
20-18 a (*Source:* 1991 Level I CFA Study Guide © 1991)
20-19 d (*Source:* 1989 Level I CFA Study Guide © 1989)
20-20 c
20-21 c
20-22 a
20-23 b
20-24 b
20-25 d

Appendix B

Answers to Selected Questions and Problems

Chapter 1

1-1 \$988
1-5 Cherry average return = 9.20%
Straw average return = 13.80%
1-9 Arithmetic average = 11.67%
Geometric average = 9.820%
1-13 Probability of doubling = 0.58%
Probability of tripling = 0.0000012%
1-17 Small company stocks = 12.69%
Long-term government bonds = 5.42%
Treasury bills = 3.72%
Inflation = 3.03%

Chapter 2

2-1 305.16 shares
2-5 \$21,818.18
2-9 Critical stock price = \$75.12
Account equity = \$22,530
2-13 \$77.14
2-17 \$1,234.60
2-21 −18.90%
2-25 Effective annual return = 18.23%

Chapter 3

3-1 Closing price = \$65.89
Round lots = 186,491
3-5 Next payment = \$126,000
Payment at maturity = \$3,126,000
3-9 Current yield = 6.62%
Treasury yield = 6.85%
3-13 −\$2,156
3-20 137.41%

Chapter 4

4-1 \$41.43
4-5 \$51.31
4-9 \$22.06; −16.73%
4-13 2.45%
4-17 9.03%
4-21 \$113,350

Chapter 5

5-1 2.21863
5-5 19.78%
5-9 3.88973
5-13 0.208594

Chapter 6

6-1 \$40.00
6-4 \$5.59
6-9 \$3.74; \$4.08
6-13 \$75.78
6-17 \$17.95
6-22 \$28.23
6-25 18.90 times
6-29 −\$30.17
6-33 ROE = 11.87%
g = 8.31%

Chapter 7

None

Chapter 8

8-2 1.232; 0.963; 0.776; 1.025; 0.862
8-6 0.4793; 0.4380; 0.3884; 0.4132; 0.3554
8-15 0.8703; 0.8901; 0.9035; 0.9120

Chapter 9

9-1 78.50%
9-5 8.30%
9-9 \$987,127.22
9-13 BEY = 5.811%
Discount yield = 5.633%
9-17 5-year STRIP = 76:06
$f_{1,5}$ = 5.589%
2-year STRIP = 89:05
$f_{2,3}$ = 5.902%
9-21 $f_{1,1}$ = 6.50%
$f_{1,2}$ = 6.91%
$f_{1,3}$ = 8.04%

Chapter 10

10-1 \$913.90
10-5 9.18%
10-9 9.75%
10-13 9.09%
10-19 11.48 years
10-21 YTM = 6.95%
Realized yield = −1.02%
10-25 \$0.606
10-29 Macaulay duration = 10.498
Modified duration = 10.143
10-33 5.33%

Chapter 11

11-1 10.80%
11-5 Roll = 17.41%
Ross = 5.96%
11-9 *a.* 7.93%
b. 0.03419; 18.49%
11-17 Standard deviation = 17.39%
Expected return = 10.30%
11-20 Standard deviation = 32.65%
Expected return = 13.05%

Chapter 12

12-1 1.32
12-5 1.155
12-9 $58.95
12-13 2.64%
12-17 1.72
12-23 Expected return = 0.645%
Standard deviation = 2.13%

Chapter 13

13-1 15.92%
13-4 Monthly standard deviation = 12.96%
Annual standard deviation = 46.73%
13-9 −44.93%
13-13 −14.10%
13-18 −121.93%
13-21 −10.78%

Chapter 14

14-1 *a.* $49,706.25
b. $872,046
c. $11,750
d. −$4,860
14-5 $16,794,515,050
14-9 $95.38
14-13 Day 1: $200,325
Day 2: $170,925
Day 3: $185,625
Day 4: $185,625
Profit = −$64,050
14-17 851.85
14-21 8,805.64
14-25 *a.* 190.55
b. 190.40

Chapter 15

15-1 $1,600
15-5 $37,500; $12,000
15-9 $82.68
15-13 $13.17
15-16 $900

Chapter 16

16-1 $14.42
16-5 $5.73
16-9 3,163
16-13 $3.48
16-17 $7.43
16-20 $5.26

Chapter 17

17-1 $46,885
17-5 P/B = 3.87 times
P/E = 11.26 times
P/CF = 8.98 times
17-9 $250,000
17-13 ROA = 16.99%
ROE = 40.11%
17-17 Maximum sales growth = 11.11%

Chapter 18

18-1 $35.71
18-5 $1,150
18-8 $79.79
18-12 Conversion value = $880
Conversion price = $47.73

Chapter 19

19-1 $3,053.67
19-5 5.78%
19-9 5.11%
19-13 $1,074.6875
19-17 4.33%

Chapter 20 (Web site only)

20-1 $1,361.74
20-5 0.4265%
20-9 $166,460.81
20-13 $56.29
20-17 50 PSA: 0.2108%
200 PSA: 0.8742%
400 PSA: 1.8423%

Appendix C

Key Equations

Chapter 1

1. Dividend yield = D_{t+1}/P_t (1.1)
2. Capital gains yield = $(P_{t+1} - P_t)/P_t$ (1.2)
3. Total return = $(D_{t+1} + P_{t+1} - P_t)/P_t$ (1.3)
4. $\text{Var}(R) = [(R_1 - \bar{R})^2 + (R_2 - \bar{R})^2 + \cdots + (R_N - \bar{R})^2]/(N - 1)$ (1.4)
5. Geometric average return = $[(1 + R_1) \times (1 + R_2) \times \cdots \times (1 + R_N)]^{1/N} - 1$ (1.5)
6. $1 + EAR = (1 + \text{holding period percentage return})^m$
7. Blume's formula: $R(T) = \frac{T-1}{N-1} \times \text{Geometric average} + \frac{N-T}{N-1} \times \text{Arithmetic average}$

Chapter 2

1. $\text{Margin} = \frac{\text{Account equity}}{\text{Value of stock}}$

   Buying on margin:

2. Maintenance margin $= \frac{\text{Number of shares} \times P^* - \text{Amount borrowed}}{\text{Number of shares} \times P^*}$

   In equation 2:

3. $P^* = \frac{\text{Amount borrowed/Number of shares}}{1 - \text{Maintenance margin}}$ (2.1)

   Short selling:

4. Maintenance margin $= \frac{\text{Initial margin deposit} + \text{Short proceeds} - \text{Number of shares} \times P^*}{\text{Number of shares} \times P^*}$

   In equation 4:

5. $P^* = \frac{(\text{Initial margin deposit} + \text{Short proceeds})/\text{Number of shares}}{1 + \text{Maintenance margin}}$

Chapter 3

1. $EAR = [1 + (APR/m)]^m - 1$

Chapter 4

1. $\text{Net asset value} = \frac{\text{Asset value}}{\text{Number of shares outstanding}}$

Chapter 5

1. $\text{Price-weighted index level} = \frac{\text{Sum of stock prices}}{\text{Divisor}}$

Chapter 6

1. $P_0 = \frac{D_1}{(1+k)} + \frac{D_2}{(1+k)^2} + \frac{D_3}{(1+k)^3} + \cdots + \frac{D_T}{(1+k)^T}$ (6.1)
2. $P_0 = \frac{D_0(1+g)}{k-g}$ (6.2)
3. $P_0 = \frac{D_1}{k-g}$ (6.3)
4. $g = \left[\frac{D_N}{D_0}\right]^{1/N} - 1$
5. Payout ratio = D/EPS
6. Sustainable growth rate = ROE × Retention ratio (6.7)
   = ROE × (1 − Payout ratio)
7. Return on equity (ROE) = Net Income/Equity (6.8)
8. The two-stage dividend growth model:
   $$P_0 = \frac{D_0(1+g_1)}{k-g_1} \times \left[1 - \left(\frac{1+g_1}{1+k}\right)^T\right] + \left(\frac{1+g_1}{1+k}\right)^T \times \frac{D_0(1+g_2)}{k-g_2} \quad (6.9)$$
9. Discount rate = U.S. T-bill rate + (Stock beta × Stock market risk premium) (6.15)

   In this equation:

   U.S. T-bill rate = Return on 90-day U.S. T-bills

   Stock beta = Risk relative to an average stock

   Stock market risk premium = Risk premium for an average stock

10. $$P_0 = B_0 + \frac{EPS_1 - B_0 \times k}{(1+k)^1} + \frac{EPS_2 - B_1 \times k}{(1+k)^2} + \frac{EPS_3 - B_2 \times k}{(1+k)^3} + \cdots \quad (6.16)$$
11. $P_0 = B_0 + \frac{EPS_0(1+g) - B_0 \times k}{k-g}$ (6.17)
12. $P_0 = \frac{EPS_1 - B_0 \times g}{k-g}$ (6.18)
13. $D_1 = EPS_1 + B_0 - B_1 = EPS_1 + B_0 - B_0(1+g) = EPS_1 - B_0 \times g$ (6.19)
14. Expected price = Historical P/E ratio × Projected EPS
    = Historical P/E ratio × Current EPS × (1 + Projected EPS growth rate)
15. Expected price = Historical P/CF ratio × Projected CFPS
    = Historical P/CF ratio × Current CFPS × (1 + Projected CFPS growth rate)
16. Expected price = Historical P/S ratio × Projected SPS
    = Historical P/S ratio × Current SPS × (1 + Projected SPS growth rate)

Chapter 7

1. Abnormal return = Observed return − Expected return (7.1)

Chapter 8

1. Market Sentiment Index (MSI)

$$= \frac{\text{Number of bearish investors}}{\text{Number of bullish investors} + \text{Number of bearish investors}}$$

2. $$\text{Arms} = \frac{\text{Declining Volume/Declining Issue}}{\text{Advancing Volume/Advancing Issues}} \quad (8.1)$$

Chapter 9

1. $\text{Future value} = \text{Present value} \times (1 + r)^N$ (9.1)

2. $\text{Present value} = \dfrac{\text{Future value}}{(1 + r)^N}$ (9.3)

3. $\text{Present value} = \text{Future value} \times (1 + r)^{-N}$ (9.4)

4. Current price

$$= \text{Face value} \times \left(1 - \frac{\text{Days to maturity}}{360} \times \text{Discount yield}\right) \quad (9.5)$$

5. Bond equivalent yield

$$= \frac{365 \times \text{Discount yield}}{360 - \text{Days to maturity} \times \text{Discount yield}} \quad (9.6)$$

6. Bill price

$$= \frac{\text{Face value}}{1 + \text{Bond equivalent yield} \times \text{Days to maturity}/365} \quad (9.7)$$

7. $1 + EAR = \left(1 + \dfrac{APR}{m}\right)^m$ (9.8)

8. Real interest rate = Nominal interest rate − Inflation rate (9.11)

9. $\text{STRIPS price} = \dfrac{\text{Face value}}{(1 + YTM/2)^{2M}}$

10. $YTM = 2 \times \left[\left(\dfrac{\text{Face value}}{\text{STRIPS price}}\right)^{\frac{1}{2M}} - 1\right]$

11. $f_{1,1} = \dfrac{(1 + r_2)^2}{1 + r_1} - 1$

12. NI = RI + IP + RP + LP + DP (9.13)

In this equation:
- NI = Nominal interest rate
- RI = Real interest rate
- IP = Inflation premium
- RP = Interest rate risk premium
- LP = Liquidity premium
- DP = Default premium

Chapter 10

1. $\text{Coupon rate} = \dfrac{\text{Annual coupon}}{\text{Par value}}$ (10.1)

2. $\text{Current yield} = \dfrac{\text{Annual coupon}}{\text{Bond price}}$ (10.2)

3. Bond price

$$= \frac{C}{YTM}\left[1 - \frac{1}{(1 + YTM/2)^{2M}}\right] + \frac{FV}{(1 + YTM/2)^{2M}} \quad (10.3)$$

In this formula:
- C = Annual coupon, the sum of two semiannual coupons
- FV = Face Value
- M = Maturity in years
- YTM = Yield to maturity

4. Premium bonds: Coupon rate > Current yield > Yield to maturity

5. Discount bonds: Coupon rate < Current yield < Yield to maturity

6. Par value bonds: Coupon rate = Current yield = Yield to maturity

7. Callable bond price

$$= \frac{C}{YTC}\left[1 - \frac{1}{(1 + YTC/2)^{2T}}\right] + \frac{CP}{(1 + YTC/2)^{2T}} \quad (10.4)$$

In this formula:
- C = Constant annual coupon
- CP = Call price of the bond
- T = Time in years until earliest possible call date
- YTC = Yield to call assuming semiannual coupons

8. $\text{Percentage change in bond price} \approx -\text{Duration} \times \dfrac{\text{Change in } YTM}{(1 + YTM/2)}$ (10.5)

9. $\text{Modified duration} = \dfrac{\text{Macaulay duration}}{(1 + YTM/2)}$ (10.6)

10. Percentage change in bond price ≈ −Modified duration × Change in YTM (10.7)

11. Par value bond duration

$$= \frac{(1 + YTM/2)}{YTM}\left[1 - \frac{1}{(1 + YTM/2)^{2M}}\right] \quad (10.8)$$

In this formula:
- M = Bond maturity in years
- YTM = Yield to maturity assuming semiannual coupons

12. Duration

$$= \frac{1 + YTM/2}{YTM} - \frac{(1 + YTM/2) + M(CPR - YTM)}{YTM + CPR[(1 + YTM/2)^{2M} - 1]} \quad (10.9)$$

In this formula:
- CPR = Constant annual coupon rate
- M = Bond maturity in years
- YTM = Yield to maturity assuming semiannual coupons

13. Dollar value of an 01 ≈ Modified duration × Bond price × 0.0001 (10.10)

14. $\text{Yield value of a 32nd} \approx \dfrac{1}{32 \times \text{Dollar value of an 01}}$ (10.11)

Chapter 11

1. Risk premium = Expected return − Risk-free rate (11.1)
   $\text{Risk premium} = E(R_j) - R_f$

2. Portfolio return for an "N" asset portfolio:
   $E(R_P) = x_1 \times E(R_1) + x_2 \times E(R_2) + \cdots + x_n \times E(R_n)$ (11.2)

3. Portfolio variance for two asset portfolio:
   $\sigma_P^2 = x_A^2\sigma_A^2 + x_B^2\sigma_B^2 + 2x_Ax_B\sigma_A\sigma_B\text{Corr}(R_A, R_B)$ (11.3)

4. Portfolio variance for three asset portfolio:
   $$\sigma_P^2 = x_A^2\sigma_A^2 + x_B^2\sigma_B^2 + x_C^2\sigma_C^2 + 2x_Ax_B\sigma_A\sigma_B\text{Corr}(R_A, R_B) + 2x_Ax_C\sigma_A\sigma_C\text{Corr}(R_A, R_C) + 2x_Bx_C\sigma_B\sigma_C\text{Corr}(R_B, R_C) \quad (11.4)$$

5. The weight in asset A in the minimum variance portfolio:
   $$x_A^* = \frac{\sigma_B^2 - \sigma_A\sigma_B\text{Corr}(R_A, R_B)}{\sigma_A^2 + \sigma_B^2 - 2\sigma_A\sigma_B\text{Corr}(R_A, R_B)} \quad (11.5)$$

6. Portfolio return for three asset portfolio:
   $R_P = x_FR_F + x_SR_S + x_BR_B$ (11.6)

7. Portfolio variance for three asset portfolio when all correlations are zero:
   $\sigma_P^2 = x_F^2\sigma_F^2 + x_S^2\sigma_S^2 + x_B^2\sigma_B^2$ (11.7)

Chapter 12

1. Total return − Expected return = Unexpected return (12.1)
   $R - E(R) = U$

2. Announcement = Expected part + Surprise (12.2)

3. $R - E(R)$ = Systematic portion + Unsystematic portion (12.3)

4. $R - E(R) = U = m + \epsilon$ (12.4)

5. Total risk = Systematic risk + Unsystematic risk (12.5)

6. $\dfrac{E(R_A) - R_f}{\beta_A} = \dfrac{E(R_B) - R_f}{\beta_B}$ (12.6)

7. SML slope $= \dfrac{E(R_M) - R_f}{\beta_M} = \dfrac{E(R_M) - R_f}{1} = E(R_M) - R_f$

8. $E(R_i) = R_f + [E(R_M) - R_f] \times \beta_i$ (12.7)

9. $R - E(R) = m + \epsilon$ (12.8)

10. $m = [R_M - E(R_M)] \times \beta$ (12.9)

11. $R - E(R) = m + \epsilon = [R_M - E(R_M)] \times \beta + \epsilon$ (12.10)

12. $\beta_i = \text{Corr}(R_i, R_M) \times \sigma_i / \sigma_M$ (12.11)

Chapter 13

1. Sharpe ratio $= \dfrac{R_p - R_f}{\sigma_p}$ (13.1)

2. Treynor ratio $= \dfrac{R_p - R_f}{\beta_p}$ (13.2)

3. $E(R_p) = R_f + [E(R_M) - R_f] \times \beta_p$ (13.3)

4. $\alpha_p = R_p - E(R_p)$
$= R_p - \{R_f + [E(R_M) - R_f] \times \beta_p\}$ (13.4)

5. $\dfrac{E(R_p) - R_f}{\sigma_p} = \dfrac{x_S E(R_S) + x_B E(R_B) - R_f}{\sqrt{x_S^2 \sigma_S^2 + x_B^2 \sigma_B^2 + 2 x_S x_B \sigma_S \sigma_B \text{Corr}(R_S, R_B)}}$ (13.5)

6. $E(R_{p,T}) = E(R_p) \times T$ (13.6)

7. $\sigma_{p,T} = \sigma_p \times \sqrt{T}$ (13.7)

8. Value-at-Risk:
$\text{Prob}[R_{p,T} \le E(R_p) \times T - 2.326 \times \sigma_p \sqrt{T}] = 1\%$
$\text{Prob}[R_{p,T} \le E(R_p) \times T - 1.96 \times \sigma_p \sqrt{T}] = 2.5\%$ (13.8)
$\text{Prob}[R_{p,T} \le E(R_p) \times T - 1.645 \times \sigma_p \sqrt{T}] = 5\%$

Chapter 14

1. Basis = Cash price − Futures price (14.1)

2. Spot-futures parity: $F_T = S(1 + r)^T$ (14.3)

3. Spot-futures parity (with dividend yield):
$F_T = S(1 + r - d)^T$ (14.6)

4. Number of index futures contracts, N, needed to change equity portfolio beta: (14.7)
$N = (\beta_D - \beta_P) \times \dfrac{V_P}{V_F}$

5. Number of U.S. Treasury note futures contracts, N, needed to hedge a bond portfolio: (14.8)
$N = \dfrac{D_P \times V_P}{D_F \times V_F}$

6. Duration of an interest rate futures contract (rule of thumb): $D_F = D_U + M_F$ (14.9)

Chapter 15

1. Call option intrinsic value = MAX($S - K$,0) (15.1)

2. Put option intrinsic value = MAX($K - S$,0) (15.2)

3. The put-call parity relationship: $C - P = S_0 - K/(1 + r_f)^T$ (15.6)

4. The put-call parity relationship (with dividends):
$C - P = S_0 - \text{Div} - K/(1 + r_f)^T$ (15.8)

Chapter 16

1. Delta, One Period Binomial Model:
$\Delta = \dfrac{C_u - C_d}{Su - Sd}$

2. Call Value, One Period Binomial Model: (16.2)
$C = \dfrac{\Delta S(1 + r - u) + C_u}{1 + r}$

3. Black-Scholes Call Option Pricing Model: (16.3)
$C = SN(d_1) - Ke^{-rT} N(d_2)$

4. Black-Scholes Put Option Pricing Model: (16.4)
$P = Ke^{-rT} N(-d_2) - SN(-d_1)$
Where, in the Black-Scholes formula, d_1 and d_2 are:

5. $d_1 = \dfrac{\ln(S/K) + (r + \sigma^2/2)T}{\sigma\sqrt{T}}$

6. $d_2 = d_1 - \sigma\sqrt{T}$

7. Call option delta $= N(d_1) > 0$

8. Put option delta $= -N(-d_1) < 0$

9. A useful option hedging equation:
Change in stock price × shares = Option delta × Number of options

10. Number of stock options needed to hedge an equity portfolio:
Number of option contracts (16.7)
$= \dfrac{\text{Portfolio beta} \times \text{Portfolio value}}{\text{Option delta} \times \text{Option contract value}}$

11. Black-Scholes-Merton call option formula:
$C = Se^{-yT} N(d_1) - Ke^{-rT} N(d_2)$ (16.8)
Where, in the Black-Scholes-Merton call option formula, d_1 and d_2 are:

12. $d_1 = \dfrac{\ln(S/K) + (r - y + \sigma^2/2)T}{\sigma\sqrt{T}}$

13. $d_2 = d_1 - \sigma\sqrt{T}$

Chapter 17

Profitability ratios:

1. Gross margin $= \dfrac{\text{Gross profit}}{\text{Net sales}}$

2. Operating margin $= \dfrac{\text{Operating income}}{\text{Net sales}}$

3. Return on assets (ROA) $= \dfrac{\text{Net income}}{\text{Total assets}}$

4. Return on equity (ROE) $= \dfrac{\text{Net income}}{\text{Shareholder equity}}$

Per share calculations:

5. Book value per share (BVPS) $= \dfrac{\text{Shareholder equity}}{\text{Shares outstanding}}$

6. Earnings per share (EPS) $= \dfrac{\text{Net income}}{\text{Shares outstanding}}$

7. Cash flow per share (CFPS) $= \dfrac{\text{Operating cash flow}}{\text{Shares outstanding}}$

Price ratios:

8. Price-book (P/B) $= \dfrac{\text{Stock price}}{\text{BVPS}}$

9. Price-earnings (P/E) $= \dfrac{\text{Stock price}}{\text{EPS}}$

10. Price-cash flow (P/CF) $= \dfrac{\text{Stock price}}{\text{CFPS}}$

Two-stage residual income model (RIM):

11. $P_0 = BVPS_0 + \dfrac{EPS_0(1 + g_1) - BVPS_0 \times k}{k - g_1}\left[1 - \left(\dfrac{1 + g_1}{1 + k}\right)^T\right]$
$+ \dfrac{EPS_0(1 + g_1)^T(1 + g_2) - BVPS_0(1 + k)^T k}{(k - g_2)/(1 + k)^T}$ (17.3)

Chapter 18

Convertible bond to stock conversion formulas:

1. Conversion ratio = Number of stock shares acquired by conversion
2. Conversion price $= \dfrac{\text{Bond par value}}{\text{Conversion ratio}}$
3. Conversion value = Price per share of stock × Conversion ratio

Chapter 19

1. STRIPS price $= \dfrac{\text{Face value}}{(1 + (YTM/2))^{2N}}$
2. STRIPS yield $= 2\left[\left(\dfrac{\text{Face value}}{\text{Price}}\right)^{\frac{1}{2N}} - 1\right]$
3. Bond Price $= \dfrac{\text{Annual Coupon}}{YTM} \times \left[1 - \dfrac{1}{(1 + YTM/2)^{2M}}\right] + \dfrac{\text{Face Value}}{(1 + YTM/2)^{2M}}$
4. Equivalent taxable yield = Tax-exempt yield / (1 − Marginal tax rate)
5. After-tax yield = Taxable yield × (1 − Marginal tax rate)
6. Critical marginal tax rate = 1 − (tax-exempt yield/taxable yield)

Name Index

Page numbers followed by n indicate notes.

K

L

M

N

O

P

R

S

T

V

W

Y

Equation Index

Page numbers followed by n indicate notes.

A

B

C

D

E

F

G

H

I

Subject Index

Page numbers followed by n indicate notes; by f, figures; by t, tables.

A

B

C

D

E

F

G

H

I

J

K

L

M

N

O

P

Q

R

S

T

U

V

W

X

Y

Z

With the purchase of a New Book*

You Can Access the Real Financial Data that the Experts Use!

*Access is available to purchasers of new books only. If you purchased a used book, the site ID may have expired.

This card entitles the purchaser of a new textbook to a semester of access to the Educational Version of Standard & Poor's Market Insight®, a rich online resource featuring hundreds of the most often researched companies in the Market Insight database.

For 1,000 companies, this website provides you:

- Access to six years' worth of fundamental financial data from the renowned Standard & Poor's COMPUSTAT® database
- 12 Excel Analytics Reports, including balance sheets, income statements, ratio reports and cash flow statements; adjusted prices reports, and profitability; forecasted values and monthly valuation data reports
- Access to Financial Highlights Reports including key ratios
- S & P Stock Reports that offer fundamental, quantitative and technical analysis
- EDGAR reports updated throughout the day
- Industry Surveys, written by S & P's Equity analysts
- News feeds (updated hourly) for companies and industries.

STANDARD & POOR'S

McGraw-Hill Irwin

Exclusive partnership!

See other side for your unique site ID access code.

Welcome to the Educational Version of Market Insight!

www.mhhe.com/edumarketinsight

Check out your textbook's website for details on how this special offer enhances the value of your purchase!

1. To get started, use your web browser to go to **www.mhhe.com/edumarketinsight**
2. Enter your site ID exactly as it appears below.
3. You may be prompted to enter the site ID for future use—please keep this card.

Your site ID is:

ah187425

STANDARD & POOR'S

ISBN 978-0-07-336382-0
MHID 0-07-336382-0

McGraw-Hill Irwin

*If you purchased a used book, this site ID may have expired.

Chapter Learning Objectives

Chapter 1: A Brief History of Risk and Return

In this chapter, you will learn:

1. How to calculate the return on an investment using different methods.
2. The historical returns on various important types of investments.
3. The historical risks on various important types of investments.
4. The relationship between risk and return.

Chapter 2: Buying and Selling Securities

In this chapter, you will learn:

1. The various types of securities brokers and brokerage accounts.
2. How to calculate initial and maintenance margin.
3. The workings of short sales.
4. The importance of investor objectives, constraints, and strategies.

Chapter 3: Overview of Security Types

In this chapter, you will learn:

1. Various types of interest-bearing assets.
2. Equity securities.
3. Futures contracts.
4. Option contracts.

Chapter 4: Mutual Funds

In this chapter, you will learn:

1. The different types of mutual funds.
2. How mutual funds operate.
3. How to find information about how mutual funds have performed.
4. The workings of Exchange-Traded Funds.

Chapter 5: The Stock Market

In this chapter, you will learn:

1. The difference between primary and secondary stock markets.
2. The workings of the New York Stock Exchange.
3. How NASDAQ operates.
4. How to calculate index returns.

Chapter 6: Common Stock Valuation

In this chapter, you will learn:

1. The basic dividend discount model.
2. The two-stage dividend growth model.
3. The residual income model.
4. Price ratio analysis.

Chapter 7: Stock Price Behavior and Market Efficiency

In this chapter, you will learn:

1. The foundations of market efficiency.
2. The implications of the forms of market efficiency.
3. Market efficiency and the performance of professional money managers.
4. What stock market anomalies, bubbles, and crashes mean for market efficiency.

Chapter 8: Behavioral Finance and the Psychology of Investing

In this chapter, you will learn:

1. Prospect theory.
2. The implications of investor overconfidence and misperceptions of randomness.
3. Sentiment-based risk and limits to arbitrage.
4. The wide array of technical analysis methods used by investors.

Chapter 9: Interest Rates

In this chapter, you will learn:

1. Money market prices and rates.
2. Rates and yields on fixed-income securities.
3. Treasury STRIPS and the term structure of interest rates.
4. Nominal versus real interest rates.

Chapter 10: Bond Prices and Yields

In this chapter, you will learn:

1. How to calculate bond prices and yields.
2. The importance of yield to maturity.
3. Interest rate risk and Malkiel's theorems.
4. How to measure the impact of interest rate changes on bond prices.